T0212758

Lecture Notes in Computer Science 9558

More information about this series at http://www.springer.com/series/7410

Soonhak Kwon · Aaram Yun (Eds.)

Information Security and Cryptology – ICISC 2015

18th International Conference Seoul, South Korea, November 25–27, 2015 Revised Selected Papers

Springer

Editors
Soonhak Kwon
Sungkyunkwan University
Suwon, Gyeonggi
Korea (Republic of)

Aaram Yun
UNIST
Ulsan
Korea (Republic of)

ISSN 0302-9743 ISSN 1611-3349 (electronic)
Lecture Notes in Computer Science
ISBN 978-3-319-30839-5 ISBN 978-3-319-30840-1 (eBook)
DOI 10.1007/978-3-319-30840-1

Library of Congress Control Number: 2016932355

LNCS Sublibrary: SL4 – Security and Cryptology

Printed on acid-free paper

This Springer imprint is published by Springer Nature
The registered company is Springer International Publishing AG Switzerland

Preface

ICISC 2015, the 18th International Conference on Information Security and Cryptology, was held in Seoul, Korea, during November 25–27, 2015. This year, the conference was hosted by KIISC (Korea Institute of Information Security and Cryptology) jointly with NSR (National Security Research Institute).

The aim of this conference is to provide an international forum for the latest results of research, development, and applications in the field of information security and cryptology. This year we received 84 submissions, and were able to accept 23 papers from 13 countries, with the acceptance rate of 27.4 %. The review and selection processes were carried out by the Program Committee (PC) members, 56 prominent experts world wide, via the IACR review system. First, each paper was blind reviewed, by at least three PC members for most cases. Second, for resolving conflicts on the reviewers' decisions, the individual review reports were open to all PC members, and detailed interactive discussions on each paper were followed.

The conference featured two invited talks: "Discrete Logarithm-Based Zero-Knowledge Arguments" by Jens Groth, and "Multilinear Maps and Their Cryptanalysis" by Jung Hee Cheon. We thank the invited speakers for their kind acceptance and interesting presentations. We would like to thank all authors who submitted their papers to ICISC 2015 and all 56 PC members. It was a truly nice experience to work with such talented and hard-working researchers. We also appreciate the external reviewers for assisting the PC members in their particular areas of expertise.

Finally, we would like to thank all attendees for their active participation and the Organizing Committee members who expertly managed this conference. We look forward to seeing you again at the next year's ICISC.

November 2015

Soonhak Kwon
Aaram Yun

Organization

General Chairs

Kwang Ho Kim	National Security Research Institute, Korea
ChoonSik Park	Seoul Women's University, Korea

Organizing Committee

Chair

Heuisu Ryu	Gyeongin National University of Education, Korea

Committee Members

Dooho Choi	ETRI, Korea
Junbeom Hur	Korea University, Korea
Howon Kim	Pusan University, Korea
Jongsung Kim	Kookmin University, Korea
Sang Choon Kim	Kangwon National University, Korea
Daesung Kwon	National Security Research Institute, Korea
Kihyo Nam	Umlogics, Korea
SangHwan Park	KISA, Korea
Okyeon Yi	Kookmin University, Korea

Program Committee

Co-chairs

Soonhak Kwon	Sungkyunkwan University, Korea
Aaram Yun	UNIST, Korea

Committee Members

Yoo-Jin Baek	Woosuk University, Korea
Joonsang Baek	Khalifa University of Science, Technology and Research (KUSTAR), UAE
Lejla Batina	Radboud University, The Netherlands
Andrey Bogdanov	Technical University of Denmark, Denmark
Zhenfu Cao	East China Normal University, China
Donghoon Chang	IIIT-Delhi, India
Paolo D'Arco	University of Salerno, Italy
Rafael Dowsley	Karlsruhe Institute of Technology, Germany
Dong-Guk Han	Kookmin University, Korea
Swee-Huay Heng	Multimedia University, Malaysia

Seokhie Hong	Korea University, Korea
Jung Yeon Hwang	ETRI, Korea
David Jao	University of Waterloo, Canada
Howon Kim	Pusan National University, Korea
Huy Kang Kim	Korea University, Korea
Jihye Kim	Kookmin University, Korea
So Jeong Kim	National Security Research Institute, Korea
Jin Kwak	Ajou University, Korea
Taekyoung Kwon	Yonsei University, Korea
Changhoon Lee	Seoul National University of Science and Technology, Korea
Hyang-Sook Lee	Ewha Womans University, Korea
Hyung Tae Lee	Nanyang Technological University, Singapore
JongHyup Lee	Gachon University, Korea
Jooyoung Lee	Sejong University, Korea
Kwangsu Lee	Korea University, Korea
Moon Sung Lee	Seoul National University, Korea
Mun-Kyu Lee	Inha University, Korea
Pil Joong Lee	POSTECH, Korea
Jiqiang Lu	Institute for Infocomm Research, Singapore
Sjouke Mauw	University of Luxembourg, Luxembourg
Florian Mendel	Graz University of Technology, Austria
Atsuko Miyaji	JAIST, Japan
DaeHun Nyang	Inha University, Korea
Katsuyuki Okeya	Hitachi Ltd., Japan
Blazy Olivier	XLim, Université de Limoges, France
Rolf Oppliger	eSECURITY Technologies, Switzerland
Jong Hwan Park	Sangmyung University, Korea
Young-Ho Park	Sejong Cyber University, Korea
Souradyuti Paul	Indian Institute of Technology, Gandhinagar, India
Christian Rechberger	DTU Compute, Denmark
Bimal Roy	Indian Statistical Institute, India
Kouichi Sakurai	Kyushu University, Japan
Jae Hong Seo	Myongji University, Korea
Sang Uk Shin	Pukyong National University, Korea
Taeshik Shon	Ajou University, Korea
Rainer Steinwandt	Florida Atlantic University, USA
Hung-Min Sun	National Tsing Hua University, Taiwan
Willy Susilo	University of Wollongong, Australia
Tsuyoshi Takagi	Kyushu University, Japan
Marion Videau	Quarkslab and Loria, France
Yongzhuang Wei	Guilin University of Electronic Technology, China
Wenling Wu	Institute of Software, Chinese Academy of Sciences, China
Toshihiro Yamauchi	Okayama University, Japan
Wei-Chuen Yau	Multimedia University, Malaysia
Ching-Hung Yeh	Far East University, Taiwan
Dae Hyun Yum	Myongji University, Korea

Information Security and Cryptology — ICISC 2015

The 18th International Conference on Information Security and Cryptology

R & D Center, Chung-Ang University, Seoul, Korea
November 25–27, 2015

Hosted by
Korea Institute of Information Security and Cryptology (KIISC)
& National Security Research Institute (NSR)

Sponsored by
Electronics and Telecommunications Research Institute (ETRI) & LG Hitachi

Contents

Protocols

Security

Side-Channel Attacks

Digital Signatures

A General Framework for Redactable Signatures and New Constructions

David Derler[1(✉)], Henrich C. Pöhls[2], Kai Samelin[3,4], and Daniel Slamanig[1]

[1] IAIK, Graz University of Technology, Graz, Austria
{david.derler,daniel.slamanig}@tugraz.at
[2] Institute of IT-Security and Security Law and Chair of IT-Security, University of Passau, Passau, Germany
hp@sec.uni-passau.de
[3] IBM Research – Zurich, Rüschlikon, Switzerland
ksa@zurich.ibm.com
[4] TU Darmstadt, Darmstadt, Germany

Abstract. A redactable signature scheme (RSS) allows *removing* parts of a signed message by any party without invalidating the respective signature. State-of-the-art constructions thereby focus on messages represented by one specific data-structure, e.g., lists, sets or trees, and adjust the security model accordingly. To overcome the necessity for this myriad of models, we present a general framework covering arbitrary data-structures and even more sophisticated possibilities. For example, we cover fixed elements which must not be redactable and dependencies between elements. Moreover, we introduce the notion of designated redactors, i.e., the signer can give some extra information to selected entities which become redactors. In practice, this often allows to obtain more efficient schemes. We then present two RSSs; one for sets and one for lists, both constructed from any EUF-CMA secure signature scheme and indistinguishable cryptographic accumulators in a black-box way and show how the concept of designated redactors can be used to increase the efficiency of these schemes. Finally, we present a black-box construction of a designated redactor RSS by combining an RSS for sets with non-interactive zero-knowledge proof systems. All the three constructions presented in this paper provide transparency, which is an important property, but quite hard to achieve, as we also conceal the length of the original message and the positions of the redactions.

1 Introduction

A redactable signature scheme (RSS) allows any party to *remove* parts of a signed message such that the corresponding signature σ can be updated without

The full version of this paper is available as IACR ePrint Report 2015/1059.

D. Derler, H.C. Pöhls and D. Slamanig are supported by EU H2020 project PRISMACLOUD, grant agreement no. 644962.
H.C. Pöhls is also supported by EU FP7 project RERUM, grant agreement no. 609094.
K. Samelin is supported by EU FP7 project FUTUREID, grant agreement no. 318424.

S. Kwon and A. Yun (Eds.): ICISC 2015, LNCS 9558, pp. 3–19, 2016.
DOI: 10.1007/978-3-319-30840-1_1

the signers' secret key sk. The so derived signature σ' then still verifies under the signer's public key pk. Hence, RSSs partially solve the "digital message sanitization problem" [28]. This separates RSSs from standard digital signatures, which prohibit *any* alteration of signed messages. Such a primitive comes in handy in use-cases where only parts of the signed data are required, but initial origin authentication must still hold and re-signing is not possible or too expensive. One real-world application scenario is privacy-preserving handling of patient data [4,7,35,37]. For instance, identifying information in a patient's record can be redacted for processing during accounting.

State-of-the-Art. RSSs have been introduced in [21,36]. Their ideas have been extended to address special data-structures such as trees [8,33] and graphs [23]. While the initial idea was that redactions are public, the notion of accountable RSSs appeared recently [30]. Here, the redactor becomes a designated party which can be held accountable for redactions. Further, RSSs with dependencies between elements have been introduced and discussed in [4]. Unfortunately, their work neither introduces a formal security model nor provides a security analysis for their construction. Consecutive redaction control allows intermediate redactors to prohibit further redactions by subsequent ones [26,27,34].

Much more work on RSSs exists. However, they do not use a common security model and most of the presented schemes do not provide the important security property denoted as transparency [8]. As an example, [20,23,37] are not transparent in our model. In such non-transparent constructions, a third party can potentially deduce statements about the original message from a redacted message-signature pair. In particular, their schemes allow to see where a redaction took place. Hence, they contradict the very intention of RSSs being a tool to increase or keep data privacy [8].

Ahn et al. [1] introduced the notion of statistically unlinkable RSSs as a stronger privacy notion. Their scheme only allows for quoting instead of arbitrary redactions, i.e., redactions are limited to the beginning and the end of an ordered list. Moreover, [1] only achieves the weaker and less common notion of selective unforgeability. Lately, even stronger privacy notions have been proposed in [2,3] in the context of the framework of $\mathcal{P}$-homomorphic signatures. There also exists a huge amount of related yet different signature primitives, where we refer the reader to [16] for a comprehensive overview of the state-of-the-art.

Motivation. RSSs have many applications. In particular, minimizing signed data before passing it to other parties makes RSSs an easy to comprehend privacy enhancing tool. However, the need for different security models and different data structures prohibits an easy integration into applications that require such privacy features, as RSSs do not offer a flexible, widely applicable framework. While the model of RSSs for sets (e.g. [26]) can protect unstructured data such as votes, it is, e.g., unclear if it can be used for multi-sets. For ordered lists (such as a text) this already becomes more difficult: should one only allow quoting (i.e., redactions at the beginning and/or the end of a text) or general redactions?

For trees (such as data-bases, XML or JSON), we have even more possibilities: only allow leaf-redactions [8], or leaves and inner nodes [23], or even allow to alter the structure [31]. Furthermore, over the years more sophisticated features such as dependencies, fixed elements and redactable structure appeared. They complicate the specialized models even more.

We want to abandon the necessity to invent specialized security models tailored to specific use-cases and data-structures. Namely, we aim for a framework that generalizes away details and covers existing approaches. Thereby, we want to keep the model compact, understandable and rigid. We aim at RSSs to become generally applicable to the whole spectrum of existing use-cases. In addition, we explicitly want to support the trend to allow the signer to limit the power of redactors [14,18,22]. To prove the applicability of our framework, we present three new constructions which hide the length of the original message, the positions of redactions, and the fact that a redaction has even happened.

Contribution. Our contribution is manifold. (1) Existing work focuses on messages representations in only a specific data-structure, whereas our model is generally applicable (even for data-structures not yet considered for RSSs in the literature). Our general framework also captures more sophisticated redaction possibilities such as dependencies between redactable parts, fixed parts and consecutive redaction control. (2) We introduce the notion of designated redactors. While this concept might seem similar to the concept of accountable RSSs [30], we are not interested in accountability, but only want to allow to hand an extra piece of information to the redactor(s). This often allows to increase the efficiency of the respective scheme. (3) We present two RSSs, one for sets and one for lists, constructed in a black-box way from digital signatures and indistinguishable cryptographic accumulators. We show that existing constructions of RSSs are instantiations of our generic constructions but tailored to specific instantiations of accumulators (often this allows to optimize some of the parameters of the schemes). (4) We present a black-box construction of RSSs with designated redactors for lists from RSSs for sets and non-interactive zero-knowledge proof systems. We stress that all three proposed constructions provide transparency, which is an important property, but quite hard to achieve.

Notation. We use $\lambda \in \mathbb{N}$ to denote a security parameter and assume that all algorithms implicitly take 1^λ as an input. We write $y \leftarrow A(x)$ to denote the assignment of the output of algorithm A on input x to y. If we want to emphasize that A receives explicit random coins r, we write $y \leftarrow A(x;r)$. If S is a finite set, then $s \xleftarrow{R} S$ means that s is assigned a value chosen uniformly at random from S. We call an algorithm efficient, if it runs in probabilistic polynomial time (PPT) in the size of its input. Unless stated otherwise, all algorithms are PPT and return a special error symbol $\bot \notin \{0,1\}^*$ during an exception. A function $\epsilon : \mathbb{N} \rightarrow \mathbb{R}_{\geq 0}$ is negligible, if it vanishes faster than every inverse polynomial. That is, for every $k \in \mathbb{N}$ there exists a $n_0 \in \mathbb{N}$ such that $\epsilon(n) \leq n^{-k}$ for all $n > n_0$. If the message M is a list, i.e., $M = (m_1, m_2, \ldots, m_{|M|})$, where $m_i \in \{0,1\}^*$, we call m_i a block. $|M| \in \mathbb{N}$ then denotes the number of blocks in the message M.

2 Generic Formalization of Redactable Signatures

This section presents our generalized definitions for RSSs.

2.1 The Generalized Framework

We use the formalization by *Brzuska* et al. [8] as a starting point. In contrast to their model, however, ours is not specifically tailored to trees, but is generally applicable to all kinds of data. The resulting model is rigid, i.e., it is more restrictive than the ones introduced in the original works [21,36], while it is not as restrictive as [1–3,9,10,12]. We think that the security model introduced in [8] is sufficient for most use cases, while the ones introduced in [1–3,9,10,12] seem to be overly strong for real world applications. Namely, we require an RSS to be correct, unforgeable, private, and transparent. We explicitly do not require unlinkability and its derivatives (constituting even stronger privacy notations), as almost all messages (documents) occurring in real world applications contain data usable to link them, e.g., unique identifiers.[1] Moreover, we do not formalize accountability, as this notion can easily be achieved by applying the generic transformation presented in [30] to constructions being secure in our model.[2]

In the following, we assume that a message M is some arbitrarily structured piece of data and for the general framework we use the following notation. ADM is an abstract data structure which describes the admissible redactions and may contain descriptions of dependencies, fixed elements or relations between elements. MOD is used to actually describe how a message M is redacted. Next, we define how ADM, MOD and the message M are tangled, for which we introduce the following notation: $\mathsf{MOD} \overset{\mathsf{ADM}}{\preceq} M$ means that MOD is a valid redaction description with respect to ADM and M. $\mathsf{ADM} \preceq M$ denotes that ADM matches M, i.e., ADM is valid with respect to M. By $M' \overset{\mathsf{MOD}}{\longleftarrow} M$, we denote the derivation of M' from M with respect to MOD. Clearly, how MOD, ADM, $\overset{\mathsf{ADM}}{\preceq}$, $\overset{\mathsf{MOD}}{\longleftarrow}$ and $\preceq$ are implemented depends on the data structure in question and on the features of the concrete RSS. Let us give a simple example for sets without using dependencies or other advanced features: then, MOD and ADM, as well as M, are sets. A redaction $M' \overset{\mathsf{MOD}}{\longleftarrow} M$ simply would be $M' \leftarrow M \setminus \mathsf{MOD}$. This further means that $\mathsf{MOD} \overset{\mathsf{ADM}}{\preceq} M$ holds if $\mathsf{MOD} \subseteq \mathsf{ADM} \subseteq M$, while $\mathsf{ADM} \preceq M$ holds if $\mathsf{ADM} \subseteq M$. We want to stress that the definitions of these operators also define how a redaction is actually performed, e.g., if a redacted block leaves a visible special symbol $\perp$ or not.

Now, we formally define an RSS within our general framework.

Definition 1. *An* RSS *is a tuple of four efficient algorithms* (KeyGen, Sign, Verify, Redact)*, which are defined as follows:*

KeyGen(1^λ): *On input of a security parameter* λ*, this probabilistic algorithm outputs a keypair* (sk, pk).

[1] However, we stress that our model can be extended in a straightforward way.

[2] Our model could also be extended to cover accountability in a straightforward way.

$\mathsf{Sign}(\mathsf{sk}, M, \mathsf{ADM})$: *On input of a secret key* sk, *a message* M *and* ADM, *this (probabilistic) algorithm outputs a message-signature pair* (M, σ) *together with some auxiliary redaction information* red.[3]

$\mathsf{Verify}(\mathsf{pk}, \sigma, M)$: *On input of a public key* pk, *a signature* σ *and a message* M, *this deterministic algorithm outputs a bit* $b \in \{0, 1\}$.

$\mathsf{Redact}(\mathsf{pk}, \sigma, M, \mathsf{MOD}, \mathsf{red})$: *This (probabilistic) algorithm takes a public key* pk, *a valid signature* σ *for a message* M, *modification instructions* MOD *and auxiliary redaction information* red *as input. It returns a redacted message-signature pair* (M', σ') *and an updated auxiliary redaction information* red$'$.[4]

We also require that Sign returns $\perp$, if $\mathsf{ADM} \npreceq M$, while Redact also returns $\perp$, if $\mathsf{MOD} \overset{\mathsf{ADM}}{\npreceq} M$. We will omit this explicit check in our constructions. Note that red can also be $\emptyset$ if no auxiliary redaction information is required.

2.2 Security Properties

The security properties for RSSs have already been formally treated for tree data-structures in [8]. We adapt them to our general framework.

Correctness. Correctness requires that all honestly computed/redacted signatures verify correctly. More formally this means that $\forall \lambda \in \mathbb{N}$, $\forall n \in \mathbb{N}$, $\forall M$, $\forall \mathsf{ADM} \preceq M, \forall (\mathsf{sk}, \mathsf{pk}) \leftarrow \mathsf{KeyGen}(1^\lambda)$, $\forall ((M_0, \sigma_0), \mathsf{red}_0) \leftarrow \mathsf{Sign}(\mathsf{sk}, M, \mathsf{ADM})$, $[\forall \mathsf{MOD}_i \overset{\mathsf{ADM}}{\preceq} M_i,\ \forall ((M_{i+1}, \sigma_{i+1}), \mathsf{red}_{i+1}) \leftarrow \mathsf{Redact}(\mathsf{pk}, \sigma_i, M_i, \mathsf{MOD}_i, \mathsf{red}_i)]_{0 \leq i < n}$ it holds that for $0 \leq i \leq n : \mathsf{Verify}(\mathsf{pk}, \sigma_i, M_i) = 1$, where $[S_i]_{0 \leq i < n}$ is shorthand for $S_0, \ldots, S_{n-1}$.

Unforgeability. Unforgeability requires that without a signing key sk, it should be infeasible to compute a valid signature σ on a message M, which is not a valid redaction of any message obtained by adaptive signature queries.

Definition 2 (Unforgeability). *An* RSS *is unforgeable, if for all PPT adversaries* $\mathcal{A}$ *there exists a negligible function* $\epsilon(\cdot)$ *such that*

$$\Pr\left[\begin{matrix}(\mathsf{sk}, \mathsf{pk}) \leftarrow \mathsf{KeyGen}(1^\lambda), (M^*, \sigma^*) \leftarrow \mathcal{A}^{\mathcal{O}^{\mathsf{Sign}}(\mathsf{sk}, \cdot, \cdot)}(\mathsf{pk}) : \\ \mathsf{Verify}(\mathsf{pk}, M^*, \sigma^*) = 1 \ \wedge \ M^* \notin \mathcal{Q}_{\mathsf{Sign}}\end{matrix}\right] \leq \epsilon(\lambda)$$

holds. $\mathcal{O}^{\mathsf{Sign}}$ *denotes a signing oracle and we define* $\mathcal{Q}_{\mathsf{Sign}} \leftarrow \bigcup_{i=1}^{q} \{M' \mid M' \xleftarrow{\mathsf{MOD}_j} M_i \ \forall\ \mathsf{MOD}_j \overset{\mathsf{ADM}_i}{\preceq} M_i\}$. *Here,* $q \in \mathbb{N}$ *is the number of signing queries and* M_i *and* ADM_i *denote the respective input to* $\mathcal{O}^{\mathsf{Sign}}$.

Note that an adversary can perform redactions on its own (also transitively).

---

[3] We assume that ADM can always be correctly and unambiguously derived from any valid message-signature pair. Also note that ADM may change after a redaction.

[4] Note that this algorithm may either explicitly or implicitly alter ADM in an unambiguous way.

Privacy. For anyone except the involved signers and redactors, it should be infeasible to derive information on redacted message parts when given a redacted message-signature pair.

Definition 3 (Privacy). *An* RSS *is private, if for all PPT adversaries $\mathcal{A}$ there exists a negligible function $\epsilon(\cdot)$ such that*

$$\Pr\left[\begin{matrix}(\mathsf{sk},\mathsf{pk}) \leftarrow \mathsf{KeyGen}(1^\lambda), b \xleftarrow{R} \{0,1\}, \mathcal{O} \leftarrow \{\mathcal{O}^{\mathsf{Sign}}(\mathsf{sk},\cdot,\cdot), \\ \mathcal{O}^{\mathsf{LoRRedact}}((\mathsf{sk},\mathsf{pk}),\cdot,\cdot,\cdot,\cdot,\cdot,\cdot,b)\}, b^* \leftarrow \mathcal{A}^{\mathcal{O}}(\mathsf{pk}) : b = b^*\end{matrix}\right] \leq \frac{1}{2} + \epsilon(\lambda)$$

holds. $\mathcal{O}^{\mathsf{Sign}}$ *is defined as before and* $\mathcal{O}^{\mathsf{LoRRedact}}$ *is defined as follows:*

$\mathcal{O}^{\mathsf{LoRRedact}}((\mathsf{sk},\mathsf{pk}), M_0, \mathsf{MOD}_0, M_1, \mathsf{MOD}_1, \mathsf{ADM}_0, \mathsf{ADM}_1, b)$:
1: *Compute* $((M_c, \sigma_c), \mathsf{red}_c) \leftarrow \mathsf{Sign}(\mathsf{sk}, M_c, \mathsf{ADM}_c)$ *for* $c \in \{0,1\}$.
2: *Let* $((M'_c, \sigma'_c), \mathsf{red}'_c) \leftarrow \mathsf{Redact}(\mathsf{pk}, \sigma_c, M_c, \mathsf{MOD}_c, \mathsf{red}_c)$ *for* $c \in \{0,1\}$.
3: *If* $M'_0 \neq M'_1$, *return* $\perp$.
4: *Return* (M'_b, σ'_b).

Note that the oracle returns $\perp$ *if any of the algorithms returns* $\perp$.

In our privacy definition, we allow the adversary to provide distinct values for ADM_0 and ADM_1 to the signing oracle. While this guarantees the required flexibility to support arbitrary data structures, it yields a rather strong definition of privacy. There is existing work, which introduces an additional abort condition in $\mathcal{O}^{\mathsf{LoRRedact}}$ [31] (it is easy to see that security in our model implies security in their model). While such a notion is sufficient for certain implementations of RSSs (such as the one in [31]), we believe that our definition is required for a general model as we propose it.

Transparency. It should be infeasible to decide whether a signature directly comes from the signer (i.e., is a fresh signature) or has been generated using the Redact algorithm, for anyone except the signer and the possibly involved redactor(s). More formally, this means:

Definition 4 (Transparency). *An* RSS *is transparent, if for all PPT adversaries $\mathcal{A}$ there exists a negligible function $\epsilon(\cdot)$ such that*

$$\Pr\left[\begin{matrix}(\mathsf{sk},\mathsf{pk}) \leftarrow \mathsf{KeyGen}(1^\lambda), b \xleftarrow{R} \{0,1\}, \mathcal{O} \leftarrow \{\mathcal{O}^{\mathsf{Sign}}(\mathsf{sk},\cdot,\cdot), \\ \mathcal{O}^{\mathsf{Sign/Redact}}((\mathsf{sk},\mathsf{pk}),\cdot,\cdot,\cdot,b)\}, b^* \leftarrow \mathcal{A}^{\mathcal{O}}(\mathsf{pk}) : b = b^*\end{matrix}\right] \leq \frac{1}{2} + \epsilon(\lambda)$$

holds. Here $\mathcal{O}^{\mathsf{Sign}}$ *is as in Definition 2 and* $\mathcal{O}^{\mathsf{Sign/Redact}}$ *is defined as follows:*

$\mathcal{O}^{\mathsf{Sign/Redact}}((\mathsf{sk},\mathsf{pk}), M, \mathsf{MOD}, \mathsf{ADM}, b)$:
1: *Compute* $((M, \sigma), \mathsf{red}) \leftarrow \mathsf{Sign}(\mathsf{sk}, M, \mathsf{ADM})$.
2: *Compute* $((M', \sigma_0), \mathsf{red}') \leftarrow \mathsf{Redact}(\mathsf{pk}, \sigma, M, \mathsf{MOD}, \mathsf{red})$.
3: *Compute* $((M', \sigma_1), \mathsf{red}'') \leftarrow \mathsf{Sign}(\mathsf{sk}, M', \mathsf{ADM}')$
4: *Return* (M', σ_b).

Note, ADM' *is extracted from* (M', σ_0) *and the oracle returns* $\perp$ *if any of the algorithms returns* $\perp$*.*

We call an RSS secure, if it is correct, unforgeable, private, and transparent.

We want to emphasize that additionally returning auxiliary redaction information red in Sign and Redact does not contradict transparency or privacy, as the "final" verifier never sees any red (which is why the privacy and transparency games do not return red for the challenge message-signature pair). Intuitively, only if an intermediate redactor exists, red is given away by the signer to selected designated entities that become redactors.[5]

Relations Between Security Properties. The relations between the different security properties do not change compared to the work done in [8]. Namely, transparency implies privacy, while privacy does not imply transparency. Furthermore, unforgeability is independent of privacy and transparency. We prove these statements in the extended version of this paper.

Notes on Our Model. In a nutshell, our generalized framework leaves the concrete data-structure—and, thus, also the definition of ADM, MOD, and red—open to the instantiation. For clarity, let us match our framework to already existing definitions. In particular, consider the model of [8]. It does not explicitly define ADM, but implicitly assumes that only leaves of a given tree are redactable, i.e., MOD may only contain changes which are possible with recursive leaf-redaction. *Pöhls* et al. [31] explicitly define ADM as the edges between different nodes in their model for RSS for trees, while allowing arbitrary redactions, i.e., MOD may contain any set of nodes in the tree (including the tree's root), as well as edges.

Finally, we note that our model also covers consecutive redaction control [26,27,34] via ADM. Recall that ADM is contained in all signatures and Redact may also change ADM.

3 Building Blocks

In this section we provide the definitions of the required building blocks.

Digital Signature Schemes. We start by defining digital signatures.

Definition 5 (Digital Signatures). *A digital signature scheme* DSS *is a triple* $(\mathsf{DKeyGen}, \mathsf{DSign}, \mathsf{DVerify})$ *of PPT algorithms:*

[5] This also distinguishes designated redactors from accountable redactable signatures [30]. Namely, the additional information red can be given to any redactor, while the redactor is a fixed entity in accountable RSSs. Hence, in our notion, the redactors can even form a chain, and can be pinpointed in an ad-hoc manner.

$\mathsf{DKeyGen}(1^\lambda)$: *This probabilistic algorithm takes a security parameter λ as input and outputs a secret (signing) key* sk *and a public (verification) key* pk *with associated message space $\mathcal{M}$.*[6]

$\mathsf{DSign}(\mathsf{sk}, m)$: *This (probabilistic) algorithm takes a message $m \in \mathcal{M}$ and a secret key* sk *as input, and outputs a signature σ.*

$\mathsf{DVerify}(\mathsf{pk}, m, \sigma)$: *This deterministic algorithm takes a signature σ, a message $m \in \mathcal{M}$ and a public key* pk *as input, and outputs a bit $b \in \{0, 1\}$.*

A DSS is secure, if it is correct and EUF-CMA secure. The formal security definitions are provided in the extended version of this paper.

Cryptographic Accumulators. Cryptographic accumulators [5] represent a finite set $\mathcal{X}$ as a single succinct value $\mathsf{acc}_\mathcal{X}$ and for each $x \in \mathcal{X}$ one can compute a witness wit_x, certifying membership of x in $\mathcal{X}$. We use the formal model from [17] which assumes a trusted setup, i.e., a TTP generates the accumulator keypair $(\mathsf{sk}_\mathsf{acc}, \mathsf{pk}_\mathsf{acc})$ and discards sk_acc. We, however, note that in some constructions sk_acc improves efficiency, which is a useful feature if the party maintaining the accumulator is trusted (as it is the case in our schemes).[7]

In the formal model below, we omit some additional features of accumulators as they are not required here (cf. [17]).

Definition 6 (Accumulator). *An accumulator* Acc *is a tuple of algorithms* (AGen,AEval,AWitCreate, AVerify) *which are defined as follows:*

$\mathsf{AGen}(1^\lambda, t)$: *This probabilistic algorithm takes a security parameter λ and a parameter t as input. If $t \neq \infty$, then t is an upper bound for the number of accumulated elements. It returns a key pair $(\mathsf{sk}_\mathsf{acc}, \mathsf{pk}_\mathsf{acc})$, where $\mathsf{sk}_\mathsf{acc} = \emptyset$ if no trapdoor exists.*

$\mathsf{AEval}((\mathsf{sk}^\sim_\mathsf{acc}, \mathsf{pk}_\mathsf{acc}), \mathcal{X})$: *This (probabilistic) algorithm takes a key pair $(\mathsf{sk}^\sim_\mathsf{acc}, \mathsf{pk}_\mathsf{acc})$ and a set $\mathcal{X}$ to be accumulated as input and returns an accumulator $\mathsf{acc}_\mathcal{X}$ together with some auxiliary information* aux.

$\mathsf{AWitCreate}((\mathsf{sk}^\sim_\mathsf{acc}, \mathsf{pk}_\mathsf{acc}), \mathsf{acc}_\mathcal{X}, \mathsf{aux}, x)$: *This (probabilistic) algorithm takes a key pair $(\mathsf{sk}^\sim_\mathsf{acc}, \mathsf{pk}_\mathsf{acc})$, an accumulator $\mathsf{acc}_\mathcal{X}$, auxiliary information* aux *and a value x as input. It returns $\perp$, if $x \notin \mathcal{X}$, and a witness wit_x for x otherwise.*

$\mathsf{AVerify}(\mathsf{pk}_\mathsf{acc}, \mathsf{acc}_\mathcal{X}, \mathsf{wit}_x, x)$: *This deterministic algorithm takes a public key pk_acc, an accumulator $\mathsf{acc}_\mathcal{X}$, a witness wit_x and a value x as input and outputs a bit $b \in \{0, 1\}$.*

An accumulator Acc is secure if it is correct, collision free, and indistinguishable. We recall the formal security definitions of these properties in the extended version of this paper and refer to [17] for an overview of concrete instantiations. Henceforth, we use Dom(acc) to denote the accumulation domain.

[6] We usually omit to mention the message space $\mathcal{M}$ and assume that it is implicit in the public key.

[7] Such a trapdoor sk_acc, when used, does not influence the output distributions of the algorithms, but improves efficiency of some algorithms.

Non-interactive Commitments. We also require non-interactive commitment schemes, which we define below.

Definition 7 (Non-interactive Commitment). *A non-interactive commitment scheme* Com *is a tuple of PPT algorithms* $(\mathsf{Gen}, \mathsf{Commit}, \mathsf{Open})$, *which are defined as follows:*

$\mathsf{Gen}(1^\lambda)$: *This probabilistic algorithm takes as input a security parameter* λ *and outputs the public parameters* pp *(subsequently, we omit* pp *for the ease of notation and assume that it is implicit input to all algorithms).*

$\mathsf{Commit}(m)$: *This (probabilistic) algorithm takes as input a message* m *and outputs a commitment* C *together with a corresponding opening information* O *including the randomness* r *used by* Commit.

$\mathsf{Open}(C, O)$: *This deterministic algorithm takes as input a commitment* C *with corresponding opening information* O *and outputs message* $m' \in m \cup \bot$.

A non-interactive commitment scheme Com is secure, if it is correct, (computationally) binding and (computationally) hiding. We provide a formal definition of the security properties in the extended version of this paper. We call a commitment scheme homomorphic if for any m, m' we have $\mathsf{Commit}(m \oplus m') = \mathsf{Commit}(m) \otimes \mathsf{Commit}(m')$ for some binary operations $\oplus$ and $\otimes$. We emphasize that any perfectly correct $\mathsf{IND\text{-}CPA}$ secure public key encryption schemes yields perfectly binding commitments, e.g., ElGamal [19], which is also homomorphic.

Non-interactive Proof Systems. Now, we introduce non-interactive proofs for an **NP**-language with witness relation $R: L_R = \{x \mid \exists\, w : R(x, w) = 1\}$.

Definition 8 (Non-interactive Proof System). *A non-interactive proof system* Π *is a tuple of algorithms* $(\mathsf{Gen}_{\mathsf{crs}}, \mathsf{Proof}, \mathsf{Verify})$, *which are defined as follows:*

$\mathsf{Gen}_{\mathsf{crs}}(1^\lambda)$: *This probabilistic algorithm takes a security parameter* λ *as input, and outputs a common reference string* crs.

$\mathsf{Proof}(\mathsf{crs}, x, w)$: *This probabilistic algorithm takes a common reference string* crs, *a statement* x, *and a witness* w *as input, and outputs a proof* π.

$\mathsf{Verify}(\mathsf{crs}, x, \pi)$: *This deterministic algorithm takes a common reference string* crs, *a statement* x, *and a proof* π *as input, and outputs* 1 *if* π *is valid and* 0 *otherwise.*

In our context, a non-interactive proof system Π is secure, if it is complete, sound, and adaptively zero-knowledge. We provide formal security definitions in the extended version of this paper. Concrete instantiations of non-interactive proof systems, tailored to our requirements, are given in Sect. 5.

4 Redactable Signatures for Sets

For our RSS for sets (cf. Scheme 1), we compute an accumulator representing the set to be signed and then sign the accumulator using any digital signature

$\mathsf{KeyGen}(1^\lambda)$: This algorithm fixes a standard digital signature scheme DSS and an indistinguishable accumulator scheme $\mathsf{Acc} = \{\mathsf{AGen}, \mathsf{AEval}, \mathsf{AWitCreate}, \mathsf{AVerify}\}$, runs $(\mathsf{sk_{DSS}}, \mathsf{pk_{DSS}}) \leftarrow \mathsf{DKeyGen}(1^\lambda)$, $(\mathsf{sk_{acc}}, \mathsf{pk_{acc}}) \leftarrow \mathsf{AGen}(1^\lambda, \infty)$ and returns $(\mathsf{sk}, \mathsf{pk}) \leftarrow ((\mathsf{sk_{DSS}}, \mathsf{sk_{acc}}, \mathsf{pk_{acc}}), (\mathsf{pk_{DSS}}, \mathsf{pk_{acc}}))$.

$\mathsf{Sign}(\mathsf{sk}, M, \mathsf{ADM})$: This algorithm computes $(\mathsf{acc}_M, \mathsf{aux}) \leftarrow \mathsf{AEval}((\mathsf{sk_{acc}}, \mathsf{pk_{acc}}), M)$, and for all $m_i \in M$: $\mathsf{wit}_{m_i} \leftarrow \mathsf{AWitCreate}((\mathsf{sk_{acc}}, \mathsf{pk_{acc}}), \mathsf{acc}_M, \mathsf{aux}, m_i)$. Finally, it computes $\sigma_{\mathsf{DSS}} \leftarrow \mathsf{DSign}(\mathsf{sk_{DSS}}, \mathsf{acc}_M || \operatorname{ord}(\mathsf{ADM}))$ and returns (M, σ) and red, where $\sigma \leftarrow (\sigma_{\mathsf{DSS}}, \mathsf{acc}_M, \{\mathsf{wit}_{m_i}\}_{m_i \in M}, \mathsf{ADM})$ and $\mathsf{red} \leftarrow \emptyset$.

$\mathsf{Verify}(\mathsf{pk}, \sigma, M)$: This algorithms checks whether $\mathsf{DVerify}(\mathsf{pk_{DSS}}, \mathsf{acc}_M || \operatorname{ord}(\mathsf{ADM}), \sigma_{\mathsf{DSS}}) = 1$, and for all $m_i \in M$: $\mathsf{AVerify}(\mathsf{pk_{acc}}, \mathsf{acc}_M, \mathsf{wit}_{m_i}, m_i) = 1$. Furthermore, it checks whether $\mathsf{ADM} \cap M = \mathsf{ADM}$. It returns 1 if all checks hold and 0 otherwise.

$\mathsf{Redact}(\mathsf{pk}, \sigma, M, \mathsf{MOD}, \mathsf{red})$: This algorithm parses σ as $(\sigma_{\mathsf{DSS}}, \mathsf{acc}_M, \mathsf{WIT}, \mathsf{ADM})$, computes $M' \leftarrow M \setminus \mathsf{MOD}$, sets $\mathsf{WIT}' \leftarrow \mathsf{WIT} \setminus \{\mathsf{wit}_{m_i}\}_{m_i \in \mathsf{MOD}}$ and returns (M', σ') and red', where $\sigma' \leftarrow (\sigma_{\mathsf{DSS}}, \mathsf{acc}_M, \mathsf{WIT}', \mathsf{ADM})$ and $\mathsf{red}' \leftarrow \emptyset$.

$\operatorname{ord}(\mathsf{ADM})$: This operator takes a set ADM, applies some unique ordering (e.g., lexicographic) to the elements in ADM and returns the corresponding sequence.

Scheme 1. A RSS for sets

scheme. For verification, one simply provides witnesses for each element in the set and it is verified whether the digital signature on the accumulator as well as the witnesses are valid. Redaction amounts to simply throwing away witnesses corresponding to redacted elements. To maintain transparency, while still allowing the signer to determine which blocks (i.e., elements) of the message (i.e., the set) are redactable, we model ADM as a set containing all blocks which must not be redacted. We also parametrize the scheme by an operator $\operatorname{ord}(\cdot)$, which allows to uniquely encode ADM as a sequence. MOD is modeled as a set containing all blocks of the message to be redacted. We note that one can straightforwardly extend Scheme 1 to support multi-sets by concatenating a unique identifier to each set element. In the extended version of this paper we prove the following:

Theorem 1. *If* Acc *and* DSS *are secure, then Scheme 1 is secure.*

4.1 Observations and Optimizations

Depending on the properties of the used accumulator scheme, one can reduce the signature size from $\mathcal{O}(n)$ to $\mathcal{O}(1)$. The required properties are as follows:

(1) The accumulator scheme needs to support batch-membership verification. Formally, this means that there are two additional algorithms AWitCreateB and AVerifyB, which are defined as follows:
   $\mathsf{AWitCreateB}((\mathsf{sk}^{\sim}_{\mathsf{acc}}, \mathsf{pk_{acc}}), \mathsf{acc}_{\mathcal{X}}, \mathsf{aux}, \mathcal{Y})$ is an deterministic algorithm that takes a key pair $(\mathsf{sk}^{\sim}_{\mathsf{acc}}, \mathsf{pk_{acc}})$, an accumulator $\mathsf{acc}_{\mathcal{X}}$, auxiliary information aux and a set $\mathcal{Y}$. It returns $\perp$, if $\mathcal{Y} \nsubseteq \mathcal{X}$, and a witness $\mathsf{wit}_{\mathcal{Y}}$ for $\mathcal{Y}$ otherwise.

$\mathsf{AVerifyB}(\mathsf{pk_{acc}}, \mathsf{acc}_{\mathcal{X}}, \mathsf{wit}_{\mathcal{Y}}, \mathcal{Y})$ is a deterministic algorithm that takes a public key $\mathsf{pk_{acc}}$, an accumulator $\mathsf{acc}_{\mathcal{X}}$, a witness $\mathsf{wit}_{\mathcal{Y}}$ and a set $\mathcal{Y}$. It returns `true` if $\mathsf{wit}_{\mathcal{Y}}$ is a witness for $\mathcal{Y} \subseteq \mathcal{X}$ and `false` otherwise.

(2) The accumulator scheme fulfills the quasi-commutativity property, i.e., with ρ being a fixed randomness it holds that

$$\begin{aligned}&\forall\ (\mathsf{sk}^{\sim}_{\mathsf{acc}}, \mathsf{pk_{acc}}) \leftarrow \mathsf{AGen}(1^{\lambda}), \forall\ \mathcal{X}, \forall\ x \in \mathcal{X}, \forall\ \mathcal{Y} \subset \mathcal{X}\\ &(\mathsf{acc}_{\mathcal{X}}, \mathsf{aux}) \leftarrow \mathsf{AEval}((\mathsf{sk}^{\sim}_{\mathsf{acc}}, \mathsf{pk_{acc}}), \mathcal{X}; \rho) :\\ &\mathsf{AEval}((\mathsf{sk}^{\sim}_{\mathsf{acc}}, \mathsf{pk_{acc}}), \mathcal{X} \setminus \mathcal{Y}; \rho) = \mathsf{AWitCreateB}((\mathsf{sk}^{\sim}_{\mathsf{acc}}, \mathsf{pk_{acc}}), \mathsf{acc}_{\mathcal{X}}, \mathsf{aux}, \mathcal{Y}).\end{aligned}$$

(3) It is possible to publicly add values to an accumulator.

Refer to [17, Table 1] for a list of accumulators providing the required properties. From (1), (2), and (3) it is straightforward to derive the following corollary:

Corollary 1. *For schemes fulfilling (1), (2), and (3), it holds that* $\forall\{x, y\} \subseteq \mathcal{X}$*, one can use* $\mathsf{wit}_{\{x\}\cup\{y\}}$ *and* $\mathsf{acc}_{\mathcal{X}}$ *to attest that* x *is a member of* $\mathsf{acc}_{\mathcal{X}\setminus\{y\}}$*. Furthermore, one can efficiently compute* $\mathsf{wit}_{\{x\}\cup\{y\}}$ *from* $\mathsf{wit}_{\{x\}}$ *and* y*.*

Then, only a single witness needs to be stored and verification is performed with respect to this witness. Redaction is performed by publicly updating the witness (can be interpreted as removing elements from the accumulator). Such a scheme generalizes the RSS for sets from [32], which builds upon the RSA accumulator. For accumulator schemes where (3) does not hold, one can still obtain constant size signatures by setting $\mathsf{red} \leftarrow \mathsf{aux}$. Upon Redact, red is not updated.

Our construction may look similar to the one in [29]. However, in contrast to our construction, they require a rather specific definition of accumulators, which they call trapdoor accumulators. Trapdoor accumulators differ from conventional accumulators regarding their features and security properties. In particular, they need to support updates of the accumulated set without modifying the accumulator itself. Further, they require a non-standard property denoted as strong collision resistance, which can be seen as a combination of conventional collision resistance and indistinguishability. Clearly, such a specific accumulator model limits the general applicability.

5 Redactable Signatures for Linear Documents

We build our RSS for linear documents upon the RSS for sets presented in the previous section. From an abstract point of view, moving from sets to linear documents means to move from an unordered message to an ordered one. A naive approach to assign an ordering to the message blocks would be to concatenate each message block with its position in the message and insert these extended tuples into the accumulator. However, such an approach trivially contradicts transparency, since the positions of the messages would reveal if redactions have taken place. Thus, inspired by [15], we choose some indistinguishable accumulator scheme and use accumulators to encode the positions. More precisely, with n being the number of message blocks, we draw a sequence of n uniformly random

$\mathsf{KeyGen}(1^\lambda)$: This algorithm fixes a redactable signature scheme $\mathbf{RS}(\text{ord}) = \{\mathbf{KeyGen}, \mathbf{Sign}, \mathbf{Verify}, \mathbf{Redact}\}$ for sets (with ord(·) as defined below) and an indistinguishable accumulator scheme $\mathsf{Acc} = \{\mathsf{AGen}, \mathsf{AEval}, \mathsf{AWitCreate}, \mathsf{AVerify}\}$, runs $(\mathsf{sk}_{\mathsf{acc}}, \mathsf{pk}_{\mathsf{acc}}) \leftarrow \mathsf{AGen}(1^\lambda, \infty)$, $(\mathbf{sk}, \mathbf{pk}) \leftarrow \mathbf{KeyGen}(1^\lambda)$ and returns $(\mathsf{sk}, \mathsf{pk}) \leftarrow ((\mathbf{sk}, \mathsf{sk}_{\mathsf{acc}}, \mathsf{pk}_{\mathsf{acc}}), (\mathbf{pk}, \mathsf{pk}_{\mathsf{acc}}))$.

$\mathsf{Sign}(\mathsf{sk}, M, \mathsf{ADM})$: This algorithm chooses $(r_i)_{i=1}^{|M|} \xleftarrow{R} \mathsf{Dom}(\mathsf{acc})^{|M|}$, sets $M' \leftarrow \emptyset$ and computes for all r_i:

$$(\mathsf{acc}_i, \mathsf{aux}) \leftarrow \mathsf{AEval}((\mathsf{sk}_{\mathsf{acc}}, \mathsf{pk}_{\mathsf{acc}}), \cup_{j=1}^{i}\{r_j\}), \mathsf{WIT}_i \leftarrow (\mathsf{wit}_{i_j})_{j=1}^{i}, \text{ where } \mathsf{wit}_{i_j} \leftarrow \mathsf{AWitCreate}((\mathsf{sk}_{\mathsf{acc}}, \mathsf{pk}_{\mathsf{acc}}), \mathsf{acc}_i, \mathsf{aux}, r_j).$$

Then it computes $\hat{\sigma} \leftarrow \mathbf{Sign}(\mathbf{sk}, \bigcup_{i=1}^{|M|}\{(m_i||\mathsf{acc}_i||r_i)\}, \mathsf{ADM})$. Finally, it returns (M, σ) and red, where $\sigma \leftarrow (\hat{\sigma}, (\mathsf{acc}_i)_{i=1}^{|M|}, (\mathsf{WIT}_i)_{i=1}^{|M|}, (r_i)_{i=1}^{|M|})$ and $\mathsf{red} \leftarrow \emptyset$.

$\mathsf{Verify}(\mathsf{pk}, \sigma, M)$: This algorithm checks whether $\mathbf{Verify}(\mathbf{pk}, \bigcup_{i=1}^{|M|}\{(m_i||\mathsf{acc}_i||r_i)\}, \hat{\sigma}) = 1$. Furthermore, it verifies for all $1 \leq i \leq |M|$ whether $(\mathsf{AVerify}(\mathsf{pk}_{\mathsf{acc}}, \mathsf{acc}_i, \mathsf{wit}_{i_j}, r_j) = 1)_{j=1}^{i}$. Finally it checks whether $\mathsf{ADM} \in \text{span}_{\vdash}(M)$. If all checks hold it returns 1 and 0 otherwise.

$\mathsf{Redact}(\mathsf{pk}, \sigma, M, \mathsf{MOD}, \mathsf{red})$: This algorithm sets $\mathsf{MOD}' \leftarrow \emptyset$ and for all $m_i \in \mathsf{MOD}$: $\mathsf{MOD}' \leftarrow \mathsf{MOD}' \cup \{(m_i||\mathsf{acc}_i||r_i)\}$ runs $(\cdot, \hat{\sigma}') \leftarrow \mathbf{Redact}(\mathbf{pk}, \hat{\sigma}, \bigcup_{i=1}^{|M|}\{(m_i||\mathsf{acc}_i||r_i)\}, \mathsf{MOD}')$. Then for all $m_i \in \mathsf{MOD}$ it removes the corresponding entries from M, $(\mathsf{acc}_i)_{i=1}^{|M|}, (\mathsf{WIT}_i)_{i=1}^{|M|}$ and $(r_i)_{i=1}^{|M|}$ and obtains M', $(\mathsf{acc}_i)_{i=1}^{|M'|}, (\mathsf{WIT}_i)_{i=1}^{|M'|}$ and $(r_i)_{i=1}^{|M'|}$. Finally, it returns (M', σ') and red', where $\sigma' \leftarrow (\hat{\sigma}', (\mathsf{acc}_i)_{i=1}^{|M'|}, (\mathsf{WIT}_i)_{i=1}^{|M'|}, (r_i)_{i=1}^{|M'|})$ and $\mathsf{red}' \leftarrow \emptyset$.

---

ord(ADM): This operator returns ADM.

Scheme 2. A RSS for linear documents

numbers $(r_j)_{j=1}^{n}$ from the accumulation domain. Then, for each message block m_i, $1 \leq i \leq n$, an accumulator acc_i containing $(r_j)_{j=1}^{i}$ is computed (i.e., acc_i contains i randomizers). Finally, for each m_i, one appends $\mathsf{acc}_i||r_i$ and signs the so obtained set $\bigcup_{j=1}^{n}\{(m_i||\mathsf{acc}_i||r_i)\}$ using the RSS for sets. Upon verification, one simply verifies the signature on the set and checks for each i whether one can provide i valid witnesses for $(r_j)_{j=1}^{i}$ with respect to acc_i. Redaction again amounts to throwing away witnesses corresponding to redacted message blocks.

Here, $M = (m_i)_{i=1}^{n}$ is a sequence of message blocks m_i, ADM is the corresponding sequence of fixed message blocks, and the operator ord(·) for the underlying RSS for sets simply returns ADM without modification. All possible valid redactions, forming the transitive closure of a message M, with respect to Redact, are denoted as $\text{span}_{\vdash}(M)$, following [15,34]. Note that for ADM it must hold that $\mathsf{ADM} \in \text{span}_{\vdash}(M)$. MOD is modeled as a sequence of message blocks to be redacted and we assume an encoding that allows to uniquely match message block with its corresponding message block in the original message.

Theorem 2. *If* Acc *and* **RS** *are secure, then Scheme 2 is secure.*

We prove Theorem 2 in the extended version of this paper.

5.1 Observations and Optimizations

Depending on the used accumulator scheme, it is possible to reduce the signature size from $\mathcal{O}(n^2)$ to $\mathcal{O}(n)$. Let us assume that (1), (2), and (3) from Sect. 4.1 hold, which means that also Corollary 1 holds. Then, due to (1), one only needs to store one witness $\mathsf{wit}_{\bigcup_{k=1}^{i}\{r_k\}}$ per message block, where i is the position of the block in the message. Furthermore, upon redaction of message block i with corresponding randomizer r_i, one can update the witnesses $\mathsf{wit}_{\bigcup_{k=1}^{j}\{r_j\}}$ for all $i > j \leq |M|$ by computing $\mathsf{wit}'_{r_j} \leftarrow \mathsf{wit}_{\bigcup_{k=1}^{j}\{r_j\}\cup\{r_i\}}$ and removing witness $\mathsf{wit}_{\bigcup_{k=1}^{i}\{r_i\}}$ and randomizer r_i from the signature, which boils down to removing r_i from all accumulators. The so-obtained construction then essentially generalizes the approach of [15], which make (white-box) use of the RSA accumulator. If (3) does not hold, one can use a similar strategy as in Sect. 4.1.

5.2 RSS for Linear Documents with Designated Redactors

The signature size and computational complexity of RSSs can often be improved by explicitly considering the possibility to allow red to be non-empty. In Scheme 3 we follow this approach and present such a generic construction of RSSs for linear documents. Basically, the idea is to compute commitments to the positions of the messages blocks and concatenate them to the respective message blocks. Then, one signs the so obtained set of concatenated messages and commitments using an RSS for sets. Additionally, one includes a non-interactive zero-knowledge proof of an order relation on the committed positions for attesting the correct order of the message blocks. The information red then represents the randomness used to compute the single commitments. Redacting message blocks then simply amounts to removing the single blocks from the signature of the RSS for sets and recomputing a non-interactive proof for the ordering on the remaining commitments. Since redaction control via ADM can straightforwardly be achieved as in Scheme 2, we omit it here for simplicity, i.e., we assume $\mathsf{ADM} = \infty$. Also note that without ADM the operator ord$(\cdot)$ is not required. MOD is defined as in Scheme 2. We emphasize that one can easily obtain constant size red by pseudorandomly generating the randomizers $(r_i)_{i=1}^{|M|}$ and storing the seed for the PRG in red instead of the actual randomizers.

Instantiating proof system Π for R_{ord} can be done straightforwardly by using zero-knowledge set membership proofs. Below, we briefly discuss the efficiency of the instantiations of Scheme 3, when based on three common techniques. We note that the below Σ-protocols can all easily be made non-interactive (having all the required properties) using the Fiat-Shamir transform.

Square Decomposition. An efficient building block for range proofs in hidden order groups is a proof that a secret integer x is positive [6, 24], which is sufficient for our instantiation. Technically, therefore we need an homomorphic integer commitment scheme and R_{ord} for Π is as follows:

$$((C_1, C_2), (x, r)) \in R_{\mathsf{ord}} \iff C_2 - C_1 = \mathsf{Commit}(x; r) \;\wedge\; x \geq 0.$$

$\mathsf{KeyGen}(1^\lambda)$: This algorithm fixes a redactable signature scheme for sets $\mathbf{RS} = \{\mathbf{KeyGen}, \mathbf{Sign}, \mathbf{Verify}, \mathbf{Redact}\}$, a commitment scheme $\mathsf{Com} = (\mathsf{Gen}, \mathsf{Commit}, \mathsf{Open})$ as well as a non-interactive zero-knowledge proof system $\Pi = (\mathsf{Gen}_{\mathsf{crs}}, \mathsf{Proof}, \mathsf{Verify})$ for the following **NP**-relation R_{ord} with $O_i = (x_i, r_i)$:

$$((C_1, C_2), (O_1, O_2)) \in R_{\mathsf{ord}} \iff C_1 = \mathsf{Commit}(x_1; r_1) \ \wedge \ C_2 = \mathsf{Commit}(x_2; r_2) \ \wedge \ x_1 \leq x_2.$$

It runs $(\mathbf{sk}, \mathbf{pk}) \leftarrow \mathbf{KeyGen}(1^\lambda)$, $\mathsf{pp} \leftarrow \mathsf{Gen}(1^\lambda)$, $\mathsf{crs} \leftarrow \mathsf{Gen}_{\mathsf{crs}}(1^\lambda)$, sets $(\mathsf{sk}, \mathsf{pk}) \leftarrow ((\mathbf{sk}, \mathsf{pp}, \mathsf{crs}), (\mathbf{pk}, \mathsf{pp}, \mathsf{crs}))$ and returns $(\mathsf{sk}, \mathsf{pk})$.

$\mathsf{Sign}(\mathsf{sk}, M, \mathsf{ADM})$: If $\mathsf{ADM} \neq \infty$, this algorithm returns $\perp$. Otherwise, it sets $D \leftarrow \emptyset$ and computes for $1 \leq i \leq |M|$: $(C_i, O_i) \leftarrow \mathsf{Commit}(\mathsf{pp}, i)$, $D \leftarrow D \cup \{(C_i || m_i)\}$ and for $1 \leq i < |M|$: $\pi_i \leftarrow \mathsf{Proof}(\mathsf{crs}, (C_i, C_{i+1}), (O_i, O_{i+1}))$. Then, it computes $\hat{\sigma} \leftarrow \mathbf{Sign}(\mathbf{sk}, D, \infty)$ and returns (M, σ), where $\sigma \leftarrow (\hat{\sigma}, (C_i)_{i=1}^{|M|}, (\pi_i)_{i=1}^{|M|-1})$ as the signature and $\mathsf{red} \leftarrow (O_i)_{i=1}^{|M|}$ as private information for the redactor.[a]

$\mathsf{Verify}(\mathsf{pk}, \sigma, M)$: This algorithms sets $D \leftarrow \emptyset$ and for all $m_i \in M : D \leftarrow D \cup \{(C_i || m_i)\}$. It checks whether $\mathbf{Verify}(\mathbf{pk}, D, \hat{\sigma}) = 1$. Furthermore, for $1 \leq i < |M|$ it checks whether $\mathsf{Verify}(\mathsf{crs}, (C_i, C_{i+1}), \pi_i) = 1$. If any of the checks fails it returns 0 and 1 otherwise.

$\mathsf{Redact}(\mathsf{pk}, \sigma, M, \mathsf{MOD}, \mathsf{red})$: This algorithm sets $\mathsf{MOD}' \leftarrow \emptyset$ and for all $m_i \in \mathsf{MOD} : \mathsf{MOD}' \leftarrow \mathsf{MOD}' \cup \{(C_i || m_i)\}$. Then it runs $(\cdot, \hat{\sigma}') \leftarrow \mathbf{Redact}(\mathbf{pk}, \hat{\sigma}, \bigcup_{i=1}^{|M|}\{(C_i || m_i)\}, \mathsf{MOD}')$. Then for all $m_i \in \mathsf{MOD}$ it removes the corresponding entries from M, $(C_i)_{i=1}^{|M|}$ and $(O_i)_{i=1}^{|M|}$ to obtain M', $(C_i)_{i=1}^{|M'|}$ and $(O_i)_{i=1}^{|M'|}$. In the end, it computes for $1 \leq i < |M'|$: $\pi_i \leftarrow \mathsf{Proof}(\mathsf{crs}, (C_i, C_{i+1}), (O_i, O_{i+1}))$, sets $\sigma' \leftarrow (\hat{\sigma}', (C_i)_{i=1}^{|M'|}, (\pi_i)_{i=1}^{|M'|-1})$, $\mathsf{red}' \leftarrow (O_i)_{i=1}^{|M'|}$ and returns (M', σ') and red'.

[a] We note that we set $\mathsf{red} \leftarrow (O_i)_{i=1}^{|M|} = (m_i, r_i)_{i=1}^{|M|}$ for notational convenience, while one would only require $\mathsf{red} \leftarrow (r_i)_{i=1}^{|M|}$.

Scheme 3. A designated redactor RSS for linear documents

This approach yields $O(n)$ signature generation cost, signature size and verification cost and has a constant size public key. It, however, only works in a hidden order group setting.

For the subsequent two approaches we need to introduce an upper bound k on the number of message blocks which will be a parameter of Scheme 3.

Multi-Base Decomposition. This technique for range proofs works by decomposing the secret integer $x = \sum_{i=1}^{n} G_i \cdot b_i$ with $b_i \in [0, u-1]$ into a (multi)-base representation and then proving that every b_i belongs to the respective small set ([25], cf. [13] for an overview). It also works in the prime order group setting. Here, the relation R_{ord} for Π is as follows:

$$((C_1, C_2), (x, r)) \in R_{\mathsf{ord}} \iff C_2 - C_1 = \mathsf{Commit}(x; r) \ \wedge \ 0 \leq x < k.$$

This approach yields $O(n \log k)$ signature generation costs, signature size and verification costs and a constant size public key.

Signature-Based Approach. This technique [11] pursues the idea of signing every element in the interval[8] using a suitable signature scheme (DKeyGen, DSign, DVerify). In our application let the interval be $[0, k[$ and let us denote the corresponding public signatures by $\sigma = (\sigma_0, \sigma_1, \ldots, \sigma_{k-1})$. Now, proving membership of x in $[0, k[$ amounts to the relation R_{ord} under crs being σ and the respective public key pk_σ (public parameters):

$$((C_1, C_2), (x, r)) \in R_{\mathsf{ord}} \iff C_2 - C_1 = \mathsf{Commit}(x; r) \;\wedge \; \exists\, i \in [0, k[\; : \mathsf{DVerify}(\mathsf{pk}_\sigma, x, \sigma_i) = 1.$$

This approach yields $O(n)$ signature generation cost, signature size and verification cost. The crs representing the public signatures and the verification key may be included into the public key of **RS**, yielding a public key of size $O(k)$.

Finally, we prove Theorem 3 in the extended version of this paper.

Theorem 3. *If* Com, *Π, and* **RS** *are secure, then Scheme 3 is secure.*

References

1. Ahn, J.H., Boneh, D., Camenisch, J., Hohenberger, S., Shelat, A., Waters, B.: Computing on authenticated data. In: Cramer, R. (ed.) TCC 2012. LNCS, vol. 7194, pp. 1–20. Springer, Heidelberg (2012)
2. Attrapadung, N., Libert, B., Peters, T.: Computing on authenticated data: new privacy definitions and constructions. In: Wang, X., Sako, K. (eds.) ASIACRYPT 2012. LNCS, vol. 7658, pp. 367–385. Springer, Heidelberg (2012)
3. Attrapadung, N., Libert, B., Peters, T.: Efficient completely context-hiding quotable and linearly homomorphic signatures. In: Kurosawa, K., Hanaoka, G. (eds.) PKC 2013. LNCS, vol. 7778, pp. 386–404. Springer, Heidelberg (2013)
4. Bauer, D., Blough, D.M., Mohan, A.: Redactable signatures on data with dependencies and their application to personal health records. In: WPES, pp. 91–100 (2009)
5. Benaloh, J.C., de Mare, M.: One-way accumulators: a decentralized alternative to digital signatures. In: Helleseth, T. (ed.) EUROCRYPT 1993. LNCS, vol. 765, pp. 274–285. Springer, Heidelberg (1994)
6. Boudot, F.: Efficient proofs that a committed number lies in an interval. In: Preneel, B. (ed.) EUROCRYPT 2000. LNCS, vol. 1807, pp. 431–444. Springer, Heidelberg (2000)
7. Brown, J., Blough, D.M.: Verifiable and redactable medical documents. In: AMIA (2012)
8. Brzuska, C., et al.: Redactable signatures for tree-structured data: definitions and constructions. In: Zhou, J., Yung, M. (eds.) ACNS 2010. LNCS, vol. 6123, pp. 87–104. Springer, Heidelberg (2010)
9. Brzuska, C., Fischlin, M., Lehmann, A., Schröder, D.: Unlinkability of Sanitizable Signatures. In: Nguyen, P.Q., Pointcheval, D. (eds.) PKC 2010. LNCS, vol. 6056, pp. 444–461. Springer, Heidelberg (2010)

[8] Actually, [11] also propose a combination of this approach with a (multi)-base decomposition, which we do not consider here for brevity.

10. Brzuska, C., Pöhls, H.C., Samelin, K.: Efficient and perfectly unlinkable sanitizable signatures without group signatures. In: Katsikas, S., Agudo, I. (eds.) EuroPKI 2013. LNCS, vol. 8341, pp. 12–30. Springer, Heidelberg (2014)
11. Camenisch, J.L., Chaabouni, R., Shelat, A.: Efficient protocols for set membership and range proofs. In: Pieprzyk, J. (ed.) ASIACRYPT 2008. LNCS, vol. 5350, pp. 234–252. Springer, Heidelberg (2008)
12. Camenisch, J., Dubovitskaya, M., Haralambiev, K., Kohlweiss, M.: Composable & modular anonymous credentials: definitions and practical constructions. IACR Cryptology ePrint Archive 2015, 580 (2015). http://eprint.iacr.org/2015/580
13. Canard, S., Coisel, I., Jambert, A., Traoré, J.: New results for the practical use of range proofs. In: Katsikas, S., Agudo, I. (eds.) EuroPKI 2013. LNCS, vol. 8341, pp. 47–64. Springer, Heidelberg (2014)
14. Canard, S., Jambert, A.: On extended sanitizable signature schemes. In: Pieprzyk, J. (ed.) CT-RSA 2010. LNCS, vol. 5985, pp. 179–194. Springer, Heidelberg (2010)
15. Chang, E.-C., Lim, C.L., Xu, J.: Short redactable signatures using random trees. In: Fischlin, M. (ed.) CT-RSA 2009. LNCS, vol. 5473, pp. 133–147. Springer, Heidelberg (2009)
16. Demirel, D., Derler, D., Hanser, C., Pöhls, H.C., Slamanig, D., Traverso, G.: PRISMACLOUD D4.4: overview of functional and malleable signature schemes. Technical report, H2020 Prismacloud (2015). www.prismacloud.eu
17. Derler, D., Hanser, C., Slamanig, D.: Revisiting cryptographic accumulators, additional properties and relations to other primitives. In: Nyberg, K. (ed.) CT-RSA 2015. LNCS, vol. 9048, pp. 127–144. Springer, Heidelberg (2015)
18. Derler, D., Slamanig, D.: Rethinking privacy for extended sanitizable signatures and a black-box construction of strongly private schemes. In: Au, M.-H., Miyaji, A. (eds.) ProvSec 2015. LNCS, vol. 9451, pp. 455–474. Springer, Heidelberg (2015). Full Version: IACR Cryptology ePrint Report 2015/843
19. El Gamal, T.: A public key cryptosystem and a signature scheme based on discrete logarithms. In: Blakely, G.R., Chaum, D. (eds.) CRYPTO 1984. LNCS, vol. 196, pp. 10–18. Springer, Heidelberg (1985)
20. Haber, S., Hatano, Y., Honda, Y., Horne, W.G., Miyazaki, K., Sander, T., Tezoku, S., Yao, D.: Efficient signature schemes supporting redaction, pseudonymization, and data deidentification. In: ASIACCS, pp. 353–362 (2008)
21. Johnson, R., Molnar, D., Song, D., Wagner, D.: Homomorphic signature schemes. In: Preneel, B. (ed.) CT-RSA 2002. LNCS, vol. 2271, pp. 244–262. Springer, Heidelberg (2002)
22. Klonowski, M., Lauks, A.: Extended sanitizable signatures. In: Rhee, M.S., Lee, B. (eds.) ICISC 2006. LNCS, vol. 4296, pp. 343–355. Springer, Heidelberg (2006)
23. Kundu, A., Bertino, E.: Privacy-preserving authentication of trees and graphs. Int. J. Inf. Sec. **12**(6), 467–494 (2013)
24. Lipmaa, H.: On diophantine complexity and statistical zero-knowledge arguments. In: Laih, C.-S. (ed.) ASIACRYPT 2003. LNCS, vol. 2894, pp. 398–415. Springer, Heidelberg (2003)
25. Lipmaa, H., Asokan, N., Niemi, V.: Secure vickrey auctions without threshold trust. In: Blaze, M. (ed.) FC 2002. LNCS, vol. 2357, pp. 87–101. Springer, Heidelberg (2002)
26. Miyazaki, K., Hanaoka, G., Imai, H.: Digitally signed document sanitizing scheme based on bilinear maps. In: ASIACCS, pp. 343–354 (2006)
27. Miyazaki, K., Iwamura, M., Matsumoto, T., Sasaki, R., Yoshiura, H., Tezuka, S., Imai, H.: Digitally signed document sanitizing scheme with disclosure condition control. IEICE Trans. **88–A**(1), 239–246 (2005)

28. Miyazaki, K., Susaki, S., Iwamura, M., Matsumoto, T., Sasaki, R., Yoshiura, H.: Digital documents sanitizing problem. IEICE Technical report, ISEC2003-20 (2003)
29. Pöhls, H.C., Samelin, K.: On updatable redactable signatures. In: Boureanu, I., Owesarski, P., Vaudenay, S. (eds.) ACNS 2014. LNCS, vol. 8479, pp. 457–475. Springer, Heidelberg (2014)
30. Pöhls, H.C., Samelin, K.: Accountable redactable signatures. In: ARES, pp. 60–69 (2015)
31. Pöhls, H.C., Samelin, K., de Meer, H., Posegga, J.: Flexible redactable signature schemes for trees - extended security model and construction. In: SECRYPT 2012, pp. 113–125 (2012)
32. Pöhls, H.C., Samelin, K., Posegga, J., de Meer, H.: Length-hiding redactable signatures from one-way accumulators in $O(n)$ (MIP-1201). Technical report (2012)
33. Samelin, K., Pöhls, H.C., Bilzhause, A., Posegga, J., de Meer, H.: On structural signatures for tree data structures MIP-1201. In: Bao, F., Samarati, P., Zhou, J. (eds.) ACNS 2012. LNCS, vol. 7341, pp. 171–187. Springer, Heidelberg (2012)
34. Samelin, K., Pöhls, H.C., Bilzhause, A., Posegga, J., de Meer, H.: Redactable signatures for independent removal of structure and content. In: Ryan, M.D., Smyth, B., Wang, G. (eds.) ISPEC 2012. LNCS, vol. 7232, pp. 17–33. Springer, Heidelberg (2012)
35. Slamanig, D., Rass, S.: Generalizations and extensions of redactable signatures with applications to electronic healthcare. In: De Decker, B., Schaumüller-Bichl, I. (eds.) CMS 2010. LNCS, vol. 6109, pp. 201–213. Springer, Heidelberg (2010)
36. Steinfeld, R., Bull, L., Zheng, Y.: Content extraction signatures. In: Kim, K. (ed.) ICISC 2001. LNCS, vol. 2288, pp. 285–304. Springer, Heidelberg (2002)
37. Wu, Z.Y., Hsueh, C.W., Tsai, C.Y., Lai, F., Lee, H.C., Chung, Y.: Redactable signatures for signed CDA documents. J. Med. Syst. **36**(3), 1795–1808 (2012)

On the Security of the Schnorr Signature Scheme and DSA Against Related-Key Attacks

Hiraku Morita[1,2](✉), Jacob C. N. Schuldt[2], Takahiro Matsuda[2], Goichiro Hanaoka[2], and Tetsu Iwata[1]

[1] Nagoya University, Nagoya, Japan
h_morita@echo.nuee.nagoya-u.ac.jp, iwata@cse.nagoya-u.ac.jp
[2] National Institute of Advanced Industrial Science and Technology (AIST), Tokyo, Japan
{jacob.schuldt,t-matsuda,hanaoka-goichiro}@aist.go.jp

Abstract. In the ordinary security model for signature schemes, we consider an adversary that may forge a signature on a new message using only his knowledge of other valid message and signature pairs. To take into account side channel attacks such as tampering or fault-injection attacks, Bellare and Kohno (Eurocrypt 2003) formalized related-key attacks (RKA), where stronger adversaries are considered. In RKA for signature schemes, the adversary can also manipulate the signing key and obtain signatures for the modified key. This paper considers RKA security of two established signature schemes: the Schnorr signature scheme and (a well-known variant of) DSA. First, we show that these signature schemes are secure against a weak notion of RKA. Second, we demonstrate that, on the other hand, neither the Schnorr signature scheme nor DSA achieves the standard notion of RKA security, by showing concrete attacks on these. Lastly, we show that a slight modification of both the Schnorr signature scheme and (the considered variant of) DSA yields fully RKA secure schemes.

Keywords: Related-key attacks · Schnorr signatures · DSA

1 Introduction

1.1 Background

A signature scheme is a cryptographic public key primitive which guarantees validity of messages. Up until now, many schemes have been proposed such as the ElGamal signature scheme [15], the Schnorr signature scheme [28], and DSA [1].The commonly accepted security notion for a signature scheme is existential unforgeability against chosen message attacks, which guarantees that even if an adversary can obtain signatures on arbitrarymessages of its choice, the adversary cannot forge a valid signature on a new message. The Schnorr signature scheme,

J.C.N. Schuldt—Supported by JSPS KAKENHI Grant Number 15K16006.

S. Kwon and A. Yun (Eds.): ICISC 2015, LNCS 9558, pp. 20–35, 2016.
DOI: 10.1007/978-3-319-30840-1_2

and two variants of DSA were proven to satisfy this notion in the random oracle model [25,26], under the discrete logarithm (DL) assumption.

Related-key attacks (RKA), stronger attacks, were formalized by Bellare and Kohno [5]. RKA security captures security against practical attacks such as tampering or fault injection, which enable adversaries to alter a hardware-stored secret key and observe the output of the algorithm using the modified key. Thus, RKA security captures practical attacks which might cause security issues in practice. Therefore, it is an important question whether primitives are secure against RKA attacks even if they are already shown to be secure against ordinary attacks.

RKA for signature schemes allows an adversary to obtain not only valid message and signature pairs, but also signatures under a modified key. RKA security is defined with respect to the related-key deriving (RKD) functions with which an adversary is allowed to modify the secret key. For example, we consider linear functions, affine functions, and polynomial functions. Since RKA considers a broader class of attacks than ordinary attacks, security against RKA is much stronger than ordinary security.

However, only a few generic constructions for achieving RKA secure signatures have been proposed. Bellare, Cash, and Miller [4] studied relations between RKA secure primitives, and in particular showed that an RKA secure pseudorandom function (PRF) can be used to convert a signature scheme secure against ordinary attacks, into a scheme providing RKA security. The conversion is relatively simple: before generating the verification and signing key, apply the PRF to the randomness used by the key generation algorithm, and then store the randomness instead of the generated signing key. Now, since the signing key of the original scheme is no longer stored, this has to be re-generated whenever a message is signed. This is done by applying the PRF to the stored randomness, and then re-running the key generation algorithm. Bellare, Cash, and Miller [4] showed that, via this conversion, it is possible to lift the RKA security of the PRF to the signature scheme. Used in combination with the recently proposed RKA secure PRF by Abdalla et al. [2], which is shown to be secure under the q-Diffie Hellman Inversion assumption, this allows the conversion of any (ordinary) signature scheme to a scheme which is RKA secure with respect to polynomial functions.

Goyal et al. [21] showed a similar conversion for achieving RKA secure signatures, but based on a correlated-input secure (CIS) hash function. Furthermore, Goyal et al. constructed a very efficient CIS hash function secure under the q-Diffie Hellman Inversion assumption, which would lead to signatures that are RKA secure with respect to polynomials. However, this construction only achieves selective security; a weak and non-adaptive security notion that requires the adversary to submit the RKD functions before seeing the verification key of the signature scheme.

Building upon the work on non-malleable key derivation functions (nm-KDFs) [17], Qin et al. [27] introduced the notion of continuous nm-KDFs, and used these in a similar conversion to the above to construct an RKA secure signature scheme with respect to polynomial functions under standard assumptions. The proposed construction of an nm-KDF can furthermore be extended to provide security with respect to any RKD function class that has the properties the authors denote "high output entropy" and "input-output collision resistant". Interestingly, the transformation into RKA-secure primitives shown in [12] can be understood as applying an nm-KDF [17,27] to the secret key.

Since a signature scheme is an essential cryptographic primitive, clarifying the RKA security of various constructions is of interest from both a practical and a theoretical point of view. Specifically, studying the RKA security of well-known signatures such as the Schnorr signature scheme and DSA is important due to their widespread use, in particular in the case of DSA, which is employed in many practical implementations. However, besides the negative result by Bao et al. [3], who showed that the Schnorr signature scheme and DSA are not RKA secure against bit flipping attack, it is not known whether either scheme can provide any form of RKA security. Furthermore, simply applying the above transformations might not always be desirable due to the relatively high performance penalties these conversions imply.

1.2 Our Contributions

In this paper, we first show that both the Schnorr signature scheme and a DSA variant are secure against a weak notion of RKA (wRKA) that does not allow messages queried to the RKA signing oracle to be a part of a forgery. Second, we show that the Schnorr signature scheme and the original DSA are vulnerable to the standard notion of simple linear RKA. We then construct (standard) RKA secure signature schemes based on the Schnorr signature scheme and DSA. Specifically, as our main technical results, we show the following four results:

- The Schnorr signature scheme is secure against wRKA with respect to polynomial functions.
- A well-known variant of DSA by [26] is secure against wRKA with respect to polynomial functions.
- Slightly modifying the signing and verification algorithms of the Schnorr signature scheme yields an RKA secure scheme with respect to polynomial functions.
- Slightly modifying the signing and verification algorithms of DSA yields an RKA secure scheme with respect to polynomial functions.

In other words, the Schnorr signature scheme, which is secure against wRKA with respect to polynomial functions, but not RKA secure even for weak attacks with respect to linear functions, can achieve full RKA security with respect to polynomial functions by slightly modifying the scheme. While DSA is not RKA secure with respect to linear functions, the DSA variant from [26] is secure against wRKA, and by slightly modifying this scheme, full RKA security with respect to polynomial functions can be achieved. Both the improved Schnorr signature scheme and the improved DSA variant are proven to be RKA secure with respect to polynomial functions in the random oracle model, under the d-strong discrete logarithm (d-SDL) assumption. As a corollary, the improved signature schemes are RKA secure with respect to affine functions under the standard discrete logarithm (DL) assumption, since the 1-SDL assumption is equivalent to the DL assumption, and polynomials of degree 1 are affine functions.

Note that our modifications of the Schnorr signature scheme and DSA only increase the computational cost of signing with a single exponentiation, while the computational cost of verification, signature size, and key sizes remain unchanged. Hence, in contrast to using a conversion based on continuous nm-KDF [17,27] or RKA secure PRFs [2,4], our modifications maintain the efficiency of the Schnorr signature scheme and DSA. Furthermore, unlike all of the above mentioned conversions for achieving RKA security, our modifications of the Schnorr signature scheme and DSA do not require the verification and signing key to change. This is a virtue for schemes which are already deployed, such as DSA, since key management and verification key certificates remain unchanged. Lastly, we would like to emphasize that in our proofs of security for our improved Schnorr signature scheme and the improved DSA, we do not restrict the number of RKA signing oracle queries or rely on a "self-destruct" mechanism [16,17] which prevents the adversary from making any further queries once it is detected that the signing key has been tampered with.

1.3 Related Work

Gennaro et al. [18] show how to recover the key of almost any cryptographic primitive assuming the adversary can tamper arbitrarily with the key of the primitive. This implies that RKA security cannot be achieved for every set of RKD functions. On the other hand, Damgård et al. [11,12] showed that in a security model which restricts the number of RKA queries that an adversary is allowed to make, it is possible to achieve security for arbitrary RKD functions. In contrast to this model, which is denoted the bounded leakage and tampering model, we will in this paper consider unrestricted adversaries which are allowed to make an arbitrary number of RKA signing oracle queries. Since Dziembowski, Pietrzak, and Wichs introduced non-malleable codes [14], they have been studied and found to have a good application in the construction of RKA secure cryptosystems. While non-malleable codes in themselves are not sufficient to provide full RKA security, continuous non-malleable codes, which were initiated in [16], enables this. However, the security of the constructions presented in [16] relies on a self-destruct mechanism that will prevent an attacker from interacting with the system once it has been detected that the internal state of the systems is being tampered with. In contrast, the continuous nm-KDF proposed by Qin et al. [27] does not require a self-destruct mechanism, and can be used to construct RKA secure public key primitives for a large class of RKD functions. Jafargholi and Wichs [22] defined two factors which yield four levels of security of continuous nm-KDF depending on (I) whether tampering is applied to the original secret key persistently or applied to the changed secret key (classified by "persistent" and "non-persistent"), (II) whether tampering to an invalid codeword causes a "self-destruct" or not. Lastly, Bellare, Cash, and Miller [4] showed how any RKA secure identity-based encryption scheme leads to an RKA secure signature scheme, and Goyal et al. [21]

showed that the Boneh-Boyen signature scheme [10] satisfied RKA security with respect to a class of certain polynomial RKD functions.

We note that the signature schemes EdDSA by Bernstein et al. [7] and ECDSA+ by Koblitz and Menezes [24] resemble our schemes provided in Sects. 5.1 and 6.1, respectively, in the sense that one of the inputs to the hash function is the verification key. However, the schemes in [7,24] are proposed for a different context and RKA security is not considered.

2 Preliminaries

Here, we review basic notation and definitions of terminology.

2.1 Notation

Throughout the paper, we will use the following notation: For the set of natural numbers $\mathbb{N}$, let $\lambda \in \mathbb{N}$ be a security parameter. Let $\mathbb{G}$ be a group of prime order q, where q is a λ-bit prime. Let g be a generator of $\mathbb{G}$. Let $\mathbb{Z}_q^* = \mathbb{Z}_q \setminus \{0\}$. A function $F : \mathbb{N} \to \mathbb{R}$ is negligible if it vanishes faster than the inverse of any polynomial. We write $\Pr[A : B]$ to denote a probability that the predicate A is true after the event B occurred. $\mathcal{O}(\cdot)$ denotes an order.

2.2 *d*-Strong Discrete Logarithm Assumption

We recall the d-strong discrete logarithm (d-SDL) assumption introduced by Goyal et al. [21]. Let d be a natural number. The d-SDL problem is to compute x given an input $(g, g^x, g^{x^2}, \ldots, g^{x^d}) \in \mathbb{G}^{d+1}$, where $x \xleftarrow{\$} \mathbb{Z}_q$.

For an adversary $\mathcal{A}$ that solves the d-SDL problem over $\mathbb{G}$, we define the advantage as follows:

$$\mathrm{Adv}_{\mathcal{A},\mathbb{G}}^{d\text{-sdl}}(\lambda) = \Pr\left[x' = x : \begin{array}{l} x \xleftarrow{\$} \mathbb{Z}_q \\ x' \leftarrow \mathcal{A}(g, g^x, g^{x^2}, \ldots, g^{x^d}) \end{array}\right].$$

The d-SDL assumption over $\mathbb{G}$ says that the advantage $\mathrm{Adv}_{\mathcal{A},\mathbb{G}}^{d\text{-sdl}}(\lambda)$ is negligible for any polynomial time algorithm $\mathcal{A}$.

It is clear that the 1-SDL assumption is equivalent to the standard DL assumption. Similar to the d-Strong Diffie-Hellman problem [10], the d-SDL problem is easier than the standard DL problem. In particular, more efficient solving algorithms, similar to Jao and Yoshida's algorithm [23] for the d-Strong Diffie-Hellman problem, can likely be constructed for the d-SDL problem.

2.3 Signature

We recall the syntax of signature schemes, introduce functions with respect to which RKA security is considered, and lastly define RKA security for a signature scheme.

Signature Scheme. A signature scheme Σ consists of three algorithms: key generation algorithm, signing algorithm, and verification algorithm. We write

$$\Sigma = (\text{KeyGen}, \text{Sign}, \text{Verify}),$$

where these algorithms have the following interfaces:

$$\begin{aligned}(sk, vk) &\leftarrow \text{KeyGen}(1^\lambda),\\ \sigma &\leftarrow \text{Sign}(m, sk),\\ 1/0 &\leftarrow \text{Verify}(m, \sigma, vk),\end{aligned}$$

and sk, vk, and σ are a signing key, a verification key and a signature, respectively. For any message m and any key pair (sk, vk) generated by KeyGen, the following correctness should be satisfied:

$$\text{Verify}(m, \text{Sign}(m, sk), vk) = 1.$$

Related-Key Attack. In the ordinary attack model, an adversary is allowed to obtain signatures on arbitrary messages of its choice. In the RKA model, an adversary is also allowed to modify the signing key and obtain signatures on arbitrary messages of its choice under the modified signing key.

The RKA model, for instance, captures a realistic attack in which an adversary manipulates a hardware-stored secret key by electromagnetic radiation and obtains the outputs of the signing algorithm. This is called tampering or a fault injection attack. RKA is formalized as a security game that also allows an adversary to obtain signatures for modified keys. Thus, an adversary is allowed to query related-key deriving (RKD) functions [5] as well as messages to the signing oracle.

An RKD function is a function $\phi : K \to K$, where K is the signing key space. Let Φ be a class of RKD functions. The RKD function class Φ consists of operations by which an adversary is allowed to manipulate a signing key. Normally, Φ is assumed to contain the identity function id so that RKA security implies standard EUF-CMA [20]. We assume that it is easy to check whether a function is contained in a class Φ, and that RKD functions are efficiently computable.

Following [6], we consider three types of RKD functions: linear functions, affine functions, and polynomial functions. In the following, K is assumed to have an appropriate algebraic structure (group or finite field). In this paper, we will consider signature schemes whose signing key space is $\mathbb{Z}_q$ with prime q, which constitutes a field, as required.

Linear functions. Assume that $(K, *)$ is a group. The class of linear functions is defined as follows: $\Phi^{\text{lin}} = \{\phi_\Delta \mid \Delta \in K\}$, where $\phi_\Delta(k) = k * \Delta$ for a key $k \in K$. Note that "$*$" represents addition or multiplication depending on the group that is considered.

Affine functions. Assume that K is a finite field. The class of affine functions is defined as follows: $\Phi^{\text{aff}} = \{\phi_{\alpha,\beta} \mid \alpha, \beta \in K\}$, where $\phi_{\alpha,\beta}(k) = \alpha \cdot k + \beta$ for a key $k \in K$.

Polynomial functions. Assume that K is a finite field. The class of polynomial functions is defined as follows: $\Phi^{\text{poly(d)}} = \{\phi_f \mid f \in K_d[x]\}$, where $K_d[x]$ is the set of polynomials over K with degree at most d, and $\phi_f(k) = f(k)$ for a key $k \in K$.

RKA security is getting stronger and harder to achieve, as it moves from linear functions to affine functions to polynomial functions. In this paper, we only consider such algebraic operations.

Φ-EUF-CM-RKA [4]. We recall existential unforgeability under chosen message and RKA defined by RKD function class Φ. This security of a signature scheme, which we will denote by Φ-EUF-CM-RKA, is formalized by the following game between an adversary $\mathcal{A}$ and a challenger $\mathcal{B}$.

Initialization. The challenger $\mathcal{B}$ runs KeyGen(1^λ) to obtain a signing key sk and a verification key vk. $\mathcal{B}$ sets a list $M \leftarrow \emptyset$. Then, $\mathcal{B}$ gives vk to $\mathcal{A}$.

RKA signing oracle query. For adaptive queries (m_i, ϕ_i) by $\mathcal{A}$, $\mathcal{B}$ returns the signatures $\sigma_i \leftarrow \text{Sign}(m_i, \phi_i(sk))$, where $\phi_i \in \Phi$. If $\phi_i(sk) = sk$, $\mathcal{B}$ records m_i in the list M.

Output. Suppose that $\mathcal{A}$ outputs (m^*, σ^*). If Verify$(m^*, \sigma^*, vk) = 1$ and $m^* \notin M$, then $\mathcal{B}$ outputs 1. Otherwise, $\mathcal{B}$ outputs 0.

Let F be the event that $\mathcal{B}$'s output is 1 in the above game. We define the advantage of $\mathcal{A}$ against Φ-EUF-CM-RKA security as

$$\text{Adv}_{\mathcal{A},\Sigma}^{\Phi\text{-euf-cm-rka}}(\lambda) := \Pr[F].$$

If the advantage $\text{Adv}_{\mathcal{A},\Sigma}^{\Phi\text{-euf-cm-rka}}(\lambda)$ is negligible for any probabilistic polynomial time algorithm $\mathcal{A}$, a signature scheme Σ is said to be Φ-EUF-CM-RKA secure.

We note that the security definition is strong in the sense that the adversary can reuse the message m_i as the forgery even if (m_i, ϕ_i) has been queried to the RKA signing oracle as long as $\phi_i(sk) \neq sk$.

Φ-wEUF-CM-RKA. We also consider a weaker variant of the above notion following the traditional weak existential unforgeability against adaptive chosen-message attacks [20] and the weak existential unforgeability of message authentication codes against RKA [8]. By requiring that the adversary in the above security experiment, produces a forgery on a message m^* which has not previously been submitted to the RKA signing oracle, we obtain the weaker security notion Φ-wEUF-CM-RKA.

Although it can be argued that, in some scenarios, the weaker notion Φ-wEUF-CM-RKA is sufficient to guarantee security, we note that the standard notion used in the literature, corresponds to the stronger notion Φ-EUF-CM-RKA defined above. We will show that the Schnorr signature scheme is $\Phi^{\text{poly(d)}}$-wEUF-CM-RKA secure, but the scheme is vulnerable with respect to Φ^{lin}-EUF-CM-RKA as we demonstrate in Sect. 4.1. The improved Schnorr signature scheme presented in Sect. 5.1 will be proven to be $\Phi^{\text{poly(d)}}$-EUF-CM-RKA secure. We furthermore show that one of the DSA variants from [26] is $\Phi^{\mathrm{poly(d)}}$-wEUF-CM-RKA secure, but the original DSA is vulnerable with respect to Φ^{lin}-EUF-CM-RKA as we demonstrate in Sect. 4.2. Note that it is not known whether the DSA variant is vulnerable to $\Phi^{\mathrm{poly(d)}}$-EUF-CM-RKA, but the improved DSA presented in Sect. 6.1 will be proven to be $\Phi^{\mathrm{poly(d)}}$-EUF-CM-RKA secure. For further details, see Sects. 4, 5, and 6.

We note that, stronger models of RKA security that is often called fault attacks have been considered for round-based symmetric encryption schemes [9,13,19]. These models allow the adversary to introduce faults (i.e. modification of the input or the internal state) in the individual rounds of the encryption algorithm, which, for example, lead to recovering a secret key. A similar extension, in which the adversary can choose when in the execution of the signing algorithm it would like to modify the signing key, could be considered for the RKA security of signature schemes. However, in this paper, we focus on the standard RKA notion (and its weaker variant) introduced above.

2.4 Schnorr Signature Scheme

The Schnorr signature scheme was proposed by Schnorr in 1989 [28] and was proven to be secure in the random oracle model based on the discrete logarithm assumption [25]. Recall that $\mathbb{G}$ is a group of prime order q, and g is a generator. The three algorithms, key generation, signing, and verification algorithms, are defined as follows.

- KeyGen: This algorithm takes 1^λ as input, and generates a signing key sk and a verification key vk as follows.
  1. Choose $x \xleftarrow{\$} \mathbb{Z}_q$ and let $y \leftarrow g^x$.
  2. Choose a hash function $H : \{0,1\}^* \to \mathbb{Z}_q$.
  3. Output $sk = x, vk = (y, H)$.
- Sign: This algorithm takes a message $m \in \{0,1\}^*$ and the signing key sk as input, and generates a signature σ as follows.
  1. Choose $t \xleftarrow{\$} \mathbb{Z}_q$ and let $r \leftarrow g^t$.
  2. Let $h \leftarrow H(m \,\|\, r)$.
  3. Let $s \leftarrow x \cdot h + t \mod q$.
  4. Output $\sigma \leftarrow (h, s)$.
- Verify: This algorithm takes a message m, a signature σ, and the verification key vk as input, and verifies the signature as follows.
  1. Let $r' \leftarrow g^s y^{-h}$.
  2. Let $h' \leftarrow H(m \,\|\, r')$.
  3. If $h' = h$, return 1, otherwise return 0.

2.5 DSA

DSA was proposed as the US Digital Signature Standard [1] in 1994. First, we recall the original DSA scheme.

Let p and q be primes, where q is a prime factor of $p - 1$. Let $g \in \mathbb{Z}_p^*$ be a generator of prime order q. DSA is defined by the following three algorithms:

- KeyGen: This algorithm takes 1^λ as input, and generates a signing key sk and a verification key vk as follows.
  1. Choose $x \xleftarrow{\$} \mathbb{Z}_q^*$ and let $y \leftarrow g^x \mod p$.
  2. Choose a hash function $H : \{0,1\}^* \to \mathbb{Z}_q$.
  3. Output $sk = x, vk = (y, H)$.
- Sign: This algorithm takes a message $m \in \{0,1\}^*$ and the signing key sk as input, and generates a signature σ as follows.
  1. Choose $t \xleftarrow{\$} \mathbb{Z}_q^*$ and let $r \leftarrow (g^t \mod p) \mod q$.
  2. Let $s \leftarrow t^{-1}(H(m) + x \cdot r) \mod q$.
  3. Output $\sigma \leftarrow (r, s)$.
- Verify: This algorithm takes a message m, a signature $\sigma = (r, s)$, and the verification key $vk = (y, H)$ as input, and verifies the signature as follows.
  1. Let $r' \leftarrow (g^{H(m)/s} y^{r/s} \mod p) \mod q$.
  2. If $r' = r$, output 1, otherwise output 0.

Variants of DSA. While the original scheme has not been proven to be secure, Pointcheval and Vaudenay [26] proved that two variants of DSA are secure in the sense of standard security in the random oracle model. The first DSA variant uses one additional random oracle H', and the first step of signing algorithm computes $r \leftarrow H'(g^t \mod p)$. The second DSA variant's main difference is that a hash function takes as input not only a message but also the value r. Looking ahead, we will consider a slight modified version of this second variant of DSA in Sect. 6.

On the Collision Resistance of the DSA Mapping from $\mathbb{Z}_p^*$ to $\mathbb{Z}_q$. Note that in Step 1 of the signing algorithm of DSA, we have to map an element $g^t \in \mathbb{Z}_p^*$ to an element $r \in \mathbb{Z}_q$. In [26], Pointcheval and Vaudenay considered this mapping an abstract function from $\mathbb{G}$ to $\mathbb{Z}_q$, where $\mathbb{G}$ is a subgroup of $\mathbb{Z}_p^*$ of order q. To prove security of their second variant of DSA, Pointcheval and Vaudenay made the assumption that this function has a certain collision resistance property. In this paper, we take a similar approach as [26], and assume this function, which we will denote $F_{p,q}$, has the following property:

Let $F_{p,q} : \mathbb{G} \to \mathbb{Z}_q$ be the mapping defined by $\overline{g} \mapsto \overline{g} \mod q$, where $\overline{g} \in \mathbb{G}$, and $\mathbb{G}, q, p$ are the parameters of the group over which DSA is constructed (i.e. $\mathbb{G}$ is a subgroup of $\mathbb{Z}_p^*$ of order q). We say that $F_{p,q}$ is ϵ-collision-resistant if no probabilistic polynomial time algorithm $\mathcal{A}$ can find two distinct elements $\overline{g}_1, \overline{g}_2 \in \mathbb{G}$ such that $F_{p,q}(\overline{g}_1) = F_{p,q}(\overline{g}_2)$ with probability more than ϵ. When ϵ is negligible in the security parameter, we simply say that $F_{p,q}$ is collision resistant.

3 wRKA Security of Signature Schemes

In this section, we show that the Schnorr signature scheme and the second variant of DSA from [26] are $\Phi^{\mathrm{poly}(d)}$-wEUF-CM-RKA secure. We remind the reader that $\Phi^{\mathrm{poly}(d)}$-wEUF-CM-RKA security requires that the message m^* in the forgery must be new and that it has not been submitted to the RKA signing oracle.

First, we show the following theorem regarding the Schnorr signature scheme.

Theorem 1. *Let d be a positive integer. Under the d-SDL assumption over $\mathbb{G}$, the Schnorr signature scheme is $\Phi^{poly(d)}$-wEUF-CM-RKA secure in the random oracle model.*

More precisely, for any probabilistic polynomial time algorithm $\mathcal{A}$ with running time $t_{\mathcal{A}}$, making q_S RKA signing oracle queries, and q_H random oracle queries to H, there exists a probabilistic polynomial time algorithm $\mathcal{B}$ with running time $t_{\mathcal{B}} = 2t_{\mathcal{A}} + \mathcal{O}(q_S + q_H)$ that satisfies the following equation:

$$\mathrm{Adv}_{\mathcal{A},\Sigma}^{\Phi^{poly(d)}\text{-euf-cm-rka}}(\lambda) \leq \left((q_H + q_S)\left(\mathrm{Adv}_{\mathcal{B},\mathbb{G}}^{d\text{-sdl}}(\lambda) + \frac{2q_S + 1}{q}\right)\right)^{1/2}.$$

We leave the proof for the full version of the paper.

Next, we show the following theorem regarding the second DSA variant from [26].

Theorem 2. *Let d be a positive integer, and assume the mapping $F_{p,q}$ is collision resistant. Under the d-SDL assumption over $\mathbb{G}$, the second DSA variant is $\Phi^{poly(d)}$-wEUF-CM-RKA secure in the random oracle model.*

More precisely, assume that $F_{p,q}$ is ϵ-collision-resistant. Then, for any probabilistic polynomial time algorithm $\mathcal{A}$ with running time $t_{\mathcal{A}}$, making q_S RKA signing oracle queries, and q_H random oracle queries to H, there exists a probabilistic polynomial time algorithm $\mathcal{B}$ with running time $t_{\mathcal{B}} = 2t_{\mathcal{A}} + \mathcal{O}(q_S + q_H)$ that satisfies the following equation:

$$\mathrm{Adv}_{\mathcal{A},\Sigma}^{\Phi^{poly(d)}\text{-euf-cm-rka}}(\lambda) \leq \left((q_H + q_S)\left(\mathrm{Adv}_{\mathcal{B},\mathbb{G}}^{d\text{-sdl}}(\lambda) + \frac{1}{q} + \frac{2\epsilon}{q_H + q_S}\right)\right)^{1/2}.$$

We leave the proof for the full version of the paper.

4 Related-Key Attacks Against Signature Schemes

In this section, we show related-key attacks against the Schnorr signature scheme and DSA. As mentioned in Sect. 2.3, linear functions as RKD functions can be described as addition or multiplication depending on the group used as the signing key space.

4.1 Related-Key Attack Against Schnorr Signature

We show that the Schnorr signature scheme is not RKA secure with respect to linear functions or addition by providing a simple and efficient attack. That is, we show that the Schnorr signature scheme is not Φ^{lin}-EUF-CM-RKA secure.

An adversary $\mathcal{A}$ forges a signature as follows.

1. Choose an arbitrary message $m' \in \{0,1\}^*$ and an arbitrary value $b \in \mathbb{Z}_q^*$.
2. Query $(m', \phi(x) = x - b)$ to the RKA signing oracle and obtain the signature (h', s') as a response.
3. Output a message m' and forgery $(h', s' + b \cdot h')$.

Now, let us confirm that the forgery is valid. First, the reply from the RKA signing oracle, (h', s'), must have been computed by the following procedure:

- Choose $t' \xleftarrow{\$} \mathbb{Z}_q$ and let $r' \leftarrow g^{t'}$.
- Let $h' \leftarrow H(m' \,\|\, r')$.
- Let $s' \leftarrow (x - b) \cdot h' + t' \mod q$.

The forged signature $(h', s' + b \cdot h')$ on the message m' is verified as follows.

$$r'' = g^{s'+b\cdot h'} y^{-h'} = g^{(x-b)\cdot h'+t'+b\cdot h'} y^{-h'} = g^{(x-b)\cdot h'+t'+b\cdot h'-x\cdot h'} = g^{t'} = r'.$$

4.2 Related-Key Attack Against DSA

We next show that DSA is not RKA secure with respect to linear functions or multiplication by providing a simple and efficient attack. That is, we show that DSA is not Φ^{lin}-EUF-CM-RKA secure.

An adversary $\mathcal{A}$ forges a signature as follows.

1. Choose two distinct messages $m_0, m_1 \in \{0,1\}^*$ and let $z_0 \leftarrow H(m_0), z_1 \leftarrow H(m_1)$.
2. Let $a \leftarrow \dfrac{z_1}{z_0} \mod q$.
3. Query $(m_1, \phi(x) = ax)$ to the RKA signing oracle and obtain the signature $(r, s = t^{-1}(z_1 + axr))$.
4. Output a message $m^* = m_0$ and the signature $(r^*, s^*) = (r, \dfrac{s}{a} \mod q)$.

Note that even if a is 1, the attack still works.

The forged signature $(r, \dfrac{s}{a} \mod q)$ on the message m_0 will be verified as follows.

First, we compute $w^* = (s^*)^{-1} = a/s = ta/(z_1 + axr) = ta/(a \cdot z_0 + axr) = t/(z_0 + xr)$. Then, we compute $u_1 = w^* z_0 \mod q$ and $u_2 = rw^* \mod q$. Now we can check

$$\begin{aligned} r' &= (g^{H(m_0)/s^*} y^{r^*/s^*} \mod p) \mod q = (g^{u_1} y^{u_2} \mod p) \mod q \\ &= (g^{w^* z_0} y^{rw^*} \mod p) \mod q = (g^{w^* z_0 + xrw^*} \mod p) \mod q \\ &= (g^{w^*(z_0+xr)} \mod p) \mod q = (g^t \mod p) \mod q = r. \end{aligned}$$

Thus, the forgery output by $\mathcal{A}$ is valid.

5 Improved Schnorr Signature Scheme and Its RKA Security

As described in Sect. 4.1, the original Schnorr signature scheme is not RKA secure with respect to linear functions. In this section, we show that a slight modification yields an RKA-secure signature scheme with respect to polynomial functions. We refer to this scheme as the improved Schnorr signature scheme.

5.1 Construction

Our slight modification of the Schnorr signature scheme is as follows. The hash function is modified to take an extra input, which will correspond to a recalculated value of the verification key. Suppose that $\mathbb{G}$ is a group of prime order q, and g is a generator. The improved Schnorr signature scheme is defined as follows:

- KeyGen: This algorithm takes 1^λ as input, and generates a signing key sk and a verification key vk as follows.
  1. Choose $x \xleftarrow{\$} \mathbb{Z}_q$ and let $y \leftarrow g^x$.
  2. Choose a hash function $H : \{0,1\}^* \to \mathbb{Z}_q$.
  3. Output $sk = x$ and $vk = (y, H)$.
- Sign: This algorithm takes a message $m \in \{0,1\}^*$ and the signing key sk as input, and generates a signature σ as follows.
  1. Choose $t \xleftarrow{\$} \mathbb{Z}_q$ and let $r \leftarrow g^t$.
  2. Let $\psi \leftarrow g^x$.
  3. Obtain $h \leftarrow H(m \,\|\, r \,\|\, \psi)$.
  4. Let $s \leftarrow x \cdot h + t \mod q$.
  5. Output $\sigma \leftarrow (h, s)$.
- Verify: This algorithm takes a message m, a signature σ, and the verification key vk as input, and verifies the signature as follows.
  1. Let $r' \leftarrow g^s y^{-h}$.
  2. Let $h' \leftarrow H(m \,\|\, r' \,\|\, y)$.
  3. If $h' = h$, output 1, otherwise output 0.

Note that the second step of the signing algorithm, computation of $\psi \leftarrow g^x$, should not be altered to simply use the verification key y as ψ. That is, the signing algorithm computes $\psi = g^x$ each time it computes a signature.

Given that the verification key is recomputed from the signing key, one might wonder whether RKA security can be achieved simply by comparing the recomputed verification key with the original (assuming that the original verification key is available to the signing algorithm). However, for this to work, the additional assumption that the original verification key is stored and remains unchanged, is required. In the RKA setting, this seems unlikely to hold since the adversary is assumed to be capable of modifying the signing key, which should be better protected than the verification key. Furthermore, if the adversary is capable of modifying the stored signing key, a similar attack to Sects. 4.1 and 4.2 will be possible: an attacker queries $(m', \phi(x) = x - b)$ under the modified verification key yg^{-b} in the second step of the attack. In contrast, our schemes provided in this section and in Sect. 6.1 can be shown RKA secure without any additional assumptions regarding stored values.

5.2 Theorem Statement

We prove the following theorem about the improved Schnorr signature scheme.

Theorem 3. *Let d be a positive integer. Under the d-SDL assumption over $\mathbb{G}$, the signature scheme in Sect. 5.1 is $\Phi^{poly(d)}$-EUF-CM-RKA secure in the random oracle model.*

More precisely, for any probabilistic polynomial time algorithm $\mathcal{A}$ with running time $t_{\mathcal{A}}$, making q_S RKA signing oracle queries, and q_H random oracle queries to H, there exists a probabilistic polynomial time algorithm $\mathcal{B}$ with running time $t_{\mathcal{B}} = 2t_{\mathcal{A}} + \mathcal{O}(q_S + q_H)$ that satisfies the following equation:

$$\mathrm{Adv}_{\mathcal{A},\Sigma}^{\Phi^{poly(d)}\text{-euf-cm-rka}}(\lambda) \leq \left((q_H + q_S)\left(\mathrm{Adv}_{\mathcal{B},\mathbb{G}}^{d\text{-sdl}}(\lambda) + \frac{2q_S + 1}{q}\right)\right)^{1/2}. \quad (1)$$

The proof is given in the full version of the paper.

The 1-SDL assumption is equivalent to the ordinary DL assumption, which leads to the following result.

Corollary 1. *The improved Schnorr signature scheme is RKA secure with respect to affine functions in the random oracle model under the DL assumption over $\mathbb{G}$.*

6 Improved DSA and Its RKA Security

As described in Sect. 4.2, the original DSA is not RKA secure with respect to linear functions. In this section, we show that a slight modification yields an RKA-secure signature scheme with respect to polynomial functions. We refer to this scheme as the improved DSA.

6.1 Construction

Based on one of DSA variants (introduced as "second variant" in [26]), we construct an RKA secure variant of DSA with respect to polynomial functions. The slight modification of DSA variant is as follows. The hash function is modified to take an extra input, which will correspond to a recalculated value of the verification key. Suppose that q is a prime, p is a prime such that $p-1 \mod q = 0$, and $\mathbb{G} \subseteq \mathbb{Z}_p^*$ is a group of prime order q. Let $g \in \mathbb{G}$ be a generator. Let $F_{p,q} : \mathbb{G} \to \mathbb{Z}_q$ be the mapping defined by $\overline{g} \mapsto \overline{g} \mod q$, where $\overline{g} \in \mathbb{G}$, and $\mathbb{G}, q, p$ are the parameters of the group.

The improved DSA is defined as follows:

- KeyGen: This algorithm takes 1^λ as input, and generates the signing key sk and the verification key vk as follows.
  1. Choose $x \xleftarrow{\$} \mathbb{Z}_q^*$ and let $y \leftarrow g^x \mod p$.
  2. Choose a hash function $H : \{0,1\}^* \to \mathbb{Z}_q$.
  3. Output $sk = x$ and $vk = (y, H)$.
- Sign: This algorithm takes a message $m \in \{0,1\}^*$, the verification key vk, and the signing key sk as input, and generates a signature σ as follows.

1. Choose $t \xleftarrow{\$} \mathbb{Z}_q^*$ and let $r \leftarrow F_{p,q}(g^t \mod p)$.
2. Let $\psi \leftarrow g^x \mod p$.
3. Let $s \leftarrow t^{-1}(H(m \,\|\, r \,\|\, \psi) + x \cdot r) \mod q$.
4. Output $\sigma \leftarrow (r, s)$.

- Verify: This algorithm takes a message m, a signature σ, and the verification key vk as input, and verifies the signature as follows.
  1. Let $r' \leftarrow F_{p,q}(g^{H(m \,\|\, r \,\|\, y)/s} y^{r/s} \mod p)$.
  2. If $r' = r$, output 1, otherwise output 0.

Note that the computation of a hash function at the third step of the signing algorithm takes as input not only a message and the value r, but also $\psi = g^x$. This computation is different from that of the second DSA variant [26].

6.2 Theorem Statement

We prove the following theorem about the improved DSA.

Theorem 4. *Let d be a positive integer, and assume the mapping $F_{p,q}$ is collision resistant. Under the d-SDL assumption over $\mathbb{G}$, the signature scheme in Sect. 6.1 is $\Phi^{\mathrm{poly}(d)}$-EUF-CM-RKA secure in the random oracle model.*

More precisely, assume that $F_{p,q}$ is ϵ-collision-resistant. Then, for any probabilistic polynomial time algorithm $\mathcal{A}$ with running time $t_{\mathcal{A}}$, making q_S RKA signing oracle queries, and q_H random oracle queries to H, there exists a probabilistic polynomial time algorithm $\mathcal{B}$ with running time $t_{\mathcal{B}} = 2t_{\mathcal{A}} + \mathcal{O}(q_S + q_H)$ that satisfies the following equation:

$$\mathrm{Adv}_{\mathcal{A},\Sigma}^{\Phi^{\mathrm{poly}(d)}\text{-euf-cm-rka}}(\lambda) \leq \left((q_H + q_S) \left(\mathrm{Adv}_{\mathcal{B},\mathbb{G}}^{d\text{-sdl}}(\lambda) + \frac{1}{q} + \frac{2\epsilon}{q_H + q_S} \right) \right)^{1/2}. \quad (2)$$

The proof is given in the full version of the paper.

The 1-SDL assumption is equivalent to the ordinary DL assumption, which leads to the following result.

Corollary 2. *If the DL assumption over $\mathbb{G}$ holds and the function $F_{p,q}$ is collision-resistant, then the improved DSA is RKA secure with respect to affine functions in the random oracle model.*

7 Conclusions

We analyzed the RKA security of the Schnorr signature scheme and DSA. We showed that the Schnorr signature scheme and the second DSA variant from [26] are weak RKA secure with respect to polynomial functions ($\Phi^{\mathrm{poly}(d)}$-wEUF-CM-RKA), but the Schnorr signature scheme and the original DSA are not fully secure against relatively weak attacks based on linear functions (Φ^{lin}-EUF-CM-RKA). It is not known whether the second DSA variant is vulnerable with respect to $\Phi^{\mathrm{poly}(d)}$-EUF-CM-RKA. We leave this as an open problem. However, we proved that simple modifications yield schemes, the improved Schnorr signature scheme and the improved DSA scheme, which are RKA secure with respect to polynomial functions ($\Phi^{\mathrm{poly}(d)}$-EUF-CM-RKA) in the random oracle model. The RKA security with respect to polynomial functions is proven under the d-SDL assumption. Interestingly, considering the case of $d = 1$, our results show that our improved Schnorr scheme and the improved DSA are RKA secure with respect to affine functions in the random oracle model under the ordinary DL assumption. Moreover, our simple modification of the original Schnorr scheme and the considered DSA variant does not require the public or private key from the original schemes to change, and only increases the computational cost of the signing algorithm with a single exponentiation while no other computational cost or the signature size will increase. However, the improved schemes do not address bit-flipping attacks, such as those highlighted by Bao et al. [3]. It remains future work to construct schemes which are provably secure against these attacks.

References

1. National Institute of Standards AND Technology (NIST), FIPS Publication 186: Digital Signature Standards (DSS) (1994)
2. Abdalla, M., Benhamouda, F., Passelègue, A., Paterson, K.G.: Related-key security for pseudorandom functions beyond the linear barrier. In: Garay, J.A., Gennaro, R. (eds.) CRYPTO 2014, Part I. LNCS, vol. 8616, pp. 77–94. Springer, Heidelberg (2014)
3. Bao, F., Deng, R.H., Han, Y., Jeng, A.B., Narasimhalu, A.D., Ngair, T.: Breaking public key cryptosystems on tamper resistant devices in the presence of transient faults. In: Christianson, B., Crispo, B., Lomas, M., Roe, M. (eds.) Security Protocols. LNCS, vol. 1361, pp. 115–124. Springer, Heidelberg (1997)
4. Bellare, M., Cash, D., Miller, R.: Cryptography secure against related-key attacks and tampering. In: Lee, D.H., Wang, X. (eds.) ASIACRYPT 2011. LNCS, vol. 7073, pp. 486–503. Springer, Heidelberg (2011)
5. Bellare, M., Kohno, T.: A theoretical treatment of related-key attacks: RKA-PRPs, RKA-PRFs, and applications. In: Biham, E. (ed.) EUROCRYPT 2003. LNCS, vol. 2656, pp. 491–506. Springer, Heidelberg (2003)
6. Bellare, M., Paterson, K.G., Thomson, S.: RKA security beyond the linear barrier: IBE, encryption and signatures. In: Wang, X., Sako, K. (eds.) ASIACRYPT 2012. LNCS, vol. 7658, pp. 331–348. Springer, Heidelberg (2012)
7. Bernstein, D.J., Duif, N., Lange, T., Schwabe, P., Yang, B.-Y.: High-speed high-security signatures. In: Preneel, B., Takagi, T. (eds.) CHES 2011. LNCS, vol. 6917, pp. 124–142. Springer, Heidelberg (2011)
8. Bhattacharyya, R., Roy, A.: Secure message authentication against related-key attack. In: Moriai, S. (ed.) FSE 2013. LNCS, vol. 8424, pp. 305–324. Springer, Heidelberg (2014)
9. Biham, E., Shamir, A.: Differential fault analysis of secret key cryptosystems. In: Kaliski Jr., B.S. (ed.) CRYPTO 1997. LNCS, vol. 1294, pp. 513–525. Springer, Heidelberg (1997)
10. Boneh, D., Boyen, X.: Short signatures without random oracles. In: Cachin, C., Camenisch, J.L. (eds.) EUROCRYPT 2004. LNCS, vol. 3027, pp. 56–73. Springer, Heidelberg (2004)

11. Damgård, I., Faust, S., Mukherjee, P., Venturi, D.: Bounded tamper resilience: how to go beyond the algebraic barrier. In: Sako, K., Sarkar, P. (eds.) ASIACRYPT 2013, Part II. LNCS, vol. 8270, pp. 140–160. Springer, Heidelberg (2013)
12. Damgård, I., Faust, S., Mukherjee, P., Venturi, D.: The chaining lemma and its application. In: Lehmann, A., Wolf, S. (eds.) ICITS 2015. LNCS, vol. 9063, pp. 181–196. Springer, Heidelberg (2015)
13. Dusart, P., Letourneux, G., Vivolo, O.: Differential fault analysis on A.E.S. IACR Cryptology ePrint Archive 2003, 10 (2003)
14. Dziembowski, S., Pietrzak, K., Wichs, D.: Non-malleable codes. In: ICS 2010, pp. 434–452 (2010)
15. El Gamal, T.: A public key cryptosystem and a signature scheme based on discrete logarithms. In: Blakely, G.R., Chaum, D. (eds.) CRYPTO 1984. LNCS, vol. 196, pp. 10–18. Springer, Heidelberg (1985)
16. Faust, S., Mukherjee, P., Nielsen, J.B., Venturi, D.: Continuous non-malleable codes. In: Lindell, Y. (ed.) TCC 2014. LNCS, vol. 8349, pp. 465–488. Springer, Heidelberg (2014)
17. Faust, S., Mukherjee, P., Venturi, D., Wichs, D.: Efficient non-malleable codes and key-derivation for poly-size tampering circuits. In: Nguyen, P.Q., Oswald, E. (eds.) EUROCRYPT 2014. LNCS, vol. 8441, pp. 111–128. Springer, Heidelberg (2014)
18. Gennaro, R., Lysyanskaya, A., Malkin, T., Micali, S., Rabin, T.: Algorithmic tamper-proof (ATP) security: theoretical foundations for security against hardware tampering. In: Naor, M. (ed.) TCC 2004. LNCS, vol. 2951, pp. 258–277. Springer, Heidelberg (2004)
19. Giraud, C.: DFA on AES. In: Dobbertin, H., Rijmen, V., Sowa, A. (eds.) AES 2005. LNCS, vol. 3373, pp. 27–41. Springer, Heidelberg (2005)
20. Goldwasser, S., Micali, S., Rivest, R.L.: A digital signature scheme secure against adaptive chosen-message attacks. SIAM J. Comput. **17**(2), 281–308 (1988)
21. Goyal, V., O'Neill, A., Rao, V.: Correlated-input secure hash functions. In: Ishai, Y. (ed.) TCC 2011. LNCS, vol. 6597, pp. 182–200. Springer, Heidelberg (2011)
22. Jafargholi, Z., Wichs, D.: Tamper detection and continuous non-malleable codes. In: Dodis, Y., Nielsen, J.B. (eds.) TCC 2015, Part I. LNCS, vol. 9014, pp. 451–480. Springer, Heidelberg (2015)
23. Jao, D., Yoshida, K.: Boneh-Boyen signatures and the strong Diffie-Hellman problem. In: Shacham, H., Waters, B. (eds.) Pairing 2009. LNCS, vol. 5671, pp. 1–16. Springer, Heidelberg (2009)
24. Koblitz, N., Menezes, A.J.: The random oracle model: a twenty-year retrospective. Des. Codes Crypt. **77**(2–3), 587–610 (2015)
25. Pointcheval, D., Stern, J.: Security proofs for signature schemes. In: Maurer, U.M. (ed.) EUROCRYPT 1996. LNCS, vol. 1070, pp. 387–398. Springer, Heidelberg (1996)
26. Pointcheval, D., Vaudenay, S.: On provable security for digital signature algorithms. Technical report, Ecole Normale Superieure, LIENS (1996)
27. Qin, B., Liu, S., Yuen, T.H., Deng, R.H., Chen, K.: Continuous non-malleable key derivation and its application to related-key security. In: Katz, J. (ed.) PKC 2015. LNCS, vol. 9020, pp. 557–578. Springer, Heidelberg (2015)
28. Schnorr, C.P.: Efficient identification and signatures for smart cards. In: Brassard, G. (ed.) CRYPTO 1989. LNCS, vol. 435, pp. 239–252. Springer, Heidelberg (1990)

Attribute-Based Two-Tier Signatures: Definition and Construction

Hiroaki Anada[1,2(✉)], Seiko Arita[2], and Kouichi Sakurai[1,3]

[1] Institute of Systems, Information Technologies and Nanotechnologies, 7F, 2–1–22, Momochihama, Sawara–ku, Fukuoka 814–0001, Japan
anada@isit.or.jp

[2] Institute of Information Security, 2–14–1 Tsuruya–cho, Kanagawa–ku, Yokohama 221–0835, Japan
arita@iisec.ac.jp

[3] Department of Informatics, Graduate School and Faculty of Information Science and Electrical Engineering, Kyushu University, W2–712, 744 Motooka, Nishi–ku, Fukuoka 819–0395, Japan
sakurai@inf.kyushu-u.ac.jp

Abstract. Attribute-based signature scheme (ABS) is a functional variant of digital signature scheme proposed in 2008 by Maji et al. The two basic requirements of ABS (and a hard task to achieve) is collusion resistance and attribute privacy. In this paper, we employ the two-tier signature (TTS) technique to achieve the collusion resistance. Here TTS was proposed in 2007 by Bellare et al., where a signer receives two tier secret keys sequentially. The secondary secret key is served as a one-time key at the timing of signing. First, we propose a definition of an attribute-based two-tier signature scheme (ABTTS). Then we provide ABTTS concretely that enjoys existential unforgeability against chosen-message attacks, collusion resistance and attribute privacy, in the standard model. For the construction, enhancing the Camenisch-Lysyanskaya signature, we construct signature bundle schemes that are secure under the Strong RSA assumption and the Strong Diffie-Hellman assumption, respectively. These signature bundle schemes enable ABTTS to achieve attribute privacy. Then, using the signature bundle as a witness in the Σ-protocol of the boolean proof, we obtain attribute-based identification schemes (ABIDs). Finally, by applying the TTS technique to ABIDs, we achieve ABTTSs. A feature of our construction is that ABTTS in the RSA setting is pairing-free.

Keywords: Digital signature · Attribute-based · Two-tier keys

1 Introduction

Digital signature scheme is one of the most widely recognized cryptographic primitives. Since its invention, functional variants have been proposed, which include *attribute-based signature schemes* (ABS) developed by Guo and Zeng [12]

S. Kwon and A. Yun (Eds.): ICISC 2015, LNCS 9558, pp. 36–49, 2016.
DOI: 10.1007/978-3-319-30840-1_3

and Maji et al. [14] in 2008. In ABS, a message m is associated with a signing policy f that is described as a boolean formula over signers' attributes. Then only signers with attributes that satisfy f can make a legitimate signature σ on m. A verifier can check whether the signature σ is valid in accordance with the signing policy f. The two basic requirements of ABS (and a hard task to achieve) is collusion resistance against collecting secret keys and attribute privacy. Intuitively, ABS is called to have attribute privacy if any cheating verifier cannot distinguish two distributions of signatures each of which is generated by different satisfying attribute set.

A two-tier signature scheme (TTS) is a digital signature scheme proposed in 2007 by Bellare and Shoup [3], in which a signer receives two tier secret keys sequentially, the latter of which is served as a one-time signing key at the timing of signing. Accordingly, two tier public keys are issued sequentially. These two-tier keys fit the Fiat-Shamir signature scheme and enable it to achieve existential unforgeability against chosen-message attacks (EUF-CMA) in the standard model.

Our Contribution. Our first contribution is to define the syntax of an attribute-based two-tier signature scheme (ABTTS) for the first time. The reason why we introduce ABTTS (in a construction of ABS) is to achieve the collusion resistance by employing the TTS technique. The issuer of a secondary secret key can check integrity of components in a primary secret keys so that the issuer can avoid collusion attacks.

Our second contribution is to provide ABTTS concretely that enjoys existential unforgeability against chosen-message attacks, collusion resistance and attribute privacy, in the standard model. It is interesting from the view point of theory (and also efficiency) that our ABTTS in the RSA setting is pairing-free.

Our Approach to Concrete Construction. First, enhancing the Camenisch-Lysyanskaya signature, we construct signature bundle schemes that are secure under the Strong RSA assumption and the Strong Diffie-Hellman assumption, respectively. These signature bundle schemes later enable ABTTS to achieve attribute privacy. Then, using the signature bundle as a witness in the Σ-protocol of the boolean proof, we obtain attribute-based identification schemes (ABIDs). Finally, by applying the TTS technique to ABIDs, we achieve ABTTSs.

Comparison: Security, Functionality and Signature Length. We compare our ABTTS with previously proposed schemes from the view point of security, functionality and signature length. The comparison is summarized in Table 1 with notations as follows. A prime of bit length λ (the security parameter in the discrete logarithm setting) is denoted by p. Though a pairing map e should be analysed for the asymmetric bilinear groups [11], we simply evaluate the symmetric case in which both source groups are $\mathbb{G}_p$ of order p. We assume that an element of $\mathbb{G}_p$ is represented by 2λ bits. l and r mean the number of rows and columns of the share-generating matrix for monotone access formula f (that is, an access structure), respectively. CR means the collision resistance of an employed hash function. q-SDH means the Strong Diffie-Hellman assumption with q-type input for bilinear groups [4]. DLIN means the Decisional Linear assumption for bilinear groups [16]. DDH means the Decisional Diffie-Hellman assumption for a cyclic group [8]. DLog means the Discrete Logarithm assumption for a cyclic group [8]. q-SRSA means the Strong RSA assumption with q-type input [13]. DDH in $QR(N)$ means the Decisional Diffie-Hellman assumption for quadratic residues modulo N (the RSA modulus) [13]. "info." means information-theoretic security and "comp." means computational security. λ_{rsa} means the security parameter in the RSA setting, and $\hat{\lambda}$ means the security parameter in either the RSA setting or the discrete logarithm setting.

Table 1. Comparison of security, functionality and signature length.

Scheme	Security Model	Assumption	Access Formula	Pairing -Free	Attribute Privacy	Length of Signature
Maji et al. [14]	Std.	q-SDH $\wedge$DLIN	Mono.	-	✓(info.)	$(2\lambda)\times$ $(51l + 2r + 18\lambda l)$
OT [16]	Std.	DLIN $\wedge$CR	Non-m.	-	✓(info.)	$(2\lambda)\times$ $(9l + 11)$
Herranz [13]	R.O.	q-SRSA$\wedge$[DDH in $QR(N)$]$\wedge$CR	Mono.	✓	✓(comp.)	$\lambda_{\mathrm{rsa}}(5 + \frac{\kappa}{\lambda_{\mathrm{rsa}}})l$ $+\lambda_{\mathrm{rsa}}3 - \kappa(\theta - 1)$
Ghadafi et al. [8]	R.O.	q-SDH$\wedge$DDH$\wedge$ DLog$\wedge$CR	Mono.	-	-	$(2\lambda)(3l + r + 3)$ $+\lambda(8l + 4)$
Anada et al. [2]	R.O.	[DLog$\vee$RSAInv] $\wedge$CR	Mono.	✓	-	$(2\hat{\lambda})l$ $+\hat{\lambda}(4l - 1)$
Our ABTTS	Std.	[q-SRSA$\vee q$-SDH] $\wedge$CR	Mono.	✓	✓(info.)	$(2\hat{\lambda})2l$ $+\hat{\lambda}2l$

First, note that our scheme assumes the secondary secret key and the secondary public key are issued as one-time keys at the timing of signing. This means the signer and the verifier should be on-line and they need to verify a certificate of the secondary public key. One possibility of executing such a process is to use Online Certificate Status Protocol (OCSP) by RFC 6990 [9].

The scheme of [16] has advantages in the security model, access formula and information-theoretically secure attribute privacy, whereas our ABS realizes shorter length of signature (less than a half). The scheme of [13] is in the RSA setting and its security parameter λ_{rsa} is almost 10 times longer than λ in the DLog setting. For example, $\lambda_{\mathrm{rsa}} = 2048$ is almost equivalent to $\lambda = 224$-bit security [17]. (θ is the threshold value of the threshold-type access structure. κ is explained in the work [13].) Therefore, our ABS in the DLog setting realizes shorter length of a signature.

2 Preliminaries

The security parameter is denoted as λ. Bit length of a string x is denoted as $|x|$. The expression "$a \stackrel{?}{=} b$" returns a value 1 if $a = b$ and 0 otherwise. The expression "$a \stackrel{?}{\in} S$" returns a value 1 if $a \in S$ and 0 otherwise.

Σ-protocol [6,7]. A Σ-protocol on a binary NP relation R is a public coin 3-move protocol between interactive PPT algorithms $\mathcal{P}$ and $\mathcal{V}$ on initial input $(x, w) \in R$ for $\mathcal{P}$ and x for $\mathcal{V}$. x and w are called a statement and a witness, respectively. $\mathcal{P}$ sends the first message called a commitment $\textsc{Cmt}$, then $\mathcal{V}$ sends a random bit string called a challenge $\textsc{Cha}$, and $\mathcal{P}$ answers with a third message called a response $\textsc{Res}$. Then $\mathcal{V}$ applies a decision test on $(x, \textsc{Cmt}, \textsc{Cha}, \textsc{Res})$ to return accept (1) or reject (0). If $\mathcal{V}$ accepts, then the triple $(\textsc{Cmt}, \textsc{Cha}, \textsc{Res})$ is said to be an *accepting conversation*. $\textsc{Cha}$ is chosen uniformly at random from the challenge space $\textsc{ChaSp}(1^\lambda) := \{1, 0\}^{l(\lambda)}$ with $l(\cdot)$ being a super-log function.

The Σ-protocol is written by a PPT algorithm $\mathbf{\Sigma}$ as follows. $\textsc{Cmt} \leftarrow \mathbf{\Sigma}^1(x, w)$: the process of selecting the first message $\textsc{Cmt}$ according to the protocol $\mathbf{\Sigma}$ on input $(x, w) \in R$. Similarly we denote $\textsc{Cha} \leftarrow \mathbf{\Sigma}^2(1^\lambda)$, $\textsc{Res} \leftarrow \mathbf{\Sigma}^3(x, w, \textsc{Cmt}, \textsc{Cha})$ and $b \leftarrow \mathbf{\Sigma}^{\mathrm{vrfy}}(x, \textsc{Cmt}, \textsc{Cha}, \textsc{Res})$. The Σ-protocol must possess the three properties: *completeness*, *special soundness* and *honest-verifier zero-knowledge* [6,7]. As a zero-knowledge proof-of-knowledge system, we denote $\mathbf{\Sigma}$ as $\mathbf{ZKPK}[\gamma : \Gamma]$, where γ is a knowledge to be proved and Γ is the condition that γ should satisfy.

Signature Bundle Scheme [14]. A signature bundle (a credential bundle in [14]) scheme SB is an extended notion of a signature scheme. It consists of three PPTs: $\mathsf{SB} = (\mathbf{SB.KG}, \mathbf{SB.Sign}, \mathbf{SB.Vrfy})$.
$\mathbf{SB.KG}(1^\lambda) \rightarrow (\mathrm{PK}, \mathrm{SK})$. Given 1^λ as input, it returns a public key PK and a secret key SK.
$\mathbf{SB.Sign}(\mathrm{PK}, \mathrm{SK}, (m_i)_{i=1}^n) \rightarrow (\tau, (\sigma_i)_{i=1}^n)$. Given PK, SK and messages $(m_i)_{i=1}^n$, it returns a *tag* τ and signatures $(\sigma_i)_{i=1}^n$. n is bounded by a polynomial in λ.
$\mathbf{SB.Vrfy}(\mathrm{PK}, (m_i)_{i=1}^n, (\tau, (\sigma_i)_{i=1}^n)) \rightarrow 1/0$. Given PK, messages $(m_i)_{i=1}^n$, a tag τ and signatures $(\sigma_i)_{i=1}^n$, it returns 1 or 0.

A PPT adversary $\mathcal{F}$ tries to make a forgery $((m_i^*)_{i=1}^{n^*}, (\tau^*, (\sigma_i^*)_{i=1}^{n^*}))$. Here τ^* is called a *target tag*. *An existential forgery by a chosen-message attack* is defined by:

$$\mathbf{Expr}^{\text{euf-cma}}_{\mathsf{SB},\mathcal{F}}(1^\lambda, \mathcal{U})$$
$$(\mathrm{PK}, \mathrm{SK}) \leftarrow \mathbf{SB.KG}(1^\lambda), ((m_i^*)_{i=1}^{n^*}, (\tau^*, (\sigma_i^*)_{i=1}^{n^*})) \leftarrow \mathcal{F}^{\mathcal{SBSIGN}}(\mathrm{PK})$$
$$\text{If } \mathbf{SB.Vrfy}(\mathrm{PK}, (m_i^*)_{i=1}^{n^*}, (\tau^*, (\sigma_i^*)_{i=1}^{n^*})) = 1$$
$$\text{then Return } \textsc{Win} \text{ else Return } \textsc{Lose}$$

Giving a vector of messages $(m_i)_{i=1}^n$, $\mathcal{F}$ queries $\mathcal{SBSIGN}(\mathrm{PK}, \mathrm{SK}, \cdot)$ for a valid signature bundle $(\tau, (\sigma_i)_{i=1}^n)$. τ^* should be different from any queried tag τ, or, whenever τ^* is equal to a queried tag τ, it should hold that $\{m_i^*\}_{i=1}^{n^*} \not\subseteq \{m_i\}_{i=1}^n$ for any queried $(m_i)_{i=1}^n$. The *advantage* of $\mathcal{F}$ over SB in the experiment of existential forgery by chosen-message attack is defined as $\mathbf{Adv}^{\text{euf-cma}}_{\text{SB},\mathcal{F}}(\lambda,\mathcal{U}) \stackrel{\text{def}}{=} \Pr[\mathbf{Expr}^{\text{euf-cma}}_{\text{SB},\mathcal{F}}(1^\lambda,\mathcal{U}) \text{ returns } \textsc{Win}]$.

Definition 1. *SB is called existentially unforgeable against chosen-message attack if, for any PPT $\mathcal{F}$, $\mathbf{Adv}^{euf\text{-}cma}_{SB,\mathcal{F}}(\lambda,\mathcal{U})$ is negligible in λ.*

Access Structure [10]. Let $\mathcal{U} = \{\mathtt{at}_i\}_{i=1}^{u}$ be an attribute universe. $|\mathcal{U}| = u$ is bounded by a polynomial in λ ($\mathcal{U}$ is called a small universe).

Let $f = f(X_{\mathtt{at}_1},\dots,X_{\mathtt{at}_a})$ be a monotone boolean formula over $U = \{X_{\mathtt{at}}\}_{\mathtt{at}}$, where boolean connectives are AND-gate ($\wedge$) and OR-gate ($\vee$). In this paper, we assume that no NOT-gate ($\neg$) appears in f. In other words, we consider only a *monotone* access formula f.[1] We denote the set of subscripts (that is, attributes) $\{\mathtt{at}_1,\dots,\mathtt{at}_a\}$ as $\mathrm{At}(f)$ and the arity a as $\mathrm{arity}(f)$, respectively. For $S \in 2^{\mathcal{U}}$, we evaluate the boolean value of f at S as: $f(S) \stackrel{\text{def}}{=} f\big(X_{\mathtt{at}} \leftarrow [\mathtt{at} \stackrel{?}{\in} S]; \mathtt{at} \in \mathrm{At}(f)\big) \in \{1,0\}$. We call a boolean formula f with this map an *access formula* over $\mathcal{U}$. An access formula corresponds to a signing policy in the case of attribute-based signatures.

An access formula f can be represented by a finite binary tree $\mathcal{T}_f$. Each inner node corresponds to an AND-gate ($\wedge$) or OR-gate ($\vee$) in f. Each leaf node l corresponds to a term $X_{\mathtt{at}}$ (not a variable $X_{\mathtt{at}}$) in f in one-to-one way. For a finite binary tree $\mathcal{T}$, we denote the root node, the set of all nodes, the set of all leaf nodes, the set of all inner nodes (all nodes excluding leaf nodes) and the set of all tree-nodes (all nodes excluding the root node) as $r(\mathcal{T})$, $\mathrm{Node}(\mathcal{T})$, $\mathrm{Leaf}(\mathcal{T})$, $\mathrm{iNode}(\mathcal{T})$ and $\mathrm{tNode}(\mathcal{T})$, respectively. Then an attribute map $\rho(\cdot)$ is defined as: $\rho : \mathrm{Leaf}(\mathcal{T}) \to \mathcal{U},\ \rho(l) \stackrel{\text{def}}{=} (\mathtt{at}$ that corresponds to $l)$. If ρ is not injective, then we call the case *multi-use* of attributes.

Attribute-Based Identification Scheme [1]. An attribute-based identification scheme, ABID, consists of four PPT algorithms: (**ABID.Setup**, **ABID.KG**, $\mathcal{P}$, $\mathcal{V}$).

ABID.Setup$(1^\lambda,\mathcal{U}) \to$ **(PK,MSK)**. Given the security parameter 1^λ and an attribute universe $\mathcal{U}$, it returns a public key PK and a master secret key MSK.

ABID.KG(PK,MSK,S**)** $\to$ **SK**$_S$. Given the public key PK, the master secret key MSK and an attribute set $S \subset \mathcal{U}$, it returns a secret key SK_S that corresponds to S.

$\mathcal{P}$**(PK,SK**$_S$**) and** $\mathcal{V}$**(PK,**f**).** $\mathcal{P}$ and $\mathcal{V}$ are interactive algorithms called a *prover* and a *verifier*, respectively. $\mathcal{P}$ takes as input the public key PK and the secret key SK_S. Here the secret key SK_S is given to $\mathcal{P}$ by an authority. $\mathcal{V}$ takes as input the public key PK and an access formula f. $\mathcal{P}$ is provided $\mathcal{V}$'s access formula f by the first move. $\mathcal{P}$ and $\mathcal{V}$ interact with each other for at most constant rounds. Then, $\mathcal{V}$ returns its decision 1 or 0. When it is 1, we say that $\mathcal{V}$ *accepts* $\mathcal{P}$ for f. When it is 0, we say that $\mathcal{V}$ *rejects* $\mathcal{P}$ for f. We demand correctness of ABID that for any λ, for any S and for any f such

[1] This limitation can be removed by adding *negation attributes* to $\mathcal{U}$ for each attribute in the original $\mathcal{U}$ though the size of the attribute universe $|\mathcal{U}|$ doubles.

that $f(S) = 1$, $\Pr[(\mathrm{PK}, \mathrm{MSK}) \leftarrow \mathrm{Setup}(1^\lambda, \mathcal{U}); \mathrm{SK}_S \leftarrow \mathrm{KG}(\mathrm{PK}, \mathrm{MSK}, S); b \leftarrow \langle \mathcal{P}(\mathrm{PK}, \mathrm{SK}_S), \mathcal{V}(\mathrm{PK}, f)\rangle : b = 1] = 1$.

An adversary $\mathcal{A}$ tries to make a verifier $\mathcal{V}$ accept with an access formula f^* of his choice. Here f^* is called a *target access formula. A concurrent attack* is defined by:

$$\mathbf{Exprmt}^{\mathrm{ca}}_{\mathtt{ABID},\mathcal{A}}(1^\lambda, \mathcal{U})$$

$$(\mathrm{PK}, \mathrm{MSK}) \leftarrow \mathbf{ABID.Setup}(\lambda, \mathcal{U}),\ (f^*, st) \leftarrow \mathcal{A}^{\mathcal{KG}, \mathcal{P}_j|_{j=1}^{q_{\mathrm{prv}}}}(\mathrm{PK}, \mathcal{U})$$

$$b \leftarrow \langle \mathcal{A}(st), \mathcal{V}(\mathrm{PK}, f^*)\rangle,\ \text{If } b = 1 \text{ then Return } \textsc{Win} \text{ else Return } \textsc{Lose}$$

Giving an attribute set S_i, $\mathcal{A}$ queries $\mathcal{KG}(\mathrm{PK}, \mathrm{MSK}, \cdot)$ for the secret key SK_{S_i}. In addition, $\mathcal{A}$ invokes provers $\mathcal{P}_j(\mathrm{PK}, \mathrm{SK}_\cdot)$, $j = 1, \ldots, q'_{\mathrm{prv}}, \ldots, q_{\mathrm{prv}}$, by giving a pair (S_j, f_j). Acting as a verifier with an access formula f_j, $\mathcal{A}$ interacts with each $\mathcal{P}_j(\mathrm{PK}, \mathrm{SK}_{S_j})$ concurrently. In the above we consider the *adaptive target* f^*. In key-extraction queries, each attribute set S_i must satisfy $f^*(S_i) = 0$. In interactions with each prover, $f^*(S_j) = 0$. The *advantage* of $\mathcal{A}$ over ABID in the game of concurrent attack is defined as $\mathbf{Adv}^{\mathrm{ca}}_{\mathtt{ABID},\mathcal{A}}(\lambda) \stackrel{\mathrm{def}}{=} \Pr[\mathbf{Exprmt}^{\mathrm{ca}}_{\mathtt{ABID},\mathcal{A}}(1^\lambda, \mathcal{U}) \text{ returns } \textsc{Win}]$. ABID is called *secure against concurrent attacks* if, for any PPT $\mathcal{A}$, $\mathbf{Adv}^{\mathrm{ca}}_{\mathtt{ABID},\mathcal{A}}(\lambda)$ is negligible in λ.

Strong RSA Assumption [5]**.** Let $p = 2p' + 1$ denote a *safe prime* (p' is also a prime). Let N denote the *special RSA modulus*; that is, $N = pq$ where $p = 2p' + 1$ and $q = 2q' + 1$ are two safe primes such that $|p'| = |q'| = \lambda - 1$. We denote the probabilistic algorithm that generates such N at random on input 1^λ as RSAmod. Let $QR_N \subset \mathbb{Z}_N^*$ denote the set of quadratic residues modulo N; that is, elements $a \in \mathbb{Z}_N^*$ such that $a \equiv x^2 \mod N$ for some $x \in \mathbb{Z}_N^*$. The strong RSA assumption [5] states that for any PPT $\mathcal{A}$, the following advantage is negligible in λ: $\mathbf{Adv}^{\mathrm{srsa}}_{\mathtt{RSAmod},\mathcal{S}}(\lambda, \mathcal{U}) := \Pr[N \leftarrow \mathtt{RSAmod}(1^\lambda), g \stackrel{\$}{\leftarrow} QR_N, (V, e) \leftarrow \mathcal{A}(N, g) : e > 1 \wedge V^e \equiv g \mod N]$.

Strong Diffie-Hellman Assumption [4]**.** Let p denote a prime of bit length λ. Let $e : \mathbb{G}_1 \times \mathbb{G}_2 \rightarrow \mathbb{G}_T$ denote bilinear groups of order p, where $\mathbb{G}_1$ is generated by g, $\mathbb{G}_2$ is generated by h and $\mathbb{G}_T$ is generated by $e(g, h) \neq 1_{\mathbb{G}_T}$. We denote the probabilistic algorithm that generates such parameters $\mathrm{params} := (p, \mathbb{G}_1, \mathbb{G}_2, \mathbb{G}_T, e)$ on input 1^λ as BlGrp. Let q denote a number that is less than a fixed polynomial in λ. The strong Diffie-Hellman assumption [4] states that for any PPT $\mathcal{A}$, the following advantage is negligible in λ: $\mathbf{Adv}^{\mathrm{sdh}}_{\mathtt{BlGrp},\mathcal{S}}(\lambda, \mathcal{U}) := \Pr[\mathrm{params} \leftarrow \mathtt{BlGrp}(1^\lambda), \alpha \stackrel{\$}{\leftarrow} \mathbb{Z}_p,\ (u, e) \leftarrow \mathcal{A}(\mathrm{params}, (g, g^\alpha, g^{\alpha^2}, \ldots, g^{\alpha^q}, h, h^\alpha)) : u^{\alpha + e} = g]$.

3 Syntax of Attribute-Based Two-Tier Signature Scheme

In this section, we propose a definition of syntax of an attribute-based two-tier signature scheme (ABTTS). Then, we define a chosen-message attack (CMA) on ABTTS where an adversary makes an existential forgery, and we define the existential unforgeability (EUF) against CMA.

3.1 Definition: Syntax of ABTTS

An attribute-based two-tier signature scheme, ABTTS, consists of five PPTs: ABTTS= (**ABTTS.Setup**, **ABTTS.KG**, **ABTTS.SKG**, **ABTTS.Sign**, **ABTTS.Vrfy**).

ABTTS.Setup$(1^\lambda, \mathcal{U}) \to (\mathrm{MSK}, \mathrm{PK})$. Given the security parameter 1^λ and the attribute universe $\mathcal{U}$, it returns a master secret key MSK and a public key PK.

ABTTS.KG$(\mathrm{MSK}, \mathrm{PK}, S) \to \mathrm{SK}_S$. Given the master secret key MSK, the public key PK and an attribute set $S \subset \mathcal{U}$, it returns a secret key SK_S that corresponds to S.

ABTTS.SKG$(\mathrm{MSK}, \mathrm{PK}, \mathrm{SK}_S, f) \to (\mathrm{SSK}_{S,f}, \mathrm{SPK}_f)$. Given the master secret key MSK, the public key PK, a secret key SK_S and an access formula f, it returns a pair $(\mathrm{SSK}_{S,f}, \mathrm{SPK}_f)$ of a secondary secret key and a secondary public key.

ABTTS.Sign$(\mathrm{PK}, \mathrm{SK}_S, \mathrm{SSK}_{S,f}, \mathrm{SPK}_f, (m, f)) \to \sigma$. Given the public key PK, a secret key SK_S, a secondary secret key $\mathrm{SSK}_{S,f}$, a secondary public key SPK_f and a pair (m, f) of a message $m \in \{1, 0\}^*$ and an access formula f, it returns a signature σ.

ABTTS.Vrfy$(\mathrm{PK}, \mathrm{SPK}_f, (m, f), \sigma) \to 1/0$. Given the public key PK, a secondary public key SPK_f, a pair (m, f) of a message and an access formula and a signature σ, it returns a decision 1 or 0. When it is 1, we say that $((m, f), \sigma)$ is *valid*. When it is 0, we say that $((m, f), \sigma)$ is *invalid*. We demand correctness of ABTTS that, for any λ, any $\mathcal{U}$, any $S \subset \mathcal{U}$ and any (m, f) such that $f(S) = 1$, $\Pr[(\mathrm{MSK}, \mathrm{PK}) \leftarrow$ **ABTTS.Setup** $(1^\lambda, \mathcal{U})$, $\mathrm{SK}_S \leftarrow$ **ABTTS.KG**$(\mathrm{MSK}, \mathrm{PK}, S)$, $(\mathrm{SSK}_{S,f}, \mathrm{SPK}_f) \leftarrow$ **ABTTS.SKG** $(\mathrm{MSK}, \mathrm{PK}, \mathrm{SK}_S, f)$, $\sigma \leftarrow$ **ABTTS.Sign**$(\mathrm{SK}_S, \mathrm{PK}, \mathrm{SSK}_{S,f}, \mathrm{SPK}_f, (m, f))$, $b \leftarrow$ **ABS.Vrfy**$(\mathrm{PK}, \mathrm{SPK}_f, (m, f), \sigma) : b = 1] = 1$.

3.2 Security Against Chosen-Message Attacks on ABTTS

A PPT adversary $\mathcal{F}$ tries to make a forgery $((m^*, f^*), \sigma^*)$ that consists of a message, a target access formula and a signature. The following experiment $\mathbf{Expr}^{\text{euf-cma}}_{\mathtt{ABTTS},\mathcal{F}}(1^\lambda, \mathcal{U})$ of a forger $\mathcal{F}$ defines the *chosen-message attack making an existential forgery*.

$\mathbf{Expr}^{\text{euf-cma}}_{\mathtt{ABTTS},\mathcal{F}}(1^\lambda, \mathcal{U})$:
$(\mathrm{PK}, \mathrm{MSK}) \leftarrow$ **ABTTS.Setup**$(1^\lambda, \mathcal{U})$
$((m^*, f^*), \sigma^*) \leftarrow \mathcal{F}^{\mathcal{ABTTSKG}, \mathcal{ABTTSSPK}, \mathcal{ABTTSSIGN}}(\mathrm{PK})$
If **ABTTS.Vrfy**$(\mathrm{PK}, \mathrm{SPK}_f, (m^*, f^*), \sigma^*) = 1$
then Return Win else Return Lose

In the experiment, $\mathcal{F}$ issues key-extraction queries to its oracle $\mathcal{ABTTSKG}$, secondary public key queries to its oracle $\mathcal{ABTTSSPK}$ and signing queries to its oracle $\mathcal{ABTTSSIGN}$. Giving an attribute set S_i, $\mathcal{F}$ queries $\mathcal{ABTTSKG}(\mathrm{MSK}, \mathrm{PK}, \cdot)$

for a secret key SK_{S_i}. Giving an attribute set S and an access formula f, $\mathcal{F}$ queries $\mathcal{ABTTSSPK}(\mathrm{MSK}, \mathrm{PK}, \mathrm{SK}_{\cdot}, \cdot)$ for a secondary public key SPK_f. Giving an attribute set S_j and a pair (m_j, f_j) of a message and an access formula, $\mathcal{F}$ queries $\mathcal{ABTTSSIGN}(\mathrm{PK}, \mathrm{SK}_{\cdot}, \mathrm{SSK}_{\cdot,\cdot}, \mathrm{SPK}_{\cdot}, (\cdot,\cdot))$ for a valid signature σ when $f(S_j) = 1$. As a rule of the two-tier signature, each published secondary public key SPK_f can be used only once to obtain a signature [3].

f^* is called a *target access formula* of $\mathcal{F}$. Here we consider the *adaptive target* case in the sense that $\mathcal{F}$ is allowed to choose f^* after seeing PK and issuing three queries. Two restrictions are imposed on $\mathcal{F}$: (1) $f^*(S_i) = 0$ for all S_i in key-extraction queries; (2) (m^*, f^*) was never queried in signing queries. The numbers of key-extraction queries and signing queries are at most q_{ke} and q_{sig}, respectively, which are bounded by a polynomial in λ. The *advantage* of $\mathcal{F}$ over ABTTS is defined as $\mathbf{Adv}^{\text{euf-cma}}_{\text{ABTTS},\mathcal{F}}(\lambda, \mathcal{U}) \stackrel{\text{def}}{=} \Pr[\mathbf{Expr}^{\text{euf-cma}}_{\text{ABTTS},\mathcal{F}}(1^\lambda, \mathcal{U}) \text{ returns } \textsc{Win}]$.

Definition 2 (EUF-CMA of ABTTS). *ABTTS is called existentially unforgeable against chosen-message attacks if, for any PPT $\mathcal{F}$ and any $\mathcal{U}$, $\mathbf{Adv}^{\text{euf-cma}}_{\text{ABTTS},\mathcal{F}}(\lambda, \mathcal{U})$ is negligible in λ.*

Then we define *attribute privacy* of ABTTS.

Definition 3 (Attribute Privacy of ABTTS). *ABTTS is called to have attribute privacy if, for all $(PK, MSK) \leftarrow$ $\mathbf{ABTTS.Setup}(1^\lambda, \mathcal{U})$, for all message m, for all attribute sets S_1 and S_2, for all signing keys $SK_{S_1} \leftarrow$ $\mathbf{ABTTS.KG}(PK, MSK, S_1)$ and $SK_{S_2} \leftarrow \mathbf{ABTTS.KG}(PK, MSK, S_2)$, for all secondary keys $(SSK_{S_1,f}, SPK_f) \leftarrow \mathbf{ABTTS.SKG}(MSK, PK, SK_{S_1}, f)$ and $(SSK_{S_2,f}, SPK_f) \leftarrow \mathbf{ABTTS.SKG}(MSK, PK, SK_{S_2}, f)$ and for all access formula f such that $[f(S_1) = 1 \wedge f(S_2) = 1] \vee [f(S_1) \neq 1 \wedge f(S_2) \neq 1]$, two distributions*
$\sigma_1 \leftarrow \mathbf{ABTTS.Sign}(PK, SK_{S_1}, SSK_{S_1,f}, SPK_f, (m, f))$ and
$\sigma_2 \leftarrow \mathbf{ABTTS.Sign}(PK, SK_{S_2}, SSK_{S_2,f}, SPK_f, (m, f))$ are identical.

4 Σ-protocol for Monotone Access Formula

In this section, we enhance the identification protocol by Okamoto [15] to the boolean proof system $\boldsymbol{\Sigma}_f$ proposed by Anada et al. [2].

4.1 Our Language L_f

We assume R to be an NP-relation. Let $R(\cdot,\cdot) : (\{1,0\}^*)^2 \to \{1,0\}$ denote the relation-function which returns $(x, w) \stackrel{?}{\in} R$. Let $f = f((X_{i_j})_{j=1}^a)$ be a boolean formula over boolean variables $\{X_i\}_i$.

Definition 4 (Language for f). *The relation R_f and the corresponding language L_f for a boolean formula f are:*

$$R_f \stackrel{def}{=} \{(x = (x_{i_j})_{j=1}^a, w = (w_{i_j})_{j=1}^a) \in \{1,0\}^* \times \{1,0\}^*; f(R(x_{i_j}, w_{i_j})_{j=1}^a) = 1\},$$

$$L_f \stackrel{def}{=} \{x \in \{1,0\}^*; \exists w, (x, w) \in R_f\}.$$

We consider hereafter the case that w is divided into $(w_{i_j})_{j=1}^{a} = (e_{i_j}, s_{i_j})_{j=1}^{a}$. (In/after the next section, we will consider the special case that $e_{i_j}, j = 1, \ldots, a$, are all equal to a single element e. The common component e will be a tag τ of a signature bundle.)

4.2 Our Σ-protocol $\mathbf{\Sigma}_f$ for L_f

Our Σ-protocol $\mathbf{\Sigma}_f$ is a zero-knowledge proof-of-knowledge $\mathbf{ZKPK}[w := (w_{\rho(l)})_l := (e_{\rho(l)}, s_{\rho(l)})_l, l \in \mathrm{Leaf}(\mathcal{T}_f) : x := (\text{equations})]$ for the language L_f, where the equations are for all the leaf nodes:

$$Z_{\rho(l)} = Z_{\rho(l),1}^{e_{\rho(l)}} Z_{\rho(l),2}^{s_{\rho(l)}}, \; l \in \mathrm{Leaf}(\mathcal{T}_f). \tag{1}$$

In the above equation, $Z_{\rho(l)}$ is represented by $(e_{\rho(l)}, s_{\rho(l)})$ to the base $(Z_{\rho(l),1}, Z_{\rho(l),2})$. A prover $\mathcal{P}(x, w, f)$ and a verifier $\mathcal{V}(x, f)$ execute our Σ-protocol in the following way.

$\underline{\mathcal{P}(x, w, f)}$. To prove the knowledge of those representations $(e_{\rho(l)}, s_{\rho(l)})$, $\mathcal{P}$ computes the first message, a commitment $(\mathrm{CMT}_l)_l$, as follows. Let $\bar{\mathbb{Z}}$ be the exponent domain for the above expression. To do the computation honestly at a leaf l, $\mathcal{P}$ chooses $\eta_{e,l}, \eta_{s,l} \overset{\$}{\leftarrow} \bar{\mathbb{Z}}$, and puts $\mathrm{CMT}_l := Z_{\rho(l),1}^{\eta_{e,l}} Z_{\rho(l),2}^{\eta_{s,l}}$. To simulate the computation at a leaf l, $\mathcal{P}$ chooses $\eta_{e,l}, \theta_{s,l} \overset{\$}{\leftarrow} \bar{\mathbb{Z}}$, and in addition, $(c_n)_n, c_n \in \bar{\mathbb{Z}}$. Here $(c_n)_n$ are chosen in accordance with the so called boolean proof system of Anada et al. [2]. Then $\mathcal{P}$ puts for each leaf l $\theta_{e,l} := \eta_{e,l} + c_l e_{\rho(l)}$, and $\mathrm{CMT}_l := Z_{\rho(l)}^{-c_l} Z_{\rho(l),1}^{\theta_{e,l}} Z_{\rho(l),2}^{\theta_{s,l}}$. $\mathcal{P}$ sends $(\mathrm{CMT}_l)_l$ to a verifier $\mathcal{V}$.

$\underline{\mathcal{V}(x, f)}$. Receiving $(\mathrm{CMT}_l)_l$, $\mathcal{V}(x, f)$ chooses the second message: a challenge $\mathrm{CHA} \overset{\$}{\leftarrow} \bar{\mathbb{Z}}$, uniformly at random, and sends CHA to $\mathcal{P}$.

$\underline{\mathcal{P}(x, w, f)}$. Receiving CHA, $\mathcal{P}$ completes to compute the third message; that is, $\mathcal{P}$ completes the division $(\mathrm{CHA}_n := c_n)_n$ such that $\mathrm{CHA}_{r(\mathcal{T}_f)} = \mathrm{CHA}$, and a response $(\mathrm{RES}_l := (\theta_{e,l}, \theta_{s,l}))_l$ with $\theta_{e,l} := \eta_{e,l} + c_l e_{\rho(l)}$, $\theta_{s,l} := \eta_{s,l} + c_l s_{\rho(l)}$. $\mathcal{P}$ sends $(\mathrm{CHA}_l)_l$ and $(\mathrm{RES}_l)_l$ to $\mathcal{V}$.

$\underline{\mathcal{V}(x, f)}$. Receiving $(\mathrm{CHA}_l)_l$ and $(\mathrm{RES}_l)_l$, $\mathcal{V}$ checks the integrity of the division $(\mathrm{CHA}_l)_l$. Then $\mathcal{V}$ verifies:

$$\mathrm{CMT}_l \overset{?}{=} Z_{\rho(l)}^{-c_l} Z_{\rho(l),1}^{\theta_{e,l}} Z_{\rho(l),2}^{\theta_{s,l}}, \; l \in \mathrm{Leaf}(\mathcal{T}_f). \tag{2}$$

According to the division rule of Anada et al. [2], the integrity of $(\mathrm{CHA}_l = c_l)_l$ can be checked as follows: From the leaves to the root, and at every inner node $n \in \mathrm{iNode}(\mathcal{T}_f)$ as well as its two children ch_1, ch_2;

- If n is an AND node($\wedge$), then verify $c_{ch_1} \overset{?}{=} c_{ch_2}$. If so, put $c_n := c_{ch_1}$.
- Else if n is an OR node ($\vee$), then just put$c_n := c_{ch_1} + c_{ch_2}$.
- If n is the root node, then verify $c_n \overset{?}{=} \mathrm{CHA}$.
- Repeat until all $n \in \mathrm{iNode}(\mathcal{T}_f)$ are verified.

Our $\mathbf{\Sigma}_f$ can be shown to possess the three requirements of Σ-protocol: completeness, special soundness and honest-verifier zero-knowledge.

5 Signature Bundle Scheme in RSA

In this section, we propose a signature bundle scheme in the RSA setting by extending the Camenisch-Lysyanskaya signature scheme [5]. We first construct the scheme. Then we discuss its EUF-CMA security. (The scheme in the discrete logarithm setting is proposed in Appendix A).

5.1 Construction of Our SB in RSA

Our signature bundle scheme SB = (**SB**.**KG**, **SB**.**Sign**, **SB**.**Vrfy**) is described as follows. Let $l_{\mathcal{M}}$ be a parameter. The message space $\mathcal{M}$ consists of all binary strings of length $l_{\mathcal{M}}$. Let $n = n(\lambda)$ denote the maximum number of messages made into a bundle, which is a polynomial in λ.
SB.**KG**$(1^\lambda) \to (\mathrm{PK}, \mathrm{SK})$. Given 1^λ, it chooses a special RSA modulus $N = pq$ of length $l_N = \lambda$, where $p = 2p' + 1$ and $q = 2q' + 1$ are safe primes. For $i = 1$ to n, it chooses $g_{i,0}, g_{i,1}, g_{i,2} \xleftarrow{\$} QR_N$. It puts $\mathrm{PK} := (N, (g_{i,0}, g_{i,1}, g_{i,2})_{i=1}^n)$ and $\mathrm{SK} = p$, and returns $(\mathrm{PK}, \mathrm{SK})$.
SB.**Sign**$(\mathrm{PK}, \mathrm{SK}, (m_i)_{i=1}^n) \to (\tau, (\sigma_i)_{i=1}^n)$. Given PK, SK and messages $(m_i)_{i=1}^n$ each of which is of length $l_{\mathcal{M}}$, it chooses a prime e of length $l_e = l_{\mathcal{M}} + 2$ at random. For $i = 1$ to n, it chooses an integer s_i of length $l_s = l_N + l_{\mathcal{M}} + l$ at random, where l is a security parameter, and it computes the value A_i:

$$A_i := (g_{i,0} g_{i,1}^{m_i} g_{i,2}^{s_i})^{\frac{1}{e}}. \tag{3}$$

It puts $\tau = e$ and $\sigma_i = (s_i, A_i)$ for each i and returns $(\tau, (\sigma_i)_{i=1}^n)$.
SB.**Vrfy**$(\mathrm{PK}, (m_i)_{i=1}^n, (\tau, (\sigma_i)_{i=1}^n)) \to 1/0$. Given PK, $(m_i)_{i=1}^n$ and a signature bundle $(\tau, (\sigma_i)_{i=1}^n)$, it verifies whether the following holds: $e := \tau$ is of length l_e and for $i = 1$ to n: $A_i^e = g_{i,0} g_{i,1}^{m_i} g_{i,2}^{s_i}$.

5.2 Security of Our SB in RSA

Theorem 1 (EUF-CMA of Our SB in RSA). *Our signature bundle scheme SB is existentially unforgeable against chosen-message attacks under the Strong RSA assumption.*

6 Attribute-Based ID Scheme in RSA

In this section, we combine two building blocks to obtain our attribute-based identification scheme; that is, the Σ-protocol $\mathbf{\Sigma}_f$ in Sect. 4.2 and the signature bundle scheme SB in Sect. 5.1.

6.1 Construction of Our ABID in RSA

ABID.Setup$(1^\lambda, \mathcal{U}) \to (\mathrm{MSK}, \mathrm{PK})$. Given the security parameter 1^λ and an attribute universe $\mathcal{U}$, it chooses a special RSA modulus $N = pq, p = 2p' + 1, q = 2q' + 1$ of length $l_N = 2\lambda$. For $\mathsf{at} \in \mathcal{U}$, it chooses $g_{\mathsf{at},0}, g_{\mathsf{at},1}, g_{\mathsf{at},2} \stackrel{\$}{\leftarrow} QR_N$ and a hash key $\mu \stackrel{\$}{\leftarrow} \mathit{Hashkeysp}(1^\lambda)$ of a hash function Hash_μ with the value in $\mathbb{Z}_{\phi(N)}$. It puts $\mathrm{PK} := (N, (g_{\mathsf{at},0}, g_{\mathsf{at},1}, g_{\mathsf{at},2})_{\mathsf{at}\in\mathcal{U}}, \mu, \mathcal{U})$ and $\mathrm{MSK} := p$. It returns PK and MSK.

ABID.KG$(\mathrm{MSK}, \mathrm{PK}, S) \to \mathrm{SK}_S$. Given PK, MSK and an attribute subset S, it chooses a prime e of length l_e. For $\mathsf{at} \in S$, it computes $a_{\mathsf{at}} \leftarrow \mathit{Hash}_\mu(\mathsf{at})$, $s_{\mathsf{at}} \stackrel{\$}{\leftarrow} \mathbb{Z}$ of length l_e, $A_{\mathsf{at}} := (g_{\mathsf{at},0} g_{\mathsf{at},1}^{a_{\mathsf{at}}} g_{\mathsf{at},2}^{s_{\mathsf{at}}})^{\frac{1}{e}}$. It puts $\mathrm{SK}_S := (e, (s_{\mathsf{at}}, A_{\mathsf{at}})_{\mathsf{at}\in S})$.

$\mathcal{P}(\mathrm{SK}_S, \mathrm{PK}, f)$ and $\mathcal{V}(\mathrm{PK}, f)$ execute $\boldsymbol{\Sigma}_f$ with the following precomputation. For $\mathsf{at} \in \mathrm{At}(f)$, $\mathcal{P}$ chooses $r_{\mathsf{at}} \stackrel{\$}{\leftarrow} \mathbb{Z}$ of length l_e. If $\mathsf{at} \in S$ then $s'_{\mathsf{at}} := s_{\mathsf{at}} + e r_{\mathsf{at}}$, $A'_{\mathsf{at}} := A_{\mathsf{at}} g_{\mathsf{at},2}^{-r_{\mathsf{at}}}$. Else $s'_{\mathsf{at}} \stackrel{\$}{\leftarrow} \mathbb{Z}$ of length l_e, $A'_{\mathsf{at}} \stackrel{\$}{\leftarrow} \mathbb{Z}_N^*$. $\mathcal{P}$ puts $Z_{\mathsf{at}} := g_{\mathsf{at},0} g_{\mathsf{at},1}^{a_{\mathsf{at}}}$, $Z_{\mathsf{at},1} := A'_{\mathsf{at}}$, $Z_{\mathsf{at},2} := g_{\mathsf{at},2}$. Then the statement for $\boldsymbol{\Sigma}_f$ is $x := (x_{\mathsf{at}} := (Z_{\mathsf{at}}, Z_{\mathsf{at},1}, Z_{\mathsf{at},2}))_{\mathsf{at}}$ and the witness is $w := (\tau := e, (w_{\mathsf{at}} := s'_{\mathsf{at}})_{\mathsf{at}})$, where $\mathsf{at} \in \mathrm{At}(f)$ for x and w. $\mathcal{P}$ sends the randomized values $(A'_{\mathsf{at}})_{\mathsf{at}}$ to $\mathcal{V}$ for $\mathcal{V}$ to be able to compute the statement x.

After the above precomputation, $\mathcal{P}$ and $\mathcal{V}$ can execute $\boldsymbol{\Sigma}_f$ for the language L_f. In other words, $\mathcal{P}$ and $\mathcal{V}$ execute $\mathbf{ZKPK}[(e, s'_{\rho(l)})_l, l \in \mathrm{Leaf}(\mathcal{T}_f) : \text{equations}]$, for the language L_f, where equations are: $Z_{\rho(l)} = Z_{\rho(l),1}^{e} Z_{\rho(l),2}^{s'_{\rho(l)}}, l \in \mathrm{Leaf}(\mathcal{T}_f)$. Note that $\mathcal{V}$ verifies whether the following verification equations hold or not for all the leaf nodes:

$$\mathrm{CMT}_l \stackrel{?}{=} Z_{\rho(l)}^{-c_l} Z_{\rho(l),1}^{\theta_{e,l}} Z_{\rho(l),2}^{\theta_{s',l}}, l \in \mathrm{Leaf}(\mathcal{T}_f). \tag{4}$$

$\mathcal{V}$ returns 1 or 0 accordingly.

6.2 Security of Our ABID in RSA

Claim 1 (Concurrent Security of Our ABID Under a Single Tag). *Our* `ABID` *is secure against concurrent attacks if our signature bundle scheme* `SB` *is existentially unforgeable against chosen-message attacks and if the extracted values e by the extractor of the underlying Σ-protocol $\boldsymbol{\Sigma}_f$ is a single value.*

Note that Claim 1 is needed only as intermediate result. That is, the assumption that the extracted value e is a single value is assured by the two-tier keys issuer, **ABTTS.SKG**, in the next section.

7 Attribute-Based Two-Tier Signature Scheme in RSA

In this section, we construct our ABTTS concretely. By applying the method of two-tier keys to our ABID in the last section, we attain the ABTTS scheme.

Our ABTTS enjoys EUF-CMA, collusion resistance and attribute privacy, in the standard model.

The critical point is that the secondary key generator **ABTTS.SKG** can issue a legitimate statement x for the boolean proof system $\mathbf{\Sigma}_f$. Hence our ABTTS can avoid collusion attacks on secret keys.

7.1 Construction of Our ABTTS in RSA

ABTTS.Setup$(1^\lambda, \mathcal{U}) \rightarrow (\mathrm{MSK}, \mathrm{PK})$. Given the security parameter 1^λ and an attribute universe $\mathcal{U}$, it chooses a special RSA modulus $N = pq, p = 2p' + 1$, $q = 2q' + 1$ of length $l_N = 2\lambda$. For $\mathsf{at} \in \mathcal{U}$, it chooses $g_{\mathsf{at},0}, g_{\mathsf{at},1}, g_{\mathsf{at},2} \overset{\$}{\leftarrow} QR_N$ and a hash key $\mu \overset{\$}{\leftarrow} \mathit{Hashkeysp}(1^\lambda)$ of a hash function Hash_μ with the value in $\mathbb{Z}_{\phi(N)}$. It puts $\mathrm{PK} := (N, (g_{\mathsf{at},0}, g_{\mathsf{at},1}, g_{\mathsf{at},2})_{\mathsf{at} \in \mathcal{U}}, \mu, \mathcal{U})$ and $\mathrm{MSK} := p$. It returns PK and MSK.

ABTTS.KG$(\mathrm{MSK}, \mathrm{PK}, S) \rightarrow \mathrm{SK}_S$. Given PK, MSK and an attribute subset S, it chooses a prime e of length l_e. For $\mathsf{at} \in S$, it computes $a_{\mathsf{at}} \leftarrow \mathit{Hash}_\mu(\mathsf{at})$, $s_{\mathsf{at}} \overset{\$}{\leftarrow} \mathbb{Z}$ of length l_e, $A_{\mathsf{at}} := (g_{\mathsf{at},0} g_{\mathsf{at},1}^{a_{\mathsf{at}}} g_{\mathsf{at},2}^{s_{\mathsf{at}}})^{\frac{1}{e}}$. It puts $\mathrm{SK}_S := (e, (s_{\mathsf{at}}, A_{\mathsf{at}})_{\mathsf{at} \in S})$ and returns SK_S.

ABTTS.SKG$(\mathrm{MSK}, \mathrm{PK}, \mathrm{SK}_S, f) \rightarrow (\mathrm{SSK}_{S,f}, \mathrm{SPK}_f)$. Given MSK, PK, the secret key SK_S and an access formula f, it first checks whether the components $e_{\rho(l)}$ in SK_S, $\rho(l) \in S$, are equal to a single value e or not. If it is false, then it aborts. Then it computes the statement for $\mathbf{\Sigma}_f$, $x := (x_{\mathsf{at}} := (Z_{\mathsf{at}}, Z_{\mathsf{at},1}, Z_{\mathsf{at},2}))_{\mathsf{at}}$, and the witness $w := (\tau := e, (w_{\mathsf{at}} := s'_{\mathsf{at}})_{\mathsf{at}})$, where $\mathsf{at} \in \mathrm{At}(f)$ for x and w. Then it runs the prover $\mathcal{P}$ according to $\mathbf{\Sigma}_f$ as $((\mathrm{CMT}_l)_l, st) \leftarrow \mathcal{P}(\mathrm{SK}_S, \mathrm{PK}, f)$. Then it puts $\mathrm{SSK}_{S,f} := (w, (\mathrm{CMT}_l)_l \| st)$ and $\mathrm{SPK}_f := (x, (\mathrm{CMT}_l)_l)$. It returns $\mathrm{SSK}_{S,f}$ and SPK_f.

ABTTS.Sign$(\mathrm{PK}, \mathrm{SK}_S, \mathrm{SSK}_{S,f}, \mathrm{SPK}_f, (m, f)) \rightarrow \sigma$. Given PK, SK_S, the secondary secret key $\mathrm{SSK}_{S,f}$, the secondary public key SPK_f, and a pair (m, f) of a message in $\{1,0\}^{l_{\mathcal{M}}}$ and an access formula f, it computes $\mathrm{CHA} \leftarrow \mathit{Hash}_\mu((A'_{\mathsf{at}})_{\mathsf{at}} \| (\mathrm{CMT}_l)_l \| m)$. Then, it runs the prover $\mathcal{P}$ according to $\mathbf{\Sigma}_f$ as $((\mathrm{CHA}_l)_l (\mathrm{RES}_l)_l \leftarrow \mathcal{P}((\mathrm{CMT}_l)_l \| \mathrm{CHA} \|, st)$. Finally, it returns the signature $\sigma := ((A'_{\mathsf{at}})_{\mathsf{at}}, (\mathrm{CMT}_l)_l, (\mathrm{CHA}_l)_l, (\mathrm{RES}_l)_l)$.

ABTTS.Vrfy$(\mathrm{PK}, \mathrm{SPK}_f, (m, f), \sigma) \rightarrow 1/0$. Given PK, the secondary public key SPK_f, a pair (m, f) and a signature σ, it first computes the statement for $\mathbf{\Sigma}_f$, $x := (x_{\mathsf{at}} := (Z_{\mathsf{at}}, Z_{\mathsf{at},1}, Z_{\mathsf{at},2}))_{\mathsf{at}}$, and the witness $w := (\tau := e$, $(w_{\mathsf{at}} := s'_{\mathsf{at}})_{\mathsf{at}})$, where $\mathsf{at} \in \mathrm{At}(f)$ for x and w. Then it computes $\mathrm{CHA} \leftarrow \mathit{Hash}_\mu((A'_{\mathsf{at}})_{\mathsf{at}} \| (\mathrm{CMT}_l)_l \| m)$. Then, it runs the verifier $\mathcal{V}$ according to $\mathbf{\Sigma}_f$ as acc or $0 \leftarrow \mathcal{V}(\mathrm{PK}, f, (\mathrm{CMT}_l)_l \| CHA \| (\mathrm{RES}_l)_l)$. It returns 1 or 0 accordingly.

7.2 Security of Our ABTTS in RSA

Theorem 2 (EUF-CMA of Our ABTTS in RSA). *Our attribute-based two-tier signature scheme ABTTS is existentially unforgeable against chosen-message attacks under the Strong RSA assumption in the standard model.*

Theorem 3 (Attribute Privacy of Our ABTTS in RSA). *Our attribute-based two-tier signature scheme ABTTS has attribute privacy.*

8 Conclusions

We defined the attribute-based two-tier signature scheme (ABTTS). Then we provided ABTTS concretely that enjoys EUF-CMA, collusion resistance and attribute privacy, in the standard model.

Acknowledgements. Concerning the first and the second authors, this work is partially supported by Grants-in-Aid for Scientific Research; Research Project Number:15K00029.

Appendix A Signature Bundle Scheme in Discrete Log

Our pairing-based signature bundle scheme, SB = (**SB.KG**, **SB.Sign**, **SB.Vrfy**), is described as follows.

SB.KG$(1^\lambda) \rightarrow (\mathrm{PK}, \mathrm{SK})$. Given 1^λ, it executes a group generator $\mathtt{BlGrp}(1^\lambda)$ to get $(p, \mathbb{G}_1, \mathbb{G}_2, \mathbb{G}_T, e(\cdot,\cdot))$. For $i = 1$ to n, it chooses $g_{i,0}, g_{i,1}, g_{i,2} \xleftarrow{\$} \mathbb{G}_1, h_0 \xleftarrow{\$} \mathbb{G}_2, \alpha \xleftarrow{\$} \mathbb{Z}_p$ and it puts $h_1 := h_0^\alpha$. It puts $\mathrm{PK} := ((g_{i,0}, g_{i,1}, g_{i,2})_{i=1}^n, h_0, h_1)$ and $\mathrm{SK} := \alpha$, and returns $(\mathrm{PK}, \mathrm{SK})$.

SB.Sign$(\mathrm{PK}, \mathrm{SK}, (m_i)_{i=1}^n) \rightarrow (\tau, (\sigma_i)_{i=1}^n)$. Given PK, SK and messages $(m_i)_{i=1}^n$ each of which is of length $l_{\mathcal{M}}$, it chooses $e \xleftarrow{\$} \mathbb{Z}_p$. For $i = 1$ to n, it chooses $s_i \xleftarrow{\$} \mathbb{Z}_p$, and it computes the value A_i:

$$A_i := (g_{i,0} g_{i,1}^{m_i} g_{i,2}^{s_i})^{\frac{1}{\alpha+e}}. \tag{5}$$

It puts $\tau = e$ and $\sigma_i = (s_i, A_i)$ for each i and returns $(\tau, (\sigma_i)_{i=1}^n)$.

SB.Vrfy$(\mathrm{PK}, (m_i)_{i=1}^n, (\tau, (\sigma_i)_{i=1}^n)) \rightarrow 1/0$. Given PK, $(m_i)_{i=1}^n$ and $(\tau, (\sigma_i)_{i=1}^n)$, it verifies whether the following holds: $e(A_i, h_0^e h_1) = e(g_{i,0} g_{i,1}^{m_i} g_{i,2}^{s_i}, h_0), breaki = 1, \ldots, n$.

Theorem 4 (EUF-CMA of Our SB in Discrete Log). *Our signature bundle scheme SB is existentially unforgeable against chosen-message attack under the Strong Diffie-Hellman assumption.*

Our ABID and ABTTS in the discrete logarithm setting will be given in the full version.

References

1. Anada, H., Arita, S., Handa, S., Iwabuchi, Y.: Attribute-based identification: definitions and efficient constructions. In: Boyd, C., Simpson, L. (eds.) ACISP. LNCS, vol. 7959, pp. 168–186. Springer, Heidelberg (2013)
2. Anada, H., Arita, S., Sakurai, K.: Attribute-based signatures without pairings via the fiat-shamir paradigm. In: ASIAPKC2014. ACM-ASIAPKC, vol. 2, pp. 49–58. ACM (2014)
3. Bellare, M., Shoup, S.: Two-tier signatures, strongly unforgeable signatures, and fiat-shamir without random oracles. In: Okamoto, T., Wang, X. (eds.) PKC 2007. LNCS, vol. 4450, pp. 201–216. Springer, Heidelberg (2007)
4. Boneh, D., Boyen, X.: Efficient selective-id secure identity-based encryption without random oracles. In: Cachin, C., Camenisch, J.L. (eds.) EUROCRYPT 2004. LNCS, vol. 3027, pp. 223–238. Springer, Heidelberg (2004)
5. Camenisch, J.L., Lysyanskaya, A.: A signature scheme with efficient protocols. In: Cimato, S., Galdi, C., Persiano, G. (eds.) SCN 2002. LNCS, vol. 2576, pp. 268–289. Springer, Heidelberg (2003)
6. Cramer, R.: Modular designs of secure, yet practical cyptographic protocols. Ph.D thesis, University of Amsterdam, Amsterdam, The Netherlands (1996)
7. Damgård, I.: On σ-protocols. In: Course Notes (2011). https://services.brics.dk/java/courseadmin/CPT/documents
8. El Kaafarani, A., Chen, L., Ghadafi, E., Davenport, J.: Attribute-based signatures with user-controlled linkability. In: Gritzalis, D., Kiayias, A., Askoxylakis, I. (eds.) CANS 2014. LNCS, vol. 8813, pp. 256–269. Springer, Heidelberg (2014)
9. I. E. T. Force.: Request for comments: 6960. http://tools.ietf.org/html/rfc6960
10. Goyal,V., Pandey, O., Sahai, A., Waters, B.: Attribute-based encryption for fine-grained access control of encrypted data. In: ACM-CCS 2006, vol. 263, pp. 89–98. ACM (2006)
11. Granger, R., Kleinjung, T., Zumbrägel, J.: Breaking '128-bit secure' supersingular binary curves. In: Garay, J.A., Gennaro, R. (eds.) CRYPTO 2014, Part II. LNCS, vol. 8617, pp. 126–145. Springer, Heidelberg (2014)
12. Guo, S., Zeng, Y.: Attribute-based signature scheme. In: ISA 2008, pp. 509–511. IEEE (2008)
13. Herranz, J.: Attribute-based signatures from RSA. Theoret. Comput. Sci. **527**, 73–82 (2014)
14. Maji, H.K., Prabhakaran, M., Rosulek, M.: Attribute-based signatures. In: Kiayias, A. (ed.) CT-RSA 2011. LNCS, vol. 6558, pp. 376–392. Springer, Heidelberg (2011)
15. Okamoto, T.: Provably secure and practical identification schemes and corresponding signature schemes. In: Brickell, E.F. (ed.) CRYPTO 1992. LNCS, vol. 740, pp. 31–53. Springer, Heidelberg (1993)
16. Okamoto, T., Takashima, K.: Efficient attribute-based signatures for non-monotone predicates in the standard model. In: Catalano, D., Fazio, N., Gennaro, R., Nicolosi, A. (eds.) PKC 2011. LNCS, vol. 6571, pp. 35–52. Springer, Heidelberg (2011)
17. Yasuda, M., Shimoyama, T., Kogure, J., Izu, T.: On the strength comparison of the ECDLP and the IFP. In: Visconti, I., De Prisco, R. (eds.) SCN 2012. LNCS, vol. 7485, pp. 302–325. Springer, Heidelberg (2012)

Public-Key Cryptography

Ciphertext-Policy Attribute-Based Broadcast Encryption with Small Keys

Benjamin Wesolowski[1] and Pascal Junod[2(✉)]

[1] EPFL, Lausanne, Switzerland
benjamin.wesolowski@epfl.ch
[2] University of Applied Sciences and Arts Western Switzerland (HES-SO/HEIG-VD), Yverdon-les-Bains, Switzerland
pascal.junod@heig-vd.ch

Abstract. Broadcasting is a very efficient way to securely transmit information to a large set of geographically scattered receivers, and in practice, it is often the case that these receivers can be grouped in sets sharing common characteristics (or attributes). We describe in this paper an efficient ciphertext-policy attribute-based broadcast encryption scheme (CP-ABBE) supporting negative attributes and able to handle access policies in conjunctive normal form (CNF). Essentially, our scheme is a combination of the Boneh-Gentry-Waters broadcast encryption and of the Lewko-Sahai-Waters revocation schemes; the former is used to express attribute-based access policies while the latter is dedicated to the revocation of individual receivers. Our scheme is the first one that involves a public key and private keys having a size that is independent of the number of receivers registered in the system. Its selective security is proven with respect to the Generalized Diffie-Hellman Exponent (GDHE) problem on bilinear groups.

Keywords: Attribute-based encryption · Broadcast encryption

1 Introduction

Broadcast channels allow transmitting information to a large set of geographically scattered receivers in a very efficient way. When this information is of high value, such as a high-definition Pay-TV stream or when delivered by a military geolocation system, for instance, one needs technical ways to enforce the signal reception by authorized receivers only. More than twenty years ago, the problem of securing a broadcast channel has began to attract cryptographers: the first works were the ones of Berkovits [2] and of Fiat and Naor [15], who coined the term "broadcast encryption". The underlying idea is that the broadcasting center sends an encrypted message to a set of non-revoked receivers, which is a

This work was supported by the EUREKA-Celtic+ H2B2VS project and by the University of Applied Sciences and Arts Western Switzerland (HES-SO). It was performed while the first author was working at HES-SO/HEIG-VD.

S. Kwon and A. Yun (Eds.): ICISC 2015, LNCS 9558, pp. 53–68, 2016.
DOI: 10.1007/978-3-319-30840-1_4

subset of all receivers. Obviously, revoked receivers (or other entities) spying the broadcast channel must not be able to decrypt a ciphertext, even if they collude together by sharing their private key material.

Precisely, if we denote by $\mathcal{U}$, with $n = |\mathcal{U}|$, the set of users (or receivers) and by $\mathcal{R}$, with $\ell = |\mathcal{R}|$, the set of revoked receivers, respectively, a *broadcast encryption scheme* is often meant to allow the secure transmission of information to an arbitrary set of receivers, *i.e.*, when $n - \ell \ll n$, while *revocation systems* are designed to exclude a small set of rogue receivers, *i.e.* when $\ell \ll n$.

A key characteristic of broadcast encryption and revocation schemes is the fact that no synchronism is assumed between the broadcasting center and the receivers, besides the initial key setup procedure: one speaks from *stateless* receivers. It means that, once each receiver is provisioned with its decryption key material, all the information required to decrypt a ciphertext must be contained in that ciphertext. Many stateless broadcast encryption schemes have been proposed in the past, being in the secret-key [18,20,34]) or in the public-key settings [6–8,12,13,17,27,37], while a large body of literature tackling the same problem, but for *stateful* receivers, this time, is available; we refer the reader to [9] and the references therein.

Attribute-Based Encryption. In practice, it is often the case that the receivers in a system can be grouped by common characteristics (or *attributes*). If we stick to a scenario around Pay-TV, receivers could be categorized by geographical location ("receivers located in California", "receivers located in a rural zone"), by technical capabilities ("receivers supporting HD content", "receivers supporting 4 K content", "receivers having an OS with patch level 3.14.159"), by subscription type ("receivers having access to the XYZ sport channels package", "receivers having access to the FGH adult channels package"), etc. Ideally, a broadcaster might then be willing to grant access to receivers according to a complicated access equation, such as to all "receivers having access to XYZ sport channels package, having an OS with patch level 3.14.159, but *not* located in California".

The idea of attribute-based encryption (ABE) has been proposed by Sahai and Waters in [41], as a generalization of identity-based encryption [5,42]; it was then formalized by Goyal and his co-authors in [19], who proposed the concepts of *ciphertext-policy (CP-ABE)* and *key-policy (KP-ABE)* encryption schemes. In the CP-ABE and KP-ABE models, the access policies are embedded in the ciphertext and in the private key, respectively. Since then, numerous variants of CP- and KP-ABE schemes have been published; see for instance [3,10,16,21,22, 26,28,29,35,38,40,43].

Attribute-Based Broadcast Encryption. Transforming an ABE encryption scheme for using it in a broadcast scenario is a natural question, as in practice, broadcasters are most of the time addressing sets of receivers sharing the same characteristics, instead of individual ones. An exception where a receiver might be addressed individually is when a key update is necessary, for example. This operation is rather costly in terms of bandwidth, as synchronism comes into play. It means that the individual key update messages have to be broadcast sufficiently many times on a sufficiently long period to guarantee their reception with high probability. This explains why addressing individual receivers is not possible in practice to enforce access equations in a broadcast setting and why efficient stateless broadcast encryption schemes are so useful.

The key difference between an *attributed-based broadcast encryption (ABBE)* scheme and an ABE one is the additional possibility to revoke individual receivers in an efficient way. Given an ABE scheme, it is possible to create a revocation system by defining a dedicated unique attribute for each receiver and to specify an access policy which rejects the revoked receivers. Unfortunately, this is in general not efficient, since in an ABE scheme, the length of the keys or ciphertexts depend often in a linear way from the number of attributes. This can become unpractical when the number of receivers is large. Concretely, one could use an ABE supporting negative attributes, such as [35], and assign individual attributes to each receivers. A ciphertext can then be sent to the non-revoked receiver identities by conjunctively adding the AND of negations of revoked receivers attributes to the access policy. Implementing this idea with [35], this would imply an acceptable overhead of $O(\ell)$ group elements in the ciphertext, with $\ell = |\mathcal{R}|$, but the private key would involve $O(n)$ attributes, where n is the total number of receivers. Furthermore, this scheme would not be dynamic in the sense of [12], i.e., one cannot easily add receivers in the system without sending individual messages to the receivers, which is, as mentionned above, costly in terms of bandwidth in a broadcast setting.

In a context where the number of receivers is way larger than the number of attributes, one is therefore interested in splitting the revocation system from the access structure. Motivated by this fact, a line of research has focused on designing ABE schemes allowing to efficiently revoke individual receivers. In other words, revoking a receiver is implemented conjunctively, meaning that even if that receiver possesses compatible attributes for a given access equation, but it belongs to the revoked receivers set $\mathcal{R}$, it will not be able to correctly decrypt the ciphertext.

Lubicz and Sirvent [33] have proposed a scheme allowing to express access policies in disjunctive normal form (DNF), *i.e.*, with disjunctions (OR) of conjunctions (AND), and able to handle negative attributes (NOT). Then, Attrapadung and Imai [1] proposed another approach, namely using a separate broadcast encryption scheme on the top of an ABE scheme, and they constructed both ciphertext-policy and key-policy variants. Since then, other designs have been published as well, see e.g. [24,32,45].

Finally, we note that attribute-based broadcast encryption schemes have numerous applications besides the Pay-TV or the geolocation satellites scenarios mentionned above. For instance, applications involving ABBE have been proposed in the context of secure storage of personal health records [31], of securing smart grids [14], and, more generally, in any data outsourcing systems requiring privacy [23].

Our Contributions. In this paper, we describe an efficient ciphertext-policy attribute-based broadcast encryption scheme (CP-ABBE) able to handle access policies in conjunctive normal form (CNF), *i.e.*, as conjunctions of disjunctions of attributes, and supporting negative attributes. Essentially, our scheme is a combination of the Boneh-Gentry-Waters broadcast encryption scheme [6] and of the Lewko-Sahai-Waters revocation system [27]. The former is used to express attribute-based access policies while the latter is dedicated to the revocation of individual receivers.

Denoting by $\mathcal{B}$ the set of attributes, our scheme requires a public key and private keys of size $O(N)$, where $N = |\mathcal{B}|$ is the total number of attributes. Ciphertexts are of size $O(\bar{\nu}+\ell)$, where $\ell = |\mathcal{R}|$ is the number of revoked receivers and $\bar{\nu}$ is the number of clauses in the access policy. We note that $\bar{\nu}$, N and ℓ are quantities independent of the number n of receivers registered in the system. As a consequence, and to the best of our knowledge, our proposal is the first ABBE scheme whose public and private key sizes *do not depend on the number of receivers in the system*, while the ciphertext length keeps linear in the size of the access policy and in the number of revoked receivers. This property is especially important in scenarios involving large numbers of users, such as large-scale Pay-TV or cloud-based storage systems, for instance.

Eventually, we prove the selective security of our scheme with respect to the Generalized Diffie-Hellman Exponent (GDHE) problem on bilinear groups [4], and we derive security bounds in the generic group model.

This paper is organized as follows: in Sect. 2, we recall the formal definition of attribute-based broadcast encryption schemes, their underlying security model as well as other mathematical preliminaries. Then, we describe our new scheme Sect. 3 and we prove its security in Sect. 4. Finally, we compare its characteristics to other existing ABBE schemes and we discuss some of its practical aspects in Sect. 6.

2 Mathematical Preliminaries

Let $\mathcal{U}$ denote a set of receivers (or users), $\mathcal{R} \subset \mathcal{U}$ the set of revoked receivers and $\mathcal{B}$ a set of attributes. Furthermore, let λ be a security parameter. A ciphertext-policy attribute-based broadcast encryption (CP-ABBE) scheme consists of the following four algorithms:

- $\mathsf{Setup}(\lambda) \to (\mathsf{pk}, \mathsf{msk})$ is a randomized algorithm which takes a security parameter λ as input and outputs the public key pk and a master key msk.
- $\mathsf{KeyGen}(u, \omega, \mathsf{msk}, \mathsf{pk}) \to \mathsf{dk}_u$ is a randomized algorithm that takes as input a receiver $u \in \mathcal{U}$, a set of attributes $\omega \subset \mathcal{B}$, the master key msk and the public key pk. It outputs a private, individual decryption key $\mathsf{dk}_{(u,\omega)}$ for the receiver u. $\mathsf{dk}_{(u,\omega)}$ will be simply denoted dk_u if it is clear from the context that u has set of attributes ω.
- $\mathsf{Encrypt}(\mathcal{R}, \mathbb{A}, \mathsf{pk}) \to (\mathsf{hdr}, \mathsf{k})$ is a randomized algorithm that takes as input a set of revoked receivers $\mathcal{R} \subset \mathcal{U}$, a Boolean access policy $\mathbb{A}$ expressed in conjonctive normal form and the public key pk. It outputs a header hdr as well as a session key k.

- $\mathsf{Decrypt}(\mathsf{hdr}, (\mathcal{R}, \mathbb{A}), \mathsf{dk}_{(u,\omega)}, (u, \omega), \mathsf{pk}) \rightarrow \mathsf{k}$ or $\perp$ is an algorithm taking as input a header hdr, a set of revoked receivers $\mathcal{R}$, an access policy $\mathbb{A}$, a decryption key $\mathsf{dk}_{(u,\omega)}$ for receiver u equipped with attributes ω as well as the public key pk. It outputs the session key k if and only if ω satisfies $\mathbb{A}$ and u is not in $\mathcal{R}$; otherwise, it outputs $\perp$.

The *selective security* notion for CP-ABBE is defined by the following probabilistic game:

- **Setup.** The adversary chooses a distribution of attributes $\mathfrak{B} : \mathcal{U} \rightarrow \mathcal{P}(\mathcal{B})$, declares a set of revoked receivers $\mathcal{R}^* \subset \mathcal{U}$ and an access policy $\mathbb{A}^*$. The challenger runs the Setup algorithm and gives the public key pk to the adversary $\mathcal{A}$.
- **Query phase 1.** The adversary is allowed to (adaptively) issue queries to the challenger for private keys dk_u for receivers $u \in \mathcal{U}$ such that either $u \in \mathcal{R}^*$ or $\mathfrak{B}(u)$ does not satisfy the policy $\mathbb{A}^*$, *i.e.*, receivers not able to decrypt a ciphertext.
- **Challenge.** After having run the encryption algorithm $\mathsf{Encrypt}(\mathcal{R}^*, \mathbb{A}^*, \mathsf{pk})$, the challenger gets a header hdr and a session key k. Next, he draws a bit b uniformly at random, sets $\mathsf{k}_b = \mathsf{k}$ and picks k_{1-b} uniformly at random in the space of possible session keys. He finally gives the triple $(\mathsf{hdr}, \mathsf{k}_0, \mathsf{k}_1)$ to the adversary.
- **Query phase 2.** The adversary is again allowed to (adaptively) issue queries for private keys dk_u for receivers $u \in \mathcal{U}$ such that either $u \in \mathcal{R}^*$ or $\mathfrak{B}(u)$ does not satisfy the policy $\mathbb{A}^*$.
- **Guess.** The adversary outputs a guess bit b'.

The adversary wins the game if $b = b'$ and its advantage is defined as

$$\mathrm{Adv}^{\mathrm{ind}}(\lambda, \mathcal{U}, \mathcal{B}, \mathcal{A}) = |2\Pr[b = b'] - 1| .$$

The set of receivers u for which $\mathcal{A}$ requested the private keys is the set of *colluding receivers*. Hence, selective security ensures semantic security against colluding receivers if the advantage of the adversary is negligible.

We note that in the selective security model, the attacker must output the access policy *before* seeing the public parameters. A stronger model, named full security, has been proposed in [30]. While selective security is not the strongest model one might hope for our scheme, we think that it is stronger than what one could expect in practice, as the list of revoked nodes and the access equations are typically defined by the broadcaster.

Now, let us recall the notion of bilinear group. Let $\mathbb{G}$ and $\mathbb{G}_T$ be two (multiplicative) cyclic groups, and g a generator of $\mathbb{G}$. A map $e : \mathbb{G} \times \mathbb{G} \rightarrow \mathbb{G}_T$ is a *symmetric, non-degenerate pairing* if it is bilinear, *i.e.* for any $u, v \in \mathbb{G}$ and $a, b \in \mathbb{Z}$, we have $e(u^a, v^b) = e(u, v)^{ab}$, and if it is non-degenerate, *i.e.* $e(g, g) \neq 1$. Endowed with such a pairing, $\mathbb{G}$ is called a *bilinear group.* For practical purposes, let us further assume that in a bilinear group $\mathbb{G}$, both the action of $\mathbb{G}$ and the pairing e are efficiently computable. Finally, we recall the *Generalized Diffie-Hellman Exponent (GDHE) Problem* [4].

Definition 1 (GDHE Decisional Problem). *Let $\mathbb{G}$ and $\mathbb{G}_T$ be two groups of prime order p, g a generator of $\mathbb{G}$, and $e : \mathbb{G} \times \mathbb{G} \longrightarrow \mathbb{G}_T$ a non-degenerate bilinear map. Let $f \in \mathbb{F}_p[X_1, \ldots, X_n]$ be a polynomial in n variables over $\mathbb{F}_p$, the finite field with p elements, and $P, Q \subset \mathbb{F}_p[X_1, \ldots, X_n]$ be two sets of polynomials, both containing 1. Choose $x_1, \ldots, x_n \in \mathbb{F}_p$ and $U \in \mathbb{G}_T$ uniformly at random. Given the elements*

$$g^{\pi(x_1,\ldots,x_n)} \text{ and } e(g,g)^{\rho(x_1,\ldots,x_n)}$$

for each $\pi \in P$ and $\rho \in Q$, the Generalized Diffie-Hellman Exponent (GDHE) Decisional Problem *is the problem of distinguishing $e(g,g)^{f(x_1,\ldots,x_n)}$ from U.*

Observe that in this setting, the classical Decisional Diffie-Hellman (DDH) problem reduces to an easy instance of the GDHE Decisional problem: let $P = \{1, a, b\}$, $Q = \{1\}$ and $f = ab$. Given g^a and g^b, we can distinguish g^{ab} from a uniform random element $h \in \mathbb{G}$ by observing that $e(g^a, g^b) = e(g^{ab}, g)$. This fact justifies the following definition, as in this example, (P, Q) and f are *dependent functions.*

Definition 2 (Dependent Functions). *A function f is said to be* dependent *on the sets P and Q if there exist constants $a_{\pi,\pi'}$ with $\pi, \pi' \in P$ and c_ρ with $\rho \in Q$ such that*

$$f = \sum_{\pi,\pi' \in P} a_{\pi,\pi'} \pi\pi' + \sum_{\rho \in Q} c_\rho \rho.$$

With this independence notion, it is proven that the (P, Q, f)-GDHE Decisional Problem is difficult in the generic group model.

Theorem 1 (Boneh et al. [4, Theorem A.2]**).** *Let*

$$d = \max\{2\deg(\pi), \deg(\rho), \deg(f) \mid \pi \in P, \rho \in Q\},$$

and $s = \max\{|P|, |Q|\}$ If f is independent of P and Q, then for any adversary $\mathcal{A}$ that makes a total of at most q queries to the oracle computing the group operations in $\mathbb{G}$, $\mathbb{G}_T$ and the pairing e, we have

$$|2\Pr[\mathcal{A} \text{ outputs } 0] - 1| \leq \frac{(q + 2s + 2)^2 \cdot d}{p}.$$

3 The New Scheme

Basically, our new scheme is a secure combination of the Boneh-Gentry-Waters (BGW) broadcast encryption scheme [6] and the Lewko-Sahai-Waters (LSW) [27] revocation system. This design strategy, which is similar to the one of Junod and Karlov [24], is motivated as follows.

3.1 High-Level Description

The BGW scheme targets arbitrary sets of priviledged receivers and involves ciphertexts with a constant size, if, as customary, one omits bandwidth consumed by the description of the set of priviledged receivers to be addressed; its public and private keys have a size depending on the number of receivers; note that, with the BGW scheme, one needs the public key to decrypt. Hence, we use it to express arbitrary access equations, that typically depend on a small number of attributes when compared to the total number of receivers. On its side, the LSW revocation scheme has ciphertexts whose size depends on the number of revoked receivers; however, its encryption and decryption keys are independant of the total number of users in the system. In systems potentially involving millions of receivers, this is a decisive practical advantage.

Given an access structure in CNF form $\mathbb{A} = \beta_1 \wedge \cdots \wedge \beta_N$ and a revocation set $\mathcal{R}$, our idea is to associate to each clause β_i a fragment of the session key k_i which can be computed only by a receiver satisfying the corresponding clause, and a fragment k_0 computable by non-revoked receivers. Then, the session key k can be derived out of the k_i's.

This alone would not resist to an attack from colluding receivers: if receiver u is revoked but satisfies $\mathbb{A}$, he can compute k_i for $i = 1, \ldots, N$, and v is not revoked but does not satisfy $\mathbb{A}$, he can compute k_0; together, u and v can compute k. To prevent this, we do not allow a receiver u to compute k_i directly, but rather an blinded value $\mathsf{k}_i^{\varepsilon_u}$ thereof, where ε_u is a secret exponent unique for each receiver u. Then, k can be derived from any collection $(\mathsf{k}_i^{\varepsilon_u})_{i=1}^n$. If u can compute $\mathsf{k}_i^{\varepsilon_u}$ for $i = 1, \ldots, N$ and v can compute $\mathsf{k}_0^{\varepsilon_v}$, they cannot derive k.

3.2 Formal Definitions

Let us write $\mathcal{B}^* = \mathcal{B} \cup \neg\mathcal{B}$ the set of all attributes $\mathcal{B}$ and their negations $\neg\mathcal{B}$. Let $\mathfrak{B} : \mathcal{U} \to \mathcal{P}(\mathcal{B}^*)$ be a *distribution of attributes*, *i.e.*, a map such that for any receiver $u \in \mathcal{U}$ and attribute $a \in \mathcal{B}$, either $a \in \mathfrak{B}(u)$ or $\neg a \in \mathfrak{B}(u)$, but not both. Let $\mathrm{id} : \mathcal{U} \to (\mathbb{Z}/p\mathbb{Z})^*$ be a public injection, and $\imath : \mathcal{B}^* \to \{2, 4, 6, \ldots, t-1\}$ be a public bijection where $t = 4N + 1$.

$\mathsf{Setup}(\lambda) \to (\mathsf{pk}, \mathsf{msk})$ According to the security parameter λ, choose two groups $\mathbb{G}$ and $\mathbb{G}_T$ of prime order $p > 2^\lambda$ as well as a non-degenerate bilinear pairing $e : \mathbb{G} \times \mathbb{G} \to \mathbb{G}_T$. Additionnaly, choose two non-zero elements $g, h = g^\xi \in \mathbb{G}$ and seven random exponents $\alpha, \gamma, b, \beta, \delta, r$ and r' in $\mathbb{Z}/p\mathbb{Z}$. Finally, let $g_i = g^{\alpha^i}$. The public key pk consists of the elements of $\mathbb{G}$ g, $g_n^{\gamma r'}$, g^r, $g_{n+1}^{rr'}$, $g_{n+1}^{rr'b}$, $g_{n+1}^{rr'b^2}$, $h^{b\alpha^{n+1}r'r}$, $g^{\delta r}$, g_n, $\left(g_{\imath(a)}^r\right)_{a \in \mathcal{B}^*}$, and the two elements of $\mathbb{G}_T$ $e(g_1, g_n)^{rr'\beta\gamma}$ and $e(g_1, g_n)^{r\beta}$. The authority keeps the exponents secret.

$\mathsf{KeyGen}(u, \mathfrak{B}(u), \mathsf{msk}, \mathsf{pk}) \to \mathsf{dk}_u$ Let $u \in \mathcal{U}$. Choose two random elements $\sigma_u, \varepsilon_u \in \mathbb{Z}/p\mathbb{Z}$. Define

$$D_{u,0} = \left(g^\gamma g^{b^2\sigma_u}\right)^{\varepsilon_u}, D_{u,1} = \left(g^{b \cdot \mathrm{id}(u)} h\right)^{\sigma_u\varepsilon_u}, D_{u,2} = g^{-\sigma_u\varepsilon_u}, D_{u,3} = g_1^{r(\beta+\varepsilon_u)}.$$

The private key of receiver u is

$$\mathsf{dk}_u = \left((D_{u,k})_{k=0}^3, \left(g_{\imath(a)}^{\varepsilon_u}\right)_{a \in \mathcal{B}^*}, \left(g_{n+1+\imath(a)}^{\varepsilon_u}\right)_{a \in \mathcal{B}^*}, \left(g_{\imath(a)}^{\delta\varepsilon_u}\right)_{a \in \mathfrak{B}(u)} \right).$$

$\mathsf{Encrypt}(\mathcal{R}, \mathbb{A}, \mathsf{pk}) \rightarrow (\mathsf{hdr}, \mathsf{k})$ Given an access policy $\mathbb{A} = \beta_1 \wedge \ldots \wedge \beta_N$, with $\beta_i = \beta_{i,1} \vee \ldots \vee \beta_{i,M_i}$ (modeled as $\beta_{i,j} \subseteq \mathcal{B} \cup \neg\mathcal{B}$) and a revocation set $\mathcal{R} \subset \mathcal{U}$, one chooses $s_0, \ldots, s_N \in \mathbb{Z}/p\mathbb{Z}$ at random and one defines $s = \gamma r' s_0 + \sum_{i=1}^N s_i$ (which needs not be computed). Also, one splits $s_0 = \sum_{u \in \mathcal{R}} s_u$. Let us define

$$C = g_n^s = \left(g_n^{\gamma \cdot r'}\right)^{s_0} g_n^{\left(\sum_{i=1}^N s_i\right)}.$$

For all $i = 1, \ldots, N$, one defines the elements $C_{i,0} = g^{rs_i}$ and

$$C_{i,1} = \left(g^{r\delta} \prod_{a \in \beta_i} g_{n+1-\imath(a)}^r \right)^{s_i},$$

as well as the corresponding N parts of the header $\mathsf{hdr}_i = (C_{i,0}, C_{i,1})$. One defines $C_0 = g_{n+1}^{rr's_0}$, and for each $u \in \mathcal{R}$,

$$C_{u,1} = g_{n+1}^{rr'bs_u} \text{ and } C_{u,2} = \left(g^{b^2 \mathrm{id}(u)} h^b\right)^{\alpha^{n+1} rr's_u}.$$

Let $\mathsf{hdr}_0 = (C_0, (C_{u,1})_{u \in \mathcal{R}}, (C_{u,2})_{u \in \mathcal{R}})$ and $\mathsf{hdr} = (C, \mathsf{hdr}_0, \ldots, \mathsf{hdr}_N)$. The global session key k is given by

$$\mathsf{k} = e(g_1, g_n)^{r\beta s} = \left(e(g_1, g_n)^{rr'\beta\gamma}\right)^{s_0} \cdot e\left(g_1^r, g_n^\beta\right)^{\left(\sum_{i=1}^N s_i\right)}$$

$\mathsf{Decrypt}(\mathsf{hdr}, (\mathcal{R}, \mathbb{A}), \mathsf{dk}_u, (u, \omega), \mathsf{pk}) \rightarrow \mathsf{k}$ or $\perp$ If $u \in \mathcal{R}$ or if there exists $i \in \{1, \ldots, N\}$, such that $\beta_i \cap \mathfrak{B}(u) = \emptyset$, return $\perp$. For $i = 1, \ldots, N$, choose one satisfying attribute $a \in \beta_i \cap \mathfrak{B}(u)$ and compute

$$\mathsf{k}_i^{\varepsilon_u} = \frac{e(g_{\imath(a)}^{\varepsilon_u}, C_{i,1})}{e\left(g_{\imath(a)}^{\delta\varepsilon_u} \prod_{a' \in \beta_i \setminus \{a\}} g_{n+1-\imath(a')+\imath(a)}^{\varepsilon_u}, C_{i,0}\right)}.$$

Also compute $\mathsf{k}_0^{\varepsilon_u}$ as

$$e(D_{u,0}, C_0) e\left(D_{u,1}, \prod_{u' \in \mathcal{R}} C_{u',1}^{1/(\mathrm{id}(u)-\mathrm{id}(u'))}\right)^{-1} e\left(D_{u,2}, \prod_{u' \in \mathcal{R}} C_{u',2}^{1/(\mathrm{id}(u)-\mathrm{id}(u'))}\right)^{-1}.$$

We have $\mathsf{k}_0^{\varepsilon_u} = e(g_1, g_n)^{rr's_0\varepsilon_u\gamma}$ and $\mathsf{k}_i^{\varepsilon_u} = e(g_1, g_n)^{rs_i\varepsilon_u}$ for $i = 1, \ldots, N$. Eventually, we can recover k as

$$\mathsf{k} = \frac{e(D_{u,3}, C)}{\prod_{i=0}^N \mathsf{k}_i^{\varepsilon_u}} = e(g_1, g_n)^{r\beta s}.$$

One can observe that the public-key size depends only on the total number of attributes defined in the system, and that the same holds for the decryption keys. The header size linearly depends only on the number of revoked rogue receivers.

If the number of attributes does not change during the lifetime of the system, we note that our new ABBE scheme is fully dynamic in the sense of [12]. Indeed, the deployment of new receivers does not imply to change the encryption or the decryption keys of other receivers, which is a desirable property for a stateless scheme.

At first sight, the system of attributes might look a bit less flexible in the sense that all receivers decryption keys include elements depending on all positive and negative attributes defined in the system. It means that the definition of new attributes after the system start arrives with the necessity of transmitting them to all receivers in a individual way, which comes with significant bandwidth issues in a system involving millions of receivers. However, this burden keeps acceptable if one considers the fact that one can define sufficiently many attributes at the start of the system and thus easily keep the set of attributes completely static during the system lifetime.

4 Security Analysis

To prove the security of our scheme, and similarly to the approach taken in [12], we show that the CP-ABBE selective security of this scheme reduces to an instance of a (P, Q, f)-GDHE problem [4]. We then prove that (P, Q) and f are independent, which implies in particular that the corresponding problem is difficult in the generic group model. This leads to a security reduction in the standard model, and a proof of security in the generic group model. Thereafter, all the polynomials considered are from the polynomial ring

$$\mathbb{F}_p[\alpha, \beta, \gamma, \delta, \xi, b, r, r', s_i, s_u, \sigma_u, \varepsilon_u : i \in \mathbb{N}, u \in \mathcal{U}].$$

Let $\mathcal{A}$ be an adversary for the CP-ABBE selective security game. It declares a distribution of attributes $\mathfrak{B} : \mathcal{U} \to \mathcal{P}(\mathcal{B}^*)$, an access structure $\mathbb{A}$ and a set $\mathcal{R}$ of revoked receivers. Let $\mathcal{C}$ be the set of all receivers which do not satisfy the policy $\mathbb{A}$, and/or are revoked. Let P be the list of polynomials consisting of 1, and all the following elements corresponding to the information in pk, hdr, and dk_u for all the receivers $u \in \mathcal{C}$.

1. Contribution of pk: the set P_{pk} of polynomials 1, $\alpha^n \gamma r'$, r, $\alpha^{n+1} r r'$, $\alpha^{n+1} r r' b$, $\alpha^{n+1} r r' b^2$, $\xi b \alpha^{n+1} r r'$, δr, α^n and for $a \in \mathcal{B}^*$, the element $\alpha^{\imath(a)} r$.
2. Contribution of dk_u, for any $u \in \mathcal{C}$: the set P_{dk_u} of polynomials $\varepsilon_u(\gamma + b^2 \sigma_u)$, $\sigma_u \varepsilon_u (b \cdot \mathrm{id}(u) + \xi)$, $\sigma_u \varepsilon_u$, $\alpha r(\beta + \varepsilon_u)$, for each $a \in \mathcal{B}^*$, $\alpha^{\imath(a)} \varepsilon_u$, $\alpha^{n+1+\imath(a)} \varepsilon_u$, and for each $a \in \mathfrak{B}(u)$, $\alpha^{\imath(a)} \delta \varepsilon_u$;
3. Contribution of hdr: the set P_{hdr} of polynomials $\alpha^n s$, $\alpha^{n+1} r r' s_0$, for each $i = 1, \ldots, N$, $r s_i$, $r s_i \left(\delta + \sum_{a \in \beta_i} \alpha^{n+1-\imath(a)}\right)$, and for each revoked receiver $u \in \mathcal{R}$, $\alpha^{n+1} r r' b s_u$, $\alpha^{n+1} r r' s_u (b^2 \cdot \mathrm{id}(u) + \xi b)$.

The list Q is simply $(1, \alpha^{n+1}rr'\beta\gamma, \alpha^{n+1}r\beta)$ and $f = \alpha^{n+1}rs\beta$.

Lemma 1. *If the adversary $\mathcal{A}$ solves the CP-ABBE selective security game with advantage ε, then a simulator can be constructed to solve the (P,Q,f)-GDHE problem with advantage ε in polynomial time, with one oracle call to $\mathcal{A}$.*

Proof. The proof is available in the full version of this paper [44].

According to Lemma 1, an adversary for the CP-ABBE selective security game gives rise to an adversary for the (P,Q,f)-GDHE problem. It now needs to be justified that the (P,Q,f)-GDHE problem is difficult. The end of Sect. 2 explains that we can suppose this problem to be difficult when (P,Q) and f are independent: it is proven to be difficult in the generic group model, and assumed to remain difficult in cryptographic bilinear groups. Thus, it remains to show that (P,Q) and f are indeed independent.

Lemma 2. *(P,Q) and f are independent.*

Proof. The proof is available in the full version of this paper [44].

We are now able to derive a bound on the security of our new scheme in the generic group model.

Theorem 2. *For any probabilistic algorithm $\mathcal{A}$ that totalizes at most q queries to the oracle performing group operations in $(\mathbb{G}, \mathbb{G}_T)$ and evaluations of $e(\cdot,\cdot)$, and declaring a set of revoked receivers of size at most η, as well as an access policy with at most N clauses ($\mathbb{A} = \beta_1 \wedge \cdots \wedge \beta_N$), then $\mathrm{Adv}^{\mathrm{ind}}(\lambda, \mathfrak{U}, \mathfrak{B}, \mathcal{A})$ is smaller or equal to*

$$\frac{(q + 4(N + N + \eta) + 22 + |\mathfrak{U}|(10N + 8))^2(8N + 3)}{2^{\lambda-1}}.$$

Proof. This is a direct consequence of Lemmas 1 and 2, and Theorem 1, with $|P_{\mathsf{pk}}| = 9 + 2N$, $|P_{\mathsf{dk}_u}| = 4 + 5N$, $|P_{\mathsf{hdr}}| = 2 + 2N + 2\ell$ and $d = 16N + 6$.

5 Optimizing the Bandwidth and Computational Overheads

As the number of revoked receivers grows, the computation of $\mathsf{k}_0^{\varepsilon_u}$ can become expensive for the receivers. The heavy computations are the products

$$\prod_{u' \in \mathcal{R}} C_{u',i}^{1/(\mathrm{id}(u) - \mathrm{id}(u'))}$$

for $i = 1, 2$, which require $O(\ell)$ exponentiations. This could be optimized if the $C_{u',1}$'s and $C_{u',2}$'s did not change from a message to another: those products could be computed the first time and reused, and any new revoked receiver would only require one exponentiation and multiplication for each of the receivers.

To do so, the broadcaster chooses a random $s_{u'}$ for every revoked receiver $u' \in \mathcal{R}$, and reuses it for all the following communications, thus generating the same $C_{u',1}$'s and $C_{u',2}$'s.

This optimization requires a new proof of security. We can show that even if the adversary is given access to old ciphertexts $\mathsf{hdr}^{(1)}, \ldots, \mathsf{hdr}^{(m)}$, (in addition to the challenge hdr) for which the sets of revoked receivers are subsets $\mathcal{R}^{(j)}$ of the set of revoked receivers $\mathcal{R}$ for hdr, and the access policies have $N^{(j)}$ clauses denoted $\beta_i^{(j)}$, for each $j = 1, \ldots, m$, the underlying (P, Q, f)-GDHE is still difficult (*i.e.*, (P, Q) and f are independent). We need to suppose $N^{(j)} > 0$ for each $j = 1, \ldots, m$.

This technique reduces the computational cost, but in a fully stateless situation, the broadcaster still needs to send all the $C_{u',1}$'s and $C_{u',2}$'s with each message. In a context where it is possible to maintain a synchronized state, via a two-way connection with a possibly very limited bandwidth, it is possible for the broadcaster to send with each ciphertext only the $C_{u',1}$'s and $C_{u',2}$'s for the newly revoked receivers. Then, the ciphertexts' lengths drop from $O(N + \ell)$ to $O(N + |\Delta\mathcal{R}|)$ (where $\Delta\mathcal{R}$ is the set of newly revoked receivers, for example those revoked during the last day or the last week).

The only thing we have to change from the setting of the original security proof is to add to P the contribution of the ciphertexts $\mathsf{hdr}^{(1)}, \ldots, \mathsf{hdr}^{(m)}$, where the secret exponents of $\mathsf{hdr}^{(j)}$ are denoted $s^{(j)}, s_0^{(j)}, s_i^{(j)}$ and $s_{u'}^{(j)}$ for $i = 1, \ldots, N^{(j)}$ and $u' \in \mathcal{R}^{(j)}$. This contribution consists, for each $j = 1, \ldots, m$, of the polynomials $\alpha^n s^{(j)}, \alpha^{n+1} r r' s_0^{(j)}$ and for each $i = 1, \ldots, N^{(j)}$, the polynomials

$$r s_i^{(j)}, r s_i^{(j)} \left(\delta + \sum_{a \in \beta_i^{(j)}} \alpha^{n+1-\imath(a)} \right).$$

Only a few observations are needed to adapt the original security proof to this new setting. The first thing is to notice that we now have new terms with a factor $\alpha^{n+1}\beta$. Those are, for any $j = 1, \ldots, M$ and $u \in \mathcal{C}$, $\alpha^{n+1} r s^{(j)} (\beta + \varepsilon_u)$. But those terms cannot have a non-zero coefficient in the linear combination forming f, because for each j, $\alpha^{n+1} r s^{(j)} (\beta + \varepsilon_u)$ is the only term containing the monomial $\alpha^{n+1} r s_1^{(j)} (\beta + \varepsilon_u)$, thus the later could not be canceled by any other linear combination of terms (here we use our assumption that $N^{(j)} > 0$).

The second thing to notice is that the terms which can cancel the monomials $\alpha^{n+1} r \varepsilon_u r' \gamma s_v$ for $v \in \mathcal{R}$ are now not only $\alpha^{n+1} r r' s_0 \varepsilon_u (\gamma + b^2 \sigma_u)$, but also the terms $\alpha^{n+1} r r' s_0^{(j)} \varepsilon_u (\gamma + b^2 \sigma_u)$ for all the j's such that $v \in \mathcal{R}^{(j)}$. We can then deduce that there is a linear combination of those terms such that the resulting coefficient of the monomial $\alpha^{n+1} r \varepsilon_u r' \gamma s_v$ is non-zero, and this coefficient is the same as the one of $\alpha^{n+1} r r' s_v \varepsilon_u b^2 \sigma_u$, which therefore is also non-zero. The end of the proof, consisting in showing that this coefficient of $\alpha^{n+1} r r' s_v \varepsilon_u b^2 \sigma_u$ cannot be canceled, remains unchanged. In conclusion, one can safely reuse the secret exponents s_u.

6 Practical Aspects

In this section, we compare the practical properties of our scheme to the other existing ABBE schemes listed in Table 1.

Table 1. Bandwidth and key storage complexity comparison. Denoting the set of all receivers by $\mathcal{U}$, the set of all attributes by $\mathcal{B}$, the set of revoked receivers by $\mathcal{R}$, then k_u is the number of attributes assigned to a receiver $u \in \mathcal{U}$, ν the length of the access structure, $\bar{\nu}$ the number of clauses in a CNF access structure, $N = |\mathcal{B}|$, $n = |\mathcal{U}|$ and $\ell = |\mathcal{R}|$.

Scheme	Access structure	Size of pk	Size of dk_u	Size of hdr
Attrapadung-Imai [1]	Monotone	$O(N+n)$	$O(N+n)$	$O(\nu)$
Lubicz-Sirvent [33]	AND & NOT	$O(N+n)$	$O(k_u)$	$O(\nu+\ell)$
Junod-Karlov [24]	CNF	$O(N+n)$	$O(N+n)$	$O(\bar{\nu})$
Zhou-Huang [45]	AND & NOT	$O(N+\log n)$	$O(N+\log n)$	$\approx O(\log n)$
Li-Zhang [32]	Monotone	$O(N+n)$	$O(k_u+n)$	$O(\nu)$
This paper	CNF	$O(N)$	$O(N)$	$O(\bar{\nu}+\ell)$

Size of Keys. First, we observe that our scheme is the only one where the public and private key sizes do not depend on the total number of receivers $n = |\mathcal{U}|$ registered in the system. Except for the Zhou-Huang scheme, whose dependency is of logarithmic nature, this dependence in n is linear in the competing schemes, which is highly impractical for a large scale deployment potentially involving millions of receivers, such as a Pay-TV system, for instance. The length of the keys in our scheme only depends linearly on the total number of attributes $N = |\mathcal{B}|$ defined in the system. This allows high scalability: the broadcaster can initially decide on a large set of possible receivers $\mathcal{U}$ without affecting the length of the keys. Adding new receivers to the system can be done efficiently, whereas with a key size linear in n, the broadcaster should choose the smallest possible $\mathcal{U}$ and change all the settings and keys when there are too many new receivers. This is undesirable in practice, as changing all the keys is way too expensive, especially when they are so long. In a nutshell, from the point of view of the key lengths, the Zhou-Huang scheme and our scheme are the only really practical candidates for large-scale deployment, while the Lubicz-Sirvent scheme can also be considered as acceptable since only its public key size is large, the private keys being pretty small.

Ciphertexts Size. The overhead on the ciphertext is $O(N+\ell)$ for our scheme, which is the same as the Lubicz-Sirvent scheme. The three schemes presenting a smaller overhead of size $O(N)$ have to compensate with private keys whose size is linear in n. The Zhou-Huang scheme can in theory reach an overhead as small as $O(\log n)$. This length relies on an optimization phase, which leads to an average length in $O(\log n)$ and a worst case length in $O(n)$; the worst case however occurs with small probability. This optimization phase is a Sum-of-Product Expression (SOPE) minimization, which is known to be an NP-Hard problem, so we can only hope for approximations. Finally, we would like to emphasize that ν and $\bar{\nu}$ have a somewhat different cardinality in the case of access structures involving only AND and NOT gates or in the case of complete CNF formulas. In the first case, ν represents the number of atomic variables, *i.e.*, the number of attributes or their negation, while in the case of a complete CNF formula, $\bar{\nu}$ represents the number of clauses, and it is independent of the number of atomic variables in the clauses. Hence, $\bar{\nu}$ is always smaller or equal, if not significantly smaller, than ν.

Overall Comparison. As mentionned before large-scale deployments rule out the schemes with a private key of length linear in $n = |\mathcal{U}|$. Remain the Lubicz-Sirvent and the Zhou-Huang schemes, which we will compare to ours. Compared to the Lubicz-Sirvent scheme, our scheme allows a much shorter public key; our private keys can be slightly larger, but still bounded by $O(N)$, which should not make a significant difference as long as the set of attributes remains reasonably small. The ciphertext overhead is the same. Our scheme allows a more flexible access control model via CNF formulas. The Lubicz-Sirvent only allows AND and NOT gates; one can also add OR gates, allowing access control by CNF formulas, via ciphertext concatenation, but the ciphertext overhead is then multiplied by the number of clauses. Note that, similarly to the Junod-Karlov scheme, our scheme allows to implement access policies in DNF form by concatenation as well. Overall, as long as $N = \mathcal{B}$ is of reasonable size, our scheme is more flexible and efficient than the Lubicz-Sirvent one. Compared to the Zhou-Huang scheme, the lengths of the public and private keys are similar; even though there is this additional term $\log n$ in the Zhou-Huang's scheme, there is no difference under the reasonable assumption that $N = O(\log n)$. As for the Lubicz-Sirvent scheme, the Zhou-Huang scheme only allows AND and NOT gates, and OR gates via ciphertext concatenation and a ciphertext overhead multiplied by the number of clauses. Furthermore, as mentioned above, the ciphertext overhead depends on the SOPE minimization phase, which is a NP-hard problem.

Practical Performances. We have implemented our new scheme using the C programming language and with help of the PBC library[1] for the elliptic curve arithmetic and pairings. The curve used let us work in a group of 160-bit long order and a base field of 512-bit long order, suitable for cryptographic use (it is a Type A curve, in PBC's classification). We ran an example with 5 attributes, on a 2.3 GHz Intel Core i7; the setup phase, including the generation of the public key takes 237 ms, generating the private key of a receiver takes 75 ms, the decryption of a message with 3 clauses, and without new revocations takes 25 ms, and each new revocation adds 4 ms to the first decryption after the revocation.

[1] This open-source library is freely available at http://crypto.stanford.edu/pbc/.

7 Conclusion

This paper describes, to the best of our knowledge, the first attribute-based broadcast encryption scheme for which the length of the encryption and decryption keys does not depend on the total number of users, but only on the number of attributes defined in the system. This property has been achieved by combining the Boneh-Gentry-Waters broadcast encryption scheme with the Lewko-Sahai-Waters revocation system in a secure way. Our scheme requires also a modest bandwidth, as the length of the header depends only of the number of revoked rogue receivers. The access equations can be defined in conjunctive normal form, *i.e.*, as AND of clauses involving ORs of attributes, and it supports negative attributes. We have proven the security of this scheme relatively to a GDHE problem in the standard model, which additionnaly allows us to derive corresponding security bounds in the generic group model. In summary, we are convinced that our scheme is fully practical in a number of real-life scenarios, including Pay-TV or cloud-storage ones involving millions of users.

References

1. Attrapadung, N., Imai, H.: Conjunctive broadcast and attribute-based encryption. In: Shacham, H., Waters, B. (eds.) Pairing 2009. LNCS, vol. 5671, pp. 248–265. Springer, Heidelberg (2009)
2. Berkovits, S.: How to broadcast a secret. In: Davies, D.W. (ed.) EUROCRYPT 1991. LNCS, vol. 547, pp. 535–541. Springer, Heidelberg (1991)
3. Bethencourt, J., Sahai, A., Waters, B.: Ciphertext-policy attribute-based encryption. In: Proceedings of IEEE-S&P 2007, pp. 321–334. IEEE Computer Society (2007)
4. Boneh, D., Boyen, X., Goh, E.-J.: Hierarchical identity based encryption with constant size ciphertext. In: Cramer [11], pp. 440–456
5. Boneh, D., Franklin, M.K.: Identity-based encryption from the Weil pairing. In: Kilian [25], pp. 213–229
6. Boneh, D., Gentry, C., Waters, B.: Collusion resistant broadcast encryption with short ciphertexts and private keys. In: Shoup, V. (ed.) CRYPTO 2005. LNCS, vol. 3621, pp. 258–275. Springer, Heidelberg (2005)
7. Boneh, D., Waters, B.: A fully collusion resistant broadcast, trace, and revoke system. In: Proceedings of ACM-CCS 2006, pp. 211–220. Association for Computing Machinery, New York, NY, USA (2006)
8. Boneh, D., Waters, B., Zhandry, M.: Low overhead broadcast encryption from multilinear maps. In: Garay, J.A., Gennaro, R. (eds.) CRYPTO 2014, Part I. LNCS, vol. 8616, pp. 206–223. Springer, Heidelberg (2014)
9. Burmester, M.: Group key agreement. In: van Tilborg, H.C.A., Jajodia, S. (eds.) Encyclopedia of Cryptography and Security, pp. 520–526. Springer, New York (2011)
10. Chase, M.: Multi-authority attribute based encryption. In: Vadhan, S.P. (ed.) TCC 2007. LNCS, vol. 4392, pp. 515–534. Springer, Heidelberg (2007)
11. Cramer, R. (ed.): EUROCRYPT 2005. LNCS, vol. 3494. Springer, Heidelberg (2005)

12. Delerablée, C., Paillier, P., Pointcheval, D.: Fully collusion secure dynamic broadcast encryption with constant-size ciphertexts or decryption keys. In: Takagi, T., Okamoto, E., Okamoto, T., Okamoto, T. (eds.) Pairing 2007. LNCS, vol. 4575, pp. 39–59. Springer, Heidelberg (2007)
13. Dodis, Y., Fazio, N.: Public key broadcast encryption for stateless receivers. In: Feigenbaum, J. (ed.) DRM 2002. LNCS, vol. 2696, pp. 61–80. Springer, Heidelberg (2003)
14. Fadlullah, Z.M., Kato, N., Lu, R., Shen, X., Nozaki, Y.: Toward secure targeted broadcast in smart grid. IEEE Commun. Mag. **50**(5), 150–156 (2012)
15. Fiat, A., Naor, M.: Broadcast encryption. In: Stinson, D.R. (ed.) CRYPTO 1993. LNCS, vol. 773, pp. 480–491. Springer, Heidelberg (1994)
16. Garg, S., Gentry, C., Halevi, S., Sahai, A., Waters, B.: Attribute-based encryption for circuits from multilinear maps. In: Canetti, R., Garay, J.A. (eds.) CRYPTO 2013, Part II. LNCS, vol. 8043, pp. 479–499. Springer, Heidelberg (2013)
17. Gentry, C., Waters, B.: Adaptive security in broadcast encryption systems (with short ciphertexts). In: Joux, A. (ed.) EUROCRYPT 2009. LNCS, vol. 5479, pp. 171–188. Springer, Heidelberg (2009)
18. Goodrich, M.T., Sun, J.Z., Tamassia, R.: Efficient tree-based revocation in groups of low-state devices. In: Franklin, M. (ed.) CRYPTO 2004. LNCS, vol. 3152, pp. 511–527. Springer, Heidelberg (2004)
19. Goyal, V., Jain, A., Pandey, O., Sahai, A.: Bounded ciphertext policy attribute based encryption. In: Aceto, L., Damgård, I., Goldberg, L.A., Halldórsson, M.M., Ingólfsdóttir, A., Walukiewicz, I. (eds.) ICALP 2008, Part II. LNCS, vol. 5126, pp. 579–591. Springer, Heidelberg (2008)
20. Halevy, D., Shamir, A.: The LSD broadcast encryption scheme. In: Yung, M. (ed.) CRYPTO 2002. LNCS, vol. 2442, p. 47. Springer, Heidelberg (2002)
21. Hohenberger, S., Waters, B.: Attribute-based encryption with fast decryption. In: Kurosawa, K., Hanaoka, G. (eds.) PKC 2013. LNCS, vol. 7778, pp. 162–179. Springer, Heidelberg (2013)
22. Hohenberger, S., Waters, B.: Online/offline attribute-based encryption. In: Krawczyk, H. (ed.) PKC 2014. LNCS, vol. 8383, pp. 293–310. Springer, Heidelberg (2014)
23. Hur, J., Noh, D.K.: Attribute-based access control with efficient revocation in data outsourcing systems. IEEE Trans. Parallel Distrib. Syst. **22**(7), 1214–1221 (2011)
24. Junod, P., Karlov, A.: An efficient public-key attribute-based broadcast encryption scheme allowing arbitrary access policies. In: Proceedings of DRM, pp. 13–24. ACM (2010)
25. Kilian, J. (ed.): CRYPTO 2001. LNCS, vol. 2139. Springer, Heidelberg (2001)
26. Lewko, A., Okamoto, T., Sahai, A., Takashima, K., Waters, B.: Fully secure functional encryption: attribute-based encryption and (hierarchical) inner product encryption. In: Gilbert, H. (ed.) EUROCRYPT 2010. LNCS, vol. 6110, pp. 62–91. Springer, Heidelberg (2010)
27. Lewko, A.B., Sahai, A., Waters, B.: Revocation systems with very small private keys. In: Proceedings of IEEE S&P, pp. 273–285. IEEE (2010)
28. Lewko, A.B., Waters, B.: Decentralizing attribute-based encryption. In: Paterson [36], pp. 568–588
29. Lewko, A.B., Waters, B.: Unbounded HIBE and attribute-based encryption. In: Paterson [36], pp. 547–567
30. Lewko, A.B., Waters, B.: New proof methods for attribute-based encryption: achieving full security through selective techniques. In: Safavi-Naini and Canetti [39], pp. 180–198

31. Li, M., Yu, S., Zheng, Y., Ren, K., Lou, W.: Scalable and secure sharing of personal health records in cloud computing using attribute-based encryption. IEEE Trans. Parallel Distrib. Syst. **24**(1), 131–143 (2013)
32. Li, Q., Zhang, F.: A fully secure attribute based broadcast encryption scheme. Int. J. Netw. Secur. **17**(3), 263–271 (2015)
33. Lubicz, D., Sirvent, T.: Attribute-based broadcast encryption scheme made efficient. In: Vaudenay, S. (ed.) AFRICACRYPT 2008. LNCS, vol. 5023, pp. 325–342. Springer, Heidelberg (2008)
34. Naor, D., Naor, M., Lotspiech, J.: Revocation and tracing schemes for stateless receivers. In: Kilian, J. (ed.) CRYPTO 2001. LNCS, vol. 2139, pp. 41–62. Springer, Heidelberg (2001)
35. Ostrovsky, R., Sahai, A., Waters, B.: Attribute-based encryption with non-monotonic access structures. In: Ning, P.., De Capitani di Vimercati, S., Syverson, P. F. (eds.) Proceedings of ACM-CCS, 2007 pp. 195–203. ACM (2007)
36. Paterson, K.G. (ed.): EUROCRYPT 2011. LNCS, vol. 6632. Springer, Heidelberg (2011)
37. Phan, D.-H., Pointcheval, D., Shahandashti, S.F., Strefler, M.: Adaptive CCA broadcast encryption with constant-size secret keys and ciphertexts. In: Susilo, W., Mu, Y., Seberry, J. (eds.) ACISP 2012. LNCS, vol. 7372, pp. 308–321. Springer, Heidelberg (2012)
38. Rouselakis, Y., Waters, B.: Practical constructions and new proof methods for large universe attribute-based encryption. In: Sadeghi, A.-R., Gligor, V.D., Yung, M. (eds) Proceedings of ACM-CCS 2013, pp. 463–474. ACM (2013)
39. Safavi-Naini, R., Canetti, R. (eds.): CRYPTO 2012. LNCS, vol. 7417. Springer, Heidelberg (2012)
40. Sahai, A., Seyalioglu, H., Waters, B.: Dynamic credentials and ciphertext delegation for attribute-based encryption. In: Safavi-Naini and Canetti [39], pp. 199–217
41. Sahai, A., Waters, B.: Fuzzy identity-based encryption. In: Cramer [11], pp. 457–473
42. Shamir, A.: Identity-based cryptosystems and signature schemes. In: Blakely, G.R., Chaum, D. (eds.) CRYPTO 1984. LNCS, vol. 196, pp. 47–53. Springer, Heidelberg (1985)
43. Waters, B.: Ciphertext-policy attribute-based encryption: an expressive, efficient, and provably secure realization. In: Catalano, D., Fazio, N., Gennaro, R., Nicolosi, A. (eds.) PKC 2011. LNCS, vol. 6571, pp. 53–70. Springer, Heidelberg (2011)
44. Wesolowski, B., Junod, P.: Ciphertext-policy attribute-based broadcast encryption scheme with small keys. Cryptology ePrint Archive, Report 2015/836 (2015). http://eprint.iacr.org/2015/836
45. Zhou, Z., Huang, D.: On efficient ciphertext-policy attribute based encryption, broadcast encryption: extended abstract. In: Proceedings of ACM-CCS 2010, pp. 753–755. ACM (2010)

Learning with Errors in the Exponent

Özgür Dagdelen[1(✉)], Sebastian Gajek[2,3], and Florian Göpfert[4]

[1] BridgingIT GmbH, Mannheim, Germany
oezguer.dagdelen@bridging-it.de
[2] NEC Research Labs, Heidelberg, Germany
sebastian.gajek@neclab.eu
[3] Flensburg University of Applied Sciences, Flensburg, Germany
[4] Technische Universität Darmstadt, Darmstadt, Germany
fgoepfert@cdc.informatik.tu-darmstadt.de

Abstract. The Snowden revelations have shown that intelligence agencies have been successful in undermining cryptography and put in question the exact security provided by the underlying intractability problem. We introduce a new class of intractability problems, called Learning with Errors in the Exponent (LWEE). We give a tight reduction from Learning with Errors (LWE) and the Representation Problem (RP) in finite groups, two seemingly unrelated problem, to LWEE. The argument holds in the classical and quantum model of computation.

Furthermore, we present the very first construction of a semantically secure public-key encryption system based on LWEE in groups of composite order. The heart of our construction is an error recovery "in the exponent" technique to handle critical propagations of noise terms.

Keywords: Lattice theory · Group theory · Public-key encryption · Intractability amplification

1 Introduction

Among the most carefully scrutinized cryptographic problems are probably the discrete logarithm in finite groups and factorization. Shor's celebrated theorems [1,2] curtailed for the first time the confidence of founding cryptosystems on group-theoretic assumptions. Shor showed the existence of polynomial-time solvers for integer factorization and discrete logarithm computation in the non-classical quantum computation model. Researchers have then begun to look for alternative computational problems. In this line of work Regev explored a lattice problem class known as learning with errors (LWE) [3]. Given a distribution of noisy equations $(\mathbf{a}, b = \langle \mathbf{a}, \mathbf{s} \rangle + e) \in \mathbb{Z}_q^n \times \mathbb{Z}_q$ where e is taken from a small Gaussian error distribution, the search learning with error problem states it is hard to compute the solution $\mathbf{s}$ whereas the decisional variant assumes it is hard to distinguish $(\mathbf{a}, b)$ from uniformly random elements in $\mathbb{Z}_q^n \times \mathbb{Z}_q$. Several arguments flesh out LWE's intractability [4]: First, the best known solvers run in exponential time and even quantum algorithms do not seem to help. Second,

S. Kwon and A. Yun (Eds.): ICISC 2015, LNCS 9558, pp. 69–84, 2016.
DOI: 10.1007/978-3-319-30840-1_5

learning with errors is a generalization of learning from parity with error, which is a well-studied problem in coding theory. Any major progress in LWE will most likely cause significant impact to known lower bounds of decoding random linear codes. Lastly and most importantly, breaking certain average-case problem instances of LWE breaks all instances of certain standard lattice problems [3,5–7].

Taking the findings from lattices in presence of errors into account we carry on the study of noise as a *non-black box* intractability amplification technique. Specifically, we ask if noise effects the intractability of group-theoretic problems as well? If so, is non-trivial cryptography possible in such groups? The main challenge is to handle the propagation of "noise in the exponent". Error terms require a careful treatment, because they may easily distort the cryptographic task. Apart from the theoretical interest, our work has concrete practical motivation. Recent large-scale electronic surveillance data mining programs put in question the security provided by present cryptographic mechanisms. (See also the IACR statement and mission on mass surveillance.[1]) One of the problems is that many security protocols in the wild are based on a single intractability problem and we do not know the exact security. What if somebody has found a clever way to factor numbers? This already suffices to decrypt most of the TLS-protected Internet traffic and eavesdrop emails, social network activities, and voice calls.[2] Answering the above questions in an affirmative way advertises a novel family of computationally hard problems with strong security and robustness properties in the superposition of group and lattice theory.

1.1 Our Contribution

Blending Group and Lattice Theory. The idea of blending intractability problems is not new and is subject to several Diffie-Hellman related problems in groups of composite order which assume the hardness of the discrete log or factorization problem [8,9]. In this work, we address the blending of group and lattice related problems, and introduce the notion of *Learning with Errors in the Exponent* (LWEE). The LWEE distribution consists of samples $(g^{\mathbf{a}}, g^{\langle \mathbf{a},\mathbf{s}\rangle + e}) \in \mathbb{G}^n \times \mathbb{G}$ where $\mathbf{a}$ is sampled uniformly from $\mathbb{Z}_q^n$, and $\mathbf{s} \leftarrow_R \chi_s^n$, $e \leftarrow_R \chi_e$ from some distributions χ_s, χ_e. Learning with errors in the exponent comes in two versions: The search version asks to find the secret vector $\mathbf{s}$ while in the decisional variant one is supposed to distinguish LWEE samples from uniformly random group elements. Except for the error the assumption bears reminiscence to the representation problem RP [10]. Given a tuple of uniformly sampled elements $g_1, \ldots, g_\ell, h$ from $\mathbb{G}$, the (search) representation problem (ℓ-SRP) asks to compute the "representation" $x_1, \ldots, x_\ell \leftarrow \chi$ with respect to h for χ the uniform distribution such that $\Pi_{i=1}^{\ell} g_i^{x_i} = h$. We give a tight reduction from ℓ-SRP to the search LWEE problem.

[1] http://www.iacr.org/misc/statement-May2014.html.

[2] TLS's preferred cipher suite makes use of RSA-OAEP to transport the (master) key in the key establishment process. Once the ephemeral master key for the session is known it is possible to derive session keys and decrypt all encrypted messages.

Relations between Group and Lattice Assumptions. Looking at the decisional problem, we first define the decisional variant of the representation problem (ℓ-DRP): Given a tuple $g, g_1, \ldots, g_\ell, g^{x_1}, \ldots, g^{x_\ell}, h$ from $\mathbb{G}$, where $x_1, \ldots, x_\ell \leftarrow \chi$ are sampled from some distribution χ, ℓ-DRP asks to distinguish between $\Pi_{i=1}^{\ell} g_i^{x_i} = h$ and a randomly sampled value h in $\mathbb{G}$. Note, for $\ell = 1$ and uniform distribution over $\mathbb{Z}_q$, DRP coincides with the decisional Diffie-Hellman (DDH) problem. For $\ell > 1$, we prove in the generic group model that ℓ-DRP belongs to the class of progressively harder assumptions [11]. We then show that DRP is reducible to LWEE. This implies that if we select a group $\mathbb{G}$ for which DDH is believed to be hard, the hardness carries over to an instantiation of LWEE in that group $\mathbb{G}$. It is worth mentioning that both of our reductions are tight. They hold for (potentially non-uniform) distributions χ, if the underlying RP problem is hard for representations sampled from the same distribution. Investigating the relation to lattices, we show that an algorithm solving either the search or decisional LWEE problem efficiently can be turned into a successful attacker against the search or decisional LWE problem. Our reductions are tight and hold as well for (potentially non-uniform) distribution χ if LWE is hard for secret $\mathbf{s}$ sampled from the same distribution.

A Concrete Cryptosystem. We give a first construction of a public-key encryption scheme. One may size the magnitude to which the RP and LWE intractability contribute to the security of the system. The selection of parameters (e.g., modulus, dimension) offers great flexibility to fine-tune the cryptosystem's resilience against (quantum)-computational progress in attacking the underlying intractability problems. Concretely, one may choose the parameters to obtain short keys and ciphertexts, make the scheme post-quantum secure or immunities the scheme for the case that at some point in time either the DRP or DLWE becomes computationally tractable.

Although our construction serves the sole purpose of showcasing the feasibility of cryptosystems (in practical applications, it would be preferable to split the message information-theoretically into two shares and encrypt each share with a different encryption scheme, say El-Gamal and Regev encryption) based on "errors in the exponent", learning with errors in the exponent is an interesting concept in its own right. We leave it open for future work to find novel applications and to study the instantiation based on the learning with errors assumptions in rings. We discuss related work in the full version [12].

1.2 Extensions and Open Problems

While learning with errors in the exponent is an interesting concept in its own right, it requires further inspection. Here we point out a few possible directions for future research:

- It would be interesting to cryptanalyze the assumption. This would help nail down concrete security parameters, in particular for the case of double-hardness where both underlying assum1ptions contribute to the overall security.

- We are unaware of any existential relation between the representation and learning with errors assumption neither in the classical nor quantum model of computation. In fact, any insight would require progress in solving the hidden subgroup problem (HSP) in certain finite Abelian and non-Abelian groups. Shor's discrete-log quantum algorithm crucially relies on the HSP in Abelian groups. However, efficient quantum algorithms for the HSP in non-Abelian groups are unknown as they would give an efficient algorithm for solving the unique shortest-vector problem, being a special case of the shortest vector problem (SVP) [13].
- Clearly, building further cryptosystems based on the search or decisional variant of learning with errors in the exponent is an interesting direction.

2 Preliminaries

2.1 Notation

Random Sampling, Negligibility and Indistinguishability. If $\mathcal{D}$ is a probability distribution, we denote by $d \leftarrow_R \mathcal{D}$ the process of sampling a value d randomly according to $\mathcal{D}$. If S is a set, then $s \leftarrow_R S$ means that s is sampled according to a uniform distribution over the set S. We write $[m]$ for the set $\{0, 1, \ldots, m-1\}$. The expression $\lceil x \rfloor$ denotes the nearest integer to $x \in \mathbb{R}$, i.e., $\lceil x \rfloor = \lceil x - 0.5 \rceil$.

A function $\varepsilon()$ is called *negligible* (in the security parameter κ) if it decreases faster than any polynomial $poly(\kappa)$ for some large enough κ. An algorithm $\mathcal{A}$ runs in probabilistic polynomial-time (PPT) if $\mathcal{A}$ is randomized—uses internal random coins— and for any input $x \in \{0,1\}^*$ the computation of $\mathcal{A}(x)$ terminates in at most $poly(|x|)$ steps. If the running time of an algorithm is $t' \approx t$, we mean that the distance between t' and t is negligible.

Let $X = \{X_\kappa\}_{\kappa \in \mathbb{N}}$ and $Y = \{Y_\kappa\}_{\kappa \in \mathbb{N}}$ ¡¡¡¡¡¡¡ .mine be two distribution ensembles. We say X and Y are (t, ϵ)-computationally indistinguishable if for every PPT distinguisher $\mathcal{A}$ with running time t, there exists a function $\epsilon(\kappa)$ such that $|\Pr[\mathcal{A}(X) = 1] - \Pr[\mathcal{A}(Y) = 1]| \leq \epsilon(\kappa)$ (and we write $X \approx_{(t,\epsilon)} Y$). If $\mathcal{A}$ is PPT and $\epsilon(\kappa)$ is negligible, we simply say ======= be two distribution ensembles. We say X and Y are (t, ϵ)-computationally indistinguishable (and write $X \approx_{(t,\epsilon)} Y$) if for every PPT distinguisher $\mathcal{A}$ with running time t, there exists a function $\epsilon(\kappa)$ such that $|\Pr[\mathcal{A}(X) = 1] - \Pr[\mathcal{A}(Y) = 1]| \leq \epsilon(\kappa)$. If $\mathcal{A}$ is PPT and $\epsilon(\kappa)$ is negligible, we simply say ¿¿¿¿¿¿¿ .r342 X and Y are (computationally) indistinguishable (and we write $X \approx Y$). We say a distribution ensemble $X = \{X_\kappa\}_{\kappa \in \mathbb{N}}$ has (high) min-entropy, if for all large enough κ, the largest probability of an element in X_κ is $2^{-\kappa}$. We say a distribution ensemble $X = \{X_\kappa\}_{\kappa \in \mathbb{N}}$ is well-spread, if for any polynomial $poly(\cdot)$ and all large enough κ, the largest probability of an element in X_κ is smaller than $poly(\kappa)$. (In other words, the max-entropy of distributions in X must vanish super-logarithmatically.) Under the Gaussian distribution D_σ with parameter $\sigma > 0$, the probability of sampling an integer $x \in \mathbb{Z}$ is proportional to $\exp[-x^2/(2\sigma^2)]$.

Vectors and Matrices in the Exponent. We denote vectors by bold lower case letters and matrices by bold upper case letters. The ith row of a matrix $\mathbf{A}$ is denoted by $\mathbf{A}[i]$, the jth element of a vector $\mathbf{a}$ is denoted by a_j, To ease notation we sometimes write $\mathbf{a}_i$ for the ith row vector, and $a_{i,j}$ for the element in the ith row and j^{th} column of matrix $\mathbf{A}$. Let $\mathbb{G}$ be a group of order q, g a generator of $\mathbb{G}$, $\mathbf{a}$ a vector in $\mathbb{Z}_q^n$, and $\mathbf{A}$ a matrix in $\mathbb{Z}_q^{m\times n}$. We use the notation $g^{\mathbf{a}} \in \mathbb{G}^n$ to denote the vector $g^{\mathbf{a}} \stackrel{\text{def}}{=} (g^{a_1}, \cdots, g^{a_n})$ and $g^{\mathbf{A}} \in \mathbb{G}^{m\times n}$ to denote the matrix $g^{\mathbf{A}} \stackrel{\text{def}}{=} (g^{\mathbf{a}_1}, \cdots, g^{\mathbf{a}_m})^\top$.

Computations in the Exponent. Given $g^{\mathbf{a}}$ and $\mathbf{b}$, the inner product of vectors $\mathbf{a}$ and $\mathbf{b}$ in the exponent, denoted by $g^{\langle \mathbf{a},\mathbf{b}\rangle}$, is

$$\prod_{i=1}^{n} (g^{a_i})^{b_i} = \prod_{i=1}^{n} g^{a_i \cdot b_i} = g^{\sum_{i=1}^{n} a_i \cdot b_i} = g^{\langle \mathbf{a},\mathbf{b}\rangle} .$$

Likewise, a matrix-vector product in the exponent, given a vector $\mathbf{v}$ and $g^{\mathbf{A}}$ for a matrix $\mathbf{A} = \begin{pmatrix}\mathbf{a}_1 \ \mathbf{a}_2 \ \ldots \ \mathbf{a}_n\end{pmatrix}$ can be performed by $\prod_{i=1}^{n}(g^{\mathbf{a}_i})^{v_i} = \prod_{i=1}^{n} g^{\mathbf{a}_i \cdot v_i} = g^{\sum_{i=1}^{n} \mathbf{a}_i \cdot v_i} = g^{\mathbf{A}\mathbf{v}}$. Adding (and subtracting) in the exponent is computed via element-wise multiplication (and division) of the group elements $g^{\mathbf{a}} \cdot g^{\mathbf{b}} = g^{\mathbf{a}+\mathbf{b}}$.

Quadratic Residuosity. The Legendre symbol verifies whether an integer $a \in \mathbb{Z}_p$ is a quadratic residue modulo a prime p, i.e., $x^2 \equiv a \bmod p$ for some x. If $\mathbb{L}(a,p) := a^{(p-1)/2} = 1$, this is the case; otherwise $\mathbb{L}(a,p) = -1$. More generally, for $n \geq 2$, we define $\mathbb{L}(a,p)_n := a^{(p-1)/gcd(n,p-1)}$. If the modulus N is of the form $N = p_1 \cdots p_k$ where the p_i are odd primes, one uses its generalization, namely the Jacobi symbol, which is defined as $\mathbb{J}(a,N) = \prod_{i=1}^{k} \mathbb{L}(a,p_i)$. Note that $\mathbb{J}(a,N) = 1$ does not imply that a is a quadratic residue modulo N. However, if $\mathbb{J}(a,N) = -1$, a is certainly not. The set of quadratic residues modulo N is denoted by $\mathbb{QR}_N := \{a^2 \ : \ a \in \mathbb{Z}_N^*\}$. By $\mathbb{J}_N$ we denote the subgroup of all elements from $\mathbb{Z}_N^*$ with Jacobi symbol 1, i.e., $\mathbb{J}_N = \{a \in \mathbb{Z}_N^* \ : \ \mathbb{J}(a,N) = 1\}$. Note that $\mathbb{QR}_N$ is a subgroup of $\mathbb{J}_N$. It is widely believed that one cannot efficiently decide whether an element $a \in \mathbb{J}_N$ is a quadratic residue modulo N if the prime factors of N are unknown (For more details, full version).

2.2 Standard Group-Theoretic Problems

We will make use of the rank hiding assumption introduced by Naor and Segev [14] (and later extended by Agrawal et al. [15]).[3] It was proven to be equivalent to the $\mathsf{DDH}_{\mathbb{G},\chi}$ assumption for groups of prime order and uniform χ [14].

Definition 1 (Rank Hiding). *Let $\mathbb{G}$ be a group of order q with generator g, and $i, j, n, m \in \mathbb{N}$ satisfying $i \neq j$ and $i, j \geq 1$. The Rank Hiding problem ($\mathsf{RH}_{\mathbb{G},i,j,m,n}$) is (t,ϵ)-hard if*

$$\{(\mathbb{G}, q, g, g^{\mathbf{M}}) : \mathbf{M} \leftarrow_R \mathsf{Rk}_i(\mathbb{Z}_q^{m\times n})\} \approx_{(t,\epsilon)} \{(\mathbb{G}, q, g, g^{\mathbf{M}}) : \mathbf{M} \leftarrow_R \mathsf{Rk}_j(\mathbb{Z}_q^{m\times n})\}$$

[3] The assumption was first introduced by Boneh et al. [16] under the Matrix DDH assumption.

where $\mathsf{Rk}_k(\mathbb{Z}_q^{m\times n})$ *returns an* $m \times n$ *matrix uniformly random from* $\mathbb{Z}_q^{n\times m}$ *with rank* $k \leq \min(n, m)$.

2.3 Representation Problem

The representation problem in a group $\mathbb{G}$ assumes that given l random group elements $g_1, \ldots, g_l \in \mathbb{G}$ and $h \in \mathbb{G}$ it is hard to find a representation $\mathbf{x} \in \mathbb{Z}_q^\ell$ such that $h = \prod_{i=1}^{\ell} g_i^{x_i}$ holds. Brands shows an electronic cash system based on the problem. Recently, the assumption was extensively applied to show leakage resiliency [15,17,18].

We now state a more general version of the search representation problem where vector $\mathbf{x} \leftarrow_R \chi^\ell$ is sampled from a distribution χ with (at least) min-entropy and where an adversary is given $m \geq 1$ samples instead of a single one.

Definition 2 (Search Representation Problem). *Let* χ *be a distribution over* $\mathbb{Z}_q$*, and* ℓ, m *be integers. Sample* $\mathbf{M} \leftarrow_R \mathbb{Z}_q^{m\times \ell}$ *and* $\mathbf{x} \leftarrow_R \chi^\ell$*. The Search Representation Problem* ($\mathsf{SRP}_{\mathbb{G},\chi,\ell,m}$) *is* (t, ϵ)*-hard if any algorithm* $\mathcal{A}$*, running in time* t*, upon input* $(g, g^{\mathbf{M}}, g^{\mathbf{x}}, g^{\mathbf{Mx}})$*, outputs* $\mathbf{x}' \in \mathbb{Z}_q^\ell$ *such that* $g^{\mathbf{Mx}'} = g^{\mathbf{Mx}}$ *with probability at most* ϵ*. If* χ *is the uniform distribution, we sometimes skip* χ *in the index and say that* $\mathsf{SRP}_{\mathbb{G},\ell,m}$ *is* (t, ϵ)*-hard.*

Brands proves the equivalence of the representation problem and the discrete logarithm problem for uniform χ and $m = 1$. It is easy to verify that the reduction holds for every distribution for which the discrete logarithm problem holds.

To establish relations to the learning with errors in the exponent problem (cf. Sect. 3.2), we need a decisional variant of the representation problem. To our surprise, the decisional version has not been defined before, although the assumption is a natural generalization of the decisional Diffie-Hellman problem to ℓ-tuples (similar in spirit as the ℓ-linear problem in $\mathbb{G}$ [11]). Given ℓ random group elements $g_1, \ldots, g_\ell \in \mathbb{G}$ together with $h \in \mathbb{G}$ and $g^{x_1}, \ldots, g^{x_\ell} \in \mathbb{G}$ where $x_1, \ldots, x_\ell \leftarrow_R \mathbb{Z}_q^*$, it is hard to decide if $h = \prod_{i=1}^{\ell} g_i^{x_i}$ or h is a random group element in $\mathbb{G}$. Our definition below generalizes this problem to the case, where $m \geq 1$ samples are given to an adversary and $x_1, \ldots, x_\ell$ are sampled from any min-entropy distribution χ.

Definition 3 (Decisional Representation Problem). *Let* χ *be a distribution over* $\mathbb{Z}_q^*$*, and* ℓ, m *be integers. Sample* $\mathbf{M} \leftarrow_R \mathbb{Z}_q^{m\times\ell}$*,* $\mathbf{h} \leftarrow_R \mathbb{Z}_q^m$*, and* $\mathbf{x} \leftarrow_R \chi^\ell$*. The Decisional Representation* ($\mathsf{DRP}_{\mathbb{G},\chi,\ell,m}$) *problem is* (t, ϵ)*-hard if*

$$(g, g^{\mathbf{M}}, g^{\mathbf{x}}, g^{\mathbf{Mx}}) \approx_{(t,\epsilon)} (g, g^{\mathbf{M}}, g^{\mathbf{x}}, g^{\mathbf{h}}).$$

If χ *is the uniform distribution over* $\mathbb{Z}_q^*$*, we say* $\mathsf{DRP}_{\mathbb{G},\ell,m}$ *is* (t, ϵ)*-hard.*

Remark 1. $\mathsf{DRP}_{\mathbb{G},\chi,\ell,m}$ can be stated in the framework of the Matrix-DDH assumption recently introduced by Escala et al. [19] and thus we put another class of hardness problems to the arsenal of their expressive framework.

We now give evidence that the family of $\mathsf{DRP}_{\mathbb{G},\chi,\ell,m}$ problems is a class of progressively harder problems (with increasing ℓ). Proofs of following propositions can be foound in the full version.

Proposition 1. *If $\mathsf{DRP}_{\mathbb{G},\chi,\ell,m}$ is (t,ϵ)-hard, then for any $\ell, m \geq 1$ with $t' \approx t$ and distribution χ with min-entropy $\mathsf{DRP}_{\mathbb{G},\chi,\ell+1,m}$ is (t',ϵ)-hard.*

Proposition 2. *In the generic group model $\mathsf{DRP}_{\mathbb{G},\chi,\ell+1,m}$ is hard for distribution χ with minimal entropy, even in presence of a $\mathsf{DRP}_{\mathbb{G},\chi,\ell,m}$-oracle.*

Remark 2. $\mathsf{DRP}_{\mathbb{G},\chi,1,1}$-problem with χ being the uniform distribution over $\mathbb{Z}_q$ coincides with the decisional Diffie-Hellman (DDH) problem. Hence, we obtain the corollary that for uniform distributions χ, the decisional Diffie-Hellman problem implies the representation problem $\mathsf{DRP}_{\mathbb{G},\chi,\ell,1}$ for $\ell \geq 1$. In fact, Proposition 1 suggests a stronger argument. Assuming the decisional Diffie-Hellman problem holds for well-spread and min-entropy distributions χ, then the $\mathsf{DRP}_{\mathbb{G},\chi,\ell,1}$ holds for χ and $\ell \geq 1$.

While Propositions 1 and 2 show that the DRP problem progressively increases with ℓ, the following proposition states that the problem remains hard with increasing number of samples m. More precisely, we show that $\mathsf{DRP}_{\mathbb{G},\chi,\ell,m+1}$ is hard as long as $\mathsf{DRP}_{\mathbb{G},\chi,\ell,m}$ and the Rank Hiding problem $\mathsf{RH}_{\mathbb{G},m,m+1,m+1,2\ell+1}$ (cf. Definition 1) is hard. The proof is given in the full version.

Proposition 3. *If $\mathsf{RH}_{\mathbb{G},m,m+1,m+1,2\ell+1}$ is (t,ϵ)-hard and $\mathsf{DRP}_{\mathbb{G},\chi,\ell,m}$ is (t',ϵ')-hard in a cyclic group $\mathbb{G}$ of order q, then for any distribution χ_e and any $m > 0$ with $t' \approx t$ and $\epsilon'' \leq (1-\epsilon)^{-1}\epsilon'$ $\mathsf{DRP}_{\mathbb{G},\chi,\ell,m+1}$ is (t,ϵ'')-hard.*

2.4 Learning with Errors

The learning with errors assumption comes as a search and decision lattice problem. Given a system of m linear equations with random coefficients $\mathbf{a}_i \in \mathbb{Z}_q^n$ in the n indeterminates $\mathbf{s}$ sampled from some distribution χ_s and biased with some error e_i from the error distribution χ_e, it is hard to compute vector $\mathbf{s}$ or distinguish the solution $b_i = \sum_i^n \mathbf{a}_i\mathbf{s} + e_i$ from a uniform element in $\mathbb{Z}_q$.

Definition 4 (Learning with Errors). *Let n, m, q be integers and χ_e, χ_s be distributions over $\mathbb{Z}$. For $\mathbf{s} \leftarrow_R \chi_s$, define the LWE distribution $L^{\mathsf{LWE}}_{n,q,\chi_e}$ to be the distribution over $\mathbb{Z}_q^n \times \mathbb{Z}_q$ obtained such that one first draws $\mathbf{a} \leftarrow_R \mathbb{Z}_q^n$ uniformly, $e \leftarrow_R \chi_e$ and returns $(\mathbf{a}, b) \in \mathbb{Z}_q^n \times \mathbb{Z}_q$ with $b = \langle \mathbf{a}, \mathbf{s}\rangle + e$. Let $(\mathbf{a}_i, b_i)$ be samples from $L^{\mathsf{LWE}}_{n,q,\chi_e}$ and $c_i \leftarrow_R \mathbb{Z}_q$ for $0 \leq i < m = poly(\kappa)$.*

- *The Search Learning With Errors ($\mathsf{SLWE}_{n,m,q,\chi_e}(\chi_s)$) problem is (t,ϵ)-hard if any algorithm $\mathcal{A}$, running in time t, upon input $(\mathbf{a}_i, b_i)_{i\in[m]}$, outputs $\mathbf{s}$ with probability at most ϵ.*
- *The Decisional Learning with Errors ($\mathsf{DLWE}_{n,m,q,\chi_e}(\chi_s)$) problem is (t,ϵ)-hard if*

$$(\mathbf{a}_i, b_i)_{i\in[m]} \approx_{(t,\epsilon)} (\mathbf{a}_i, c_i)_{i\in[m]}$$

for a random secret $\mathbf{s} \leftarrow_R \chi_s$.

If χ_s is the uniform distribution over $\mathbb{Z}_q$, we simply write $\mathsf{LWE}_{n,m,q,\chi_e}$.

A typical distribution for the error is a discrete Gaussian distribution with an appropriate standard deviation. There are several proposals for the distribution of the secret. While the uniform distribution is the most standard one, it is shown that setting $\chi_s = \chi_e$, known as the "normal form", retains the hardness of LWE [20,21]. We also note that the learning with errors problem where the error is scaled by a constant α relatively prime to q is as hard as the original definition [22]. The "scaled" LWE distribution then returns $(\mathbf{a}, b)$ with $\mathbf{a} \leftarrow_R \mathbb{Z}_q^n$ and $b = \langle \mathbf{a}, \mathbf{s} \rangle + \alpha e$.

3 Learning with Errors in the Exponent

3.1 Definition

For self-containment, the assumption is stated both as a search and decision problem over a group $\mathbb{G}$ of order q, and exponents sampled from distributions χ_e, χ_s over $\mathbb{Z}$. We demonstrate the versatility and general utility of the decisional version in Sect. 4.

Definition 5 (Learning with Errors in the Exponent). *Let $\mathbb{G}$ be a group of order q where g is a generator of $\mathbb{G}$. Let n, m, q be integers and χ_e, χ_s be distributions over $\mathbb{Z}$. For any fixed vector $\mathbf{s} \in \mathbb{Z}_q^n$, define the* LWEE *distribution $L^{\mathsf{LWEE}}_{\mathbb{G},n,q,\chi_e}$ to be the distribution over $\mathbb{G}^n \times \mathbb{G}$ obtained such that one first draws vector $\mathbf{a} \leftarrow_R \mathbb{Z}_q^n$ uniformly, $e \leftarrow_R \chi_e$ and returns $(g^{\mathbf{a}}, g^b) \in \mathbb{G}^n \times \mathbb{G}$ with $b = \langle \mathbf{a}, \mathbf{s} \rangle + e$. Let $(g^{\mathbf{a}_i}, g^{b_i})$ be samples from $L^{\mathsf{LWEE}}_{\mathbb{G},n,q,\chi_e}$ and c_i be uniformly sampled from $\mathbb{Z}_q^*$ for $0 \le i < m = poly(\kappa)$.*

- *The* Search Learning With Errors in the Exponent *($\mathsf{SLWEE}_{\mathbb{G},n,m,q,\chi_e}(\chi_s)$) problem is (t, ϵ)-hard if any algorithm $\mathcal{A}$, running in time t, upon input $(g^{\mathbf{a}_i}, g^{b_i})_{i \in [m]}$, outputs $\mathbf{s}$ with probability at most ϵ.*
- *The* Decision Learning With Errors in the Exponent *($\mathsf{DLWEE}_{\mathbb{G},n,m,q,\chi_e}(\chi_s)$) problem is (t, ϵ)-hard if $(g^{\mathbf{a}_i}, g^{b_i})_{i \in [m]} \approx_{(t,\epsilon)} (g^{\mathbf{a}_i}, g^{c_i})_{i \in [m]}$ for a random secret $\mathbf{s} \leftarrow_R \chi_s^n$. If χ_s is the uniform distribution over $\mathbb{Z}_q$, we write $\mathsf{DLWEE}_{\mathbb{G},n,m,q,\chi_e}$.*

We let $\mathsf{Adv}^{\mathsf{DLWEE/SLWEE}}_{\mathbb{G},n,m,q,\chi_e,\chi_s}(t)$ denote a bound on the value ϵ for which the decisional/search LWEE *problem is (t, ϵ)-hard.*

One may interpret learning with errors in the exponent in two ways. One way is to implant an error term from a distribution χ_e into the Diffie-Hellman exponent. Another way to look at LWEE is as compressing an LWE instance within some group $\mathbb{G}$ of order q.

3.2 Relations to Group and Lattice Problems

We connect the representation and learning with errors problem to learning with errors in the exponent. The essence is that there exist tight reductions from the search (resp. decision) learning with errors in the exponent problem to either the search (resp. decision) representation problem and the search (resp. decision) learning with errors problem. This has several interesting property preserving implications. As a corollary we infer that for appropriate parameter choices LWEE preserves the *hardness* and *robustness* properties of the representation and/or learning with errors problem. Essentially then LWEE boils down to the security of either of the two underlying problems. This way, the cryptosystem can be instantiated to leverage leakage resistance and post-quantum hardness thanks LWE [3,23]. On the flip side, the cryptosystem may offer short instance sizes through the underlying RP problem (when instantiated on elliptic curves). Of particular interest for many emerging applications is the partnering of the two hardness assumptions. One may choose parameters such that both RP and LWE hold. We call the case *double-hard*, which appeals to provide in some sense hedged security.

Following four propositions summarize our main results. Proofs appear in the full version.

Proposition 4. *If* $\mathsf{SRP}_{\mathbb{G},\chi_s,\ell,m}$ *is* (t,ϵ)*-hard in a cyclic group* $\mathbb{G}$ *of order* q*, then for any distribution* χ_e *and any number of samples* $m > 0$ $\mathsf{SLWEE}_{\mathbb{G},\ell,m,q,\chi_e}(\chi_s)$ *is* (t',ϵ)*-hard with* $t' \approx t$.

Proposition 5. *If* $\mathsf{SLWE}_{n,m,q,\chi_e}(\chi_s)$ *is* (t,ϵ)*-hard, then for any cyclic group* $\mathbb{G}$ *of order* q *with known (or efficiently computable) generator* $\mathsf{SLWEE}_{\mathbb{G},n,m,q,\chi_e}(\chi_s)$ *is* (t',ϵ)*-hard with* $t' \approx t$.

Proposition 6. *If* $\mathsf{DRP}_{\mathbb{G},\chi_s,\ell,m}$ *is* (t,ϵ)*-hard in a cyclic group* $\mathbb{G}$ *of order* q*, then for any distribution* χ_e *and any number of samples* $m > 0$ $\mathsf{DLWEE}_{\mathbb{G},\ell,m,\chi_e}(\chi_s)$ *is* (t',ϵ)*-hard with* $t' \approx t$.

Proposition 7. *If* $\mathsf{DLWE}_{n,m,q,\chi_e}(\chi_s)$ *is* (t,ϵ)*-hard, then for any cyclic group* $\mathbb{G}$ *of order* q *with known (or efficiently computable) generator* $\mathsf{DLWEE}_{\mathbb{G},n,m,\chi_e}(\chi_s)$ *is* (t',ϵ)*-hard with* $t' \approx t$.

3.3 On the Generic Hardness of LWEE

With Propositions 4–7 in our toolbox we conjecture LWEE to be harder than either of the underlying RP or LWE problems. The argument is heuristic and based on what is known about the hardness of each intractability problem (see full version for more details).

Fix parameters such that RP and LWE problem instances give κ bits security. The only obvious known approach today to solve the LWEE instance is to first compute the discrete logarithm of samples $(g^{\mathbf{a}_i}, g^{b_i})$ and then solve the LWE problem for samples $(\mathbf{a}_i, b_i)$. Note that an adversary must solve n^2+n many discrete logarithms because the secret vector $\mathbf{s}$ is information-theoretically hidden, if less than n samples of LWE are known. Solving $N := n^2+n$ discrete logarithms in generic groups of order q takes time $\sqrt{2Nq}$ while computing a single discrete logarithm takes time $\sqrt{\pi q/2}$ [24,25].[4] In fact, this bound is proven to be optimal

[4] Solving N-many discrete logarithms is easier than applying N times a DL solver for a single instance.

in the generic group model [26]. Note, parameters for LWEE are chosen such that computing a single discrete logarithm takes time 2^κ. Hence, in order to solve the LWEE instance for $N = \mathcal{O}(\kappa^2)$, one requires time $\frac{2}{\sqrt{\pi}}\sqrt{N} \cdot 2^\kappa + 2^\kappa > 2^{\kappa + 2\log(\kappa)}$. This shows that generically the concrete instance of LWEE is logarithmically harder in the security parameter κ.

4 Public-Key Encryption from LWEE

4.1 The High-Level Idea

The idea behind our scheme is reminiscent of Regev's public-key encryption scheme. In a nutshell, the public key is an LWEE instance $(g^{\mathbf{A}}, g^{\mathbf{A}\mathbf{s}+\mathbf{x}}) \in \mathbb{G}^{n \times n} \times \mathbb{G}^n$. Similarly to [27,28] and as opposed to Regev [3], for efficiency reason we avoid the use of the leftover hash lemma –instead we impose one further LWEE instance– and make use of a square matrix A. Ciphertexts consist of two LWEE instances $C = (\mathbf{c}_0, c_1)$ where $\mathbf{c_0} = g^{\mathbf{A}\mathbf{r}+\mathbf{e}_0}$ encapsulates a random key $\mathbf{r} \in \mathbb{Z}_q^n$ and $c_1 = g^{\langle \mathbf{b}, \mathbf{r}\rangle + e_1} \cdot g^{\alpha\mu}$ encrypts the message μ (we discuss the exact value of α below). The tricky part is the decryption algorithm. All known LWE-based encryption schemes require some technique to deal with the noise terms. Otherwise, decryption is prone to err. Regev's technique ensures small error terms. One simply rounds $c_1 - \mathbf{c}_0\mathbf{s}$ to some reference value c_b indicating the encryption of bit b. While rounding splendidly works on integers, the technique fails in our setting.

Our approach explores a considerably different path. Instead of rounding, we synthesize the pesky error terms. To this end, we adapt the trapdoor technique of Joye and Libert [29] and recover partial bits of the discrete logarithm (by making use of the Pohlig-Hellman algorithm [30]). The main idea is to tweak the modulus in a smart way. Given composite modulus $N = pq$ with p', q', such that $p = 2^k p' + 1$ and $q = 2^k q' + 1$ are prime, there exists an efficient algorithm for recovering the k least significant bits of the discrete logarithm. We choose the parameters so that the sum of all error terms in the exponent is (with high probability) at most $2^{k-\ell}$. This leads to a "gap" between error bits and those bits covert by the discrete log instance. We plant the message in this gap by shifting it to the $2^{k-\ell}$'s bit, where ℓ is the size of the message we want to decrypt. Hence, we choose $\alpha = 2^{k-\ell}$ in our construction to shift the message bits accordingly. We leave it as an interesting open problem to instantiate the scheme in prime order groups.

4.2 Our Construction

The scheme is parameterized by positive integers $n, k, \ell < k$ and Gaussian parameters σ_s, σ_e.

KeyGen: Sample prime numbers p' and q', such that $p = 2^k p' + 1$ and $q = 2^k q' + 1$ are prime. Set $N = pq$ and $M = 2^k p' q'$. Sample $\mathbf{s} \leftarrow_R \mathsf{D}^n_{\sigma_s}$, $\mathbf{A} \leftarrow_R \mathbb{Z}_M^{n \times n}$ and $\mathbf{x} \leftarrow_R \mathsf{D}^n_{\sigma_e}$ and compute $\mathbf{b} = \mathbf{A}^\top \mathbf{s} + \mathbf{x}$. Sample $g \in \mathbb{J}_N \setminus \mathbb{QR}_N$ of order M. The public key consists of $\mathsf{pk} = (g, g^{\mathbf{A}}, g^{\mathbf{b}}, N)$, and the secret key of $\mathsf{sk} = (p, \mathbf{s})$.

Algorithm 1.

Input: Generator g of a group with order $p-1=2^k p'$, p and k
Output: k least significant bits of $\log_g(h)$

```
begin
    a = 0, B = 1;
    for i ∈ {1,...,k} do
        z ← 𝕃(h,p)_{2^i} mod p;
        t ← 𝕃(g,p)^a_{2^i} mod p;
        if z ≠ t then
            a ← a + B;
        end
        B ← 2B;
    end
    return a
end
```

$\mathsf{Encrypt}(\mathsf{pk},\mu)$: To encrypt ℓ bits $\mu \in \{0,1,\dots 2^\ell - 1\}$ given public key pk choose $\mathbf{r} \leftarrow_R \mathsf{D}^n_{\sigma_s}$, $\mathbf{e}_0 \leftarrow_R \mathsf{D}^n_{\sigma_e}$ and $e_1 \leftarrow_R \mathsf{D}_{\sigma_e}$. Use $g^{\mathbf{A}}$, $\mathbf{r}$ and $\mathbf{e}_0$ to compute $g^{\mathbf{Ar}+\mathbf{e}_0}$, and $g^{\mathbf{b}}$, $\mathbf{r}$ and e_1 to compute $g^{\langle \mathbf{b},\mathbf{r}\rangle + e_1}$. The ciphertext is $\mathbf{c}_0, c_1$ with

$$\mathbf{c}_0 = g^{\mathbf{Ar}+\mathbf{e}_0}, \quad c_1 = g^{\langle \mathbf{b},\mathbf{r}\rangle + e_1} \cdot g^{2^{k-\ell}\mu}.$$

$\mathsf{Decrypt}(\mathsf{sk},(\mathbf{c}_0,c_1))$: To decrypt the ciphertext $(\mathbf{c}_0,c_1)$ given secret key $\mathsf{sk} = (p,\mathbf{s})$, first compute $g^{\langle \mathbf{s},\mathbf{Ar}+\mathbf{e}_0\rangle}$ and then $h = c_1/g^{\langle \mathbf{s},\mathbf{Ar}+\mathbf{e}_0\rangle}$. Run Algorithm 1 to synthesize $v = \log_g(h) \mod 2^k$ and return $\left\lfloor \frac{v}{2^{k-\ell-1}} \right\rceil$.

4.3 Correctness

To show correctness of our construction we build upon two facts. First, Algorithm 1 synthesizes the k least significant bits of a discrete logarithm. The algorithm's correctness for a modulus being a multiple of 2^k is proven in [29, Section 3.2]. Second, noise in the exponent does not overlap with the message. To this end, we bound the size of the noise with following lemma.

Lemma 1 (adapted from [28, Lemma 3.1]**).** *Let c, T be positive integers such that*

$$\sigma_s \cdot \sigma_e \leq \frac{\pi}{c} \frac{T}{\sqrt{n \ln(2/\delta)}} \quad \text{and} \quad \left(c \cdot \exp(\frac{1-c^2}{2})\right)^{2n} \leq 2^{-40}.$$

For $\mathbf{x},\mathbf{s} \leftarrow_R \mathsf{D}^n_{\sigma_e}, \mathbf{r}, \mathbf{r}_0 \leftarrow_R \mathsf{D}^n_{\sigma_e}, e_1 \leftarrow_R \mathsf{D}_{\sigma_e}$, we have $|\langle \mathbf{x},\mathbf{r}\rangle - \langle \mathbf{s},\mathbf{e}_0\rangle + e_1| < T$ with probability at least $1-\delta-2^{-40}$.

We are now ready to prove the following theorem.

Theorem 1. *Let c, T be as in Lemma 1. Then, the decryption is correct with probability at least $1-\delta-2^{-40}$.*

4.4 Ciphertext Indistinguishability

Theorem 2. *Let $\mathbb{G} = \langle g \rangle$ be the cyclic group of composite order generated by g. If the decisional LWEE problem $\mathsf{DLWEE}_{\mathbb{G},n,n+1,q,\mathsf{D}_{\sigma_e}}(\mathsf{D}_{\sigma_s})$ is (t,ϵ)-hard, then the above cryptosystem is $(t, 2\epsilon)$-indistinguishable against chosen plaintext attacks.*

Proof. In a high level, our proof works as follows. Instead of showing IND-CPA security via a direct argument we show that the distribution $(\mathsf{pk}, \mathbf{c}_0, c_1)$ is indistinguishable from the uniform distribution over $(\mathbb{G}^{n\times n} \times \mathbb{G}^{2n+1})$. That is, a ciphertext $(\mathbf{c}_0, c_1)$ under public key pk appears completely random to an adversary. This holds, in particular, in the IND-CPA experiment when the adversary chooses the underlying plaintext. We prove the theorem via a series of hybrid arguments, Hybrid_0 to Hybrid_2, where in each consecutive argument we make some slight changes with the provision that the adversary notices the changes with negligible probability only. In the following, we use the abbreviations $\mathbf{u} = \mathbf{A}\mathbf{r} + \mathbf{e}_0$ and $v = \langle \mathbf{b}, \mathbf{r}\rangle + e_1 + 2^{k-\ell}\mu$.

Hybrid_0**:** In this hybrid we consider the original distribution of the tuple

$$(\mathsf{pk}, (\mathbf{c}_0, \mathbf{c}_1)) = (g^{\mathbf{A}}, g^{\mathbf{b}}, g^{\mathbf{u}}, g^{v}).$$

Hybrid_1**:** In this hybrid we modify the distribution and claim

$$(g^{\mathbf{A}}, g^{\mathbf{b}}, g^{\mathbf{u}}, g^{v}) \approx_c (g^{\mathbf{A}'}, g^{\mathbf{b}'}, g^{\mathbf{A}'\mathbf{r}+\mathbf{e}_0}, g^{\langle \mathbf{b}'\cdot\mathbf{r}\rangle+e_1} \cdot g^{2^{k-\ell}\mu})$$

for a uniformly sampled elements $g^{\mathbf{A}'}, g^{\mathbf{b}'} \in \mathbb{G}^{n\times n} \times \mathbb{G}^{n}$. We argue that any successful algorithm distinguishing between Hybrid_0 and Hybrid_1 can be easily turned into a successful distinguisher $\mathcal{B}$ in the $\mathsf{DLWEE}_{\mathbb{G},n,n,q,\mathsf{D}_{\sigma_e}}(\mathsf{D}_{\sigma_s})$ problem. The DLWEE-adversary $\mathcal{B}$ is given as challenge the tuple $(g^{\mathbf{A}}, g^{\mathbf{b}})$ and is asked to decide whether there exist vectors $\mathbf{s} \leftarrow_R \mathsf{D}_{\sigma_s}$, $\mathbf{x} \leftarrow_R \mathsf{D}_{\sigma_e}^n$ such that $g^{\mathbf{b}} = g^{\mathbf{A}^\top\mathbf{s}+\mathbf{x}}$ or $g^{\mathbf{b}}$ was sampled uniformly from $\mathbb{G}^n$.
Let $\Pr[\mathsf{Hybrid}_i(t)]$ denote the probability of any algorithm with runtime t to win the IND-CPA experiment in hybrid i. Then, we have

$$\Pr[\mathsf{Hybrid}_0(t)] \le \Pr[\mathsf{Hybrid}_1(t)] + \mathsf{Adv}^{\mathsf{DLWEE}}_{\mathbb{G},n,n,q,\mathsf{D}_{\sigma_e},\mathsf{D}_{\sigma_s}}(t).$$

Hybrid_2**:** In this hybrid we modify the distribution and claim

$$(g^{\mathbf{A}'}, g^{\mathbf{b}'}, g^{\mathbf{A}'\mathbf{r}+\mathbf{e}_0}, g^{\langle \mathbf{b}'\cdot\mathbf{r}\rangle+e_1} \cdot g^{2^{k-1}\mu}) \approx_c (g^{\mathbf{A}''}, g^{\mathbf{b}''}, g^{\mathbf{u}'}, g^{v'} \cdot g^{2^{k-1}\mu})$$

for a uniformly sampled elements $g^{\mathbf{A}''}, g^{\mathbf{b}''}, g^{\mathbf{u}'}, g^{v'} \cdot g^{\mu} \in \mathbb{G}^{(n+1)\times n} \times \mathbb{G}^{n+1}$. We argue that any successful algorithm distinguishing between Hybrid_1 and Hybrid_2 can be easily turned into a successful distinguisher $\mathcal{B}$ against the $\mathsf{DLWEE}_{\mathbb{G},n,n+1,q,\mathsf{D}_{\sigma_e}}(\mathsf{D}_{\sigma_s})$ problem. Note that $g^{\mathbf{b}'}, g^{\langle \mathbf{b}'\cdot\mathbf{r}\rangle+e_1}$ is an additional sample from the LWEE distribution from which $g^{\mathbf{A}'}, g^{\mathbf{A}'\mathbf{r}+\mathbf{e}_0}$ is sampled. We have

$$\Pr[\mathsf{Hybrid}_1(t)] \le \Pr[\mathsf{Hybrid}_2(t)] + \mathsf{Adv}^{\mathsf{DLWEE}}_{\mathbb{G},n,n+1,q,\mathsf{D}_{\sigma_e},\mathsf{D}_{\sigma_s}}(t).$$

Note that now all exponents are uniformly distributed, and, in particular, independent of μ and thus, independent of b in the IND-CPA game. Hence, any algorithm has in Hybrid_2 exactly a success probability of $1/2$.

This completes the proof of semantic security.

4.5 Candidate Instantiations of Our Encryption Scheme

We give three possible instantiations to derive a system with short key sizes, post-quantum security or double hardness. Throughout this section we instantiate our scheme such that the encryption scheme from Sect. 4.2 encrypts only a single bit. Nonetheless, parameters can easily be upscaled to many bits.

Table 1. Key sizes in kilobytes (kB) for our encryption scheme basing security on DRP or LWE, respectively.

Sizes/Security	DRP-based instantiation			LWE-based instantiation		
	80-bit	128-bit	256-bit	80-bit	128-bit	256-bit
Public-key size	0.565 kB	1.500 kB	7.500 kB	235 kB	417 kB	1233 kB
Secret-key size	0.212 kB	0.563 kB	2.813 kB	0.976 kB	1.302 kB	2.237 kB
Ciphertext size	0.283 kB	0.750 kB	3.750 kB	0.980 kB	1.306 kB	2.241 kB

The Classical Way. Here, we instantiate our encryption scheme such that the underlying DRP is intractable, and neglecting the hardness of the underlying LWE. In the full version, we recall some groups where we believe DRP is hard to solve. Our encryption scheme works in the group $\mathbb{J}_N := \{x \in \mathbb{Z}_N : \mathbb{J}(x, N) = 1\}$ for $N = pq$ with p, q being k-safe primes. In fact, we can even take safe primes p, q (i.e., $k = 1$) since we do not need any noise in the exponent if we neglect the underlying LWE hardness. Thus, we embed the message to the least significant bit in the exponent. For this reason, we can sample $g \leftarrow_R \mathbb{J}_N/\mathbb{QR}_N$ where $\langle g \rangle$ has order $2p'q'$. Since the LWE instance within LWEE is not an issue here we select $n = m = 1$, $\sigma_s = \infty$ and $\sigma_e = 0$.

We obtain 80-bit security for the underlying DRP problem if we choose safe primes p and q such that $\log p = \log q = 565$ (see full version for more details). Table 1 lists possible key sizes for our encryption scheme. Recall that the public key consists of $\mathsf{pk} = (g, g^{\mathbf{A}}, g^{\mathbf{b}}, k, N)$ (i.e., 4 group elements if we fix $k = 1$) and the secret key of $\mathsf{sk} = (p, \mathbf{s})$.

The Post-Quantum Way. Here we give example instantiations of our encryption scheme when it is based on a presumably quantum-resistant LWEE assumption. That is, we select parameters such that the underlying LWE assumption is intractable without relying on the hardness of DRP. For this, we modify the scheme slightly by choosing fixed values for p' and q' instead of sampling. A good choice is $k = 15$, since it allows to choose $p' = 2$ and $q' = 5$, which are very small prime numbers such that $2^k p' + 1$ and $2^k q' + 1$ are prime. For the LWE modulus, this leads to $M = 2^k p'q' = 327680$. Like Lindner and Peikert [28], we choose the Gaussian parameter such that the probability of decoding errors is bounded by 1 %. We choose furthermore the same parameter for error and secret distribution (i.e. $\sigma_s = \sigma_e = \sigma$), since a standard argument reduces LWE with arbitrary secret to LWE with secret chosen according to the error distribution. For this choice of k, p' and q', we obtain 80-bit security by choosing $n = 240$ and $\sigma = 33.98$. Table 1 lists the key sizes when our encryption scheme is instantiated such that its security is based on LWE only (see full version for more information about the concrete hardness of LWE).

The Hardest Way (Double-Hardness). The most secure instantiation of our encryption is such that even if one of the problems DRP or LWE is efficiently solvable at some point, our encryption scheme remains semantically secure. Selecting parameters for double hardness, however, is non-trivial.

To select appropriate parameters for the case of double hardness, we apply the following approach: For a given security level (say $\kappa = 80$), we select N such that the Number Field Sieve needs at least 2^κ operations to factor N. A possible choice is $\log N = 1130$ (See full version). Since factoring N must also be hard for McKee-Pinch's algorithm, which works well when $(p-1)$ and $(q-1)$ share common factor, k must be chosen such that $N^{1/4}2^{-k} \geq 2^\kappa$, i.e. $k \leq \frac{\log(N)}{4} - \kappa$. This leads to $k = 203$. Given N and k, we can calculate the sizes of the primes $\log(p') \approx \log(q') \approx 362$ and $log(p) \approx \log(q) \approx 565$ and the LWE modulus $\log(M) \approx 927$. Taking $n = 67000$ and $\sigma = 2^{97}$, Lemma 1 shows that the algorithm decrypts correctly with high probability.

References

1. Shor, P.: Algorithms for quantum computation: discrete logarithms and factoring. In: 35th Annual Symposium on Foundations of Computer Science, 1994 Proceedings, pp. 124–134 (1994)
2. Shor, P.: Polynomial-time algorithms for prime factorization and discrete logarithms on a quantum computer. SIAM J. Comput. **26**, 1484–1509 (1997)
3. Regev, O.: On lattices, learning with errors, random linear codes, and cryptography. In: Gabow, H.N., Fagin, R. (eds.) Proceedings of the 37th Annual ACM Symposium on Theory of Computing, pp. 84–93, 22–24 May 2005. ACM, Baltimore, MD, USA (2005)
4. Regev, O.: The learning with errors problem (invited survey). In: IEEE Conference on Computational Complexity, pp. 191–204. IEEE Computer Society (2010)
5. Peikert, C.: Public-key cryptosystems from the worst-case shortest vector problem: extended abstract. In: Proceedings of the 41st Annual ACM Symposium on Theory of Computing, STOC 2009, pp. 333–342. ACM, New York (2009)
6. Lyubashevsky, V., Micciancio, D.: On bounded distance decoding, unique shortest vectors, and the minimum distance problem. In: Halevi, S. (ed.) CRYPTO 2009. LNCS, vol. 5677, pp. 577–594. Springer, Heidelberg (2009)
7. Brakerski, Z., Langlois, A., Peikert, C., Regev, O., Stehlé, D.: Classical hardness of learning with errors. In: Proceedings of the 45th Annual ACM Symposium on Symposium on Theory of Computing, pp. 575–584. ACM (2013)
8. Katz, J., Sahai, A., Waters, B.: Predicate encryption supporting disjunctions, polynomial equations, and inner products. J. Cryptology **26**, 191–224 (2013)
9. Boneh, D., Goh, E.-J., Nissim, K.: Evaluating 2-DNF formulas on ciphertexts. In: Kilian, J. (ed.) TCC 2005. LNCS, vol. 3378, pp. 325–341. Springer, Heidelberg (2005)

10. Brands, S.A.: An efficient off-line electronic cash system based on the representation problem. Technical report, Amsterdam, The Netherlands (1993)
11. Shacham, H.: A Cramer-Shoup encryption scheme from the linear assumption and from progressively weaker linear variants. Cryptology ePrint Archive, Report 2007/074 (2007). http://eprint.iacr.org/
12. Dagdelen, O., Gajek, S., Gopfert, F.: Learning with errors in the exponent. Cryptology ePrint Archive, Report 2014/826 (2014). http://eprint.iacr.org/
13. Regev, O.: Quantum computation and lattice problems. SIAM J. Comput. **33**, 738–760 (2004)
14. Naor, M., Segev, G.: Public-key cryptosystems resilient to key leakage. In: Halevi, S. (ed.) CRYPTO 2009. LNCS, vol. 5677, pp. 18–35. Springer, Heidelberg (2009)
15. Agrawal, S., Dodis, Y., Vaikuntanathan, V., Wichs, D.: On continual leakage of discrete log representations. In: Sako, K., Sarkar, P. (eds.) ASIACRYPT 2013, Part II. LNCS, vol. 8270, pp. 401–420. Springer, Heidelberg (2013)
16. Boneh, D., Halevi, S., Hamburg, M., Ostrovsky, R.: Circular-secure encryption from decision diffie-hellman. In: Wagner, D. (ed.) CRYPTO 2008. LNCS, vol. 5157, pp. 108–125. Springer, Heidelberg (2008)
17. Katz, J., Vaikuntanathan, V.: Signature schemes with bounded leakage resilience. In: Matsui, M. (ed.) ASIACRYPT 2009. LNCS, vol. 5912, pp. 703–720. Springer, Heidelberg (2009)
18. Dagdelen, Ö., Venturi, D.: A second look at Fischlin's transformation. In: Pointcheval, D., Vergnaud, D. (eds.) AFRICACRYPT. LNCS, vol. 8469, pp. 356–376. Springer, Heidelberg (2014)
19. Escala, A., Herold, G., Kiltz, E., Ràfols, C., Villar, J.: An algebraic framework for Diffie-Hellman assumptions. In: Canetti, R., Garay, J.A. (eds.) CRYPTO 2013, Part II. LNCS, vol. 8043, pp. 129–147. Springer, Heidelberg (2013)
20. Micciancio, D.: Improving lattice based cryptosystems using the Hermite normal form. In: Silverman, J.H. (ed.) CaLC 2001. LNCS, vol. 2146, pp. 126–145. Springer, Heidelberg (2001)
21. Applebaum, B., Cash, D., Peikert, C., Sahai, A.: Fast cryptographic primitives and circular-secure encryption based on hard learning problems. In: Halevi, S. (ed.) CRYPTO 2009. LNCS, vol. 5677, pp. 595–618. Springer, Heidelberg (2009)
22. Brakerski, Z., Vaikuntanathan, V.: Fully homomorphic encryption from ring-LWE and security for key dependent messages. In: Rogaway, P. (ed.) CRYPTO 2011. LNCS, vol. 6841, pp. 505–524. Springer, Heidelberg (2011)
23. Goldwasser, S., Kalai, Y., Peikert, C., Vaikuntanathan, V.: Robustness of the learning with errors assumption. In: ICS, 2010, [GPV08] [GRS08] (2008)
24. Kuhn, F., Struik, R.: Random walks revisited: extensions of Pollard's Rho algorithm for computing multiple discrete logarithms. In: Vaudenay, S., Youssef, A.M. (eds.) SAC 2001. LNCS, vol. 2259, pp. 212–229. Springer, Heidelberg (2001)
25. Hitchcock, Y., Montague, P., Carter, G., Dawson, E.: The efficiency of solving multiple discrete logarithm problems and the implications for the security of fixed elliptic curves. Int. J. Inf. Secur. **3**, 86–98 (2004)
26. Yun, A.: Generic hardness of the multiple discrete logarithm problem. Cryptology ePrint Archive, Report 2014/637 (2014). http://eprint.iacr.org/
27. Lyubashevsky, V., Palacio, A., Segev, G.: Public-key cryptographic primitives provably as secure as subset sum. In: Micciancio, D. (ed.) TCC 2010. LNCS, vol. 5978, pp. 382–400. Springer, Heidelberg (2010)

28. Lindner, R., Peikert, C.: Better key sizes (and attacks) for LWE-based encryption. In: Kiayias, A. (ed.) CT-RSA 2011. LNCS, vol. 6558, pp. 319–339. Springer, Heidelberg (2011)
29. Joye, M., Libert, B.: Efficient cryptosystems from 2^k-th power residue symbols. In: Johansson, T., Nguyen, P.Q. (eds.) EUROCRYPT 2013. LNCS, vol. 7881, pp. 76–92. Springer, Heidelberg (2013)
30. Pohlig, S., Hellman, M.: An improved algorithm for computing logarithms over GF(p) and its cryptographic significance (corresp.). IEEE Trans. Inf. Theory **24**, 106–110 (1978)

Block Cipher Cryptanalysis

Higher-Order Cryptanalysis of LowMC

Christoph Dobraunig, Maria Eichlseder(✉), and Florian Mendel

Graz University of Technology, Graz, Austria
maria.eichlseder@iaik.tugraz.at

Abstract. LowMC is a family of block ciphers developed particularly for use in multi-party computations and fully homomorphic encryption schemes, where the main performance penalty comes from non-linear operations. Thus, LowMC has been designed to minimize the total quantity of logical "and" operations, as well as the "and" depth. To achieve this, the LowMC designers opted for an incomplete S-box layer that does not cover the complete state, and compensate for it with a very dense, randomly chosen linear layer. In this work, we exploit this design strategy in a cube-like key-recovery attack. We are able to recover the secret key of a round-reduced variant of LowMC with 80-bit security, where the number of rounds is reduced from 11 to 9. Our attacks are independent of the actual instances of the used linear layers and therefore, do not exploit possible weak choices of them. From our results, we conclude that the resulting security margin of 2 rounds is smaller than expected.

Keywords: Cryptanalysis · LowMC · Higher-order cryptanalysis · Key recovery · Zero-sum distinguisher

1 Introduction

The recently proposed family of block ciphers LowMC [1] addresses the need for new block cipher structures suited for multi-party computation and fully homomorphic encryptions schemes, where the non-linear operations of a cipher contribute much more to the overall computational execution costs than the linear operations. Therefore, LowMC combines an incomplete S-box layer with a strong linear layer to reduce the multiplicative depth and size of the cipher. However, this is a quite uncommon approach and can be risky as shown for Zorro [3,9,14,17]. Therefore, LowMC comes with strong security arguments (bounds) against standard cryptanalytic attacks like differential and linear cryptanalysis. In more detail, the authors show that for the proposed instances of LowMC, no good differential and linear characteristics exist for more than 5 rounds. However, they do not provide such strong security arguments against other attack vectors including algebraic attacks.

In this work, we show that the security of LowMC against algebraic attacks is lower than expected. Our attacks are based on the ideas previously used in cube attacks [8], higher order differential cryptanalysis [13], AIDA [16], bit-pattern based integral attacks [18], or the square [6] and intergral [12] attacks. To be

S. Kwon and A. Yun (Eds.): ICISC 2015, LNCS 9558, pp. 87–101, 2016.
DOI: 10.1007/978-3-319-30840-1_6

more specific, our attacks make use of the rather low algebraic degree of one round of LowMC to construct cube testers [2]. The fact that the S-box layers are incomplete can be exploited to efficiently construct vector spaces at the input which allow to create cube testers of low dimension covering a rather high number of rounds. The incomplete S-box layer also facilitates the existence of linear relations with probability 1, which allow to attack additional rounds. This leads to attacks on round-reduced variants of LowMC with 80-bit security, where the number of rounds is reduced from 11 to 9. Note that these attacks do not exploit any specific property of the linear layers and are thus applicable for randomly chosen linear layers.

Our results show that the security margin of LowMC with 80-bit security is smaller than expected, being only 2 rounds. Therefore, we conclude that the design of primitives with an incomplete S-box layer has not been fully understood yet. Therefore, it is recommendable to be more conservative when choosing the security margin in those designs.

Related Work. In very recent independent research, Dinur et al. [7] also investigate the security of LowMC against high-order differential cryptanalysis. By developing an optimized variation of interpolation attacks for key recovery, they are able to identify large classes of weak keys for LowMC-80, and also demonstrate attacks on up to 10 of 11 rounds of LowMC-80 and on full-round LowMC-128.

2 Description of LowMC

LowMC [1] is a family of block ciphers, where each instance is characterized by several parameters: the block size n and key size k, the number m of S-boxes per substitution layer, a (logarithmic) data complexity limit d, the number of rounds r, the concrete instantiations of the linear layers f_L, and the key derivation function used in f_K.

The encryption of LowMC starts with a key whitening layer $f_K^{(0)}$, followed by r iterative applications of the round function

$$f^{(i)} = f_K^{(i)} \circ f_L^{(i)} \circ f_S,$$

consisting of the substitution layer f_S (identical for each round), the linear layer $f_L^{(i)}$, and the round-key addition $f_K^{(i)}$, as illustrated in Fig. 1.

The substitution layer is the parallel application of the same 3-bit S-box $S(a, b, c) = (a \oplus bc, a \oplus b \oplus ac, a \oplus b \oplus c \oplus ab)$ on the right-most (least significant) $3 \cdot m$ bits of the state. On the remaining $\ell = n - 3m$ bits, the identity mapping is applied. The used S-box has a maximum differential and linear probability of 2^{-2}, and algebraic degree 2 (the maximum possible degree for a 3-bit permutation).

The linear layer f_L multiplies the n-bit state with a randomly chosen and invertible $n \times n$ matrix over $\mathbb{F}_2$. The matrix differs for each round.

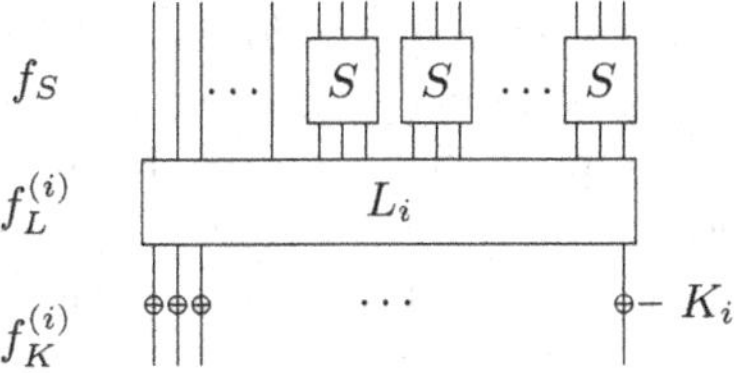

Fig. 1. The round function of LowMC: $f^{(i)} = f_K^{(i)} \circ f_L^{(i)} \circ f_S$.

In $f_K^{(i)}$, the whitening key K_0 and round keys $K_1, \ldots, K_r$ are added in the respective rounds. These round keys are generated by binary multiplications of randomly generated, full-rank $n \times k$ matrices with the master key K, followed by an addition with a randomly chosen n-bit round constant.

Albrecht et al. [1] propose two concrete instances, with the parameter sets shown in Table 2. The first set provides "PRESENT-like" security using an 80-bit key, while the second set provides "AES-like" security using a 128-bit key. To generate the used random matrices, the recommended instantiations use the Grain LSFR [10] as a source of random bits. Since our analysis does not depend on concrete instantiations of matrices, only on the parameters given in Table 2, we omit a description of the matrices.

We will denote LowMC with key size k, state size (permutation size) n and m S-boxes per round as LowMC-$k^{n,m}$. We abbreviate the recommended parameter sets as LowMC-80 = LowMC-$80^{256,49}$ ("PRESENT-like security" variant) and LowMC-128 = LowMC-$128^{256,63}$ ("AES-like security" variant).

3 Higher-Order Attacks in the Known-Key Setting

In the known-key setting [11], we assume that the round keys have known values. The attack goal is to find non-random properties of the resulting permutation. More specifically, we will focus on (families of) zero-sum distinguishers: finding sets of inputs to the permutation such that both the sum (over $\mathbb{F}_2^n$) of the inputs, as well as the sum of their outputs, equal zero. It should be remarked that LowMC's designers make no security claims for the known-key setting, and it is hardly a practical attack scenario. Rather, it serves as an introductory setting, and we will reuse and adapt the results for the secret-key setting in Sect. 4.

3.1 Basic Zero-Sum Distinguisher

A well-known result from the theory of Boolean functions is that if the algebraic degree of a vectorial Boolean function (like a permutation) is d, then the sum over the outputs of the function applied to all elements of a vector space of dimension $\geq d+1$ is zero (as is the sum of all inputs, i.e., the elements of the vector space). The same property holds for affine vector spaces of the form $\{v + c \mid v \in V\}$ for some vector space V and constant c. Therefore, in the remaining text, we also refer to affine vector spaces as vector spaces for simplicity. This property allows to exploit a low algebraic degree of cryptographic functions to create zero-sum distinguishers and has been applied, for example, to Keccak [4,5].

For this reason, the designers of LowMC included bounds for the algebraic degree of multiple rounds of the permutation in their design paper [1]. Their bounds are based on the observation (see [5]) that if the degree after r rounds (with m S-boxes per round of the n-bit permutation) is $d_r^{(n,m)}$, then the degree $d_{r+1}^{(n,m)}$ after $r+1$ rounds is bounded by

$$d_{r+1} \leq \min\left\{2 \cdot d_r, \quad m + d_r, \quad \tfrac{1}{2} \cdot (n + d_r)\right\},$$

since the degree of one round is $d_1 = 2$. The resulting bounds for up to 15 rounds are given in Table 1.

Table 1. Upper bounds for the algebraic degree $d_r^{(n,m)}$ after r rounds of the LowMC permutation on $n = 256$ bits with $m \in \{49, 63\}$ S-boxes.

r	1	2	3	4	5	6	7	8	9	10	11	12	13	14	15
$d_r^{(256,49)}$	2	4	8	16	32	64	113	162	209	232	244	250	253	254	255
$d_r^{(256,63)}$	2	4	8	16	32	64	127	190	223	239	247	251	253	254	255

Based on these numbers, the designers recommend that the number of rounds r satisfies $r \geq r_{\text{deg}} + r_{\text{outer}}$, where r_{deg} is the number of rounds necessary for a sufficiently high degree ($d_{r_{\text{deg}}} \geq d - 1$ for the logarithmic data complexity limit d), and $r_{\text{outer}} = 5$ is a heuristic estimate for the number of rounds that can be "peeled off" in the beginning and end of the cipher, based on the bounds for linear and differential cryptanalysis. This leads to the round numbers stated in Table 2 for the recommended parameter sets.

Table 2. Recommended number of rounds $r \geq r_{\text{deg}} + r_{\text{outer}}$ [1].

Key size k	Block size n	S-boxes m	Data complexity d	r_{deg}	r_{outer}	Rounds r
80	256	49	64	6	5	11
128	256	63	128	7	5	12

The degree bounds from Table 1 clearly show that 11 or 12 rounds of the unkeyed round function cannot be considered an ideal random permutation, although the complexity of a straightforward zero-sum distinguisher is far beyond the claimed security level: if we choose any subspace $V \leq \mathbb{F}_2^{256}$ with dimension ≥ 245 (resp. ≥ 252), we get

$$\sum_{v \in V} v = \sum_{v \in V} f^{11}(v) = 0$$

(resp. $\sum_{v \in V} f^{12}(v) = 0$) for LowMC-80 (resp. LowMC-128) with $m = 49$ (resp. $m = 63$) S-boxes per round, where f is the round with some fixed, known key. However, it is easy to obtain distinguishers with a much lower complexity.

3.2 Initial Structure, Direct-Sum Construction, and Partial Zero-Sums

First, since we are considering the known-key setting, we are not limited to starting computation before the first round. We can also define an initial structure as input for one of the middle rounds – say, round 7 – and compute backwards and forwards from there to again get zero-sums at input and output, with a much lower data complexity. Since LowMC uses 3-bit bijective S-boxes, the degree of the inverse S-box and thus of the inverse round function f^{-1} is also at most 2. Thus, for any subspace $V \leq \mathbb{F}_2^{256}$ with dimension ≥ 65, we get

$$\sum_{v \in V} f^{-6}(v) = \sum_{v \in V} f^{5}(v) = 0$$

(resp. $\sum_{v \in V} f^6 = 0$). The set of 2^{65} zero-sum input values $\{f^{-6}(v) \mid v \in V\}$ is below the data complexity limit d for LowMC-128, and only slightly above for LowMC-80.

Second, by choosing a vector space V of a particular structure as a starting point, we can add a free round in the middle. Assume that V is the direct sum of any subspace of $\mathbb{F}_2^{256-3\cdot m}$, and m trivial subspaces of $\mathbb{F}_2^3$ (i.e., each is either $\mathbb{F}_2^3$ or $\{(0,0,0)\}$). Since the bijective 3-bit S-box maps any trivial subspace of $\mathbb{F}_2^3$ to itself, applying the S-box layer to this vector space produces another vector space $V' \leq \mathbb{F}_2^{256}$ (of the same form). This reduces the data complexity of the distinguisher below the data complexity limit for LowMC-80: for any V of dimension ≥ 33 of the above direct-sum format and the corresponding V',

$$\sum_{v \in V} f^{-5}(v) = \sum_{v' \in V' = f_S(V)} (f^5 \circ f_K \circ f_L)(v') = 0,$$

so the set $\{f^{-5}(v) \mid v \in V\}$ is a zero-sum distinguisher for LowMC-80 with known key, with a data complexity of 2^{33}. The attack is illustrated in Fig. 2.

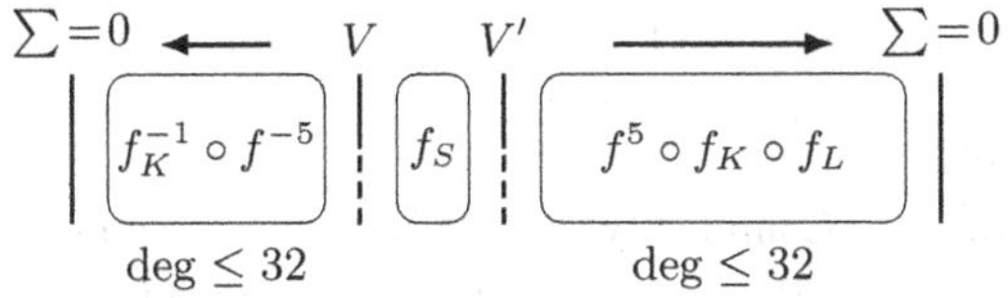

Fig. 2. Zero-sum distinguisher for $r = 11$ rounds of LowMC-80 with a data complexity of 2^{33} message blocks.

Third, we can take advantage of the special structure of the S-box layer, which only applies S-boxes to part of the state, while the rest is left unchanged by an identity map. In the inverse round f^{-1}, the linear layer is applied before the S-box layer. This means that (the leftmost/most significant) $\ell = n - 3 \cdot m$ bits of the output of each inverse round f^{-1} only depend linearly on the round input bits ($\ell = 109$ bits for LowMC-80, $\ell = 67$ bits for LowMC-128). If we add such an inverse round to a function, the degree of ℓ output bits is bounded by the same limit as the original function output, so the inverse round (corresponding to a round in the beginning of the cipher) is essentially "for free" on these bits. A similar idea can be used to also add a free forward round at the end. To compensate for the additional linear layer after the last S-box layer, however, we need to generalize the partial zero-sum property further: instead of a zero-sum property on some of the output bits, we get a zero-sum property on some (linearly independent) linear combinations of the cipher's output bits. Note that the final linear transformation $f_K \circ f_L$ can be swapped to $f_L \circ f_{K'}$ with some equivalent key K'. Since the addition of K' does not change the partial zero-sum property, the linear combination of output bits that sums to zero does not depend on the key. Since ℓ is relatively large ($\ell > k$ for LowMC-80), even a zero-sum distinguisher only for ℓ bits of the input and (linearly combined) output gives us a detectable distinguishing property. With the above approach, we get ℓ-bit partial zero-sums with 2 more rounds for free, so the dimension of V can be reduced to 17 (for LowMC-80) and 33 (for LowMC-128) to cover the recommended full round sizes, as illustrated in Fig. 3. Table 3 summarizes the best attacks for the known-key setting.

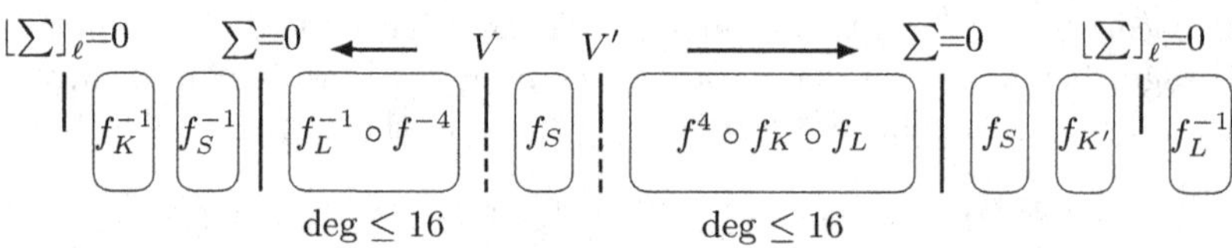

Fig. 3. Partial 109-bit zero-sum distinguisher for $r = 11$ rounds of LowMC-80 with a data complexity of 2^{17} message blocks.

Table 3. Distinguishers for LowMC in the known-key setting.

	Zero-sum		Partial zero-sum		
Target	Rounds	Complexity	Zero-sum bit size	Rounds	Complexity
LowMC-80	11/11	2^{33}	109/256	11/11	2^{17}
LowMC-128	12/12	2^{65}	67/256	12/12	2^{33}

4 Higher-Order Attacks in the Secret-Key Setting

In this section, we investigate the applicability of higher-order attacks in the secret-key setting. While the basic observations about the degree of the round functions and the zero-sum property still hold in this setting, it is no longer easily possible to define an initial structure in the middle of the cipher as in Sect. 3.2 and compute in both directions. Attack goals in the secret-key setting include output distinguishers and key recovery. For simplicity, we demonstrate our attacks for the LowMC variant LowMC-80 ("PRESENT-like security"), and only briefly discuss the applicability and complexity for LowMC-128 and more general LowMC configurations at the end of the paper.

4.1 Basic Zero-Sum Key Recovery

Based on the basic observations from Sect. 3.1, an attacker can trivially distinguish the output of up to 3, 4, or 5 rounds of LowMC-80 from random values with a data complexity of 2^9, 2^{17}, or 2^{33}, respectively (all below the logarithmic data complexity of $d = 64$): he requests the ciphertexts for all values of an (affine) vector space V of the given size, and verifies the zero-sum property of the corresponding outputs.

By choosing a vector space of the same direct-sum form as in Sect. 3.2 for V, we can add an additional free round in the beginning: the output values after applying the initial key whitening f_K and the first S-box layer f_S to all vectors in V is another (affine) vector space V' of the same direct-sum form, and the remaining added round functions f_L, f_K, both of degree ≤ 1, can be added to the following 3, 4, or 5 rounds for free, without increasing the necessary dimension of V.

Additionally, we can add another final round without increasing the data complexity, by turning the distinguishing attack into a key recovery attack: to recover the key from $r \in \{5, 6, 7\}$ rounds of LowMC-80, the attacker chooses a vector space V of the previous direct-sum form with $|V| = 2^{2^{r-2}+1}$ elements as inputs (corresponding to 2^9, 2^{17}, or 2^{33} plaintexts, respectively). As previously, the corresponding outputs after $r-1$ rounds will sum to zero. This property can be used to recover the final round key K_r in 3-bit chunks, which in turn allows to easily recover the original key K. Let $S_i^{(r-1)}$ denote the state after $r-1$ rounds applied to input $P_i \in V$, and $S_i^{(r)} = C_i$ the corresponding ciphertext obtained by the attacker, so

$$C_i = (f_K^{(r)} \circ f_L^{(r)} \circ f_S)(S_i^{(r-1)}) = (f_L^{(r)} \circ f_S)(S_i^{(r-1)}) + K_r.$$

Since the key addition $f_K^{(r)}$ and linear layer $f_L^{(r)}$ can be swapped (replacing the original K_r with a transformed K_r'), the zero-sum property translates to

$$\sum_i S_i^{(r-1)} = \sum_i f_S^{-1}\left(K_r' + {f_L^{(r)}}^{-1}(C_i)\right) = 0.$$

For the 109 bits of the identity part of f_S, this property holds irrespective of the value of the corresponding bits of K'_r. For each of the $m = 49$ S-boxes, however, the property can be checked independently for each possible value of the corresponding 3 bits of K'_r. Since we expect to require about 80 bits of K'_r to recover K_r and consequently K, we guess the keys for 27 S-boxes, which leads to an overall complexity of $2^{2^{r-2}+1}$ queries (plus $2^{2^{r-2}+1} \cdot 8 \cdot 27$ xor operations).

The approach is illustrated in Fig. 4. The complexity is 2^9 encryption queries for 5 rounds, 2^{17} for 6 rounds, and 2^{33} for 7 rounds. Note that this attack is relatively generic for SPNs with degree 2, without using any particular properties of LowMC (in particular, independent of the number m of S-boxes per layer).

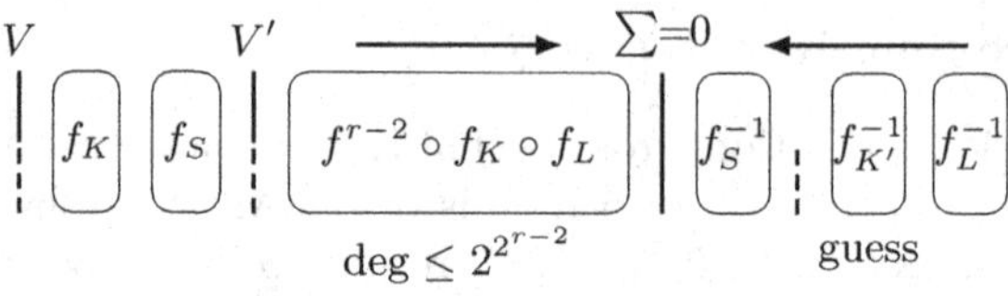

Fig. 4. Key recovery attack on $r = 5$, 6, or 7 rounds of LowMC, with a data complexity of $2^{2^{r-2}+1} = 2^9$, 2^{17}, or 2^{33} plaintexts, respectively.

4.2 Adding Rounds: Initial Key-Guessing

In addition to the generic attack strategy applied so far, we can take advantage of the special structure of LowMC's substitution layer. So far, we were able to add one free initial round by using a direct-sum construction to obtain a vector space again after applying one round f. We will now try to define an initial structure that yields a vector space after 2 rounds f^2.

Consider the first 2 rounds $f^2 = f_K \circ f_L \circ f_S \circ f_K \circ f_L \circ f_S$ of LowMC-80. The final linear components $f_K \circ f_L$ pose no constraints. Let $V = \{(0, \dots, 0)\} \times \mathbb{F}_2^{109} \leq \mathbb{F}_2^{256}$ be the vector space of elements that are zero except for the bits processed by the identity part of the substitution layer f_S. Thus, for any subspace $W \leq V$, $f_S(W) = W$. We want to find a suitable subspace $W \leq V$ that will yield another vector space W'' even after applying the second substitution layer f_S. The input space W' to the second f_S is an affine transformation of W, $W' = (f_K \circ f_L)(W)$. Ideally, this space W' would be of the same structure as W: zero (or constant) in all bits except the identity part. However, this requirement would impose 147 linear constraints (one for each S-box input bit) on the 109-dimensional space V, so we cannot expect any suitable (nontrivial) solution space W.

However, it is not actually necessary to require all S-box input bits to be zero or constant. Consider an input set where two of the input bits to an S-box are fixed, but one bit is toggled. The two different input values will produce two different output values, i.e., toggling one input bit will toggle some of the output bits. This is essentially "linear" behaviour, so the S-box is linear with respect to one input bit. Thus, an input space that allows up to one bit per S-box to be toggled (non-constant) will produce another affine space as the output of the S-box layer. Note that due to the key addition f_K just before the S-box layer, we cannot know or control the constant values of the constant bits, and thus do not know the linear behaviour of the S-box. However, we can be sure that if W is such that after the linear layer f_L, two of the three input bits to each S-box of f_S are constant, then the input space W will be mapped to another vector space by 2 rounds f^2 of LowMC-80. This corresponds to $2 \cdot 49 = 98$ linear constraints on the 109-dimensional V, so we will get a solution space W of dimension at least $109 - 98 = 11$. W can be precomputed and depends only on the matrix of the linear layer of the first round of LowMC-80. The dimension of 11 is sufficient for our previous attack on 5 rounds, which required an input space of 2^9 elements, and allows us to extend this attack to 6 rounds at no additional cost. The attack is illustrated in Fig. 5.

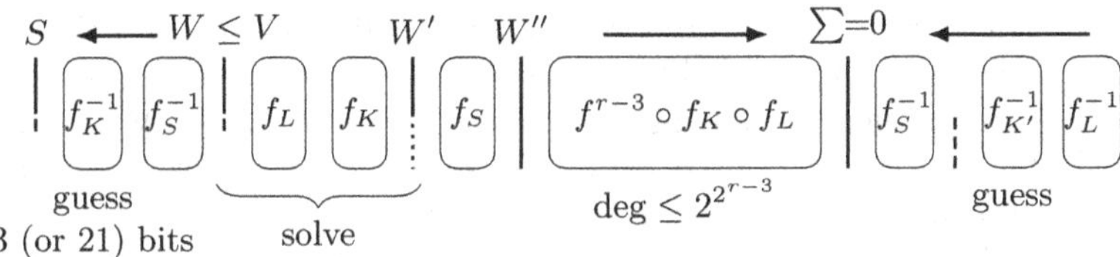

Fig. 5. Key recovery attack on $r = 6$ rounds of LowMC-80, with complexity 2^9.

Unfortunately, the dimension is too small to extend the previous attacks on 6 and 7 rounds, which required input spaces of 2^{17} and 2^{33} elements, respectively. To increase the dimension of W to 17 or higher, we need to allow for more freedom either in the first or in the second substitution layer f_S. First consider the first substitution layer. If we want to choose our inputs so as to ensure a specific vector space structure after the first substitution layer, we can achieve this trivially if the target vectors are non-constant only in the identity part. If we want specific values at the output of an S-box, we need to guess the corresponding 3 bits of the first whitening key, which is added right before the substitution layer. By guessing these 3 bits, we can increase the dimension of W by 3. Note that if we "activate" an S-box this way, the required message input set S to produce W is no longer necessarily a vector space. In particular, its elements no longer necessarily sum to zero. However, this is not required for our key recovery attacks, so the loss of the input zero-sum property is not a problem. To apply the technique to extend the previous 6-round attack of Sect. 4.1 and increase W to dimension 17, we need to activate 2 S-boxes and thus guess 6 key bits. This increases the attack complexity for the extended 7-round attack to $2^{17} \cdot 2^6 = 2^{23}$. For the previous 7-round attack of Sect. 4.1, we need dimension 33 and thus need to activate 8 S-boxes with 24 guessed key bits, and the complexity for the extended 8 rounds is $2^{33} \cdot 2^{24} = 2^{57}$.

We can, however, also consider additional freedom in the second substitution layer in order to decrease the necessary number of activated S-boxes in the first layer. We previously chose a fixed bit per S-box of the second f_S which was allowed to toggle, while the other two bits needed to remain constant. But this is not actually necessary: we have the freedom to choose any of the 3 bit positions of each S-box as the toggle-bit, so we have a total of $3^{49} \approx 2^{77.7}$ options to choose the 98 (out of the total 147) constraints imposed by the second layer. The 147 available constraints are specified by the (roughly uniformly randomly generated) rows of the linear layer matrix. In addition, we have the freedom to select the activated S-boxes of the first layer. For each option, we have a very small chance that the selection of 98 constraints is redundant (with respect to the $109 + 3s$-dimensional V, if we guess s S-box keys in the first substitution layer), and the remaining solution space has a dimension larger than $11 + 3s$.

Consider again the 8-round attack, with its required input space of $2^{33} = 2^{11} \cdot 2^{22}$ elements. To increase the dimension by 22, we had to activate $s = 8$ S-boxes. We only needed 1 bit of freedom from the last of the 8 S-boxes, but still had to guess all the corresponding 3 key bits. There is a reasonable chance that if we activate only $s = 7$ S-boxes (and start with V of dimension $109 + 7 \cdot 3 = 130$) and add the 98 constraints of the second layer, the remaining solution space has the required dimension 33 instead of the expected $130 - 98 = 32$. This is equivalent to the event that 98 randomly selected vectors from $\mathbb{F}_2^{130}$ span a subspace of dimension 97, or that a randomly selected 130×98 matrix over $\mathbb{F}_2$ has rank 97. The probability of picking a rank-r matrix uniformly random from $\mathbb{F}_2^{n \times m}$, $n \geq m$ [15] is given by

$$P(n, m, r) = \frac{\prod_{i=0}^{r-1}(2^m - 2^i) \cdot \prod_{i=0}^{r-1}(2^n - 2^i)}{\prod_{i=0}^{r-1}(2^r - 2^i) \cdot 2^{n \cdot m}},$$

so our success chance for one selection of constraints is $P(130, 98, 97) \approx 2^{-32.0}$.

Even though the available selections of constraints are not independent, we verified experimentally that the measured distribution of the rank of random selections closely matches the theoretic expectations. Thus, it is reasonable to expect that a suitable selection exists among the available choices, and that it can be efficiently found (e.g., after trying about 2^{32} random selections). Since the selection depends only on the corresponding matrix of the linear layer, it can be precomputed in advance.

The same strategy can also be applied to the 7-round attack, although at a higher precomputation cost: we activate $s = 1$ instead of $s = 2$ S-boxes in the first layer, and compensate by reducing the rank of the 98 selected constraint vectors by 3 to 95. The success chance for one selection is $P(112, 98, 95) \approx 2^{-49.4}$. The modified attack for 7 and 8 rounds is illustrated in Fig. 6. The final attack complexities are 2^9 for 6 rounds, 2^{20} (with $2^{49.4}$ precomputation) or 2^{23} (without precomputation) for 7 rounds, and 2^{54} for 8 rounds.

4.3 Adding Rounds: Final Key-Guessing

We can not only guess the round keys of the first round to increase the number of attacked rounds, but also the last round keys. We want to combine a linear

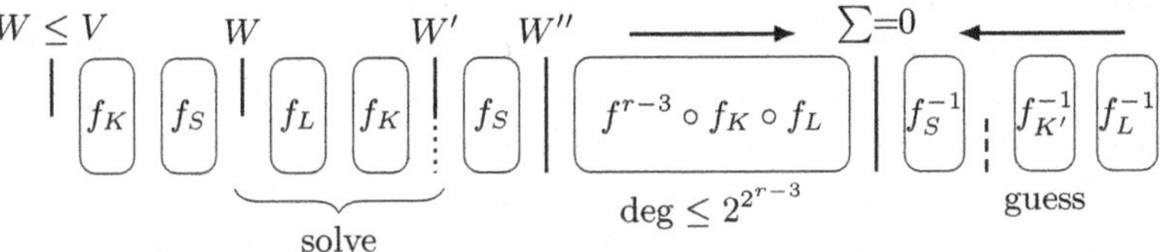

Fig. 6. Key recovery attack on $r = 7$ (or 8) rounds of LowMC-80, with complexities 2^{20} and 2^{54}, respectively.

mask for the linear layer of the second-to-last round with key guesses for some S-boxes of the last round. This combination will allow us to derive 1 bit of key information per input set, and can be repeated to learn more.

For an attack on r rounds, assume we have constructed a zero-sum attack for $r-2$ rounds, that is, we can generate sets of inputs such that their corresponding outputs after $r-2$ rounds sum to zero. If we denote the intermediate states and rearrange the key addition layer as in Sect. 4.1, we get

$$C_i = S_i^{(r)} = \left(f_L^{(r)} \circ f_{K'}^{(r)} \circ f_S \circ f_L^{(r-1)} \circ f_{K'}^{(r-1)} \circ f_S\right)\left(S_i^{(r-2)}\right).$$

Since $\sum_i S_i^{(r-2)} = 0$, we also get the partial zero-sum

$$\left\lfloor \sum_i \left(f_{K'}^{(r-1)} \circ f_S\right)\left(S_i^{(r-2)}\right) \right\rfloor_{109} = 0,$$

where $\lfloor x \rfloor_\ell$ is the value x truncated to the most significant ℓ bits, i.e., the identity part of the S-box layer. Now let

$$x_i = \left(f_{K'}^{(r-1)} \circ f_S\right)\left(S_i^{(r-2)}\right), \qquad y_i = \left(f_S^{-1} \circ {f_{K'}^{(r)}}^{-1} \circ {f_L^{(r)}}^{-1}\right)(C_i),$$

so x_i and y_i are the states right before and after the linear layer of the second-to-last round, $y_i = f_L^{(r-1)}(x_i)$.

Now assume (a, b) is a pair of consistent linear input- and output masks for $f_L^{(r-1)}$, that is, for all $x \in \mathbb{F}_2^{256}$,

$$\langle a, x \rangle = \langle b, f_L^{(r-1)}(x) \rangle.$$

We will call the mask pair (a, b) suitable if a is zero on its 147 least significant bits (i.e., all bits except the identity part of f_S), and b is zero on most of its 147 least significant bits. We refer to the S-boxes where b is non-zero on one of the corresponding 3 input bits as active.

We target mask pairs (a, b) with at most 6 active S-boxes. For a random matrix, the probability that an input mask a is mapped to an output mask b in which only 6 of 49 S-boxes are active is, by the inclusion-exclusion principle,

$$P[\leq 6 \text{ S-boxes active}] = \sum_{i=0}^{6} (-1)^i \cdot \binom{6}{i} \cdot \binom{49}{i} \cdot 2^{-3 \cdot (49-i)} \approx 2^{-105.4}.$$

Since we have a total of 2^{109} possible input masks a available, we can expect a suitable mask pair to exist. In practical experiments, we were able to find suitable masks with 6 or even fewer active S-boxes in reasonable time.

Observe that if (a, b) is a suitable mask pair, then

$$\sum_i \langle b, y_i \rangle = \sum_i \left\langle b, f_L^{(r-1)}(x_i) \right\rangle = \sum_i \langle a, x_i \rangle = \left\langle a, \sum_i x_i \right\rangle = 0,$$

since a only selects from the 109 most significant bits, and the x_i have the partial zero-sum property $\lfloor \sum_i x_i \rfloor_{109} = 0$. This modified zero-sum property of the y_i depends only on the last-round key bits (of the equivalent key K') added to the active S-boxes, i.e., for 6 active S-boxes, on 18 key bits. The other key bits are either not selected by b (inactive S-boxes), or cancel out during summation (identity part). The probability of the 1-bit property to hold for a random key guess is $\frac{1}{2}$, so applying the attack to one zero-sum input set will eliminate half of the key guesses for the 18 key bits, or win 1 bit of key information. By repeating the attack for 18 input sets S (e.g., by adding 18 different constants to the original input set), we expect to recover all 18 round key bits. The attack is illustrated in Fig. 7.

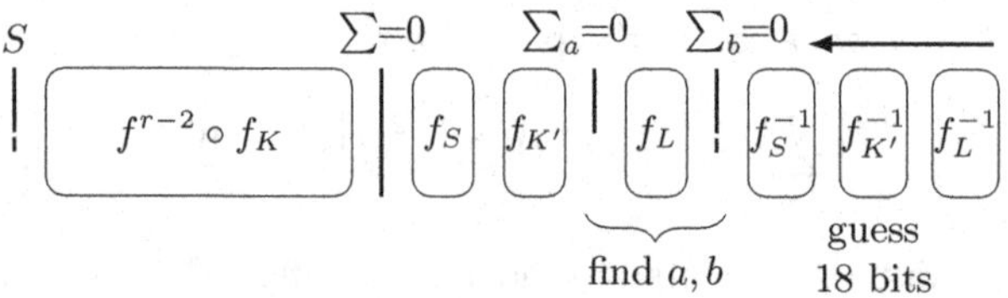

Fig. 7. Key recovery attack on $r = 7$, 8, or 9 rounds of LowMC-80, with 1-bit sums $\sum_a = \sum_i \langle a, x_i \rangle$ and $\sum_b = \sum_i \langle b, y_i \rangle$ (details of $f^{r-2} \circ f_K$ as in Fig. 6).

To learn more key bits, we need to find more linear mask pairs (a, b), with different active S-boxes. Since the previously active S-boxes with previously recovered key bits can now be active for free, finding such masks becomes easier. In addition, we can re-use the same ciphertexts for different masks, so the data complexity does not increase. In summary, after precomputing suitable mask pairs, this attack described so far allows to recover the complete key for r instead of $r-1$ rounds at an additional cost factor of $18 \approx 2^{4.2}$ data complexity and about $2^{18} \cdot 80 \approx 2^{24.3}$ computational complexity.

However, the computational complexity can be further reduced by optimizing the repeated evaluation of the modified zero-sum check. Instead of summing all inputs for each of the 2^{18} key guesses, we can precompute partial bit sums, and only combine those to compute the final sum for each of the 2^{18} key candidates. The idea is to decompose the target sum into its S-box-wise components as

$$\sum_i \langle b, y_i \rangle = \sum_i \left\langle \sum_{s=0}^{49} b_s, y_i \right\rangle = \sum_{s=0}^{49} \sum_i \langle b_s, y_i \rangle,$$

Table 4. Key-recovery attacks for LowMC-80: number of rounds with computational and data complexity (all below logarithmic data complexity limit $d = 64$).

	Basic (Sect. 4.1)		Initial key guess (Sect. 4.2)		Final key guess (Sect. 4.3)	
Cube degree	Rounds	Compl.	Rounds	Compl.	Rounds	Compl.
8 (f^3)	5/11	2^9	6/11	2^9	7/11	2^{14}
16 (f^4)	6/11	2^{17}	7/11	2^{23}	8/11	2^{28}
32 (f^5)	7/11	2^{33}	8/11	2^{54}	9/11	2^{59}

where b_s equals b on the 3 bit positions corresponding to S-box s, $1 \leq s \leq 49$ (or the 109 bits of the identity part for $s = 0$), and is zero otherwise. Then $\sum_i \langle b_s, y_i \rangle$ depends only on the 3 round key bits corresponding to S-box s (and 3 bits of $f_L^{-1}(C_i)$, see the definition of y_i), and can be precomputed in a first phase for all 2^3 possible values of these key bits, for each active S-box s. Then, in the second phase, to determine the test bit for each of the 2^{18} key candidates, it suffices to sum the 6 corresponding partial sums (of the active S-boxes). Considering that each linear layer alone needs about 2^{16} xor operations, the complexity of both phases is significantly smaller compared to the computational effort of generating all the required ciphertexts C_i. This step can be repeated 4 times with different mask pairs (a, b) to recover about $4 \cdot 18 = 72$ key bits; the remaining bits can easily be determined by brute force testing.

With this improvement, the computational complexity overhead factor incurred by this approach over the attack on $r - 1$ rounds is dominated by the data complexity increase by a factor of about $2^{4.2}$. Based on the attacks of Sect. 4.2, we get full key recovery for 7 rounds with 2^{14} complexity, for 8 rounds with 2^{28}, and for 9 rounds with 2^{59}. We summarize all attacks in Table 4.

Acknowledgments. The work has been supported in part by the Austrian Science Fund (project P26494-N15) and by the Austrian Research Promotion Agency (FFG) and the Styrian Business Promotion Agency (SFG) under grant number 836628 (SeCoS).

A Application to Other Parameter Sets

Besides the recommended versions LowMC-80 and LowMC-128, the designers also propose several alternative parameter sets for the 80-bit and 128-bit security level. For 128-bit security, the design document discusses the performance of LowMC-$128^{256,63}$ ($r = 12$ rounds, main variant) and LowMC-$128^{512,86}$ ($r = 11$ or 12 rounds), all with data complexity limit $d = 128$; for 80-bit security, LowMC-$80^{256,49}$ ($r = 11$ rounds, main variant, or $r = 10$) and LowMC-$80^{128,34}$ ($r = 11$ rounds), all with data complexity limit $d = 64$.

For LowMC-$128^{256,63}$, the attacks of Sect. 4.1 apply for the same number of rounds, with the same complexity. Furthermore, due to the increased logarithmic data complexity limit, an additional round can be added here (for a total of 8 rounds), and the data complexity increased accordingly. However, the size of the identity part, $\ell = 67$, is too small to append rounds with initial-key-guessing as in Sect. 4.2: the necessary number of about $3 \cdot 40$ guessed S-box key bits becomes prohibitive. Final-key-guessing as in Sect. 4.3, on the other hand, is applicable in a similar way. Again, the smaller identity part increases the complexity: instead of masks b with 6 active S-boxes, about 24 active S-boxes are necessary for a reasonably high probability. If the correct $3 \cdot 24$-bit subkey is recovered as described in Sect. 4.3, the computational complexity is about 2^{72} (for up to 9 rounds). However, it is possible to optimize this step at the cost of a slightly higher data complexity.

For LowMC-$128^{512,86}$, on the other hand, the size of the identity part $\ell = 254$ is almost as large as the S-box part of $3 \cdot m = 258$ bits. This allows the application of initial-key-guessing for free, and 1 active S-box is expected to be sufficient for final-key-guessing. Additionally, due to the higher logarithmic data complexity limit of $d = 128$, the core cube degree can be increased to 64 (f^6) to add another round, for a total of 10 attacked rounds (out of 11 or 12).

For LowMC-$80^{128,34}$, $\ell = 26$, so the same problems as for LowMC-$128^{256,63}$ apply. For the final-key-guessing, about 14 active S-boxes would be required to find suitable a, b, to attack a total of 8 rounds.

We want to stress that all described attacks are generic for the design of LowMC, without requiring specific instances of the linear layer f_L or the key schedule matrices. For specific "weak" choices of the random matrices, it is likely that attacks on more rounds are feasible.

References

1. Albrecht, M.R., Rechberger, C., Schneider, T., Tiessen, T., Zohner, M.: Ciphers for MPC and FHE. In: Oswald, E., Fischlin, M. (eds.) EUROCRYPT 2015. LNCS, vol. 9056, pp. 430–454. Springer, Heidelberg (2015)
2. Aumasson, J.-P., Dinur, I., Meier, W., Shamir, A.: Cube testers and key recovery attacks on reduced-round MD6 and Trivium. In: Dunkelman, O. (ed.) FSE 2009. LNCS, vol. 5665, pp. 1–22. Springer, Heidelberg (2009)
3. Bar-On, A., Dinur, I., Dunkelman, O., Lallemand, V., Keller, N., Tsaban, B.: Cryptanalysis of SP networks with partial non-linear layers. In: Oswald, E., Fischlin, M. (eds.) EUROCRYPT 2015. LNCS, vol. 9056, pp. 315–342. Springer, Heidelberg (2015)
4. Boura, C., Canteaut, A.: Zero-sum distinguishers for iterated permutations and application to KECCAK-f and Hamsi-256. In: Biryukov, A., Gong, G., Stinson, D.R. (eds.) SAC 2010. LNCS, vol. 6544, pp. 1–17. Springer, Heidelberg (2011)
5. Boura, C., Canteaut, A., De Cannière, C.: Higher-order differential properties of KECCAK and *Luffa*. In: Joux, A. (ed.) FSE 2011. LNCS, vol. 6733, pp. 252–269. Springer, Heidelberg (2011)
6. Daemen, J., Knudsen, L.R., Rijmen, V.: The block cipher Square. In: Biham, E. (ed.) FSE 1997. LNCS, vol. 1267, pp. 149–165. Springer, Heidelberg (1997)
7. Dinur, I., Liu, Y., Meier, W., Wang, Q.: Optimized interpolation attacks on LowMC. In: Iwata, T., Cheon, J.H. (eds.) ASIACRYPT 2015. LNCS, vol. 9453, pp. 535–560. Springer, Heidelberg (2015)

8. Dinur, I., Shamir, A.: Cube attacks on tweakable black box polynomials. In: Joux, A. (ed.) EUROCRYPT 2009. LNCS, vol. 5479, pp. 278–299. Springer, Heidelberg (2009)
9. Guo, J., Nikolic, I., Peyrin, T., Wang, L.: Cryptanalysis of Zorro. IACR Cryptology ePrint Archive 2013, 713 (2013). http://eprint.iacr.org/2013/713
10. Hell, M., Johansson, T., Maximov, A., Meier, W.: The Grain family of stream ciphers. In: Robshaw, M., Billet, O. (eds.) New Stream Cipher Designs. LNCS, vol. 4986, pp. 179–190. Springer, Heidelberg (2008)
11. Knudsen, L.R., Rijmen, V.: Known-key distinguishers for some block ciphers. In: Kurosawa, K. (ed.) ASIACRYPT 2007. LNCS, vol. 4833, pp. 315–324. Springer, Heidelberg (2007)
12. Knudsen, L.R., Wagner, D.: Integral cryptanalysis. In: Daemen, J., Rijmen, V. (eds.) FSE 2002. LNCS, vol. 2365, pp. 112–127. Springer, Heidelberg (2002)
13. Lai, X.: Higher order derivatives and differential cryptanalysis. In: Blahut, R.E., Costello Jr., D.J., Maurer, U., Mittelholzer, T. (eds.) Communications and Cryptography: Two Sides of One Tapestry, pp. 227–233. Kluwer Academic Publishers, Berlin (1994)
14. Rasoolzadeh, S., Ahmadian, Z., Salmasizadeh, M., Aref, M.R.: Total break of Zorro using linear and differential attacks. IACR Cryptology ePrint Archive 2014, 220 (2014). http://eprint.iacr.org/2014/220
15. van Lint, J.H., Wilson, R.M.: A Course in Combinatorics. Cambridge University Press, Cambridge (2001)
16. Vielhaber, M.: Breaking ONE.FIVIUM by AIDA an algebraic IV differential attack. IACR Cryptology ePrint Archive 2007, 413 (2007). http://eprint.iacr.org/2007/413
17. Wang, Y., Wu, W., Guo, Z., Yu, X.: Differential cryptanalysis and linear distinguisher of full-round Zorro. In: Boureanu, I., Owesarski, P., Vaudenay, S. (eds.) ACNS 2014. LNCS, vol. 8479, pp. 308–323. Springer, Heidelberg (2014)
18. Z'aba, M.R., Raddum, H., Henricksen, M., Dawson, E.: Bit-pattern based integral attack. In: Nyberg, K. (ed.) FSE 2008. LNCS, vol. 5086, pp. 363–381. Springer, Heidelberg (2008)

Integral Attack Against Bit-Oriented Block Ciphers

Huiling Zhang[1,2,3(✉)], Wenling Wu[1,2,3], and Yanfeng Wang[1,2,3]

[1] TCA Laboratory, SKLCS, Institute of Software, Chinese Academy of Sciences, Beijing, China
{zhanghuiling,wwl}@tca.iscas.ac.cn

[2] State Key Laboratory of Cryptology, P.O.Box 5159, Beijing 100878, China

[3] University of Chinese Academy of Sciences, Beijing, China

Abstract. Integral attack is an extremely important and extensively investigated cryptanalytic tool for symmetric-key primitives. In this paper, we improve the integral attack against bit-oriented ciphers. First, we propose the match-through-the-Sbox technique based on a specific property of the Sbox. Instead of computing the inverse of the Sbox in partial decryption, we independently calculate two Boolean functions which accept less input bits. The time complexity is thus reduced and the number of attacked rounds will be stretched. Second, we devise an easy-to-implement algorithm for construction of the integral distinguisher, which is then proved to be very effective for constructing lower order distinguishers. It shows SIMON 32, 48, 64, 96 and 128 has 13-, 14-, 17-, 21- and 25-round integral distinguisher, respectively, significantly improving the recent results from EUROCRYPT 2015. Finally, our techniques are applied to several ciphers. We attack one more round than the previous best integral attack for PRESENT and first evaluate the securities of SIMON family (except for SIMON 32) and RECTANGLE with integral attack.

Keywords: Bit-oriented block cipher · Integral attack · Meet-in-the-middle · Algebraic normal form · PRESENT · SIMON

1 Introduction

Integral attack was firstly proposed by Daemen et al. to evaluate the security of Square cipher [5] and then formalized by Knudsen and Wagner [7]. It consists of two phases, the integral distinguisher construction and the key recovery. An attacker starts with a set of 2^d plaintexts, which travel all values at d bit positions and take a constant value at others. If he proves that the state after r encryption rounds has a property with probability 1, e.g., the XOR of all values of the state equals to 0 at some bits which are known as *balanced* bits, a d-order integral distinguisher containing r rounds is thus achieved. Then for the second phase, the key space is reduced by checking balanced property. More specifically, the attacker guesses a part of subkeys and computes the balanced bits for every

S. Kwon and A. Yun (Eds.): ICISC 2015, LNCS 9558, pp. 102–118, 2016.
DOI: 10.1007/978-3-319-30840-1_7

Table 1. Summary of integral attack results

Target	#Rounds	Time	Data	Mem	Technique	Ref.
PRESENT-80	6	$2^{41.7}$	$2^{22.4}$	-	Bit-pattern	[14]
	9	2^{60}	$2^{20.3}$	2^{20}	7-round IND	[12]
	10	2^{35}	$2^{21.5}$	$2^{35.9}$	MTTS	Sect. 4.1
PRESENT-128	7	$2^{100.1}$	$2^{24.3}$	2^{80}	Bit-pattern	[14]
	10	$2^{99.3}$	$2^{22.4}$	2^{84}	7-round IND	[12]
	11	$2^{94.8}$	$2^{21.2}$	$2^{32.1}$	MTTS	Sect. 4.1
SIMON$(2n, m)$	19/20/21/	2^{m-1}	2^{2n-1}	$2^c c$	New IND	Sect. 4.2
	23/24/27/					
	28/32/33/34					
RECTANGLE-80	11	$2^{69.5}$	$2^{39.6}$	$2^{45.6}$	New IND and MTTS	Sect. 4.3
RECTANGLE-128	12	$2^{120.7}$	2^{45}	2^{39}	New IND and MTTS	Sect. 4.3

IND: integral distinguisher. MTTS: match-through-the-Sbox technique. $2n$: block size. m: key size. $c = 42/52/76/55/84/56/89/89/130/179$.

ciphertext by the partial decryption. If the XOR of the results is 0, the guessed value is a candidate for the right subkey, otherwise, it must be wrong.

Several techniques were proposed to optimize integral attack. In 2000, Ferguson et al. [6] introduced the *partial-sum technique*, which reduces the complexity of the partial decryption by guessing each subkey byte one after another and timely discarding the redundant data. The *meet-in-the-middle technique* for integral attack against Feistel ciphers was proposed by Sasaki et al. [8,9]. It employs the characteristic of Feistel structure and represents the balanced state by the XOR of two variables. Then, the partial decryption is separated into two independent parts, which greatly diminishes the time complexity. In 2014, Todo and Aoki applied the *FFT technique* to integral attack [11]. As the partial decryption is performed by Fast Walsh-Hadamard Transform, the time complexity does not depend on the number of chosen plaintexts, which is useful in an integral attack with enormous number of chosen plaintexts.

Recently, block ciphers which can be implemented in resource constraint environment, e.g., RFID Tags for a sensor network, have received much attention. This kind of block ciphers are called *lightweight block ciphers*. Lots of them are bit-oriented, such as PRESENT [3], PRINCE [4], PRIDE [1], RECTANGLE [15], as well as EPCBC [13] and SIMON family [2]. Traditional integral attack is less effective for these ciphers, which impels the cryptanalysts to develop new techniques. In FSE 2008, Z'aba et al. introduced a method of constructing integral distinguishers for bit-oriented ciphers [14]. Several bit-wise integral properties, denoted by *bit-patterns*, were defined and after that they showed the propagation of bit-patterns which will indicate the existence of integral distinguishers. This method requires the set of plaintexts to be ordered, and bit-patterns are easily destroyed after a few encryption rounds. Thus, the applications are limited. In EUROCRYPT 2015, Todo proposed a generalized integral property [10], named *division property*, which evaluates the sum of the outputs of a parity function. A multi-set Λ has the division property D_k^n if and only if for all Boolean functions, $f: F_2^n \rightarrow F_2$, with algebraic degree $< k$, the sum of f on Λ is always 0. It has been pointed out that the propagation characteristic of division property for the nonlinear function totally depends on the algebraic degree. Hence, ciphers with low-degree functions are vulnerable to this analysis. Another generic method is by directly evaluating the algebraic degree, which is often called "higher-order differential attack". It utilizes the facts: (1) any state bit can be computed by a Boolean function taking plaintext and key bits as variables. (2) If the degree of the Boolean function is less than d for any value of the key, this state bit is balanced for 2^d chosen plaintexts. But, unfortunately, the existing approaches of degree evaluation are mostly rough, which will result in the misjudgment of balanced bits. In 2013, Wu et al. discovered that some properties of PRESENT's Sbox help to make a more accurate evaluation of the degree and they extended the integral distinguisher to 7 rounds [12]. However, their improvement is dedicated for PRESENT. The generic approach to improve the accuracy of degree evaluation is still unavailable.

Our Contributions. In this paper, we first attempt to optimize the key recovery phase by the property of Sboxes and propose *match-through-the-Sbox* technique for bit-oriented block ciphers. In previous key recovery, attackers compute the inverse of the Sbox to get the value of balanced bits. We discover that the computation can be divided into two independent parts when the Sbox has a specific property. This leads to a great decrease of the time complexity and furthermore leads to an extension of the number of attacked rounds. Then, we propose an algorithm of constructing integral distinguishers. It is inspired by [12], however our improvement is generic. The algorithm focuses on the terms occurring in the algebraic normal form of the Boolean function mapping plaintext bits to the state bit, which shows a tighter upper-bound of the degree. Therefore, integral distinguishers can be more effectively constructed. Moreover, it can be automatically implemented, that is to say, it does not require the complicated and tedious manual deductions, such as the proof of the 7-round distinguisher for PRESENT in [12]. As applications, we prove 13-, 14-, 17-, 21- and 25-round distinguisher for SIMON 32, 48, 64, 96 and 128, which contains 4, 3, 6, 8 and 12 more rounds than the previous best result, respectively. We also reduce the order of the integral distinguisher for RECTANGLE to 36 from 56, and thus the required number of chosen plaintexts for the integral attack can be decreased 2^{20} times. Finally, our techniques are applied to the integral attacks against PRESENT, SIMON family and RECTANGLE. The comparison of the results to previous integral attacks is summarized in Table 1.

Organization. Section 2 gives a brief review of Boolean function and integral attack. The techniques for improving integral attack against bit-oriented block ciphers are proposed in Sect. 3. In Sect. 4, we apply our techniques to PRESENT, SIMON family and RECTANGLE. Finally, Sect. 5 concludes this paper.

2 Preliminaries

2.1 Boolean Function

A *Boolean function* f on n variables is a mapping from F_2^n to F_2. It can be expressed with *algebraic normal form (ANF)*, that is

$$f(x) = \bigoplus_{\Gamma \in \mathcal{P}(\mathcal{N})} a_\Gamma \prod_{k \in \Gamma} x_k,$$

where $\mathcal{P}(\mathcal{N})$ is the power set of $\mathcal{N} = \{0, 1, \cdots, n-1\}$ and $x = (x_{n-1}, \cdots, x_0) \in F_2^n$. The *algebraic degree* of f, denoted by $deg(f)$, is the number of variables in the highest order term with the nonzero coefficient. It has following properties,

$$deg(fg) \leq deg(f) + deg(g), \tag{1}$$

$$deg(f \oplus g) \leq max\{deg(f), deg(g)\}. \tag{2}$$

A *vectorial Boolean function* F is a mapping from F_2^n into F_2^m. Such function being given, the Boolean functions $f_{m-1}, \cdots, f_0$ defined, at every $x \in F_2^n$, by $F(x) = (f_{m-1}(x), \cdots, f_0(x))$, are called the *coordinate Boolean functions* of F. The *algebraic degree* of F is defined as the highest degree of its coordinate Boolean functions. And the linear combinations, with non all-zero coefficients, of the coordinate functions are called the *component functions* of F.

2.2 Integral Attack

A well-known result from the theory of Boolean functions is that if the algebraic degree of a Boolean function is less than d, then the sum over the outputs of the function applied to all elements of an affine vector space of dimension $\geq d$ is zero. This property allows to exploit the algebraic degree to create integral distinguishers.

In a key-alternating block cipher, the intermediate state X^i is iteratively computed from the plaintext X^0 as:

$$X^i = F(K^{i-1} \oplus X^{i-1}),$$

where F is the round function. We denote the j-th bit of X^i by x_j^i. Assuming the block size is l, then, x_j^i can be expressed as a Boolean function on l plaintext bits, $x_0^0, x_1^0, \cdots, x_{l-1}^0$. To construct a d-order integral distinguisher, we first choose d bits in the plaintext as variables, supposing they are $x_0^0, x_1^0, \cdots, x_{d-1}^0$ for simplicity, and then evaluate the degree of the function (treating the rest of $l-d$ plaintext bits as constants). If the degree is less than d for any key, the sum of the values of x_j^i must be zero for a plaintext set whose elements travel all values of $x_0^0, x_1^0, \cdots, x_{d-1}^0$ and have a fixed value of remaining bits, i.e., x_j^i is a balanced bit.

A generic method of the degree evaluation is by recursion. Supposing the upper-bounds of the degrees for x_t^{i-1}, $0 \leq t < l$, are known, we can evaluate the degree for x_j^i according to property (1), (2).

3 Improvements of Integral Attack

In this section, we first propose the match-through-the-Sbox technique, which is very simple and effective for integral attacks against some bit-oriented ciphers. After that, we scrutinize and improve the integral distinguisher construction described in Sect. 2.2.

3.1 Match-Through-the-Sbox Technique

A property of the Boolean function is firstly defined. Then, the match-through-the-Sbox technique based on this property is developed, which is used in the key recovery phase to reduce the time and memory complexities and even extend the number of attacked rounds.

Definition 1. *Let f be a Boolean function on n variables. If there exist two Boolean functions on less than n variables, denoted by g_1 and g_2, satisfying*

$$f = g_1 \oplus g_2$$

f is said to be a separable Boolean function. In addition, if g_1 and g_2 do not share any variable, f is completely separable.

Example 1. Suppose f is a Boolean function on 4 variables.

- Let $f = x_3x_2x_1 \oplus x_2x_1x_0 \oplus x_3x_0 \oplus 1$. f is not a separable Boolean function.
- Let $f = x_3x_2x_1 \oplus x_2x_1x_0 \oplus 1$. f is separable, while it is not completely separable.
- Let $f = x_3x_2 \oplus x_1x_0 \oplus x_0$. f is completely separable.

Separable property commonly occurs for the component functions of 4-bit Sboxes (or their inverse mappings) in lightweight block ciphers, such as PRESENT, LBlock, PRINCE, etc., because lightweight block ciphers prefer the Sbox with compact algebraic expression for the sake of low cost. We will explain how to optimize the key recovery by using this property, which is called the match-through-the-Sbox technique.

Match-Through-the-Sbox Technique. Assume that y is a balanced bit. Let f be the coordinate Boolean function of S^{-1} such that $y = f(x_3, x_2, x_1, x_0)$, where x_i is the state bit outputted from the Sbox. In previous key recovery, attackers decrypt to the values of y and check whether the sum is zero for a plaintext set (denoted by Λ). However, if f is separable and $f = g_1(x_3, x_2, x_1) \oplus g_2(x_2, x_1, x_0)$ without loss of generality, we can write the checking equation $\bigoplus_{\Lambda} y = 0$ as the equivalent form:

$$\bigoplus_{\Lambda} g_1(x_3, x_2, x_1) = \bigoplus_{\Lambda} g_2(x_2, x_1, x_0). \tag{3}$$

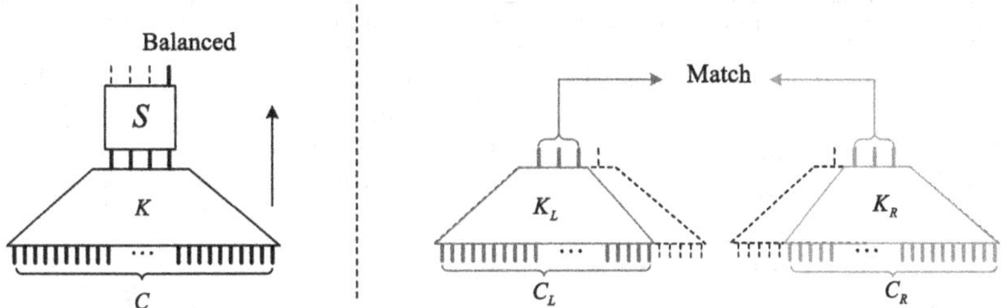

Fig. 1. Left: previous approach; right: match-through-the-Sbox technique

We then compute $x_3||x_2||x_1$ and $x_2||x_1||x_0$, independently, and finally check whether they match each other according to the Eq. (3).

The difference between the previous approach and our match-through-the-Sbox technique is depicted in Fig. 1. We now analyze their complexities without considering any optimal technique, for example, the partial-sum technique. Let K be the subkey information which needs to be guessed to obtain the value of y by partial decryption. Let C be the ciphertext bits involved in the computation of y. The previous attack costs time complexity $2^{|K|+|C|}$. Let K_L and K_R be the subkey that needs to be guessed to obtain the value of $x_3||x_2||x_1$ and $x_2||x_1||x_0$, respectively. And let C_L and C_R be the ciphertext bits involved in two partial decryption phases, respectively. Our method costs time complexity $2^{|K_L|+|C_L|} + 2^{|K_R|+|C_R|}$. Since K is the combination of K_L and K_R, we have $|K_L| < |K|$ and $|K_R| < |K|$. Similarly, $|C_L| < |C|$ and $|C_R| < |C|$ hold. Therefore, the time complexity of our method is much lower than the previous approach. Meanwhile, the cost of storing ciphertext bits will be reduced to $2^{|C_L|}|C_L| + 2^{|C_R|}|C_R|$ from $2^{|C|}|C|$. However, additional $\min\{2^{|K_L|}|K_L|, 2^{|K_R|}|K_R|\}$ bits of memory is required to find the matches.

3.2 Integral Distinguisher Construction

The traditional integral distinguisher construction, as shown in Sect. 2.2, only focuses on the upper-bound of the degree. Here we further pay attention to the terms occurring in the algebraic expression and then propose a searching algorithm.

We assume that $x_0^0, x_1^0, \cdots, x_{d-1}^0$ are chosen as d variables from l plaintext bits. The j-th bit of the state after i encryption rounds, x_j^i, is uniquely represented as a polynomial on these variables with coefficients in F_2, i.e.,

$$x_j^i = \bigoplus_{\Gamma \in \mathcal{S}(\mathcal{D})} \rho_\Gamma(k, c) \left(\prod_{t \in \Gamma} x_t^0 \right), \quad (4)$$

where $\mathcal{S}(\mathcal{D})$ denotes a subset of the power set of $\mathcal{D} = \{0, 1, \cdots, d-1\}$, k denotes the key, c is the constant in plaintext, and $\rho_\Gamma(k, c)$ either takes value 1 or else depends on k and c. The polynomial (hereinafter referred to as the "$Poly(x_j^i)$")

Algorithm 1. Construction of integral distinguishers

INDSearch$(d, l, \{t_0, t_1, \cdots, t_{d-1}\})$
$r = 0$
for $i = 0$ to $l - 1$ **do**
  $A^i \triangleq a^i_{2^d-1}||\cdots||a^i_0 = 0||\cdots||1$
end for
for $i = 0$ to $d - 1$ **do**
  $a^{t_i}_{2^i} = 1$
  $a^{t_i}_0 = 0$
end for
while $a^{l-1}_{2^d-1}\cdots a^1_{2^d-1}a^0_{2^d-1} = 0$ **do**
  for $i = 0$ to $l - 1$ **do**
    $T^i = A^i$
  end for
  $r = r + 1$
  for $i = 0$ to $l - 1$ **do**
    $A^i = \mathit{EvalFunc}(f_i, T^{l-1}, \cdots, T^0)$
  end for
end while
return $r - 1$

can be deduced from the coordinate functions of the round function by recursion, however, it is a tedious procedure since k is unknown. Therefore, we consider a collection of several monomials instead, denoted by $\Omega(x^i_j)$, which contains every term in $Poly(x^i_j)$ no matter which values k and c take. Thus if the highest order term $x^0_{d-1}\cdots x^0_1 x^0_0$ does not occur in $\Omega(x^i_j)$, it certainly has $\deg(x^i_j) < d$. The challenge is how to estimate the set $\Omega(x^i_j)$ as small as possible. We realize it by a straightforward method as follows.

Obviously, $\Omega(x^0_j)$ only contains term x^0_j if x^0_j is a variable, otherwise, it only contains constant term 1. $\Omega(x^1_t)$ can be evaluated from $\Omega(x^0_j)$, $0 \le j < l$, according to the t-th coordinate function of the round function. This process involves two basic operations, XOR and AND, which comply with the rules:

$$\Omega(x \oplus y) = \Omega(x) \cup \Omega(y) \text{ and } \Omega(xy) = \{ab | a \in \Omega(x), b \in \Omega(y)\}. \quad (5)$$

where x and y are state or key bits. By noting that $\Omega(x) = \{1\}$ when x is a key bit, we can easily prove Eq. (5). In the recursive manner, $\Omega(x^i_j)$ is evaluated.

Search Algorithm. The basic idea has been explained above. We further describe each term by a d-bit string $a_{d-1}||\cdots||a_1||a_0$, where a_s $(0 \le s < d)$ takes 1 if the variable x^0_s occurs in the term, otherwise it takes 0. Then, $\Omega(x^i_j)$ corresponds to a 2^d-bit string $a_{2^d-1}||\cdots||a_1||a_0$, where s-th bit $(0 \le s < 2^d)$ takes 1 if the term $[s]_2$ (the binary representation of s) is in the set. Thereafter, the construction of the integral distinguisher can be performed by Algorithm 1.

In the algorithm, f_i is the i-th coordinate Boolean function of the round function. And $\mathit{EvalFunc}(f_i, T^{l-1}, \cdots, T^0)$ evaluates $\Omega(x^r_i)$ from $\Omega(x^{r-1}_j)$, $0 \le j < l$, by the rules:

(1) $\Omega(x \oplus y) = (a_{2^d-1}||\cdots||a_0) \vee (b_{2^d-1}||\cdots||b_0)$, where $\vee$ is bit-wise OR.
(2) $\Omega(xy) = a'_{2^d-1}||\cdots||a'_0$, where $a'_{[i]_2 \vee [j]_2} = 1$ if $a_i = 1$ and $b_j = 1$.

for $\Omega(x) = a_{2^d-1}||\cdots||a_0$ and $\Omega(y) = b_{2^d-1}||\cdots||b_0$. The time and memory complexity is 2^{2d} simple computations and $l2^d$ bits, respectively.

Table 2. Integral distinguishers for RECTANGLE and SIMON family.

r	Orders of r-round integral distinguishers											
	RECTANGLE		SIMON32		SIMON48		SIMON64		SIMON96		SIMON128	
	[15]	Ours	[10]	Ours	[10]	Ours	[10]	Ours	[10]	Ours	[10]	Ours
6	-	-	17	1	17	-	17	-	17	-	17	-
7	56	36	25	2	29	1	33	-	33	-	33	-
8	-	-	29	8	39	3	49	1	57	-	65	-
9	-	-	31	16	44	10	57	2	77	-	97	-
10	-	-	-	23	46	21	61	8	87	1	113	-
11	-	-	-	28	47	33	63	18	92	2	121	-
12	-	-	-	31	-	42	-	31	94	8	125	1
13	-	-	-	**31**	-	47	-	44	95	18	127	2
14	-	-	-	-	-	**47**	-	54	-	31	-	8
15	-	-	-	-	-	-	-	60	-	46	-	18
16	-	-	-	-	-	-	-	63	-	62	-	31
17	-	-	-	-	-	-	-	**63**	-	76	-	46
18	-	-	-	-	-	-	-	-	-	86	-	62
19	-	-	-	-	-	-	-	-	-	92	-	78
20	-	-	-	-	-	-	-	-	-	95	-	94
21	-	-	-	-	-	-	-	-	-	**95**	-	108
22	-	-	-	-	-	-	-	-	-	-	-	118
23	-	-	-	-	-	-	-	-	-	-	-	124
24	-	-	-	-	-	-	-	-	-	-	-	127
25	-	-	-	-	-	-	-	-	-	-	-	**127**

The generic method loses too much information and thus has a rough estimation, which is improved by our approach. Hence, our algorithm can more effectively construct the integral distinguishers, especially for ciphers with simple confusion components.

Results. We apply Algorithm 1 to construct integral distinguishers for RECTANGLE and SIMON family. Since the complexities grow exponentially with d, we choose small d and get a lower order integral distinguisher, and then extend it by applying the higher order integral method as shown in [16]. The results are displayed in Table 2, where the distinguishers colored red are directly achieved, and others are constructed based on them. Note that, we built the 7-round distinguisher for RECTANGLE by extending a 4-order distinguisher with 4 rounds constructed by Algorithm 1. Besides, the distinguishers marked in bold type are free extensions of previous ones. They choose the plaintext set as $\{(R, F(R) \oplus L) | (L, R) \in \Lambda\}$, where F is the round function and Λ is a plaintext set of the previous distinguisher. Compared with the previous best known results, our distinguishers have much lower order under the same number of rounds, furthermore, the longest distinguisher for each member of SIMON family contains 4/3/6/8/12 more rounds than the distinguisher in [10] which is constructed by the division property.

4 Applications

In this section, we demonstrate several applications of our techniques. Based on the match-through-the-Sbox technique we attack one more round than the previous best integral attacks against PRESENT for both two versions. Besides, new integral distinguishers are used to launch the attacks against SIMON family and RECTANGLE.

4.1 Application to PRESENT

PRESENT is a 31-round SPN (Substitution Permutation Network) type block cipher with block size 64 bits. It supports 80- and 128-bit master key, which will be denoted by PRESENT-80 and PRESENT-128, respectively. The round function of PRESENT is the same for both versions and consists of standard operations such as subkey XOR, substitution and permutation. At the beginning of each round, 64-bit input is XORed with the subkey. Just after the subkey XOR, 16 identical 4×4 Sboxes are used in parallel as a non-linear substitution layer and finally a bit-wise permutation is performed so as to provide diffusion.

The subkeys K^i for $0 \leq i \leq 31$, where K^{31} is used for post-whitening, are derived from the master key by the key schedule. We provide the key schedule of PRESENT-80: 80-bit master key is stored in a key register and represented as $k_{79}||k_{78}||\cdots||k_0$. At i-th round, the 64 leftmost bits of actual content of the key register are extracted as the subkey K^i, that is, $K^i = k_{79}||k_{78}||\cdots||k_{16}$. After that, the key register is rotated by 61 bit positions to the left, then the Sbox is applied to left-most four bits of the key register and finally the round counter value, which is a different constant for each round, is XORed with $k_{19}k_{18}k_{17}k_{16}k_{15}$. The key schedule of PRESENT-128 is similar with PRESENT-80 except two Sboxes are applied. For more details, please refer to [3].

We denote by X^i the internal state which is the input to the i-th round and denote by Y^i its output after subkey XOR, i.e., $Y^i = X^i \oplus K^i$. We further describe 64 bits inside of X^i as $X^i = X^i[63]||\cdots||X^i[1]||X^i[0]$. A plaintext is loaded into the state X^0 and Y^{31} is produced as the ciphertext.

In 2013, Wu et al. proposed a 7-round integral distinguisher of PRESENT [12], that is, for a set of 2^{16} plaintexts where $X^0[0,\cdots,15]$ are active bits, the rightmost bit of Y^7 is balanced. We adopt this distinguisher in following attacks.

Property of the Sbox. Let $x = (x_3, x_2, x_1, x_0)$ be the input of S^{-1}, and y_0 be the rightmost bit of the output. It has

$$y_0 = x_3 x_1 \oplus x_2 \oplus x_0 \oplus 1. \tag{6}$$

Suppose that $g_1 = x_3 x_1$ and $g_2 = x_2 \oplus x_0 \oplus 1$. We get $y_0 = g_1 \oplus g_2$, which means the coordinate Boolean function of S^{-1} is completely separable.

Key Recovery Against 10-Round PRESENT-80. Choose $X^0[0,\cdots,15]$ as active bits and then $Y^7[0]$ is balanced. From Eq. (6), it has $Y^7[0] = X^8[48]X^8[16] \oplus X^8[32] \oplus X^8[0] \oplus 1$. Applying the match-through-the-Sbox technique, we need to check the following equation in the key recovery:

$$\bigoplus_{\Lambda} X^8[48]X^8[16] = \bigoplus_{\Lambda} (X^8[32] \oplus X^8[0]). \tag{7}$$

As shown in Fig. 2, the computation of $\bigoplus_{\Lambda} X^8[48]X^8[16]$ and $\bigoplus_{\Lambda}(X^8[32] \oplus X^8[0])$ involves the bits marked with red lines and black lines, respectively. One observation is that we only need to get the rightmost bit of the output from each S^{-1}, which is computed by this form: $(x_3 \oplus k_3)(x_1 \oplus k_1) \oplus (x_2 \oplus k_2) \oplus (x_0 \oplus k_0) \oplus 1$, where $k_0, \cdots, k_3$ are subkey bits. Therefore, we actually require 3-bit subkey information, $k_0 \oplus k_2, k_1, k_3$, instead of 4-bit. The details of the attack are as follows:

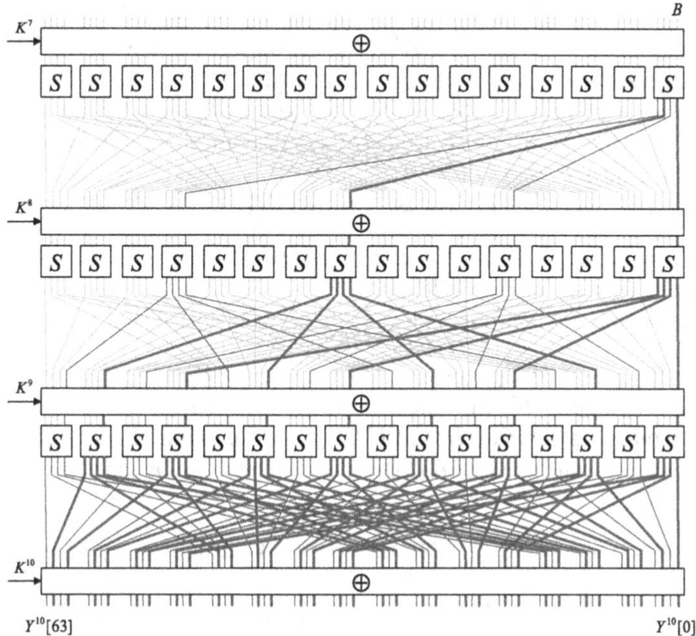

Fig. 2. 10-round key recovery (Color figure online)

1. Choose N plaintext sets, $\Lambda_0, \cdots, \Lambda_{N-1}$, satisfying the integral distinguisher, and get the ciphertexts after 10-round encryption.
2. Compute $\bigoplus_{\Lambda_s} X^8[48]X^8[16]$ for $0 \leq s < N$.
   - We guess 12-bit subkey: $K^{10}[i] \oplus K^{10}[i+32], K^{10}[i+16], K^{10}[i+48]$ for $i \in \{1, 3, 9, 11\}$, and compute the value of $Y^9[4] \oplus Y^9[36]$, $Y^9[12] \oplus Y^9[44]$ for each ciphertext. Count how many times each 14-bit value appears: $Y^9[4] \oplus Y^9[36]$, $Y^9[12] \oplus Y^9[44]$ and $Y^{10}[i] \oplus Y^{10}[i+32], Y^{10}[i+16], Y^{10}[i+48]$ for $i \in \{5, 7, 13, 15\}$, and then save the values which appear odd times in a table.
   - Guess 3 subkey bits, $K^{10}[5] \oplus K^{10}[37], K^{10}[21]$ and $K^{10}[53]$. Compress the data into 2^{12} texts of $Y^9[4] \oplus Y^9[36]$, $Y^9[20]$, $Y^9[12] \oplus Y^9[44]$ and $Y^{10}[i] \oplus Y^{10}[i+32], Y^{10}[i+16], Y^{10}[i+48]$ for $i \in \{7, 13, 15\}$.

- Guess 3 subkey bits, $K^{10}[13] \oplus K^{10}[45], K^{10}[29]$ and $K^{10}[61]$. Compress the data into 2^{10} texts of $Y^9[4] \oplus Y^9[36]$, $Y^9[20,52]$, $Y^9[12] \oplus Y^9[44]$ and $Y^{10}[i] \oplus Y^{10}[i+32], Y^{10}[i+16], Y^{10}[i+48]$ for $i \in \{7, 15\}$.
- Guess 3 subkey bits, $K^{10}[7] \oplus K^{10}[39], K^{10}[23]$ and $K^{10}[55]$. Compress the data into 2^8 texts of $Y^9[4] \oplus Y^9[36]$, $Y^9[20,28,52]$, $Y^9[12] \oplus Y^9[44]$ and $Y^{10}[15] \oplus Y^{10}[47], Y^{10}[31], Y^{10}[63]$.
- Guess 3 subkey bits, $K^{10}[15] \oplus K^{10}[47], K^{10}[31]$ and $K^{10}[63]$. Compress the data into 2^6 texts of $Y^9[4] \oplus Y^9[36]$, $Y^9[20,28,52,60]$, $Y^9[12] \oplus Y^9[44]$.
- Thanks to the key schedule, $K^9[44]$ is obtained due to previous guessed subkey bit $K^{10}[25]$, and $K^9[28] \oplus K^9[60] = K^{10}[9] \oplus K^{10}[41]$. Therefore, we only need to guess 2-bit $K^9[12,60]$, compute $Y^8[48]$ and compress the data into 2^4 texts of $Y^8[48]$, $Y^9[4] \oplus Y^9[36]$, $Y^9[20,52]$.
- Similarly, we have $K^9[36] = K^{10}[15]$ and $K^9[20] \oplus K^9[52] = K^{10}[1] \oplus K^{10}[33]$. Hence, we guess 2-bit $K^9[4,52]$, compute $Y^8[16]$ and compress the data into 2^2 texts of $Y^8[16,48]$.
- Guess 2-bit value of $K^8[16,48]$, compute $\bigoplus_{\Lambda_s} X^8[48]X^8[16]$ for $0 \leq s < N$ and save the values of 30-bit guessed subkey, K_1, in a hash table H indexed by the N-bit result.

3. Similar to Step 2, we compute $\bigoplus_{\Lambda_s}(Y^8[32] \oplus Y^8[0])$ (notice that it is $\bigoplus_{\Lambda_s}(X^8[32] \oplus X^8[0])$) for $0 \leq s < N$ by guessing 30-bit subkey K_2. The details are shown in Appendix A. Save K_2 in a hash table H' indexed by the N-bit sum.
4. Check the matches between H and H'. If the indexes match each other and the overlap information between K_1 and K_2 matches, $K_1||K_2$ is a key candidate.

Complexities. We have $|K_1| = 30$ and $|K_2| = 30$. Due to the key schedule, K_1 and K_2 overlap in 3 bits, $K^9[40,48]$ and $K^9[24] \oplus K^9[56]$. Therefore, the total guessed subkey K contains $30 + 30 - 3 = 57$ bits. 2^{57-N} candidates for K are left after checking the matches. They are then exhaustively searched together with the remaining 23 subkey bits. The time complexity of Step 2 is evaluated as

$$\begin{aligned}
&2^{12} \times 2^{16} \times 4 + 2^3 \times 2^{12} \times 2^{14} + \cdots + 2^2 \times 2^{28} \times 2^2 \\
&= 2^{30} + 2^{29} + 2^{30} + 2^{31} + 2^{32} + 2^{32} + 2^{32} + 2^{32} \\
&= 2^{34.3}
\end{aligned}$$

computations of the Sbox. The time complexity of Step 3 is 2^{35} as explained in Appendix A. For the trade-off between time and data complexity, we choose $N = 46$. Hence, the attack totally costs $(2^{34.3} + 2^{35}) \times \frac{1}{16} \times \frac{1}{10} N + 2^{80-N} = 2^{35}$ 10-round encryptions. The data complexity is $2^{16} N = 2^{21.5}$ chosen plaintexts. The memory complexity depends on the storage of two hash tables, which is $2 \times (2^{30} \times 30) = 2^{35.9}$ bits.

For the integral attack against 11-round PRESENT-128, we first guess 64-bit K^{11} and decrypt the ciphertexts to Y^{10}. After that, procedures of the partial decryption are similar with the 10-round case. Specifically, we guess 27-bit and 25-bit subkeys to compute $\bigoplus_{\Lambda} X^8[48]X^8[16]$ and $\bigoplus_{\Lambda}(Y^8[32] \oplus Y^8[0])$, respectively, as K^{11} has been guessed. They only overlap in one bit, $K^8[16]\oplus K^8[48]$, therefore, the total guessed subkey K contains $64+27+25-1=115$ bits. We analyze 38 plaintexts sets for the optimization of time complexity. The data complexity is hence $2^{21.2}$ chosen plaintexts. The memory complexity is evaluated by $2^{16}\times 64\times 38+2^{27}\times 27+2^{25}\times 25=2^{32.1}$ bits, and time complexity is $2^{64}\times(2^{32}+2^{32})\times\frac{1}{16}\times\frac{1}{11}\times 38+2^{128-38}=2^{94.8}$ 11-round encryptions.

4.2 Application to SIMON

SIMON is a family of lightweight block ciphers, optimized for performance on hardware devices, proposed by NSA. It is based on a classical Feistel construction operating on two n-bit branches. Denote the state entering i-th round by (L^i, R^i), which is further described as $(L^i[n-1]||\cdots||L^i[0],\ \ R^i[n-1]||\cdots||R^i[0])$. At each round, the round function F transforms the left branch in the following way,

$$F(L^i)=((L^i<<<8)\&(L^i<<<1))\oplus(L^i<<<2).$$

The output of F is then XORed with the subkey K^i and with the right branch to form the left input of the next round. There exist in total ten members of the SIMON family, each one characterized by different block and key size. We denote a member of the SIMON family by SIMON$(2n/m)$, where $2n$ is the block size and m is the key size. The key schedule processes different procedures depending on $\frac{m}{n}$. While, it is always linear, and the master key can be derived if any sequence of $\frac{m}{n}$ consecutive subkeys are known. For detailed description, please refer to [2].

Key Recovery Against SIMON Family. We use the longest integral distinguisher shown in Table 2 for each member. Assume that s is the number of rounds of the distinguisher. We append t rounds to the distinguisher and give the key recovery attack against $(s+t)$-round SIMON$(2n/m)$.

We only decrypt to one balanced bit for the sake of less subkey involved. Suppose it is $R^s[b]$. It has $R^s[b]=(R^{s+1}[b-1]R^{s+1}[b-8])\oplus R^{s+1}[b-2]\oplus L^{s+1}[b]\oplus K^s[b]$. Therefore, we check the following equation in key recovery:

$$\bigoplus(R^{s+1}[b-1]R^{s+1}[b-8])=\bigoplus(R^{s+1}[b-2]\oplus L^{s+1}[b]). \tag{8}$$

If Eq. (8) holds for a guessed value, it is regarded as a candidate for the right subkey, which will be exhaustively searched together with the remaining key information. To check Eq. (8), we first decrypt to $\bigoplus(R^{s+1}[b-2]\oplus L^{s+1}[b])$ by applying the partial-sum technique. After that, a hash table is achieved, which saves the values of guessed subkey indexed with the result. Then we compute $\bigoplus(R^{s+1}[b-1]R^{s+1}[b-8])$ similarly and finally we find matches in the hash table.

Now we analysis the complexities of our attack. Let K_1 and K_2 be the subkey involved in the computation of $\bigoplus(R^{s+1}[b-2]\oplus L^{s+1}[b])$ and $\bigoplus(R^{s+1}[b-1]R^{s+1}[b-8])$, respectively. Denote the total subkey guessed in key recovery phase by $K_1\cup K_2$. We count the number of bits in K_1, K_2 and $K_1\cup K_2$ for each cipher in SIMON family, without considering the key schedule.

Table 3. Size of guessed subkey for t-round key recovery against SIMON family

(2n/m)	s	t	Size of guessed subkey		
			$\|K_1\|$	$\|K_2\|$	$\|K_1 \cup K_2\|$
(32/64)	13	6	42	45	49
(48/72)	14	6	52	59	65
(48/96)	14	7	76	83	89
(64/96)	17	6	55	63	69
(64/128)	17	7	84	93	99
(96/96)	21	6	56	65	73
(96/144)	21	7	89	101	109
(128/128)	25	7	89	101	110
(128/192)	25	8	130	145	155
(128/256)	25	9	179	197	207

The results are summarized in Table 3. Then the memory complexity is calculated by $2^{|K_1|}|K_1|$. The subkey space can be reduced by 1 bit for a plaintext set, furthermore, the master key space is accordingly reduced by 1 bit since the subkeys are related with linear relations. Hence, the time complexity of exhaustive search is 2^{m-1} $(s+t)$-round encryptions, which dominates the time complexity of the entire attack. The data complexity is 2^{2n-1} chosen plaintexts.

4.3 Application to RECTANGLE

RECTANGLE is a 25-round SPN cipher with bit-slice design. The 64-bit state $X^i = (X^i[63], \cdots, X^i[1], X^i[0])$ has equivalent representation as Fig. 3. The round function consists of three steps: AddSubkey, SubColumn, ShiftRow. Denote the state after AddSubkey in i-th round by Y^i, i.e., $Y^i = X^i \oplus K^i$. SubColumn is parallel application of Sboxes to the 4 bits in the same column. ShiftRow is a left rotation by 0, 1, 12 and 13 offset for row 0, 1, 2, and 3, respectively. The key schedule is similar to the encryption with less Sboxes and different rotations. Limited by the space, please refer to [15] for the details.

$$\begin{bmatrix} X[15] & X[14] & \cdots & X[1] & X[0] \\ X[31] & X[30] & \cdots & X[17] & X[16] \\ X[47] & X[46] & \cdots & X[33] & X[32] \\ X[63] & X[62] & \cdots & X[49] & X[48] \end{bmatrix} \Leftrightarrow \begin{bmatrix} X(0f) & X(0e) & \cdots & X(01) & X(00) \\ X(1f) & X(1e) & \cdots & X(11) & X(10) \\ X(2f) & X(2e) & \cdots & X(21) & X(20) \\ X(3f) & X(3e) & \cdots & X(31) & X(30) \end{bmatrix}$$

Fig. 3. Two-dimensional representation of the state

Our search algorithm constructs a 36-order integral distinguisher containing 7 rounds, which improves the 56-order distinguisher proposed by the designers. More specifically, for a set of 2^{36} plaintexts with $X^0(i0, i2, i3, i4, i6, i7, i8, ie, if)$, $0 \leq i < 4$, being active, the state after 7 encryption rounds has 22 balanced bits: $X^7(00, 10, 20, 01, 11, 21, 31, 12, 32, 03, 04, 14, 05, 15, 16, 2b, 2c, 2d, 3d, 3e, 0f, 2f)$.

Key Recovery Against RECTANGLE. Since $Y^7(01)$ and $Y^7(11)$ are balanced bits, $\bigoplus_{\Lambda}(Y^7(01) \oplus Y^7(11)) = 0$ holds. Applying the match-through-the-Sbox technique, we have

$$\bigoplus_{\Lambda} X^8(12)X^8(01) = \bigoplus_{\Lambda} \{X^8(3e)X^8(12) \oplus X^8(3e) \oplus X^8(12)\}. \tag{9}$$

We first prepare N sets of 2^{36} plaintexts satisfying the integral distinguisher. 48 bits of the ciphertext are related to the partial decryption for $X^8(01, 12)$, and also 48 bits of the ciphertext are related to the partial decryption of $X^8(3e, 12)$. Let K_1 and K_2 be the subkey involved in the computation of $X^8(01, 12)$ and $X^8(3e, 12)$, respectively. From the key schedule, $|K_1| = 60$, $|K_2| = 61$ and they overlap in 45 bits. We first guess 20 subkey bits shared by them for saving memory. Then we independently guess the rest of bits in K_1 and K_2 and independently compute the left and right of Eq. (9). Finally, the matches between the results are checked in order to sieve the guessed keys. Due to the limitation of space, we only show the complexities. The total time complexity of the attack is evaluated by $(2^{56}+2^{72.3}+2^{71.7})N \times \frac{1}{16} \times \frac{1}{11} + 2^{80-N} = 2^{65.3}N + 2^{80-N}$ encryptions. Choose $N = 12$, and then the time complexity is optimized to $2^{69.5}$ encryptions. The memory complexity is $2^{36} \times 64N + 2^{60-20} \times 40 + 2^{61-20} \times 41 = 2^{45.6}$ bits. The data complexity is $2^{36}N = 2^{39.6}$. In a similar manner, we can attack 12-round RECTANGLE-128 with the time, memory and data complexity being $2^{120.7}$ 12-round encryptions, 2^{45} bits and 2^{39} chosen plaintexts, respectively.

5 Conclusion

In this paper, we raised the power of integral attack against bit-oriented ciphers in both aspects. We first proposed the match-through-the-Sbox technique, which reduces the time and memory for the key recovery phase by using the separable property of the Sbox. It works similarly to the meet-in-the-middle technique for integral attack against Feistel ciphers, however, its application is not restricted by the structure but by the property of the Sbox. Therefore, it can be applied to SPN ciphers, such as PRESENT and RECTANGLE. Then, we devised a generic algorithm for increasing the accuracy of the degree evaluation and thereby improving the integral distinguisher. Limited by the memory cost, it is suitable for constructing lower order distinguishers, which can be extended to more rounds by the higher order method. The effect of this algorithm was demonstrated for several ciphers. For instance, it constructed 13-, 14-, 17-, 21- and 25-round integral distinguisher for SIMON 32, 48, 64, 96 and 128, respectively, which are all the best results as we known. Besides, it reduced the order of the distinguisher for RECTANGLE to 36 from 56.

As applications, we launched the integral attack on several ciphers. For PRESENT, we can attack one more round than the previous best integral attack for two versions. Moreover, for SIMON family and RECTANGLE, we first evaluated their securities against integral attack (except for SIMON 32). Although our attacks do not pose a threat to these ciphers, it shows that the integral attack against bit-oriented ciphers has more room to be enhanced.

As we shown, both of our techniques are relevant to the property of the confusion component, for example the Sbox, hence, we conclude that integral attack is also sensitive to the Sbox for bit-oriented ciphers, except for the linear layer. Since the lightweight block ciphers is an actively discussed topic, we hope that this paper returns some useful feedback to future design and analysis.

A Details of Step 3

Compute $\bigoplus_{\Lambda_s}(Y^8[32] \oplus Y^8[0])$ for $0 \le s < N$.

- We guess 12-bit subkey: $K^{10}[i] \oplus K^{10}[i+32], K^{10}[i+16], K^{10}[i+48]$ for $i \in \{0, 2, 8, 10\}$, and compute the value of $Y^9[0] \oplus Y^9[32]$, $Y^9[8] \oplus Y^9[40]$ for each ciphertext. Count how many times each 14-bit value appears: $Y^9[0] \oplus Y^9[32]$, $Y^9[8] \oplus Y^9[40]$ and $Y^{10}[i] \oplus Y^{10}[i+32], Y^{10}[i+16], Y^{10}[i+48]$ for $i \in \{4, 6, 12, 14\}$. And then pick the values which appear odd times.
- Guess 3 subkey bits, $K^{10}[4] \oplus K^{10}[36], K^{10}[20]$ and $K^{10}[52]$. Compress the data into at most 2^{12} values of $Y^9[0] \oplus Y^9[32]$, $Y^9[16]$, $Y^9[8] \oplus Y^9[40]$ and $Y^{10}[i] \oplus Y^{10}[i+32], Y^{10}[i+16], Y^{10}[i+48]$ for $i \in \{6, 12, 14\}$, which appear odd times.
- Guess 3 subkey bits, $K^{10}[12] \oplus K^{10}[44], K^{10}[28]$ and $K^{10}[60]$. Compress the data into 2^{10} texts of $Y^9[0] \oplus Y^9[32]$, $Y^9[16, 48]$, $Y^9[8] \oplus Y^9[40]$ and $Y^{10}[i] \oplus Y^{10}[i+32], Y^{10}[i+16], Y^{10}[i+48]$ for $i \in \{6, 14\}$.
- Guess 3 subkey bits, $K^{10}[6] \oplus K^{10}[38], K^{10}[22]$ and $K^{10}[54]$. Compress the data into 2^8 texts of $Y^9[0] \oplus Y^9[32]$, $Y^9[16, 24, 48]$, $Y^9[8] \oplus Y^9[40]$ and $Y^{10}[14] \oplus Y^{10}[46], Y^{10}[30], Y^{10}[62]$.
- Guess 3 subkey bits, $K^{10}[14] \oplus K^{10}[46], K^{10}[30]$ and $K^{10}[62]$. Compress the data into 2^6 texts of $Y^9[0] \oplus Y^9[32]$, $Y^9[16, 24, 48, 56]$, $Y^9[8] \oplus Y^9[40]$.
- Guess 3 subkey bits, $K^9[0] \oplus K^{10}[32], K^{10}[16]$ and $K^{10}[48]$. Compress the data into 2^4 texts of $Y^8[0]$, $Y^9[24, 56]$, $Y^9[8] \oplus Y^9[40]$.
- Guess 3 subkey bits, $K^9[8] \oplus K^{10}[40], K^{10}[24]$ and $K^{10}[56]$. Compress the data into 2^2 texts of $Y^8[0, 32]$.
- Compute $\bigoplus_{\Lambda_s}(Y^8[32] \oplus Y^8[0])$ for $0 \le s < N$ and save the 30-bit guessed subkey K_2 in a hash table H' indexed by the corresponding N-bit result.

The time complexity is $2^{30} + 2^{29} + 2^{30} + 2^{31} + 2^{32} + 2^{33} + 2^{34} = 2^{35}$ computations of the Sbox.

References

1. Albrecht, M.R., Driessen, B., Kavun, E.B., Leander, G., Paar, C., Yalçın, T.: Block ciphers – focus on the linear layer (feat. PRIDE). In: Garay, J.A., Gennaro, R. (eds.) CRYPTO 2014, Part I. LNCS, vol. 8616, pp. 57–76. Springer, Heidelberg (2014)
2. Beaulieu, R., Shors, D., Smith, J., Treatman-Clark, S., Weeks, B., Wingers, L.: The SIMON and SPECK families of lightweight block ciphers. Cryptology ePrint Archive, Report 2013/404 (2013). http://eprint.iacr.org/
3. Bogdanov, A.A., Knudsen, L.R., Leander, G., Paar, C., Poschmann, A., Robshaw, M., Seurin, Y., Vikkelsoe, C.: PRESENT: an ultra-lightweight block cipher. In: Paillier, P., Verbauwhede, I. (eds.) CHES 2007. LNCS, vol. 4727, pp. 450–466. Springer, Heidelberg (2007)
4. Borghoff, J., Canteaut, A., Güneysu, T., Kavun, E.B., Knezevic, M., Knudsen, L.R., Leander, G., Nikov, V., et al.: PRINCE – a low-latency block cipher for pervasive computing applications. In: Wang, X., Sako, K. (eds.) ASIACRYPT 2012. LNCS, vol. 7658, pp. 208–225. Springer, Heidelberg (2012)
5. Daemen, J., Knudsen, L.R., Rijmen, V.: The block cipher SQUARE. In: Biham, E. (ed.) FSE 1997. LNCS, vol. 1267, pp. 149–165. Springer, Heidelberg (1997)
6. Ferguson, N., Kelsey, J., Lucks, S., Schneier, B., Stay, M., Wagner, D., Whiting, D.L.: Improved cryptanalysis of Rijndael. In: Schneier, B. (ed.) FSE 2000. LNCS, vol. 1978, pp. 213–230. Springer, Heidelberg (2001)
7. Knudsen, L.R., Wagner, D.: Integral cryptanalysis. In: Daemen, J., Rijmen, V. (eds.) FSE 2002. LNCS, vol. 2365, pp. 112–127. Springer, Heidelberg (2002)
8. Sasaki, Y., Wang, L.: Comprehensive study of integral analysis on 22-round LBlock. In: Kwon, T., Lee, M.-K., Kwon, D. (eds.) ICISC 2012. LNCS, vol. 7839, pp. 156–169. Springer, Heidelberg (2013)
9. Sasaki, Y., Wang, L.: Meet-in-the-middle technique for integral attacks against feistel ciphers. In: Knudsen, L.R., Wu, H. (eds.) SAC 2012. LNCS, vol. 7707, pp. 234–251. Springer, Heidelberg (2013)
10. Todo, Y.: Structural evaluation by generalized integral property. In: Oswald, E., Fischlin, M. (eds.) EUROCRYPT 2015. LNCS, vol. 9056, pp. 287–314. Springer, Heidelberg (2015)
11. Todo, Y., Aoki, K.: FFT key recovery for integral attack. In: Gritzalis, D., Kiayias, A., Askoxylakis, I. (eds.) CANS 2014. LNCS, vol. 8813, pp. 64–81. Springer, Heidelberg (2014)
12. Wu, S., Wang, M.: Integral attacks on reduced-round PRESENT. In: Qing, S., Zhou, J., Liu, D. (eds.) ICICS 2013. LNCS, vol. 8233, pp. 331–345. Springer, Heidelberg (2013)
13. Yap, H., Khoo, K., Poschmann, A., Henricksen, M.: EPCBC - a block cipher suitable for electronic product code encryption. In: Lin, D., Tsudik, G., Wang, X. (eds.) CANS 2011. LNCS, vol. 7092, pp. 76–97. Springer, Heidelberg (2011)
14. Z'aba, M.R., Raddum, H., Henricksen, M., Dawson, E.: Bit-pattern based integral attack. In: Nyberg, K. (ed.) FSE 2008. LNCS, vol. 5086, pp. 363–381. Springer, Heidelberg (2008)

15. Zhang, W., Bao, Z., Lin, D., Rijmen, V., Yang, B., Verbauwhede, I.: RECTANGLE: a bit-slice ultra-lightweight block cipher suitable for multiple platforms. Cryptology ePrint Archive, Report 2014/084 (2014). http://eprint.iacr.org/
16. Zhang, W., Su, B., Wu, W., Feng, D., Wu, C.: Extending higher-order integral: an efficient unified algorithm of constructing integral distinguishers for block ciphers. In: Bao, F., Samarati, P., Zhou, J. (eds.) ACNS 2012. LNCS, vol. 7341, pp. 117–134. Springer, Heidelberg (2012)

Single Key Recovery Attacks on 9-Round Kalyna-128/256 and Kalyna-256/512

Akshima, Donghoon Chang, Mohona Ghosh, Aarushi Goel(✉), and Somitra Kumar Sanadhya

Indraprastha Institute of Information Technology, Delhi (IIIT-D), India
{akshima12014,donghoon,mohonag,aarushi12003,somitra}@iiitd.ac.in

Abstract. The Kalyna block cipher has recently been established as the Ukranian encryption standard in June, 2015. It was selected in a Ukrainian National Public Cryptographic Competition running from 2007 to 2010. Kalyna supports block sizes and key lengths of 128, 256 and 512 bits. Denoting variants of Kalyna as Kalyna-b/k, where b denotes the block size and k denotes the keylength, the design specifies $k \in \{b, 2b\}$. In this work, we re-evaluate the security bound of some reduced round Kalyna variants, specifically Kalyna-128/256 and Kalyna-256/512 against key recovery attacks in the single key model. We first construct new 6-round distinguishers and then use these distinguishers to demonstrate 9-round attacks on these Kalyna variants. These attacks improve the previous best 7-round attacks on the same.

Our 9-round attack on Kalyna-128/256 has data, time and memory complexity of 2^{105}, $2^{245.83}$ and $2^{226.86}$ respectively. For our 9-round attack on Kalyna-256/512, the data/time/memory complexities are 2^{217}, $2^{477.83}$ and $2^{451.45}$ respectively. The attacks presented in this work are the current best on Kalyna. We apply multiset attack - a variant of meet-in-the-middle attack to achieve these results.

Keywords: Block cipher · Kalyna · Key recovery · Differential enumeration · Single key model

1 Introduction

The block cipher Kalyna proposed by Oliynykov et al. has been recently selected as Ukranian encryption standard in 2015. Kalyna block cipher adopts an SPN (substitution-permutation network) structure, similar to AES [2] but with increased MDS matrix size, a new set of four different S-boxes, pre-and post-whitening modular 2^{64} key addition and a new key scheduling algorithm.

The official version of Kalyna specification (in English) available publicly does not include any security analysis of the design. A preliminary study in [9], before this cipher was standardized, reports attack complexities for Kalyna-128/128 against various attacks such as differential, linear, integral, impossible differential, boomerang etc. and shows that upto 5 rounds of this variant can be broken. Similar results are claimed for other Kalyna variants as well. The designers of Kalyna thus claim brute force security against Kalyna for rounds ≥ 6.

S. Kwon and A. Yun (Eds.): ICISC 2015, LNCS 9558, pp. 119–135, 2016.
DOI: 10.1007/978-3-319-30840-1_8

In this work, we extend the number of rounds attacked and show the first 9-round key recovery attack against Kalyna-128/256 and Kalyna-256/512. Similar to [1], our attack is inspired from the multiset attack demonstrated by Dunkelman et al. on AES in [6]. Multiset attack is a variant of meet-in-the-middle attack presented by Demirci et al. on AES in [4]. However, Demirci et al.'s attacks suffered from a very high memory complexity. To reduce the memory complexity of Demirci et al.'s attacks on AES, Dunkelman et al. in [6], proposed multiset attack which replaces the idea of storing 256 ordered byte sequences with 256 unordered byte sequences (with multiplicity). This reduced both memory and time complexity of MITM attack on AES. They also introduced the novel idea of differential enumeration technique to significantly lower the number of parameters required to construct the multiset. Derbez et al. in [5] improved Dunkelman et al.'s attack on AES-192/256 by refining the differential enumeration technique. By using rebound-like techniques [7], they showed that the number of reachable multisets are much lower than those counted in Dunkelman et al.'s attack. Due to structural similarities between Kalyna and AES, a similar attack was applied to 7-rounds of Kalyna by AlTawy et al. in [1]. The multiset attack on AES-192/256 was further improved by Li et al. in [8] by using the concept of key sieving. Recently, in [11], Li et al. demonstrated the most efficient multiset attack on AES-256 by exploiting some more key sieving properties and clever MixColumn properties. On similar lines, we investigate the effectiveness of improved multiset attack on Kalyna in this work.

In our attacks, we examine Kalyna-128/256 and Kalyna-256/512. We construct new 6-round distinguishers for both the variants and use it to extend our attacks up to 9 rounds. For Kalyna-256/512, we significantly reduce the data and time complexities of the previous best 7-round attack on the same [1]. The key schedule algorithm of Kalyna does not allow recovery of all subkeys or the master key from one subkey only unlike AES [2]. However, it allows recovery of odd-round keys from even-round keys and vice-versa. This property will be used by us in our attacks to reduce the attack complexities. To the best of our knowledge, our attacks are the first attacks on 9-round Kalyna-128/256 and Kalyna-256/512 respectively.

Organization. In Sect. 2, we provide a brief description of Kalyna and notations used throughout the work. In Sect. 3, we give details of our 6-round distinguisher for Kalyna-128/256 followed by Sect. 4 where we present our 9-round attack on the same. In Sect. 5, we briefly describe our 6-round distinguisher for Kalyna-256/512 and report the attack complexities for our 9-round attack on the same.

Finally in Sect. 6, we conclude our work. Our results are summarized in Table 1.

Table 1. Comparison of cryptanalytic attacks on round reduced variants of Kalyna. The blank entries were not reported in [9]. (The memory complexity header represents the number of 128-bit blocks for Kalyna-128 and 256-bit blocks for Kalyna-256 required to be stored in memory.)

Algorithm	Rounds attacked	Attack type	Time complexity	Data complexity	Memory complexity	Reference
Kalyna-128/128	2 (of 10)	Interpolation	–	-	-	[9]
	3 (of 10)	Linear Attack	$2^{52.8}$	-	-	[9]
	4 (of 10)	Differential	2^{55}	-	-	[9]
	4 (of 10)	Boomerang	2^{120}	-	-	[9]
	5 (of 10)	Impossible Differential	2^{62}	-	2^{66}	[9]
	5 (of 10)	Integral	2^{97}	-	2^{33+4}	[9]
Kalyna-128/256	7 (of 14)	Meet-in-the-Middle	$2^{230.2}$	2^{89}	$2^{202.64}$	[1]
	9 (of 14)	Meet-in-the-Middle	$2^{245.83}$	2^{105}	$2^{226.86}$	This work, Sect. 4
Kalyna-256/512	7 (of 18)	Meet-in-the-Middle	$2^{502.2}$	2^{233}	2^{170}	[1]
	9 (of 18)	Meet-in-the-middle	$2^{477.83}$	2^{217}	$2^{451.45}$	This work, Sect. 5

2 Preliminaries

In this section, we describe Kalyna and mention the key notations and definitions used.

2.1 Description of Kalyna

The block cipher Kalyna-b/k has five variants namely - Kalyna-128/128, Kalyna-128/256, Kalyna-256/256, Kalyna-256/512 and Kalyna-512/512 where, b is the block size and k is the key size. The 128-bit, 256-bit and 512-bit internal states are treated as a byte matrix of 8×2 size, 8×4 size and 8×8 size respectively where, the bytes are numbered column-wise. The pre-whitening and post-whitening keys are added modulo 2^{64} to the plaintext and ciphertext respectively columnwise. Each internal round consists of 4 basic operations -*SubBytes (SB)*, *Shift Rows (SR)*, *MixColumn (MC)* and *Add Round Key (ARK)*. For detailed description of these operations, we refer the reader to [10].

Key Scheduling Algorithm. The key scheduling algorithm of Kalyna first involves splitting of the master key K into two parts - K_α and K_ω. If the block size and key size are equal, i.e., ($k = b$), then $K_\alpha = K_\omega = K$, otherwise if ($k = 2b$), then $K_\omega \mid\mid K_\alpha = K$, i.e., K_α is set as $b/2$ least significant bits of K and K_ω is set as $b/2$ most significant bits of K. Using these two parameters, an intermediate key K_σ is generated which is then used to independently generate even indexed round keys. For complete details of the key schedule algorithm, one may refer to [10]. Two properties which are important for us are as follows:

1. Recovery of a subkey does not allow recovery of master key better than brute force.

2. The keys for round i where i is an odd number can be linearly computed from the key used in round $(i-1)$ and vice- versa as follows:

$$K_i = K_{i-1} \lll (b/4 + 24) \tag{1}$$

where, $\lll$ denotes circular left shift operation.

2.2 Notations and Definitions

The following notations are followed throughout the rest of the paper.

P	: Plaintext
C	: Ciphertext
i	: Round number i, where, $0 \leq i \leq 8$
Kalyna-b	: Kalyna with state size of b-bits
Kalyna-b/k	: Kalyna with state size of b-bits and key size of k-bits
$\mathbf{K_i}$	: Subkey of round i
$\mathbf{U_i}$	: $MC^{-1}(\mathrm{K}_i)$, where MC^{-1} is the inverse MixColumn operation
$\mathbf{X_i}$	: State before SB in round i
$\mathbf{Y_i}$	: State before SR in round i
$\mathbf{Z_i}$	: State before MC in round i
$\mathbf{W_i}$	: State after MC in round i
$\mathbf{\Delta s}$	: Difference in a state s
$\mathbf{s_i[m]}$	: m^{th} byte of state s in round i, where, $0 \leq m \leq l$ and $l = 15$ for Kalyna-128/256 and $l = 31$ for Kalyna-256/512
$\mathbf{s_i[p-r]}$	: p^{th} byte to r^{th} byte (both inclusive) of state s in round i, where $0 \leq p < r \leq l$ and $l = 15$ for Kalyna-128/256 and $l = 31$ for Kalyna-256/512

In some cases we interchange the order of the *MixColumn* and *Add Round Key* operations. As these operations are linear, they can be swapped, by first xoring the intermediate state with an equivalent key and then applying the *MixColummn* operation. This is exactly similar to what one can do in AES [5]. As mentioned above, we denote the equivalent round key by $U_i = MC^{-1}(K_i)$. We utilize the following definitions for our attacks.

Definition 1 (δ-list). We define the δ-list as an ordered list of 256 16-byte (or 32-byte) distinct elements that are equal in 15 (or 31) bytes for Kalyna-128 (or Kalyna-256). Each of the equal bytes are called as passive bytes whereas the one byte that takes all possible 256 values is called the active byte [2]. We denote the δ-list as $(x^0, x^1, x^2, \ldots, x^{255})$ where x^j indicates the jth 128-bit (or 256-bit) member of the δ-list for Kalyna-128 (or Kalyna-256). As mentioned in the notations, x_i^j [m] represents the mth byte of x^j in round i.

Definition 2 (Multiset). A multiset is a set of elements in which multiple instances of the same element can appear. A multiset of 256 bytes, where each byte can take any one of the 256 possible values, can have $\binom{2^8+2^8-1}{2^8} \approx 2^{506.17}$ different values.

Definition 3 (Super S-Box). The Kalyna Super S-box (denoted as SSB) can be defined similar to AES Super S-box [3]. For each 8-byte key, it produces a mapping between an 8-byte input array to an 8-byte output array.

Two important properties that will be used in our attacks are as follows:

Property 1a (Kalyna S-box). For any given Kalyna S-box, say S_i (where, $i = 0$, 1, 2 or 3) and any non-zero input - output difference pair, say $(\Delta_{in}, \Delta_{out})$ in $F_{256} \times F_{256}$, there exists one solution in average, say y, for which the equation, $S_i(y) \oplus S_i(y \oplus \Delta_{in}) = \Delta_{out}$, holds true.

Proof. The proof of this will be provided in the extended version of the paper.

Property 1b (Kalyna Super S-box). For any given Kalyna Super S-box, say SSB and any non-zero input - output difference pair, say $(\Delta_{in}, \Delta_{out})$ in $F_{2^{64}} \times F_{2^{64}}$, the equation, $SSB(z) \oplus SSB(z \oplus \Delta_{in}) = \Delta_{out}$ has one solution in average.

Property 2 (Kalyna MixColumns). If the values (or the differences) in any eight out of its sixteen input/output bytes of the Kalyna MixColumn operation are known, then the values (or the differences) in the other eight bytes are uniquely determined and can be computed efficiently. This is similar to AES MixColumn property stated in [11].

Proof. The proof of this will be provided in the extended version of the paper.

The time complexity of the attack is measured in terms of 9-round Kalyna encryptions required. The memory complexity is measured in units of b-bit Kalyna (where, $b = 128$ or 256) blocks required.

3 Construction of Distinguisher for 6-Round Kalyna-128/256

In this section, we construct a distinguisher on the 6-inner rounds of Kalyna-128/256. Before, we proceed further, we first establish the following relation for Kalyna-128/256. According to Property 2, we can form an equation using any 11 out of 16 input-output bytes in the Kalyna MixColumn operation. For any round j, where, $0 \leq j \leq 8$:

$$\begin{aligned} \texttt{0xCA} \cdot Z_j[12] &\oplus \texttt{0xAD} \cdot 0xZ_j[13] \oplus \texttt{0x49} \cdot Z_j[14] \oplus \texttt{0xD7} \cdot Z_j[15] \\ &= \texttt{0x94} \cdot W_j[8] \oplus \texttt{0xB4} \cdot W_j[9] \oplus \texttt{0x4E} \cdot W_j[10] \oplus \texttt{0x7E} \cdot W_j[11] \\ &\quad \oplus \texttt{0xC0} \cdot W_j[13] \oplus \texttt{0xDA} \cdot W_j[14] \oplus \texttt{0xC5} \cdot W_j[15] \end{aligned} \tag{2}$$

$$\begin{aligned} \text{or,} \quad \texttt{0xCA} \cdot Z_j[12] &\oplus \texttt{0xAD} \cdot Z_j[13] \oplus \texttt{0x49} \cdot Z_j[14] \oplus \texttt{0xD7} \cdot Z_j[15] \\ &= \texttt{0x94} \cdot (K_j[8] \oplus X_{j+1}[8]) \oplus \texttt{0xB4} \cdot (K_j[9] \oplus X_{j+1}[9]) \oplus \\ &\quad \texttt{0x4E} \cdot (K_j[10] \oplus X_{j+1}[10]) \oplus \texttt{0x7E} \cdot (K_j[11] \oplus X_{j+1}[11]) \\ &\quad \oplus \texttt{0xC0} \cdot (K_j[13] \oplus X_{j+1}[13]) \oplus \texttt{0xDA} \cdot (K_j[14] \oplus X_{j+1}[14]) \\ &\quad \oplus \texttt{0xC5} \cdot (K_j[15] \oplus X_{j+1}[15]) \end{aligned} \tag{3}$$

where, $W_j = K_j \oplus X_{j+1}$. Let,

$$P_j = \texttt{0xCA} \cdot Z_j[12] \oplus \texttt{0xAD} \cdot Z_j[13] \oplus \texttt{0x49} \cdot Z_j[14] \oplus \texttt{0xD7} \cdot Z_j[15] \quad (4)$$

$$Q_j = \texttt{0x94} \cdot X_{j+1}[8] \oplus \texttt{0xB4} \cdot X_{j+1}[9] \oplus \texttt{0x4E} \cdot X_{j+1}[10] \oplus \texttt{0x7E} \cdot X_{j+1}[11] \oplus \texttt{0xC0} \cdot X_{j+1}[13] \oplus \texttt{0xDA} \cdot X_{j+1}[14] \oplus \texttt{0xC5} \cdot X_{j+1}[15]$$

$$Const = \texttt{0x94} \cdot K_j[8] \oplus \texttt{0xB4} \cdot K_j[9] \oplus \texttt{0x4E} \cdot K_j[10] \oplus \texttt{0x7E} \cdot K_j[11] \quad (5)$$

$$\oplus\, \texttt{0xC0} \cdot K_j[13] \oplus \texttt{0xDA} \cdot K_j[14] \oplus \texttt{0xC5} \cdot K_j[15] \quad (6)$$

then, Eq. 3 can be rewritten as,

$$P_j = Q_j \oplus Const \quad (7)$$

Eq. 7 will be used to establish the distinguishing property as shown next.

3.1 Distinguishing Property for Kalyna-128/256

Given, a list of 256 distinct bytes (M^0, M^1, ..., M^{255}), a function f: $\{0,1\}^{128} \mapsto \{0,1\}^{128}$ and a 120-bit constant T, we define a multiset v as follows:

$$C^i = f(T \mid\mid M^i), \text{where } (0 \le i \le 255) \quad (8)$$

$$u^i = \texttt{0x94} \cdot C^i[8] \oplus \texttt{0xB4} \cdot C^i[9] \oplus \texttt{0x4E} \cdot C^i[10] \oplus \texttt{0x7E} \cdot C^i[11] \oplus \texttt{0xC0} \cdot C^i[13] \oplus \texttt{0xDA} \cdot C^i[14] \oplus \texttt{0xC5} \cdot C^i[15] \quad (9)$$

$$v = \{u^0 \oplus u^0, u^1 \oplus u^0, \ldots, u^{255} \oplus u^0\} \quad (10)$$

Note that, ($T \mid\mid M^0$, $T \mid\mid M^1$, ..., $T \mid\mid M^{255}$) forms a δ-list and atleast one element of v (i.e., $u^0 \oplus u^0$) is always zero.

Distinguishing Property. Let us consider $\mathcal{F}$ to be a family of permutations on 128-bit. Then, given any list of 256 distinct bytes (M^0, M^1, ..., M^{255}), the aim is to find how many multisets v (as defined above) are possible when, $f \xleftarrow{\$} \mathcal{F}$ and $T \xleftarrow{\$} \{0,1\}^{120}$.

In case, when $\mathcal{F}$ = family of all permutations on 128-bit and $f \xleftarrow{\$} \mathcal{F}$. Under such setting, since in the multiset v, we have 255 values (one element is always 0) that are chosen uniformly and independently from the set {0, 1, ..., 255}, the total number of possible multisets v are at most $\binom{2^8-1+2^8-1}{2^8-1} \approx 2^{505.17}$.

In case, when $\mathcal{F}$ = 6-full rounds of Kalyna-128/256 and $f \xleftarrow{\$} \mathcal{F}$. Here, $f \xleftarrow{\$} \mathcal{F} \Leftrightarrow K \xleftarrow{\$} \{0,1\}^{256}$ and $f = E_K$. Let us consider the 6 inner rounds of Kalyna-128/256 as shown in Fig. 1. Here, C in Eq. 8 is represented by X_6 and Eq. 9 is defined as:

$$u^i = \texttt{0x94} \cdot X_6^i[8] \oplus \texttt{0xB4} \cdot X_6^i[9] \oplus \texttt{0x4E} \cdot X_6^i[10] \oplus \texttt{0x7E} \cdot X_6^i[11] \oplus \texttt{0xC0} \cdot X_6^i[13] \oplus \texttt{0xDA} \cdot X_6^i[14] \oplus \texttt{0xC5} \cdot X_6^i[15] \quad (11)$$

It is to be noted that under this setting, for each i where, $(0 \leq i \leq 255)$, Eq. 11 is same as Eq. 5 computed at round 5, i.e., $u^i = Q_5^i$. Now, we state the following *Observation 1.*

Observation 1. The multiset v is determined by the following 52 single byte parameters only :

- $X_1^0[0$ - $7]$ (8-bytes)
- $X_2^0[0$ - $15]$ (16-bytes)
- $X_3^0[0$ - $15]$ (16-bytes)
- $X_4^0[0$ - 3, 12 - $15]$ (8-bytes)
- $X_5^0[4$ - $7]$ (4-bytes)

Thus, the total number of possible multisets is $2^{52 \times 8} = 2^{416}$ since, each 52-byte value defines one sequence.

Proof. In round 0 (in Fig. 1), the set of differences $\{X_0^0[15] \oplus X_0^0[15], X_0^1[15] \oplus X_0^0[15], \ldots, X_0^{255}[15] \oplus X_0^0[15]\}$ (or, equivalently the set of differences at $X_0[15]$) is known to the attacker as there are exactly 256 differences possible. This is so, because in the plaintext we make the most significant byte as the active byte. Hence, when the pre-whitening key is added (columnwise), the carry-bit in the most significant bit is ignored limiting the possible values (and the differences) at $X_0[15]$ to 256 only. Since S-box is injective, exactly 256 values exist in the set $\{Y_0^0[15] \oplus Y_0^0[15], Y_0^1[15] \oplus Y_0^0[15], \ldots, Y_0^{255}[15] \oplus Y_0^0[15]\}$. As *Shift Row* (SR), *MixColumn* (MC) and *Add Round Key* (ARK) are linear operations, the set of differences at $X_1[0-7]$ will be known to the attacker.

Owing to the non-linearity of the S-box operation, the set of differences at $Y_1[0-7]$ cannot be computed to move forward. To allievate this problem, it is sufficient to guess $X_1^0[0-7]$, i.e., values of the active bytes of the first state (out of 256 states) at X_1 as it allows calculating the other $X_1^i[0-7]$ states (where, $1 \leq \mathrm{i} \leq 255$) and cross SB layer in round 1. Since, SR, MC and ARK operations are linear, the set of differences at $X_2[0-15]$ is known. Continuing in a similar manner as discussed above, if the attacker guesses full states $X_2^0[0-15]$ and $X_3^0[0-15]$, then the set of differences at Z_3, i.e., $\{Z_3^0 \oplus Z_3^0, Z_3^1 \oplus Z_3^0, \ldots, Z_3^{255} \oplus Z_3^0\}$ can be easily computed. Now at this stage, she can easily calculate the set of differences at W_3 [0, 1, 2, 3, 12, 13, 14, 15] which is equal to the set of differences at X_4 [0, 1, 2, 3, 12, 13, 14, 15][1]. By guessing X_4^0 [0, 1, 2, 3, 12, 13, 14, 15], the attacker can cross the SB layer in round 4 and calculate the set of differences at W_4 [4, 5, 6, 7]. By guessing X_5^0 [4, 5, 6, 7], the attacker can obtain the set of values $\{Z_5^0[12-15], Z_5^1[12-15], \ldots, Z_5^{255}[12-15]\}$. Using these, she can compute P_5^i at Z_5^i as $P_5^i = CA_x \cdot Z_5^i[12] \oplus AD_x \cdot Z_5^i[13] \oplus 49_x \cdot Z_5^i[14] \oplus D7_x \cdot Z_5^i[15]$ (according to Eq. 4) and thus the set $\{P_5^0 \oplus P_5^0, P_5^0 \oplus P_5^1, \ldots, P_5^{255} \oplus P_5^0\}$. Since, according to Eq. 7, $P_j^i \oplus P_j^0 = (Q_j^i \oplus Const) \oplus (Q_j^0 \oplus Const) = Q_j^i \oplus Q_j^0$ and $u^i = Q_5^i$ (mentioned above), the attacker can easily calculate the multiset $v = \{Q_5^0 \oplus Q_5^0, Q_5^1 \oplus Q_5^0, \ldots, Q_5^{255} \oplus Q_5^0\}$. This shows that the multiset v depends on 52 parameters and can take 2^{416} possible values. □

---

[1] In Fig. 1, byte 3 in states W_3, X_4, Y_4 and Z_4 have not been colored grey for a purpose which will be cleared when we reach *Observation 2.*

Since, there are 2^{416} possible multisets, if we precompute and store these values in a hash table, then the precomputation complexity goes higher than brute force for Kalyna-128/256. In order to reduce the number of multisets, we apply the Differential Enumeration technique suggested by Dunkelman et al. in [6] and improved by Derbez et al. in [5]. We call the improved version proposed in [5] as *Refined Differential Enumeration.*

Refined Differential Enumeration. The basic idea behind this technique is to choose a δ-set such that several of the parameters mentioned in *Observation 1* equal some pre-determined constants. To achieve so, we first construct a 6-round truncated differential trail in round 0 - round 5 (as shown in Fig. 1) where, the input difference is non-zero at one byte and output difference is non zero in 7 bytes. The probability of such a trail is 2^{-112} as follows: the one byte difference at $\Delta P[15]$ and correspondingly at $\Delta X_0[15]$ propagates to 8-byte difference in $\Delta X_1[0-7]$ and 16-byte difference in $\Delta X_2[0-15]$ and further till $\Delta Z_3[0-15]$ with probability close to 1. Next, the probability that 16-byte difference in $\Delta Z_3[0-15]$ propagates to 7-byte difference in $\Delta W_3[0-2, 12-15]$ ($= \Delta X_4[0-2, 12-15]$) is 2^{-72}. This 7-byte difference in ΔX_4 propagates to 4-byte difference in $\Delta W_4[4-7]$ followed by 7-byte difference in $\Delta W_5[8-11, 13-15]$ with a probability of 2^{-32} and 2^{-8} respectively. Thus, the overall probability of the differential from ΔP to ΔZ_5 is $2^{-(72+32+8)} = 2^{-112}$.

In other words, we require 2^{112} plaintext pairs to get a right pair. Once, we get a right pair, say (P^0, P^1), we state the following *Observation 2.*

Observation 2. Given a right pair (P^0, P^1) that follows the truncated differential trail shown in Fig. 1, the 52 parameters corresponding to P^0, mentioned in Observation 1 can take one of atmost 2^{224} fixed 52-byte values (out of the total 2^{416} possible values), where each of these 2^{224} 52-byte values are defined by each of the 2^{224} values of the following 39 parameters:

- $\Delta Z_0[7]$ (1-byte)
- $X_1^0[0-7]$ (8-bytes)
- $Y_3^0[0-15]$ (16-bytes)
- $Y_4^0[0-3, 12-15]$ (8-bytes)
- $Y_5^0[5-7]$ (3-bytes)
- $\Delta Z_5[12-14]$ (3-bytes)

Proof. Given a right pair (P^0, P^1), the knowledge of these 39 new parameters allows us to compute all the differences shown in Fig. 1. This is so because the knowledge of $\Delta Z_0[7]$ allows us to compute $\Delta X_1[0-7]$. Then, if the values of $X_1^0[0-7]$ are known, one can compute the corresponding $X_1^1[0-7]$ and cross the S-box layer in round 1 to get ΔX_2. From the bottom side, we know that $\Delta W_5[12] = \Delta Z_5[8] = \Delta Z_5[9] = \Delta Z_5[10] = \Delta Z_5[11] = 0$. Thus, if $\Delta Z_5[12, 13, 14]$ are known, then using *Property 2* (as 9 bytes are known), we can deduce $\Delta Z_5[15]$ (and $\Delta W_5[8-11, 13-15]$). Then, the knowledge of $Y_5^0[5-7]$, allows us to easily determine the corresponding $Y_5^1[5-7]$ and compute $\Delta X_5[5-7]$ (and $\Delta W_4[5-7]$). We know that $\Delta W_4[0] = \Delta W_4[1] = \Delta W_4[2] = \Delta W_4[3] = \Delta Z_4[3] = 0$. Using

Property 2, we can deduce $\Delta W_4[4]$ and hence $\Delta X_5[4]$ and since we already know $\Delta Y_5[4]$ (from $\Delta Z_5[12]$ guessed previously), using *Property 1a.* the possible values of $X_5[4]$ and $Y_5[4]$ can be computed. We can compute $\Delta Y_4[0-2, 12-15]$ from $\Delta W_4[0-7]$. By guessing $Y_4^0[0-2, 12-15]$, we can obtain $\Delta Y_3[0-15]$. Using the value of $Y_3^0[0-15]$, we can compute ΔY_2. Then using *Property 1a.*, the possible values of X_2^0 and Y_2^0 can be computed. At this stage, the total possible values of these 39 parameters are $2^{39\times 8} = 2^{312}$.

However, for each value of this 39-byte parameter, the following key bytes - $U_2[0-3, 12-15]$, $K_3[0-15]$, $K_4[0-2, 12-15]$ and $K_5[4-7]$ can be deduced as follows:

1. Knowledge of $X_1^0[0-7]$ allows us to compute the corresponding $Z_1^0[0-3, 12-15]$. Xoring these values with $X_2^0[0-3, 12-15]$ helps us in deducing $U_2[0-3, 12-15]$.
2. Knowledge of X_2^0 allows us to compute the corresponding W_2^0. Xoring W_2^0 with X_3^0 helps us in deducing K_3.
3. Similarly, knowledge of X_3^0 and $X_4^0[0-2, 12-15]$ (from $Y_4^0[0-2, 12-15]$) can be used to deduce $K_4[0-2, 12-15]$.
4. Again, knowledge of $X_4^0[0-3, 12-15]$ and $X_5^0[4-7]$ (from $Y_5^0[4-7]$) helps in deducing $K_5[4-7]$.

Now, according to the key schedule algorithm of Kalyna-128/256, from K_3, we can compute K_2 (according to Eq. 1) which allows us to compute the corresponding U_2. Thus, by comparing the computed $U_2[0-3, 12-15]$ with the deduced $U_2[0-3, 12-15]$, a sieve of 8-bytes (since matching probability is 2^{-64}) can be applied to eliminate the wrong guesses. Similarly, again from Eq. 1, knowledge of $K_5[4-7]$ allows us to compute $K_4[12]$, $K_4[13]$ and $K_4[14]$ as $K_4[12] = K_5[5]$, $K_4[13] = K_5[6]$ and $K_4[14] = K_5[7]$. This allows us a filtering of further 3-bytes. Thus by key sieving, the total possible guesses of 39-byte parameter reduces from $2^{39\times 8}$ to $2^{(39-(8+3))\times 8} = 2^{28\times 8} = 2^{224}$.

Using *Observation 1* and *Observation 2*, we state the following third *Observation 3*:

Observation 3. Given (M^0, M^1, ..., M^{255}) and $f \xleftarrow{\$} \mathcal{F}$ and $T \xleftarrow{\$} \{0,1\}^{120}$, such that $T \parallel M^0$ and $T \parallel M^j$, (where, $j \in \{1, \ldots, 255\}$) is a right pair that follows the differential trail shown in Fig. 1, then atmost 2^{224} multisets v are possible.

Proof. From *Observation 1*, we know that each 52-byte parameter defines one multiset and *Observation 2* restricts the possible values of these 52-byte parameters to 2^{224}. Thus, atmost 2^{224} multisets are only possible for Kalyna-128/256. □

As the number of multisets in case of 128-bit random permutation ($= 2^{505.17}$) is much higher than 6-round Kalyna-128/256 ($= 2^{224}$), a valid distinguisher is constructed.

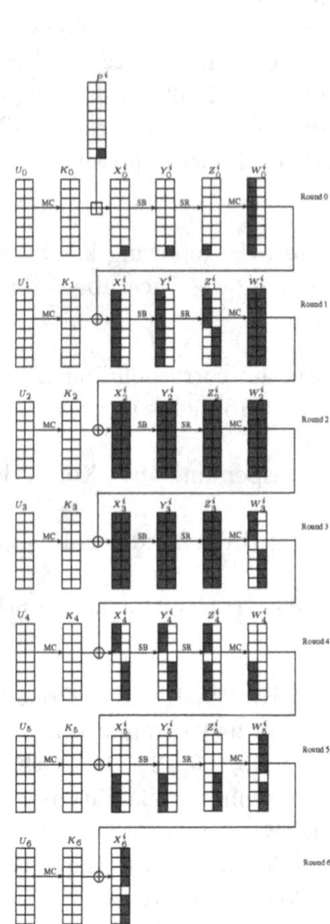

Fig. 1. 6-Round distinguisher for Kalyna-128/256. Here, P^i denotes $(T \parallel M^i)$ and X_j^i, Y_j^i, Z_j^i, W_j^i denote intermediate states corresponding to P^i in round j. The round subkeys K_j, where, $0 \leq j \leq 6$ are generated from the master key K.

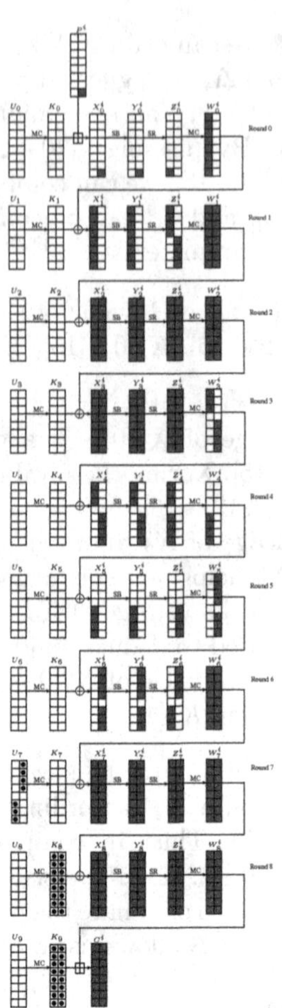

Fig. 2. 9-round attack on Kalyna-128/256. The subkey bytes guessed are shown dotted.

4 Key Recovery Attack on 9-Round Kalyna-128/256

In this section, we use our Observation 3 to launch meet-in-the-middle attack on 9-round Kalyna-128/256 to recover the key. The distinguisher is placed in round 0 to round 5, i.e., plaintext is considered as the δ-list with byte 15 being the active byte and the multiset sequence is checked at X_6 (as shown in Fig. 2). Three rounds are added at the bottom of the 6-round distinguisher. The attack consists of the following three phases:

4.1 Precomputation Phase

In this phase, we build a lookup table T to store 2^{224} sequences to be used for comparison in the online phase. The construction of this table requires us to create two more hash tables (T_0 and T_1) in the intermediate steps. The entire procedure is as follows:

1. For each K_3
   - We guess $\Delta Z_1[0-3, 12-15]||\Delta X_4[0-2, 12-15]$ to compute the difference ΔX_2 and ΔY_3 respectively. We resolve (ΔX_2 - ΔY_3) using *Property 1b* to compute the corresponding $X_2||X_3$. We then deduce K_2 from K_3 and compute the corresponding value of $Z_1[0-3, 12-15]$. Using the guessed value of $\Delta Z_1[0-3, 12-15]$ and the computed value of $Z_1[0-3, 12-15]$, we compute $\Delta Z_0[0-7]$. If $\Delta Z_0[0-6] = 0$ (which happens with a probability of 2^{-56}), we store the corresponding $X_1[0-7]||\Delta Z_1[0-3, 12-15]||X_2||X_3||W_3[12-14]||\Delta X_4[0-2, 12-15]$ at index K_3 in table T_0. There are about 2^{64} entries for each index.
2. For each guess of $\Delta Z_5[12-14]$
   - We compute $\Delta Z_5[15]$ using *Property 2*.
   - We guess $Y_5[5-7]$, compute $X_5[5-7]$ and $\Delta X_5[0-3, 5-7]$ where, $\Delta X_5[0-3] = 0$. Since, $\Delta X_5[0-3, 5-7] = \Delta W_4[0-3, 5-7]$ and we know that $\Delta Z_4[3] = 0$, thus we can compute $\Delta X_5[4]$ ($= \Delta W_4[4]$) and $\Delta Z_4[0-2, 4-7]$ again using *Property 2*. Since $\Delta Y_5[4]$ is known from $\Delta Z_5[12]$, we can resolve ($\Delta X_5[4]$-$\Delta Y_5[4]$) to get $X_5[4]$.
   - We guess $Y_4[0-3, 12-15]$ and compute corresponding $X_4[0-3, 12-15]$ in the backward direction and $W_4[4-7]$ in the forward direction. This allows us to calculate $K_5[4-7]$ and deduce the corresponding $K_4[12-14]$. We use this to compute $W_3[12-14]$.
   - We store $X_4[0-3, 12-15]||X_5[4-7]$ at index value $W_3[12-14]||\Delta X_4[0-2, 12-15]$ in table T_1. There are about 2^{32} entries for each index.
3. For each of the 2^{128} index of K_3 in table T_0, we have 2^{64} entries of W_3 $[12-14]||\Delta X_4[0-2, 12-15]$ and corresponding to each of these we have 2^{32} entries of $X_4[0-3, 12-15]||X_5[4-7]$ in table T_1. So in all, after merging T_0 and T_1, we get $2^{128+64+32} = 2^{224}$ unique set of 39-byte parameters, that are required to construct the multiset v.
4. For each of these 2^{224} 39-byte parameters, we calculate the corresponding 52-byte parameters for all the elements of the δ-list and compute the multiset $v = \{u^0 \oplus u^0,\ u^1 \oplus u^0,\ \ldots,\ u^{255} \oplus u^0\}$. We store the multiset along with the 52-byte parameters in the table T.

The time complexity to construct $T_0 = 2^{(16+8+7)\times 8} \times 2^{-2.17} = 2^{245.83}$. The time complexity to construct $T_1 = 2^{(3+3+8)\times 8} \times 2^{-2.17} = 2^{109.83}$. The time complexity to merge T_0 and $T_1 = 2^{128+64+32} = 2^{224}$. Finally, the time complexity to construct $T = 2^{224} \times 2^8 \times 2^{-0.58} = 2^{231.41}$.

4.2 Online Phase

In this phase we extend the differential trail shown Fig. 1, by adding 3 more rounds at the bottom (as shown in Fig. 2). The steps of the online phase are as follows:

1. We encrypt 2^{97} structures of 2^8 plaintexts each where byte 15 takes all possible values and rest of the bytes are constants. We store the corresponding ciphertexts in the hash table.
2. For each of the 2^{112} (P_0, P_0') plaintext pairs, do the following:
   - We guess 2^{128} values of K_9 and deduce the corresponding values of K_8 from K_9. We decrypt each of the ciphertext pairs through 2 rounds, to get X_7 and ΔX_7. Then, we deduce the corresponding ΔW_6 and ΔZ_6.
   - We filter out the keys, which do not give zero difference at $\Delta Z_6[0-4, 12-15]$. 2^{56} key guesses are expected to remain.
   - We pick one member of the pair, say P_0, create the δ-list by constructing the rest of the 255 plaintexts as $P_i = P_0 \oplus i$, where, $1 \leq i \leq 255$ and get their corresponding ciphertexts.
   - For each remaining 2^{56} key guesses of K_8 and K_9, we guess $U_7[5-11]$, compute the corresponding $Z_6[5-11]$ and $Y_6[8-11, 13-15]$ and then obtain the multiset $\{ u^0 \oplus u^0, u^1 \oplus u^0, \ldots, u^{255} \oplus u^0\}$.
   - We check whether this multiset exists in the precomputation table T or not. If not, then we discard the corresponding guesses.

The probability for a wrong guess to pass the test is $2^{224} \times 2^{-467.6} = 2^{-243.6}$.[2] Since we try only $2^{112+56} = 2^{168}$ multisets, only the right subkey should verify the test.

4.3 Recovering the Remaining Subkey Bytes

The key schedule algorithm of Kalyna does not allow recovery of master key from any subkey better than brute-force [10]. However, knowledge of all round keys enables encryption/decryption. We follow a similar approach as described in [1] to recover all the round subkeys. When a match with a multiset is found using a given plaintext-ciphertext pair, we choose one of the ciphertexts and perform the following steps:

1. We already know the corresponding K_8 and K_9 and $U_7[5-11]$.
2. We guess the remaining 9 bytes of U_7, and deduce the corresponding 2^{72} values of K_7 and K_6.
3. For each 2^{72} guesses of (K_7, K_6), from X_7 we compute X_5. We discard the key guesses for which $X_5[4-7]$ does not match with the values of $X_5[4-7]$ obtained from the corresponding matched multiset in the pre-computation table.

[2] Note that the probability of randomly having a match is $2^{-467.6}$ and not $2^{-505.17}$ since the number of ordered sequences associated to a multiset is not constant [6].

4. For the remaining $2^{72-32} = 2^{40}$ guesses of (K_9, K_8, K_7, K_6), we guess 2^{128} values of K_5. We deduce X_4 and discard the key guesses for which $X_4[0-2, 12-15]$ does not match with the values obtained corresponding to the correct multiset sequence from the precomputation table. From a total of $2^{128+40} = 2^{168}$ key guesses, 2^{112} key guesses are expected to remain.
5. We deduce K_4 from K_5 for the remaining key guesses and compute X_3. We compare this to the value obtained from the precomputation table corresponding to the correct multiset sequence and discard those that do not match. Only one value of (K_9, K_8, K_7, K_6, K_5, K_4) is expected to remain.
6. One value of K_3 and K_2 corresponding to the matching sequence is already known from the pre-computation table. We deduce X_1 for the remaining one value of (K_9, K_8, K_7, K_6, K_5, K_4, K_3, K_2).
7. We guess 2^{128} values of K_1, deduce K_0 and compute the plaintext. We compare this to the plaintext corresponding to ciphertext being decrypted. We are left with only one value of (K_9, K_8, K_7, K_6, K_5, K_4, K_3, K_2, K_1, K_0).

Complexities. The time complexity of the precomputation phase is dominated by step 1 and is $2^{248} \times 2^{-2.17} = 2^{245.83}$ Kalyna-128/256 encryptions. The time complexity of the online phase is dominated by step 1 and is $2^{112} \times 2^{128} \times 2^{-2.17} = 2^{237.83}$. The time complexity of the Subkey recovery phase is dominated by step 4 which is $2^{168} \times 2^{-3.17} = 2^{164.83}$. Clearly the time complexity of the whole attack is dominated by the time complexity of the precomputation phase, i.e., $2^{245.83}$. It was shown in [5] that each 256-byte multiset requires 512-bits space. Hence, to store each entry in table T, we require 512-bits to store the multiset and $52 \times 8 = 416$-bits to store the 52-byte parameters, i.e., a total of 928-bits ($= 2^{9.86}$). Therefore, the memory complexity of this attack is $2^{224} \times 2^{9.86-7} = 2^{226.86}$ Kalyna 128-bit blocks. The data complexity of this attack is 2^{105} plaintexts.

5 Key Recovery Attack on 9-Round Kalyna-256/512

In this section, we briefly describe our meet-in-the-middle attack on 9-round Kalyna-256/512. We first establish the following relation for Kalyna-256/512. According to Property 2, we can form an equation using any 12 out of 16 input-output bytes in the Kalyna MixColumn operation. For any round j, where, $0 \leq j \leq 8$:

$$\begin{aligned} Z_j[8] \oplus Z_j[9] \oplus Z_j[12] \oplus Z_j[13] = {} & EA_x \cdot W_j[8] \oplus 54_x \cdot W_j[9] \oplus 7D_x \cdot W_j[10] \\ & \oplus C3_x \cdot W_j[11] \oplus E0_x \cdot W_j[12] \oplus 5E_x \cdot W_j[13] \\ & \oplus 7D_x \cdot W_j[14] \oplus C3_x \cdot W_j[15] \end{aligned} \tag{12}$$

Similar to as shown in Sect. 3, since, $W_j = K_j \oplus X_{j+1}$, If

$$P_j = Z_j[8] \oplus Z_j[9] \oplus Z_j[12] \oplus Z_j[13] \quad (13)$$

$$Q_j = EA_x \cdot X_{j+1}[8] \oplus 54_x \cdot X_{j+1}[9] \oplus 7D_x \cdot X_{j+1}[10] \oplus C3_x \cdot X_{j+1}[11] \oplus E0_x \cdot X_{j+1}[12] \oplus 5E_x \cdot X_{j+1}[13] \oplus 7D_x \cdot X_{j+1}[14] \oplus C3_x \cdot X_{j+1}[15] \quad (14)$$

$$Const = EA_x \cdot K_j[8] \oplus 54_x \cdot K_j[9] \oplus 7D_x \cdot K_j[10] \oplus C3_x \cdot K_j[11] \oplus E0_x \cdot K_j[12] \oplus 5E_x \cdot K_j[13] \oplus 7D_x \cdot K_j[14] \oplus C3_x \cdot K_j[15] \quad (15)$$

then, Eq. 12 can be rewritten as,

$$P_j = Q_j \oplus Const \quad (16)$$

For Kalyna-256/512, instead of counting multisets, we count 256-byte ordered sequence as shown next.

5.1 Construction of 6-Round Distinguisher for Kalyna-256/512

Given a list of 256 distinct bytes (M^0, M^1, ..., M^{255}), a function f: $\{0,1\}^{256} \mapsto \{0,1\}^{256}$ and a 248-bit constant T, we define an ordered sequence ov as follows:

$$C^i = f(T \,||\, M^i), \text{where } (0 \leq i \leq 255) \quad (17)$$

$$ou^i = EA_x \cdot C^i[8] \oplus 54_x \cdot C^i[9] \oplus 7D_x \cdot C^i[10] \oplus C3_x \cdot C^i[11] \oplus E0_x \cdot C^i[12] \oplus 5E_x \cdot C^i[13] \oplus 7D_x \cdot C^i[14] \oplus C3_x \cdot C^i[15] \quad (18)$$

$$ov = \{ou^0 \oplus ou^0, ou^1 \oplus ou^0, \ldots, ou^{255} \oplus ou^0\} \quad (19)$$

Note that, ($T \,||\, M^0$, $T \,||\, M^1$, ..., $T \,||\, M^{255}$) forms a δ-list and the first element of ov (i.e., $ou^0 \oplus ou^0$) is always zero.

Distinguishing Property. Let us consider $\mathcal{F}$ to be a family of permutations on 256-bit. Then, given any list of 256 distinct bytes (M^0, M^1, ..., M^{255}), the aim is to find how many ordered sequences ov (as defined above) are possible when, $f \xleftarrow{\$} \mathcal{F}$ and $T \xleftarrow{\$} \{0,1\}^{248}$.

In case, when $\mathcal{F}$ = family of all permutations on 256-bit and $f \xleftarrow{\$} \mathcal{F}$. Under such setting, since, ov is a 256-byte ordered sequence in which the first byte is always zero and the rest 255 bytes are chosen uniformly and independently from the set {0, 1, ..., 255}, the total possible values of ov are $(256)^{255} = 2^{2040}$.

In case, when $\mathcal{F}$ = 6-full rounds of Kalyna-128/256 and $f \xleftarrow{\$} \mathcal{F}$. Here, $f \xleftarrow{\$} \mathcal{F} \Leftrightarrow K \xleftarrow{\$} \{0,1\}^{512}$ and $f = E_K$. Let us consider the first 6 rounds of Kalyna-256/512 as shown in Fig. 3. Here, C in Eq. 17 is represented by X_6 and Eq. 18 is defined as:

$$ou^i = EA_x \cdot X_6^i[8] \oplus 54_x \cdot X_6^i[9] \oplus 7D_x \cdot X_6^i[10] \oplus C3_x \cdot X_6^i[11] \oplus E0_x \cdot X_6^i[12] \oplus 5E_x \cdot X_6^i[13] \oplus 7D_x \cdot X_6^i[15] \oplus C3_x \cdot X_6^i[15] \quad (20)$$

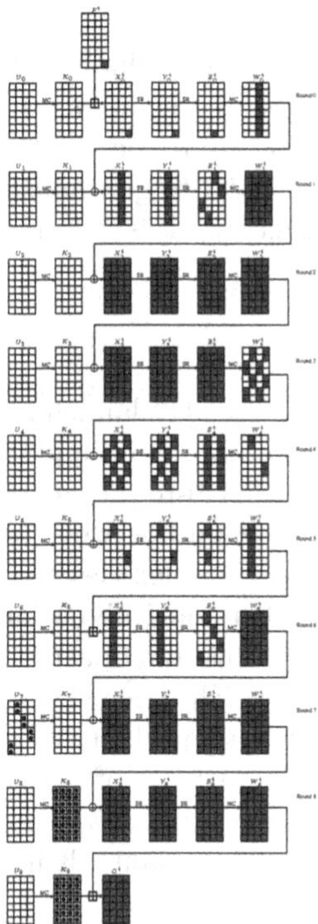

Fig. 3. 9-round attack on Kalyna-256/516. The subkey bytes guessed are shown dotted.

It is to be noted that here, for each i where, $(0 \leq i \leq 255)$, Eq. 20 is same as Eq. 14 computed at round 5, i.e., $ou^i = Q_5^i$. Under this setting, by applying differential enumeration technique [5,6] and key sieving technique [8,11], the total possible values of ordered sequence ov is $\mathbf{2^{448}}$. Due to space constraints, we are unable to provide proofs of the same in this work[3].

As the number of ordered sequences in case of 256-bit random permutation $(= 2^{2040})$ is much higher than 6-round Kalyna-256/512 $(= 2^{448})$, a valid distinguisher is constructed.

5.2 Key Recovery Attack

Following a similar approach as used in Kalyna-128/256, it is possible to launch an attack on 9-round Kalyna-256/512 (as shown in Fig. 3). Due to space limitations, we omit the full details of the key recovery attack here and just report the attack complexities[4]. The time complexity of the precomputation phase is $2^{453.83}$

[3] The details of this distinguisher will be provided in the extended version of this paper.

[4] The complete details of this attack will be provided in the extended version of this paper.

Kalyna encryptions. The time complexity of the online phase is $2^{477.83}$ and the time complexity of the Subkey recovery phase is $2^{412.83}$. Clearly the time complexity of this attack is dominated by the online phase, i.e., $2^{477.83}$. The memory complexity of this attack comes out to be $2^{451.45}$ Kalyna-256 blocks. In this attack, we require 2^{224} plaintext pairs to guarantee the existence of a right pair. Thus, the data complexity of this attack is 2^{217} plaintexts.

6 Conclusions

In this work, we utilize multiset attacks to launch key recovery attack on Kalyna-128/256 and Kalyna-256/512. We improve the previous 7-round attack on both the variants to demonstrate the first 9-round attacks on the same. Our attacks on Kalyna-256/512 even improve upon the previous 7-round attack on the same variant in terms of time and data complexities. We obtain these results by constructing new 6-round distinguishers on Kalyna and applying MITM attack on the rest of the rounds. Currently, this line of attack only works on Kalyna-b/2b variants and Kalyna variants in which block size and key size are equal appear to be safe. It would be an interesting problem to try applying multiset attacks on Kalyna-b/b. Presently, all five variants of Kalyna have been included in the Ukranian standard. However, our results as well as the previous 7-round attack show that compared to Kalyna-b/2b variants, Kalyna-b/b variants appear to be more robust.

References

1. AlTawy, R., Abdelkhalek, A., Youssef, A.M.: A meet-in-the-middle attack on reduced-round kalyna-b/2b. IACR Cryptol. ePrint Arch. **2015**, 762 (2015). http://eprint.iacr.org/2015/762
2. Joan, D., Vincent, R.: The Design of Rijndael: AES - The Advanced Encryption Standard. Information Security and Cryptography. Springer, New York (2002)
3. Daemen, J., Rijmen, V.: Understanding two-round differentials in AES. In: De Prisco, R., Yung, M. (eds.) SCN 2006. LNCS, vol. 4116, pp. 78–94. Springer, Heidelberg (2006)
4. Demirci, H., Selçuk, A.A.: A meet-in-the-middle attack on 8-round AES. In: Nyberg, K. (ed.) FSE 2008. LNCS, vol. 5086, pp. 116–126. Springer, Heidelberg (2008)
5. Derbez, P., Fouque, P.-A., Jean, J.: Improved key recovery attacks on reduced-round AES in the single-key setting. In: Johansson, T., Nguyen, P.Q. (eds.) EUROCRYPT 2013. LNCS, vol. 7881, pp. 371–387. Springer, Heidelberg (2013)
6. Dunkelman, O., Keller, N., Shamir, A.: Improved single-key attacks on 8-round AES-192 and AES-256. J. Cryptol. **28**(3), 397–422 (2015)
7. Lamberger, M., Mendel, F., Rechberger, C., Rijmen, V., Schläffer, M.: Rebound distinguishers: results on the full whirlpool compression function. In: Matsui, M. (ed.) ASIACRYPT 2009. LNCS, vol. 5912, pp. 126–143. Springer, Heidelberg (2009)
8. Li, L., Jia, K., Wang, X.: Improved single-key attacks on 9-round AES-192/256. In: Cid, C., Rechberger, C. (eds.) FSE 2014. LNCS, vol. 8540, pp. 127–146. Springer, Heidelberg (2015)

9. Oliynykov, R.: Next generation of block ciphers providing high-level security, June 2015. http://www.slideshare.net/oliynykov/next-generation-ciphers/
10. Oliynykov, R., Gorbenko, I., Kazymyrov, O., Ruzhentsev, V., Kuznetsov, O., Gorbenko, Y., Dyrda, O., Dolgov, V., Pushkaryov, A., Mordvinov, R., Kaidalov, D.: A new encryption standard of Ukraine: The Kalyna block cipher. IACR Cryptol. ePrint Arch. **2015**, 650 (2015). http://eprint.iacr.org/2015/650
11. Rongjia, L., Chenhui, J.: Meet-in-the-middle attacks on 10-round AES-256. Designs, Codes and Cryptography, pp. 1–13 (2015)

Improved Impossible Differential Attack on Reduced-Round LBlock

Ning Wang[1,2], Xiaoyun Wang[1,2,3](✉), and Keting Jia[4]

[1] Key Laboratory of Cryptologic Technology and Information Security, Ministry of Education, Shandong University, Jinan 250100, China

[2] School of Mathematics, Shandong University, Jinan 250100, China
wangning2012@mail.sdu.edu.cn

[3] Institute for Advanced Study, Tsinghua University, Beijing 100084, China
xiaoyunwang@mail.tsinghua.edu.cn

[4] Department of Computer Science and Technology, Tsinghua University, Beijing 100084, China
ktjia@tsinghua.edu.cn

Abstract. LBlock is a 32-round lightweight block cipher with a 64-bit block size and an 80-bit key. This paper presents a new impossible differential attack on LBlock by improving the previous best result for 1 more round. Based on the nibble conditions, detailed differential properties of LBlock S-Boxes and thorough exploration of subkey relations, we set up well precomputation tables to collect the data needed and propose an optimal key-guessing arrangement to effectively reduce the time complexity of the attack. With these techniques, we launch an impossible differential attack on 24-round LBlock. To the best of our knowledge, this attack is currently the best in terms of the number of rounds attacked (except for biclique attacks).

Keywords: Lightweight block cipher · LBlock · Impossible differential cryptanalysis

1 Introduction

In the past few years, the wide applications of RFID tags and sensor networks have stimulated the needs of lightweight cryptographic primitives that require very limited resources (the area size on the chip, memory, power consumption etc.) while still providing good security. In accordance with this tendency, many lightweight block ciphers were proposed, such as TWINE [19], PRESENT [4], LED [7], LBlock [23], SIMON and SPECK [2] etc. For all of them, LBlock is a relatively recent proposal and its security analysis is still under the heated discussions.

N. Wang—Supported by National Key Basic Research Program of China (Grant No. 2013CB834205), and the National Natural Science Foundation of China (Grant No. 61133013 and 61402256).

S. Kwon and A. Yun (Eds.): ICISC 2015, LNCS 9558, pp. 136–152, 2016.
DOI: 10.1007/978-3-319-30840-1_9

The LBlock block cipher was introduced by Wu and Zhang at ACNS 2011 [23] and the designers gave corresponding cryptanalysis. As a lightweight primitive, LBlock has 64-bit block size and 80-bit key length. Since its proposal, the security of LBlock has been analyzed by various cryptanalysis methods, such as differential [11], impossible differential [5,6,8,12,14,22,23], integral [16,17,23], zero-correlation linear [18,20], cube cryptanalysis [10], biclique attacks [1,21] and so on.

Impossible differential cryptanalysis was independently introduced by Knudsen [9] and Biham et al. [3], which allowed the adversary to discard wrong keys as many as possible by distinguishing the impossible differential characteristics, and exhaustively search the rest of the keys. Up to date, the impossible differential attack is a relatively effective method in terms of attacked rounds of LBlock. Boura et al. proposed the latest impossible differential result to attack 23-round LBlock with a time complexity $2^{75.36}$ and a data complexity 2^{59} [5,6]. In [6], the authors provided new generic formulas to compute the data, time and memory complexities of impossible differential attacks. As to LBlock specifically, they presented some new key-bridging techniques for discarding wrong keys and therefore improved the time and data complexities of their attack. Boura et al.'s work simplified the computation of impossible differential cryptanalysis by a general equation. By comprehensive studying on their works of LBlock and utilizing the 14-round impossible differential in [6], we further found that the time complexity could be improved.

Our Contributions. The contributions of this paper are summarized in three folds as follows:

- In this paper, we thoroughly explore the relations of the subkeys involved to find an optimal arrangement for key guessing. Based on this and some precomputations, a new key-guessing technique based on nibble is proposed to reduce the guessed key space greatly, which is similar to dynamic key-guessing technique [15] that is valid for block ciphers based on bit operations such as SIMON.
- We make a more detailed investigation of the differential properties of S-Boxes. These properties enable us to build some precomputation tables that help us to collect available plaintext (ciphertext) pairs more efficiently and simplify the operations in the online phase.
- The number of bit-conditions ascends to 88 after extending the 14-round impossible differential to attack 24-round LBlock. According to the formulas given in [6], the smallest amount of input (or output) pairs N should be approximately 2^{88} so that the 24-round attack is seemingly unavailable. We lower the high data complexity and make the 24-round attack a success with $2^{77.50}$ encryptions and 2^{59} chosen plaintexts by using our techniques.

Table 1 outlines our impossible differential attack on 24-round LBlock compared with some previous cryptanalysis.

This paper is organized as follows, Sect. 2 reviews the LBlock cipher and investigates detailed differential properties of S-Boxes used in round function.

Table 1. Summary of some main attacks on LBlock

Model	Attacks	Rounds	Time	Data	Memory	Reference
Single-key	Impossible differential	20	$2^{72.7}$	$2^{63}CP$	2^{68}	[23]
		21	$2^{73.7}$	$2^{62.5}CP$	$2^{55.5}$	[12]
		21	$2^{69.5}$	$2^{63}CP$	2^{75}	[8]
		22	$2^{79.28}$	$2^{58}CP$	2^{76}	[8]
		23	$2^{75.36}$	$2^{59}CP$	2^{74}	[6]
		24	$2^{77.50}$	$2^{59}CP$	2^{75}	Sect. 3
	Integral	22	$2^{70.54}$	$2^{64}CP$	N/A	[23]
		22	$2^{71.27}$	$2^{62.1}CP$	2^{35}	[17]
		22	2^{79}	$2^{60}CP$	2^{63}	[16]
	Zero-correlation linear	20	$2^{63.7}$	$2^{64}KP$	2^{64}	[18]
		20	$2^{39.6}$	$2^{63.6}KP$	2^{64}	[18]
		22	2^{70}	$2^{61}KP$	2^{64}	[18]
		23	2^{76}	$2^{62.1}KP$	2^{60}	[20]
	Biclique attack	32	$2^{78.4}$	$2^{52}CP$	2^{8}	[21]
		32	$2^{78.338}$	$2^{2}KP$	$2^{7}FC$	[1]
Related-key	Differential	22	2^{67}	$2^{63.1}RKCP$	N/A	[11]
	Impossible differential	22	2^{70}	$2^{47}RKCP$	N/A	[14]
		23	$2^{78.3}$	$2^{61.4}RKCP$	$2^{61.4}$	[22]

CP: Chosen Plaintext; KP: Known Plaintext; $RKCP$: Related-Key Chosen Plaintext.

We give detailed analysis on 24-round LBlock in Sect. 3. Section 4 concludes the paper.

2 Preliminaries

In the first part of this section, we make a brief description of LBlock. In the second part, we present some detailed properties about LBlock S-Boxes which are helpful to launch our impossible differential attack.

2.1 Description of LBlock

Encryption Algorithm. LBlock adopts a 64-bit block with an 80-bit key, which is a variant of 32-round Feistel network. Let $P = L_0||R_0$ be the 64-bit plaintext, $L_{i-1}||R_{i-1}$ be the input of the i-th round, $L_i||R_i$ be the output, K_i be the subkey of the i-th round, and $L_i = (X_7^i, ..., X_0^i)$, $R_i = (X_{15}^i, ..., X_8^i)$, where $X_j^i (0 \leq j \leq 15)$ are 4-bit nibbles. We denote the j-th nibble subkey of i-th round as k_j^i. Then the data processing procedure is expressed as follows.

1. For $i = 1, 2, ..., 32$, do

$$L_i = F(L_{i-1}, K_i) \oplus (R_{i-1} \lll 8),$$
$$R_i = L_{i-1}$$

2. $C = (R_{32}, L_{32})$ as the 64-bit ciphertext.

Round Function. The round function F of LBlock is composed of three basic operations: subkey addition, S-Box transformation and nibble permutation. There are 8 different 4-bit bijective S-Boxes $(S_7, S_6, ..., S_0)$ in S-Box transformation. The round function is shown in Fig. 1.

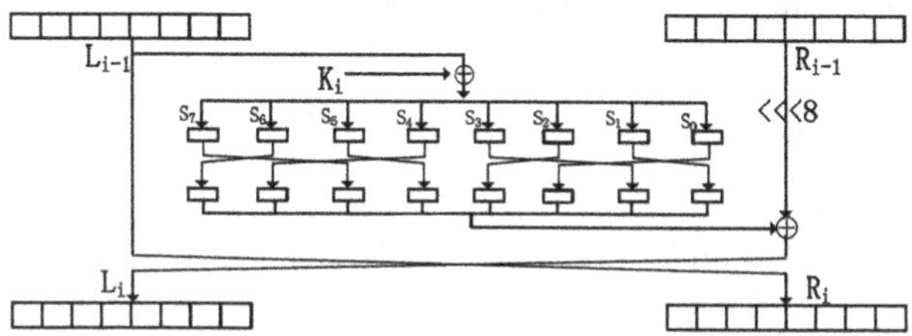

Fig. 1. Round function of LBlock

Key Schedule. The key schedule function takes an 80-bit masterkey K, and produces 32-bit subkeys for each round. Let $K^i (i = 1, ..., 32)$ be an 80-bit internal state for the key schedule function for the i-th round. Then, the 32-bit subkeys $K_i (i = 1, ..., 32)$ are derived as follows.

- $K^1 \leftarrow K$;
- $K_1 \leftarrow K^1[79, ..., 48]$;
- for $i = 2, ..., 32$ do
  - $K^i \leftarrow K^{i-1} \lll 29$;
  - $K^i[79, 78, 77, 76] \leftarrow S_9(K^i[79, 78, 77, 76])$;
  - $K^i[75, 74, 73, 72] \leftarrow S_8(K^i[75, 74, 73, 72])$;
  - $K^i[50, ..., 46] \leftarrow K^i[50, ..., 46] \oplus [i-1]_2$, where $[i-1]_2$ is the binary representation of $i-1$;
  - $K_i \leftarrow K^i[79, ..., 48]$.

2.2 Observations on Differential Properties of S-Boxes

Some differential properties of LBlock S-Boxes have been given in [5]. Let A, B be the input and output of S-Boxes, i.e. $B = S_i(A)$ $(i = 0, ..., 7)$, and $\Delta A, \Delta B$ be the input and output differences respectively. We represent $\Delta A \xrightarrow{S_i} \Delta B$ for the pair $(\Delta A, \Delta B)$ satisfying difference transition of S_i excluding $(\Delta A, \Delta B) = (0, 0)$, which is available for difference transition of S_i.

Property 1. *(from [5]) For any given ΔA and ΔB, the probability $P_r\{\Delta A \xrightarrow{S_i} \Delta B\} = \frac{96}{256} \approx 2^{-1.41}$. For each differential pair $(\Delta A, \Delta B)$ satisfying following conditions,*

$$\begin{cases} S_i(A) \oplus S_i(A \oplus \Delta A) = \Delta B, \\ (\Delta A, \Delta B) \neq (0, 0). \end{cases} \tag{1}$$

there are on average $\frac{240}{96} \approx 2^{1.32}$ values that verify condition (1).

In this paper, we further investigate the detailed differential distribution tables of S-Boxes that draw connections between differences and exact values, and give the more detailed differential properties of LBlock S-Boxes which are useful in impossible differential attack of LBlock similar to the early abort technique proposed by Lu et al. [13]. For example, the detailed differential distribution table of S_0 is given in Table 5 in Appendix A.

Property 2. *For condition (1), the following differential properties of S-Boxes are derived:*

- *If $\Delta A \neq 0$, then the probability $P_r\{\Delta A \xrightarrow{S_i} \Delta B \mid \Delta A \neq 0\} = \frac{96}{240} \approx 2^{-1.32}$. Similarly, $P_r\{\Delta A \xrightarrow{S_i} \Delta B \mid \Delta B \neq 0\} = \frac{96}{240} \approx 2^{-1.32}$.*
- *If $\Delta A \neq 0$ and $\Delta B \neq 0$, then the probability $P_r\{\Delta A \xrightarrow{S_i} \Delta B \mid \Delta A \neq 0, \Delta B \neq 0\} = \frac{96}{225} \approx 2^{-1.22}$.*
- *Furthermore, for condition (1), when input and output differences of a S-Box are known, we could directly get the input values that satisfy the differential transition of the S-Box by looking up the detailed differential distribution tables.*

Example. For the differential equation $\Delta S_1(X_1^0 \oplus k_1^1) \oplus \Delta X_{14}^0 = 0$, and the given $(\Delta X_1^0, \Delta X_{14}^0)$ make the equation hold, we could directly get about $2^{1.32}$ values of $X_1^0 \oplus k_1^1$ by accessing the detailed differential distribution table of S_1. Furthermore, if X_1^0 is known, then corresponding values of k_1^1 that satisfy the differential equation could be also obtained by one table looking up.

3 Impossible Differential Cryptanalysis of 24-Round LBlock

In this section, we describe our attack on 24-round LBlock by utilizing the 14-round impossible differential in [6]. In the remainder of this paper, we denote a zero-difference nibble by "0", nonzero-difference nibble by "1" and unknown-difference (either 0 or 1) by "*". Therefore, the 14-round impossible differential characteristic is represented as: $(00000000, 00001000) \nrightarrow (00000100, 00000000)$.

Before introducing the whole attack, we thoroughly explore the relations of the subkeys and build some precomputation tables. Based on these, we present an efficient data collection and a new key-guessing technique to mount an impossible differential attack on 24-round LBlock.

3.1 Conditions of Extended Impossible Differential Paths

We add 5 rounds to the top and bottom of the 14-round impossible differential respectively to attack 24-round LBlock (see Fig. 2). We find the sufficient nibble conditions to conform the extended 10-round differential propagation. Then,

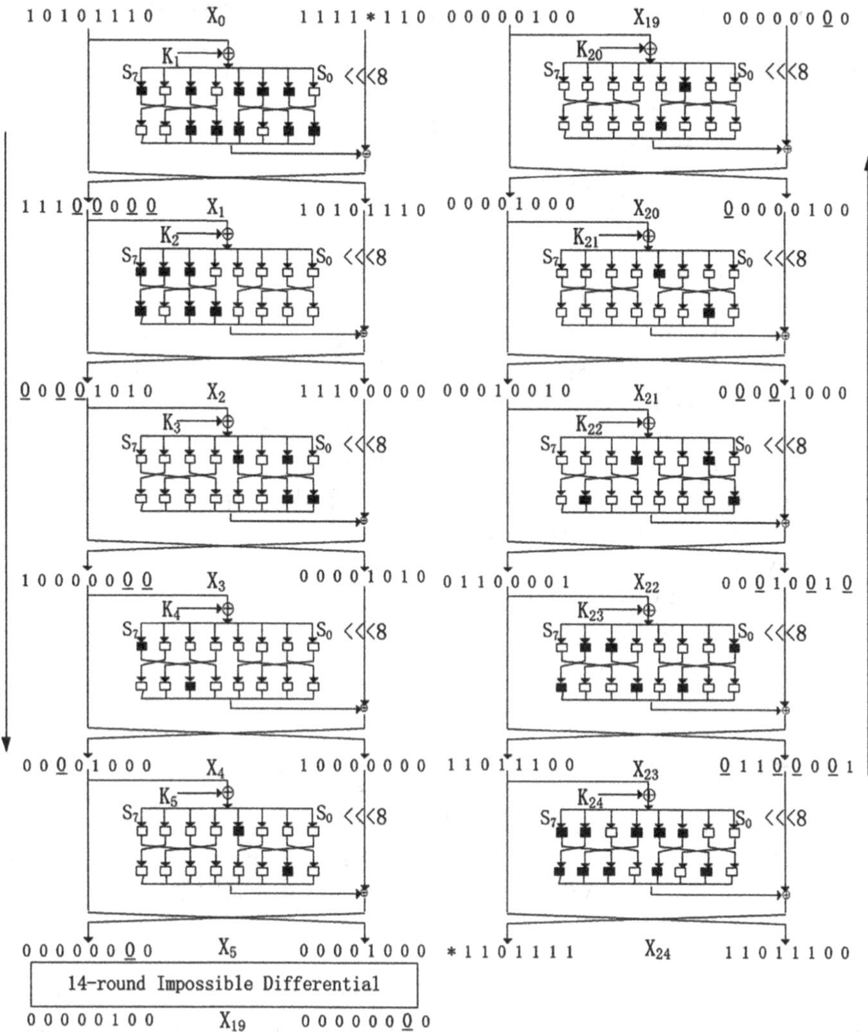

Fig. 2. Impossible differential attack against 24-round LBlock

we deduce the differential equations related to subkeys for chosen plaintext-ciphertext pairs from the nibble conditions. These equations are effective for filtering the incorrect subkey candidates. The acquired conditions, corresponding differential equations and subkeys involved in conditions are listed in Table 2. (**subkeys in bold** mean that the subkeys also involve in some other rounds).

3.2 Relationship Among Involved Subkeys

We reveal that 75 bits of key-information are well enough to deduce all the subkeys involved in the conditions by thoroughly exploring the relations among

Table 2. Differential conditions of extended impossible differential paths

Round	Nibble conditions (differential equations)	Subkeys involved in conditions	Known equations
1	$\Delta X_0^1 = 0 : \Delta S_1(X_1^0 \oplus k_1^1) \oplus \Delta X_{14}^0 = 0$	$\mathbf{k_1^1}$	
	$\Delta X_1^1 = 0 : \Delta S_3(X_3^0 \oplus k_3^1) \oplus \Delta X_{15}^0 = 0$	$\mathbf{k_3^1}$	
	$\Delta X_3^1 = 0 : \Delta S_2(X_2^0 \oplus k_2^1) \oplus \Delta X_9^0 = 0$	$\mathbf{k_2^1}$	
	$\Delta X_4^1 = 0 : \Delta S_5(X_5^0 \oplus k_5^1) \oplus \Delta X_{10}^0 = 0$	$\mathbf{k_5^1}$	
2	$\Delta X_4^2 = 0 : \Delta S_5(X_5^1 \oplus k_5^2) \oplus \Delta X_2^0 = 0$	k_5^2,$\mathbf{k_7^1}$	
	$\Delta X_5^2 = 0 : \Delta S_7(X_7^1 \oplus k_7^2) \oplus \Delta X_3^0 = 0$	k_7^2,k_6^1	$\Delta X_7^1 = \Delta X_{13}^0$
	$\Delta X_7^2 = 0 : \Delta S_6(X_6^1 \oplus k_6^2) \oplus \Delta X_5^0 = 0$	k_6^2,k_4^1	$\Delta X_6^1 = \Delta X_{12}^0$
3	$\Delta X_0^3 = 0 : \Delta S_1(X_1^2 \oplus k_1^3) \oplus \Delta X_{12}^0 = 0$	k_1^3,$\mathbf{k_3^2}$,$\mathbf{k_2^1}$	$\Delta X_1^2 = \Delta X_7^0$
	$\Delta X_1^3 = 0 : \Delta S_3(X_3^2 \oplus k_3^3) \oplus \Delta X_{13}^0 = 0$	k_3^3,k_2^2,k_0^1	$\Delta X_3^2 = \Delta X_1^0$
4	$\Delta X_5^4 = 0 : \Delta S_7(X_7^3 \oplus k_7^4) \oplus \Delta X_1^0 = 0$	k_7^4,k_6^3,k_4^2,$\mathbf{k_5^1}$,$\mathbf{k_7^1}$	$\Delta X_7^3 = \Delta X_5^1$
5	$\Delta X_1^5 = 0$	k_3^5, k_2^4, k_0^3, k_1^2,	$\Delta X_3^4 = \Delta X_7^0$
	$\Delta S_3(X_3^4 \oplus k_3^5) \oplus \Delta X_5^1 = 0$	$\mathbf{k_3^2}$, $\mathbf{k_2^1}$, $\mathbf{k_3^1}$, $\mathbf{k_1^1}$, $\mathbf{k_7^1}$	
23	$\Delta X_9^{23} = 0 : \Delta S_2(X_{10}^{24} \oplus k_2^{24}) \oplus \Delta X_3^{24} = 0$	$\mathbf{k_2^{24}}$	
	$\Delta X_{11}^{23} = 0 : \Delta S_7(X_{15}^{24} \oplus k_7^{24}) \oplus \Delta X_5^{24} = 0$	$\mathbf{k_7^{24}}$	
	$\Delta X_{12}^{23} = 0 : \Delta S_4(X_{12}^{24} \oplus k_4^{24}) \oplus \Delta X_6^{24} = 0$	$\mathbf{k_4^{24}}$	
	$\Delta X_{15}^{23} = 0 : \Delta S_3(X_{11}^{24} \oplus k_3^{24}) \oplus \Delta X_1^{24} = 0$	$\mathbf{k_3^{24}}$	
22	$\Delta X_{10}^{22} = 0 : \Delta S_5(X_{13}^{23} \oplus k_5^{23}) \oplus \Delta X_{12}^{24} = 0$	k_5^{23},$\mathbf{k_6^{24}}$	
	$\Delta X_8^{22} = 0 : \Delta S_0(X_8^{23} \oplus k_0^{23}) \oplus \Delta X_{10}^{24} = 0$	k_0^{23},k_0^{24}	$\Delta X_8^{23} = \Delta X_2^{24}$
	$\Delta X_{13}^{22} = 0 : \Delta S_6(X_{14}^{23} \oplus k_6^{23}) \oplus \Delta X_{15}^{24} = 0$	k_6^{23},k_1^{24}	$\Delta X_{14}^{23} = \Delta X_0^{24}$
21	$\Delta X_{12}^{21} = 0 : \Delta S_4(X_{12}^{22} \oplus k_4^{22}) \oplus \Delta X_0^{24} = 0$	k_4^{22},$\mathbf{k_4^{23}}$, $\mathbf{k_4^{24}}$	$\Delta X_{12}^{22} = \Delta X_{14}^{24}$
	$\Delta X_{14}^{21} = 0 : \Delta S_1(X_9^{22} \oplus k_1^{22}) \oplus \Delta X_2^{24} = 0$	k_1^{22},k_2^{23},k_5^{24}	$\Delta X_9^{22} = \Delta X_{11}^{24}$
20	$\Delta X_{15}^{20} = 0 : \Delta S_3(X_{11}^{21} \oplus k_3^{21}) \oplus \Delta X_{11}^{24} = 0$	k_3^{21},k_7^{22},k_3^{23},$\mathbf{k_7^{24}}$, $\mathbf{k_6^{24}}$	$\Delta X_{11}^{21} = \Delta X_{13}^{23}$
19	$\Delta X_9^{19} = 0$	k_2^{20},k_5^{21},k_6^{22},k_1^{23},	$\Delta X_{10}^{20} = \Delta X_{14}^{24}$
	$\Delta S_2(X_{10}^{20} \oplus k_2^{20}) \oplus \Delta X_{13}^{23} = 0$	$\mathbf{k_4^{23}}$, $\mathbf{k_4^{24}}$, $\mathbf{k_2^{24}}$, $\mathbf{k_3^{24}}$, $\mathbf{k_6^{24}}$	

subkeys. This enable us to find an optimal arrangement for key guessing in key recovery in order to reduce the time complexity of the attack. We show relations among subkeys involved in conditions and the masterkey in Table 3.

For a S-Box S and its input x, we denote the 4 output bits by $(S(x)^0$, $S(x)^1$, $S(x)^2$, $S(x)^3)$, simply as $((x)^0$, $(x)^1$, $(x)^2$, $(x)^3)$. In LBlock, a subkey bit may be both the s-th output bit of a S-Box and the boolean function of partial masterkey bits $K[i \sim j]$. On this occasion, we denote such a bit by $K(i \sim j)^s$. For example, $k_7^2 = S_9(47, 48, 49, 50)$, we denote its 4 bits by $S_9(47, 48, 49, 50)^0$, $S_9(47, 48, 49, 50)^1$, $S_9(47, 48, 49, 50)^2$, $S_9(47, 48, 49, 50)^3$ or simply $(47 \sim 50)^0$, $(47 \sim 50)^1$, $(47 \sim 50)^2$, $(47 \sim 50)^3$ without causing ambiguities.

3.3 Precomputation

Firstly, in the remainder of this paper, we refer a pair that makes an equation hold as an *available pair* for this equation. From Table 2, we observe that

Table 3. Relations among subkeys involved in conditions and masterkeys

Round	Relations between subkeys and masterkeys
1	$\mathbf{k_1^1}$: $(\mathbf{55, 54, 53, 52})$
	$\mathbf{k_3^1}$: $(\mathbf{63, 62, 61, 60})$
	$\mathbf{k_2^1}$: $(\mathbf{59, 58, 57, 56})$
	$\mathbf{k_5^1}$: $(\mathbf{71, 70, 69, 68})$
2	$(k_5^2$: $(42, 41, 40, 39)$, $\mathbf{k_7^1}$: $(\mathbf{79, 78, 77, 76}))$
	k_7^2: $S_9(47, 48, 49, 50)$, k_6^1: $(75, 74, 73, 72)$
	k_6^2: $S_8(43, 44, 45, 46)$, k_4^1: $(67, 66, 65, 64)$
3	k_1^3: $(77, 76, 75, 74)$,$\mathbf{k_3^2}$: $(\mathbf{34, 33, 32, 31})$, $\mathbf{k_2^1}$
	k_3^3: $(5, 4, 3, 2)$, k_2^2: $(30, 29, 28, 27)$, k_0^1: $(51, 50, 49, 48)$
4	k_7^4: $(S_9(69, 70, 71, 72)$, k_6^3: $(S_8(14, 15, 16, 17)$, k_4^2: $(38, 37, 36, 35)$, $\mathbf{k_5^1}, \mathbf{k_7^1}$
5	k_3^5: $(27, 26, 25, 24)$, k_2^4:$(52,51,(S_9(47, 48, 49, 50)^0,S_9(47, 48, 49, 50)^1)$,
	k_0^3: $(73, 72, 71, 70)$, k_1^2: $(26, 25, 24, 23)$, $\mathbf{k_3^2}, \mathbf{k_2^1}, \mathbf{k_3^1}, \mathbf{k_1^1}, \mathbf{k_7^1}$
23	$\mathbf{k_2^{24}}$: $((\mathbf{29 \sim 39})^\mathbf{1}, (\mathbf{29 \sim 39})^\mathbf{2}, (\mathbf{26 \sim 39})^\mathbf{0}, (\mathbf{26 \sim 39})^\mathbf{1})$
	$\mathbf{k_7^{24}}$: $\mathbf{S_9}((\mathbf{47 \sim 61})^\mathbf{0}, (\mathbf{47 \sim 61})^\mathbf{1}, (\mathbf{47 \sim 61})^\mathbf{2}, (\mathbf{47 \sim 61})^\mathbf{3})$
	$\mathbf{k_4^{24}}$: $((\mathbf{36 \sim 46})^\mathbf{0}, (\mathbf{36 \sim 46})^\mathbf{1}, (\mathbf{36 \sim 46})^\mathbf{2}, (\mathbf{33 \sim 46})^\mathbf{0})$
	$\mathbf{k_3^{24}}$: $((\mathbf{33 \sim 46})^\mathbf{1}, (\mathbf{33 \sim 46})^\mathbf{2}, (\mathbf{33 \sim 46})^\mathbf{3}, (\mathbf{29 \sim 39})^\mathbf{0})$
22	k_5^{23}: $((69 \sim 76)^0, (69 \sim 76)^1, (69 \sim 76)^2, (69 \sim 76)^3)$, $\mathbf{k_6^{24}}$: $\mathbf{S_8}((\mathbf{43 \sim 54})^\mathbf{0}, (\mathbf{43 \sim 54})^\mathbf{1}, (\mathbf{43 \sim 54})^\mathbf{2}, (\mathbf{43 \sim 54})^\mathbf{3})$
	k_0^{23}: $((51 \sim 61)^2, (51 \sim 61)^3, (47 \sim 54)^0, 47 \sim 54)^1)$, k_0^{24}: $((22 \sim 32)^2, (22 \sim 32)^3, (18 \sim 25)^0, (18 \sim 25)^1)$
	k_6^{23}: $S_8((77 \sim 3)^3, (73 \sim 76)^0, (73 \sim 76)^1, (73 \sim 76)^2)$, k_1^{24}: $(26 \sim 39)^2, (26 \sim 39)^3, (22 \sim 32)^0, (22 \sim 32)^1)$
21	k_4^{22}: $((14 \sim 21)^0$,$(14 \sim 21)^1$,$(14 \sim 21)^2$,$(11 \sim 21)^0)$, $\mathbf{k_4^{23}}$: $((\mathbf{65 \sim 72})^\mathbf{0}, (\mathbf{65 \sim 72})^\mathbf{1}, (\mathbf{65 \sim 72})^\mathbf{2}, (\mathbf{62 \sim 72})^\mathbf{0})$, $\mathbf{k_4^{24}}$
	k_1^{22}: $((4 \sim 17)^2, (4 \sim 17)^3, (0 \sim 10)^0, (0 \sim 10)^1)$, k_2^{23}: $((58 \sim 68)^1, (58 \sim 68)^2, (55 \sim 68)^0, (55 \sim 68)^1)$, k_5^{24}: $((40 \sim 50)^0, (40 \sim 50)^1, (40 \sim 50)^2, (40 \sim 50)^3)$
20	k_3^{21}: $(40 \sim 50)^1, (40 \sim 50)^2, (40 \sim 50)^3, (36 \sim 46)^0)$, k_7^{22}: $(26 \sim 39)^0, (26 \sim 39)^1, (26 \sim 39)^2, (26 \sim 39)^3)$, k_3^{23}: $(62 \sim 72)^1, (62 \sim 72)^2, (62 \sim 72)^3, (58 \sim 68)^0)$, $\mathbf{k_7^{24}}, \mathbf{k_6^{24}}$
19	k_2^{20}: $((65 \sim 72)^1, (65 \sim 72)^2, (62 \sim 72)^0, (62 \sim 72)^1)$, k_5^{21}: $((47 \sim 54)^0, (47 \sim 54)^1, (47 \sim 54)^2, (47 \sim 54)^3)$, k_6^{22}: $((22 \sim 32)^0, (22 \sim 32)^1, (22 \sim 32)^2, (22 \sim 32)^3)$, k_1^{23}: $((55 \sim 68)^2, (55 \sim 68)^3, (51 \sim 61)^0, (51 \sim 61)^1)$, $\mathbf{k_4^{23}}, \mathbf{k_4^{24}}, \mathbf{k_2^{24}}, \mathbf{k_3^{24}}, \mathbf{k_6^{24}}$

some conditions of extended impossible differential paths are closely related rather than independent. The input differences of some conditions could also be output differences of other conditions, and plaintext- (ciphertext-) differences have determined whether corresponding conditions held. Based on these, we construct well precomputation tables by combining some related conditions to provide higher efficiency for collecting available pairs. The connections between input/output differences and conditions of active S-Boxes are depicted in Fig. 3.

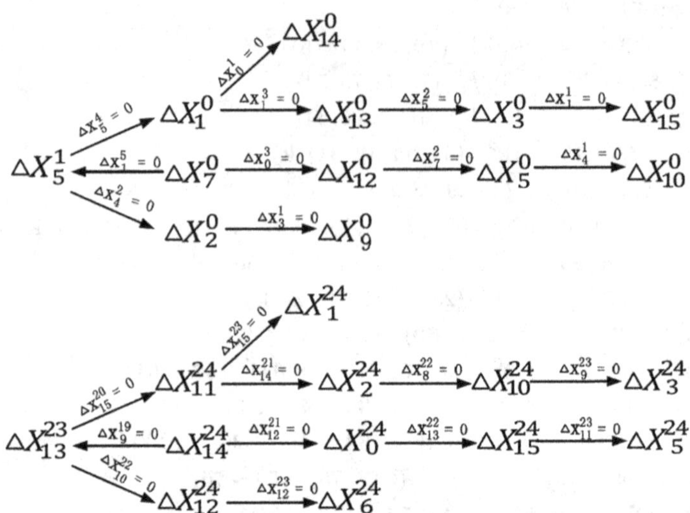

Fig. 3. Connections between input/output differences and conditions

Secondly, in order to reduce time complexity of key recovery phase, we set up five precomputation tables TK_i $(i = 1, 2, 3, 4, 5)$. When some key bits in a condition equation have been known, the other related key bits could be obtained by one table looking up rather than redundant online computations.

Precomputation Tables of Plaintext-Pairs. We first consider three conditions ($\Delta X_1^3 = 0$, $\Delta X_5^2 = 0$, $\Delta X_1^1 = 0$), and deduce follow equations,

$$\Delta S_3(X_3^2 \oplus k_3^3) \oplus \Delta X_{13}^0 = 0, \tag{2}$$

$$\Delta S_7(X_7^1 \oplus k_7^2) \oplus \Delta X_3^0 = 0, \tag{3}$$

$$\Delta S_3(X_3^0 \oplus k_3^1) \oplus \Delta X_{15}^0 = 0. \tag{4}$$

Since $\Delta X_3^2 = \Delta X_1^0$ and $\Delta X_7^1 = \Delta X_{13}^0$, the Eq. (2) holds with probability $2^{-1.41}$ for any given $(\Delta X_1^0, \Delta X_{13}^0)$ according to Property 1. When (2) holds, it is easy to verify that $\Delta X_{13}^0 \neq 0$. In this case, (3) holds with probability $2^{-1.32}$ according to Property 2. Similarly, the Eq. (4) holds with probability $2^{-1.32}$. Therefore, for any given $(\Delta X_1^0, \Delta X_{13}^0, \Delta X_3^0, \Delta X_{15}^0)$, all the three equations hold with probability $2^{-4.05}$. That is to say, for each value of $(X_1^0, X_{13}^0, X_3^0, X_{15}^0)$, there are about

$2^{11.95}$ values of $(X_1^0{\prime}, X_{13}^0{\prime}, X_3^0{\prime}, X_{15}^0{\prime})$ such that the corresponding differences $(\Delta X_1^0, \Delta X_{13}^0, \Delta X_3^0, \Delta X_{15}^0)$ make all these three equations hold.

A table T_1 on nibbles $(X_1^0, X_{13}^0, X_3^0, X_{15}^0)$ is set up. The row address of T_1 is natually

$$i = X_1^0 \| X_{13}^0 \| X_3^0 \| X_{15}^0, \tag{5}$$

the column index is

$$j = \Delta X_1^0 \| \Delta X_{13}^0 \| \Delta X_3^0 \| \Delta X_{15}^0 \tag{6}$$

where the nibble difference $(\Delta X_1^0, \Delta X_{13}^0, \Delta X_3^0, \Delta X_{15}^0)$ conforms that all the three equations hold. We store $(X_1^0 \oplus \Delta X_1^0, X_{13}^0 \oplus \Delta X_{13}^0, X_3^0 \oplus \Delta X_3^0, X_{15}^0 \oplus \Delta X_{15}^0)$ in the corresponding location of table T_1, denoted by $T_1(i,j)$. Therefore, there are 2^{16} rows, and about $2^{11.95}$ columns in each row of table T_1. The size of the table T_1 is about $2^{16} \times 2^{11.95} = 2^{27.95}$ words.

In the same way, considering the three equations

$$\Delta S_1(X_1^2 \oplus k_1^3) \oplus \Delta X_{12}^0 = 0,$$
$$\Delta S_6(X_6^1 \oplus k_6^2) \oplus \Delta X_5^0 = 0,$$
$$\Delta S_5(X_5^0 \oplus k_5^1) \oplus \Delta X_{10}^0 = 0$$

we also set up a table T_2 with $(X_7^0, X_{12}^0, X_5^0, X_{10}^0)$ as row address, index of difference $(\Delta X_7^0, \Delta X_{12}^0, \Delta X_5^0, \Delta X_{10}^0)$ satisfying the three equations as column address.

Precomputation Tables of Ciphertext-Pairs. We know that the three conditions $(\Delta X_{14}^{21} = 0, \Delta X_8^{22} = 0, \Delta X_9^{23} = 0)$ in Table 2 hold with probability $2^{-4.05}$ for any given $(\Delta X_{11}^{24}, \Delta X_2^{24}, \Delta X_{10}^{24}, \Delta X_3^{24})$. A precomputation table T_3 is set up with

$$i = \Delta X_{11}^{24} \| \Delta X_2^{24} \| \Delta X_{10}^{24} \| \Delta X_3^{24} \tag{7}$$

being index and $T_3(i) = 1$ when $(\Delta X_{11}^{24}, \Delta X_2^{24}, \Delta X_{10}^{24}, \Delta X_3^{24})$ satisfy the three conditions, otherwise $T_3(i) = 0$. There are about $2^{11.95}$ "1"s out of 2^{16} locations in table T_3. In other words, ciphertext pair (C, C') is an available pair for the characteristic in Fig. 2 only if their nibble difference satisfying $T_3(i) = 1$ where i is defined as (7).

In the same way, for $(\Delta X_{14}^{24}, \Delta X_0^{24}, \Delta X_{15}^{24}, \Delta X_5^{24})$, we also set up a table T_4.

Precomputation Tables of Key Bits. For condition $\Delta X_5^2 = 0$ in round 2, by partially decrypting 2 rounds, we deduce that

$$\begin{cases} \Delta S_7(X_7^1 \oplus k_7^2) \oplus \Delta X_3^0 = 0, \\ X_7^1 = S_6(X_6^0 \oplus k_6^1) \oplus X_{13}^0, \\ \Delta X_7^1 = \Delta X_{13}^0. \end{cases} \tag{8}$$

According to the detailed difference properties of S-Box S_7, we could set up a precomputation table TK_1 with $(\Delta X_{13}^0, \Delta X_3^0, X_6^0, X_{13}^0)$ as row address, store (k_7^2, k_6^1) satisfying (8) in the corresponding row. Therefore, there are 2^{16} rows, and about $2^{5.32}$ bytes in each row of table TK_1.

By using the same method, we also set up other precomputation tables used in key recovery phase, and list them in Table 6 in Appendix A.

3.4 Data Collection

In the data collection phase, we adopt the idea which is similar to the "preliminary sieving of pairs" in [5], but our method only needs to process those available pairs satisfying that all equations hold. By dividing the whole 2^{64} plaintexts into several sets according to some plaintext- and ciphertext-nibbles, and accessing precomputation tables T_i $(i = 1, 2, 3, 4)$, we apply the divide-and-conquer technique to collect available plaintext-ciphertext pairs such that the corresponding equations hold. This enables us to reduce the time complexity of collecting available pairs.

We demonstrate the available-pair-collecting procedure as follows.

1. Encrypt 2^n sets of plaintexts whose nibbles X_0^0, X_4^0, X_6^0, X_8^0 are constants while other nibbles traverse all 2^{48} values. We therefore acquire 2^{n+48} plaintexts P and their corresponding ciphertexts C.
2. Within each set, we collect the available pairs satisfying the extended conditions by taking the following steps:
   (a) The plaintexts/ciphertexts (P, C) of every set are divided into 2^{48} subsets according to (X_4^{24}, X_8^{24}, X_9^{24}, X_{13}^{24}, X_1^0, X_{13}^0, X_3^0, X_{15}^0, X_7^0, X_{12}^0, X_5^0, X_{10}^0). There is about 1 plaintext/ciphertext in every subset.
   (b) For every subset A, we find corresponding subset A' by accessing tables T_1, T_2, and combine each element of A with each element of A' to construct pairs. Furthermore, for each obtained pair, we verify whether this pair is available by accessing tables T_3 and T_4. Therefore, we construct about $2^{48-1} \times 2^{11.95\times2} \times 2^{-4.05\times2} \approx 2^{62.8}$ pairs for each set, and need about $(2^{48+11.95\times2}) \times 2 \approx 2^{72.9}$ times table looking-up equivalent to $2^{72.9}/(8\times24) \approx 2^{65.3}$ 24-round encryptions.
   (c) For the $2^{62.8}$ remaining pairs, we verify whether condition equations ($\Delta X_0^1 = 0$, $\Delta X_3^1 = 0$, $\Delta X_{12}^{23} = 0$, $\Delta X_{15}^{23} = 0$) in Table 2 hold by testing corresponding plaintext (ciphertext) nibble differences appeared in conditions. According to Properties 1 and 2, there are about $2^{62.8} \times 2^{-1.41\times2-1.32\times2} \approx 2^{57.34}$ pairs remaining for each set.

In data collection phase, we could collect about $2^{n+57.34}$ pairs, the complexity of the data collection is about $2^{n+65.3}$ 24-round encryptions.

3.5 Key Recovery

By thoroughly exploring the relations of subkeys, we find that many key bits are determined accordingly only by solving some simple equations after some key bits have been guessed. Based on these, we present an optimal arrangement for guessing key bits and identifying wrong guesses as early as possible. With the optimal arrangement of guessing key and precomputation tables, we effectively reduce the key-guessing space in the procedure of "wrong key filtering" to reduce the time complexity of key recovery phase. We repeatedly follow steps of "wrong key filtering" for 2^n sets to calculate and discard wrong keys as many as possible, and exhaustively search the rest of the equivalent keys. The masterkey will be recovered with the key schedule after discarding wrong keys.

Wrong Key Filtering. From the round function of LBlock, we know that the calculations of X_5^1, ΔX_5^1, X_{13}^{23} and ΔX_{13}^{23} involved in the remaining six equations in Table 2 depend on (k_7^1, k_6^{24}). Hence, we guess (k_7^1, k_6^{24}) in advance to only store pairs that satisfy these 6 conditions. For each value of guessed (k_7^1, k_6^{24}), there are about $2^{57.34-1.22\times4-1.32\times2} \approx 2^{49.82}$ pairs such that these 6 equations hold. Therefore, within each set, we have $N_1 = 2^{49.82} \times 2^8 \approx 2^{57.82}$ available pairs with their corresponding $(k_7^1,\ k_6^{24})$ satisfying that all the equations in Table 2 have solutions.

For an available pair, we further guess other subkey bits and filter wrong keys by taking the following steps.

1. For conditions $\Delta X_0^1 = 0$, we get about $2^{1.32}$ values of k_1^1 with corresponding X_0^1 by accessing differential distribution table of S_1. Similar method is applied for 9 conditions ($\Delta X_1^1 = 0$, $\Delta X_3^1 = 0$, $\Delta X_4^1 = 0$, $\Delta X_4^2 = 0$, $\Delta X_9^{23} = 0$, $\Delta X_{11}^{23} = 0$, $\Delta X_{12}^{23} = 0$, $\Delta X_{15}^{23} = 0$, $\Delta X_{10}^{22} = 0$) in rounds 1, 2, 23, and 22 one by one, and we get about $2^{1.32}$ values for k_3^1, k_2^1, k_5^1, k_5^2, k_2^{24}, k_7^{24}, k_4^{24}, k_3^{24}, k_5^{23} with corresponding X_1^1, X_3^1, X_4^1, X_4^2, X_9^{23}, X_{11}^{23}, X_{12}^{23}, X_{15}^{23}, X_{10}^{22} respectively. For 2 conditions ($\Delta X_5^2 = 0$, $\Delta X_7^2 = 0$) in round 2, we get about $2^{5.32}$ values of $(k_7^2,\ k_6^1)$ with $(X_5^2,\ X_7^1)$ and $2^{5.32}$ values of $(k_6^2,\ k_4^1)$ with $(X_7^2,\ X_6^1)$ by accessing the corresponding precomputation tables TK_1,TK_2 respectively.
2. In this step, we combine partial obtained subkeys to diminish the candidate key space. Firstly, because k_5^{23} is determined by k_7^1, k_5^1, $(k_7^2,\ k_6^1)$ according to relations among subkeys, we combine them to get $2^{(1.32\times3)}$ values of (k_7^1, k_5^1, k_7^2, k_6^1, k_5^{23}) and corresponding key information $K[47 \sim 50, 68 \sim 79]$. Secondly, we get $2^{(1.32\times5+1)}$ values of $K[43 \sim 55, 64 \sim 79]$ by combining them with k_1^1, $(k_6^2,\ k_4^1)$ and guessing $K[51]$ to verify k_6^{24}. Thirdly, We get $2^{(1.32\times8-3)}$ values of $K[43 \sim 79]$ by further combining k_2^1, k_3^1 to verify k_7^{24}. In the end, we get $2^{(1.32\times9-3)}$ values of $K[39 \sim 79]$ by combining them with k_5^2.
3. For every subkey candidate obtained in step 2, we deduce k_3^{23}, $k_3^{21}[0,1,2]$ with corresponding X_{15}^{22} by the key schedule and partial decryptions. For condition $\Delta X_{15}^{20} = 0$ in round 20, we obtain about $2^{(1.32+1)}$ values of $(k_7^{22},\ k_3^{21}[3])$ by accessing table TK_3. Therefore, we get about $2^{(1.32\times10-2)}$ values of $K[39 \sim 79]$, $K(26 \sim 39)^0$, $K(26 \sim 39)^1$, $K(26 \sim 39)^2$, $K(26 \sim 39)^3$, $K(36 \sim 46)^0$ in total.
4. Similarly, we get about $2^{(1.32\times13-6)}$ values of $K[26 \sim 79]$ by guessing 1 bit $K(26 \sim 32)^3$ and combining obtained subkeys of step 4 with k_2^{24}, k_4^{24}, k_3^{24} one by one. Then, we apply obtained values to verify condition $\Delta X_0^3 = 0$ in round 3 and get about $2^{1.32\times14-10}$ values of $K[26 \sim 79]$ with corresponding X_1^2.
5. We further compute k_1^{23}, k_4^{23}, k_5^{21}, k_2^{20} and X_{12}^{22}, X_{14}^{22} with the knowledge of the subkeys. For condition $\Delta X_9^{19} = 0$ in round 19, we get about $2^{1.32}$ values of k_6^{22} by accessing tables TK_4 for each one of guessed key and plaintext/ciphertext informations obtained. Because $K(26 \sim 32)^3$ could also be deduced from k_6^{22}, we get $2^{(1.32\times15-11)}$ values of $K[26 \sim 79]$, $K(22 \sim 32)^0$, $K(22 \sim 32)^1$, $K(22 \sim 32)^2$, $K(22 \sim 32)^3$.
6. Under each one of obtained subkeys of step 5, we deduce k_1^{24} and X_{14}^{23}. For condition $\Delta X_{13}^{22} = 0$ in round 22, and get about $2^{1.32}$ values of k_6^{23} by accessing the differential distribution table of S_6. Because k_6^{23} can also be computed from $K[73 \sim 79]$ and $(0 \sim 3)^3$ according to key schedule, we get about $2^{(1.32\times16-14)}$ values of $K[26 \sim 79]$, $K(22 \sim 32)^0$, $K(22 \sim 32)^1$, $K(22 \sim 32)^2$, $K(22 \sim 32)^3$, $K(0 \sim 3)^3$. Similar method is applied to $\Delta X_8^{22} = 0$, with repeated 2 bits of k_0^{24}, we get $2^{(1.32\times17-16)}$ values of

$K[26 \sim 79]$, $K(22 \sim 32)^0$, $K(22 \sim 32)^1$, $K(22 \sim 32)^2$, $K(22 \sim 32)^3$, $K(0 \sim 3)^3$, $K(18 \sim 25)^0$, $K(18 \sim 25)^1$.

7. We can deduce $K[22 \sim 25]$ by guessing $K(22 \sim 25)^3$ and above subkeys obtained, thus k_2^4, k_0^3 and k_1^2 and corresponding X_0^2, X_2^3, X_3^4 are known. For $\Delta X_1^5 = 0$ in round 5, we get about $2^{1.32}$ values of k_3^5 for each one of subkeys obtained by accessing the differential distribution table of S_3. Because 3 bits of k_3^5 are repeated, then we get $2^{(1.32\times18-19)}$ values of $K[22 \sim 79]$, $K(0 \sim 3)^3$, $K(18 \sim 25)^0$, $K(18 \sim 25)^1$.
8. Similarly, we can acquire key materials step by step as follows:
   (a) For equation $\Delta X_5^4 = 0$ in round 4, we get $2^{(1.32\times19-19)}$ values of $K[14 \sim 17, 22 \sim 79], K(0 \sim 3)^3, K(18 \sim 25)^0, K(18 \sim 25)^1$ by TK_5.
   (b) For $\Delta X_{12}^{21} = 0$ in round 21, we get $2^{(1.32\times20-19)}$ values of $K[14 \sim 17, 22 \sim 79], K(0 \sim 3)^3, K(18 \sim 25)^0, K(18 \sim 25)^1, K(14 \sim 21)^0, K(14 \sim 21)^1, K(14 \sim 21)^2, K(11 \sim 21)^0$.
   (c) For $\Delta X_{14}^{21} = 0$ in round 21, we get $2^{(1.32\times21-21)}$ values of $K[14 \sim 17, 22 \sim 79], K(0 \sim 3)^3, K(18 \sim 25)^0, K(18 \sim 25)^1, K(18 \sim 21)^3, K(11 \sim 21)^0, K(4 \sim 17)^2, K(4 \sim 17)^3, K(0 \sim 10)^0, K(0 \sim 10)^1$.
   (d) For $\Delta X_1^3 = 0$ in round 3, we get $2^{(1.32\times22-21)}$ values of $K[2 \sim 5, 14 \sim 17, 22 \sim 79], K(0 \sim 3)^3, K(18 \sim 25)^0, K(18 \sim 25)^1, K(18 \sim 21)^3, K(11 \sim 21)^0, K(4 \sim 17)^2, K(4 \sim 17)^3, K(0 \sim 10)^0, K(0 \sim 10)^1$.

Therefore, for each available pair, there are about $2^{1.32\times22} \times 2^{-21} \approx 2^{8.04}$ values of 75-bit keys ($K[2 \sim 5, 14 \sim 17, 22 \sim 79]$, $K(0 \sim 3)^3$, $K(18 \sim 25)^0$, $K(18 \sim 25)^1$, $K(18 \sim 21)^3$, $K(11 \sim 21)^0$, $K(4 \sim 17)^2$, $K(4 \sim 17)^3$, $K(0 \sim 10)^0$, $K(0 \sim 10)^1$) to be discarded.

Exhaustive Search. For every remaining candidate key after filtering wrong keys, we search the rest of key bits to recover the masterkey as follows.

According to key schedule, we deduce keys ($K(4 \sim 10)^3$,$K[0,1,2,3]$) from each one of candidate keys ($K(0 \sim 10)^0$, $K(0 \sim 10)^1$), $K(0 \sim 3)^3$) and guessed 2-bit ($K(0 \sim 10)^2$, $K(0 \sim 10)^3$). Because subkeys $K[2,3]$ are also involved in candidate subkeys, we get about 1 value of ($K(4 \sim 10)^3$,K[0,1]) for each remaining candidate key. Similarly, 2 values of K[18, 19, 20, 21], 1 value of ($K(7 \sim 17)^3$, $K(7 \sim 10)^3$, 6), and 2^4 values of subkeys $K[7, 8, 9, 10, 11, 12, 13]$ would be deduce in sequence.

Hence, there are 2^5 values of 80-bit masterkey left to be exhaustively searched by 24-round encryptions test for every remained candidate subkey.

3.6 Complexity Analysis

From wrong key filtering phase, there are about $2^{(1.32\times22-21)} = 2^{8.04}$ values of the 75-bit keys to be discarded for each one of available pairs. In other words, for every available pair, a key is discarded with probability $P_1 = 2^{8.04-75} = 2^{-66.96}$. Thus, we let N be the amount of available plaintext-ciphertext pairs such that all equations hold rather than the previous sense of amount of pairs only satisfying input and output differences. By repeatedly processing with N different available plaintext-ciphertext pairs, the probability that one key is kept in the candidate set is

$$P = (1 - P_1)^N \simeq e^{-N\times P_1}.$$

Table 4. Complexity in wrong key filtering

Step	Time complexity
1	$N \times (\frac{2^{1.32}\times 10}{8\times 24} + \frac{2^{5.32}\times 2}{8\times 24})$ 24-round encryptions
2	$N \times (\frac{2^{(1.32\times 3+4)}}{8\times 24} + \frac{2^{(1.32\times 5+5)}}{8\times 24} + \frac{2^{(1.32\times 8+1)}}{8\times 24} + \frac{2^{(1.32\times 9-3)}}{8\times 24})$ 24-round encryptions
3	$N \times \frac{2^{(1.32\times 9-3)}\times 4}{8\times 24}$ 24-round encryptions
4	$N \times (\frac{2^{(1.32\times 11-2)}}{8\times 24} + \frac{2^{(1.32\times 12-4)}}{8\times 24} + \frac{2^{(1.32\times 13-4)}}{8\times 24} + \frac{2^{(1.32\times 13-6)}}{8\times 24}$ 24-round encryptions
5	$N \times \frac{2^{(1.32\times 14-10)}\times 8}{8\times 24}$ 24-round encryptions
6	$N \times (\frac{2^{(1.32\times 15-11)}\times 2}{8\times 24} + \frac{2^{(1.32\times 16-14)}\times 2}{8\times 24})$ 24-round encryptions
7	$N \times \frac{2^{(1.32\times 17-15)}\times 5}{8\times 24}$ 24-round encryptions
8	$N \times (\frac{2^{(1.32\times 18-19)}}{8\times 24} + \frac{2^{(1.32\times 19-19)}}{8\times 24} + \frac{2^{(1.32\times 20-19)}}{8\times 24} + \frac{2^{(1.32\times 21-21)}}{8\times 24})$ 24-round encryptions

When $N = \frac{2^{1.86}}{P_1} = 2^{68.82}$, we calculate:

$$P \simeq e^{2^{1.86}} \approx 2^{5.23},$$
$$n = N - N_1 = 68.82 - 57.82 = 11.$$

Thus we need $C = 2^{11+48} = 2^{59}$ plaintexts. The complexity of data collection is about $2^{65.3+11} = 2^{76.3}$ 24-round encryption. The complexity of exhaustive search is about $2^{80-2^{5.76}=2^{74.77}}$ 24-round encryption tests.

In the following Table 4 , we discuss the time complexity of each step in wrong key filtering phase.

From Table 4, we know that the total time complexity of wrong key filtering is about $2^{68.82+7.4} = 2^{76.22}$ 24-round encryptions.

Therefore, the total time complexity of the impossible differential attack on 24-round LBlock is: $2^{76.3}+2^{76.22}+2^{74.77} \approx 2^{77.50}$ 24-round encryptions. Its data complexity is 2^{59} chosen plaintexts.

4 Conclusion

In this paper, we propose a 24-round impossible differential attack on LBlock, one round more than the best previous result. This attack is achieved by employing several advanced techniques including dynamic key-guessing, more detailed properties of S-Boxes, optimal key-guessing arrangement etc. This attack is, to the best of our knowledge, the best result on LBlock (except biclique attacks) in terms of the number of attacked rounds.

A Detailed Differences Distribution of S-Box and Precomoutation Tables

Table 5. Distribution of input and output differences of S_0

Input difference	Values satisfying difference propagation	Available number	Unavailable number
0	(1, 2, 3, 4, 5, 6, 7, 8, 9, 10, 11, 12, 13, 14, 15), 0, 0, 0, 0, 0, 0, 0, 0, 0, 0, 0, 0, 0, 0, 0	0	16
1	0, (6, 7, 12, 13), 0, (8, 9), 0, 0, 0, (0, 1), 0, (4, 5, 14, 15), 0, (10, 11), 0, 0, 0, (2, 3)	6	10
2	0, (0, 2, 9, 11), 0, (13, 15), 0, 0, 0, (4, 6), 0, (1, 3, 8, 10), 0, (12, 14), 0, 0, 0, (5, 7)	6	10
3	0, 0, (8, 11, 12, 15), 0, 0, 0, (1, 2, 4, 7), 0, 0, 0, (9, 10, 13, 14), 0, 0, 0, (0, 3, 5, 6), 0	4	12
4	0, 0, 0, (0, 4), (9, 10, 13, 14), (2, 6), (8, 11, 12, 15), 0, 0, 0, 0, (3, 7), 0, (1, 5), 0, 0	6	10
5	0, 0, 0, 0, (1, 2, 4, 7), (9, 12), 0, (8, 13), 0, 0, (0, 3, 5, 6), 0, 0, (10, 15), 0, (11, 14)	6	10
6	0, 0, (1, 2, 4, 7), 0, (0, 3, 5, 6), (11, 13), 0, (9, 15), 0, 0, 0, 0, 0, (8, 14), 0, (10, 12)	6	10
7	0, 0, 0, (1, 6), (8, 11, 12, 15), (0, 7), 0, 0, 0, 0, 0, (2, 5), 0, (3, 4), (9, 10, 13, 14), 0	6	10
8	0, 0, (5, 13), (3, 11), 0, 0, (6, 14), (2, 10), 0, 0, (4, 12), (1, 9), 0, 0, (7, 15), (0, 8)	8	8
9	0, 0, 0, (5, 12), 0, 0, 0, (7, 14), (1, 3, 8, 10), 0, 0, (4, 13), (0, 2, 9, 11), 0, 0, (6, 15)	6	10
10	0, (4, 5, 14, 15), (3, 9), 0, 0, 0, (0, 10), 0, 0, 0, (1, 11), 0, 0, (6, 7, 12, 13), (2, 8), 0	6	10
11	0, (1, 3, 8, 10), 0, 0, 0, 0, 0, 0, (4, 5, 14, 15), 0, 0, 0, (6, 7, 12, 13), (0, 2, 9, 11), 0, 0	4	12
12	0, 0, (6, 10), (2, 14), 0, (3, 15), (5, 9), 0, (7, 11), (0, 12), 0, 0, (4, 8), 0, 0, (1, 13)	8	8
13	0, 0, 0, (7, 10), 0, (5, 8), 0, 0, (0, 13), (6, 11), (2, 15), 0, (3, 14), 0, (1, 12), (4, 9)	8	8
14	0, 0, (0, 14), 0, 0, (4, 10), (3, 13), (5, 11), (2, 12), (7, 9), 0, (6, 8), (1, 15), 0, 0, 0	8	8
15	0, 0, 0, 0, 0, (1, 14), 0, (3, 12), (6, 9), (2, 13), (7, 8), (0, 15), (5, 10), 0, (4, 11), 0	8	8

Table 6. Precomputation tables of keys

Table	Index	Content	Size
TK_1	$(\Delta X_{13}^0, \Delta X_3^0, X_6^0, X_{13}^0)$	(k_7^2, k_6^1)	$2^{16} \times 2^{5.32}$
TK_2	$(\Delta X_{12}^0, \Delta X_5^0, X_4^0, X_{12}^0)$	(k_6^2, k_4^1)	$2^{16} \times 2^{5.32}$
TK_3	$(\Delta X_{13}^{23}, \Delta X_{11}^{24}, X_{15}^{22}, X_{13}^{23}, k_3^{21}[0,1,2])$	$(k_7^{22}, k_3^{21}[3])$	$2^{19} \times 2^{2.32}$
TK_4	$(\Delta X_{14}^{24}, \Delta X_{13}^{23}, X_{14}^{22}, X_{15}^{23} \oplus k_5^{21}, X_{12}^{22} \oplus k_2^{20})$	k_6^{22}	$2^{20} \times 2^{1.32}$
TK_5	$(\Delta X_5^1, \Delta X_1^0, X_6^2, X_5^1 \oplus k_7^4)$	k_6^3	$2^{16} \times 2^{1.32}$

References

1. AlTawy, R., Tolba, M., Youssef, A.M.: A higher order key partitioning attack with application to LBlock. In: Hajji, S.E., Nitaj, A., Carlet, C., Souidi, E.M. (eds.) C2SI 2015. LNCS, vol. 9084, pp. 215–227. Springer, Heidelberg (2015)
2. Beaulieu, R., Shors, D., Smith, J., Treatman-Clark, S., Weeks, B., Wingers, L.: The SIMON and SPECK families of lightweight block ciphers. IACR Cryptology ePrint Archive 2013/404 (2013)
3. Biham, E., Biryukov, A., Shamir, A.: Cryptanalysis of Skipjack reduced to 31 rounds using impossible differentials. In: Stern, J. (ed.) EUROCRYPT 1999. LNCS, vol. 1592, p. 12. Springer, Heidelberg (1999)

4. Bogdanov, A.A., Knudsen, L.R., Leander, G., Paar, C., Poschmann, A., Robshaw, M., Seurin, Y., Vikkelsoe, C.: PRESENT: an ultra-lightweight block cipher. In: Paillier, P., Verbauwhede, I. (eds.) CHES 2007. LNCS, vol. 4727, pp. 450–466. Springer, Heidelberg (2007)
5. Boura, C., Minier, M., Naya-Plasencia, M., Suder, V.: Improved impossible differential attacks against round-reduced LBlock. Cryptology ePrint Archive, Report 2014/279 (2014)
6. Boura, C., Naya-Plasencia, M., Suder, V.: Scrutinizing and improving impossible differential attacks: applications to CLEFIA, Camellia, LBlock and SIMON. In: Sarkar, P., Iwata, T. (eds.) ASIACRYPT 2014. LNCS, vol. 8873, pp. 179–199. Springer, Heidelberg (2014)
7. Guo, J., Peyrin, T., Poschmann, A., Robshaw, M.: The LED block cipher. In: Preneel, B., Takagi, T. (eds.) CHES 2011. LNCS, vol. 6917, pp. 326–341. Springer, Heidelberg (2011)
8. Karakoç, F., Demirci, H., Harmancı, A.E.: Impossible differential cryptanalysis of reduced-round LBlock. In: Askoxylakis, I., Pöhls, H.C., Posegga, J. (eds.) WISTP 2012. LNCS, vol. 7322, pp. 179–188. Springer, Heidelberg (2012)
9. Knudsen, L.: DEAL - a 128-bit block cipher. In: NIST AES Proposal (1998)
10. Li, Z., Zhang, B., Yao, Y., Lin, D.: Cube cryptanalysis of LBlock with noisy leakage. In: Kwon, T., Lee, M.-K., Kwon, D. (eds.) ICISC 2012. LNCS, vol. 7839, pp. 141–155. Springer, Heidelberg (2013)
11. Liu, S., Gong, Z., Wang, L.: Improved related-key differential attacks on reduced-round LBlock. In: Chim, T.W., Yuen, T.H. (eds.) ICICS 2012. LNCS, vol. 7618, pp. 58–69. Springer, Heidelberg (2012)
12. Liu, Y., Gu, D., Liu, Z., Li, W.: Impossible differential attacks on reduced-round LBlock. In: Ryan, M.D., Smyth, B., Wang, G. (eds.) ISPEC 2012. LNCS, vol. 7232, pp. 97–108. Springer, Heidelberg (2012)
13. Lu, J., Kim, J.-S., Keller, N., Dunkelman, O.: Improving the efficiency of impossible differential cryptanalysis of reduced camellia and MISTY1. In: Malkin, T. (ed.) CT-RSA 2008. LNCS, vol. 4964, pp. 370–386. Springer, Heidelberg (2008)
14. Minier, M., Naya-Plasencia, M.: A related key impossible differential attack against 22 rounds of the lightweight block cipher LBlock. Inf. Process. Lett. **112**(16), 624–629 (2012)
15. Wang, N., Xiaoyun Wang, K.: Differential attacks on reduced SIMON versions with dynamic key-guessing techniques. Cryptology ePrint Archive, Report 2014/448 (2014)
16. Sasaki, Y., Wang, L.: Comprehensive study of integral analysis on 22-round LBlock. In: Kwon, T., Lee, M.-K., Kwon, D. (eds.) ICISC 2012. LNCS, vol. 7839, pp. 156–169. Springer, Heidelberg (2013)
17. Sasaki, Y., Wang, L.: Meet-in-the-middle technique for integral attacks against feistel ciphers. In: Knudsen, L.R., Wu, H. (eds.) SAC 2012. LNCS, vol. 7707, pp. 234–251. Springer, Heidelberg (2013)
18. Soleimany, H., Nyberg, K.: Zero-correlation linear cryptanalysis of reduced-round LBlock. Des. Codes Crypt. **73**(2), 683–698 (2014)
19. Suzaki, T., Minematsu, K., Morioka, S., Kobayashi, E.: TWINE: a lightweight block cipher for multiple platforms. In: Knudsen, L.R., Wu, H. (eds.) SAC 2012. LNCS, vol. 7707, pp. 339–354. Springer, Heidelberg (2013)
20. Wang, Y., Wu, W.: Improved multidimensional zero-correlation linear cryptanalysis and applications to LBlock and TWINE. In: Susilo, W., Mu, Y. (eds.) ACISP 2014. LNCS, vol. 8544, pp. 1–16. Springer, Heidelberg (2014)

21. Wang, Y., Wu, W., Yu, X., Zhang, L.: Security on LBlock against biclique cryptanalysis. In: Lee, D.H., Yung, M. (eds.) WISA 2012. LNCS, vol. 7690, pp. 1–14. Springer, Heidelberg (2012)
22. Wen, L., Wang, M.Q., Zhao, J.Y.: Related-key impossible differential attack on reduced-round LBlock. J. Comput. Sci. Technol. **29**(1), 165–176 (2014)
23. Wu, W., Zhang, L.: LBlock: a lightweight block cipher. In: Lopez, J., Tsudik, G. (eds.) ACNS 2011. LNCS, vol. 6715, pp. 327–344. Springer, Heidelberg (2011)

Elliptic Curve Cryptography

Point Decomposition Problem in Binary Elliptic Curves

Koray Karabina(✉)

Florida Atlantic University, Boca Raton, FL 33431, USA
kkarabina@fau.edu

Abstract. We analyze the point decomposition problem (PDP) in binary elliptic curves. It is known that PDP in an elliptic curve group can be reduced to solving a particular system of multivariate non-linear equations derived from the so called Semaev summation polynomials. We modify the underlying system of equations by introducing some auxiliary variables. We argue that the trade-off between lowering the degree of Semaev polynomials and increasing the number of variables provides a significant speed-up.

Keywords: Semaev polynomials · Elliptic curves · Point decomposition problem · Discrete logarithm problem

1 Introduction

The *point decomposition problem* (PDP) in an additive abelian group $\mathbb{G}$ with respect to a *factor base* $\mathcal{B} \subset \mathbb{G}$ is the following: Given a point[1] $R \in \mathbb{G}$, find $P_i \in \mathcal{B}$ such that

$$R = \sum_{i=1}^{m} P_i$$

for some positive integer m; or conclude that R cannot be decomposed as a sum of points in $\mathcal{B}$. The *discrete logarithm problem* (DLP) in $\mathbb{G}$ with respect to a base $P \in \mathbb{G}$ is the following: Given P and $Q = aP \in \mathbb{G}$ for some secret integer a, compute a. DLP can be solved using the *index calculus algorithm* in two main steps. In the *relation collection* step, fix a factor base $\mathcal{B}$, and find a set of points $R_i = a_iP + b_iQ$ for some randomly chosen integers a_i, b_i, such that R_i can be decomposed with respect to $\mathcal{B}$, i.e.,

$$R_i = \sum_{j} P_{ij},\ P_{ij} \in \mathcal{B}.$$

Here, we may assume for convenience that P_{ij} are not necessarily distinct. Note that each decomposition induces a modular linear dependence on the discrete

[1] We prefer to use *point* rather than *element* because elliptic curve group elements are commonly called points.

S. Kwon and A. Yun (Eds.): ICISC 2015, LNCS 9558, pp. 155–168, 2016.
DOI: 10.1007/978-3-319-30840-1_10

logarithms of $Q \in \mathbb{G}$ and $P_{ij} \in \mathcal{B}$ with respect to the base P. After collecting sufficiently many relations[2], *linear algebra* step solves for the discrete logarithm of $Q \in \mathbb{G}$, as well as the discrete logarithms of the factor base elements. Clearly, the success probability and the running time of the index calculus algorithm heavily depend on the decomposition probability of a random element in $\mathbb{G}$, the cost of the decomposition step, and the size of the factor base. In particular, the overall cost of the relation collection and the linear algebra steps must be optimized with a non-trivial success probability.

In 2004, Semaev [11] showed that solving PDP in an elliptic curve group is equivalent to solving a particular system of multivariate non-linear equations derived from the so called *Semaev summation polynomials*. Semaev's work triggered the possibility of the existence of an index calculus type algorithm which is more efficient than the Pollard's rho algorithm to solve the discrete logarithm problem in elliptic curves defined over $\mathbb{F}_{q^n}$, which we denote ECDLP(q, n). Note that Pollard's rho algorithm is a general purpose algorithm that solves DLP in a group $\mathbb{G}$, and runs in time $\mathcal{O}(\sqrt{|\mathbb{G}|})$. Gaudry [7] showed that, for a fixed n, Semaev summation polynomials can be effectively used to solve ECDLP(q, n) in heuristic time $\mathcal{O}(q^{2-\frac{2}{n}})$, where the constant in $\mathcal{O}(\cdot)$ is exponential in n. For example, Gaudry's algorithm and Pollard's rho algorithm solve ECDLP$(q, 3)$ in time $\mathcal{O}(q^{1.33})$ and $\mathcal{O}(q^{1.5})$, respectively. Due to the exponential in n constant in the running time of Gaudry's algorithm, his attack is expected to be more effective than Pollard's rho algorithm if $n \geq 3$ is relatively small and q is large. Diem [2] rigorously showed that ECDLP(q, n) can be solved in an expected subexponential time when $a(\log q)^{\alpha} \leq n \leq b(\log q)^{\beta}$ for some $a, b, \alpha, \beta > 0$. On the other hand, Diem's method has expected exponential running time $\mathcal{O}(e^{n(\log n)^{1/2}})$ for solving ECDLP$(2, n)$. As a result, the index calculus type algorithms presented in [2,7] do not yield ECDLP solvers which are more effective than Pollard's rho method when $q = 2$ and n is prime. The ideas for choosing an appropriate factor base in [2] have been adapted in [5,10], and the complexity of the relation collection step have been analyzed. In both papers [5] and [10], a positive integer m, which we call the *decomposition constant*, is fixed to represent the number of points in the decomposition of a random point in the relation collection step. The factor base consists of elliptic curve points whose x-coordinates belong to an n'-dimensional subspace $V \subset \mathbb{F}_{2^n}$ over $\mathbb{F}_2$, where n' is chosen such that $mn' \approx n$. We refer to PDP in this setting by PDP(n, m, n') throughout the rest of this paper.

Faugère et al. [5] showed, under a certain assumption, that ECDLP$(2, n)$ can be solved in time $\mathcal{O}(2^{\omega n/2})$, where $2.376 \leq \omega \leq 3$ is the linear algebra constant. The running time analysis in [5] considers the linearization technique to solve the system of multivariate nonlinear of equations which are derived from the $(m+1)$'st Semaev polynomial S_{m+1} during the relation collection step to solve PDP(n, m, n'). Faugère et al. further argue that, Groebner basis techniques may improve the running time by a factor m in the exponent, where m is the decomposition constant. This last claim has been confirmed in the experiments in [5] for elliptic curves defined over $\mathbb{F}_{2^n}$ with $n \in \{41, 67, 97, 131\}$ and $m = 2$.

[2] This is roughly when the number of relations exceeds $|\mathcal{B}|$.

Petit and Quisquater's heuristic analysis in [10] claims that ECDLP$(2, n)$ can asymptotically be solved in time $\mathcal{O}(2^{cn^{2/3}\log n})$ for some constant $0 < c < 2$. The subexponential running time in [10] is based on a rather strong assumption on the behavior of the systems of equations that arise from Semaev polynomials. In particular, it is assumed in [10] that the degree of regularity D_{reg} and the first fall degree $D_{\mathsf{FirstFall}}$ of the underlying polynomial systems to solve PDP(n, m, n') are approximately equal. The analysis in [10] also assumes that $n' = n^{\alpha}$ and $m = n^{1-\alpha}$ for some positive constant α. Experiments with a very limited set of parameters (n, m, n'), $n \in \{11, 17\}$, $m \in \{2, 3\}$, $n' = \lceil n/m \rceil$ were conducted in [10] in the favor of their assumption.

A recent paper by Shantz and Teske [13] presented some extended experimental results on solving PDP(n, m, n') for the same setting as in the Petit and Quisquater's paper [10]. In particular, [13] validates the degree of regularity assumption in [10] for the set of parameters (n, m, n') such that $n \in \{11, 13, 15, 17, 19, 23, 29\}$, $m = 2$, $n' = \lceil n/m \rceil$; and for (n, m, n') such that $n \in \{11, 13, 15, 17, 19, 21\}$, $m = 3$, $n' = \lceil n/m \rceil$. Shantz and Teske [13] were able to extend their experimental data for the parameters (n, m, n', Δ), $n \leq 48$, $m = 2$, and where $\Delta = n - mn'$ is chosen appropriately to possibly improve the running time of ECDLP$(2, n)$. In another recent paper [8], Huang et al. exploit the symmetry in Semaev polynomials, and improve on the running time and memory requirements of the PDP(n, m, n') solver in [5]. The efficiency of the method in [8] is tested for parameters (n, m, n') such that $n \leq 53$, $m = 3$, $n' = 3, 4, 5, 6$.

Petit and Quisquater's heuristic analysis [10] claims that index calculus methods for solving ECDLP$(2, n)$ is more effective than the Pollard's rho method for $n > 2000$, $m \geq 4$ and $mn' \approx n$. However, all the experiments reported so far on solving PDP(n, m, n') for the set of parameters (n, m, n', Δ) with $\Delta = n - mn' \leq 1$ and $m = 3$ are limited to $n \leq 19$; see [8,13]. Similarly, all the experiments for the set of parameters (n, m, n', Δ) with $m = 3$ are limited to $n' \leq 6$, which forces $\Delta \geq 2$ for $n \geq 20$. In general, it is desired to have n' increasing as a function of n, rather than having some upper bound on n', so that $n \approx mn'$ as assumed in the running time analysis of ECDLP$(2, n)$ solvers in [5,10]. Therefore, it remains a challenge to run experiments on an extensive set of parameters (n, m, n') with larger prime n values, $m \geq 4$, and $mn' \approx n$. For example, it is stated in [8, Sect. 4.1] that

> On the other hand, the method appears unpractical for $m = 4$ even for very small values of n because of the exponential increase with m of the degrees in Semaev's polynomials.

In a more recent paper [6], Galbraith and Gebregiyorgis introduce a new choice of variables and a new choice of factor base, and they are able to solve PDP with various $n \geq 17$, $m = 4$, $n' = 3, 4$ using Groebner basis algorithms; and also with various $n \geq 17$, $m = 4$, $n' \leq 7$ using SAT solvers.

In this paper, we modify the system of equations, that are derived from Semaev polynomials, by introducing some auxiliary variables. We show that

PDP(n, m, n') can be solved by finding a solution to a system of equations derived from several third Semaev polynomials S_3 each of which has at most three variables. For a comparison, PDP(n, m, n') in $E(\mathbb{F}_{2^n})$ with decomposition constant $m = 5$ would be traditionally attacked via considering the Semaev polynomial S_6 with 5 variables, which is likely to have a root in V^5, where $V \subset \mathbb{F}_{2^n}$ is a subspace of dimension $n' = \lfloor n/5 \rfloor$. On the other hand, when $m = 5$, our polynomial system consists of third Semaev polynomials $S_{3,i}$ $(i = 1, 2, 3, 4)$, and a total of 8 variables which is likely to have a root in $V^5 \times \mathbb{F}_{2^n}^3$, where $V \subset \mathbb{F}_{2^n}$ is a subspace of dimension $\lfloor n/5 \rfloor$. As a result, our technique overcomes the difficulty of dealing with the $(m+1)$'st Semaev polynomial S_{m+1} when solving PDP(n, m, n') with $m \geq 4$. We should emphasize that choosing $m \geq 4$ is desirable for an index calculus based ECDLP$(2, n)$ solver to be more effective than a generic DLP solver such as Pollard's rho algorithm. Our method introduces an overhead of introducing some auxiliary variables. However, we argue that the trade-off between lowering the degree of Semaev polynomials and increasing the number of variables provides a significant speed-up. In particular, we present some experimental results on solving PDP(n, m, n') for the following parameters:

- $n \leq 19$, $m = 4, 5$, and $n' = \lfloor n/m \rfloor$. We are not aware of any previous experimental data for $n > 15$ and $m = 5$.
- $n \leq 26$, $m = 3$, $n' = \lfloor n/m \rfloor$. We are not aware of any previous experimental data for $n > 21$, $m = 3$, and $\Delta = n - mn' \leq 2$.

We observe in our experiments that regularity degrees of the underlying systems are relatively low. We also observe that running time and memory requirement of algorithms can be improved significantly if the Groebner basis computations are first performed on a subset of polynomials and if the ReductionHeuristic parameter in Magma is set to be a small number; see Sect. 5 for more detail. We would like to emphasize that these techniques are applied for the first time in this paper to solve the point decomposition problem. As a result, we gain significant improvement over the recently published experimental results [12]. For a comparison, we are able to solve PDP(15, 5, 3) instances in about 7 s (with 256 MB memory). Note that, PDP(15, 5, 3) is solved in about 175 s (with 2635 MB memory) in [12]. In general, our experimental findings with $m = 3, 4, 5$ extend and improve on the recently reported results in [8,12,13].

The rest of this paper is organized as follows. In Sect. 2, we recall Semaev polynomials and their application to ECDLP$(2, n)$. In Sect. 3, we describe and analyze a new method to solve PDP(n, m, n') in $E(\mathbb{F}_{2^n})$. In Sect. 4, we present our experimental results. In Sect. 5, we extend our results from Sect. 3.

2 Semaev Polynomials and ECDLP

Let $\mathbb{F}_{2^n} = \mathbb{F}_2[\sigma]/\langle f(\sigma)\rangle$ be a finite field with 2^n elements, where $f(\sigma)$ is a monic irreducible polynomial of degree n over the field $\mathbb{F}_2 = \{0, 1\}$. Let E be a non-singular elliptic curve defined by the short Weierstrass equation

$$E/\mathbb{F}_{2^n} : \; y^2 + xy = x^3 + ax^2 + b, \; a, b \in \mathbb{F}_{2^n}.$$

We denote the identity element of E by ∞. The i'th Semaev polynomial associated with E is defined as follows:

$$S_i(x_1, x_2, \ldots, x_i) = \begin{cases} (x_1x_2 + x_1x_3 + x_2x_3)^2 + x_1x_2x_3 + b & \text{if } i = 3 \\ \mathrm{Res}_X(S_{i-j}(x_1, \ldots, x_{i-j-1}, X), S_{j+2}(x_{i-j}, \ldots, x_i, X)) & \text{if } i \geq 4, \end{cases} \tag{1}$$

where $1 \leq j \leq i - 3$.

For $n' \leq n$, let

$$V = \{a_0 + a_1\sigma + \cdots + a_{n'-1}\sigma^{n'-1} : \; a_i \in \mathbb{F}_2\} \subset \mathbb{F}_{2^n}$$

and define the factor base

$$\mathcal{B} = \{P = (x, y) \in E : \; x \in V\}.$$

Recall that in PDP(n, m, n'), we are looking for $P_i = (x_i, y_i) \in \mathcal{B}$ such that

$$P_1 + \cdots + P_m = R, \tag{2}$$

for some given point $R = (x_R, y_R) \in E$. We refer to (2) as an m-decomposition of R in $\mathcal{B}$. We expect that, on average, a random point $R \in E$ has an m-decomposition in $\mathcal{B}$ with probability $2^{mn'}/2^n m!$ simply because $|\mathcal{B}| \approx 2^{n'}$ and permuting P_i does not change the sum $\sum P_i$ (see [7]). As described in Sect. 1, the DLP in E can be solved via an index-calculus based approach by computing about $|\mathcal{B}|$ explicit m-decompositions and solving a sparse linear system of about $|\mathcal{B}|$ equations. Therefore, the cost of solving ECDLP$(2, n)$ may be estimated as

$$2^{n'} \frac{2^n m!}{2^{mn'}} C_{n,m,n'} + 2^{\omega' n'}, \tag{3}$$

where $C_{n,m,n'}$ is the cost of solving PDP(n, m, n'), and $\omega' = 2$ is the sparse linear algebra constant. Semaev [11] showed that a decomposition of the form (2) exists if and only if the x-coordinates of P_i and R are zeros of the $(m+1)$'st Semaev polynomial, that is, $S_{m+1}(x_1, \ldots, x_m, x_R) = 0$. In the rest of this paper, we focus on solving PDP(n, m, n') (and estimating $C_{n,m,n'}$) via modifying the equation induced by S_{m+1}.

3 A New Approach to Solve the Point Decomposition Problem

Let $E/\mathbb{F}_{2^n}$, V, and $\mathcal{B}$ be as defined in Sect. 2. Recall that an m-decomposition of a point

$$R = P_1 + \cdots + P_m,$$

where $R = (x_R, y_R) \in E$, $P_i = (x_i, y_i) \in \mathcal{B}$, can be computed (if exists) by identifying a tuple $(x_1, \ldots, x_m) \in V^m$ that satisfies

$$S_{m+1}(x_1, \ldots, x_m, x_R) = 0 \tag{4}$$

Note that x_i belong to an n'-dimensional subspace of $\mathbb{F}_{2^n}$. Therefore, (4) defines a system Sys_1 of a single equation over $\mathbb{F}_{2^n}$ in m variables. In [5,10], the Weil descent technique is applied, and a second system Sys_2 of n equations over $\mathbb{F}_2$ in mn' boolean variables is derived from Sys_1. The cost $C_{n,m,n'}$ of solving $\mathrm{PDP}(n, m, n')$ in [5,10] is estimated through the analysis of solving Sys_2 using linearization and Groebner basis techniques. Next, we describe a new approach to derive another system Sys_3 of boolean equations such that a solution of Sys_3 yields an m-decomposition of a point R.

Notation. Throughout the rest of this paper, we distinguish between two classes Semaev polynomials. The first class of Semaev polynomials is denoted by $S_{m,1}(x_1, \ldots, x_m)$, which represents the m'th Semaev polynomial with m variables. The second class of Semaev polynomials is denoted by $S_{m,2}(x_1, \ldots, x_{m-1}, x_R)$, which represents the m'th Semaev polynomial with $m - 1$ variables (i.e., the last variable x_m is evaluated at a number x_R).

3.1 The Case: $m = 3$

Let $R = (x_R, y_R) \in E$. Notice that there exist $P_i \in \mathcal{B}$ such that

$$P_1 + P_2 + P_3 - R = \infty$$

if and only if there exist $P_i \in \mathcal{B}$ and $P_{12} \in E$ such that

$$\begin{cases} P_1 + P_2 - P_{12} = \infty \\ P_3 + P_{12} - R = \infty \end{cases} \tag{5}$$

Therefore, a 3-decomposition of $R = P_1 + P_2 + P_3$ may be found as follows:

1. Define the following system of equations derived from Semaev polynomials

$$\begin{cases} S_{3,1}(x_1, x_2, x_{12}) = 0 \\ S_{3,2}(x_3, x_{12}, x_R) = 0. \end{cases} \tag{6}$$

   Note that this system is defined over $\mathbb{F}_{2^n}$ and has 4 variables x_1, x_2, x_3, x_{12}.
2. Introduce boolean variables $x_{i,j}$ such that

$$x_i = \sum_{j=0}^{n'-1} x_{i,j}\sigma^j,$$

   for $i = 1, 2, 3$, and

$$x_{12} = \sum_{j=0}^{n} x_{12,j}\sigma^j.$$

   Apply the Weil descent technique to (6) and define an equivalent system of $2n$ equations over $\mathbb{F}_2$ with $3n' + n$ boolean variables

$$\{x_{i,j} : \ i = 1, 2, 3, \ j = 0, \ldots n' - 1\} \cup \{x_{12,j} : \ j = 0, \ldots n - 1\}.$$

Solve this new system of boolean equations and recover $x_1, x_2, x_3 \in \mathbb{F}_{2^n}$ from $x_{i,j} \in \mathbb{F}_2$.

Note that the proposed method solves a system of $2n$ equations over $\mathbb{F}_2$ with $3n' + n$ boolean variables rather than solving a system of n equations over $\mathbb{F}_2$ with $3n'$ boolean variables.

3.2 The Case: $m = 4$

Let $R = (x_R, y_R) \in E$. Notice that there exist $P_i \in \mathcal{B}$ such that

$$P_1 + P_2 + P_3 + P_4 - R = \infty$$

if and only if there exist $P_i \in \mathcal{B}$ and $P_{12} \in E$ such that

$$\begin{cases} P_1 + P_2 - P_{12} = \infty \\ P_3 + P_4 + P_{12} - R = \infty \end{cases} \tag{7}$$

Therefore, a 4-decomposition of $R = P_1 + P_2 + P_3 + P_4$ may be found as follows:

1. Define the following system of equations derived from Semaev polynomials

$$\begin{cases} S_{3,1}(x_1, x_2, x_{12}) = 0 \\ S_{4,2}(x_3, x_4, x_{12}, x_R) = 0 \end{cases} \tag{8}$$

   Note that this system is defined over $\mathbb{F}_{2^n}$ and has 5 variables $x_1, x_2, x_3, x_4, x_{12}$.
2. Introduce boolean variables $x_{i,j}$ such that

$$x_i = \sum_{j=0}^{n'-1} x_{i,j} \sigma^j,$$

   for $i = 1, 2, 3, 4$, and

$$x_{12} = \sum_{j=0}^{n} x_{i,j} \sigma^j.$$

   Apply the Weil descent technique to (8) and define an equivalent system of $2n$ equations over $\mathbb{F}_2$ with $4n' + n$ boolean variables

$$\{x_{i,j} : \ i = 1, 2, 3, 4 \ j = 0, \dots n' - 1\} \cup \{x_{12,j} : \ j = 0, \dots n - 1\}.$$

   Solve this new system of boolean equations and recover $x_1, x_2, x_3, x_4 \in \mathbb{F}_{2^n}$ from $x_{i,j} \in \mathbb{F}_2$.

Note that the proposed method solves a system of $2n$ equations over $\mathbb{F}_2$ with $4n' + n$ boolean variables rather than solving a system of n equations over $\mathbb{F}_2$ with $4n'$ boolean variables.

3.3 The Case: $m = 5$

Let $R = (x_R, y_R) \in E$. Notice that there exist $P_i \in \mathcal{B}$ such that

$$P_1 + P_2 + P_3 + P_4 + P_5 - R = \infty$$

if and only if there exist $P_i \in \mathcal{B}$ and $P_{123} \in E$ such that

$$\begin{cases} P_1 + P_2 + P_3 - P_{123} = \infty \\ P_4 + P_5 + P_{123} - R = \infty \end{cases} \tag{9}$$

Therefore, a 5-decomposition of $R = P_1 + P_2 + P_3 + P_4 + P_5$ may be found as follows:

1. Define the following system of equations derived from Semaev polynomials

$$\begin{cases} S_{4,1}(x_1, x_2, x_3, x_{123}) = 0 \\ S_{4,2}(x_4, x_5, x_{123}, x_R) = 0 \end{cases} \tag{10}$$

   Note that this system is defined over $\mathbb{F}_{2^n}$ and has 6 variables $x_1, x_2, x_3, x_4, x_5, x_{123}$.
2. Introduce boolean variables $x_{i,j}$ such that

$$x_i = \sum_{j=0}^{n'-1} x_{i,j}\sigma^j,$$

   for $i = 1, 2, 3, 4, 5$, and

$$x_{123} = \sum_{j=0}^{n} x_{123,j}\sigma^j.$$

   Apply the Weil descent technique to (10) and define an equivalent system of $2n$ equations over $\mathbb{F}_2$ with $5n' + n$ boolean variables

$$\{x_{i,j} : \ i = 1, 2, 3, 4, 5 \ j = 0, \ldots n' - 1\} \cup \{x_{123,j} : \ j = 0, \ldots n - 1\}.$$

   Solve this new system of boolean equations and recover $x_1, x_2, x_3, x_4, x_5 \in \mathbb{F}_{2^n}$ from $x_{i,j} \in \mathbb{F}_2$.

Note that the proposed method solves a system of $2n$ equations over $\mathbb{F}_2$ with $5n' + n$ boolean variables rather than solving a system of n equations over $\mathbb{F}_2$ with $5n'$ boolean variables.

3.4 Analysis of the New Polynomial Systems

One of the methods to solve a system of multivariate non-linear equations is to compute the Groebner basis of the underlying ideal. Groebner basis computations can be performed using Faugère's algorithms [3,4], which reduce the problem to Gaussian elimination of Macaulay-type matrices M_d of degree d. The Macaulay matrix M_d encodes degree (at most) d polynomials, that are generated during Groebner basis computation. Therefore, the cost of solving a system of equations is determined by the maximal degree D (also known as the degree of regularity of the system) reached during the computation. If N is the number of variables in the system, then the cost is estimated as $O\left(\binom{N+D-1}{D}^{\omega}\right)$, where $\binom{N+D-1}{D}$ is the maximum number of columns in M_D and ω is the linear algebra constant. In general, it is hard to estimate D. In the recent paper [10], it is conjectured that the degree of regularity D_{reg} of systems arising from PDP(n, m, n') satisfies $D_{\mathsf{reg}} = D_{\mathsf{FirstFall}} + o(1)$, where $D_{\mathsf{FirstFall}}$ is the first fall degree of the system and defined as follows.

Definition 1. [10] Let R be a polynomial ring over a field K. Let $F := \{f_1, \ldots, f_\ell\} \subset R$ be a set of polynomials of degrees at most $D_{\mathsf{FirstFall}}$. The first fall degree of F is the smallest degree $D_{\mathsf{FirstFall}}$ such that there exist polynomials $g_i \in R$ with $\max_i (\deg(f_i) + \deg(g_i)) = D_{\mathsf{FirstFall}}$, satisfying $\deg(\sum_{i=1}^{\ell} g_i f_i) < D_{\mathsf{FirstFall}}$ but $\sum_{i=1}^{\ell} g_i f_i \neq 0$.

Experimental studies in recent papers [10,13] give supporting evidence that $D_{\mathsf{reg}} \approx D_{\mathsf{FirstFall}}$. However, experimental data is yet very limited (see Sect. 1) to verify this conjecture. In this section, we compute the first fall degree of the systems proposed in Sects. 3.1, 3.2, and 3.3. Our experimental results in Sect. 4 support that $D_{\mathsf{reg}} \approx D_{\mathsf{FirstFall}}$.

$D_{\mathsf{FirstFall}}$ of the system when $m = 3$. In this case, one needs to solve the system of $2n$ equations over $\mathbb{F}_2$ with $3n' + n$ boolean variables. The system of equations is derived by applying Weil descent to (6) that consists of two Semaev polynomials $S_{3,1}$ and $S_{3,2}$. The monomial set of $S_{3,1}(x_1, x_2, x_{12})$ is

$$\{1, x_1^2 x_2^2, x_1^2 x_{12}^2, x_2^2 x_{12}^2, x_1 x_2 x_{12}\}.$$

Therefore, the Weil descent of $S_{3,1}(x_1, x_2, x_{12})$ yields a $2n' + n$ variable polynomial set $\{f_i\}$ over $\mathbb{F}_2$ such that $\max_i(\deg(f_i)) = 3$. On the other hand, the monomial set of $x_1 \cdot S_{3,1}(x_1, x_2, x_{12})$ is

$$\{x_1, x_1^3 x_2^2, x_1^3 x_{12}^2, x_2^2 x_{12}^2, x_1^2 x_2 x_{12}\}.$$

Therefore, the Weil descent of $x_1 \cdot S_{3,1}(x_1, x_2, x_{12})$ yields a polynomial set $\{F_i\}$ over $\mathbb{F}_2$ such that $\max_i(\deg(F_i)) = 3$. It follows from the definition that $D_{\mathsf{FirstFall}}(S_{3,1}) \leq 4$ because the maximum degree of polynomials obtained from the Weil descent of x_1 is 1. Similarly, the monomial set of $S_{3,2}(x_3, x_{12}, x_R)$ is

$$\{1, x_3^2 x_{12}^2, x_3^2, x_{12}^2, x_3 x_{12}\}.$$

Therefore, the Weil descent of $S_{3,2}(x_3, x_{12}, x_R)$ yields a $n' + n$ variable polynomial set $\{f_i\}$ over $\mathbb{F}_2$ such that $\max_i(\deg(f_i)) = 2$. On the other hand, the monomial set of $x_3^3 \cdot S_{3,2}(x_3, x_{21}, x_R)$ is

$$\{x_3^3, x_3^5 x_{12}^2, x_3^5, x_3^3 x_{12}^2, x_3^4 x_{12}\}.$$

Therefore, the Weil descent of $x_3^3 \cdot S_{3,2}(x_3, x_{12}, x_R)$ yields a polynomial set $\{F_i\}$ over $\mathbb{F}_2$ such that $\max_i(\deg(F_i)) = 3$. It follows from the definition that $D_{\mathsf{FirstFall}}(S_{3,2}) \leq 4$ because the maximum degree of polynomials obtained from the Weil descent of x_3^3 is 2. We conclude that $D_{\mathsf{FirstFall}} \leq 4$.

$D_{\mathsf{FirstFall}}$ of the system when $m = 4$. In this case, one needs to solve the system of $2n$ equations over $\mathbb{F}_2$ with $4n' + n$ boolean variables. The system of equations is derived by applying Weil descent to (8) that consists of two Semaev polynomials $S_{3,1}$ and $S_{4,2}$. From our above discussion, $D_{\mathsf{FirstFall}}(S_{3,1}) \leq 4$. Now, analyzing the monomial set of $S_{4,2}(x_3, x_4, x_{123}, x_R)$, we can see that the Weil descent of $S_{4,2}(x_3, x_4, x_{123}, x_R)$ yields a $2n' + n$ variable polynomial set $\{f_i\}$ over $\mathbb{F}_2$ such that $\max_i(\deg(f_i)) = 6$ (this follows from the Weil descent of the monomial $(x_3x_4x_{123})^3$). On the other hand, analyzing the monomial set of $x_3 \cdot S_{4,2}(x_3, x_4, x_{123}, x_R)$, we see that the Weil descent of $x_3 \cdot S_{4,2}(x_3, x_4, x_{123}, x_R)$ yields a polynomial set $\{F_i\}$ over $\mathbb{F}_2$ such that $\max_i(\deg(F_i)) = 6$. It follows from the definition that $D_{\mathsf{FirstFall}}(S_{4,2}) \leq 7$ because the maximum degree of polynomials obtained from the Weil descent of x_3 is 1. We conclude that $D_{\mathsf{FirstFall}} \leq 7$.

$D_{\mathsf{FirstFall}}$ of the system when $m = 5$. In this case, one needs to solve the system of $2n$ equations over $\mathbb{F}_2$ with $5n' + n$ boolean variables. The system of equations is derived by applying Weil descent to (10) that consists of two Semaev polynomials $S_{4,1}$ and $S_{4,2}$. From our above discussion, $D_{\mathsf{FirstFall}}(S_{4,2}) \leq 7$. Now, analyzing the monomial set of $S_{4,1}(x_1, x_2, x_3, x_{123})$, we can see that the Weil descent of $S_{4,1}(x_1, x_2, x_3, x_{123})$ yields a $3n' + n$ variable polynomial set $\{f_i\}$ over $\mathbb{F}_2$ such that $\max_i(\deg(f_i)) = 8$ (this follows from the Weil descent of the monomial $(x_1x_2x_3x_{123})^3$). On the other hand, analyzing the monomial set of $x_3 \cdot S_{4,1}(x_1, x_2, x_3, x_{123})$, we see that the Weil descent of $x_3 \cdot S_{4,1}(x_1, x_2, x_3, x_{123})$ yields a polynomial set $\{F_i\}$ over $\mathbb{F}_2$ such that $\max_i(\deg(F_i)) = 8$. It follows from the definition that $D_{\mathsf{FirstFall}}(S_{4,1}) \leq 9$ because the maximum degree of polynomials obtained from the Weil descent of x_3 is 1. We conclude that $D_{\mathsf{FirstFall}} \leq 9$.

4 Experimental Results

We implemented the methods proposed in Sect. 3 on a desktop computer (Intel(R) Xeon(R) CPU E31240 3.30GHz) using Groebner basis algorithms in Magma [1]. For each parameter set (n, m, n'), we solved 5 random instances of PDP over a randomly chosen elliptic curve $E/\mathbb{F}_{2^n}$. In Table 1, we report on our experimental results for solving PDP$(n, m, n' = \lfloor n/m \rfloor)$ with $m = 3, 4, 5$. In particular, for each of these 5 computations, we report on the maximum CPU time (seconds) and memory (MB) required for solving PDP. We also report on the maximum of the maximum step degrees D in the Groebner basis computations. Recall that in Sect. 3, we estimated $D_{\mathsf{FirstFall}} \leq 4$ when $m = 3$; $D_{\mathsf{FirstFall}} \leq 7$ when $m = 4$; and $D_{\mathsf{FirstFall}} \leq 9$ when $m = 5$. In our experiments, we observe that $D_{\mathsf{reg}} = 4$ when $m = 3$; $D_{\mathsf{reg}} = 7$ when $m = 4$; and $D_{\mathsf{reg}} \leq 8$ when $m = 5$.

Let $m = 5$ and $n' = \lfloor n/m \rfloor$. Based on our experimental data, it is tempting to assume that the underlying system of polynomial equations has $D_{\mathsf{reg}} \leq 9$.

Table 1. Experimental results on solving PDP($n, m, n' = \lfloor n/m \rfloor$). Time in seconds; Memory in MB; D is the maximum step degree.

	$m = 3$			$m = 4$			$m = 5$		
n	Time	Memory	D	Time	Memory	D	Time	Memory	D
11							0.520	25.8	7
12							0.670	33.0	7
13							0.890	42.8	7
14							4.260	126.7	8
15							350.100	1839.5	8
16				414.320	5100.7	7	408.270	2633.9	8
17	1.690	38.8	4	1395.170	5632.8	7	506.340	4050.3	8
18	26.680	264.5	4	497.770	5632.8	7	920.790	6186.9	8
19	15.270	321.8	4	509.330	5634.1	7	1265.090	8282.9	8
20	49.350	397.6	4						
21	163.100	1228.3	4						
22	126.290	1413.2	4						
23	248.820	1668.7	4						
24	1266.610	5142.2	4						
25	1623.180	6363.8	4						
26	1645.78	6596.9	4						

Moreover, the system has $N = 5n' + n \approx 2n$ boolean variables. Therefore, when $m = 5$, we may estimate the cost of solving ECDLP($2, n$) (see (3)) as

$$\begin{aligned} & 2^{n'} \frac{2^n m!}{2^{mn'}} \binom{N + D_{\mathsf{reg}} - 1}{D_{\mathsf{reg}}}^w + 2^{w'n'} \\ & \approx 2^{n/5} m! (2n)^{9w} + 2^{w'n/5} \\ & \approx 2^{34} 2^{n/5} n^{27} + 2^{2n/5}, \end{aligned}$$

where we assume $w = 3$ and $w' = 2$. For example, when $n \approx 1200$, the cost of solving ECDLP($2, n$) is estimated to be 2^{550} which is significantly smaller than the cost 2^{600} of square-root time algorithms.

5 Extensions and Optimization

In Sect. 3, we introduced a single auxiliary variable to lower the degree of Semaev polynomials. The degree of polynomials can further be lowered by introducing more auxiliary variables. As an example, we consider the case $m = 5$. Let $R = (x_R, y_R) \in E$, as before. Notice that there exist $P_i \in \mathcal{B}$ such that

$$P_1 + P_2 + P_3 + P_4 + P_5 - R = \infty$$

if and only if there exist $P_i \in \mathcal{B}$ and $P_{12}, P_{34}, P_{50} \in E$ such that

$$\begin{cases} P_1 + P_2 - P_{12} = \infty \\ P_3 + P_4 - P_{34} = \infty \\ P_5 - P_{50} - R = \infty \\ P_{12} + P_{34} + P_{50} = \infty \end{cases} \tag{11}$$

Therefore, a 5-decomposition of $R = P_1 + P_2 + P_3 + P_4 + P_5$ may be found as follows:

1. Define the following system of equations derived from Semaev polynomials

$$\begin{cases} S_{3,1}(x_1, x_2, x_{12}) = 0 \\ S_{3,1}(x_3, x_4, x_{34}) = 0 \\ S_{3,2}(x_5, x_{50}, x_R) = 0 \\ S_{3,1}(x_{12}, x_{34}, x_{50}) = 0 \end{cases} \tag{12}$$

   Note that this system is defined over $\mathbb{F}_{2^n}$ and has 8 variables $x_1, x_2, x_3, x_4, x_5, x_{12}, x_{34}, x_{50}$.
2. Introduce boolean variables $x_{i,j}$ such that

$$x_i = \sum_{j=0}^{n'-1} x_{i,j}\sigma^j,$$

   for $i = 1, 2, 3, 4, 5$, and

$$x_{i,j} = \sum_{k=0}^{n} x_{i,j}\sigma^j,$$

   for $i = 12, 34, 50$. Apply the Weil descent technique to (12) and define an equivalent system of $4n$ equations over $\mathbb{F}_2$ with $5n' + 3n$ boolean variables

$$\{x_{i,j} : i = 1, 2, 3, 4, 5\ j = 0, \ldots n'-1\} \cup \{x_{i,j} : i = 12, 34, 50,\ j = 0, \ldots n-1\}.$$

   Solve this new system of boolean equations and recover $x_1, x_2, x_3, x_4, x_5 \in \mathbb{F}_{2^n}$ from $x_{i,j} \in \mathbb{F}_2$.

Note that the proposed method solves a system of $4n$ equations over $\mathbb{F}_2$ with $5n' + 3n$ boolean variables rather than solving a system of n equations over $\mathbb{F}_2$ with $5n'$ boolean variables. Similar to the analysis in Sect. 3, we can show that $D_{\mathsf{FirstFall}} \leq 4$.

In Table 2, we report on our experimental results for solving $\mathrm{PDP}(n, m, n' = \lfloor n/m \rfloor)$ with $m = 5$ deploying only the third Semaev polynomials; see (12). The time and memory results in the second and third column of Table 2 are obtained using the Groebner basis implementation of Magma with the grevlex ordering of monomials. We observe that the maximum step degree is $D_{\mathsf{reg}} = 4$ for $11 \leq n \leq 19$. The time and memory results in the last two columns of Table 2 are

Table 2. Experimental results on solving $\mathrm{PDP}(n, m, n' = \lfloor n/m \rfloor)$. Time in seconds; Memory in MB; D is the maximum step degree; $D_{\mathsf{Heuristic}}$ is set to be 4 in Groebner basis computations.

	$D_{\mathsf{Heuristic}} = 4$				
	$m = 5$			$m = 5$	
n	Time	Memory	D	Time	Memory
11	2.380	58	4		
12	4.150	116.7	4		
13	6.390	124.1	4		
14	9.510	245.2	4		
15	393.170	6421.9	4	7.130	256.3
16	242.500	5911.7	4	6.900	320.4
17	365.460	7063.8	4	6.660	320.4
18	836.080	8619.4	4	11.700	394.6
19	531.420	8864.2	4	45.570	2505.3

obtained using the Groebner basis implementation of Magma with the grevlex ordering of monomials in a boolean ring. We also introduced two modifications in the computations: We set the ReductionHeuristic parameter in Magma to 4; and we first computed Groebner bases of partial systems described by single equations in (12), and merged them later. These two techniques yield non-trivial optimization both in time and memory. For a comparison, when $n = 15$ and $m = 3$, (Time, Memory) values decrease from $(393.170, 6421.9)$ to $(7.130, 256.3)$ when this modification is deployed in the computation; see Table 2. For the same parameters ($n = 15$ and $m = 3$), (Time, Memory) values are reported as $(174.47, 2635.4)$ in [12].

Based on our experimental data, it is tempting to assume that the underlying system of polynomial equations has $D_{\mathsf{reg}} \leq 4$ for all n. Moreover, the system has $N = 5n' + 3n \approx 4n$ boolean variables. Therefore, when $m = 5$, we may estimate the cost of solving $\mathrm{ECDLP}(2, n)$ (see (3)) as

$$\begin{aligned} & 2^{n'} \frac{2^n m!}{2^{mn'}} \binom{N + D_{\mathsf{reg}} - 1}{D_{\mathsf{reg}}}^{w} + 2^{w'n'} \\ & \approx 2^{n/5} m! (4n)^{4w} + 2^{w'n/5} \\ & \approx 2^{31} 2^{n/5} n^{12} + 2^{2n/5}, \end{aligned}$$

where we assume $w = 3$ and $w' = 2$. This running time outperforms square-root methods when $n > 457$. For example, when $n \approx 550$, the cost of solving $\mathrm{ECDLP}(2, n)$ is estimated to be 2^{250} which is significantly smaller than the cost 2^{275} of square-root time algorithms.

Acknowledgment. I would like to acknowledge two recent papers [9,12]. Semaev [12] claims a new complexity bound $2^{c(\sqrt{n \ln n})}$ for solving ECDLP$(2, n)$ under the assumption that the degree of regularity in Groebner computations of particular polynomial systems is $D_{\mathsf{reg}} \leq 4$. Semaev also shows that ECDLP$(2, n)$ can be solved in time $2^{o(c\sqrt{n \ln n})}$ under a weaker assumption that $D_{\mathsf{reg}} = o(\sqrt{n/\ln n})$ The techniques used in [12] and in this paper are similar. In [9], Kosters and Yeo provide experimental evidence that the degree of regularity of the underlying polynomial systems is likely to increase as a function of n, whence the conjecture $D_{\mathsf{reg}} \approx D_{\mathsf{FirstFall}}$ may be false.

I would like to thank Michiel Kosters and Igor Semaev for their comments on the first version of this paper.

References

1. Bosma, W., Cannon, J., Playoust, C.: The Magma algebra system I: the user language. J. Symbolic Comput. **24**, 235–265 (1997)
2. Diem, C.: On the discrete logarithm problem in elliptic curves II. Algebra Number Theory **7**, 1281–1323 (2013)
3. Faugère, J.-C.: A new efficient algorithm for computing Groebner bases (F4). J. Pure Appl. Algebra **139**, 61–68 (1999)
4. Faugère, J.-C.: A new efficient algorithm for computing Groebner bases without reduction to zero (F5). In: International Symposium on Symbolic and Algebraic Computation, pp. 75–83 (2002)
5. Faugère, J.-C., Perret, L., Petit, C., Renault, G.: Improving the complexity of index calculus algorithms in elliptic curves over binary fields. In: Pointcheval, D., Johansson, T. (eds.) EUROCRYPT 2012. LNCS, vol. 7237, pp. 27–44. Springer, Heidelberg (2012)
6. Galbraith, S.D., Gebregiyorgis, S.W.: Summation polynomial algorithms for elliptic curves in characteristic two. In: Meier, W., Mukhopadhyay, D. (eds.) Progress in Cryptology – INDOCRYPT 2014. LNCS, vol. 8885, pp. 409–427. Springer, Berlin (2014)
7. Gaudry, P.: Index calculus for abelian varieties of small dimension and the elliptic curve discrete logarithm problem. J. Symbolic Comput. **44**, 1690–1702 (2009)
8. Huang, Y.-J., Petit, C., Shinohara, N., Takagi, T.: Improvement of Faugère *et al.*'s Method to Solve ECDLP. In: Terada, M., Sakiyama, K. (eds.) IWSEC 2013. LNCS, vol. 8231, pp. 115–132. Springer, Heidelberg (2013)
9. Kosters, M., Yeo, S.: Notes on summation polynomials (2015). arXiv:1503.08001
10. Petit, C., Quisquater, J.-J.: On polynomial systems arising from a Weil descent. In: Wang, X., Sako, K. (eds.) ASIACRYPT 2012. LNCS, vol. 7658, pp. 451–466. Springer, Heidelberg (2012)
11. Semaev, I.: Summation polynomials and the discrete logarithm problem on elliptic curves, Cryptology ePrint Archive: Report/031 (2004)
12. Semaev, I.: New algorithm for the discrete logarithm problem on elliptic curves, Cryptology ePrint Archive: Report 2015/310 (2015)
13. Shantz, M., Teske, E.: Solving the elliptic curve discrete logarithm problem using Semaev polynomials, Weil descent and Gröbner basis methods – an experimental study. In: Fischlin, M., Katzenbeisser, S. (eds.) Buchmann Festschrift. LNCS, vol. 8260, pp. 94–107. Springer, Heidelberg (2013)

Faster ECC over $\mathbb{F}_{2^{521}-1}$ (feat. NEON)

Hwajeong Seo[1], Zhe Liu[2], Yasuyuki Nogami[3], Taehwan Park[1], Jongseok Choi[1], Lu Zhou[4], and Howon Kim[1](✉)

[1] School of Computer Science and Engineering, Pusan National University, San-30, Jangjeon-Dong, Geumjeong-Gu, Busan 609–735, Republic of Korea
{hwajeong,pth5804,jschoi85,howonkim}@pusan.ac.kr

[2] Laboratory of Algorithmics, Cryptology and Security (LACS), University of Luxembourg, 6, rue R. Coudenhove-Kalergi, L-1359 Luxembourg-Kirchberg, Luxembourg
zhe.liu@uni.lu

[3] Graduate School of Natural Science and Technology, Okayama University, 3-1-1, Tsushima-naka, Kita, Okayama 700-8530, Japan
yasuyuki.nogami@okayama-u.ac.jp

[4] School of Computer Science and Technology, Shandong University, Jinan, China

Abstract. In this paper, we present high speed parallel multiplication and squaring algorithms for the Mersenne prime $2^{521}-1$. We exploit 1-level Karatsuba method in order to provide asymptotically faster integer multiplication and fast reduction algorithms. With these optimization techniques, ECDH on NIST's (and SECG's) curve P-521 requires 8.1/4 M cycles on an ARM Cortex-A9/A15, respectively. As a comparison, on the same architecture, the latest OpenSSL 1.0.2d's ECDH speed test for curve P-521 requires 23.8/18.7 M cycles for ARM Cortex-A9/A15, respectively.

Keywords: Elliptic Curve Cryptography · P-521 · Karatsuba · SIMD · NEON

1 Introduction

Multi-precision modular multiplication and squaring are performance-critical building blocks of Elliptic Curve Cryptography (ECC). Since the algorithm is a computation-intensive operation, it demands careful optimizations to achieve

This work was partly supported by Institute for Information & communications Technology Promotion (IITP) grant funded by the Korea government (MSIP) (No. 10043907, Development of high performance IoT device and Open Platform with Intelligent Software) and the MSIP (Ministry of Science, ICT and Future Planning), Korea, under the ITRC(Information Technology Research Center) support program (IITP-2015-H8501-15-1017) supervised by the IITP(Institute for Information & communications Technology Promotion).

S. Kwon and A. Yun (Eds.): ICISC 2015, LNCS 9558, pp. 169–181, 2016.
DOI: 10.1007/978-3-319-30840-1_11

acceptable performance particularly over embedded processors. Recently, an increasing number of embedded processors started to employ Single Instruction Multiple Data (SIMD) instructions to perform massive body of multimedia workloads. In order to exploit the parallel computing power of SIMD instructions, traditional cryptography software needs to be rewritten into a vectorized format. The most well known approach is a reduced-radix representation for a better handling of the carry propagations [6]. The redundant representation reduces the number of active bits per register. Keeping the final result within remaining capacity of a register can avoid a number of carry propagations. In [2], vector instructions on the CELL microprocessor are used to perform multiplication on operands represented with a radix of 2^{16}. At CHES 2012, Bernstein and Schwabe adopted the reduced radix and presented an efficient modular multiplication on Curve25519. At HPEC 2013, a multiplicand reduction method in the reduced-radix representation was introduced for the NIST curves [8]. At CHES 2014, the Curve41417 implementation adopts 2-level Karatsuba multiplication in the redundant representation as well as a clever method to reduce inputs to the required multiplications rather than outputs [1]. Recently efficient Karatsuba multiplication algorithm for P-521 by Granger and Scott is proposed at PKC'15 which requires as few word-by-word multiplications as is needed for squaring, while incurring very little overhead from extra additions [4]. The algorithm shows high performance over 64-bit SISD architecture but it is not favorable for 32-bit ARM-NEON SIMD platforms because 32-bit SIMD architecture does not conduct 64-bit wise multiplication efficiently and needs to group the operands for parallel computations. Until now, there is relatively few studied on NIST's (and SECG's) curve P-521 for ARM-NEON architecture. Since the curve is NIST standard and ARM-NEON is the most well known smart phone processor, the efficient implementation of P-521 over ARM-NEON processor should be deserved. In this paper, we present speed record of P-521 over ARM-NEON platform. We exploit 1-level Karatsuba method in order to provide asymptotically faster integer multiplication and fast reduction algorithms.

The remainder of this paper is organized as follows. In Sect. 2, we recap the P-521 curve. In Sect. 3, we propose the efficient implementations of P-521 curve. In Sect. 4, we evaluate the performance of proposed methods in terms of clock cycles. Finally, Sect. 5 concludes the paper.

2 NIST Curve P-521

The Weierstrass form NIST curve P-521 as standardized in [3, 7] and the finite field $\mathbb{F}_p$ is defined by:

$$p = 2^{521} - 1$$

The curve $E : y^2 = x^3 + ax + b$ over $\mathbb{F}_p$ is defined by:

$a =$ 01FF FFFFFFFF FFFFFFFF FFFFFFFF FFFFFFFF FFFFFFFF FFFFFFFF
FFFFFFFF FFFFFFFF FFFFFFFF FFFFFFFF FFFFFFFF FFFFFFFF FFFFFFFF
FFFFFFFF FFFFFFFF FFFFFFFC

$b =$ 0051 953EB961 8E1C9A1F 929A21A0 B68540EE A2DA725B 99B315F3 B8B48991 8EF109E1 56193951 EC7E937B 1652C0BD 3BB1BF07 3573DF88 3D2C34F1 EF451FD4 6B503F00

and group order is defined by:

$n =$ 01FF FFFFFFFF FFFFFFFF FFFFFFFF FFFFFFFF FFFFFFFF FFFFFFFF FFFFFFFF FFFFFFFA 51868783 BF2F966B 7FCC0148 F709A5D0 3BB5C9B8 899C47AE BB6FB71E 91386409

Using Jacobian projective coordinates, for $P_1 = (X_1, Y_1, Z_1)$ the point $2P_1 = (X_3, Y_3, Z_3)$ is computed as follows:

$$T_1 \leftarrow Z_1^2,\ T_2 \leftarrow Y_1^2,\ T_3 \leftarrow X_1 \cdot T_2,\ T_4 \leftarrow X_1 + T_1,\ T_5 \leftarrow X_1 - T_1,$$
$$T_6 \leftarrow T_4 \cdot T_5,\ T_4 \leftarrow 3 \cdot T_6,\ T_5 \leftarrow T_4^2,\ T_6 \leftarrow 8 \cdot T_3,\ X_3 \leftarrow T_5 - T_6,$$
$$T_5 \leftarrow Y_1 + Z_1,\ T_6 \leftarrow T_5^2,\ T_5 \leftarrow T_6 - T_1,\ Z_3 \leftarrow T_5 - T_2,\ T_5 \leftarrow 4 \cdot T_3,$$
$$T_6 \leftarrow T_5 - X_3,\ T_5 \leftarrow T_4 \cdot T_6,\ T_6 \leftarrow T_2^2,\ T_4 \leftarrow 8 \cdot T_6,\ Y_3 \leftarrow T_5 - T_4$$

For a point $P_2 = (X_2, Y_2, 1)$ which is affine point and not equal to P_1, let $P_3 = (X_3, Y_3, Z_3) = P_1 + P_2$. Then P_3 is computed as follows:

$$T_1 \leftarrow Z_1^2,\ T_2 \leftarrow T_1 \cdot Z_1,\ T_1 \leftarrow T_1 \cdot X_2,\ T_2 \leftarrow T_2 \cdot Y2,\ T_1 \leftarrow T_1 - X_1$$
$$T_2 \leftarrow T_2 - Y_1,\ Z_3 \leftarrow Z_1 \cdot T_1,\ T_3 \leftarrow T_1^2,\ T_4 \leftarrow T_3 \cdot T_1,\ T_3 \leftarrow T_3 \cdot X_1$$
$$T_1 \leftarrow 2 \cdot T_3,\ X_3 \leftarrow T_2^2,\ X_3 \leftarrow X_3 - T_1,\ X_3 \leftarrow X_3 - T_4,\ T_3 \leftarrow T_3 - X_3$$
$$T_3 \leftarrow T_3 \cdot T_2,\ T_4 \leftarrow T_4 \cdot Y_1,\ Y_3 \leftarrow T_3 - T_4$$

For a point P_2 which is projective point (X_2, Y_2, Z_2) and not equal to P_1, let $P_3 = (X_3, Y_3, Z_3) = P_1 + P_2$. Then P_3 is computed as follows:

$$T_1 \leftarrow Z_2^2,\ U_1 \leftarrow X_1 \cdot T_1,\ T_2 \leftarrow Z_1^2,\ U_2 \leftarrow X_2 \cdot T_2,\ T_3 \leftarrow Y_1 \cdot Z_2$$
$$S_1 \leftarrow T_3 \cdot T_1,\ T_4 \leftarrow Y_2 \cdot Z_1,\ S_2 \leftarrow T_4 \cdot T_2,\ H \leftarrow U_2 - U_1,\ R \leftarrow S_2 - S_1$$
$$T_1 \leftarrow R^2,\ T_2 \leftarrow H^2,\ T_3 \leftarrow T_2 \cdot H,\ T_4 \leftarrow U_1 \cdot T_2,\ T_1 \leftarrow T_1 - T_3$$
$$T_2 \leftarrow 2 \cdot T_4,\ X_3 \leftarrow T_1 - T_2,\ T_3 \leftarrow S_1 \cdot T_3 T_4 \leftarrow T_4 - X_3,\ T_4 \leftarrow R \cdot T_4$$
$$Y_3 \leftarrow T_4 - T_3,\ T_1 \leftarrow Z_1 \cdot Z_2,\ Z_3 \leftarrow H \cdot T_1$$

3 Proposed Method

3.1 Multiplication

The prime of P-521 curve is $2^{521} - 1$. This representation can be written in $2^{522} - 2$ by following the idea of Langley in OpenSSL 1.0.0e approach. We choose 27/26-radix and this divides 522-bit into 20-limb as follows: (27, 26, 26, 26, 26, 26, 26, 26, 26, 26 || 27, 26, 26, 26, 26, 26, 26, 26, 26, 26). Since the lower and

Algorithm 1. Karatsuba-based multiplication mod p_{521}

Require: Integer a, b satisfying $1 \leq a, b \leq p-1$.
Ensure: Results $z = a \cdot b \bmod p$.

1: $a_L \leftarrow a\ mod\ 2^{261}$
2: $a_H \leftarrow a\ div\ 2^{261}$
3: $b_L \leftarrow b\ mod\ 2^{261}$
4: $b_H \leftarrow b\ div\ 2^{261}$
5: $r_L \leftarrow a_L \cdot b_L$
6: $t \leftarrow (r_L - a_H \cdot b_H \cdot 2^{261})\ mod\ p$ {`direct reduction`}
7: $t_H \leftarrow t\ div\ 2^{261}$
8: $t_L \leftarrow t\ mod\ 2^{261}$
9: $t_{HL} \leftarrow t_H - t_L$
10: $a_K \leftarrow a_L + a_H$
11: $b_K \leftarrow b_L + b_H$
12: $ab_K \leftarrow (t_{HL} \cdot 2^{261} + t_L - 2 \cdot t_H + a_K \cdot b_K \cdot 2^{261})\ mod\ p$ {`direct reduction`}
13: **return** ab_K

higher 261-bit wise operands share identical radix representation, we applied 1-level of Karatsuba multiplication which replaces the one 522-bit multiplication complexity to three 261-bit multiplications with some addition and subtraction operations. In this paper, we further improve the ordinary 1 level of Karatsuba multiplication particularly over $2^{522} - 2$. The detailed descriptions are available in Algorithm 1. For starter, both operands are divided into lower and higher parts from Steps $1-4$. In Step 5, lower part of operands are multiplied each other. In Step 6, higher parts are multiplied and then subtracted from the results of Step 5. Since the intermediate results exceed the 522-bit length, we directly reduce the intermediate results into range of modulus[1]. In Steps $7-9$, the results are divided into higher and lower parts and then lower parts are subtracted from higher parts. In Steps 10 and 11, higher and lower parts of operands are added each other. In Step 12, remaining several addition, subtraction and multiplication operations are conducted with direct reduction techniques. Finally, in Step 13, we obtained the results.

This approach introduces two advantages. First NEON engine over ARMv7 provides only 16 128-bit wise registers. For 261-bit multiplication, we need 5 registers for both 20-limb of 32-bit operands and 10 for 20-limb of 64-bit intermediate results and 1 for temporal registers. If we retain whole 522 multiplication results without reduction, the intermediate results exceed the size of general purpose registers, which introduces a number of memory load and store operations. Second this method follows basic concept of refined Karatsuba algorithm which reduces the one time of addition operation.

For 261-bit multiplication of 10-limb operand in (27, 26, 26, 26, 26, 26, 26, 26, 26, 26) representation, we can conduct multiplication as follows. The variables ($a_0 \sim a_9$ and $b_0 \sim b_9$) indicate the both operands and the other variables ($c_0 \sim c_{18}$) represents the intermediate results. The equation shows that some

[1] We discuss the detailed direct reduction techniques in following section.

of the partial product needs doubling the intermediate results to align the bit position. For example, the partial products including a_0b_2 and a_1b_1 are stored in same destination (c_2) but one (a_0b_2) is placed in 53-th and the other one (a_1b_1) is 52-th bit. In order to store the results in right bit position, we should conduct doubling on the partial product (a_1b_1) and get the doubled result ($2a_1b_1$) which is finally located in 53-th bit as like opponent (a_0b_2). The bit-aligned multiplication on 26/27 radix is as follows.

$$
\begin{aligned}
c_0 &\leftarrow a_0b_0\\
c_1 &\leftarrow a_0b_1 + a_1b_0\\
c_2 &\leftarrow a_0b_2 + a_2b_0 + 2a_1b_1\\
c_3 &\leftarrow a_0b_3 + a_3b_0 + 2(a_1b_2 + a_2b_1)\\
c_4 &\leftarrow a_0b_4 + a_4b_0 + 2(a_1b_3 + a_3b_1 + a_2b_2)\\
c_5 &\leftarrow a_0b_5 + a_5b_0 + 2(a_1b_4 + a_4b_1 + a_2b_3 + a_3b_2)\\
c_6 &\leftarrow a_0b_6 + a_6b_0 + 2(a_1b_5 + a_5b_1 + a_2b_4 + a_4b_2 + a_3b_3)\\
c_7 &\leftarrow a_0b_7 + a_7b_0 + 2(a_1b_6 + a_6b_1 + a_2b_5 + a_5b_2 + a_3b_4 + a_4b_3)\\
c_8 &\leftarrow a_0b_8 + a_8b_0 + 2(a_1b_7 + a_7b_1 + a_2b_6 + a_6b_2 + a_3b_5 + a_5b_3 + a_4b_4)\\
c_9 &\leftarrow a_0b_9 + a_9b_0 + 2(a_1b_8 + a_8b_1 + a_2b_7 + a_7b_2 + a_3b_6 + a_6b_3 + a_4b_5 + a_5b_4)\\
c_{10} &\leftarrow 2(a_1b_9 + a_9b_1 + a_2b_8 + a_8b_2 + a_3b_7 + a_7b_3 + a_4b_6 + a_6b_4 + a_5b_5)\\
c_{11} &\leftarrow a_2b_9 + a_9b_2 + a_3b_8 + a_8b_3 + a_4b_7 + a_7b_4 + a_5b_6 + a_6b_5\\
c_{12} &\leftarrow a_3b_9 + a_9b_3 + a_4b_8 + a_8b_4 + a_5b_7 + a_7b_5 + a_6b_6\\
c_{13} &\leftarrow a_4b_9 + a_9b_4 + a_5b_8 + a_8b_5 + a_6b_7 + a_7b_6\\
c_{14} &\leftarrow a_5b_9 + a_9b_5 + a_6b_8 + a_8b_6 + a_7b_7\\
c_{15} &\leftarrow a_6b_9 + a_9b_6 + a_7b_8 + a_8b_7\\
c_{16} &\leftarrow a_7b_9 + a_9b_7 + a_8b_8\\
c_{17} &\leftarrow a_8b_9 + a_9b_8\\
c_{18} &\leftarrow a_9b_9
\end{aligned}
$$

However, the aligned multiplication should be re-written in a SIMD friendly form. Particularly, the NEON architecture supports 2-way 32-bit wise multiplication, which means two consecutive 32-bit multiplications are computed and the store the two consecutive 64-bit results in one 128-bit register. For this reason, the alignments in the 128-bit register should be concerned in order to accumulate the multiplication results into correct destinations. We group the two adjacent partial product results as follows: $(c_1, c_0), (c_3, c_2), (c_5, c_4), (c_7, c_6), (c_9, c_8), (c_{11}, c_{10}), (c_{13}, c_{12}), (c_{15}, c_{14}), (c_{17}, c_{16})$. After then we re-arrange the partial products that need doubling the results to correct bit position. Since the doubling process can be computed together with multiplication by using instruction set (`vqdmull`), we can avoid one time of shift operation per each doubling operation. However, all partial products aren't grouped at once properly. We re-locate the intermediate results by conducting the shift to left by word size. This aligns the intermediate results as follows: $(c_2, c_1), (c_4, c_3), (c_6, c_5), (c_8, c_7)$,

$(c_{10}, c_9), (c_{12}, c_{11}), (c_{14}, c_{13}), (c_{16}, c_{15}), (c_{18}, c_{17})$ and conducts the vectorized partial products.

$$
\begin{aligned}
(c_1, c_0) &\leftarrow (a_0b_1, a_0b_0) \\
(c_3, c_2) &\leftarrow (a_0b_3, a_0b_2) + (a_3b_0, a_2b_0) \\
(c_5, c_4) &\leftarrow (a_0b_5, a_0b_4) + 2(a_2b_3, a_2b_2) + (a_5b_0, a_4b_0) \\
(c_7, c_6) &\leftarrow (a_0b_7, a_0b_6) + 2(a_2b_5, a_2b_4) + 2(a_4b_3, a_4b_2) + (a_7b_0, a_6b_0) \\
(c_9, c_8) &\leftarrow (a_0b_9, a_0b_8) + 2(a_2b_7, a_2b_6) + 2(a_4b_5, a_4b_4) + 2(a_6b_3, a_6b_2) + (a_9b_0, a_8b_0) \\
(c_{11}, c_{10}) &\leftarrow (a_2b_9, 2a_2b_8) + (a_4b_7, 2a_4b_6) + (a_6b_5, 2a_6b_4) + (a_8b_3, 2a_8b_2) \\
(c_{13}, c_{12}) &\leftarrow (a_4b_9, a_4b_8) + (a_6b_7, a_6b_6) + (a_8b_5, a_8b_4) \\
(c_{15}, c_{14}) &\leftarrow (a_6b_9, a_6b_8) + (a_8b_7, a_8b_6) \\
(c_{17}, c_{16}) &\leftarrow (a_8b_9, a_8b_8) \\
c &\leftarrow c \ll word \\
(c_2, c_1) &\leftarrow (2a_1b_1, a_1b_0) \\
(c_4, c_3) &\leftarrow 2(a_1b_3, a_1b_2) + 2(a_3b_1, a_2b_1) \\
(c_6, c_5) &\leftarrow 2(a_1b_5, a_1b_4) + 2(a_3b_3, a_3b_2) + 2(a_5b_1, a_4b_1) \\
(c_8, c_7) &\leftarrow 2(a_1b_7, a_1b_6) + 2(a_3b_5, a_3b_4) + 2(a_5b_3, a_5b_2) + 2(a_7b_1, a_6b_1) \\
(c_{10}, c_9) &\leftarrow 2(a_1b_9, a_1b_8) + 2(a_3b_7, a_3b_6) + 2(a_5b_5, a_5b_4) + 2(a_7b_3, a_7b_2) + 2(a_9b_1, a_8b_1) \\
(c_{12}, c_{11}) &\leftarrow (a_3b_9, a_3b_8) + (a_5b_7, a_5b_6) + (a_7b_5, a_7b_4) + (a_9b_3, a_9b_2) \\
(c_{14}, c_{13}) &\leftarrow (a_5b_9, a_5b_8) + (a_7b_7, a_7b_6) + (a_9b_5, a_9b_4) \\
(c_{16}, c_{15}) &\leftarrow (a_7b_9, a_7b_8) + (a_9b_7, a_9b_6) \\
(c_{18}, c_{17}) &\leftarrow (a_9b_9, a_9b_8)
\end{aligned}
$$

In Step 6 of Algorithm 1, it conducts the partial product of $a_H \cdot b_H$ together with direct modular reduction. Since the reduction on our P-521 representation $(2^{522} - 2)$ only requires double addition/subtraction with values over 2^{522}, we conduct multiplication and double addition/subtraction with variables by calling `vqdmlal` and `vqdmlsl` instructions, respectively. The lower part of multiplication $(a_H \cdot b_H)$ is subtracted from intermediate results from c_{10} to c_{19}. Since the higher part of multiplication $(a_H \cdot b_H)$ is larger than modulus $(2^{522} - 2)$, we directly conduct reduction on intermediate results from c_0 to c_9. More in detail, firstly intermediate results are grouped in $(c_2, c_1), (c_4, c_3), (c_6, c_5), (c_8, c_7), (c_{10}, c_9), (c_{12}, c_{11}), (c_{14}, c_{13}), (c_{16}, c_{15}), (c_{18}, c_{17})$. After then the lower parts of multiplication $(a_H \cdot b_H)$ are subtracted from intermediate results $(c_{11} \sim c_{19})$. The higher parts of multiplication $(a_H \cdot b_H)$ are directly subtracted from intermediate results $(c_0 \sim c_9)$. After then intermediate results are shift to right by word size and then conduct the remaining partial products in following group order: $(c_1, c_0), (c_3, c_2), (c_5, c_4), (c_7, c_6), (c_9, c_8), (c_{11}, c_{10}), (c_{13}, c_{12}), (c_{15}, c_{14}), (c_{17}, c_{16})$.

$$
\begin{aligned}
(a_9 \sim a_0) &\leftarrow (a_{19} \sim a_{10}) \\
(b_9 \sim b_0) &\leftarrow (b_{19} \sim b_{10}) \\
(c_{12}, c_{11}) &\leftarrow (c_{12}, c_{11}) - (2a_1b_1, a_1b_0)
\end{aligned}
$$

$$(c_{14}, c_{13}) \leftarrow (c_{14}, c_{13}) - 2(a_1b_3, a_1b_2) - 2(a_3b_1, a_2b_1)$$
$$(c_{16}, c_{15}) \leftarrow (c_{16}, c_{15}) - 2(a_1b_5, a_1b_4) - 2(a_3b_3, a_3b_2) - 2(a_5b_1, a_4b_1)$$
$$(c_{18}, c_{17}) \leftarrow (c_{18}, c_{17}) - 2(a_1b_7, a_1b_6) - 2(a_3b_5, a_3b_4) - 2(a_5b_3, a_5b_2) - 2(a_7b_1, a_6b_1)$$
$$(t_1, t_0) \leftarrow (4a_1b_9, 2a_1b_8) - (4a_3b_7, 2a_3b_6) - (4a_5b_5, 2a_5b_4) - (4a_7b_3, 2a_7b_2) - (4a_9b_1, 2a_8b_1)$$
$$c_{19} \leftarrow c_{19} - t_0$$
$$c_0 \leftarrow c_0 - t_1$$
$$(c_2, c_1) \leftarrow (c_2, c_1) - 2(a_3b_9, a_3b_8) - 2(a_5b_7, a_5b_6) - 2(a_7b_5, a_7b_4) - 2(a_9b_3, a_9b_2)$$
$$(c_4, c_3) \leftarrow (c_4, c_3) - 2(a_5b_9, a_5b_8) - 2(a_7b_7, a_7b_6) - 2(a_9b_5, a_9b_4)$$
$$(c_6, c_5) \leftarrow (c_6, c_5) - 2(a_7b_9, a_7b_8) - 2(a_9b_7, a_9b_6)$$
$$(c_8, c_7) \leftarrow (c_8, c_7) - 2(a_9b_9, a_9b_8)$$
$$c \leftarrow c \gg word$$
$$(c_{11}, c_{10}) \leftarrow (c_{11}, c_{10}) - (a_0b_1, a_0b_0)$$
$$(c_{13}, c_{12}) \leftarrow (c_{13}, c_{12}) - (a_0b_3, a_0b_2) - (a_3b_0, a_2b_0)$$
$$(c_{15}, c_{14}) \leftarrow (c_{15}, c_{14}) - (a_0b_5, a_0b_4) - 2(a_2b_3, a_2b_2) - (a_5b_0, a_4b_0)$$
$$(c_{17}, c_{16}) \leftarrow (c_{17}, c_{16}) - (a_0b_7, a_0b_6) - 2(a_2b_5, a_2b_4) - 2(a_4b_3, a_4b_2) - (a_7b_0, a_6b_0)$$
$$(c_{19}, c_{18}) \leftarrow (c_{19}, c_{18}) - (a_0b_9, a_0b_8) - 2(a_2b_7, a_2b_6) - 2(a_4b_5, a_4b_4) - 2(a_6b_3, a_6b_2) - (a_9b_0, a_8b_0)$$
$$(t_1, t_0) \leftarrow (2a_2b_9, 4a_2b_8) - (2a_4b_7, 4a_4b_6) - (2a_6b_5, 4a_6b_4) - (2a_8b_3, 4a_8b_2)$$
$$c_0 \leftarrow c_0 - t_0$$
$$c_1 \leftarrow c_1 - t_1$$
$$(c_3, c_2) \leftarrow (c_3, c_2) - 2(a_4b_9, a_4b_8) - 2(a_6b_7, a_6b_6) - 2(a_8b_5, a_8b_4)$$
$$(c_5, c_4) \leftarrow (c_5, c_4) - 2(a_6b_9, a_6b_8) - 2(a_8b_7, a_8b_6)$$
$$(c_7, c_6) \leftarrow (c_7, c_6) - 2(a_8b_9, a_8b_8)$$

3.2 Squaring

Multi-precision squaring can be utilized with ordinary multiplication methods. However, squaring method has two advantages over the multiplication methods. Both partial products $A[i] \times A[j]$ and $A[j] \times A[i]$ output the identical results. By taking accounts of these features, the parts are multiplied with doubled form (i.e. $2 \times A[i] \times A[j]$) which provides the same results of conventional multiplication (i.e. $A[i] \times A[j] + A[j] \times A[i]$). We applied squaring on 261-bit wise operand as follows. Unlike multiplication operation, squaring can eliminate the almost half of partial product with doubling but this introduces quadrupled results. In order to resolve this matter, we firstly doubled the operands and preserve both original and doubled operands in the registers. This is possible approach, because squaring only needs one operand and remaining registers can retain the doubled operands. This ensures the quadrupled multiplication with doubled operands and double multiplication instruction such as `vqdmull`.

$$
\begin{aligned}
c_0 &\leftarrow a_0a_0\\
c_1 &\leftarrow 2(a_0a_1)\\
c_2 &\leftarrow 2(a_0a_2 + a_1a_1)\\
c_3 &\leftarrow 2(a_0a_3) + 4(a_1a_2)\\
c_4 &\leftarrow 2(a_0a_4 + a_2a_2) + 4(a_1a_3)\\
c_5 &\leftarrow 2(a_0a_5) + 4(a_1a_4 + a_2a_3)\\
c_6 &\leftarrow 2(a_0a_6 + a_3a_3) + 4(a_1a_5 + a_2a_4)\\
c_7 &\leftarrow 2(a_0a_7) + 4(a_1a_6 + a_2a_5 + a_3a_4)\\
c_8 &\leftarrow 2(a_0a_8 + a_4a_4) + 4(a_1a_7 + a_2a_6 + a_3a_5)\\
c_9 &\leftarrow 2(a_0a_9) + 4(a_1a_8 + a_2a_7 + a_3a_6 + a_4a_5)\\
c_{10} &\leftarrow 2(a_5a_5) + 4(a_1a_9 + a_2a_8 + a_3a_7 + a_4a_6)\\
c_{11} &\leftarrow 2(a_2a_9 + a_3a_8 + a_4a_7 + a_5a_6)\\
c_{12} &\leftarrow 2(a_3a_9 + a_4a_8 + a_5a_7) + a_6a_6\\
c_{13} &\leftarrow 2(a_4a_9 + a_5a_8 + a_6a_7)\\
c_{14} &\leftarrow 2(a_5a_9 + a_6a_8) + a_7a_7\\
c_{15} &\leftarrow 2(a_6a_9 + a_7a_8)\\
c_{16} &\leftarrow 2(a_7a_9) + a_8a_8\\
c_{17} &\leftarrow 2(a_8a_9)\\
c_{18} &\leftarrow a_9a_9
\end{aligned}
$$

Similar with SIMD multiplication, squaring operation also needs to group the two intermediate results in SIMD friendly way. Squaring has one more advantage over that of multiplication. The whole squaring operation can be executed in following representation (c_1, c_0), (c_3, c_2), (c_5, c_4), (c_7, c_6), (c_9, c_8), (c_{11}, c_{10}), (c_{13}, c_{12}), (c_{15}, c_{14}), (c_{17}, c_{16}). Since squaring reduces the duplicated partial products, single group representation can cover the whole partial products without re-arrangements.

$$
\begin{aligned}
(c_1, c_0) &\leftarrow (2a_0a_1, a_0a_0)\\
(c_3, c_2) &\leftarrow 2(a_0a_3, a_0a_2) + (4a_1a_2, 2a_1a_1)\\
(c_5, c_4) &\leftarrow 2(a_0a_5, a_0a_4) + 4(a_1a_4, a_1a_3) + (4a_2a_3, 2a_2a_2)\\
(c_7, c_6) &\leftarrow 2(a_0a_7, a_0a_6) + 4(a_1a_6, a_1a_5) + 4(a_2a_5, a_2a_4) + (4a_3a_4, 2a_3a_3)\\
(c_9, c_8) &\leftarrow 2(a_0a_9, a_0a_8) + 4(a_1a_8, a_1a_7) + 4(a_2a_7, a_2a_6) +\\
&\quad 4(a_3a_6, a_3a_5) + (4a_4a_5, 2a_4a_4)\\
(c_{11}, c_{10}) &\leftarrow (2a_2a_9, 4a_1a_9) + (2a_3a_8, 4a_2a_8) + (2a_4a_7, 4a_3a_7) + (2a_5a_6, 4a_4a_6)\\
(c_{13}, c_{12}) &\leftarrow 2(a_4a_9, a_3a_9) + 2(a_5a_8, a_4a_8) + 2(a_6a_7, a_5a_7)\\
(c_{15}, c_{14}) &\leftarrow 2(a_6a_9, a_5a_9) + 2(a_7a_8, a_6a_8)
\end{aligned}
$$

$$(c_{17}, c_{16}) \leftarrow 2(a_8a_9, a_7a_9)$$
$$(t_1, t_0) \leftarrow (a_6a_6, 2a_5a_5)$$
$$(t_3, t_2) \leftarrow (a_8a_8, a_7a_7)$$
$$t_4 \leftarrow a_9a_9$$
$$c_{10} \leftarrow c_{10} + t_0$$
$$c_{12} \leftarrow c_{12} + t_1$$
$$c_{14} \leftarrow c_{14} + t_2$$
$$c_{16} \leftarrow c_{16} + t_3$$
$$c_{18} \leftarrow c_{18} + t_4$$

We also applied the direct reduction techniques described in Steps 6 and 12 in Algorithm 1 for the squaring method as well. Firstly intermediate results are grouped in $(c_1, c_0), (c_3, c_2), (c_5, c_4), (c_7, c_6), (c_9, c_8), (c_{11}, c_{10}), (c_{13}, c_{12}), (c_{15}, c_{14}), (c_{17}, c_{16})$. After then the lower part of multiplication $(a_H \cdot a_H)$ is subtracted from intermediate results $(c_{11} \sim c_{19})$. The higher part of multiplication $(a_H \cdot a_H)$ is directly subtracted from intermediate results $(c_0 \sim c_9)$.

$$(a_9 \sim a_0) \leftarrow (a_{19} \sim a_{10})$$
$$(c_{11}, c_{10}) \leftarrow (c_{11}, c_{10}) - (2a_0a_1, a_0a_0)$$
$$(c_{13}, c_{12}) \leftarrow (c_{13}, c_{12}) - 2(a_0a_3, a_0a_2) - (4a_1a_2, 2a_1a_1)$$
$$(c_{15}, c_{14}) \leftarrow (c_{15}, c_{14}) - 2(a_0a_5, a_0a_4) - 4(a_1a_4, a_1a_3) - (4a_2a_3, 2a_2a_2)$$
$$(c_{17}, c_{16}) \leftarrow (c_{17}, c_{16}) - 2(a_0a_7, a_0a_6) - 4(a_1a_6, a_1a_5) - 4(a_2a_5, a_2a_4) - (4a_3a_4, 2a_3a_3)$$
$$(c_{19}, c_{18}) \leftarrow (c_{19}, c_{18}) - 2(a_0a_9, a_0a_8) - 4(a_1a_8, a_1a_7) - 4(a_2a_7, a_2a_6) - 4(a_3a_6, a_3a_5) - (4a_4a_5, 2a_4a_4)$$
$$(c_1, c_0) \leftarrow (c_1, c_0) - (4a_2a_9, 8a_1a_9) - (4a_3a_8, 8a_2a_8) - (4a_4a_7, 8a_3a_7) - (4a_5a_6, 8a_4a_6)$$
$$(c_3, c_2) \leftarrow (c_3, c_2) - 4(a_4a_9, a_3a_9) - 4(a_5a_8, a_4a_8) - 4(a_6a_7, a_5a_7)$$
$$(c_5, c_4) \leftarrow (c_5, c_4) - 4(a_6a_9, a_5a_9) - 4(a_7a_8, a_6a_8)$$
$$(c_7, c_6) \leftarrow (c_7, c_6) - 4(a_8a_9, a_7a_9)$$
$$(t_1, t_0) \leftarrow (2a_6a_6, 4a_5a_5)$$
$$(t_3, t_2) \leftarrow 2(a_8a_8, a_7a_7)$$
$$t_4 \leftarrow 2a_9a_9$$
$$c_0 \leftarrow c_{10} - t_0$$
$$c_2 \leftarrow c_{12} - t_1$$
$$c_4 \leftarrow c_{14} - t_2$$
$$c_6 \leftarrow c_{16} - t_3$$
$$c_8 \leftarrow c_{18} - t_4$$

3.3 Inversion

Constant-time inversion is performed by powering by $p_{521} - 2 = 2^{521} - 3$. The inverse can be computed at a cost of 520S + 13M by following Algorithm 2.

Algorithm 2. Fermat-based inversion mod p_{521}

Require: Integer a_1 satisfying $1 \leq a_1 \leq p-1$.
Ensure: Inverse $z = a_1^{p-2} \bmod p = a_1^{-1} \bmod p$.

$a_2 \leftarrow a_1^{2} \cdot a_1$ {cost: 1S+1M}
$a_3 \leftarrow a_2^{2} \cdot a_1$ {cost: 1S+1M}
$a_6 \leftarrow a_3^{2^3} \cdot a_3$ {cost: 3S+1M}
$a_7 \leftarrow a_6^{2} \cdot a_1$ {cost: 1S+1M}
$a_8 \leftarrow a_7^{2} \cdot a_1$ {cost: 1S+1M}
$a_{16} \leftarrow a_8^{2^8} \cdot a_8$ {cost: 8S+1M}
$a_{32} \leftarrow a_{16}^{2^{16}} \cdot a_{16}$ {cost: 16S+1M}
$a_{64} \leftarrow a_{32}^{2^{32}} \cdot a_{32}$ {cost: 32S+1M}
$a_{128} \leftarrow a_{64}^{2^{64}} \cdot a_{64}$ {cost: 64S+1M}
$a_{256} \leftarrow a_{128}^{2^{128}} \cdot a_{128}$ {cost: 128S+1M}
$a_{512} \leftarrow a_{256}^{2^{256}} \cdot a_{256}$ {cost: 256S+1M}
$a_{519} \leftarrow a_{512}^{2^7} \cdot a_7$ {cost: 7S+1M}
$a_1^{2^{521}-3} \leftarrow a_{519}^{2^2} \cdot a_1$ {cost: 2S+1M}
return $a_1^{2^{521}-3}$

3.4 Addition and Subtraction

Addition and subtraction over redundant representations do not introduce the carry or borrow propagations from least significant word to most significant word. Since SIMD instruction conducts the four different addition or subtraction operations with single instruction, we conduct 20 26/27-radix addition/subtraction with five times of 32-bit wise vector addition/subtraction operations. For point addition and doubling, several addition variants such as integer doubling, tripling, quadrupling, octupling are required. We also exploit the vector addition by 1, 2, 2, 3 times for doubling, tripling, quadrupling and octupling operations, respectively. Since the tripling, quadrupling and octupling operations may generate the overflows in very next step, we conduct reduction right after the operations.

3.5 Radix Adjustments

The multiplication and squaring computations produce a product of the 63-bit 20 limbs for intermediate results. We then use a sequence of carries to bring each limb down to 26 or 27 bits. We vectorized between a carry $c_0 \rightarrow c_1$ and $c_{10} \rightarrow c_{11}$, between a carry $c_1 \rightarrow c_2$ and $c_{11} \rightarrow c_{12}$. The computation order is as follows: $(c_{10}, c_0) \rightarrow (c_{11}, c_1)$, $(c_{11}, c_1) \rightarrow (c_{12}, c_2)$, $(c_{12}, c_2) \rightarrow (c_{13}, c_3)$, $(c_{13}, c_3) \rightarrow (c_{14}, c_4)$, $(c_{14}, c_4) \rightarrow (c_{15}, c_5)$, $(c_{15}, c_5) \rightarrow (c_{16}, c_6)$, $(c_{16}, c_6) \rightarrow (c_{17}, c_7)$, $(c_{17}, c_7) \rightarrow (c_{18}, c_8)$, $(c_{18}, c_8) \rightarrow (c_{19}, c_9)$, $(c_{19}, c_9) \rightarrow (c_0, c_{10})$, $(c_{10}, c_0) \rightarrow (c_{11}, c_1)$. The computations output 20 limbs of results (27, 27, 26, 26, 26, 26, 26, 26, 26, 26 || 27, 27, 26, 26, 26, 26, 26, 26, 26, 26) (Table 1).

The addition and subtraction computations carry out the 31-bit wise 20 limbs. Similarly, we use a sequence of carries to bring each limb down to 26 or

27 bits. The computation order is as follows: $(c_{19}, c_9) \rightarrow (c_0, c_{10})$, $(c_{10}, c_0) \rightarrow (c_{11}, c_1)$, $(c_{11}, c_1) \rightarrow (c_{12}, c_2)$, $(c_{12}, c_2) \rightarrow (c_{13}, c_3)$, $(c_{13}, c_3) \rightarrow (c_{14}, c_4)$, $(c_{14}, c_4) \rightarrow (c_{15}, c_5)$, $(c_{15}, c_5) \rightarrow (c_{16}, c_6)$, $(c_{16}, c_6) \rightarrow (c_{17}, c_7)$, $(c_{17}, c_7) \rightarrow (c_{18}, c_8)$, $(c_{18}, c_8) \rightarrow (c_{19}, c_9)$. This computation outputs 20 limbs as follows (27, 26, 26, 26, 26, 26, 26, 26, 26, 27 || 27, 26, 26, 26, 26, 26, 26, 26, 26, 27). Unlike multiplication case, we firstly conduct the radix adjustment on the most significant group (c_{19}, c_9) which can reduce the one time of adjustment.

Table 1. Prime-field ECC timings from `openssl speed ecdh` on Cortex-A9 and Cortex-A15 devices where Cortex-A9 with OpenSSL 1.0.2d on a Odroid-X2 development board running at 1.7 GHz and Cortex-A15 with OpenSSL 1.0.2d on a Odroid-XU development board running at 1.6 GHz

Curve	A9 op/s	Cycles	A15 op/s	Cycles
`secp160r1`	1014.4	1,700,000	1258.8	1,280,000
`nist192`	718.2	2,380,000	951.0	1,760,000
`nist224`	489.2	3,400,000	701.4	2,240,000
`nist256`	475.5	3,570,000	574.9	2,720,000
`nist384`	154.6	11,050,000	223.0	7,200,000
`nist521`	71.2	23,800,000	85.3	18,720,000

3.6 Scalar Multiplication

Constant time scalar multiplication is computed with the window method. This consists of pre-computation of point and scalar multiplication by window width. For unknown point, we tested over three different window sizes including 4, 5 and 6. For window size 4, pre-computation needs 1 time of doubling and 7 times of addition. For window size 5, pre-computation needs 1 time of doubling and 15 times of addition. For window size 6, pre-computation needs 1 time of doubling and 31 times of addition. Without point pre-computation, scalar multiplication needs (131A+520D), (105A+520D), (87A+516D) for 4, 5, 6 window methods. Total (138A+521D), (120A+521D), (118A+517D) are needed for 4, 5, 6 window methods. For fixed point we conduct the comb window method. Since fixed point can take advantages of online pre-computation which reduces the number of point doubling, total overheads for 4, 5, 6 window methods are calculated in (131A+130D), (105A+104D), (87A+86D), respectively.

4 Evaluation

There are several works done over lower security levels including Curve41417 and Ed448-Goldilocks [1,5]. However it is hard to retrieve the fair performance evaluations due to different parameters. One obvious difference is that smaller curve

Table 2. Clock cycles for scalar multiplication

Target	Unknown point			Fixed point			ECDH
	w=4	w=5	w=6	w=4	w=5	w=6	
Cortex-A9	6,291,936	6,098,946	6,011,768	3,056,410	2,527,714	2,147,404	8,159,172
Cortex-A15	3,097,904	3,003,728	2,970,976	1,503,661	1,243,027	1,056,902	4,027,878

Table 3. Clock cycles for finite field multiplication, squaring and inversion; point addition and doubling

Target	Finite field arithmetic			Point operation	
	MUL	SQR	INV	ADD	DBL
Cortex-A9	708	578	311,451	12,453	8,036
Cortex-A15	350	276	149,208	6,176	3,962

only requires small number of general purpose registers which utilizes the more number of temporal registers than longer curve. Furthermore target modulus prime is different to each other which introduces totally different radix representations and fast reduction algorithms. For this reason, we evaluate the obvious candidate, latest OpenSSL 1.0.2d implementations using the command `openssl speed ecdh`. On the same architecture, OpenSSL 1.0.2d reports 71.2 and 85.3 operations per second for A9 and A15, which implies a count of approximately 23.8 M and 18.7 M cycles per ECDH. On the other hand, our implementations described in Table 2 only require 8.1 M and 4.0 M cycles per ECDH for A9 and A15, respectively. In Table 3, the detailed clock cycles for basic operations are drawn where the clock cycles of finite field operations include reduction operation and the point addition and doubling is calculated over Jacobian representations.

5 Conclusion

In this paper, we show efficient implementations of P-521 over ARM-NEON processor. We conduct 1-level of Karatsuba multiplication together with direct modular reduction on $(2^{522} - 2)$. By taking advantages of several optimization techniques, we improve the modular multiplication on P-521 significantly. Same technique is also applied to squaring and reduces the complexities in similar manner. Finally, we outperform the latest OpenSSL 1.0.2d over both A9 and A15 ARM processors.

References

1. Bernstein, D.J., Chuengsatiansup, C., Lange, T.: Curve41417: karatsuba revisited. In: Batina, L., Robshaw, M. (eds.) CHES 2014. LNCS, vol. 8731, pp. 316–334. Springer, Heidelberg (2014)

2. Bos, J.W., Kaihara, M.E.: Montgomery multiplication on the cell. In: Wyrzykowski, R., Dongarra, J., Karczewski, K., Wasniewski, J. (eds.) PPAM 2009, Part I. LNCS, vol. 6067, pp. 477–485. Springer, Heidelberg (2010)
3. Standard for Efficient Cryptography Group: Recommended elliptic curve domain parameters (2000)
4. Granger, R., Scott, M.: Faster ECC over $\mathbb{F}_{2^{521}-1}$. In: Katz, J. (ed.) PKC 2015. LNCS, vol. 9020, pp. 539–553. Springer, Heidelberg (2015)
5. Hamburg, M.: Ed448-goldilocks, a new elliptic curve
6. Intel Corporation.: Using streaming SIMD extensions (SSE2) to perform big multiplications, Application note AP-941 (2000). http://software.intel.com/sites/default/files/14/4f/24960
7. U.D. of Commerce/N.I.S.T. Federal information processing standards publication 186–2 fipps 186–2 digital signature standard
8. Pabbuleti, K.C., Mane, D.H., Desai, A., Albert, C., Schaumont, P.: SIMD acceleration of modular arithmetic on contemporary embedded platforms. In: High Performance Extreme Computing Conference (HPEC), pp. 1–6. IEEE (2013)

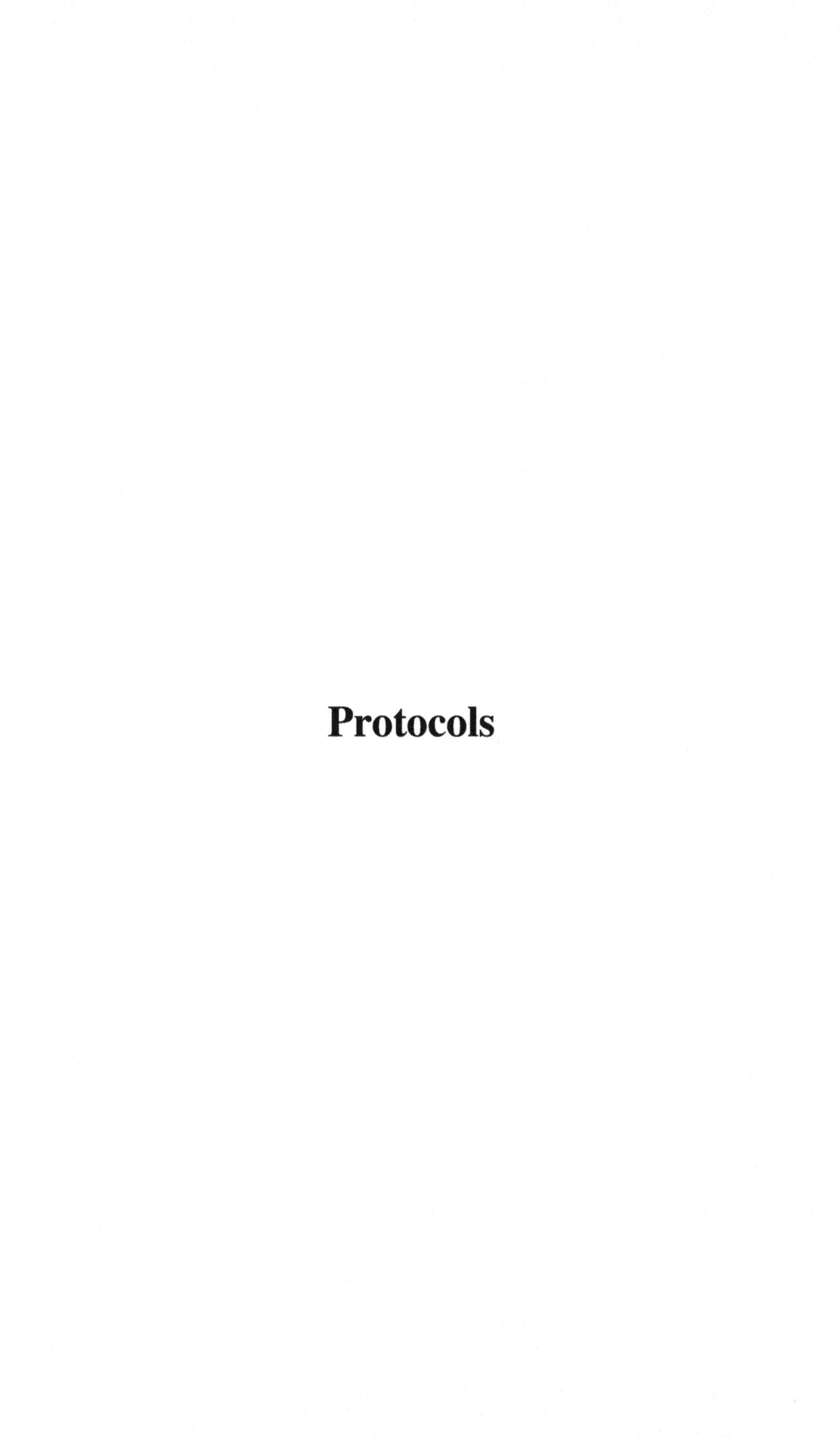

Protocols

On the (In)Efficiency of Non-Interactive Secure Multiparty Computation

Maki Yoshida[1(✉)] and Satoshi Obana[2]

[1] NICT, Tokyo, Japan
maki-yos@nict.go.jp
[2] Hosei University, Tokyo, Japan
obana@hosei.ac.jp

Abstract. Secure multi-party computation (MPC) enables multiple players to cooperatively evaluate various functions in the presence of adversaries. In this paper, we consider *non-interactive* MPC (NIMPC) against honest-but-curious adversaries in the information-theoretic setting, which was introduced by Beimel et al. in CRYPTO 2014. Their main focus is to realize stronger security while completely avoiding interaction, and succeeded to show that every function admits a fully robust NIMPC protocol. A drawback of this positive result is the communication complexity, which is linear in the size of the input domain (i.e., exponential in the input length). We first prove that this inefficiency is essentially unavoidable by deriving a lower bound on the communication complexity. However, there is an exponential gap between the derived lower bound and the previous construction. We then reduce the gap between the lower and upper bounds to quadratic in the input length by presenting a much more efficient construction of an important building block, which is an NIMPC protocol for indicator functions.

Keywords: Multiparty computation · Information theoretical setting · Non-interactive · Communication complexity · Lower bound · Upper bound

1 Introduction

Secure multi-party computation (MPC) aims to enable multiple players to cooperatively compute various functions in the presence of adversaries. MPC was first introduced by Yao [10] and because of its importance in cryptography, there have been presented many variants so far [3–5, 7–9]. In CRYPTO 2014 [2], Beimel et al. have introduced a novel type of MPC, called *non-interactive* MPC (NIMPC), against honest-but-curious adversaries in the information theoretical setting, which completely avoids interaction while realizing as strong security as possible. They have succeeded to obtain unconditional positive results for some special cases of interest. In particular, they have presented fully robust protocols for various classes of functions including the class of arbitrary functions. The fully robustness here means that any set of corrupted players cannot obtain

S. Kwon and A. Yun (Eds.): ICISC 2015, LNCS 9558, pp. 185–193, 2016.
DOI: 10.1007/978-3-319-30840-1_12

Table 1. The communication complexity of n-player NIMPC protocols for a family of functions $h : \mathcal{X} \to \{0,1\}^m$ where $\mathcal{X} = \mathcal{X}_1 \times \cdots \times \mathcal{X}_n$ and $d' \le |\mathcal{X}_i| \le d$ for all $1 \le i \le n$.

	Arbitrary functions	Indicator functions ($m = 1$)
Previous protocols in [2]	$\lvert\mathcal{X}\rvert \cdot m \cdot d^2 \cdot n$	$d^2 \cdot n$
Lower bound (Sect. 3)	$\lvert\mathcal{X}\rvert \cdot m$	$\log_2 d' \cdot n$
Our protocols (Sect. 4)	$\lvert\mathcal{X}\rvert \cdot m \cdot \lceil \log_2(d+1) \rceil^2 \cdot n$	$\lceil \log_2(d+1) \rceil^2 \cdot n$

any information other than those obtained by an oracle access to the function restricted to the input values of uncorrupted players. However, except for special functions like the summation in an abelian group, the communication complexity is not less than polynomial in the size of the input domain (i.e., exponential in the input length) (Table 1).

The question we ask is whether there is a room to reduce the communication complexity of NIMPC. Unfortunately, relatively less has been known about limitations on the communication complexity of MPC. Recently, the research to tackle the difficult problem of lower bounds for communication in MPC becomes active like Data et al. in CRYPTO 2014 [6]. They have developed novel information-theoretic tools to prove lower bounds on the communication complexity in the traditional (i.e., *interactive*) model involving 3-parties.

In this paper, we study the communication complexity of NIMPC defined in [2]. As a result, we show that the inefficiency on communication of NIMPC is essentially unavoidable except for special classes of functions. The contributions of this paper are as follows.

Communication complexity of NIMPC for the set of any functions: We derive the first lower bound on the communication complexity of NIMPC for any set of functions. The derived lower bound is the logarithm of the size of the function set. In particular, for the set of arbitrary functions $f : \mathcal{X} \to \{0,1\}^m$ where $\mathcal{X}$ is the input domain and m is the output length, the lower bound is $|\mathcal{X}| \cdot m$, i.e., exponential in the input length.

Communication complexity for the set of indicator functions: On the other hand, for the set of indicator functions, where the number of functions is linear in the input and output length, we have a significantly small lower bound. However, the communication complexity of the previous NIMPC protocol for indicator functions in [2] is exponential in the input length. This gap implies an exponential gap between the lower and upper bounds of NIMPC protocols for arbitrary functions because the NIMPC protocol for indicator functions is used as a building block.

Efficient NIMPC protocol for indicator functions: We then reduce the exponential gap between the lower and upper bounds on the communication complexity to quadratic by constructing a much more efficient NIMPC protocol for indicator functions. Specifically, we present a construction of NIMPC protocols for indicator functions whose communication complexity is quadratic in the input length.

Our technique for deriving lower bounds is quite simple and useful for approximating the amount of communication. For the target class of functions, we first assume the existence of a *correct* NIMPC protocol with some communication complexity and show a method for a server to send data to a client by encoding data into a function and evaluating the function with the use of the NIMPC protocol. Thus, the communication complexity is bounded by the size of target class. If the assumed communication complexity is smaller than the logarithm of the size of the target class, the contradiction is implied. Thus, the communication complexity is lower bounded by the logarithm of the size of the target class. A similar technique is used in [1] for proving *impossibility* of multiplicative secret sharing rather than derivation of lower bounds.

2 Preliminaries

We recall the notations and definitions of NIMPC introduced in [2]. For an integer n, let $[n]$ be the set $\{1, 2, \ldots, n\}$. For a set $\mathcal{X} = \mathcal{X}_1 \times \cdots \times \mathcal{X}_n$ and $T \subseteq [n]$, we denote $\mathcal{X}_T \triangleq \prod_{i \in T} \mathcal{X}_i$. For $x \in \mathcal{X}$, we denote by x_T the restriction of x to $\mathcal{X}_T$, and for a function $h : \mathcal{X} \to \Omega$, a subset $T \subseteq [n]$, and $x_{\overline{T}} \in \mathcal{X}_{\overline{T}}$, we denote by $h|_{\overline{T}, x_{\overline{T}}} : \mathcal{X} \to \Omega$ the function h where the inputs in $\mathcal{X}_{\overline{T}}$ are fixed to $x_{\overline{T}}$. For a set S, let $|S|$ denote its size (i.e., cardinality of S).

An NIMPC protocol for a family of functions $\mathcal{H}$ is defined by three algorithms: (1) a randomness generation function GEN, which given a description of a function $h \in \mathcal{H}$ generates n correlated random inputs $R_1, \ldots, R_n$, (2) a local encoding function ENC_i $(1 \leq i \leq n)$, which takes an input x_i and a random input R_i and outputs a message, and (3) a decoding algorithm DEC that reconstructs $h(x_1, \ldots, x_n)$ from the n messages. The formal definition is given as follows:

Definition 1 (NIMPC: Syntax and Correctness). *Let $\mathcal{X}_1, \ldots, \mathcal{X}_n$, $\mathcal{R}_1, \ldots$, $\mathcal{R}_n$, $\mathcal{M}_1, \ldots, \mathcal{M}_n$ and Ω be finite domains. Let $\mathcal{X} \triangleq \mathcal{X}_1 \times \cdots \times \mathcal{X}_n$ and let $\mathcal{H}$ be a family of functions $h : \mathcal{X} \to \Omega$. A non-interactive secure multi-party computation (NIMPC) protocol for $\mathcal{H}$ is a triplet $\Pi = (\mathsf{GEN}, \mathsf{ENC}, \mathsf{DEC})$ where*

- $\mathsf{GEN} : \mathcal{H} \to \mathcal{R}_1 \times \cdots \times \mathcal{R}_n$ *is a random function,*
- ENC *is an n-tuple deterministic functions* $(\mathsf{ENC}_1, \ldots, \mathsf{ENC}_n)$*, where* $\mathsf{ENC}_i : \mathcal{X}_i \times \mathcal{R}_i \to \mathcal{M}_i$*,*
- $\mathsf{DEC} : \mathcal{M}_1 \times \cdots \times \mathcal{M}_n \to \Omega$ *is is a deterministic function satisfying the following correctness requirement: for any $x = (x_1, \ldots, x_n) \in \mathcal{X}$ and $h \in \mathcal{H}$,*

$$\Pr[R = (R_1, \ldots, R_n) \leftarrow \mathsf{GEN}(h) : \mathsf{DEC}(\mathsf{ENC}(x, R)) = h(x)] = 1, \quad (1)$$

where $\mathsf{ENC}(x, R) \triangleq (\mathsf{ENC}_1(x_1, R_1), \ldots, \mathsf{ENC}_n(x_n, R_n))$.

The individual communication complexity of Π is the maximum of $\log |\mathcal{R}_1|, \ldots,$ $\log |\mathcal{R}_n|$, $\log |\mathcal{M}_1|, \ldots,$ $\log |\mathcal{M}_n|$. *The total communication complexity of Π is the summation of* $\log |\mathcal{R}_1|, \ldots,$ $\log |\mathcal{R}_n|$, $\log |\mathcal{M}_1|, \ldots,$ $\log |\mathcal{M}_n|$.

We next show the definition of robustness for NIMPC, which states that a coalition can only learn the information they should. In the above setting, a coalition T can repeatedly encode any inputs for T and decode h with the new encoded inputs and the original encoded inputs of $\overline{T}$. Thus, the following robustness requires that they learn no other information than the information obtained from oracle access to $h|_{\overline{T},x_{\overline{T}}}$.

Definition 2 (NIMPC: Robustness). *For a subset $T \subseteq [n]$, we say that an NIMPC protocol Π for $\mathcal{H}$ is T-*robust *if there exists a randomized function Sim_T (a "simulator") such that, for every $h \in \mathcal{H}$ and $x_{\overline{T}} \in \mathcal{X}_{\overline{T}}$, we have $Sim_T(h|_{\overline{T},x_{\overline{T}}}) \equiv (M_{\overline{T}}, R_T)$, where R and M are the joint randomness and messages defined by $R \leftarrow \mathsf{GEN}(h)$ and $M_i \leftarrow \mathsf{ENC}_i(x_i, R_i)$.*

*For an integer $0 \leq t \leq n$, we say that Π is t-*robust *if it is T-robust for every $T \subseteq [n]$ of size $|T| \leq t$. We say that Π is* fully robust *(or simply refer to Π as an NIMPC for $\mathcal{H}$) if Π is n-robust. Finally, given a concrete function $h : \mathcal{X} \to \Omega$, we say that Π is a (t-robust) NIMPC protocol for h if it is a (t-robust) NIMPC for $\mathcal{H} = \{h\}$.*

As the same simulator Sim_T is used for every $h \in \mathcal{H}$ and the simulator has only access to $h|_{\overline{T},x_{\overline{T}}}$, NIMPC hides both h and the inputs of $\overline{T}$. An NIMPC protocol is 0-robust if it is $\emptyset$-robust. In this case, the only requirement is that the messages $(M_1, \ldots, M_n)$ reveal $h(x)$ and nothing else.

An NIMPC protocol is also described in the language of protocols in [2]. Such a protocol involves n players $P_1, \ldots, P_n$, each holding an input $x_i \in \mathcal{X}_i$, and an external "output server," a player P_0 with no input. The protocol may have an additional input, a function $h \in \mathcal{H}$.

Definition 3 (NIMPC: Protocol Description). *For an NIMPC protocol Π for $\mathcal{H}$, let* $\mathrm{P}(\Pi)$ *denote the protocol that may have an additional input, a function $h \in \mathcal{H}$, and proceeds as follows.*

Protocol $\mathrm{P}(\Pi)(h)$

- **Offline preprocessing:** *Each player P_i, $1 \leq i \leq n$, receives the random input $R_i \triangleq \mathsf{GEN}(h)_i \in \mathcal{R}_i$.*
- **Online messages:** *On input R_i, each player P_i, $1 \leq i \leq n$, sends the message $M_i \triangleq \mathsf{ENC}_i(x_i, R_i) \in \mathcal{M}_i$ to P_0.*
- **Output:** *P_0 computes and outputs $\mathsf{DEC}(M_1, \ldots, M_n)$.*

Informally, the relevant properties of protocol $\mathrm{P}(\Pi)$ are given as follows:

- For any $h \in \mathcal{H}$ and $x \in \mathcal{X}$, the output server P_0 outputs, with probability 1, the value $h(x_1, \ldots, x_n)$.
- Fix $T \subseteq [n]$. Then, Π is T-robust if in $\mathrm{P}(\Pi)$ the set of players $\{P_i\}_{i \in T} \cup \{P_0\}$ can simulate their view of the protocol (i.e., the random inputs $\{R_i\}_{i \in T}$ and the messages $\{M_i\}_{i \in \overline{T}}$) given oracle access to the function h restricted by the other inputs (i.e., $h|_{\overline{T},x_{\overline{T}}}$).

- Π is 0-robust if and only if in $\mathrm{P}(\Pi)$ the output server P_0 learns nothing but $h(x_1, \ldots, x_n)$.

We show a claim in [2] stating that for functions outputting more than one bit, we can compute each output bit separately. Based on this fact, in [2], a fully robust NIMPC protocol for the set of indicator functions was first constructed, and then NIMPC protocols for the set of arbitrary functions are constructed based on it.

Proposition 1 (Claim 7 in [2]). *Let $\mathcal{X} \triangleq \mathcal{X}_1 \times \cdots \times \mathcal{X}_n$, where $\mathcal{X}_1, \ldots, \mathcal{X}_n$ are some finite domains. Fix an integer $m > 1$. Suppose $\mathcal{H}$ is a family of boolean functions $h : \mathcal{X} \to \{0,1\}$ admitting an NIMPC protocol with communication complexity δ. Then, the family of functions $\mathcal{H}^m = \{h : \mathcal{X} \to \{0,1\}^m | h = h_1 \circ \cdots \circ h_m, h_i \in \mathcal{H}\}$ admits an NIMPC protocol with communication complexity $\delta \cdot m$.*

Definition 4 (Indicator Functions). *Let $\mathcal{X}$ be a finite domain. For n-tuple $a = (a_1, \ldots, a_n) \in \mathcal{X}$, let $h_a : \mathcal{X} \to \{0,1\}$ be the function defined by $h_a(a) = 1$, and $h_a(x) = 0$ for all $a \neq x \in \mathcal{X}$. Let $h_0 : \mathcal{X} \to \{0,1\}$ be the function that is identically zero on $\mathcal{X}$. Let $\mathcal{H}_{\text{ind}} \triangleq \{h_a\}_{a \in \mathcal{X}} \cup \{h_0\}$ be the set of all indicator functions together with h_0.*

Note that every function $h : \mathcal{X} \to \{0,1\}$ can be expressed as the sum of indicator functions, namely, $h = \sum_{a \in \mathcal{X}, h(a)=1} h_a$.

We review the previous results on upper bounds on the *individual* communication complexity of NIMPC. As described above, the NIMPC protocols in [2] are constructed from NIMPC for $\mathcal{H}_{\text{ind}}$. Thus, the previous upper bounds depend on the upper bound for $\mathcal{H}_{\text{ind}}$. This means we have a better upper bound if we obtain a more efficient NIMPC protocol for $\mathcal{H}_{\text{ind}}$.

Proposition 2 (Arbitrary Functions $\mathcal{H}_{\text{all}}$, Proof of Theorem 10 in [2]). *Fix finite domains $\mathcal{X}_1, \ldots, \mathcal{X}_n$ such that $|\mathcal{X}_i| \leq d$ for all $1 \leq i \leq n$ and let $\mathcal{X} \triangleq \mathcal{X}_1 \times \cdots \times \mathcal{X}_n$. Let $\mathcal{H}_{\text{all}}$ be the set of all functions $h : \mathcal{X} \to \{0,1\}^m$. If there exists an NIMPC protocol for $\mathcal{H}_{\text{ind}}$ with individual communication complexity δ, then there exists an NIMPC protocol for $\mathcal{H}$ with individual (resp. total) communication complexity $|\mathcal{X}| \cdot m \cdot \delta$ (resp. $|\mathcal{X}| \cdot m \cdot \delta \cdot n$).*

3 Lower Bounds on the Communication Complexity

We derive a lower bound on the *total* communication complexity for any finite set of functions, $\mathcal{H}_{\text{all}}$, and $\mathcal{H}_{\text{ind}}$, respectively.

As described in the introduction, the total communication complexity is bounded by the size of target class. In other words, the total communication complexity cannot be smaller than the logarithm of the size of the target class.

Theorem 1 (Lower bound for any Finite Set of Functions). *Fix finite domains $\mathcal{X}_1, \ldots, \mathcal{X}_n$ and Ω. Let $\mathcal{X} \triangleq \mathcal{X}_1, \ldots, \mathcal{X}_n$ and $\mathcal{H}$ a set of functions $h : \mathcal{X} \to \Omega$. Then, any fully robust NIMPC protocol Π for $\mathcal{H}$ satisfies*

$$\sum_{i=1}^{n} \log |\mathcal{R}_i| \geq \log |\mathcal{H}|, \tag{2}$$

$$\sum_{i=1}^{n} \log |\mathcal{M}_i| \geq \log |\Omega|. \tag{3}$$

Proof. We first prove Eq. (2). Let $H = |\mathcal{H}|$. Let φ be a one-to-one mapping from $\mathcal{H}$ to $\{0, 1, \ldots, H-1\}$. (That is, all functions in $\mathcal{H}$ are numbered on some rule.) Suppose a server holding a random number $a \in \{0, \ldots, H-1\}$ aims to send a to a client. Suppose also that there is an NIMPC protocol (GEN, ENC, DEC) for $\mathcal{H}$ that satisfies $\sum_{i=1}^{n} \log |\mathcal{R}_i| < \log H$. For the function $h = \varphi(a)$, the server executes $R \leftarrow \mathsf{GEN}(h)$ and sends R to the client. The client obtains a by executing ENC and DEC for all possible inputs $x \in \mathcal{X}$ and identifying the function h. We conclude that the server can communicate any $a \in \{0, \ldots, H-1\}$ to the client using $R = (R_1, \ldots, R_n)$ of which domain size $\prod_{i=1}^{n} |\mathcal{R}_i|$ is smaller than H, that is impossible. Thus, we have $\sum_{i=1}^{n} \log |\mathcal{R}_i| \geq \log H$.

In a similar way, we next prove Eq. (3). Suppose a server holding a random element $b \in \Omega$ and aiming to send b to a client and that there is an NIMPC protocol (GEN, ENC, DEC) for $\mathcal{H}$ that satisfies $\sum_{i=1}^{n} \log |\mathcal{M}_i| < \log |\Omega|$. For a function $h \in \mathcal{H}$ and an element $a \in \mathcal{X}$ such that $h(a) = b$, the server executes $R \leftarrow \mathsf{GEN}(h)$ and $M \leftarrow \mathsf{ENC}(a, R)$, and sends M to the client. The client obtains b by executing DEC. We conclude that the server can communicate any $b \in \Omega$ to the client using $M = (M_1, \ldots, M_n)$ of which domain size $\prod_{i=1}^{n} |\mathcal{M}_i|$ is smaller than $|\Omega|$, that is impossible. Thus, we have $\sum_{i=1}^{n} \log |\mathcal{M}_i| \geq \log |\Omega|$. □

The following corollary shows a lower bound on the *total* communication complexity of NIMPC for the set of arbitrary functions. The lower bounds indicate the impossibility of reducing the communication complexity to polynomial in the input length.

Corollary 1 (Lower bound for Arbitrary Functions). *Fix finite domains $\mathcal{X}_1, \ldots, \mathcal{X}_n$ such that $|\mathcal{X}_i| \geq d$ for all $1 \leq i \leq n$. Let $\mathcal{X} \triangleq \mathcal{X}_1 \times \cdots \times \mathcal{X}_n$ and $\mathcal{H}_{\text{all}}$ the set of all functions $h : \mathcal{X} \to \{0,1\}^m$. Any NIMPC protocol Π for $\mathcal{H}_{\text{all}}$ satisfies*

$$\sum_{i=1}^{n} \log |\mathcal{R}_i| \geq m \cdot |\mathcal{X}| \geq d^n \cdot m, \tag{4}$$

$$\sum_{i=1}^{n} \log |\mathcal{M}_i| \geq m. \tag{5}$$

Proof. The proof is obvious from Theorem 1 by setting $\mathcal{H} = \mathcal{H}_{\text{all}}$. A function maps each input value to some output value. Thus, $|\mathcal{H}|$ is given by multiplying the number of all possible input values by the number of all possible output values, i.e., $2^{m \cdot |\mathcal{X}|}$. Then, $\sum_{i=1}^{n} \log |\mathcal{R}_i| \geq \log |\mathcal{H}| = m \cdot |\mathcal{X}|$. □

The following corollary shows a lower bounds on the *total* communication complexity of NIMPC for $\mathcal{H}_{\text{ind}}$. The gap between this lower bound (linear in the input length) and the previous upper bound (exponential in the input length) is large. In the next section, we will present an efficient NIMPC protocol for $\mathcal{H}_{\text{ind}}$ with individual (resp. total) communication complexity $O(n \cdot \log^2 d)$ (resp. $O(n^2 \cdot \log^2 d)$).

Corollary 2 (Lower bound for Indicator Functions). *Fix finite domains $\mathcal{X}_1, \ldots, \mathcal{X}_n$ such that $|\mathcal{X}_i| \geq d$ for all $1 \leq i \leq n$ and let $\mathcal{X} \triangleq \mathcal{X}_1 \times \cdots \times \mathcal{X}_n$. Then, any NIMPC protocol Π_{ind} for $\mathcal{H}_{\text{ind}}$ satisfies*

$$\sum_{i=1}^{n} \log |\mathcal{R}_i| \geq \log |\mathcal{X}| \geq n \cdot \log d. \tag{6}$$

Though the proof is obvious from Theorem 1, we give a more constructive proof, which need not to assume an existence of a one-to-one mapping ϕ.

Proof. Suppose a server holding a random vector $a = (a_1, \ldots, a_n) \in \mathcal{X}$ and aiming to send a to a client. Suppose that there is an NIMPC protocol (GEN, ENC, DEC) for $\mathcal{H}_{\text{ind}}$ that satisfies $\sum_{i=1}^{n} \log |\mathcal{R}_i| < \log |\mathcal{X}|$. The server executes $R \leftarrow \mathsf{GEN}(h_a)$ and sends R to the client. The client obtains a by executing ENC and DEC for all possible inputs $a' \in \mathcal{X}$ and checking whether the output is 1 or not. The input a' for which the output is 1 is considered as a. We conclude that the server can communicate any $a \in \mathcal{X}$ to the client using $R = (R_1, \ldots, R_n)$ of which domain size $\prod_{i=1}^{n} |\mathcal{R}_i|$ is smaller than $|\mathcal{X}|$, that is impossible. Thus, we have $\sum_{i=1}^{n} \log |\mathcal{R}_i| \geq \log |\mathcal{X}|$. □

4 Efficient Constructions

We now present an efficient construction of NIMPC for $\mathcal{H}_{\text{ind}}$. In the previous construction in [2], all the possible input values are encoded in a *unary* way, and thus the communication complexity depends on the size of the input domain. Specifically, each possible input value is represented by a single vector over $\mathbb{F}_2$ so that the summation of vectors corresponding to $a = (a_1, \ldots, a_n)$ is equal to the zero vector while the other combination is linearly independent to satisfy the robustness. Our idea to reduce the communication complexity is to encode all the possible input values in a *binary* way. Specifically, for each bit in the binary representation, two vectors representing "0" and "1" are generated so that the summation of all vectors over the binary representation of a is equal to zero. Since the proposed encoding reduces the required dimension of vectors, the communication complexity of resulting NIMPC is greatly reduced, too.

The detailed description of the protocol is as follows. For $i \in [n]$, let $d_i = |\mathcal{X}_i|$ and ϕ_i a one-to-one mapping from $\mathcal{X}_i$ to $[d_i]$. Let $l_i = \lceil \log_2(d_i + 1) \rceil$ and $s = \sum_{i=1}^{n} l_i$. Fix a function $h \in \mathcal{H}_{\text{ind}}$ that we want to compute.

The proposed NIMPC $P(\Pi_{\text{ind}})(h)$

- **Offline preprocessing:** If $h = h_0$, then choose s linearly independent random vectors $\{m_{i,j}\}_{i \in [n], j \in [l_i]}$ in $\mathbb{F}_2^s$. If $h = h_a$ for some $a = (a_1, \ldots, a_n) \in \mathcal{X}$,

denote the binary representation of $\phi_i(a_i)$ by $b_i = (b_{i,1}, \ldots, b_{i,l_i})$ and define a set of indices I_i by $I_i = \{j \in [l_i] \mid b_{i,j} = 1\}$. Choose s random vectors $\{m_{i,j}\}_{i \in [n], j \in [l_i]}$ in $\mathbb{F}_2^s$ under the constraint that $\sum_{i=1}^{n} \sum_{j \in I_i} m_{i,j} = 0$ and there are no other linear relations between them (that is, choose all the vectors $m_{i,j}$ except $m_{n,\max I_n}$, as random linear independent vectors and set $m_{n,\max I_n} = -\sum_{i=1}^{n-1} \sum_{j \in I_i} m_{i,j} - \sum_{j \in I_n \setminus \{\max I_n\}} m_{n,j}$). Define $\mathsf{GEN}(h) = R = (R_1, \ldots, R_n)$, where $R_i = \{m_{i,j}\}_{j \in [l_i]}$.
- **Online messages:** For an input x_i, let $\hat{b}_i = (\hat{b}_{i,1}, \ldots, \hat{b}_{i,l_i})$ be the binary representation of $\phi_i(x_i)$. Let $\hat{I}_i$ be the set of indices defined by $\hat{I}_i = \{j \in [l_i] \mid \hat{b}_{i,j} = 1\}$. $\mathsf{ENC}(x, R) = (M_1, \ldots, M_n)$ where $M_i = \sum_{j \in \hat{I}_i} m_{i,j}$.
- **Output** $h(x_1, \ldots, x_n)$: $\mathsf{DEC}(M_1, \ldots, M_n) = 1$ if $\sum_{i=1}^{n} M_i = \mathbf{0}$.

Theorem 2. *Fix finite domains $\mathcal{X}_1, \ldots, \mathcal{X}_n$ such that $|\mathcal{X}_i| \le d$ for all $1 \le i \le n$ and let $\mathcal{X} \triangleq \mathcal{X}_1 \times \cdots \times \mathcal{X}_n$. Then, there is an NIMPC protocol Π_{ind} for $\mathcal{H}_{\text{ind}}$ with individual (resp. total) communication complexity at most $\lceil \log_2(d+1) \rceil^2 \cdot n$ (resp. $\lceil \log_2(d+1) \rceil^2 \cdot n^2$).*

Proof. For the correctness, note that $\sum_{i=1}^{n} M_i = \sum_{i=1}^{n} \sum_{j \in \hat{I}_i} m_{i,j}$. If $h = h_a$ for $a \in \mathcal{X}$, this sum equals 0 if and only if $I_i = \hat{I}_i$ for all $i \in [n]$, i.e., $a = x$. If $h = h_0$, this sum is never zero, as all vectors were chosen to be linearly independent in this case.

To prove robustness, fix a subset $T \subset [n]$ and $x_{\overline{T}} \in \mathcal{X}_{\overline{T}}$. The encodings $M_{\overline{T}}$ of $\overline{T}$ consist of the vectors $\{M_i\}_{i \in \overline{T}}$. The randomness R_T consists of the vectors $\{m_{i,j}\}_{i \in [n], j \in [l_i]}$. If $h|_{\overline{T}, x_{\overline{T}}} \equiv 0$, then these vectors are uniformly distributed in $\mathbb{F}_2^s$ under the constraint that they are linearly independent. If $h|_{\overline{T}, x_{\overline{T}}}(x_T) = 1$ for some $x_T \in \mathcal{X}_T$, then $\sum_{i \in \overline{T}} M_i + \sum_{i \in T} \sum_{j \in \hat{I}_i} m_{i,j} = 0$ and there are no other linear relations between them. Formally, to prove the robustness, we describe a simulator Sim_T: the simulator queries $h|_{\overline{T}, x_{\overline{T}}}$ on all possible inputs in $\mathcal{X}_T$. If all answers are zero, this simulator generates random independent vectors. Otherwise, there is an $x_T \in \mathcal{X}_T$ such that $h|_{\overline{T}, x_{\overline{T}}}(x_T) = 1$, and the simulator outputs random vectors under the constrains described above, that is, all vectors are independent with the exception that $\sum_{i \in T} M_i + \sum_{i \in \overline{T}} \sum_{j \in \hat{I}_j} m_{i,j} = 0$.

The correlated randomness R_i is composed of $l_i \le \lceil \log_2(d+1) \rceil$ binary vectors of length $s \le \lceil \log_2(d+1) \rceil \cdot n$ and the encoding is the summation of some of them. Hence, the communication complexity is at most $\lceil \log_2(d+1) \rceil^2 \cdot n$. □

Corollary 3. *Fix finite domains $\mathcal{X}_1, \ldots, \mathcal{X}_n$ such that $|\mathcal{X}_i| \le d$ for all $1 \le i \le n$ and let $\mathcal{X} \triangleq \mathcal{X}_1 \times \cdots \times \mathcal{X}_n$. Then, there is an NIMPC protocol for $\mathcal{H}_{\text{all}}$ with individual (resp. total) communication complexity at most $|\mathcal{X}| \cdot m \cdot \lceil \log_2(d+1) \rceil^2 \cdot n$ (resp. $|\mathcal{X}| \cdot m \cdot \lceil \log_2(d+1) \rceil^2 \cdot n^2$).*

From Proposition 2 and Theorem 1, it is obvious.

5 Conclusion

We have presented the first lower bound on the communication complexity of n-player NIMPC protocols for any set of functions including the set of arbitrary functions and the set of indicator functions. We have constructed novel NIMPC protocols for the set of arbitrary functions and the set of indicator functions. The proposed protocols are much more efficient than the previous protocols. For example, for the set of arbitrary functions, while the previous best known protocol in [2] requires $|\mathcal{X}| \cdot m \cdot d^2 \cdot n$ communication complexity, the communication complexity of the proposed construction is only $|\mathcal{X}| \cdot m \cdot \lceil \log_2(d+1) \rceil^2 \cdot n$, where $\mathcal{X}$ denote the (total) input domain, d is the maximum domain size of a player, and m is the output length. By this result, the gap between the lower and upper bounds on the communication complexity is significantly reduced from $d^2 \cdot n$ to $\lceil \log_2(d+1) \rceil^2 \cdot n$, that is, from the exponential in the input length to the quadratic.

The lower bounds in this paper are derived from the correctness property of NIMPC. While this approach is useful for approximating the communication complexity, there may be a room to improve the lower bounds by taking the robustness property into account. Thus, a possible future work is to derive a tighter lower bound and present an optimum construction of NIMPC.

References

1. Barkol, O., Ishai, Y., Weinreb, E.: On *d*-multiplicative secret sharing. J. cryptol. **23**(4), 580–593 (2010)
2. Beimel, A., Gabizon, A., Ishai, Y., Kushilevitz, E., Meldgaard, S., Paskin-Cherniavsky, A.: Non-interactive secure multiparty computation. In: Garay, J.A., Gennaro, R. (eds.) CRYPTO 2014, Part II. LNCS, vol. 8617, pp. 387–404. Springer, Heidelberg (2014)
3. Ben-Or, M., Goldwasser, S., Wigderson, A.: Completeness theorems for non-cryptographic fault-tolerant distributed computation. In: Proceedings of the 20th Annual ACM Symposium on Theory of Computing, STOC 1988, pp. 1–10 (1988)
4. Chaum, D., Crèpeau, C., Damgård, I.: Multiparty unconditionally secure protocols. In: Proceedings of the 20th Annual ACM Symposium on Theory of Computing, STOC 1988, pp. 11–19 (1988)
5. Cramer, R., Damgård, I.B., Maurer, U.M.: General secure multi-party computation from any linear secret-sharing scheme. In: Preneel, B. (ed.) EUROCRYPT 2000. LNCS, vol. 1807, pp. 316–335. Springer, Heidelberg (2000)
6. Data, D., Prabhakaran, M.M., Prabhakaran, V.M.: On the communication complexity of secure computation. In: Garay, J.A., Gennaro, R. (eds.) CRYPTO 2014, Part II. LNCS, vol. 8617, pp. 199–216. Springer, Heidelberg (2014)
7. Hirt, M., Maurer, U.: Player Simulation and General Adversary Structures in Perfect Multiparty Computation. J. Cryptology **13**(1), 31–60 (2000)
8. Maurer, U.M.: Secure multi-party computation made simple. In: Cimato, S., Galdi, C., Persiano, G. (eds.) SCN 2002. LNCS, vol. 2576, pp. 14–28. Springer, Heidelberg (2003)
9. Rabin, T., Ben-Or, M.: Verifiable secret sharing and multiparty protocols with honest majority. In: Proceedings of the 21st Annual ACM Symposium on Theory of Computing, STOC 1989, pp. 73–85 (1989)
10. Yao, A.C.: Protocols for secure computations. In: Proceedings of the 23rd Annual Symposium on Foundations of Computer Science, FOCS 1982, pp. 160–164 (1982)

Apollo: End-to-End Verifiable Voting Protocol Using Mixnet and Hidden Tweaks

Donghoon Chang[1], Amit Kumar Chauhan[1(✉)], Muhammed Noufal K[1], and Jinkeon Kang[2]

[1] Indraprastha Institute of Information Technology, Delhi (IIIT-D), New Delhi, India
{donghoon,amitc,muhammed1207}@iiitd.ac.in
[2] Center for Information Security Technologies (CIST), Korea University, Seoul, Korea
jinkeon.kang@gmail.com

Abstract. Fair conduct of elections is essential for the smooth existence of democratic societies. In order to response voting security concerns, security researchers have developed tamper-resistant and voter verifiable methods. These end-to-end voting schemes are unique because they give voters the option to both verify the voting scheme's functionality and to check that their votes have been recorded after leaving the polling booth. Helios and Prêt á voter are the most usable voter verifiable, end-to-end voting schemes using mixnet. Helios is a web-based open-audit voting system utilizing mixnet and secure cryptographic primitives. It satisfies almost all the security properties like privacy, individual and universal verifiability, and mixnet integrity etc. However, the proof of mixnet integrity is complex to understand and costly in terms of computations that effects conducting large-scale elections. For a voter, it is rarely impossible to verify the correctness of election results without trusting on election administrator and the candidates for the correctness of election result. In this paper, we address this issue by presenting a simple and fast method for conducting end-to-end voting and allowing public verification of the correctness of the announced vote tallying results. Our method is based on existing Helios structure, we call it Apollo that facilitates a direct proof of mixnet integrity, and also satisfies all the security properties.

Keywords: E-voting · Re-encryption · Mixnet integrity · Verifiability

1 Introduction

Electronic voting systems are being introduced, or trialled, in several countries to provide more efficient voting procedures. The trustworthiness of voting scheme is crucial to record people consensus correctly. It should allow voters and election observers to verify, independently of the hardware and software running the election, that votes have been recorded, tallied and declared correctly. However, in a large-scale implementation, it is very hard for an election authority to enforce

S. Kwon and A. Yun (Eds.): ICISC 2015, LNCS 9558, pp. 194–209, 2016.
DOI: 10.1007/978-3-319-30840-1_13

these procedures. For a voter, it is impractical to verify that authorities followed all the correctness measures and procedures, and there is no simple way to ensure that his vote is properly included in the final tally. This makes voters trust on election authority and rely on machinery as crucial components in the successful conduct of an election. It can lead to creating doubts among voters about the integrity of an election, and have the potential to break the smooth running of democratic systems. To avoid such situations, researchers come up with a new kind of election system, where the correctness of each and every step is verifiable while preserving the voters' privacy. Such type of schemes is known as end-to-end verifiable voting schemes. The concept of election or end-to-end verifiability that has emerged in the academic literature, e.g. [2,9] etc. aims to address this problem.

In end-to-end verifiable voting schemes, an individual voter has the ability to verify that his intended vote has been properly cast, recorded and tallied into the election result. In this direction, Ben Adida [2] proposed Helios 1.0 that is a web-based open-audit voting scheme. The main idea of Helios is based on verifiable election schemes proposed by Benaloh [4]. However, the proof of mixnet integrity is not directly verifiable, and the cost of verification in zero-knowledge interactive proof setting is very high which is an obstruction to perform large-scale elections. In this paper, we firstly explain the mixnet-based Helios structure in detail, and then, motivated by Helios, we propose a new voting scheme called Apollo that facilitates easy proof of mixnet integrity. Moreover, Apollo is significantly fast in terms of computations during mixing in comparison to Helios.

1.1 Other Related Work

In [6], Chaum suggested for the first time that anonymous communication can lead to voting systems with individual verifiability, i.e., the voters can verify that their votes were counted correctly. In [19], Sako and Killian introduced explicitly the notion of universal verifiability, that is, the ability for anyone to verify that the election result derives from the cast votes.

The first end-to-end verifiable voting scheme was proposed by Cohen and Fischer in 1985 [10], where election integrity was verifiable, but the government was able to read any vote. Later on, researchers came up with several such schemes [5,11,12,14,18,19]. Prêt à Voter [9], Scantegrity [7], ThreeBallot [20] and Helios [2] are the recent major proposals. Prêt à voter [9] was proposed by Peter YA Ryan in 2004 and it is a paper-based scheme uses mixnet using onion encryption for voter privacy. It is an end-to-end verifiable scheme that gives the voters a receipt when they submit their vote to verify that their votes were never modified. Scantegrity [7] was proposed by David Chaum in 2008 and later gone through several major modification. The current version is known as Scantegrity II. It can be implemented using existing optical scan voting system infrastructure. ThreeBallot [20] was proposed by Rivest in 2006, it is purely paper-based, without using any cryptographic tools. But later, it turned out that ThreeBallot is vulnerable to several attacks [13,15].

1.2 Our Contribution

We introduce an improved version of Helios 1.0 voting scheme, so-called Apollo. We model voting protocol in end-to-end verifiability using mixnet and introduce the concept of hidden tweaks in existing Helios 1.0 for easy and straightforward proof of mixnet integrity. The consideration of direct proof of mixnet integrity is particularly interesting as it provides an assurance that the election outcome corresponds to votes legitimately cast and hence provides an easy mechanism to detect ballot stuffing. We also provide proof sketches for various security properties required for a secret voting scheme.

1.3 Comparison of our Results

Summary of Comparison. Our comparison includes the most relevant electronic voting schemes based on mixnet implementation. A detailed comparison for security properties has been shown in Table 1 below.

Table 1. Comparison between mixnet voting schemes. A: attacks found, C: claimed achieved requirement, P: proved achieved requirement, S: supposed achieved requirement, Complex: complex proof of mixnet integrity, Easy: easy proof of mixnet integrity.

Security properties	Voting protocols and schemes (using mixnet)								
	OMA [17]	LBD [16]	Web [21]	HS [14]	Abe [1]	ALBD [3]	Prêt à voter [9]	Helios 1.0 [2]	Apollo (this paper)
Completeness	-	-	-	-	-	-	C	C	C
Soundness	A	C	C	C	-	C	C	C	C
Robustness	A	C	C	C	P	C	C	C	C
Privacy	C	P	C	C	P	C	C	C	C
Unreusability	C	C	C	S	-	C	-	C	C
Eligibility	C	-	C	S	-	C	-	C	C
Fairness	C	C	C	C	-	C	C	C	C
Receipt-freeness	A	C	C	C	-	C	C	C	C
Individual verifiability	C	-	A	C	-	-	C	C	C
Universal verifiability	A	C	C	C	P	C	C	C	C
Proof of mixnet integrity	-	-	-	-	-	-	-	Complex	Easy

1.4 Outline of the Paper

In Sect. 2, we put forward the preliminaries such as notations and definitions of a secret e-voting schemes. In Sect. 3, we introduce Helios 1.0 voting scheme and analyze Helios 1.0 for mixnet integrity. In Sect. 4, we propose a new end-to-end verifiable e-voting scheme called Apollo. In Sect. 5, we show the comparison of the computational efficiency for Helios 1.0 and Apollo. In Sect. 6, we analyze the security of proposed voting protocol Apollo. In Sect. 7, we conclude our results.

2 Preliminaries

2.1 Notations

Throughout this work, we take λ to be a security parameter and p, q to be large primes such that $q|(p-1)$. Let $\mathcal{Z}_n^* = \{x \in \mathcal{Z}_n \mid \mathsf{gcd}(x, n) = 1\}$. (Note that if p is prime, $\mathcal{Z}_p^* = \mathcal{Z}_p \backslash \{0\}$). We denote a cyclic group generated $\mathcal{Z}_p^*$ by a group element g by $\mathbb{Z}_p^* = \langle g \rangle$ satisfying $\mathsf{Ord}_p(g) = q$. Selecting a uniform and independently distributed variable x from a set X is denoted by $x \xleftarrow{\$} X$. We say a probability function $\epsilon : \mathcal{R}_{\geq 0} \rightarrow \mathcal{R}_{\geq 0}$ is negligible if $\epsilon(\lambda)$ is smaller than all polynomial fractions for sufficiently large λ. Other notations used in this paper are as follows:

N : the number of voters
V_i : the voter i
v_i : the vote of voter V_i
c_i : the encrypted vote of voter V_i
r_i : one-time secret random number generated for voter V_i
n : the number of mix-servers in mixnet
M_j : j^{th} mix-server in mixnet
c_i^j : i^{th} output from mix-server M_j
s_i^j : a random number used for re-encryption of ith ciphertext by mix-server M_j
d_i^j : i^{th} output from j^{th} shadow mix-server.

2.2 Security of Secret Voting Scheme

In this paper, we discuss security of secret voting scheme in following definition.

Definition 1. *We say that the secret voting scheme is secure if we have the following:*

- ***Completeness.*** *All valid votes are counted correctly.*
- ***Soundness.*** *The dishonest voter cannot disrupt the voting.*
- ***Robustness.*** *No coalition of voters can disrupt the election and any cheating voter will be detected.*
- ***Privacy.*** *All votes must be secret.*
- ***Unreusability.*** *No voter can vote twice.*
- ***Eligibility.*** *No one who isn't allowed to vote can vote.*
- ***Fairness.*** *Nothing must affect the voting.*
- ***Receipt-freeness.*** *A voter may not be able to create a receipt, i.e., any information that can be used to convince an attacker or a coercer that he voted in a specific manner.*
- ***Verifiability.*** *No one can falsify the result of the voting.*
- ***Universal Verifiability.*** *Anyone can verify the validity of individual votes and of the final tally of the election.*
- ***Individual Verifiability.*** *Each voter can verify that his own vote was correctly included in the final result.*

2.3 ElGamal Encryption

Given $G = \langle g \rangle$ where $o(g) = q$ and q is a prime, private key x and public key $y = g^x \mod p$, the encryption of message m is defined as

$$\mathsf{Enc}(m) = (g^\alpha, y^\alpha m) \text{ where } \alpha \stackrel{\$}{\leftarrow} \mathbb{Z}_p.$$

We also define a special instance of reblinding denoted by Reblind and works as

$$\mathsf{Reblind}(\mathsf{Enc}(m)) = (g^\alpha, y^\beta(y^\alpha m)) = (g^\alpha, y^{\alpha+\beta} m) \text{ where } \beta \stackrel{\$}{\leftarrow} \mathbb{Z}_p.$$

2.4 Re-encryption Mixnet

A mix network or mixnet is a cryptographic construction that invokes a set of servers to establish private communication channels. One type of mix networks accepts as input a collection of ciphertexts, and outputs the corresponding plaintexts in a randomly permuted order. The main privacy property desired of such a mixnet is that the permutation matching inputs to outputs should be known only to the mixnet, and no one else. In particular, an adversary should be unable to guess which input ciphertext corresponds to an output plaintext any more effectively than by guessing at random.

One common variety of mixnet known as a re-encryption mixnet relies on a public key encryption scheme, such as ElGamal, that allows for re-encryption of ciphertexts. For a given public key, a ciphertext C' is said to represent a re-encryption of C if both ciphertexts decrypt to the same plaintext. In a re-encryption mixnet, inputs are submitted encrypted under the public key of the mixnet. The batch of input ciphertexts is processed sequentially by each mix-server. Each server in turn takes the set of ciphertexts output by the previous server, and re-encrypts and mixes them. The set of ciphertexts produced by the last server may be decrypted by a quorum of mix-servers to yield plaintext outputs. Privacy in the mixnet construction derives from the fact that ciphertext pair (C, C') is indistinguishable from a pair (C, R) for a random ciphertext R to any adversary without knowledge of the private key.

In voting protocols using mixnets, mix-servers are authorities and each of them possesses a public key and a corresponding secret key (or more). The ballots have to be prepared before the elections using the mix-servers' public keys. During the election stage, each ballot is cast and passed through the mixnet to be decrypted by the successive mix-servers' secret keys before the final tally.

2.5 Mixnet Integrity

During mixnet operations, each mix-server receives a set of ciphertexts and generates another set of ciphertexts after re-encryption and permutation. To remove the relation between input and output sets of ciphertexts, the re-encryption factors and permutations are kept secret by mix-server. So, each mix-server act as a black box for non-participating observers (spectators). How do spectators know that the mixnet servers really have permuted the original ciphertexts, without adding new ciphertexts, deleting old ones, or modifying any of the original ciphertexts?

A mixnet is called to preserve its integrity if it has respected the integrity goal while maintaining the voter's anonymity/privacy.

3 Helios 1.0 [2]

Helios 1.0 [2] is a web-based open-audit voting system released in 2008 by Ben Adida. Helios makes use of cryptographic tools such as ElGamal encryption, ElGamal re-encryption and Sako-Killian mixnet [19]. It also allows independent verification by voters and observers of election results. The implementation of Helios follows web server-client architecture. For explaining in a modular way, we divide the whole voting process into five stages: initialization, registration, voting, mixing and tallying stages.

- **Initialization Stage:** The election administrator A sets up an ElGamal cryptosystem.
  - A chooses a private key $x \stackrel{\$}{\leftarrow} \mathbb{Z}_q^*$.
  - A computes a public key $y \leftarrow g^x \mod p$.
  - (p, q, g, y) are published for registered voters.
- **Registration Stage:** Each voter V_i gets a credential from administrator A.
  - A generates a unique credential (password) $z_i \stackrel{\$}{\leftarrow} \mathbb{Z}_q$ for each eligible voter V_i, and send it to him via his corresponding email address through an untappable channel (Fig. 1).
- **Voting Stage:** Each voter V_i submits his encrypted vote with his credential and keeps the fingerprint of encrypted vote with himself. (H is a hash function.)
  - V_i chooses his vote v_i from a set of possible votes.
  - Helios ballot preparation system (BPS) generates a random number r_i.
  - Helios BPS encrypts the message $m_i = v_i || r_i$ using ElGamal encryption as $\alpha \stackrel{\$}{\leftarrow} \mathbb{Z}_p$, $c_i \stackrel{\mathsf{def}}{=} (g^\alpha, y^\alpha m_i)$.
  - Helios BPS returns the fingerprint of c_i as $\mathsf{H}(c_i)$ to the voter V_i.

  (Ballot Auditing). Each voter V_i can audit the ballot as many times as he wants until he gains the assurance on Helios BPS.
  - V_i chooses the ballot audit option.
  - Helios BPS reveals all the randomness used for the ballot encryption to the voter V_i.
  - V_i can verify the correctness of the ballot encryption in Helios BPS by repeating encryption process in his trusted environment.

  (Ballot Casting). After ballot auditing, Helios BPS discards all random values used before and encrypt the ballot with a new random number. Once voter V_i authenticates himself with password credential received on email, Helios BPS sends the encrypted ballot to Helios server and server stores this in a database.

- **Mixing Stage:** To preserve the anonymity, Helios uses mixnet, a set of mix-servers each managed by different authorities. Each mix-server re-encrypts and permutes the set of encrypted votes to remove the relation between a voter and the corresponding vote. Shuffling is a procedure which on the input of N ciphertexts $(c_1^{j-1}, c_2^{j-1}, \ldots, c_N^{j-1})$, outputs N ciphertexts $(c_1^j, c_2^j, \ldots, c_N^j)$ where:
  - There exists a permutation $\pi \in \mathsf{Perm}(\lambda)$ such that $D(c_i^j) = D(c_{\pi^{-1}(i)}^{j-1})$ for all i, $1 \leq i \leq N$. Here, D is a decryption algorithm for ciphertexts, and $\mathsf{Perm}(\lambda)$ be the set of all permutations on $\{0,1\}^\lambda$.
  - Without the knowledge of D or π, $(c_1^{j-1}, c_2^{j-1}, \ldots, c_N^{j-1})$ and $(c_1^j, c_2^j, \ldots, c_N^j)$ reveal no information on the permutation π.

  Since we make use of ElGamal cryptosystem with public keys (p, q, g, y) and private key $x \in \mathbb{Z}_q$ such that $y = g^x \mod p$, therefore, given N ciphertexts $\{c_i^{j-1}\} = \{(g_i^{j-1}, m_i^{j-1})\}$ where all $\{g_i^{j-1}\}$ and $\{m_i^{j-1}\}$ have the order q, shuffled ciphertexts $\{c_i^j\} = \{(g_i^j, m_i^j)\}$ can be obtained by using randomly chosen number $\{s_i^j\}$ from $\mathbb{Z}_p$,

$$g_i^j = g^{s_i^j} g_{\pi^{-1}(i)} \mod p \tag{1}$$

$$m_i^j = y^{s_i^j} m_{\pi^{-1}(i)} \mod p \tag{2}$$

  - Thus, each M_j receives a batch of encrypted ballots from M_{j-1}. M_j re-encrypts each ballot like described above and then permutes them before handling them to M_{j+1}.
- **Tallying Stage:** Talliers verify the votes (by checking the proofs), and publish the valid ballots. At last, ballots are decrypted and counted.
  - For each shuffled and encrypted vote, write $\{c_i^n\}$ as $\{(g_i^n, m_i^n)\} = \{(g^{s_i^n} g_{\pi^{-1}(i)}^{n-1}, y^{s_i^n} m_{\pi^{-1}(i)}^{n-1})\}$.
  - Administrator A using his secret key x, compute $(g^{s_i^n} g_{\pi^{-1}(i)}^{n-1})^x$ and then use it to divide $(y^{s_i^n} m_{\pi^{-1}(i)}^{n-1})$ to get m_i. Now since $m_i = v_i || r_i$, he finally gets the vote v_i cast for a candidate, and counts.

Remark 1 (A Note on Proof of Mixnet Integrity in Helios 1.0). *The proof of mixnet integrity in Helios 1.0 is based on zero-knowledge proof. There are two approaches - one is interactive and the other is non-interactive. In both approaches, prover needs to generate few shadow mixes for proving the mixnet integrity whenever questioned by verifier. However, these proofs are not easily verifiable, and costly in terms of computations because of the generation of shadow mixes. In another way, we can say that the proof of mixnet integrity is not easy for Helios 1.0. To make it straightforward and easy to verify, we present a new variant of Helios 1.0 which we call Apollo.*

4 Our Proposed Voting Scheme: Apollo

We propose a new tweak-based scheme for the efficient verification of mixnet integrity. The core idea is adding a hidden tweak in ElGamal ciphertext before

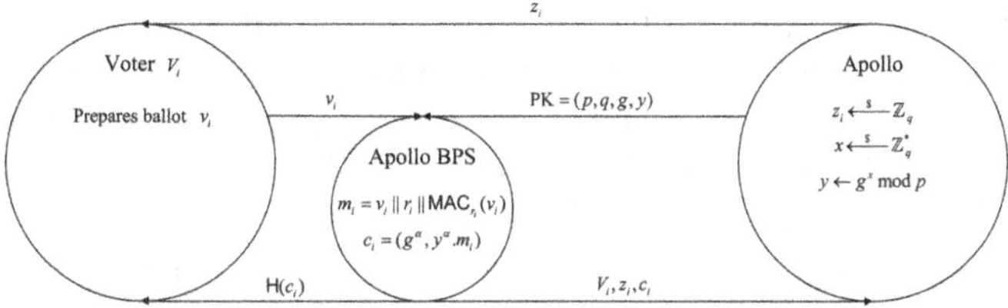

Fig. 1. Initialization, registration and voting stage of Apollo voting protocol

passing through mixnet so that mix-server or anybody else cannot add a valid ciphertext into the set of encrypted ballots. Any attempt to replace a genuine ciphertext vote with a new ciphertext vote can be detected once decryption is done. We divide the whole voting process into five stages: initialization, registration, voting, mixing and tallying stages. Moreover, mixing stage consists of two phases: mix-and-tweak network phase, and mixnet phase. The Apollo voting scheme works as follows:

- **Initialization Stage:** The election administrator A sets up an ElGamal cryptosystem.
  - A chooses a private key $x \xleftarrow{\$} \mathbb{Z}_q$.
  - A computes a public key $y \leftarrow g^x \mod p$.
  - (p, q, g, y) are published for registered voters.
- **Registration Stage:** Each voter V_i gets a credential from administrator A.
  - A generates a unique credential (password) $z_i \xleftarrow{\$} \mathbb{Z}_q$ for each eligible voter V_i, and send it to him via his corresponding email address through an untappable channel.
- **Voting Stage:** Each voter V_i submits his encrypted vote with his credential and keeps fingerprint of encrypted vote with himself. (H is a hash function.)
  - V_i chooses his vote v_i from a set of possible votes.
  - Apollo ballot preparation system (BPS) generates a random number r_i.
  - Apollo BPS generates the message $m_i = v_i || r_i || \mathsf{MAC}_{r_i}(v_i)$ where $\mathsf{MAC}(\cdot)$ is a message authentication generation algorithm. (The additional MAC is added for verification of valid votes to nullify the generation of invalid votes that may be added in between by adversary (malicious mix-server).
  - Apollo BPS encrypts the message m_i using ElGamal encryption as $\alpha \xleftarrow{\$} \mathbb{Z}_p$, $c_i \stackrel{\mathsf{def}}{=} (g^\alpha, y^\alpha m_i)$.
  - Apollo BPS returns the fingerprint of c_i as $\mathsf{H}(c_i)$ to the voter V_i.

  (Ballot Auditing). Each voter V_i can audit the ballot as many times as he wants until he gains the assurance on Apollo BPS.
  - V_i chooses the ballot audit option.
  - Apollo BPS reveals all randomness used for ballot encryption to V_i.
  - V_i can verify the correctness of the ballot encryption in Apollo BPS by repeating encryption process in his trusted environment.

(Ballot Casting). After ballot auditing, Apollo BPS discards all random values used before and encrypt the ballot with a new random number. Once voter V_i has authenticated himself with authenticated credential received by email, Apollo BPS sends the encrypted ballot to Apollo server and server stores this in a database.

- **Mixing Stage:** To preserve the anonymity, Apollo uses mix-and-tweak operations and mixnet, a set of mix-servers each managed by different authorities. Each mix-server re-encrypts and permutes the set of encrypted votes to remove the relation between a voter and the corresponding vote. This is again a two steps procedure. We separately describe both these steps.
i. (Mix-and-Tweak Network Phase). To shuffle the set of ciphertexts received from Apollo server, we use this mix-and-tweak procedure. Mix-server does this by ElGamal encryptions and reblinding for each of the ciphertexts in the obtained set. Thus, on the input of a set of N ciphertexts $(c_1^0, c_2^0, \ldots, c_N^0)$, mix-server outputs N ciphertexts $(c_1^n, c_2^n, \ldots, c_N^n)$ by performing: for $j = 1$ to n, each mix-server M_j does the following: on the input of N ciphertexts $(c_1^{j-1}, c_2^{j-1}, \ldots, c_N^{j-1})$, the mix-server M_j outputs N ciphertexts $(c_1^j, c_2^j, \ldots, c_N^j)$ where:
  - there exists a permutation $\pi \in \mathsf{Perm}(\lambda)$ such that $D(c_i^j) = D(c_{\pi^{-1}(i)}^{j-1})$ for all i, $1 \leq i \leq N$. Here, D is a decryption algorithm for ciphertexts, and $\mathsf{Perm}(\lambda)$ be the set of all permutations on $\{0,1\}^\lambda$.
  - without the knowledge of D or π, $(c_1^{j-1}, c_2^{j-1}, \ldots, c_N^{j-1})$ and $(c_1^j, c_2^j, \ldots, c_N^j)$ reveal no information on the permutation π.

Since we make use of ElGamal and tweaked ElGamal encryptions with public keys (p, q, g, y) and private key $x \in \mathbb{Z}_q$ such that $y = g^x \mod p$, therefore, given N ciphertexts $\{c_i^{j-1}\} = \{(g_i^{j-1}, m_i^{j-1})\}$ where all $\{g_i^{j-1}\}$ and $\{m_i^{j-1}\}$ have the order q, the shuffled ciphertexts $\{c_i^j\} = \{(g_i^j, m_i^j)\}$ can be obtained by using randomly chosen numbers $\{s_i^j\}$ and β from $\mathbb{Z}_p$,

$$g_i^j = g^{s_i^j} g_{\pi^{-1}(i)}^{j-1} \mod p \tag{3}$$

$$m_i^j = y^\beta (y^{s_i^j} m_{\pi^{-1}(i)}^{j-1}) \mod p \tag{4}$$

  - Thus, each M_j receives a batch of encrypted ballots from M_{j-1}. M_j re-encrypts each ballot, permutes and Reblind before handling them to M_{j+1}.
  - At the end of mix-and-tweak stage, we obtain a new set of ciphertexts $(c_1^n, c_2^n, \ldots, c_N^n)$. We denote this set of ciphertexts by $(\hat{c}_1^0, \hat{c}_2^0, \ldots, \hat{c}_N^0)$.

ii. (Mixnet Phase). We again mix the set of ciphertexts obtained at the end of step 1. (This step is same as Helios mixing stage, however, it is different from step 1 in the sense that we remove the Tweaked-Elgamal part). Thus, on input of a set of N ciphertexts $(\hat{c}_1^0, \hat{c}_2^0, \ldots, \hat{c}_N^0)$, mixnet outputs N ciphertexts $(\hat{c}_1^n, \hat{c}_2^n, \ldots, \hat{c}_N^n)$ by performing: for $j = 1$ to n, each mix-server M_j does the following: on input of N ciphertexts $(\hat{c}_1^{j-1}, \hat{c}_2^{j-1}, \ldots, \hat{c}_N^{j-1})$, the mix-server M_j outputs N ciphertexts $(\hat{c}_1^j, \hat{c}_2^j, \ldots, \hat{c}_N^j)$ where:

– There exists a permutation $\pi \in \mathsf{Perm}(\lambda)$ such that $D(\hat{c}_i^j) = D(\hat{c}_{\pi^{-1}(i)}^{j-1})$ for all i, $1 \leq i \leq N$. Here, D is a decryption algorithm for ciphertexts, and $\mathsf{Perm}(\lambda)$ be the set of all permutations on $\{0,1\}^\lambda$.
– Without the knowledge of D or π, $(\hat{c}_1^{j-1}, \hat{c}_2^{j-1}, \ldots, \hat{c}_N^{j-1})$ and $(\hat{c}_1^j, \hat{c}_2^j, \ldots, \hat{c}_N^j)$ reveal no information on the permutation π.

Since we make use of ElGamal cryptosystem with public keys (p, q, g, y) and private key $x \in \mathbb{Z}_q$ such that $y = g^x \mod p$, therefore, given N ciphertexts $\{\hat{c}_i^{j-1}\} = \{(\hat{g}_i^{j-1}, \hat{m}_i^{j-1})\}$ where all $\{\hat{g}_i^{j-1}\}$ and $\{\hat{m}_i^{j-1}\}$ have order q, shuffled ciphertexts $\{\hat{c}_i^j\} = \{(\hat{g}_i^j, \hat{m}_i^j)\}$ can be obtained by using randomly chosen numbers $\{\hat{s}_i^j\}$ from $\mathbb{Z}_p$,

$$\hat{g}_i^j = \hat{g}^{\hat{s}_i^j} \hat{g}_{\pi^{-1}(i)} \mod p \tag{5}$$

$$\hat{m}_i^j = y^{\hat{s}_i^j} \hat{m}_{\pi^{-1}(i)} \mod p \tag{6}$$

– Thus, each M_j receives a batch of encrypted ballots from M_{j-1}. M_j re-encrypts each ballot like described above and then permutes them before handling them to M_{j+1}.

Finally, it outputs the set of shuffled ciphertexts $(\hat{c}_1^n, \hat{c}_2^n, \ldots, \hat{c}_N^n)$.
After mixing stage, the administrator A publishes this set of ciphertexts obtained in step 2 on the final bulletin board (which is public).

- **Tallying Stage:** Talliers verify the votes (by checking the proofs), and publish the valid ballots. At last, ballots are decrypted and counted.
  1. **(Revealing Mix-and-tweak Variables).** The variables used for the mix-and-tweak operation are re-encryption exponents, permutations, and tweak values. Now, since the operations performed inside mix-and-tweak network are transparent, therefore, anybody can detect the malfunction occurred while mixing.
  2. **(Removing Tweak Variable).** In this step, the system will remove all tweak values added by the mix-and-tweak operation. Let $\hat{c} = (\hat{c}_1, \hat{c}_2)$ be the tweaked ElGamal ciphertext and $\beta \in \mathbb{Z}_q$ be the secret tweak value added earlier during the tweaked-encryption. The removal of the tweak value is done as follows: compute $y' = (y^\beta)^{-1} \mod p$, and then get $c = (\hat{c}_1, y'.\hat{c}_2)$. We apply this tweak removal process for all ciphertexts and for each mix-servers.
  3. **(Decrypting the Encrypted Votes)**
     – For each shuffled and encrypted vote, write $\{\hat{c}_i^n\}$ as $\{(\hat{g}_i^n, \hat{m}_i^n)\} = \{(\hat{g}^{\hat{s}_i^n} \hat{g}_{\pi^{-1}(i)}^{n-1}, y^{\hat{s}_i^n} \hat{m}_{\pi^{-1}(i)}^{n-1})\}$.
     – Administrator A using his secret key x, compute $(\hat{g}^{\hat{s}_i^n} \hat{g}_{\pi^{-1}(i)}^{n-1})^x$ and then use it to divide $(y^{\hat{s}_i^n} \hat{m}_{\pi^{-1}(i)}^{n-1})$ to get m_i. Now since $m_i = v_i || r_i || \mathsf{MAC}_{r_i}(v_i)$, he checks the whether $\mathsf{MAC}_{r_i}(v_i)$ is valid or invalid for obtained v_i and r_i, and then he finally gets the vote v_i cast for a candidate.
  4. **(Counting the Votes).** Administrator counts the votes received by decrypting in step 3 above.

4.1 Proof of Correctness for Decryption in Apollo

Once an ElGamal ciphertext is decrypted, this decryption can be proven using the Chaum-Pedersen protocol [8] for proving discrete logarithm equality. Specifically, given a ciphertext $c = (a, b)$ and claimed plaintext m, the prover shows that $\log_g(y) = \log_a(b/m)$:

- The prover selects $\omega \in \mathbb{Z}_p$ and sends $A = g^\omega$, $B = a^\omega$ to the verifier.
- The verifier challenges with $c \in \mathbb{Z}_p$.
- The prover responds with $s = xc + \omega$.
- The verifier checks that $g^s = Ay^c$ and $a^s = B(b/m)^c$.

It is clear that, given c and s, A and B can be easily computed, thus providing for simulated transcripts of such proofs indicating Honest-Verifier Zero-Knowledge. It is also clear that, if one could rewind the protocol and obtains prover's responses for two challenge values against the same A and B, the value of x would be easily solvable, thus indicating that this is a proof of knowledge of the discrete logarithm and that $\log_g(y) = \log_A(b/m)$.

4.2 Proof of Mixnet Integrity in Apollo

In general, the integrity goal is that the decryption of the ciphertexts at the input to the mixnet should yield the same (multi-) set of plaintexts as the decryption of the ciphertexts at the output to the mixnet. The proof of mixnet integrity [2] in Helios is based on Sako-Killian Shuffle and proof [19].

Unlike Helios, the mixing stage of our scheme consists of 2 phases: mix-and-tweak network phase and mixnet phase. In this section, we want to show how to defeat the adversarial behavior trying to destroy the integrity of the mixing stage in a straightforward way.

First, the mix-and-tweak server can behave maliciously. However, after mixing stage, all mix-and-tweak servers reveal the variables (re-encryption exponents, permutations, and tweak values) used in the mix-and-tweak network phase. It makes all the operations performed in the mix-and-tweak network transparent. So if any malfunction occurred during mix-and-tweak network phase, it can be detected.

Second, the mix-servers in mixnet phase can manipulate the integrity of input and output set of ciphertexts. Next, we justify the proof of mixnet integrity in Apollo by following three claims.

- *Claim (i)* : If a malicious mix-server adds or removes ballot, this can be easily detected by comparing the number of input/output set in mixnet phase.
- *Claim (ii)* : If a malicious mix-server replaces an existing ballot with another existing ballot, this can be easily detected by checking the duplicated ballot after decryption. The duplicated ballot may occur when the voter chose the same choice and the same random number was generated. But its probability is almost negligible.

- *Claim (iii)* : If a malicious mix-server replaces an existing ballot with another ballot, it can be detected with high probability by checking the validity of ballots in the tallying phase after the revelation of mix-and-tweak phase secret factors (re-encryption exponents, tweaks as reblind factors). Now suppose a particular $c_0 = (g^\alpha, y^\alpha m)$ is re-encrypted and reblinded by mix-server in the mix-and-tweak network phase to $c_1 = (g^{\alpha+u}, y^{\alpha+u+\beta}m)$ for $u, \beta \xleftarrow{\$} \mathbb{Z}_p$, and then it is re-encrypted by mix-server in the mixnet phase to $c_2 = (g^{\alpha+u+v}, y^{\alpha+u+\beta+v}m)$ for $v \xleftarrow{\$} \mathbb{Z}_p$. Two possible cases can be executed by the malicious mix-server:
  - Case (i) : Suppose malicious mix-server in the mixnet phase replaces an existing vote by a valid vote. Now since it does not know the mix-and-teak secret factors, it cannot generate a valid ciphertext which is the output of mixnet.
  - Case (ii) : Consider malicious mix-server of mixnet phase modifies the ciphertext c_2 to $c_2' = (g^{\alpha+u+v}, y^{\alpha+u+\beta+v}mk)$ by multiplying some constant k to second factor of the ciphertext, then in the tallying phase, mix-and-tweak secret factors are revealed and removed, the new ciphertext c_2'' will be $c_2'' = (g^{\alpha+v}, y^{\alpha+v}mk)$. Now when server will decrypt the ciphertext c_2'' using his secret key x, it will be decrypted to km. Let's say $m' = km$, i.e., $m' = (v_i' || r_i' || \mathsf{MAC}_{r_i'}(v_i'))$. But since r_i is not known to the malicious server, so even if v_i' may be valid, the chances of a valid $\mathsf{MAC}_{r_i'}(v_i')$ are very low. That is, if the output size of MAC is t-bits, then the probability of generating a valid vote for a malicious server is $\frac{1}{2^t}$ which is negligible for a sufficiently large value of t.

5 Efficiency Comparison of Proposed Apollo with Helios

In this section, we compare computational requirement of proposed scheme with mixnet-based Helios scheme. The major change in proposed schemes from Helios 1.0 is on proof of mixnet integrity part. So our comparison is mainly focused on proof of mixnet integrity part only. The detailed comparison is given in Table 2 below. In Fig. 2, we draw a graph for computation costs in Helios and Apollo.

6 Security of the Proposed Scheme: Apollo

In this section, we briefly sketch the proof that the scheme presented in Sect. 4 has the essential properties of a secure e-voting scheme.

Theorem 1 (Completeness). *The ballot of an honest voter is accepted by the honest candidate and is counted with probability close to one.*

Proof. For a valid vote, all the checks are performed by Apollo server and candidates in the tallying stage of the voting process on the final bulletin board. It ensures that the valid ballot will always be accepted by candidates and is counted by Apollo server with probability close to 1. Therefore, the result of the casting is trustable.

Table 2. Comparison of costs for proof of mixnet integrity for Helios 1.0 and Apollo. Re-enc: re-encryptions using ElGamal, Exp: number of modulo exponentiations, Reblind: reblinding using ElGamal, N: number of voters, n: number of mix-servers, t: number of shadows, λ: maximum number of mix-servers used in mixnet.

Number of mix-servers (n)	Helios 1.0				Apollo				
	Plain mixes		Shadow mixes		Plain mixes		Mix-and-tweak		
	# Re-enc	# Exp	# Re-enc	# Exp	# Re-enc	# Exp	# Re-enc	# Reblind	# Exp
$n = 1$	N	$2N$	Nt	$2Nt$	N	$2N$	N	N	$3N$
$n = 2$	$2N$	$4N$	$2Nt$	$4Nt$	$2N$	$4N$	$2N$	$2N$	$6N$
$n = 3$	$3N$	$6N$	$3Nt$	$6Nt$	$3N$	$6N$	$3N$	$3N$	$9N$
...	...	...	...	...	...	...	...	...	...
$n = \lambda$	λN	$2\lambda N$	λNt	$2\lambda Nt$	λN	$2\lambda N$	λN	λN	$3\lambda N$
$t = 80$	λN	$2\lambda N$	$80\lambda N$	$160\lambda N$	λN	$2\lambda N$	λN	λN	$3\lambda N$
Verifiability	Zero Knowledge [(Non-) Interactive]				Direct				

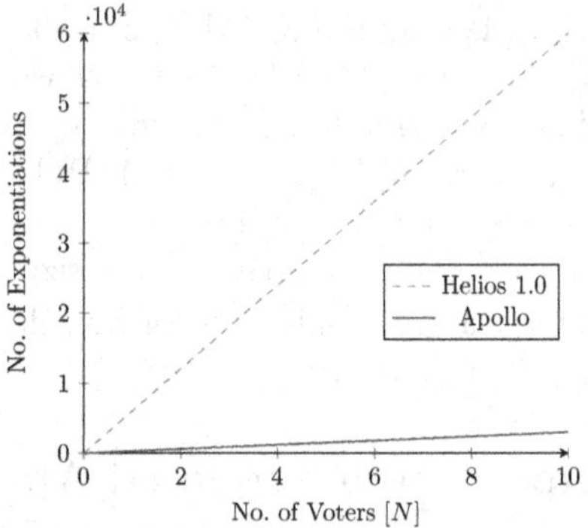

Fig. 2. Cost of mixing in Helios 1.0 and Apollo. Here, we fix the mixnet parameters like $n = 100$, $t = 80$. If mix-server succeeds at responding all challenges in Helios, then primary mix is correct with probability $(1 - 2^{-t})$, so if $t = 80$, it guarantees integrity with overwhelming probability. This graph clearly shows that cost of computations (exponentiations) during mixing in Apollo is relatively low in comparison to Helios 1.0.

Theorem 2 (Robustness). *If the Apollo server is honest and mixnet integrity is preserved, then no one (a small set of voters or mix-servers) cannot disrupt the election.*

Proof (Sketch). One way to disrupt the election is for voters to send invalid votes, Apollo server will not pass forward these invalid votes to the counter if Apollo server is honest. Another way to disrupt the election is modifying the encrypted votes by mix-servers, but again, Apollo server will reject these votes during verification in tallying phase. Hence, cheating by mix-server can also be caught. In any case, no one can disrupt the election.

Theorem 3 (Privacy). *Even if all the participants (the administrator, the Apollo server, the counter, and the candidates) conspire, they cannot detect the relationship between vote v_i and voter V_i, i.e., the privacy of the votes is preserved.*

Proof (Sketch). Assume that the Apollo server is honest and trustworthy, and one of the mix-server in mixnet is also honest to maintain the anonymity in the network. The relationship between the voters and their identity is firstly hidden by ElGamal encryption when it is sent to Apollo server. Furthermore, it is again mixed by mix-and-tweak network operations (re-encryption and reblinding) and re-encryption mixnets. In the opening stage, when the counter doesn't list the voter's ballot, the voter only show the pair $(v_i, \mathsf{H}(c_i))$ to claim the disruption. So, he can claim the disruption with keeping hs vote v_i secret. This ensures the voter's privacy.

Theorem 4 (Unreusability). *Given that Apollo server is honest, no voter can vote more than once.*

Proof (Sketch). To vote more than once, a voter must have valid tuples of the ballot, password credential. This means that he has obtained one password credential from Apollo server through the proper procedures, and created extra password credential himself. But when he sends his cast vote to Apollo server along with password credential, this cheating will be caught during the authenticity check by just matching with already stored password credential corresponds to the identity of the voter. Thus, the voter cannot vote more than once.

Theorem 5 (Fairness). *The counting of votes does not affect the voting.*

Proof (Sketch). Fairness means no information that can influence voter's decision should be revealed before finishing voting phase. In Apollo, since counting is done after the voting stage is completed, so it is impossible that the counting of the voted affect the voting. (In Apollo, partial counting is not allowed before the completion of voting, i.e., each voter has cast his vote).

Theorem 6 (Eligibility). *Under the assumption that the Apollo server is honest, only the eligible voters are able to vote.*

Proof (Sketch). Assume that a dishonest person can vote. Administrator checks the list of voters who have the right to vote. So the dishonest person must create a valid pair of the ballot and a password credential himself, and then vote is accepted. This contradicts that Apollo server is honest.

Theorem 7 (Receipt-freeness). *The voter must neither obtain nor be able to construct a receipt which can prove to a third party that he had cast a particular vote.*

Proof (Sketch). To achieve receipt-freeness, one-time secret random number r_i is used while ballot encryption in Apollo BPS so that the voter cannot repeat the ballot encryption by himself without knowing r_i. The only data the voter can obtain is the fingerprint of his encrypted ballot, therefore, he cannot demonstrate his choice to a third party.

Theorem 8 (Verifiability). *Assume that the Apollo server is honest, the encryption scheme is secure, and mixnet integrity is preserved. Then the published tally is equal to the actual result of the election. In other words, a voting system is said to be verifiable if all voters can verify that their vote was counted.*

Proof (Sketch). Once a voter has decided to cast the ballot, he is asked to authenticate himself using password credential. After a successful authentication, the ballot is sent to the server. The cast ballots are published in hashed form on a bulletin board after the voting stage is finished. Each individual voter can verify that the Apollo server stored his ballot is same as what he had cast. After a bulletin board published in public, any observer can verify the validity of the vote result. These encrypted ballots are now first sent through verifiable mix-and-tweak and then decrypted and tallied by a trusted Apollo server. So we need the proof of mix-and-tweak integrity (Sect. 4.2) and the proof of correctness for decryption(Sect. 4.1). Through these proofs, any observer guaranteed that there is no malfunction during tallying stage and validity of the vote result is preserved.

7 Conclusion

The major advantage of end-to-end verifiable voting schemes over traditional voting schemes is, anybody can verify the integrity of election result. The Helios is one of the latest and popular end-to-end verifiable voting scheme implemented using mixnet. In this work, we proposed an improved Helios, called Apollo. The main contribution to Apollo was introducing tweaks in hidden form, later on, these hidden tweaks were being released during the tallying stage. This modification gives two advantages - one that the proof of mixnet integrity is straightforward, i.e., directly verifiable, and second is that the cost of verification is significantly reduced. Due to this, our proposed scheme becomes practical for conducting large public elections as well.

References

1. Abe, M.: Mix-networks on permutation networks. In: Lam, K.-Y., Okamoto, E., Xing, C. (eds.) ASIACRYPT 1999. LNCS, vol. 1716, pp. 258–273. Springer, Heidelberg (1999)
2. Adida, B.: Helios: web-based open-audit voting. In: Proceedings of the 17th USENIX Security Symposium, San Jose, CA, USA, pp. 335–348. 28 July–1 August 2008
3. Aditya, R., Lee, B., Boyd, C., Dawson, E.: An efficient mixnet-based voting scheme providing receipt-freeness. In: Katsikas, S.K., López, J., Pernul, G. (eds.) TrustBus 2004. LNCS, vol. 3184, pp. 152–161. Springer, Heidelberg (2004)
4. Benaloh, J.: Simple verifiable elections. In: USENIX/ACCURATE Electronic Voting Technology Workshop, EVT 2006, Vancouver, BC, Canada, 1 August 2006
5. Benaloh, J.C., Tuinstra, D.: Receipt-free secret-ballot elections (extended abstract). In: Proceedings of the Twenty-Sixth Annual ACM Symposium on Theory of Computing, Montréal, Québec, Canada, pp. 544–553. 23–25 May 1994

6. Chaum, D.: Untraceable electronic mail, return addresses, and digital pseudonyms. Commun. ACM **24**(2), 84–88 (1981)
7. Chaum, D., Essex, A., Carback, R., Clark, J., Popoveniuc, S., Sherman, A., Vora, P.: Scantegrity: end-to-end voter-verifiable optical-scan voting. IEEE Secur. Priv. **6**(3), 40–46 (2008)
8. Chaum, D., Pedersen, T.P.: Wallet databases with observers. In: Brickell, E.F. (ed.) CRYPTO 1992. LNCS, vol. 740, pp. 89–105. Springer, Heidelberg (1993)
9. Chaum, D., Ryan, P.Y.A., Schneider, S.: A practical voter-verifiable election scheme. In: di Vimercati, S.C., Syverson, P.F., Gollmann, D. (eds.) ESORICS 2005. LNCS, vol. 3679, pp. 118–139. Springer, Heidelberg (2005)
10. Cohen, J.D., Fischer, M.J.: A robust and verifiable cryptographically secure election scheme (extended abstract). In: 26th Annual Symposium on Foundations of Computer Science, Portland, Oregon, USA, pp. 372–382. 21–23 October 1985
11. Cramer, R., Gennaro, R., Schoenmakers, B.: A secure and optimally efficient multi-authority election scheme. Eur. Trans. Telecommun. **8**(5), 481–490 (1997)
12. Fujioka, A., Okamoto, T., Ohta, K.: A practical secret voting scheme for large scale elections. In: Zheng, Y., Seberry, J. (eds.) AUSCRYPT 1992. LNCS, vol. 718, pp. 244–251. Springer, Heidelberg (1993)
13. Henry, K., Stinson, D.R., Sui, J.: The effectiveness of receipt-based attacks on threeballot. IEEE Trans. Inf. Forensics Secur. **4**(4), 699–707 (2009)
14. Hirt, M., Sako, K.: Efficient receipt-free voting based on homomorphic encryption. In: Preneel, B. (ed.) EUROCRYPT 2000. LNCS, vol. 1807, pp. 539–556. Springer, Heidelberg (2000)
15. Küsters, R., Truderung, T., Vogt, A.: Clash attacks on the verifiability of e-voting systems. In: IEEE Symposium on Security and Privacy, SP 2012, San Francisco, California, USA, pp. 395–409. 21–23 May 2012
16. Lee, B., Boyd, C., Dawson, E., Kim, K., Yang, J., Yoo, S.: Providing receipt-freeness in mixnet-based voting protocols. In: Lim, J.-I., Lee, D.-H. (eds.) ICISC 2003. LNCS, vol. 2971, pp. 245–258. Springer, Heidelberg (2004)
17. Ohkubo, M., Miura, F., Abe, M., Fujioka, A., Okamoto, T.: An improvement on a practical secret voting scheme. In: Zheng, Y., Mambo, M. (eds.) ISW 1999. LNCS, vol. 1729, pp. 225–234. Springer, Heidelberg (1999)
18. Okamoto, T.: An electronic voting scheme. In: Terashima, N., Altman, E. (eds.) Advanced IT Tools. The International Federation for Information Processing, pp. 21–30. Springer, US (1996)
19. Sako, K., Kilian, J.: Receipt-free mix-type voting scheme. In: Guillou, L.C., Quisquater, J.-J. (eds.) EUROCRYPT 1995. LNCS, vol. 921, pp. 393–403. Springer, Heidelberg (1995)
20. Smith, W.D.: Three voting protocols: threeballot, vav, and twin. In: 2007 USENIX/ACCURATE Electronic Voting Technology Workshop, EVT 2007, Boston, MA, USA, 6 August 2007
21. Weber, S.: A coercion-resistant cryptographic voting protocol - evaluation and prototype implementation. Master's thesis, Darmstadt University of Technology (2006)

On Differentially Private Online Collaborative Recommendation Systems

Seth Gilbert, Xiao Liu(✉), and Haifeng Yu

School of Computing, National University of Singapore, Singapore, Singapore
{seth.gilbert,liuxiao,haifeng}@comp.nus.edu.sg

Abstract. In collaborative recommendation systems, privacy may be compromised, as users' opinions are used to generate recommendations for others. In this paper, we consider an online collaborative recommendation system, and we measure users' privacy in terms of the standard notion of differential privacy. We give the first quantitative analysis of the trade-offs between recommendation quality and users' privacy in such a system by showing a lower bound on the best achievable privacy for any algorithm with non-trivial recommendation quality, and proposing a near-optimal algorithm. From our results, we find that there is actually little trade-off between recommendation quality and privacy, as long as non-trivial recommendation quality is to be guaranteed. Our results also identify the key parameters that determine the best achievable privacy.

Keywords: Differential privacy · Collaborative recommendation system · Lower bound · Online algorithm

1 Introduction

In this paper we consider an *online collaborative recommendation system* that attempts to predict which objects its users will like. Imagine, for example, a news website which publishes articles every day. When a user enjoys an article, he/she votes on the article (e.g., upvotes it, likes it, +1s it, etc.). Users can also ask the system for a recommendation, i.e., to suggest an article that they might like. After reading the recommended article, the user gives the system feedback on the recommendation so that it can improve its recommendation quality. In this paper, we work with a simplified, abstract version of this very common paradigm.

Due to the way it works, a collaborative recommendation system has the risks of leaking its users' privacy. Clearly, there are trade-offs between recommendation quality and privacy: a system that gives completely random recommendations certainly leaks no one's privacy, but it is also useless; in contrast, a recommendation system that gives high quality recommendations has to make "full use" of its users' data, which is more prone to privacy leakage.

A full version [21] of this paper is available at http://arxiv.org/abs/1510.08546. This research was supported by MOE ARC-2 grant MOE2014-T2-1-157.

S. Kwon and A. Yun (Eds.): ICISC 2015, LNCS 9558, pp. 210–226, 2016.
DOI: 10.1007/978-3-319-30840-1_14

In this paper, we adopt ϵ-differential privacy [17] as our formal definition of privacy, and we give the first quantitative analysis of these trade-offs for online collaborative recommendation systems. Prior to this paper, the topic of differentially private recommendation systems has primarily been examined under *offline matrix* models [12,13,23,24,28,32,42]. From the theoretical perspective, our recommendation model can be viewed as a variant of an *online learning* problem. Currently, there are only a limited number of existing papers on differentially private online learning [18,26,41], and their privacy models do not fit the recommendation problem (see Sect. 3 for more details).

We first study the best achievable privacy for a fixed recommendation quality by showing a near-tight lower bound on the privacy parameter ϵ (smaller ϵ means better privacy). For example, if we were to guarantee a trivial recommendation quality only, then we can achieve "perfect privacy" (i.e., $\epsilon = 0$) by ignoring users' opinions on objects and recommending randomly. As we set better and better target recommendation quality, it might be expected that the best achievable ϵ smoothly gets larger and larger. However, we show that the transition is sharp: although $\epsilon = 0$ is achievable for the trivial recommendation quality, the lower bound of ϵ rises to a certain level as long as non-trivial recommendation quality is to be guaranteed, and it remains essentially the same (up to a logarithmic factor) as the target recommendation quality increases.

We then propose a novel ϵ-differentially private algorithm. Our algorithm's ϵ is within a logarithmic factor to the aforementioned lower bound, and meanwhile its recommendation quality is also near-optimal up to a logarithmic factor, even when compared to algorithms providing no privacy guarantee.

Our near matching results surprisingly imply that there are actually little trade-offs between recommendation quality and privacy — an inherent "amount of privacy" (up to a logarithmic factor) must be "leaked" for *any* algorithm with non-trivial recommendation quality. Our results also identify the key parameters that fundamentally determine the best achievable recommendation quality and privacy. We provide more details about our results in Sect. 4.

2 Model and Problem Statement

2.1 Recommendation System Model

We now describe the model in more detail, abstracting away some of the complications in the scenario above in order to focus on the fundamental trade-offs.

We consider an online collaborative recommendation system that contains *voters*, *clients* and *objects*, and it repeatedly recommends objects to clients based on voters' opinions on objects. A voter/client either *likes* or *dislikes* an object. Voters submit their opinions on objects to the system in the form of *votes*, where a vote by voter i on object j indicates that voter i likes object j; clients receive recommendations from the system and provide *feedback* to the system which tells whether they like the recommended objects or not. Since every client has his/her own personalized preferences, the system will serve each client separately.

We now describe how the model operates for a particular client C. The system runs for T *rounds*. In each round $t \in \{1, \ldots, T\}$, a set of m *new* candidate objects arrives in the system, out of which the client C likes at least one of them. We assume that m is a constant, and totally the system has mT objects over all the T rounds. Let $\mathcal{U}$ denote the set of all the voters, and $\mathcal{B}_t$ denote the set of candidate objects in the tth round. After $\mathcal{B}_t$ arrives, each voter $i \in \mathcal{U}$ votes on one object in $\mathcal{B}_t$; the system then recommends one object $b_t \in \mathcal{B}_t$ to the client C (based on the voters' votes and the previous execution history), and C responses the system with his/her feedback which tells whether he/she likes b_t or not. The system proceeds into the next round after that.

We measure the recommendation quality by *loss*, which is defined as the number of objects that the algorithm recommends to the client C but C dislikes.

A client C is fully characterized by specifying C's preferences on every object. However, in a recommendation system, whether a client C likes an object j or not is unknown until the system has recommended j to C and gotten the feedback.

We denote the votes of all the voters in $\mathcal{U}$ by $\mathcal{V}\langle\mathcal{U}\rangle$, and we call $\mathcal{V}\langle\mathcal{U}\rangle$ the *voting pattern of* $\mathcal{U}$, or simply a *voting pattern* when $\mathcal{U}$ is clear from the context. Given a client C and a voting pattern $\mathcal{V}\langle\mathcal{U}\rangle$, a (randomized) recommendation algorithm $\mathcal{A}$ maps the pair $(C, \mathcal{V}\langle\mathcal{U}\rangle)$ to a (random) sequence of objects in $\mathcal{B}_1 \times \cdots \times \mathcal{B}_T$. We call a particular sequence in $\mathcal{B}_1 \times \cdots \times \mathcal{B}_T$ a *recommendation sequence.*

2.2 Differential Privacy in Recommendation Systems

Voters' votes are assumed to be securely stored by the system, which are not accessible from the public. Nevertheless, a curious client may still try to infer voters' votes by analyzing the recommendation results. In this paper, we adopt *differential privacy* [17] as our definition of privacy. Roughly speaking, differential privacy protects privacy by ensuring that the outputs are "similar" for two voting patterns $\mathcal{V}\langle\mathcal{U}\rangle$ and $\mathcal{V}\langle\mathcal{U}'\rangle$ if they differ by one voter. Such a pair of voting patterns are called *adjacent voting patterns*, and they are formally defined as:

Definition 1 (Adjacent Voting Patterns). Two voting patterns $\mathcal{V}\langle\mathcal{U}\rangle$ and $\mathcal{V}\langle\mathcal{U}'\rangle$ are adjacent voting patterns iff i) $|\mathcal{U} \triangle \mathcal{U}'| = 1$, and ii) for any voter $i \in \mathcal{U} \cap \mathcal{U}'$ and in any round $t \in \{1, \ldots, T\}$, i always votes on the same object in both $\mathcal{V}\langle\mathcal{U}\rangle$ and $\mathcal{V}\langle\mathcal{U}'\rangle$.

Generalizing Definition 1, we say that two voting patterns $\mathcal{V}\langle\mathcal{U}\rangle$ and $\mathcal{V}\langle\mathcal{U}'\rangle$ are *k-step adjacent*, if there exists a sequence of $k+1$ voting patterns $\mathcal{V}\langle\mathcal{U}_0\rangle = \mathcal{V}\langle\mathcal{U}\rangle, \mathcal{V}\langle\mathcal{U}_1\rangle, \ldots, \mathcal{V}\langle\mathcal{U}_{k-1}\rangle, \mathcal{V}\langle\mathcal{U}_k\rangle = \mathcal{V}\langle\mathcal{U}'\rangle$ such that $\mathcal{V}\langle\mathcal{U}_\ell\rangle$ and $\mathcal{V}\langle\mathcal{U}_{\ell+1}\rangle$ are adjacent for any $\ell = 0, \ldots, k-1$.

Having defined adjacent voting patterns, we can then apply the standard differential privacy in [17] to our setting:

Definition 2 (ϵ-Differential Privacy). A recommendation algorithm $\mathcal{A}$ preserves ϵ-differential privacy if for any client C, any pair of adjacent voting patterns $\mathcal{V}\langle\mathcal{U}\rangle, \mathcal{V}\langle\mathcal{U}'\rangle$, and any subset $S \subseteq \mathcal{B}_1 \times \cdots \times \mathcal{B}_T$,

$$\Pr[\mathcal{A}(C, \mathcal{V}\langle\mathcal{U}\rangle) \in S] \leq e^\epsilon \Pr[\mathcal{A}(C, \mathcal{V}\langle\mathcal{U}'\rangle) \in S],$$

where the probabilities are over $\mathcal{A}$'s coin flips.

2.3 Attack Model, Power of the Adversary

As indicated by Definitions 1 and 2, we protect voters' privacy against the client. We do not need to protect the client's privacy because voters receive nothing from the system.

Our research goal is to study the theoretical hardness of the aforementioned recommendation problem, therefore we assume that there is an adversary with unlimited computational power who controls how the voters vote and which objects the client likes. The adversary tries to compromise our algorithm's loss/privacy by feeding the algorithm with "bad" inputs. From the perspective of game theory, our recommendation model can be viewed as a repeated game between the algorithm, who chooses the objects to recommend, and the adversary, who chooses the client's preferences on objects and the voting pattern. For our lower bounds, we consider an *oblivious adversary* that chooses the client's preferences on objects and the voting patterns in advance; for our upper bounds, we consider an *adaptive adversary* whose choice in time t can depend on the execution history prior to time t. By doing so, our results are only strengthened.

2.4 Notations

Next we introduce some notations that characterize the system. Some of them are also the key parameters that determine the best achievable loss/privacy.

The Client's Diversity of Preferences. A client C's *diversity of preferences* D_C is defined to be the number of rounds in which C likes more than one objects.

The Client's Peers. Inherently, a collaborative recommendation system is able to achieve small loss only if some voters have similar preferences to the client. Let the *distance* between a client C and a voter i be the total number of objects that are voted on by i but are disliked by C. Given a radius parameter $R \in \{0, \ldots, T\}$, we define a voter i to be a client C's *peer* if their distance is within R. Given a client C, a voting pattern $\mathcal{V}\langle\mathcal{U}\rangle$ and a radius parameter R, we can count the number of C's peers in $\mathcal{U}$, and we denote it by $P_{C,\mathcal{V}\langle\mathcal{U}\rangle,R}$.

Other Notations. We define n to be an upper bound of $|\mathcal{U}|$ (i.e., the number of voters), D to be an upper bound of D_C (i.e., the client's diversity of preferences), and P to be a lower bound of $P_{C,\mathcal{V}\langle\mathcal{U}\rangle,R}$ (i.e., the number of the client's peers). The reader may wonder why these parameters are defined as upper/lower bounds. The purpose is to give a succinct presentation. Take n as an example: since differential privacy needs to consider two voting patterns with different numbers of voters, if we define n as the number of voters, it would be unclear which voting pattern we are referring to. The reader can verify that by choosing the right directions for the parameters (e.g., we define n to be an upper bound, and P to be a lower bound), our definition does not weaken our results.

In general, we consider a large system that consists of many voters, many objects (over all the rounds), and runs for a long time. That is, n and T can be very large. In this paper, we also impose a (quite loose) requirement that $n = O(\text{poly}(T))$, i.e., n is not super large compared to T.

In reality, a client shall find more peers as more voters join the system. Otherwise, the client has an "esoteric tastes" and it is inherently hard for any collaborative system to help him/her. Thus, in this paper, we consider the case that $P \geq 6m$, i.e., the client has at least a constant number of peers.

2.5 Loss/Privacy Goal

In this paper, we consider the *worst-case expected loss* of the algorithm, that is, we aim to bound the algorithm's expected loss for any client C and any voting pattern $\mathcal{V}\langle\mathcal{U}\rangle$ such that $|\mathcal{U}| \leq n$, $D_C \leq D$ and $P_{C,\mathcal{V}\langle\mathcal{U}\rangle,R} \geq P$. Notice that $O(T)$ loss can be trivially achieved by ignoring voters' votes and recommending objects randomly. However, such an algorithm is useless, and hence we consider the more interesting case when *non-trivial* loss (i.e., $o(T)$ worst-case expected loss) is to be guaranteed. It can be shown that the worst-case expected loss is $\Omega(R)$ for any algorithm (Theorem 3). Therefore, sub-linear loss is achievable only when R is sub-linear. In this paper, we focus on the case when $R = O(T^{\nu})$ for some constant $\nu < 1$.[1]

For the privacy, we aim to preserve ϵ-differential privacy. We study the best achievable ϵ-differential privacy for any given target loss.

3 Related Work

Recommendation Systems and Online Learning. The research on recommendation systems has a long history [1,40]. A classic recommendation model is the *offline matrix-based* model, in which the user-object relation is represented by a matrix. In this paper, we consider a very different *online* recommendation model. From the theoretical perspective, our model can be viewed as a variant of the "Prediction with Expert Advice" (PEA) problem in online learning [9]. Such an approach that models the recommendation systems as online learning problems has been adopted by other researchers as well, e.g., in [2,31,33,37,43].

Differential Privacy. There has been abundant research [14–16,18,20] on differential privacy. Much of the early research focused on answering a single query on a dataset. Progress on answering multiple queries with non-trivial errors was made later on, for both offline settings [4,19,25,38] (where the input is available in advance), and online settings [5,10,11,18,26,29,41] (where the input continuously comes). We will introduce the work on *differentially private online learning* in [18,26,41] with more details soon after, as they are most related to this paper.

[1] Technically, the assumptions that $n = O(\text{polylog}(T))$, $P \geq 6m$ and $R = O(T^{\nu})$ are only for showing the near-optimality of our lower bound. Our lower bound itself remains to hold without these assumptions.

Protecting Privacy in Recommendation Systems. People are well aware of the privacy risks in collaborative recommendation systems. Two recent attacks were demonstrated in [34] (which de-anonymized a dataset published by Netflix) and [6] (which inferred users' historical data by combining passive observation of a recommendation system with auxiliary information). The research in [34] even caused the second Netflix Prize competition to be cancelled.

Many of the existing privacy-preserving recommendation systems adopted privacy notions other than differential privacy (e.g., [3,7,8,35,36,39]). For studies on *differentially private* recommendation systems, prior to our paper, most of them were for *offline matrix-based* models. Some experimentally studied the empirical trade-offs between loss and privacy (e.g., [13,32,42]); the others focused on techniques that manipulate matrices in privacy-preserving ways (e.g., [12,23,24,28]). In a recent work [22], the authors proposed a modified version of differential privacy (called distance-based differential privacy), and they showed how to implement distance-based differential privacy in matrix-based recommendation systems.

Differentially Private Online Learning. This paper is most related to *differentially private online learning*, as our recommendation model is a variant of the PEA problem in online learning. Currently, only a limited number of studies have been done on this area [18,26,41]. In [18], Dwork et al. proposed a differentially private algorithm for the PEA problem by plugging privacy-preserving online counters into "Follow the Perturbed Leader" algorithm [27]. In [26,41], differential privacy was considered under a more general online learning model called "Online Convex Programming."

Despite the similarity between our recommendation model and the learning models in [18,26,41], there is an important difference. Since their research is not for recommendation systems, they considered somewhat different notions of privacy from ours. Roughly speaking, if interpreting their models as recommendation problems, then their privacy goal is to ensure that each *voter* is "followed" with similar probabilities when running the algorithm with two adjacent voting patterns. Such a guarantee is not sufficient for a recommendation system. For example, an algorithm that always "follows" voter Alice is perfectly private in terms of their privacy definition, but completely discloses Alice's private votes.[2] Besides the difference in privacy definition, we provide both lower bound and upper bound results, while [18,26,41] only have upper bound results.

4 Our Results and Contributions

Main Results. Our first result is a lower bound on the best achievable privacy:

[2] On the other hand, our privacy definition does not imply their definitions either. Therefore these two types of privacy models are incomparable.

Theorem 1. *For any recommendation algorithm that guarantees $L = O(T^\eta)$ worst-case expected loss ($\eta < 1$ is a constant) and preserves ϵ-differential privacy, $\epsilon = \Omega(\frac{1}{P}(D+R+\log\frac{T}{L})) = \Omega(\frac{1}{P}(D+R+\log T))$, even for an oblivious adversary.*

Our second result is a near-optimal algorithm (the p-REC algorithm in Sect. 7.2):

Theorem 2. *The p-REC algorithm guarantees $O((R+1)\log\frac{n}{P})$ worst-case expected loss, and it preserves $O(\frac{1}{P}(D+R+1)\log\frac{T}{R+1})$-differential privacy, even for an adaptive adversary.*

It can be shown that the worst-case expected loss is $\Omega(R+\log\frac{n}{P})$ even for algorithms with no privacy guarantee (Theorem 3). Thus, p-REC's worst-case expected loss is within a logarithmic factor to the optimal. Recall that $R = O(T^\nu)$ for a constant $\nu < 1$ and $\log n = O(\log T)$, hence p-REC's worst-case expected loss is within $O(T^\eta)$ for some constant $\eta < 1$ too. Then, by Theorem 1, p-REC's privacy is also within a logarithmic factor to the optimal.

Discussion of our Results. Theorem 1 shows that a minimal amount of "privacy leakage" is inevitable, even for the fairly weak $O(T^\eta)$ target loss.

Moreover, unlike many other systems in which the utility downgrades linear to the privacy parameter ϵ, the loss in an online recommendation system is much more sensitive to ϵ: according to Theorem 2, we can achieve near-optimal loss for an $\epsilon = O(\frac{1}{P}(D+R+1)\log\frac{T}{R+1})$; meanwhile, only trivial loss is achievable for just a slightly smaller $\epsilon = o(\frac{1}{P}(D+R+\log T))$. In other words, the trade-offs between loss and privacy are rather little — the best achievable ϵ is essentially the same (up to a logarithmic factor) for *all* the algorithms with $O(T^\eta)$ worst-case expected loss.[3] For this reason, instead of designing an algorithm that has a tunable privacy parameter ϵ, we directly propose the p-REC algorithm that simultaneously guarantees both near-optimal loss and privacy.

From our results, we identify the key parameters D, P and R that determine the best achievable loss and/or privacy.

The parameter R characterizes the correlation between the client and the voters, and it is not surprised that the best achievable loss is inherently limited by R, because a basic assumption for any collaborative system is the existence of correlation in the data (e.g., the low-rank assumption in matrix-based recommendation systems), and the system works by exploring/exploiting the correlation.

We notice that a larger P gives better privacy. This is consistent with our intuition, as an individual's privacy is obtained by hiding oneself in a population.

We also notice that the best achievable privacy linearly depends on the client's diversity of preferences D and the radius parameter R. The parameter D looks to be unnatural at the first sight, and no prior research on recommendation systems has studied it. The reason might be that most of the prior research

[3] This statement actually holds for all the algorithms with $o(T)$ loss. In Theorem 1, we choose $O(T^\eta)$ target loss to get a clean expression for the lower bound on ϵ, and a similar (but messier) lower bound on ϵ holds for $o(T)$ target loss too.

focused on the loss, and D has no impact on the loss (the loss should only be smaller if a client likes more objects). Nevertheless, in this paper, we discover that D is one of the fundamental parameters that determine the best achievable privacy. We provide an intuitive explanation of ϵ's linear dependence on D and R with an illustrative example in Sect. 7.1.

5 Preliminaries

Let $\mathcal{P}$ and $\mathcal{Q}$ be two distributions over sample space Ω. The *relative entropy* between $\mathcal{P}$ and $\mathcal{Q}$ is defined as $\sum_{\omega\in\Omega}\mathcal{P}(\omega)\ln\frac{\mathcal{P}(\omega)}{\mathcal{Q}(\omega)}$, where $\mathcal{P}(\omega)$ and $\mathcal{Q}(\omega)$ is the probability of ω in $\mathcal{P}$ and $\mathcal{Q}$, respectively. We adopt the conventions that $0\log\frac{0}{0}=0$, $0\log\frac{0}{x}=0$ for any $x>0$ and $x\log\frac{x}{0}=\infty$ for any $x>0$. It is well known that relative entropy is always non-negative [30].

In this paper, we often simultaneously discuss two executions $\mathcal{A}(C,\mathcal{V}\langle\mathcal{U}\rangle)$ and $\mathcal{A}(C,\mathcal{V}\langle\mathcal{U}'\rangle)$ for some algorithm $\mathcal{A}$, some client C and two voting patterns $\mathcal{V}\langle\mathcal{U}\rangle$ and $\mathcal{V}\langle\mathcal{U}'\rangle$. As a notation convention, we will use $\Pr[\cdot]$ and $\Pr'[\cdot]$ to denote the probability of some event in the execution of $\mathcal{A}(C,\mathcal{V}\langle\mathcal{U}\rangle)$ and $\mathcal{A}(C,\mathcal{V}\langle\mathcal{U}'\rangle)$, respectively. For any recommendation sequence $b=(b_1,\ldots,b_T)\in\mathcal{B}_1\times\cdots\times\mathcal{B}_T$ and any round t, we define the random variables $\mathcal{E}_t(b)=\ln\frac{\Pr[b_t|b_1,\ldots,b_{t-1}]}{\Pr'[b_t|b_1,\ldots,b_{t-1}]}$ and $\mathcal{E}(b)=\ln\frac{\Pr[b]}{\Pr'[b]}$. It then follows that $\mathcal{E}(b)=\sum_{t=1}^{T}\mathcal{E}_t(b)$. We also define random variable $\mathcal{L}_t$ to be the loss of execution $\mathcal{A}(C,\mathcal{V}\langle\mathcal{U}\rangle)$ in the tth round.

Finally, we list the following lower bound for the worst-case expected loss. Theorem 3 can be proved by constructing a client with random opinions on objects. Please see the full version [21] of this paper for its proof.

Theorem 3. *The worst-case expected loss of any recommendation algorithm is $\Omega(R+\log\frac{n}{P})$, even for an algorithm providing no privacy guarantee and an oblivious adversary.*

6 The Special Setting Where $D=R=0$

In order to better explain our ideas, we start by discussing the simple setting where $D=R=0$. That is, the client likes exactly one object in every round, and the client's peers never vote on any object that the client dislikes. We discuss the general setting where $D+R\geq 0$ in the next section.

6.1 Lower Bound

When $D=R=0$, we have the following lower bound on the privacy:

Theorem 4. *For any recommendation algorithm that guarantees $L=o(T)$ worst-case expected loss and preserves ϵ-differential privacy, if $D=R=0$, then $\epsilon=\Omega(\frac{1}{P}\log\frac{T}{L})$, even for an oblivious adversary.*

Proof (Sketch). Due to the limitation of space, here we provide a proof sketch of Theorem 4. The reader can refer to [21] for the full proof of this theorem. Our proof consists two main steps. In the first step, we consider a particular round t and two clients Alice and Bob who have different preferences in the tth round. Since the algorithm has to provide good recommendations to both Alice and Bob, the output distributions must be very different. Meanwhile, we carefully construct Alice's and Bob's executions, such that their voting patterns are $O(P)$-step adjacent to each other, hence the output distributions cannot be much different. From this dilemma we can establish a lower bound for the tth round. In the second step, we then extend this lower bound to all the T rounds using mathematical induction.

6.2 Algorithm

We propose the following Algorithm 1 for the simple setting where $D = R = 0$. As we will see, it is a special case of the general p-REC algorithm in Sect. 7.2. Therefore, we call it the p-REC$_{\text{sim}}$ algorithm ("sim" is short for "simple").

The p-REC$_{\text{sim}}$ algorithm maintains a weight value $\mathtt{weight}[i]$ for each voter i, and it recommends objects according to voters' weight in each round by invoking the procedure `RecommendByWeight()`. When it receives the client's feedback, it invokes the procedure `UpdateWeight()` to update voters' weight. In p-REC$_{\text{sim}}$, each voter's weight is either 1 or 0. A voter with 0 weight has no impact on the algorithm's output, and once a voter's weight is set to 0, it will never be reset to 1. Therefore, we can think of that `UpdateWeight()` works by "kicking out" voters from the system. We call the voters who have not been kicked out (i.e., those who have non-zero weight) *surviving voters.*

The p-REC$_{\text{sim}}$ algorithm shares a similar structure to the classic Weighted Average algorithm for the PEA problem [9], as they both introduce weight to voters and output according to the weight. Our core contribution is the dedicated probability of recommending objects. In each round t, p-REC$_{\text{sim}}$ recommends object j with probability $\gamma \cdot \frac{1}{m} + (1-\gamma) \cdot \frac{\phi(x_{j,t})}{\sum_{k \in \mathcal{B}_t} \phi(x_{k,t})}$, where $x_{j,t}$ is the fraction of surviving voters voting on object j in round t. We have:

Theorem 5. *If $D = R = 0$, then the p-REC$_{sim}$ algorithm guarantees $O(\log \frac{n}{P})$ worst-case expected loss and it preserves $O(\frac{1}{P} \log T)$-differential privacy, even for an adaptive adversary.*

According to Theorem 3, p-REC$_{\text{sim}}$'s loss is within a constant factor to the optimal. Then by Theorem 4, p-REC$_{\text{sim}}$'s ϵ is also within a constant factor to the optimal ϵ among all the algorithms that guarantee $O(T^{\eta})$ worst-case expected loss. We prove p-REC$_{\text{sim}}$'s loss bound in [21]. Here we briefly introduce the main steps to analyze p-REC$_{\text{sim}}$'s privacy.

Consider the executions p-REC$_{\text{sim}}(C, \mathcal{V}\langle\mathcal{U}\rangle)$ and p-REC$_{\text{sim}}(C, \mathcal{V}\langle\mathcal{U}'\rangle)$, where C is any client and $\mathcal{V}\langle\mathcal{U}\rangle$ and $\mathcal{V}\langle\mathcal{U}'\rangle$ are any pair of adjacent voting patterns ($\mathcal{U}$ contains one more voter than $\mathcal{U}'$). To show that p-REC$_{\text{sim}}$ preserves $O(\frac{1}{P} \log T)$-differential privacy, it is sufficient to show that $|\mathcal{E}(b)| = O(\frac{1}{P} \log T)$ for any

Input : A client C, a voting pattern $\mathcal{V}\langle\mathcal{U}\rangle$
Output : Recommend an object from $\mathcal{B}_t$ to client C in each round t
Initialization: $\gamma \leftarrow \frac{m}{3T-1}$, $\lambda \leftarrow 2m \ln T$, $\rho \leftarrow \frac{1}{2m}$, weight$[i] \leftarrow 1$ for each $i \in \mathcal{U}$

Procedure `Main()`
  foreach *round* $t = 1, \ldots, T$ **do**
    obj $\leftarrow$ `RecommendByWeight`(weight[ ]);
    Recommend object obj to the client C;
    feedback $\leftarrow$ the client C's feedback on object obj;
    `UpdateWeight`(weight[ ], obj, feedback);

Procedure `RecommendByWeight`(weight[ ])
  foreach *object* $j \in \mathcal{B}_t$ **do**
    $x_{j,t} \leftarrow \frac{\sum_{i \in \mathcal{U}_{j,t}} \text{weight}[i]}{\sum_{i \in \mathcal{U}} \text{weight}[i]}$, where $\mathcal{U}_{j,t}$ is the set of voters who vote on object j in round t;
  Independently draw a Bernoulli random variable Z_t with $\Pr[Z_t = 1] = \gamma$;
  if $Z_t = 1$ **then**
    Independently draw an object obj from $\mathcal{B}_t$ uniformly at random;
  else
    Independently draw an object obj from $\mathcal{B}_t$ according to the following distribution: each object $j \in \mathcal{B}_t$ is drawn with probability proportional to $\phi(x_{j,t})$, where $\phi(x) = \begin{cases} 0 & \text{if } x \leq \rho, \\ e^{\lambda x} - e^{\lambda \rho} & \text{otherwise;} \end{cases}$
  return obj;

Procedure `UpdateWeight`(weight[ ], obj, feedback)
  if feedback = *"dislike"* **then**
    weight$[i] \leftarrow 0$ for every voter i who votes on object obj;
  else
    weight$[i] \leftarrow 0$ for every voter i who does not vote on object obj;

Algorithm 1. The p-REC$_{\text{sim}}$ algorithm.

recommendation sequence $b = (b_1, \ldots, b_T)$. From now on, we will consider a fixed b, a fixed C and a fixed pair of $\mathcal{V}\langle\mathcal{U}\rangle$ and $\mathcal{V}\langle\mathcal{U}'\rangle$.

Given $b = (b_1, \ldots, b_T)$, let $W_t(b) = \sum_{i \in \mathcal{U}} \text{weight}[i]$ be the number of surviving voters at the beginning of round t in execution p-REC$_{\text{sim}}(C, \mathcal{V}\langle\mathcal{U}\rangle)$, conditioned on that the recommendations in the first $t-1$ rounds are $b_1, \ldots, b_{t-1}$. Since p-REC$_{\text{sim}}$ never kicks out the client's peers, $W_t(b) \geq P \geq 6m$.

First, we upper-bound the "privacy leakage" in each single round:

Lemma 6. *For any round* t, $|\mathcal{E}_t(b)| \leq 3\lambda \cdot \frac{1}{W_t(b)}$.

Lemma 6 can be shown by a straightforward but rather tedious calculation, see the full version [21] of this paper for the proof.

Next, we show that a constant fraction of surviving voters are kicked out whenever there is non-zero "privacy leakage:"

Lemma 7. *For any round t, if $|\mathcal{E}_t(b)| \neq 0$, then $W_{t+1}(b) \leq W_t(b) \cdot (1 - \frac{1}{3m})$.*

Proof. Notice that $|\mathcal{E}_t(b)| \neq 0$ iff $\Pr[b_t|b_1, \ldots, b_{t-1}] \neq \Pr'[b_t|b_1, \ldots, b_{t-1}]$. Let x and x' be the fraction of surviving voters voting on the recommended object b_t in execution p-REC$_{\text{sim}}(C, \mathcal{V}\langle\mathcal{U}\rangle)$ and p-REC$_{\text{sim}}(C, \mathcal{V}\langle\mathcal{U}'\rangle)$, respectively. Since there are $W_t(b)$ surviving voters, $|x - x'| \leq \frac{1}{W_t(b)} \leq \frac{1}{P} \leq \frac{1}{6m}$.

We claim that $x > \frac{1}{3m}$. Assume for contradiction that $x \leq \frac{1}{3m}$. Since $|x - x'| \leq \frac{1}{6m}$, both x and x' will be no larger than $\frac{1}{3m} + \frac{1}{6m} = \frac{1}{2m} = \rho$. Notice that $\phi(\zeta) = 0$ for any variable $\zeta \leq \rho$, it then follows that $\phi(x) = \phi(x') = 0$ and $\Pr[b_t|b_1, \ldots, b_{t-1}] = \Pr'[b_t|b_1, \ldots, b_{t-1}] = \gamma \cdot \frac{1}{m}$, contradiction.

If the clients dislikes the recommended object b_t, by p-REC$_{\text{sim}}$'s rule of updating weight, $x > \frac{1}{3m}$ fraction of surviving voters will be kicked out.

If the clients likes b_t, then there must exist another object $\xi \in \mathcal{B}_t$ which is different from b_t, such that $\Pr[\xi|b_1, \ldots, b_{t-1}] \neq \Pr'[\xi|b_1, \ldots, b_{t-1}]$. Otherwise, if all the other objects are recommended with the same probability in executions p-REC$_{\text{sim}}(C, \mathcal{V}\langle\mathcal{U}\rangle)$ and p-REC$_{\text{sim}}(C, \mathcal{V}\langle\mathcal{U}'\rangle)$, so will be b_t, contradiction. By similar arguments, there are at least $\frac{1}{3m}$ fraction of surviving voters voting on the object ξ in both p-REC$_{\text{sim}}(C, \mathcal{V}\langle\mathcal{U}\rangle)$ and p-REC$_{\text{sim}}(C, \mathcal{V}\langle\mathcal{U}'\rangle)$. Since p-REC$_{\text{sim}}$ kicks out all the voters who do not vote on b_t (including those who vote on ξ), again we get the desired result. □

Lemma 6 states that $|\mathcal{E}_t(b)|$ is $O(\frac{\lambda}{W_t(b)}) = O(\frac{1}{P} \log T)$. Lemma 7 implies that there can be at most $O(\log \frac{n}{P})$ rounds with $|\mathcal{E}_t(b)| \neq 0$. A combination of these two lemmas immediately shows that overall we have $O(\frac{1}{P} \log T \cdot \log \frac{n}{P})$-differential privacy. With a bit more careful analysis, we can remove the extra $\log \frac{n}{P}$ factor. We leave the details to [21].

7 The General Setting Where $D + R \geq 0$

7.1 Lower Bound

In this section, we prove Theorem 1. If $0 \leq D + R < 6 \ln T$ and the target loss $L = O(T^\eta)$, then $\Omega(\log \frac{T}{L}) = \Omega(D + R + \log \frac{T}{L})$ and hence Theorem 1 is implied by Theorem 4. When $D + R \geq 6 \ln T$, we have the following Theorem 8. Theorem 1 is then proved because $\Omega(D + R) = \Omega(D + R + \log \frac{T}{L})$ if $D + R \geq 6 \ln T$.

Theorem 8. *For any recommendation algorithm that guarantees $L = o(T)$ worst-case expected loss and preserves ϵ-differential privacy, if $D + R \geq 6 \ln T$, then $\epsilon = \Omega(\frac{1}{P}(D + R))$, even for an oblivious adversary.*

Before proving Theorem 8, we first explain the intuition behind the proof by a simple illustrative example. Imagine that there is one client Alice, and two voting patterns $\mathcal{V}_1$ and $\mathcal{V}_2$. Both $\mathcal{V}_1$ and $\mathcal{V}_2$ contain only one voter named Bob, but Bob may vote differently in $\mathcal{V}_1$ and $\mathcal{V}_2$. We let Bob be Alice's peer in both $\mathcal{V}_1$ and $\mathcal{V}_2$. For simplicity let us set $R = 0$, so Bob never votes on any object that Alice dislikes. By Definition 1, $\mathcal{V}_1$ and $\mathcal{V}_2$ are 2-step voting patterns.

Now consider a particular round t with two candidate objects. If Alice likes only one of the objects, then there is only one way for Bob to cast vote; otherwise Bob will no longer be a peer of Alice. However, if Alice likes both objects, then Bob can vote on different objects in $\mathcal{V}_1$ and $\mathcal{V}_2$ without breaking the promise that he is Alice's peer. Since Bob is the only information source of the system, an recommendation algorithm $\mathcal{A}$ has to somehow "follow" Bob, and hence the distributions of the executions $\mathcal{A}(\text{Alice}, \mathcal{V}_1)$ and $\mathcal{A}(\text{Alice}, \mathcal{V}_2)$ will be different. If Alice's diversity of preferences is D, then this situation can happen for D times, which results an $\epsilon \propto D$. The linear dependency of ϵ on R is for a similar reason.

Proof (Sketch of Theorem 8). Due to the limitation of space, we provide a proof sketch in the main text. The full proof can be found in [21].

We first prove Theorem 8 for the case where $P = 1$ and $6 \ln T \leq D + R \leq T$. To show Theorem 8 for the case where $P = 1$, it is sufficient to show that for any given algorithm $\mathcal{A}$, we can construct a client C and a pair of 2-step adjacent voting patterns $\mathcal{V}\langle\mathcal{U}\rangle, \mathcal{V}\langle\mathcal{U}'\rangle$, such that $\ln \frac{\Pr[b]}{\Pr'[b]} = \Omega(D + R)$ for some recommendation sequence $b \in \mathcal{B}_1 \times \cdots \times \mathcal{B}_T$.

We construct the client C by setting C's preferences on objects. We will always ensure that C likes multiple objects in at most D rounds. For the voting pattern $\mathcal{V}\langle\mathcal{U}\rangle$ and $\mathcal{V}\langle\mathcal{U}'\rangle$, we let each of them contain one voter U and U', respectively. We construct the voting patterns by setting U and U''s votes in each round. We will always ensure that both U and U' vote on at most R objects that are disliked by the client C, hence U and U' are both the client C's peers.

We construct C, $\mathcal{V}\langle\mathcal{U}\rangle$ and $\mathcal{V}\langle\mathcal{U}'\rangle$ round by round. Imagine that we are in the beginning of the tth round, with the previous recommendation history being $b_{<t} = (b_1, \ldots, b_{t-1})$. In order to better demonstrate our ideas, let us temporarily assume an adaptive adversary who can also see the recommendation history $b_{<t}$. The adversary can then set C's preferences on objects and U and U''s votes based on the algorithm $\mathcal{A}$'s behavior:

- *Case 1*: $\mathcal{A}$ "follows" voter U with probability ≤ 0.75. In this case, the adversary let C like exactly one object in round t, and it let U vote on the only object that C likes. It then follows that $\mathbb{E}[\mathcal{L}_t | b_{<t}] \geq 1 - 0.75 = 0.25$, i.e., the expected loss in round t is at least a constant.
- *Case 2.a*: $\mathcal{A}$ "follows" voter U with probability > 0.75, but it "follows" the voter U' with probability ≤ 0.5. In this case, if the adversary let U and U' vote *identically*, then the distributions $\Pr[\cdot | b_{<t}]$ and $\Pr'[\cdot | b_{<t}]$ will be different. In particular, we can show that the relative entropy $\mathbb{E}[\mathcal{E}_t | b_{<t}] \geq 0.13$, i.e., the expected "privacy leakage" in round t is at least a constant.
- *Case 2.b*: $\mathcal{A}$ "follows" voter U with probability ≥ 0.75, and it "follows" voter U' with probability > 0.5. This case is symmetric to *Case 2.a*, and hence the adversary can force $\mathbb{E}[\mathcal{E}_t | b_{<t}] \geq 0.13$ by letting U and U' vote *differently*. However, it is worth noting that during the entire execution of $\mathcal{A}$, the adversary can let U and U' vote differently for at most $D + R$ times due to the constraints imposed by D and R (see the full proof for more details).

It can be shown that with the above adaptive construction, $\mathbb{E}[\mathcal{E}] = \Omega(D+R)$ for any algorithm $\mathcal{A}$, which implies the existence of one recommendation sequence b such that $\mathcal{E}(b) = \ln \frac{\Pr[b]}{\Pr'[b]} = \Omega(D+R)$. To see why $\mathbb{E}[\mathcal{E}] = \Omega(D+R)$, we first notice that there cannot be too many rounds in *Case 1* on expectation, because $\mathcal{A}$ has to ensure $o(T)$ expected loss. Therefore most of the rounds must be in *Case 2.a* or *Case 2.b*. If there are many rounds in *Case 2.a*, then $\mathbb{E}[\mathcal{E}]$ must be large because $\mathbb{E}[\mathcal{E}_t|b_{<t}] \geq 0.13$ in every *Case 2.a* round, and $\mathbb{E}[\mathcal{E}_t|b_{<t}] \geq 0$ in all the other rounds (relative entropy is non-negative [30]). Otherwise, there must be many rounds in *Case 2.b*. In this case, the adversary can force $\mathbb{E}[\mathcal{E}_t|b_{<t}] \geq 0.13$ for $\Omega(D+R)$ times, and we have $\mathbb{E}[\mathcal{E}] = \Omega(D+R)$.

The aforementioned adaptive adversary chooses a "bad setting" for the algorithm $\mathcal{A}$ in each round based on which case $\mathcal{A}$ is in. We point out that this is actually not necessary: we still have $\mathbb{E}[\mathcal{E}] = \Omega(D+R)$ if the adversary randomly chooses a "bad setting" in each round with a proper distribution. Such a (random) adversary is oblivious, and it implies the existence of a "bad input" that does not depend on $\mathcal{A}$'s execution. This finishes the proof in the case of $P = 1$.

Finally, we prove Theorem 8 for the cases where $D + R > T$ and/or $P > 1$. These proofs are just simple extensions of the above basic proof. □

7.2 Algorithm

We propose the following p-REC algorithm for the general setting where $D+R \geq 0$. The p-REC algorithm is a generalized version of the p-REC$_{\text{sim}}$ algorithm, and it shares a similar structure as that of p-REC$_{\text{sim}}$, except that the procedure `UpdateWeight()` is replaced by `UpdateCreditAndWeight()`. In fact, we can get back the p-REC$_{\text{sim}}$ algorithm by setting $D = R = 0$ in the p-REC algorithm.

Theorem 2 summarizes p-REC's loss and privacy. According to the lower bounds in Theorems 1 and 3, both its loss and privacy are within logarithmic factors to the optimal.

In the beginning of the p-REC algorithm, each voter $i \in \mathcal{U}$ is initialized with two *credit* values $\mathsf{credit}^{(D)}[i] = 2D$ (which we call *D-credit*) and $\mathsf{credit}^{(R)}[i] = 2R + 1$ (which we call *R-credit*). In each round t, the algorithm recommends objects by invoking the `RecommendByWeight()` procedure. After it receives the client's feedback, the algorithm updates each voter's credit and then calculate his/her weight by invoking the `UpdateCreditAndWeight()` procedure.

To see the intuition behind the p-REC algorithm, let us analyze why the p-REC$_{\text{sim}}$ algorithm fails in the general setting where $D + R \geq 0$. If we run p-REC$_{\text{sim}}$ in the general setting, we may end up with a situation where all the client's peers are kicked out from the system. A client's peer can be (wrongly) kicked out in two scenarios:

- when the client likes more than one objects in some round, the peer votes on one such object, but another such object is recommended;
- when the peer votes on an object that the client dislikes, and that object is recommended to the client.

```
Input          : A client C, a voting pattern V⟨U⟩
Output         : Recommend an object from B_t to client C in each round t
Initialization: γ ← m/((3T/(R+1))−1); λ ← 2m ln (T/(R+1)); ρ ← 1/(2m); for each i ∈ U:
                credit^(D)[i] ← 2D, credit^(R)[i] ← 2R + 1, weight[i] ← 1
Procedure Main()
    foreach round t = 1,...,T do
        obj ← RecommendByWeight(weight[ ]);
        Recommend object obj to the client C;
        feedback ← the client C's feedback on object obj;
        UpdateCreditAndWeight(credit^(D)[ ], credit^(R)[ ], weight[ ], obj,
        feedback);
Procedure UpdateCreditAndWeight(credit^(D)[ ], credit^(R)[ ], weight[ ], obj,
feedback)
    if feedback = "dislike" then
        credit^(R)[i] ← credit^(R)[i] − 1 for every voter i who votes on obj;
    else
        credit^(D)[i] ← credit^(D)[i] − 1 for every voter i who does not vote on obj;
    foreach voter i ∈ U do
        if credit^(R)[i] > 0 and credit^(D)[i] + credit^(R)[i] > 0 then
            weight[i] ← 1;
        else
            weight[i] ← 0;
```

Algorithm 2. Privacy-preserving RECommendation (p-REC) algorithm.

However, since these two scenarios can happen for at most $D + R$ times, a natural idea is to give a voter $D+R$ more "chances" before we kick out him/her. Motivated by this, we could initialize each voter i with $D + R + 1$ credit, and deduct i's credit by 1 when i is caught to vote on an object the client dislikes, or when the client likes the recommended object but i does not vote on it. We kick out a voter only when he/she has no credit.

For some technical reasons, p-REC needs to introduce two types of credit (D-credit and R-credit), and deducts different types of credit in different situations. It also initializes each voter with $2D$ (instead of D) D-credit and $2R + 1$ (instead of $R + 1$) R-credit. The analysis of the p-REC algorithm is similar in spirit to that of the p-REC$_{\text{sim}}$ algorithm, and we leave the details to [21].

References

1. Adomavicius, G., Tuzhilin, A.: Toward the next generation of recommender systems: a survey of the state-of-the-art and possible extensions. IEEE Trans. Knowl. Data Eng. **17**(6), 734–749 (2005)
2. Awerbuch, B., Hayes, T.P.: Online collaborative filtering with nearly optimal dynamic regret. In: Proceedings of the 19th Annual ACM Symposium on Parallelism in Algorithms and Architectures, pp. 315–319. ACM (2007)

3. Berkovsky, S., Eytani, Y., Kuflik, T., Ricci, F.: Enhancing privacy and preserving accuracy of a distributed collaborative filtering. In: Proceedings of the 2007 ACM Conference on Recommender Systems. pp. 9–16. ACM (2007)
4. Blum, A., Ligett, K., Roth, A.: A learning theory approach to non-interactive database privacy. In: Proceedings of the 40th Annual ACM Symposium on Theory of Computing, pp. 609–618. ACM (2008)
5. Bolot, J., Fawaz, N., Muthukrishnan, S., Nikolov, A., Taft, N.: Private decayed predicate sums on streams. In: Proceedings of the 16th International Conference on Database Theory, pp. 284–295. ACM (2013)
6. Calandrino, J., Kilzer, A., Narayanan, A., Felten, E.W., Shmatikov, V., et al.: "You might also like:" privacy risks of collaborative filtering. In: Proceedings of the 2011 IEEE Symposium on Security and Privacy, pp. 231–246. IEEE (2011)
7. Canny, J.: Collaborative filtering with privacy. In: Proceedings of the 2002 IEEE Symposium on Security and Privacy, pp. 45–57. IEEE (2002)
8. Canny, J.: Collaborative filtering with privacy via factor analysis. In: Proceedings of the 25th Annual International ACM SIGIR Conference on Research and Development in Information Retrieval, pp. 238–245. ACM (2002)
9. Cesa-Bianchi, N., Lugosi, G.: Prediction, Learning, and Games. Cambridge University Press, New York (2006)
10. Chan, T.-H.H., Li, M., Shi, E., Xu, W.: Differentially private continual monitoring of heavy hitters from distributed streams. In: Fischer-Hübner, S., Wright, M. (eds.) PETS 2012. LNCS, vol. 7384, pp. 140–159. Springer, Heidelberg (2012)
11. Chan, T.H.H., Shi, E., Song, D.: Private and continual release of statistics. ACM Trans. Inf. Syst. Secur. **14**(3), 26 (2011)
12. Chaudhuri, K., Sarwate, A.D., Sinha, K.: A near-optimal algorithm for differentially-private principal components. J. Mach. Learn. Res. **14**(1), 2905–2943 (2013)
13. Chow, R., Pathak, M.A., Wang, C.: A practical system for privacy-preserving collaborative filtering. In: Proceedings of the 12th IEEE International Conference on Data Mining Workshops (ICDMW), pp. 547–554. IEEE (2012)
14. Dwork, C.: Differential privacy: a survey of results. In: Agrawal, M., Du, D.-Z., Duan, Z., Li, A. (eds.) TAMC 2008. LNCS, vol. 4978, pp. 1–19. Springer, Heidelberg (2008)
15. Dwork, C.: The differential privacy frontier (extended abstract). In: Reingold, O. (ed.) TCC 2009. LNCS, vol. 5444, pp. 496–502. Springer, Heidelberg (2009)
16. Dwork, C.: A firm foundation for private data analysis. Commun. ACM **54**(1), 86–95 (2011)
17. Dwork, C., McSherry, F., Nissim, K., Smith, A.: Calibrating noise to sensitivity in private data analysis. In: Halevi, S., Rabin, T. (eds.) TCC 2006. LNCS, vol. 3876, pp. 265–284. Springer, Heidelberg (2006)
18. Dwork, C., Naor, M., Pitassi, T., Rothblum, G.N.: Differential privacy under continual observation. In: Proceedings of the 42nd ACM Symposium on Theory of Computing, pp. 715–724. ACM (2010)
19. Dwork, C., Naor, M., Reingold, O., Rothblum, G.N., Vadhan, S.: On the complexity of differentially private data release: efficient algorithms and hardness results. In: Proceedings of the 41st Annual ACM Symposium on Theory of Computing, pp. 381–390. ACM (2009)
20. Dwork, C., Smith, A.: Differential privacy for statistics: what we know and what we want to learn. J. Priv. confidentiality **1**(2), 2 (2010)
21. Gilbert, S., Liu, X., Yu, H.: On differentially private online collaborative recommendation systems. ArXiv e-prints (2015). arxiv:1510.08546

22. Guerraoui, R., Kermarrec, A.M., Patra, R., Taziki, M.: D2P: distance-based differential privacy in recommenders. Proc. VLDB Endowment **8**(8), 862–873 (2015)
23. Hardt, M., Roth, A.: Beating randomized response on incoherent matrices. In: Proceedings of the 44th annual ACM Symposium on Theory of Computing, pp. 1255–1268. ACM (2012)
24. Hardt, M., Roth, A.: Beyond worst-case analysis in private singular vector computation. In: Proceedings of the 45th annual ACM Symposium on Theory of Computing, pp. 331–340. ACM (2013)
25. Hardt, M., Rothblum, G.N.: A multiplicative weights mechanism for privacy-preserving data analysis. In: Proceedings of the 51th Annual IEEE Symposium on Foundations of Computer Science, pp. 61–70. IEEE (2010)
26. Jain, P., Kothari, P., Thakurta, A.: Differentially private online learning. In: Proceedings of the 25th Annual Conference on Learning Theory, pp. 24.1–24.34 (2011)
27. Kalai, A., Vempala, S.: Efficient algorithms for online decision problems. J. Comput. Syst. Sci. **71**(3), 291–307 (2005)
28. Kapralov, M., Talwar, K.: On differentially private low rank approximation. In: Proceedings of the 24th Annual ACM-SIAM Symposium on Discrete Algorithms, pp. 1395–1414. SIAM (2013)
29. Kellaris, G., Papadopoulos, S., Xiao, X., Papadias, D.: Differentially private event sequences over infinite streams. Proc. VLDB Endowment **7**(12), 1155–1166 (2014)
30. Kullback, S.: Information Theory and Statistics. Courier Corporation, New York (1968)
31. Lee, W.S.: Collaborative learning for recommender systems. In: Proceedings of the 18th International Conference on Machine Learning, pp. 314–321 (2001)
32. McSherry, F., Mironov, I.: Differentially private recommender systems: building privacy into the net. In: Proceedings of the 15th ACM SIGKDD International Conference on Knowledge Discovery and Data Mining, pp. 627–636. ACM (2009)
33. Nakamura, A., Abe, N.: Collaborative filtering using weighted majority prediction algorithms. In: Proceedings of the 15th International Conference on Machine Learning, pp. 395–403 (1998)
34. Narayanan, A., Shmatikov, V.: Robust de-anonymization of large sparse datasets. In: Proceedings of the 2008 IEEE Symposium on Security and Privacy, pp. 111–125. IEEE (2008)
35. Polat, H., Du, W.: Privacy-preserving collaborative filtering. Int. J. Electron. Commer. **9**(4), 9–35 (2003)
36. Polat, H., Du, W.: SVD-based collaborative filtering with privacy. In: Proceedings of the 2005 ACM Symposium on Applied Computing, pp. 791–795. ACM (2005)
37. Resnick, P., Sami, R.: The influence limiter: provably manipulation-resistant recommender systems. In: Proceedings of the 2007 ACM Conference on Recommender Systems, pp. 25–32. ACM (2007)
38. Roth, A., Roughgarden, T.: Interactive privacy via the median mechanism. In: Proceedings of the 42nd ACM Symposium on Theory of Computing, pp. 765–774. ACM (2010)
39. Shokri, R., Pedarsani, P., Theodorakopoulos, G., Hubaux, J.P.: Preserving privacy in collaborative filtering through distributed aggregation of offline profiles. In: Proceedings of the 2009 ACM Conference on Recommender Systems, pp. 157–164. ACM (2009)
40. Su, X., Khoshgoftaar, T.M.: A survey of collaborative filtering techniques. Adv. Artif. Intell. **2009**, Article ID 421425, 19 (2009). Doi:10.1155/2009/421425

41. Thakurta, A.G., Smith, A.: (Nearly) optimal algorithms for private online learning in full-information and bandit settings. In: Advances in Neural Information Processing Systems, pp. 2733–2741 (2013)
42. Xin, Y., Jaakkola, T.: Controlling privacy in recommender systems. In: Advances in Neural Information Processing Systems, pp. 2618–2626 (2014)
43. Yu, H., Shi, C., Kaminsky, M., Gibbons, P.B., Xiao, F.: Dsybil: optimal sybil-resistance for recommendation systems. In: Proceedings of the 2009 IEEE Symposium on Security and Privacy, pp. 283–298. IEEE (2009)

Security

Stack Layout Randomization with Minimal Rewriting of Android Binaries

Yu Liang[1], Xinjie Ma[2], Daoyuan Wu[3], Xiaoxiao Tang[3], Debin Gao[3], Guojun Peng[1](✉), Chunfu Jia[2], and Huanguo Zhang[1]

[1] Wuhan University, Wuhan, China
{liangyu,guojpeng,liss}@whu.edu.cn
[2] Nankai University, Tianjin, China
{mxjnkcs,cfjia}@nankai.edu.cn
[3] Singapore Management University, Singapore, Singapore
{dywu.2015,xxtang.2013,dbgao}@smu.edu.sg

Abstract. Stack-based attacks typically require that attackers have a good understanding of the stack layout of the victim program. In this paper, we leverage specific features on ARM architecture and propose a practical technique that introduces randomness to the stack layout when an Android application executes. We employ *minimal* binary rewriting on the Android app that produces randomized executable of the same size which can be executed on an unmodified Android operating system. Our experiments on applying this randomization on the most popular 20 free Android apps on Google Play show that the randomization coverage of functions increases from 65 % (by a state-of-the-art randomization approach) to 97.6 % with, on average, 4 and 7 bits of randomness applied to each 16-bit and 32-bit function, respectively. We also show that it is effective in defending against stack-based memory vulnerabilities and real-world ROP attacks.

Keywords: Memory layout randomization · Android security

1 Introduction

Stack plays an essential part in maintaining and managing runtime data of an execution, e.g., context of function invocation, parameters, and local variables. Many attacks are based on disclosure or modification of such information on the stack. Examples include traditional code injection attacks that overwrite sensitive data, e.g., return addresses and function pointers, to execute the injected malicious code [1], and more recent code reuse attacks that chain existing code gadgets together to perform malicious activities [2–5].

A common requirement of such stack-based attacks is a good understanding of the stack layout by attackers. Applications with predictable stack layout are typically exposed to the high risks of such attacks. This requirement of knowing the stack layout becomes more critical in recent Return-Oriented Programming

S. Kwon and A. Yun (Eds.): ICISC 2015, LNCS 9558, pp. 229–245, 2016.
DOI: 10.1007/978-3-319-30840-1_15

(ROP) attacks because an attacker needs to put more efforts in arranging data on the stack to chain various code gadgets together [2,6–9].

Randomizing the stack layout is a natural response to make it more difficult for attackers to locate critical data. Modifications have been proposed to operating systems to introduce such randomness. For example, Address Space Layout Randomization (ASLR) randomizes the base address of many code/data segments, and is widely used in both x86 and mobile platforms [10–12]. However, researchers have been questioning such randomization techniques with modified operating systems in their effectiveness (or amount of randomness) [13,14], completeness [15–17], and many claim that they can be circumvented with advanced attacking techniques like Return-Oriented Programming [5,8].

Randomness could also be introduced to the application alone without modifications to the operating system [18–20]. However, this has since been considered as a less favorable solution mainly due to the difficulty in binary rewriting the application as well as the relatively low applicability and amount of randomness [21]. Binary rewriting an executable could be problematic especially when the size of a function in the resulting binary increases, which means that all instructions in the subsequent functions have to be shifted and all jump targets affected have to be recalculated. This can sometimes be avoided with tricks like re-ordering of functions [13], but is in general an unsolved problem that puts heavy stress on its applicability.

In this paper, we explore how far we can go in terms of introducing randomness into the stack layout with some *minimal* rewriting to the executable binary without any operating system support. By *minimal* binary rewriting, we exercise the restriction that no insertion or deletion of instructions is allowed, which also implies that the program size will remain unchanged.

We show that a reasonable amount of randomness of up to 7 bits to many functions is possible by leveraging special features of the ARM architecture when binary rewriting Android applications. Our solution does not require any modification to the Android operating system. The main idea is to randomize the set of registers to be pushed onto the stack at prologue of a function (and the corresponding registers to be popped). For example, a function might be surrounded with `push {r3,r4,r5,lr}` and `pop {r3,r4,r5,pc}` to store registers used in the caller function. Our technique randomly chooses a superset of the registers, e.g., `{r1,r3,r4,r5,r8,r9,lr}`, to be pushed onto (and popped off) the stack. This change effectively adds a random amount of data on the stack and shifts all other data on the stack frame by a random offset. The intuition behind such a design is that this change requires a simple mutation to the `push` and `pop` instructions which change neither the length of the instructions nor the overall size of the app on ARM architecture.

We implement a proof-of-concept binary rewriter to automatically apply this randomization to Android apps. We show that many existing code reuse attacks no longer work with our randomized Android apps. Our experiments with the most popular 20 free Android apps on Google Play also show that the randomization successfully applies to more than 97.6 % of the functions, a noticeable increase from 65 % achievable by previous state-of-the-art randomization techniques [15]. Every function receives, on average, 7 bits of randomness to their location on the stack when it uses 32-bit ARM/Thumb instructions or 4 bits of randomness if it uses 16-bit Thumb instructions. Experiments on a format-string vulnerability and a real-world ROP attack show that our proposed randomization is effective in defending against real-world attacks.

2 Background and Threat Model

As our proposed technique deals with binary rewriting of Android apps to be executed on ARM devices, we first briefly present some necessary background of ARM instructions and registers. We also present the threat model under which our proposed solution works.

Any ARM binary (containing native code from shared libraries or Dalvik bytecode compilation) may contain both ARM and Thumb-2 instructions. ARM is a 32-bit fixed-length instruction set. Thumb-2, developed from 16-bit Thumb instructions, constitutes an instruction set with 16-bit and 32-bit instructions intermixed. This brings flexibility and performance; however, the difference in instruction length also makes binary analysis and rewriting more difficult.

ARM architecture provides 16 core registers of 32-bit length for ARM and Thumb-2 instructions. These registers are labeled `r0` to `r15`. Registers from `r12` to `r15` are also known as the `ip`, `sp`, `lr`, and `pc` register. During a function call, registers from `r0` to `r3` are used to store parameters if needed, `lr` is used to store the return address, and `r0` is used to keep the return value. A function typically uses some but not all registers.

We assume a threat model in which the adversary has a copy of the original application (without randomization) and understands the full details of our randomization algorithm. The adversary may also have multiple copies of the randomized app; although he/she does not have the specific randomized copy that the victim is using. We also assume that the app might contain some exploitable vulnerabilities that the adversary is aware of.

3 Randomizing Stack Layout and Application Scenarios

Recall that our objective is to introduce randomness to the stack layout when an Android app executes, and to do so with *minimal* binary rewriting without operating system support. In this section, we present the high-level idea of our design and a few scenarios in which our proposed solution might be applied.

3.1 Randomization Design

Figure 1 shows the native code of a function in an Android app and the corresponding stack layout when it executes. The function first pushes registers `r4`, `r5`, `r6`, and `lr` onto the stack, performs its execution during which `r4`, `r5`, and r6 are used as temporary storage, and finally pops data out of the stack into r4, r5, r6, and pc. Randomizing this stack layout is to make the location of data on the stack frame unpredictable from the attacker. Considering possible ways of doing so with binary rewriting only (recall that we do not want to modify the operating system), one could introduce random padding to the base (as done in one of the previous state-of-the-art randomization techniques [10]), or to introduce the random padding among data objects in the stack frame [15,16].

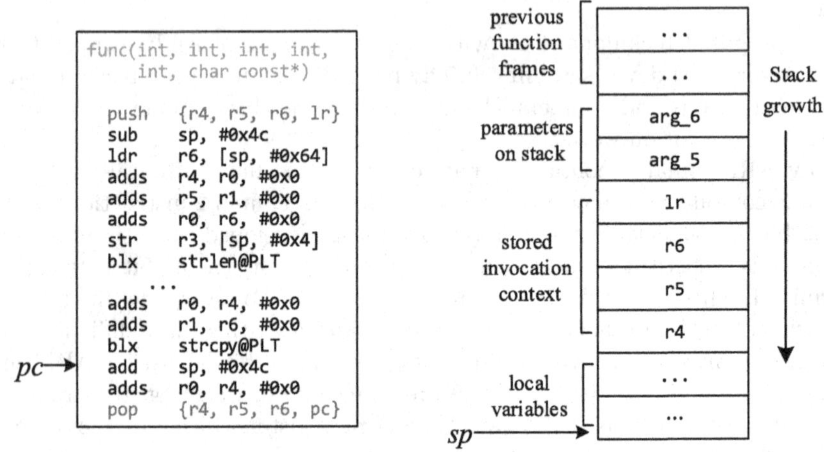

Fig. 1. An example of native code execution

However, we will not be able to introduce padding among the various data objects due to our requirement of doing *minimal* binary rewriting without addition or deletion of instructions. What we could do, though, is to modify the push instruction to have a random set of additional registers pushed, as shown in Fig. 2, effectively randomizing the base of the stack frame. In this example, we additionally push r2 and r7. In general, for 16-bit Thumb instructions, the set of general registers that can be pushed and popped includes 8 registers r0 to r7. For ARM and 32-bit Thumb instructions, the set contains 13 registers r0 to r12. Besides them, lr and pc can also appear on the list.

This design of pushing and popping a random set of registers satisfies our requirement of *minimal* binary rewriting because ARM architecture uses a single push or pop instruction to push or pop any number of registers, and the instructions to push/pop different sets of registers are of the same length — a feature that is very different from the x86 platform.

To maintain semantic equivalence with the original app for proper execution, there are a few things we have to take note. First, the same set of registers are to be pushed and popped; otherwise our modification could have modified the execution context of the caller function. Second, any references to memory locations on the stack frame between the push and pop instructions are to be

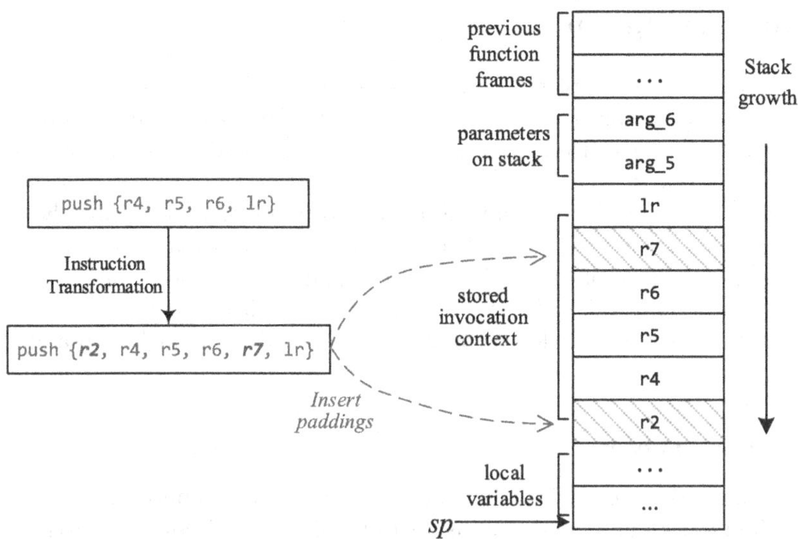

Fig. 2. Randomized set of registers pushed onto the stack

updated with the modified offsets. Lastly, note that `r0` cannot be added to the set of padding registers when it is used to store the return value, since popping `r0` would overwrite the return value stored.

3.2 Application Scenarios

Our system can be implemented as a third-party Android app to introduce randomization to the subject app (and potentially re-package it and re-sign it). This satisfies our requirement of not modifying the operating system while achieving the objective of randomizing stack layout. However, there are a few ways in which we can gain better user experience and security.

We can perform the binary rewriting right after app installation. The binary to be rewritten could be the original native code included in the installation package or the `oat` file compiled during installation (when ART runtime is used). This would not require re-packaging of the rewritten app.

We could also perform the binary rewriting every time the app starts its execution. This has the advantage that a new and different randomization is used every time the app is loaded, making it even harder for an attacker to predict the stack layout.

In either case, minimal changes are needed to the Android application installer or loader, and the binary rewriting becomes completely transparent to the end user. Also note that our proposed randomization can be used in conjunction with other existing security mechanisms, e.g., ASLR on Android.

4 Implementation

As a proof-of-concept implementation, our automatic binary rewriting has been implemented in Python with about 2000 LOC. It takes as input any Android app and outputs the randomized app ready for installation and execution on Android 4.0 or later. We first extract the binary files from the Android app, disassemble them, and discover functions and the `push` and `pop` instruction pairs. For each pair identified, we flip a coin and apply our randomization design to change the set of registers accordingly. After that, we update the offset of operands in affected instructions to be consistent with the randomization applied. In the rest of this section, we present details of our implementation in each step and show the complexity involved.

4.1 Static Analysis

In this step, we discover all functions that are candidates of applying our randomization, find out all `push` and `pop` instruction pairs, and discover all instructions for which the offsets need to be updated. We use Hopper[1], a powerful disassembler, to disassemble the binary file.

However, the mixture of ARM instructions (32-bit) and Thumb instructions (16-bit and 32-bit) and the existence of embedded constants between instructions sometimes make Hopper incorrect in disassembling all instructions. We use analysis results from Hopper as a reference and conduct more in-depth analysis to ensure the completeness and correctness of static analysis.

Function Discovery. Our analysis performs recursive disassembling of instructions and functions by starting with functions listed in the exported function table and tracing control flow targets of `blx` and `bl`. Hopper fails to recognize `blx` and `bl` proceeded functions when the target of `blx` or `bl` is a function that never returns back to its caller, e.g., when the target is an exception handler. Listing 1 in Appendix A shows an example of this case.

We solve this problem by recognizing the multiple prologue instructions in a function recognized by Hopper which signals the identification of a new function.

Push/Pop Instructions. For each function discovered, we need to find *all* epilogue instructions to apply the randomization to ensure correct execution and semantic equivalence. Here are some cases that require special attention.

CASE 1: Multiple Epilogue Instructions. It is not uncommon for a function to have multiple returns and the corresponding (multiple) epilogue instructions (Listing 2 in Appendix B shows an example). It is important that we identify and change *all* these epilogue instructions to maintain balance of the stack. We make sure not to miss any epilogue instructions by constructing the intra-procedure control flow graph for each function and identifying all leaf nodes.

[1] Hopper Disassembler: http://www.hopperapp.com.

*CASE 2: **Push**-Proceeded Prologue.* There could be additional `push` instructions before a function prologue (Listing 3 in Appendix B shows an example). For simplicity, we randomize only the `push` and `pop` instructions pairs involving register `lr`.

*CASE 3: Unmatched **Push** and **Pop**.* There are scenarios in which the set of registers pushed and popped in a function prologue and epilogue does not match (Listings 4 and 5 in Appendix B are two examples). To maximize the opportunities of randomization, we go ahead and apply our binary rewriting in both cases. We exercise extra care in these cases, though, to make sure that the *sequence* (not just the set) of registers pushed and popped maintain the same one-to-one mapping before and after randomization (see the examples in Appendix B).

4.2 Randomization and Updating Offsets

We flip a coin here to determine the set of registers to be pushed in addition to those included in the original prologue and epilogue. The candidate set of registers from which we can choose includes `r1` to `r11` for ARM instructions and `r1` to `r7` for Thumb (16-bit and 32-bit) instructions excluding those in the original prologue and epilogue. Exception goes to some ARM instructions that use a special constant encoding as explained below.

As discussed in Sect. 3.1, we have to modify instructions in the randomized function to make sure that they can access the correct data on the stack which is now shifted by a random offset. This typically applies to data addressed with the stack pointer `sp` (or directly via `r11`). Figure 8 in Appendix B shows data in four different regions that require different treatment in our updating.

With the exception of local variables, instructions involving access to data including stored invocation context, function parameters, and data from the previous stack frames need to be updated by adding to the original offset the randomized amount of padding introduced. A complexity arises when trying to update the offset to a number that cannot be properly represented in the ARM instruction. This is due to the design of using only 12 bits of instruction space to represent a useful set of 32-bit constants. If the new offset cannot be properly represented in the 12-bit "rotation" format, we simply exclude the corresponding set of registers from the randomization candidate. Note that the required offset could potentially be represented with (multiple) alternative instructions; we do not explore this option due to the *minimal* binary rewriting requirement.

5 Evaluation and Discussions

Our evaluation focuses on the security effectiveness in defending against stack-based memory attacks. In this section, we present our analysis on the function coverage, amount of randomness introduced, and demonstrate our capability in mitigating real-world attacks. To put our analysis into the context of real-world applications, we pick the top 20 free Android apps on Google Play as in Jan 2015 and apply our randomization on the native code included in these application packages. One of these twenty apps, QRCode Reader, does not include any native code in its application package, and we therefore did not include it in our analysis; however, as discussed in Sect. 3, our randomization could also be applied to the native code compiled at load time or installation time with some engineering effort. Our experiments include some widely used native libraries, e.g., `libffmpeg.so` and `libcocos2dcpp.so`. We directly execute every randomized app on a Google Nexus 5 phone with Android 4.4.4 to make sure that our modification maintains the semantics and correctness of execution.

In terms of performance (not the focus of our evaluation in this section), since there is no extra instruction inserted while performing the instruction randomization and *minimal* binary rewriting, there is no observable performance overhead at runtime.

5.1 Function Coverage and Amount of Randomness

Our first evaluation focuses on the number of functions that can be randomized and the amount of randomness obtained with our proposed scheme. Functions that cannot be randomized are those with their prologue and epilogue originally covering all candidate registers, i.e., when `r0-r7` were all pushed/popped in a 16-bit Thumb function or when `r0-r11` were all pushed/popped in an ARM or 32-bit Thumb function.

Figure 3 shows the percentage of functions that have various numbers of registers for randomization (0 means that the function cannot be randomized). Our evaluation shows that the percentage of functions that cannot be randomized is 0.8 % and 2.4 % for 16-bit and 32-bit functions, respectively, which are both small. We also notice that many functions have large (≥ 6 for 16-bit functions and ≥ 10 for 32-bit functions) randomization opportunities, average of which account for 32.75 % and 30.28 % of all 16-bit and 32-bit functions, respectively.

Here we compare our function coverage with another state-of-the-art stack layout randomization technique that does not require operating system support as well. Bhatkar et al. proposed to introduce a randomized padding between the base of stack frame and the local variables by modifying instructions that create the space for local variables, typically `sub esp, #0x100` for example [15]. They reported a function coverage of 65 % – 80 %. We apply Bhatkar's idea on the 19 Android apps in our experiment and obtain even worse results with an average function coverage of 9.94 % function. This relatively low coverage is mainly because only functions with at least one local variable would have instructions like `sub esp, #immediate`. Android, however, has more general-purpose registers and applications typically favors using them rather than local variables. With many functions not using local variable, the applicability of Bhatkar's approach on Android applications is low.

We also count the number of available registers for randomization as it tells us the number of bits of the randomness we introduce for a function frame. Our evaluation results show that 16-bit and 32-bit functions enjoy an average

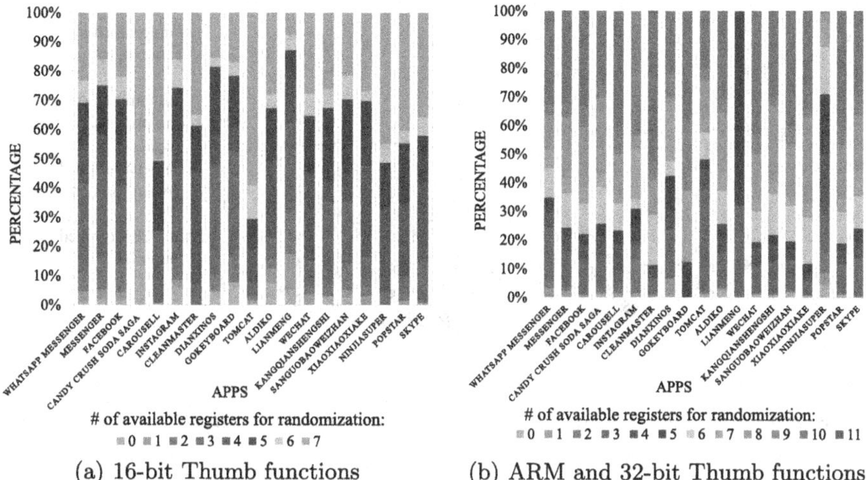

(a) 16-bit Thumb functions (b) ARM and 32-bit Thumb functions

Fig. 3. Percentage of functions with various number of registers for randomization

of 4 bits and 7 bits of randomness, respectively, out of the maximum amount of randomness of 8 (for the entire set of registers r0 to r7) and 12 (for the entire set of registers r0 to r11) for 16-bit and 32-bit functions, respectively[2]. Note that this is the amount of randomness applied to *each individual function* (independently). Functions usually use only a small subset of the registers with the rest being available for our introducing randomness.

5.2 Randomness Among Objects Inside a Function

The previous subsection evaluates the function coverage of our scheme and the amount of randomness introduced. In this subsection, we walk *inside* each function and see the amount of randomness applied to *various objects* inside a function. In particular, we count the distribution of data objects over four different stack regions in Fig. 4. We find that most of data objects that are accessed by the current function residing in regions that can be randomized. These include invocation context, parameters, and previous function frames. Only 4.83 % of data objects on average reside in non-randomized invocation context and location variable regions.

5.3 Defending Against Stack-Based Vulnerabilities

As shown earlier, our approach can randomize stack data objects with a wide randomness coverage to defend against stack-based memory vulnerabilities (e.g.,

[2] We utilized one fewer bit as we chose not to include r0 for simplicity since it usually carries the return value; however, it could be included if the function does not return anything.

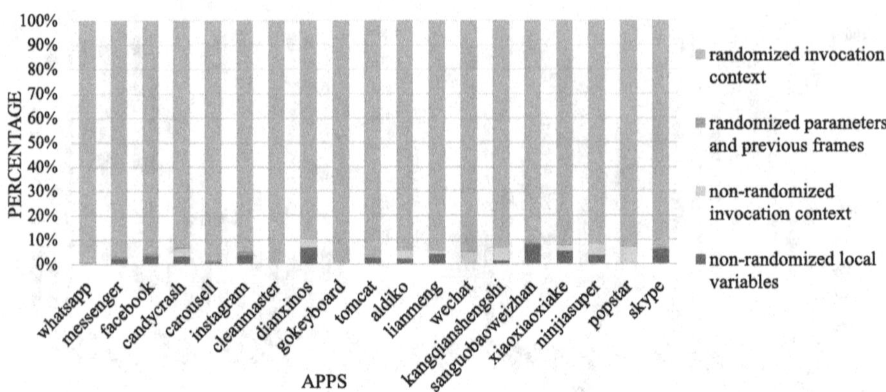

Fig. 4. How data objects are randomized and distributed in stack regions

buffer overflows). Here we further demonstrate this capability using a concrete example. Figure 5 presents a self-designed format string vulnerability that causes stack data leakage. `sprintf` in function `vulnerable(char* fmt)` enables the attacker to insert an evil format-control string (e.g., `"%s"`+4×`"%p"`) to retrieve security-critical data `key` by supplying four more `"%p"`. Our experiment demonstrates that such a working exploit fails to succeed with our randomized app. This is because our approach inserts random padding between objects on the stack and changes the relative distance as shown in Fig. 5. These random padding `r7,r2,r3` successfully relocate the previous function frames in stack and randomize locate the security-critical data `key`.

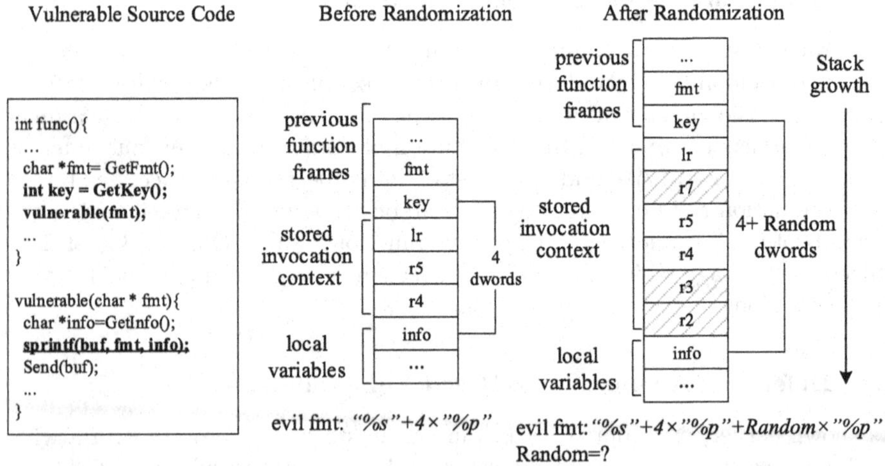

Fig. 5. Our randomization in defending against a format string vulnerability

5.4 Mitigating ROP-Based Attacks

Our approach also randomizes gadgets that are potentially employed in building the execution path of an ROP attack. ROP attacks prefer using indirect branch instructions residing in functions' epilogue as gadgets to construct and drive the malicious control flow. Our approach randomizes functions' epilogue, effectively lowering the attacker's knowledge about gadgets and making ROP attacks more difficult. We use a recent famous Android system vulnerability, CVE-2014-7911 [22,23], as an example. This vulnerability can lead to arbitrary code execution and be exploited to obtain the system privilege [24,25].

We test and analyze its publicly available exploit code [25]. In Fig. 6, we show the gadgets used by this exploit and the pivoted stack constructed by attackers (using the stack pivoting technique [26]).

By analyzing the four major gadgets shown in Fig. 6, we can find that two of them are randomized by our approach. More specifically, the `pop` instructions (marked in red color) in gadget ❷ and ❸ are added with random registers. Consequently, the attacker-intended stack layout (for entering gadget ❹) is changed, and the original control flow from gadget ❸ to ❹ will be disrupted. The exploit code thus fails to invoke the `system` function. It is worth noting that besides

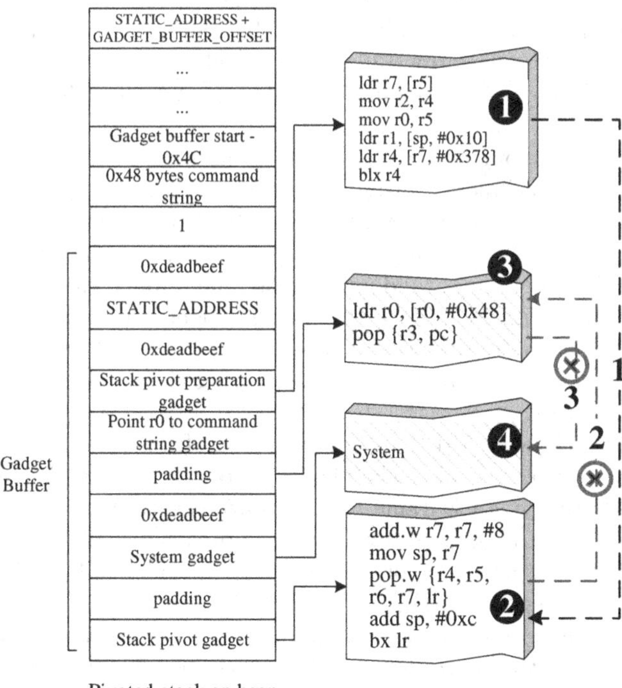

Fig. 6. The real-world exploit [25] for CVE-2014-7911, and it major gadgets (Color figure online).

pop-based instructions, some sp-based data-addressing instructions are randomized (see Sect. 4.2).

5.5 Limitations

Although our proposed technique is simple and effective in many aspects, there are potential attacks that could circumvent our randomization. In particular, an attacker might want to make use of memory leakage vulnerabilities to find out the randomized set of registers pushed onto the stack, or the effective additional offset introduced. The recently proposed Just-In-Time code reuse attack [5] might seem to be a reasonable strategy in achieving this. However, to the best of our knowledge, this type of attacks have only shown to be possible on applications that support scripting environment to which most Android applications are immune.

6 Related Work

Address space layout randomization (ASLR) is probably the most widely deployed randomization technique to make memory attacks more difficult. The traditional coarse-grained ASLR [10] randomizes the base address of data/code segments for each program, providing relatively small entropy for randomization especially on a 32-bit platform [13]. Fine-grained ASLR techniques [18,21,27] proposed recently focus on randomizing code segments to defend against code reuse technique.

In-place code randomization [21] permutes and substitutes instructions for basic blocks. Our technique, instead, substitutes instructions to randomize the memory layout rather than randomizing the code. STIR [18] randomizes addresses of basic blocks at load-time with a focus on the code segment. Our technique, on the other hand, randomizes more fine-grained elements in memory layout of programs and focuses on the data segment. In addition to that, our work is much easier to implement and has a higher chance to get user acceptance due to the *minimal* binary rewriting by leveraging the fixed instruction length on ARM architecture.

One of the advanced ASLR techniques, stack frame padding proposed by Bhatkar et al. [15], is probably the closest to our work. Bhatkar et al. introduce padding within a stack frame to randomize the base address by inserting additional code into the original binary. Our approach achieves the same objective without inserting new code or deleting existing code while achieving higher function coverage (see Sect. 5.1).

There are other randomization techniques proposed for improving security, e.g., instruction set randomization [28,29] and control flow randomization [30]. There is also a wide body of research that defend against stack disclosure and modification without randomization [10,31–33]. Being very different from these techniques, our work reallocates different types of data on the stack frame and could defend against more general memory attacks.

7 Conclusion

In this paper, we introduce a novel stack data randomization method which is achieved by a lightweight ARM-specific instruction randomization strategy. By randomly updating the number of registers in the operand of function's prologue `push` and epilogue `pop` instructions, randomized padding is inserted between function's invocation context. Evaluation on real-world applications shows that out technique covers more than 97.6 % functions in an application and introduces on average 4 and 7 bits of randomness to 16-bit and 32-bit functions, respectively. More than 95 % of objects in functions are randomized with a new address. We also show the effectiveness of our approach in defending against stack-based memory vulnerabilities and real-world ROP attacks.

Acknowledgments. We would like to thank the anonymous reviewers for providing valuable feedback on our work. This research was partially supported by the National Science Foundation of China (Grant No. 61202387, 61332019, and 61373168) and the National Key Basic Research Program of China (Grant No. 2014CB340600).

Appendix

A Missing Functions in Static Analysis

Listing 1: Failure in discovering blx and bl proceeded functions

```
sub_7c893c:
007c893c  push {r4, r5, r6, lr}
007c8940  mov  r4, r0
...
007c8990  mov  r1, r5
007c8994  pop  {r4, r5, r6, lr}
...
007c899c  bl   sub_7a35e8
--------------------------------
007c89a0  push {r4, r5, r6, r7, r8, r9,
          r10, lr}
007c89a4  sub  sp, sp,
....
007c89e8  mov  r0, r5
007c89ec  add  sp, sp, #0x208
007c89f0  pop  {r4, r5, r6, r7, r8, r9,
          r10, pc}
--------------------------------
...
...
--------------------------------
sub_7a35e8:
007a35e8 push {r3, r4, r11, lr}
007a35ec mov   r0, #0x4
007a35f0 add   r11, sp, #0xc
007a35f4 ldr   r4, = 0x1f34a4
007a35f8 bl    __cxa_allocate_exception
007a35fc ldr   r3, = 0xfffffd60
007a3600 add   r4, pc, r4
007a3604 ldr   r3, [r4, r3]
007a3608 add   r3, r3, #0x8
007a360c str   r3, [r0]
007a3610 ldr   r3, = 0xfffffd64
007a3614 ldr   r1, [r4, r3]
007a3618 ldr   r3, = 0xfffffd68
007a361c ldr   r2, [r4, r3]
007a3620 bl    __cxa_throw
```

In this example, jump target `sub_7a35e8` is an exception handler that does not return as a normal function would do, and Hopper fails in recognizing the `bl`-proceeded function at `0x7c89a0`.

B Complexities in Identifying Push/Pop Instructions

Listing 2: A function with multiple returns

```
000287bc push  {r4, lr}
000287c0 subs  r4, r0, #0x0
000287c4 mov   r3, r1
000287c8 beq   0x28814
000287cc ldr   r0, [r4, #0x14]
000287d0 cmp   r1, r0
...
000287e0 bne   0x28808
000287e4 ldr   r1, [r4, #0x10]
000287e8 mov   r0, #0x1
...
00028804 pop   {r4, pc}
------------------------------
00028808 blx   0x449b4
0002880c mov   r0, #0x0
00028810 pop   {r4, pc}
------------------------------
00028814 blx   0x44944
00028818 mov   r0, r4
0002881c pop   {r4, pc}
```

Listing 3: A function with push-proceeded prologue

```
 _Z12formatStringPKcz:
0045f628 push  {r1, r2, r3}
0045f62a push  {r4, r5, lr}
0045f62c sub.w sp, sp, #0x410
....
0045f640 ldr   r1, [r2], #0x4
0045f646 str   r2, [sp, #0x8]
0045f648 str.w r3, [sp, #0x40c]
0045f64c blx   vsprintf@PLT
0045f650 add   r2, sp, #0x4
...
0045f662 cmp   r2, r3
0045f664 beq   0x45f66a
0045f666 blx __stack_chk_fail@PLT
------------------------------
0045f66a add.w sp, sp, #0x410
0045f66e pop.w {r4, r5, lr}
0045f672 add   sp, #0xc
0045f674 bx    lr
```

In Listing 2, instructions at `0x28804`, `0x28810`, and `0x2881c` are epilogue instructions corresponding to the prologue instruction at `0x287bc`.

Listing 3 shows an example in which there is another `push` instruction before the prologue instruction that pushes register `lr`. Correspondingly, the last three instructions first pop out whatever was pushed at `0x45f62a`, adjust `sp` to offload whatever was pushed at `0x45f628`, and, in the end, use a direct branch instruction `bx lr` to return back to its caller.

Listing 4: Different registers in prologue and epilogue

```
VTestURadio10cellCreateEi:
0045fc68  push {r0, r1, r4, lr}
0045fc6a  adds  r1, #0x1
...
0045fc84  add    r0, sp, #0x4
0045fc86  blx    0x7d3ca4
0045fc8a  mov    r0, r4
0045fc8c  pop  {r2, r3, r4, pc}
```

Listing 5: Different number of registers in prologue and epilogue

```
sub_46724:
004616d4  push {r0,r1,r4,r5,lr}
004616d6  mov     r4, r0
004616d8  ldrb.w r3,[r0,#0x1a8]
004616dc  cbz     r3, 0x46171c
...
0046171c  add     sp, #0x8
0046171e  pop   {r4, r5,  pc}
```

Listing 4 shows an example where the same number of registers are pushed and popped, but they are of different registers. Listing 5 shows another example where different numbers of registers are pushed and popped.

Figure 7 presents examples of correct and incorrect randomization results for the original function which is similar with the function shown in Listing 5.

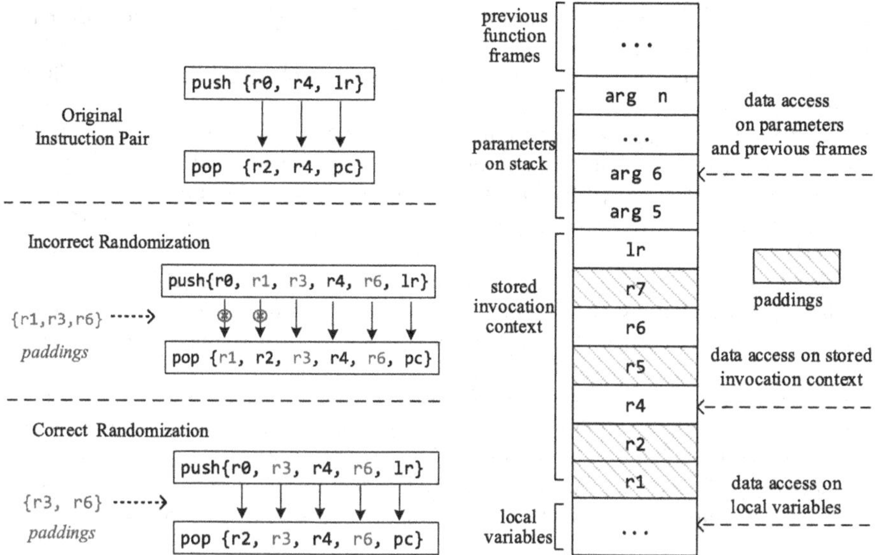

Fig. 7. Correct and incorrect randomization examples for unmatched push and pop

Fig. 8. Data on stack with new offsets

References

1. One, A.: Smashing the stack for fun and profit. Phrack Magazine (1996)
2. Shacham, H.: The geometry of innocent flesh on the bone: return-into-libc without function calls (on the x86). In: Proceedings of the ACM CCS (2007)
3. Checkoway, S., Davi, L., Dmitrienko, A., Sadeghi, A.R., Shacham, H., Winandy, M.: Return-oriented programming without returns. In: Proceedings of the ACM CCS (2010)
4. Bletsch, T., Jiang, X., Freeh, V.W., Liang, Z.: Jump-oriented programming: a new class of code-reuse attack. In: Proceedings of the ACM ASIACCS (2011)
5. Snow, K.Z., Monrose, F., Davi, L., Dmitrienko, A., Liebchen, C., Sadeghi, A.R.: Just-in-time code reuse: on the effectiveness of fine-grained address space layout randomization. In: Proceedings of the IEEE Symposium on Security and Privacy (2013)
6. Davi, L., Sadeghi, A.R., Lehmann, D., Monrose, F.: Stitching the gadgets: on the ineffectiveness of coarse-grained control-flow integrity protection. In: Proceedings of the USENIX Security (2014)
7. Carlini, N., Wagner, D.: Rop is still dangerous: breaking modern defenses. In: Proceedings of the USENIX Security (2014)
8. Buchanan, E., Roemer, R., Shacham, H., Savage, S.: When good instructions go bad: generalizing return-oriented programming to RISC. In: Proceedings of the ACM CCS (2008)
9. Francillon, A., Castelluccia, C.: Code injection attacks on harvard-architecture devices. In: Proceedings of the ACM CCS (2008)

10. Team, P.: Pax address space layout randomization(ASLR) (2003). https://pax.grsecurity.net/docs/aslr.txt
11. Apple: iOS securityguide (2014).https://www.apple.com/business/docs/iOS_Security_Guide.pdf
12. Google: security enhancements in android 1.5through 4.1. https://source.android.com/devices/tech/security/enhancements/enhancements41.html
13. Shacham, H., Page, M., Pfaff, B., Goh, E.J., Modadugu, N., Boneh, D.: On the effectiveness of address-space randomization. In: Proceedings of the ACM CCS (2004)
14. Durden, T.: Bypassing pax ALSR protection. Phrack Magazine (2002)
15. Bhatkar, S., DuVarney, D.C., Sekar, R.: Address obfuscation: an efficient approach to combat a broad range of memory error exploits. In: Proceedings of the USENIX Security (2003)
16. Chen, X., Slowinska, A., Andriesse, D., Bos, H., Giuffrida, C.: StackArmor: comprehensive protection from stack-based memory error vulnerabilities for binaries. In: Proceedings of the ISOC NDSS (2015)
17. Bhatkar, S., Sekar, R., DuVarney, D.C.: Efficient techniques for comprehensive protection from memory error exploits. In: Proceedings of the USENIX Security (2005)
18. Wartell, R., Mohan, V., Hamlen, K.W., Lin, Z.: Binary stirring: self-randomizing instruction addresses of legacy x86 binary code. In: Proceedings of the ACM CCS (2012)
19. Zhang, C., Wei, T., Chen, Z., Duan, L., Szekeres, L., McCamant, S., Song, D., Zou, W.: Practical control flow integrity and randomization for binary executables. In: Proceedings of the IEEE Symposium on Security and Privacy (2013)
20. O'Sullivan, P., Anand, K., Kotha, A., Smithson, M., Barua, R., Keromytis, A.D.: Retrofitting security in COTS software with binary rewriting. In: Camenisch, J., Fischer-Hübner, S., Murayama, Y., Portmann, A., Rieder, C. (eds.) SEC 2011. IFIP AICT, vol. 354, pp. 154–172. Springer, Heidelberg (2011)
21. Pappas, V., Polychronakis, M., Keromytis, A.: Smashing the gadgets: hindering return-oriented programming using in-place code randomization. In: Proceedings of the IEEE Symposium on Security and Privacy (2012)
22. Horn, J.: CVE-2014-7911 (2014). http://cve.mitre.org/cgi-bin/cvename.cgi?name=CVE-2014-7911
23. Horn, J.: CVE-2014-7911: Android < 5.0 Privilege Escalation using ObjectInputStream (2014). http://seclists.org/fulldisclosure/2014/Nov/51
24. Lavi, Y., Markus, N.: CVE-2014-7911: A deep dive analysis of android system service vulnerability and exploitation (2015). http://goo.gl/XMCM2J
25. retme7: Local root exploit for Nexus5 Android 4.4.4 (KTU84p) (2015).https://github.com/retme7/CVE-2014-7911_poc
26. Li, X.: Emerging stack pivoting exploits bypass common security (2013). https://goo.gl/4FbVlF
27. Hiser, J., Nguyen-Tuong, A., Co, M., Hall, M., Davidson, J.W.: Ilr: where'd my gadgets go?. In: Proceedings of the IEEE Symposium on Security and Privacy (2012)
28. Kc, G.S., Keromytis, A.D., Prevelakis, V.: Countering code-injection attacks with instruction-set randomization. In: Proceedings of the ACM CCS (2003)
29. Barrantes, E.G., Ackley, D.H., Palmer, T.S., Stefanovic, D., Zovi, D.D.: Randomized instruction set emulation to disrupt binary code injection attacks. In: Proceedings of the ACM CCS (2003)

30. Davi, L., Liebchen, C., Sadeghi, A.R., Snow, K.Z., Monrose, F.: Isomeron: code randomization resilient to (just-in-time) return-oriented programming. In: Proceedings of the ISOC NDSS (2015)
31. Microsoft: /GS (buffer security check). https://msdn.microsoft.com/en-us/library/8dbf701c.aspx
32. Cowan, C., Beattie, S., Johansen, J., Wagle, P.: Pointguard tm: protecting pointers from buffer overflow vulnerabilities. In: Proceedings of the USENIX Security (2003)
33. Vendicator: stack shield (2000). http://www.angelfire.com/sk/stackshield/

Improving Fuzzing Using Software Complexity Metrics

Maksim O. Shudrak(✉) and Vyacheslav V. Zolotarev

IT Security Department, Siberian State Aerospace University, Krasnoyarsky Rabochy Av. 31, 660014 Krasnoyarsk, Russia
mxmssh@gmail.com, amida@land.ru

Abstract. Vulnerable software represents a tremendous threat to modern information systems. Vulnerabilities in widespread applications may be used to spread malware, steal money and conduct target attacks. To address this problem, developers and researchers use different approaches of dynamic and static software analysis; one of these approaches is called fuzzing. Fuzzing is performed by generating and sending potentially malformed data to an application under test. Since first appearance in 1988, fuzzing has evolved a lot, but issues which addressed to effectiveness evaluation have not fully investigated until now.

In our research, we propose a novel approach of fuzzing effectiveness evaluation and improving, taking into account semantics of executed code along with a quantitative assessment. For this purpose, we use specific metrics of source code complexity assessment specially adapted to perform analysis of machine code. We conducted effectiveness evaluation of these metrics on 104 wide-spread applications with known vulnerabilities. As a result of these experiments, we were able to identify the best metrics that is more suitable to find bugs. In addition we proposed a set of open-source tools for improving fuzzing effectiveness. The experimental results of effectiveness assessment have shown viability of our approach and allowed to reduce time costs for fuzzing campaign by an average of 26–28 % for 5 well-known fuzzing systems.

Keywords: Fuzzing · Metrics · Complexity · Code coverage · Machine code

1 Introduction

Nowadays each software product should meet a number of conditions and requirements to be useful and successful on the market. Despite this fact, software engineers and developers keep making mistakes (bugs) during software development. In turn, these bugs can create favorable conditions for emergence of serious vulnerabilities. This is particularly relevant for network applications because vulnerabilities in this type of software create great opportunities for an attacker, such as remote code execution or DoS attack. However, practice has shown that vulnerabilities in local applications may also present a serious threat

S. Kwon and A. Yun (Eds.): ICISC 2015, LNCS 9558, pp. 246–261, 2016.
DOI: 10.1007/978-3-319-30840-1_16

to information systems if they allow to execute arbitrary code in the context of vulnerable application. This severely endangers commercial success of the product and can considerably decrease the security rate of infrastructure as well. Critical vulnerabilities in widespread products deserve special attention because they are often a target for mass malware attacks and persistent threats. Suffice it to say that in 2014, US National Vulnerability Database registered 26 new vulnerabilities per day on average [1].

There are two fundamentally different approaches for bugs detection in binary executables: static and dynamic analysis. Static analysis is aimed at finding bugs in applications without execution, while dynamic analysis performs bugs detection at runtime.

In our research, we consider only binary code of the program. Binary code (machine code, executable code) is a code (a set of instructions) executed directly by a CPU. The reason of this is due to the presence of proprietary software that is distributed in binary form only. The second problem related to transformations performed by compilers and optimizer tools that may significantly change actual behavior of the program in the binary form. This problem is called What You See Is Not What You eXecute [2].

In the paper, we will use technique of dynamic analysis called fuzzing. Fuzzing is performed by generating and sending potentially malformed data to an application. The first appearance of fuzzing in software testing dates back to 1988 by Professor Barton Miller [7]; since then the fuzzing has evolved a lot and it is now used for vulnerabilities detection and bugs finding in a large number of different applications. There are a lot of instruments for fuzzing, such as Sulley [3], Peach [4], SAGE [5] and many others. However, issues which addressed to effectiveness evaluation have not fully investigated until now.

Today researchers often use several basic criteria for effectiveness evaluation: the number of errors found, the number of executed instructions, basic blocks or syscalls as well as cyclomatic complexity or attack surface exposure [6–9].

During the last several decades, the theory of software reliability has proposed a wide range of different metrics to assess source code complexity and the probability of errors. The general idea of this assessment is that more complex code has more bugs. In this paper, our hypothesis is that source code complexity assessment metrics could be adapted to use them for binary code analysis. Thus it would allow to perform analysis based on semantics of executed instructions as well as their interaction with input data.

We will provide an overview of technique, architecture, implementation, and effectiveness evaluation of our approach. We will carry out separate tests to compare effectiveness of 25 complexity metrics on 104 wide-spread applications with known vulnerabilities. Moreover, we will perform assessment of our approach to reduce time costs of fuzzing campaigns for 5 different well-known fuzzers.

The purpose of this research was to increase effectiveness of the fuzzing technique in general, regardless of the specific solutions. Thus, we did not develop our own fuzzer, but focused on flexibility of our tools by making them easy to use with any fuzzers. Thus we did not try to improve test cases generation or mutation to find more bugs but we try to make fuzzing campaign more efficient in terms of time costs required to detect bugs in software.

The contributions of this paper are the following:

1. We adapted a set of source code complexity metrics to perform fuzzing effectiveness evaluation by estimating complexity of executable code.
2. We conducted the comparative experimental evaluation of proposed metrics and identified the most appropriate ones to detect bugs in executable code.
3. We implemented a set of tools for executable code complexity evaluation and executable trace analysis. In addition, we also made our tools and experimental results accessible for everyone in support of open science [28].

The paper is structured as follows. In Sect. 2 we illustrate short overview of fuzzing and problems of its effectiveness evaluation. Section 3 covers details of metrics adaptation. Then, Sect. 4 provides an in-depth description of system implementation. Detailed results of metrics effectiveness evaluation and their comparison are presented in Sect. 5. Section 6 used to present experimental results of system integration with well-known fuzzers. Further, we outline related works in Sect. 7 and describe the direction of our future research in Sect. 8. Finally, we use Sect. 9 to present conclusions.

2 Problem Statement

In Sect. 1, we mentioned that fuzzing is performed by generating and sending potentially malformed data to an application. Nowadays, fuzzing is used for testing different types of input interfaces such as: network protocols [10], file formats [11], in-memory fuzzing [12], drivers and many others software and hardware products that process input data. Moreover, fuzzing is not limited to pseudorandom data generation or mutation, but includes a mature formal data description protocol and low-level analysis of binary code for generating data and monitoring results. However, the question still remains: *How can we evaluate fuzzing effectiveness?* Of course, we can assess it by the number of bugs detected in an application. But this is not a flexible approach, since it does not provide any information on how well the testing data was generated or mutated in case when the analysis showed no errors at all. On the other hand, for this purpose, we can use code coverage, assuming that the higher is code coverage, the more effective the testing. Code coverage is a measure used to describe the degree to which the code of a program is tested by a particular test suite. In most cases, researchers assess code coverage by calculating the total number of instructions, basic blocks or routines that have been executed in the application under test. However, they do not take into account the complexity of tested code. For example, different code paths may have equal values of code coverage but their complexity may be different. Let us consider the example in Fig. 1.

Listing A	Listing B
push eax	push eax
push 0Ah	push offset Format
lea eax, [ebp+Source]	call scanf
push eax	add esp, 8
call fgets	mov eax, [ebp+b]
add esp, 0Ch	imul eax, 6
lea eax, [ebp+Source]	add eax, 3
push eax	mov ecx, [ebp+b]
lea ecx, [ebp+Format]	imul ecx, 6
push ecx	add ecx, 3
call strcpy	imul eax, ecx
add esp, 8	add eax, [ebp+a]
cmp [ebp+var_34], 0	mov [ebp+a], eax
jnz short loc_4135B6	jnz short loc_4135AD

Fig. 1. Two different code blocks with equal code coverage measure

The code in Listing A handles user data and may contain buffer overflow, whereas the code in Listing B reads an integer and performs some calculations by using this value. Code coverage for these examples is the same, but the code in Listing A is more interesting for analysis.

Basili [13], Khoshgoftaar [14], Olague [15] and other researchers have shown that in general, increasing of code complexity leads to increase in the probability of an error. This contention is supported by experimental results [6–9].

In this paper, we propose to adapt source code complexity assessment metrics so as to take into account semantics of binary code. We propose the following hypothesis: *"There is a more effective complexity metric for fuzzing effectiveness assessment than the number of executed instructions, basic blocks and routines, as well as than cyclomatic complexity"*. Thus, we need to adapt complexity metrics for binary code and then perform analysis of their effectiveness in comparison with traditional metrics.

In our research, we consider the following types of errors: buffer and heap overflows, format string errors, read and write to invalid or incorrect memory address, null pointer dereferences, use after free, as well as use of uninitialized memory.

3 Metrics Adaptation

In the article, we adapted 25 metrics of source code complexity assessment. Without getting into description of each metric, let us describe symbols and references to the authors of each measure.

- Lines of code count (*LOC*), basic blocks count (*BBLs*), procedure calls count (*CALLS)*;
- Jilb metric (*Jilb*) [16], ABC metric (*ABC*), Cyclomatic complexity (*CC*) [17], Modified cyclomatic complexity (*CC_mod*)[16], density of CFG (*R*) [18], Pivovarsky metric (*Pi*) [16], Halstead metrics for code volume (*H.V*), length and calculated length (*H.N*, *H.N**), difficulty (*H.D*), effort (*H.E*), the number of delivered bugs (*H.B*) [19];

- Harrison and Magel metric (*Harr*) [20], boundary values metric (*Bound*), span metric (*Span*), Henry and Cafura metric (*H&C*) [21], Card and Glass metric (*C&G*) [22], Oviedo metric (*Oviedo*) [23], Chapin metric (*Chapin*) [24];
- Cocol metric (*Cocol*) [16].

The detailed description of each adapted metric is also given in the Appendix A. Metrics that take into account high level information such as source code comments, name of variables or some object oriented information were excluded from the scope of this analysis.

It should be noted that for most of the metrics we need to perform conversion of routines code into control flow graph (CFG). CFG has only one entry and one exit. A path in the CFG can be represented as an ordered sequence of node numbers. In terms of binary code analysis, graph nodes are represented as a basic block of instructions and edges describe control flow transfer between basic blocks. Basic block (linear block) is a set of machine instructions without conditional or unconditional jumps excluding function calls. Algorithm 1 allows to perform such conversion.

Algorithm 1. Routine to CFG translation

```
Data: Address of the first instruction, an empty set of links
Result: A set of nodes, A set of edges
while not end of routine do
    Read instruction;
    if First instruction in the node then
        Save instruction address as the first address of the node;
    Get links of the instriction;
    if Number of links > 0 then
        Save instruction address as the last address of the node;
        Save edges in a set of edges;
    Move the pointer to the next instruction;
```

The algorithm passes through all basic blocks in the routine. A link is conditional or unconditional jump to some address within routine code. Note that the link is not considered for call instructions. Each instruction at some address may have from 0 up to n outgoing links. Unconditional jump always has two links, the first one refers to the address of unconditional jump, and the second one is the link to the address following immediately after jump instruction. Thus each node is associated with the following information: address of the head, address of the end, edge address 1 (optional) and edge address 2 (optional).

Note that bugs may arise from the use of unsafe library functions, such as *strcpy*, *strcat*, *lstrcat*, *memcpy* and etc. These functions are banned or not recommended to use, since they may cause overflows in the memory. Efficient fuzzing campaign should take into account this fact and firstly cover the routines that call these functions. In the article, we propose to use the following experimental measure based on Halstead B metric (rationale for the choice of this metric is proposed in Sect. 5):

$$Exp = H.B \times \sum_{i=1}^{n}(v_i + 1) \quad (1)$$

n - a total number of banned or not recommended functions used in the routine. v_i is calculated as the total number of calls of banned or not recommended functions in the routine, multiplied by the coefficient of the potential danger associated with this syscall. This coefficient calculated by using the banned functions list proposed by Microsoft within their secure development lifecycle concept [25]. In our research, a function can take only two values: 0.5 for dangerous and 1 for banned syscalls. It should be noted that multiplication is used to prioritize routines that calls unsafe functions.

4 System Overview

4.1 Fuzzing Strategy

Let's describe all basic blocks in a program as an ordered set of nodes: $CFG = \{node_0, node_1,...,node_n\}$, where *node* is a basic block and n - total number of basic blocks. Let's define an array of test data as $TD = [td_0, td_1,...,td_\nu]$, ν- an array size and *td* - one instance of test data (file, network packet, etc.) to make one fuzzing iteration. Then code coverage for one test iteration may be written as:

$$Cover = [cov_0, ..., cov_\nu] \quad (2)$$

Then, let's assign weight for each test case and sort them in descending order of weight. Weights for test cases is assigned using complexity of trace which is calculated using metrics described above. Further we will send test cases according with their position in the sorted array.

In the case of adding new test data in TD without associated coverages, new instances take the highest priority with respect to existing elements, and passed to the program in random order before existing test cases.

4.2 Trace Analysis

As it was noted in the second section, we need to save addresses of instructions, basic blocks or routines to assess complexity of code that has been executed during analysis. In this research, we used technique called dynamic binary instrumentation to perform code coverage analysis. Dynamic Binary Instrumentation (DBI) is a technique of analyzing the behavior of a binary application at runtime through the injection of instrumentation code. The main advantage of DBI is the ability to perform binary code instrumentation without switching the processor context, which significantly improves performance. In our research we use DBI framework called Pin [26]. Pin provides API to create the dynamic binary analysis tools called PinTools. Pin performs dynamic translation of each instruction and adds instrumentation code, if it required. Note that dynamic translator performs code translation without intermediate stages in the same architectures (IA32 to IA32, ARM to ARM and etc.).

4.3 Metrics Evaluation Module

Let us describe basic scheme of the tool for binary code complexity assessment in Fig. 2.

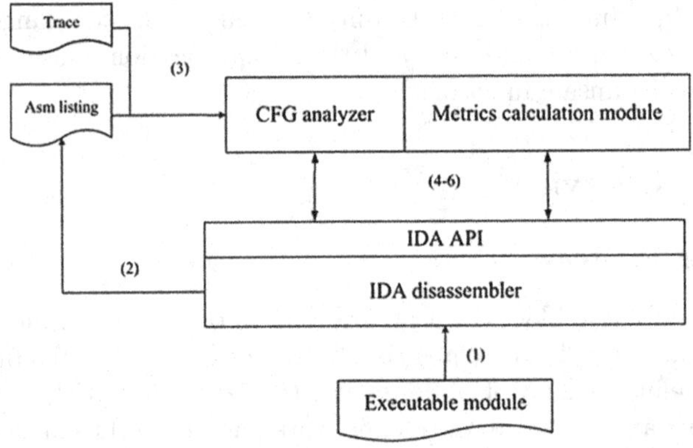

Fig. 2. Scheme of the tool for binary code complexity assessment

At the first stage, we use IDA disassembler to perform preliminary analysis and disassembling of executable module. Then assembler listing and trace is passed to the module of CFG analysis that sequentially iterates through each executed basic block in the program. The routine parser performs analysis of interconnections between basic blocks on the basis of which the tool builds graph of a routine. This graph is used in the module of metrics calculation that performs analysis and evaluation of each complexity measure for each required metric. Where necessary, this module also uses the binary code translation to get information required for some metrics. For example, the total number of assignments could be in turn obtained by using high level listing obtained by the translator, where operations like $eax = eax + 1$ may be considered as an assignment.

5 Metrics Effectiveness Evaluation

In Sect. 2, it was mentioned that we need to perform effectiveness comparison between adapted and traditional metrics. To meet this challenge, we decided to

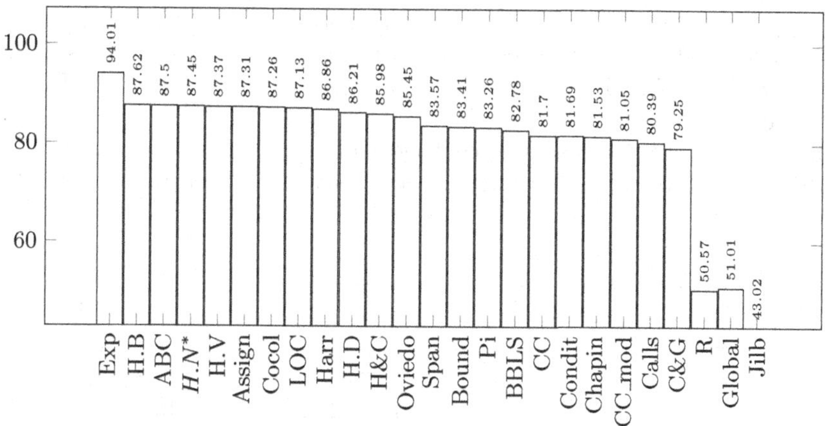

Fig. 3. Average effectiveness of each metric. Experimental metric demonstrates maximum effectiveness. Y - percent interval.

use open database with vulnerable applications called exploit-db supported by Offensive Security [27]. In our experiment, we randomly selected 104 different vulnerable applications. This is minimum sample size which is required to evaluate the effectiveness of all the metrics in the 95 % confidence interval within an error no more than 3 %. As a result we randomly selected the following types of applications: video and audio players; FTP, HTTP, SMTP, IMAP and media servers; network tools; scientific applications; computer games; auxiliary tools (downloaders, torrent-clients, development tools and etc.); libraries (converters, data parsers and etc.); readers (PDF, DJVU, JPEG and etc.); archivers and etc. For details please visit [28].

Then exploit has been found for each program which allowed to locate vulnerable routine in the application. Each application was in turn analyzed by the tool of code complexity assessment. Complexity of each metric has been obtained for each routine in each vulnerable application. Then obtained measures were ranked in descending order. Lastly, we selected ranks of all vulnerable routines in each application (The results for each application may be found at [28]). Obviously that obtained results do not allow to assess and compare effectiveness of metrics, since they do not take into account total number of routines in the application.*An effective metric is a metric that takes a maximum complexity value for vulnerable routines.* Thus the following formula was used to solve this problem:

$$PR = (1 - \frac{frang}{TF}), \tag{3}$$

$frang$ - a routine rank and TF - a total number of routines. This expression enables to answer the following question: *How many routines in a program have metric values less than for a vulnerable routine?* This value in percent may be obtained for each metric in each application. Now, it's possible to calculate average measures for each metric (Fig. 3).

According to Fig. 3, *Jilb*, *Global* and *R* metrics showed the lowest average values. Let's exclude these metrics from further analysis. Also, it makes sense to exclude $H.D$, $H.V$ and $H.N^*$ metrics, since they're used to calculate $H.B$ and showed comparable results.

Let us compare metrics using coefficient of variation (Fig. 4). Coefficient of variation is used to show the extent of variability in relation to the mean of the value.

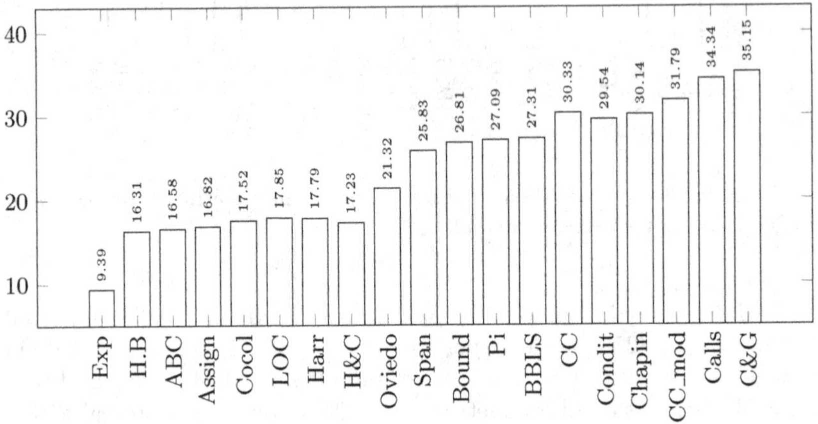

Fig. 4. Coefficients of variation for metrics (less is better). Y axis - coefficient of variation. Cyclomatic complexities, Chapin and Card & Glass demonstrate high level of variation.

The obtained statistical results have shown that experimental metric exceeds metrics based on cyclomatic complexity (by 12,31 %) the number of basic blocks (by 11,23 %), calls (by 13,62 %), LOC (6.88 %) and at the same time has the lowest coefficient of variation 9.4 %. Note that the statistical error for the experimental metric is 2,54 % at 95 % confidence interval. Thus, all of these data prove that hypothesis proposed in the Sect. 2 is correct.

In Sect. 3 it was noted that the basis of experimental metric is Halstead B measure. We use this measure because Halstead B demonstrated the best effectiveness compared to other known metrics.

6 Experiments

6.1 Code Coverage Analysis

According to Sect. 5, the system is based on 2 modules: module of metrics calculation and module of trace analysis. Let's describe the general scheme of the system integration with fuzzer in Fig. 5.

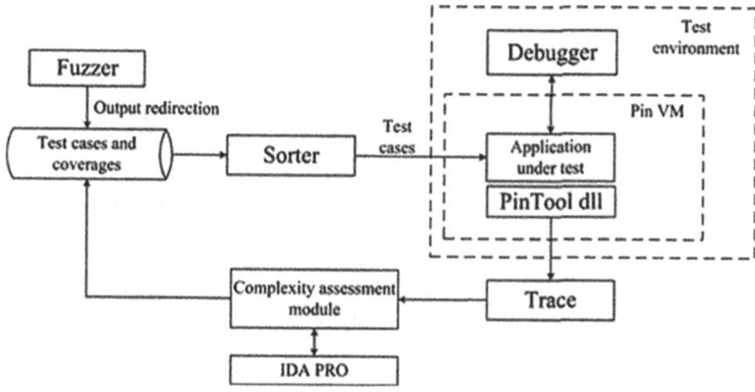

Fig. 5. General scheme of the system

The output of the fuzzer is redirected first in the database to perform test cases prioritization according to fuzzing strategy. Then the system starts fuzzing and executable code instrumentation. For each test case the system evaluates new code coverage using obtained trace. Calculated coverages are written in the database (to use them further) and results are visualized on the screen. It should be noted that the process of complexity evaluation is performed in parallel with fuzzing to increase performance of the system. The tools were developed taking into account support of several platforms, thus making them easy to port across different operating systems with minimal changes.

6.2 Experiments

For experimental analysis of proposed approach, it was decided to estimate time costs for fuzzing campaign before and after integration of our system with 5 well-known fuzzers. We randomly selected 14 popular applications with known bugs from exploit-db, so as to include each type of bug that is considered in the article (stratification technique was used). Also we added 4 randomly selected applications (2 for Linux and 2 for Windows) from exploit-db with two and more bugs in one application to analyze capability of the system reduce time costs for several bug detections. Each software product was deployed in the private virtual environments within the following configurations: Windows 7 x64 (Intel Core i7 2.4 GHz with 2 Gb RAM), Windows Server 2008 SP2 x64 (Intel Core i7 2.4 GHz with 4 Gb RAM), Ubuntu Linux 12.10 (Intel Core i7 2.4 GHz with 4 Gb RAM). Experimental results presented in Fig. 6.

Thus experimental results have shown that proposed system allowed to reduce time costs for testing by an average of 26–28 % for any considered fuzzer. Detailed results may be found at [29].

7 Related Works

There are a lot of researches which performs fuzzing using some knowledge about testing application (white box fuzzing) to improve future tests generation, such as: symbolic execution or taint analysis [32–35]. Also, in several

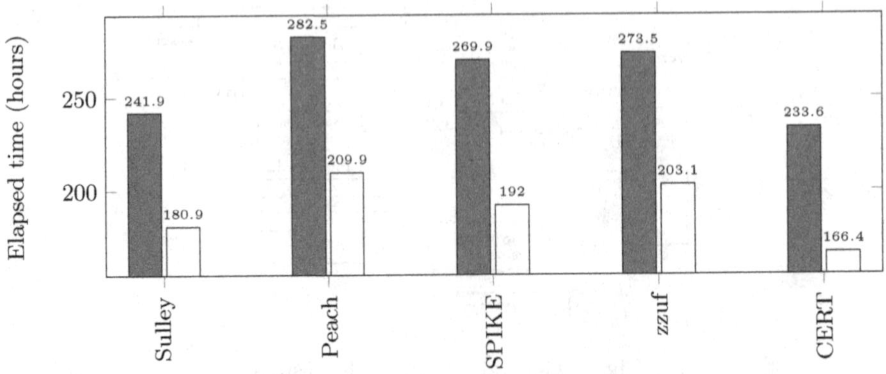

Fig. 6. The total time costs for fuzzing campaigns before and after integration of proposed system. The ordinate represents the total number of hours spent on testing all programs. White bar represents fuzzing campaign with proposed system. Zzuf [30], CERT fuzzer [31]

researches, authors try to use evolution algorithms [6,36,37] for effective data generation and increasing code coverage. Often, as an indicator of effectiveness is used the following metrics: the number of detected bugs, executed instructions, basic blocks and dangerous syscalls [6–9,37–42]. Moreover, authors may apply special coverage criteria such as statements, decisions, and condition coverage [12,38,39]. In other case, researchers use input-based coverage criteria based on using input domain partitions and their boundary values [40].

In some way, our approach has certain features in common with this paper [37]. Authors used a set of variables based on disassembly attribute information and application for procedure, such as the number and size of function arguments and local variables, the number of assembler code lines, procedure frame stack size and also cyclomatic complexity. In [41], author uses cyclomatic complexity metric to perform in-memory fuzzing for more complex functions finding to increase a probability of bugs detection. In [12] author mentions about opportunity to apply cyclomatic complexity as a metric of effectiveness evaluation of the fuzzing technique. In [42] authors use basic blocks coverage to pick seed files to maximize the total number of bugs found during a fuzz campaign. In addition to coverage, they also consider other attributes, such as speed of execution, file size, etc. In [8] authors provide analysis of effective fuzzing strategies by using targeted taint driving fuzzing. Researchers used a different set of complexity metrics, such as cyclomatic complexity, attack surface exposure or static analysis for potentially vulnerable syscalls. The basic difference of our approach is that we use specially adapted metrics that take into account semantics of executed instructions as well as their interaction with input data.

8 Discussion and Future Work

While implementing the metrics evaluation module, we limited ourselves to only general-purpose x86 instructions. Thus, in future, the module should also support co-processor group of instructions as well as applications for x64 and ARM architectures. Also we did not consider obfuscated executables since analysis of obfuscated code is a separate direction of research.

Secondly, we plan to start using metrics to automatically improve the efficiency level of data generation. For example, it makes sense to perform in-memory fuzzing for routines that have the highest level of complexity. It is also possible to generate data using evolutionary algorithms, in which we could use our set of efficiency assessment metrics as parameters for the data fitness function to improve data generation. Certainly, this approach needs to be confirmed experimentally.

It should be noted that the limitation of our approach is the fact that to reduce time costs, we need to have coverages array for each test case even before fuzzing. However if we do not have such coverages, reducing of time costs is only achieved at the second fuzzing campaign. This is justified when the system is being integrated within existed secure development life cycle [25], when fuzzing is performed on the regular basis after new patch or functionality has been released. The system is also may be useful when existed set of test cases is applied for similar type of applications. Such fuzzing strategy makes sense, demonstrates positive results and is considered in this research [42].

9 Conclusion

In this article, we propose the novel approach to reduce time costs of fuzzing campaign. We adapted 25 source code complexity assessment metrics to perform analysis in binary code. Our experiments on the 104 vulnerable applications have shown that Halstead B metric demonstrates maximum effectiveness to find vulnerable routines in comparison with other metrics. We also proposed our own metric based on Halsted B which shows more stable results. The experimental results of effectiveness assessment have shown viability of our approach and allowed to reduce time costs for fuzzing campaign by an average of 26–28 % for 5 well-known fuzzing systems. We have implemented our approach as a set of open-source tools that allows test cases prioritization, binary code complexity evaluation as well as performs code coverage analysis and results visualization.

This article is based upon work supported by the Russian Fund of Fundamental Research, research project 14-07-31350. This work was also supported by the research grant for young Russian scientists 14.Z56.15.6012-MK.

A Appendix: Adapted Metrics List

Metric	Symbol	Formula	Description
Halstead metric	H.V	$H.V = N \times log_2 n$	Program volume $N = N_1 + N_2$ N_1 - the total number of operators. N_2 - the total number of operands. $n = n_1 + n_2$ n_1 - the total number of unique operators. n_2 - the total number of unique operands.
	$H.N^*$	$H.N^* = n_1 \times log_2 n_1 + n_2 \times log_2 n_2$	Calculated program length.
	$H.D$	$H.D = \frac{n_1}{2} \times \frac{N_2}{n_2}$	Program complexity.
	$H.B.$	$H.B = \frac{E^{\frac{2}{3}}}{3000}$	The number of delivered bugs. $E = H.D \times H.B$
Jilb's metric	Jilb	$cl = \frac{CL}{n}$	CL - the total number of condition operators (jmp, jxx, etc.). N - the total number of operators.
ABC metric	ABC	$ABC = \sqrt{A^2 + B^2 + C^2}$	A - assignments count. B - branches count. C - calls count.
Cyclomatic com-plexity	CC	$CC = e - v + 2$	e the number of edges;. v - the number of nodes (basic blocks).
Modified cycl. com-plex.	CC_mod	$CC\_mod = e - v^* + 2$	v^* - the number of nodes (switch cases are considered as one node).
Pivovarskiy metric	Pi	$Pi = CC\_mod + \sum_{i=0}^{n} p_i$	p_i - nesting level of predicate node i. n - the total number of predicate nodes.
Harrison & Magel metric	H&M	$H\&M = \sum_{i=0}^{n} c_i$	c_i - node complexity. n - the total number of predicate nodes.

Boundary values metric	Bound	$Bound = 1 - \frac{(n-1)}{S_a}$	n - the total number of nodes. $S_a = \sum_i^n v_i$ - routine complexity $v_i = e_i - e_o$, e_i - the total number of input edges. e_o - the total number of output edges.
Span metric	Span	$Span = \sum_{i=0}^{n} s_i$	s_i - the number of statements containing the identifier. n - the total number of unique operators.
Henry & Cafura metric	H&C	$H\&C = LOC \times (fan_{in} + fan_{out})^2$	fan_{in} - the total number of input data flows. fan_{out} - the total number of output data flows.
Card & Glass metric	C&G	$C\&G = S + D$	$S = fan_{out}^2$, $D = \frac{v}{(fan_{out}+1)}$ v - the total number of input and output arguments.
Oviedo metric	Oviedo	$Oviedo = \sum_{i=0}^{n} DEF(V_j)$	$DEF(V_j)$ - a number of occurrences of variable V_j from $R(i)$ set. n - a set of variables which is used in R(i). $R(i)$ - a set of local variables defined in a node i first time.
Chapin metric	Chapin	$Chapin = P + 2M + 3C$	P - the total number of output variables. M - the total number of local variables. C - the total number of variables which are used to manage CFG, such as: *cmp/test var* and then *jxx*.
Cocol metric	Cocol	$Cocol = H.B + LOC + CC$	

References

1. NIST National Vulnerability Database. http://nvd.nist.gov
2. Balakrishnan, G., Reps, T., Melski, D., Teitelbaum, T.: WYSINWYX: what you see is not what you execute. In: Meyer, B., Woodcock, J. (eds.) VSTTE 2005. LNCS, vol. 4171, pp. 202–213. Springer, Heidelberg (2008)
3. Sulley Fuzzing Framework. http://code.google.com/p/sulley/
4. Peach Fuzzing Framework. http://peachfuzzer.com/

5. Godefroid, P., Levin, M.Y., Molnar, D.: SAGE: whitebox fuzzing for security testing. Queue **10**(1), 20 (2012)
6. Miller, C.: Fuzz by number. In: CanSecWest (2008)
7. Woo, M., Cha, S.K., Gottlieb, S., Brumley, D.: Scheduling black-box mutational fuzzing. In: Proceedings of the 2013 ACM SIGSAC Conference on Computer & Communications Security, pp. 511–522. ACM (2013)
8. Duran, D., Weston, D., Miller, M.: Targeted taint driven fuzzing using software metrics. In: CanSecWest (2011)
9. Weber, I.M.: Evaluation. In: Weber, I.M. (ed.) Semantic Methods for Execution-level Business Process Modeling. LNBIP, vol. 40, pp. 203–225. Springer, Heidelberg (2009)
10. Banks, G., Cova, M., Felmetsger, V., Almeroth, K.C., Kemmerer, R.A., Vigna, G.: SNOOZE: toward a stateful NetwOrk prOtocol fuzZEr. In: Katsikas, S.K., López, J., Backes, M., Gritzalis, S., Preneel, B. (eds.) ISC 2006. LNCS, vol. 4176, pp. 343–358. Springer, Heidelberg (2006)
11. Kim, H.C., Choi, Y.H., Lee, D.H.: Efficient file fuzz testing using automated analysis of binary file format. J. Syst. Architect. **57**(3), 259–268 (2011)
12. Takanen, A., Demott, J.D., Miller, C.: Fuzzing for Software Security Testing and Quality Assurance. Artech House, Norwood (2008)
13. Basili, V.R., Perricone, B.T.: Software errors and complexity: an empirical investigation. Commun. ACM **27**(1), 42–52 (1984)
14. Khoshgoftaar, T.M., Munson, J.C.: Predicting software development errors using software complexity metrics. IEEE J. Sel. Areas Commun. **8**(2), 253–261 (1990)
15. Olague, H.M., Etzkorn, L.H., Gholston, S., Quattlebaum, S.: Empirical validation of three software metrics suites to predict fault-proneness of object-oriented classes developed using highly iterative or agile software development processes. IEEE Trans. Softw. Eng. **33**(6), 402–419 (2007)
16. Abran, A.: Software Metrics and Software Metrology. Wiley-IEEE Computer Society, Hoboken (2010)
17. McCabe, T.J.: A complexity measure. IEEE Trans. Softw. Eng. **4**, 308–320 (1976)
18. Fenton, N.E., Ptleeger, S.L., Metrics, S.: A Rigorous and Practical Approach, 2nd edn, p. 647. International Thomson Computer Press, London (1997)
19. Halstead, M.H.: Elements of Software Science, p. 127. Elsevier North-Holland Inc., Amsterdam (1977)
20. Harrison, W.A., Magel, K.I.: A complexity measure based on nesting level. ACM SIGPLAN Not. **16**(3), 63–74 (1981)
21. Henry, S., Kafura, D.: Software structure metrics based on information flow. IEEE Trans. Softw. Eng. **5**, 510–518 (1981)
22. Card, D., Glass, R.: Measuring Software Design Quality. Prentice Hall, Englewood Cliffs (1990)
23. Oviedo, E.I.: Control flow, data flow and program complexity. In: Shepperd, M. (ed.) Software Engineering Metrics I, pp. 52–65. McGraw-Hill, Inc., New York (1993)
24. Chapin, N.: An entropy metric for software maintainability. In: Vol. II: Software Track, Proceedings of the Twenty-Second Annual Hawaii International Conference on System Sciences, vol. 2, pp. 522–523. IEEE (1989)
25. Lifecycle, S.D.: List of banned syscalls. https://msdn.microsoft.com/en-us/library/bb288454.aspx
26. Intel Pin: A Dynamic Binary Instrumentation Tool. http://software.intel.com/en-us/articles/pin-a-dynamic-binary-instrumentation-tool

27. Vulnerable applications, exploits database. http://www.exploit-db.com/
28. The set of tools, experimental results, the list of selected applications. https://github.com/MShudrak/ida-metrics
29. Detailed results of experiments for each application. https://goo.gl/3dRMEx
30. Zzuf fuzzer. http://caca.zoy.org/wiki/zzuf
31. CERT fuzzer. https://www.cert.org/vulnerability-analysis/tools/bff.cfm?
32. Newsome, J., Song, D.: Dynamic taint analysis for automatic detection, analysis, and signature generation of exploits on commodity software (2005)
33. Godefroid, P., Kiezun, A., Levin, M.Y.: Grammar-based whitebox fuzzing. ACM SIGPLAN Not. **43**(6), 206–215 (2008). ACM
34. Schwartz, E.J., Avgerinos, T., Brumley, D.: All you ever wanted to know about dynamic taint analysis and forward symbolic execution (but might have been afraid to ask). In: 2010 IEEE Symposium on Security and Privacy (SP), pp. 317–331. IEEE (2010)
35. Ganesh, V., Leek, T., Rinard, M.: Taint-based directed whitebox fuzzing. In: IEEE 31st International Conference on Software Engineering, ICSE 2009, pp. 474–484. IEEE (2009)
36. Sparks, S., Embleton, S., Cunningham, R., Zou, C.: Automated vul-nerability analysis: leveraging control flow for evolutionary input crafting. In: Twenty-Third Annual Computer Security Applications Conference, ACSAC 2007, pp. 477–486. IEEE (2007)
37. Seagle Jr., R.L.: A framework for file format fuzzing with genetic algorithms. Ph.D. thesis, University of Tennessee, Knoxville (2012)
38. Myers, G.J., Sandler, C., Badgett, T.: The Art of Software Testing. Wiley, Hoboken (2011)
39. Clarke, L.A., Podgurski, A., Richardson, D.J., Zeil, S.J.: A formal evaluation of data flow path selection criteria. IEEE Trans. Softw. Eng. **15**(11), 1318–1332 (1989)
40. Tsankov, P., Dashti, M.T., Basin, D.: Semi-valid input coverage for fuzz testing. In: Proceedings of the 2013 International Symposium on Software Testing and Analysis, pp. 56–66. ACM (2013)
41. Iozzo, V.: 0-knowledge fuzzing. http://resources.sei.cmu.edu/assetfiles/WhitePaper/2010_019_001_53555.pdf
42. Rebert, A., Cha, S.K., Avgerinos, T., Foote, J., Warren, D., Grieco, G., Brumley, D.: Optimizing seed selection for fuzzing. In: Proceedings of the USENIX Security Symposium, pp. 861–875 (2014)

Uncloaking Rootkits on Mobile Devices with a Hypervisor-Based Detector

Julian Vetter(✉), Matthias Junker-Petschick, Jan Nordholz, Michael Peter, and Janis Danisevskis

Technische Universität Berlin, Berlin, Germany
{julian,matthias,jnordholz,peter,janis}@sec.t-labs.tu-berlin.de

Abstract. Cell phones have evolved into general purpose computing devices, which are tightly integrated into many IT infrastructures. As such, they provide a potential malware entry point that cannot be easily dismissed if attacks by determined adversaries are considered. Most likely, such targeted attacks will employ rootkit technologies so as to hide their presence for as long as possible.

We have designed a rootkit detector that will allow to inspect the complete state of a smart phone, turning up a rootkit if present. Our solution draws on the strong isolation provided by virtualization to protect our detector from attempts to disable it. In comparison to mainstream hypervisors such as Xen and KVM, our hypervisor consist of only 7.000 SLOC, allowing for systems with a small trusted computing base. We implemented a full prototype using a low-cost embedded board and a full Android stack and validated its effectiveness against an exemplary rootkit that employs advanced countermeasures. Also, various benchmark measurements of the prototype proved that the performance degradation incurred by our design, while noticable, is not prohibitive.

Keywords: Hypervisor · Virtualization · ARM · Advanced persistent threats (APT) · Kernel rootkit

1 Introduction

Over the last several years, the market for mobile devices, most of which are ARM-based, has seen strong growth. The decreasing manufacturing costs and the advances in computing and communication hardware has allowed smart phones to evolve into general purpose computing devices. To support the increasing complexity of software and hardware on smart phones, the operating system (OS) has evolved in a similar fashion. Modern smart phones typically run general purpose OS with tens of millions of lines of source code. This complexity has rendered them vulnerable to malware, not unlike their desktop cousins before. F-Secure's mobile threat report [10] showed that 275 new threat families, including new variants of known ones, were found for the Android OS during the first quarter of 2014 alone.

S. Kwon and A. Yun (Eds.): ICISC 2015, LNCS 9558, pp. 262–277, 2016.
DOI: 10.1007/978-3-319-30840-1_17

Although most attention related to mobile security centers on rather unsophisticated app-based threats, the potential risk of smart phones being used in a targeted attack should not be dismissed. A targeted attack is a threat whereby a determined attacker seeks to compromise the IT infrastructure of its victim with the goal of ensuring long-term access, rather than immediate gains. Usual targets encompass government agencies and high-tech industries such as finance, pharmaceutical, or defence. The attacker, for its part, is well resourced and possesses enough stamina for long campaigns, involving a series of failed attempts before a successful exploit is used to establish a beachhead in the targeted system and widen it over time. As the goals of advanced persistent threats (APT) emphasize long-term goals, it is critical for them to evade detection. That is where rootkits come into play, programs that use stealth to maintain a persistent and undetectable presence. Rootkits are a special form of malware that strive to maintain control over a victim system while hiding its presence from the owner of the device. Commonly rootkits are used to hide malicious user space processes, install keyloggers, and disable firewalls and virus scanners.

Under the assumption that an adversary succeeds in implanting a kernel rootkit into a system, the chances of reliably detecting and removing it in a conventional – that is, non-virtualized – system are low. The underlying fundamental reason is that within a monolithic kernel, modularization is by convention only. An attacker who has managed to gain access to the kernel, e.g. by loading a kernel module, cannot be prevented from modifying kernel code and data structures with the goal of thwarting any detection and removal attempt. Virtualization offers a solution to that dilemma, providing strongly isolated virtual machines (VMs). For all its advantages, virtualization has struggled to gain traction on mobile devices because of their resource limitations. However, previous work [3,6,22] has shown that when carefully constructed, virtualization can be a useful means to address security issues on mobile devices.

In this paper, we show that a rootkit detector can be constructed with off-the-shelf smart phone hardware using virtualization technologies. In particular, we make the following new contributions:

- We discuss the challenges of modern detection systems in the context of the latest rootkits (e.g. hardware-supported rootkits).
- We present a hypervisor-based security architecture. The underlying hypervisor provides a snapshotting capability whereby the complete system state (memory and architectural register state) of a supervised VM can be captured. Detectors running in dedicated virtual machines can then analyze these snapshots to the extent deemed necessary without the need to halt the supervised VM.
- We design and implement a hypervisor that is suitable for the proposed architecture. While virtualization is a technology widely recognized for its contributions to system security, it is important to ensure that the virtualization layer does not itself introduce new vulnerabilities into the system. With ~7000 SLOC, our hypervisor is much smaller than mainstream hypervisors such as KVM and Xen, providing a firm foundation for systems that aim at a small trusted computing base.

- We develop a rootkit detector on top of the snapshot mechanism that is capable of detecting an extensive range of sophisticated rootkits. We validate the effectiveness of our solution on an exemplary rootkits with advanced capabilities.
- We evaluate our results on a low-cost embedded development board. We run a full Android stack on top of our hypervisor to show the feasibility of our approach. A wide range of benchmarks indicate that the performance overhead incurred due to the virtualization is not prohibitively large.

The rest of the paper is structured as follows. In Sect. 2 we provide background information on malware and rootkits. In Sect. 3 we describe the our system design, which will then be used to built a rootkit detector (Sect. 4). We evaluate our system in Sect. 5. Related work is discussed in Sect. 6. Finally, in Sect. 7, we discuss future work and draw a conclusion.

2 Rootkit Background

The term rootkit as defined by Hoglund [16] is a *kit* consisting of small programs that allow an attacker to gain (and maintain) *root*, the most powerful user in a (Unix-like) system. The principle nowadays also applies to non-Unix systems, such as Windows, but the name has stuck.

2.1 Operation

Broadly speaking, the activities surrounding a rootkit infection fall into four categories: infection, hiding its presence, staying in control, and hiding other malicious activities of its conspirators.

In the infection phase, attackers first exploit vulnerabilities in applications or services on the system to gain root privileges and then abuse these privileges to install the rootkit. Rootkits typically infect the system by loading themselves as a module into the kernel. Even though module loading is disabled on many contemporary systems, the tendency towards kernels that run on more than one device may revert this trend. Alternatively, an attacker may implant a rootkit by modifying kernel data structures directly in kernel memory, e.g., through interfaces such as `/dev/mem` and `/dev/kmem` [29,31]).

Once the OS has been successfully infected, a rootkit may take steps to hide its presence. The particulars are system specific. For example, a rootkit loaded as a kernel module may remove its module instance from the list of loaded modules. This operation, which is only meant to be executed for modules being unloaded, hides it from module listings. Another approach is to inject code in other kernel modules [18]. A rootkit needs to make sure that it reliably gains control to implement its functionality. It can use two techniques for that. First, it can overwrite kernel code. This may affect specific kernel functions or generic code such as the entry vector code. Alternatively, it can change existing indirection mechanisms, the syscall table being the most prominent one. Also of note is that an indirection mechanism may also include hardware features, as shown in [7]. Finally, a rootkit provides cover for other unauthorized activities. To that end, it may conceal selected processes, network connections, and files. Also, it may provide a remote access mechanism, also known as *backdoor*.

Rootkit countermeasures may target any of the four sub-activities. However, the infection stage is related to any sufficiently severe kernel vulnerability and is thus beyond the scope of this paper; we assume that an attacker has succeeded in putting a rootkit into the kernel. The detector we describe below will find control flow manipulations. Moreover, it will detect hidden processes and network connections.

2.2 Mobile Rootkits

The landscape of rootkits for mobile devices is relatively uncharted. Still, we want to elaborate on various techniques used by actual mobile rootkits. We also discuss attack vectors that are platform-independent and threats that might arise in the future.

Table 1. List of existing rootkits and the features they use. (* Source code available)

Name	Comment	Arch.	Module loading	Module hiding	Arch. state manipulation	Use raw socket	Process hiding	Syscall table manipulation
Cloaker (POC)	- Academic rootkit	ARM			X			
knark*	- Very old (kernel v2.2)	x86	X	X		X	X	
	- Already provided many *modern* features							
Phrack rootkit I*	- Concepts described in Phrack magazine issue 58	x86						X
Phrack rootkit II*	- Concepts described in Phrack magazine issue 68	ARM			X			X
Suterusu*	- Modern rootkit (kernel v3.x)	ARM/x86/	X				X	
	- Can hide network ports	x86_64						
	- Can disable LKM							
XOR.DDoS (rootkit component)	- One of the latest *wild* rootkits	ARM/x86/	X	X		X	X	
	- Binary only	x86_64						

Table 1 gives an overview of rootkits. Rootkits such as Suterusu use well-understood techniques to hide themselves (e.g. process hiding, LKM hiding etc.). *XOR.DDoS* [28], first spotted in September 2014, consists of a malware core with an *optional* rootkit extension. It tries to determine the Linux kernel version it is currently running on. This information is transmitted to a command-and-control server, which then tries to build a module for this specific kernel. If it is successful, the compiled module is sent back and loaded into the victims kernel; otherwise *XOR.DDoS* operates just as user space malware. If *XOR.DDoS* is able to inject the module, it provides the classical rootkit features (process hiding, file/directory hiding, LKM hiding, etc.).

Several concepts that are known today have not been spotted in real-world rootkits, yet. However, once described in academia, it is not difficult for adversaries to pick up the concepts. For example, the Cloaker malware [7] uses ARM's alternative vectors page address to hide its presence from rootkit scanners. Other ideas to utilize the architecture state of the processor for a different purpose are described in [4,12]. In both cases, special purpose registers (e.g. debugging or NEON SIMD registers) are used to store key material (for encryption/decryption). However, a rootkit could make use of the concept to either hide its presence, or to store its own encryption/decryption keys, thwarting simple signature-based scanners. It could then only store an encrypted copy of its code in memory. Such a rootkit would be very hard to spot.

3 System Architecture

Before we present our rootkit detector in the next section, we will describe our system architecture. Our architecture is based on a Type-I hypervisor. In recognition of the security vulnerabilities in mainstream hypervisors [21], we decided to develop our own with an emphasis on simplicity at the expense of features not needed for our use case. Possibly the most important simplification is the adoption of a static model, that is, VMs and the resources they are granted are created at boot time and cannot be changed dynamically. Since the hypervisor does not contain device drivers, access to devices is selectively granted to virtual machines, which then are responsible for providing virtualized device interfaces to other VMs. As our platform does not provide IOMMUs, the hypervisor cannot prevent VMs with access to DMA-capable devices from using DMA to access system memory arbitrarily. In terms of code size, with ~7.000 SLOC, our system is significantly smaller than XEN's ARM port with ~30.000 SLOC [26]. In addition to simplifying code audits, the small size of our hypervisor may make possible the application of formal methods. Formal proofs of small kernels [19] stressed the importance a small code size, with 10.000 SLOC commonly assumed as the largest feasible size for the object under examination beyond which the problem becomes soon intractable.

We run two virtual machines under control of the hypervisor: the *supervised VM*, a full Android stack, and the *detector VM*, a minimal Linux with a special cross-VM inspection driver and our inspection tools. The detector VM can initiate a state snapshot of the supervised VM, which is stored in a dedicated memory

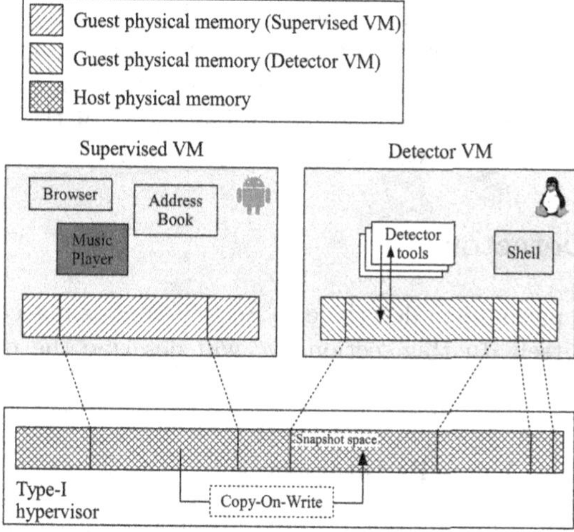

Fig. 1. System architecture.

region, the snapshot space. The snapshot buffer appears as special (guest physical) memory region in the detector VM, from where a kernel driver maps it into the rootkit detectors, which run as user-space processes. Note that the right to take a snapshot does not entail the privilege to change the state of the supervised VM. The architecture is shown in Fig. 1.

Since taking a memory snapshot involves copying several hundreds MB, we use a copy-on-write(COW) mechanism to incrementally copy the entire memory of the supervised VM, that is, taking the snapshot and the execution of the supervised VM are interleaved. That way, the operation of the supervised VM is only slightly slowed, but not suspended for an appreciable duration, which would result in undesirable starts and glitches. Our implementation leverages the fact that under ARM VE the page table that translates guest physical to host physical addresses, the Stage 2 page table[1], can specify access rights. To initiate a snapshot, the access rights in the Stage 2 page table of the supervised VM are set to *read only* while it keeps executing. Whenever a (guest) physical page for which no snapshot copy is taken yet is modified, an abort is raised in the hypervisor, which makes a copy and sets the Stage 2 permissions to *read-write*. Also, the detector VM can issue a hypercall that copies a page and sets it *read-write* in the Stage 2 page table unless that page is already copied due to a COW. These operations, which have to be repeated until a complete snapshot is taken, are executed in the context of the detector VM and accounted to its processing time by the system scheduler. Relying exclusively on a COW strategy does not produce a full memory dump though, as the active memory working set of the supervised VM is usually much smaller than its available memory. We

[1] Similar concepts are known as *nested page table* (NPT) or *extended page table* (EPT) on x86 systems.

therefore complement this with a separate copy thread in the hypervisor which completes the snapshot regardless of the memory access pattern of the target.

In addition to the memory snapshot, we also take a snapshot of the architecture state. This gives us access to control registers of the target which are crucial in reconstructing the system state, e. g. `TTBCR`, `TTBR0`, and `SCTLR`.

4 Rootkit Detector

The snapshotting mechanism described in Sect. 3 alone is not capable of detecting a rootkit by itself. In this section, we will describe the detector we have developed.

4.1 Checking the Kernel's Integrity

As described in Sect. 2.1, a rootkit will divert selected kernel operations. In this section, we examine the details of how such an attack can be mounted on the ARM architecture, using the example of the Linux kernel.

In Linux, a process denotes a request syscall by loading a value into a designated register[2] before trapping into the kernel. There the value is used as an index into a table, the syscall table, that holds function pointers to the kernel functions implementing the requested syscall. Modifying the syscall table is thus a convenient attack vector for an adversary. The address of the syscall table can be either determined based on the kernel image or retrieved at runtime by examining the entry path starting from the vectors page [13, 31]. To prevent this form of attack, we save a hash of the initial syscall table and check the memory snapshot for changes. On ARM, every privilege transition from PL0 to PL1[3] involves a control flow transfer to the so called *vectors page*. Since syscalls also use that mechanism, redirecting the control flow by changing the vectors page would allow an attacker to get into control for each syscall. Hence, to detect rootkits performing this kind of attack, we need to monitor the vectors page, too. The virtual address of the vectors page is controlled through `SCTLR` and `VBAR`. An attacker may try to relocate it to another address under its control [7]. In order to counter this form of rootkit, our snapshot comprises the general purpose registers, as well as all privileged architectural registers, which include `SCTLR` and `VBAR`.

Finally, the rootkit could opt to overwrite selected functions in the kernel so as to redirect the control flow. Such manipulations can be detected by comparing the kernel text section in the snapshot with an unmodified original. To simplify the operation, the comparison can be performed on a cryptographic hash sum computed over the text section. However, in certain configurations, the Linux kernel might patch its text section during startup as part of its normal operation. This renders precomputed hashes of the vmlinux file useless. Under the

[2] The ARM EABI uses r7.

[3] PL0 denotes *USR*, the only unpriviled processor state, whereas PL1 subsumes all privileged processor states (*SVC, SYS, IRQ, FIQ, ABT, UND*).

assumption that the bootloader checks the integrity of the kernel, we trust the kernel to send a notification to the detector after it has set up itself. The detector then computes a checksum over the text section, which is then later used for comparison.

4.2 Reconstructing Hidden Kernel Objects

Aside from detecting the rootkit itself as described in the previous section, undoing the cloaking that is performed by the rootkit might be another goal of a detector. In this section, we describe which hidden objects can be recovered by our detector.

Modules. A common way whereby rootkits infect the kernel is loading a kernel module. Naturally, they seek to hide the module's presence afterwards. To do so, attackers can overwrite entries in the *inode_operations* structure belonging to the module *sysfs_dirent* structure. Our detector works in three steps. First, it searches through the memory snapshot based on specific patterns to identify all modules in the `/sys/module` folder. It then iterate over the memory snapshot again and searches for a pattern that matches the *module* data structure. Finally, it verifies that the inode operations for the *module* are correct and have not been overwritten.

Processes. A wide range of Linux rootkits, such as [20,27,31], modify the functionality of the *proc* filesystem (procfs) to hide select processes, e.g., a hidden ssh server. To that end, they usually divert procfs operations by overwriting the file operations structure of the *procfs* root node. Our detector bypasses the procfs and searches directly in the memory snapshot for task structures. Our detection method encompasses two passes: first we look for potentially kernel stacks. Each kernel stack is contains a *thread_info* structure, in which, among other things, the address limits of the user-accessible portion of the address space are stored. Since the thread_info structure resides at a fixed offset in the aligned kernel stack, we only need to check one value for each 2 KB chunk. Second, we check if a candidate holds a pointer to a *task_structs*, which in turn contains a pointer to the *thread_info* structure.

Sockets. Given the goal of long-term intelligence gathering, an advanced rootkit is likely to communicate with an outside party over a network socket. This socket needs to be hidden as well. Using the previously reconstructed *task_struct* list, we are able to identify open file descriptors, including those denoting sockets. By looking up the kernel *socket_file_ops* and comparing it with the actual *f_ops* of the currently investigated file descriptor, we are able to distinguish between socket and file handles. If the entry refers to a socket, the *socket* structure provides us with information about the network connection. Alternatively, open sockets can also be found by reconstructing the procfs content. That way, the file operations of the procfs top level directory, which may be compromised, are bypassed.

Files. Typically, rootkits serve as a means of hiding the infiltration of a system and ensure its persistence. Often, further activities require data to be deposited in the file system in an undetectable way. Instead of changing the entries for the relevant syscalls – which is easily detected –, an attacker may choose to replace function pointers in *struct file_operations* pointed to by *struct file* [20]. For the attacker, this approach has the advantage that file objects are dynamically allocated, which makes their detection more complicated.

5 Evaluation

The evaluation section is split into three parts. First up is a test as to how reliably our detector can detect a rootkit In the second part (Sect. 5.2), we measured the time the detector needs for a reconstruction of specific elements. We performed multiple Android benchmarks as well as LMBench to measure the virtualization overhead and the overhead induced by the snapshotting mechanism (Sect. 5.3). All experiments were conducted on a Cubietruck (Allwinner A20, 2xCortex A7@1.06 GHz CPU, 2 GB RAM) running Android 4.4.2 on a Linux 3.4.0 kernel.

5.1 Detector Efficacy

To test the efficacy of our solution, we have tested it against two exemplary rootkits: Suterusu [20] and nameless proof of concept [8] that started off as a class project. The results are shown in Table 2a and b.

Our detector picks up manipulation to and relocation of the vectors page. Since neither of the two specimen under test manipulates the vectors page, we tested this ability with a small extension to Suterusu. Also, changes to the syscall table are detected. Function hooking, overwriting function code, causes changes in the checksum of the kernel text section, which our detector notices. Although the integrity of genuine kernel modules is not checked in our system, standard

Table 2. Detector efficiency.

(a) Kernel integrity.

	Suterusu	PoC Rootkit	Detector
vector page manipulation			x
vector page relocation			x
syscall table manipulation		x	x
function hooking	x		x
function pointer manipulation	x		(x)

(b) Object reconstruction.

	Suterusu	PoC Rootkit	Detector
module hiding	x	x	x
process hiding	x		x
connection hiding	x		x
file hiding	x	x	

techniques such as whitelisting of cryptographic hash of trusted modules or signature schemes could easily be used.

Function pointer manipulations are detected to the extent this attack vector is used by the exemplary rootkits. However, the currently used mechanism is not generic enough to detect arbitrary function pointer manipulations. Unlike the processes and connections, for which the underlying kernel data structures are guaranteed to be memory resident, file-associated data structures may or may not reside in memory. As such, our detector cannot guarantee to reconstruct them from a snapshot of the guest's physical memory.

5.2 Kernel Object Reconstruction

Table 3 gives a short description for each tool we used in our analyses to describe its purpose and examined property, as well as listing the required runtime to extract the respective properties. The reconstruction of some kernel structures is rather costly because we have to iterate through the memory snapshot multiple times.

Table 3. Runtime of tools to extract specific information from the memory snapshot.

Tool	Description	Time (in sec.)
gsnps_procfs	Check *procfs* `fops`	0.3790
gsnps_proc	Extract `task_struct` process list	0.1350
gsnps_sysfs	Extract *sysfs* module list	20.1980
gsnps_mod	Extract `module` structures	17.3520
gsnps_sock	Extract `socket` list	0.2130
gsnps_exec	Hash kernel `.text` section	0.5689

To check the integrity of the kernel text section, we used the mbed TLS library [2] and compute a SHA1 hash over the text section.

5.3 Application Benchmarks

To measure the snapshotting overhead, we used the established LMBench suite for Linux and two Android benchmarking suites: Antutu [1](v5.7) and Geekbench (v3.3.2). In the measurement results, *Baseline* refers to benchmarks run on the device without a hypervisor.

As for LMBench (v3), we only ran the relevant latency and bandwidth benchmarks. The results are shown in Fig. 2a and b. In most of the benchmarks, the virtualized scenarios show only slightly inferior results. While a snapshot is in progress, the bandwidth benchmark still show constantly stable and comparable results. This is due to the fact that the bulk of copy operations is performed by the second CPU core, i. e. by the copy thread instead of as a reaction to

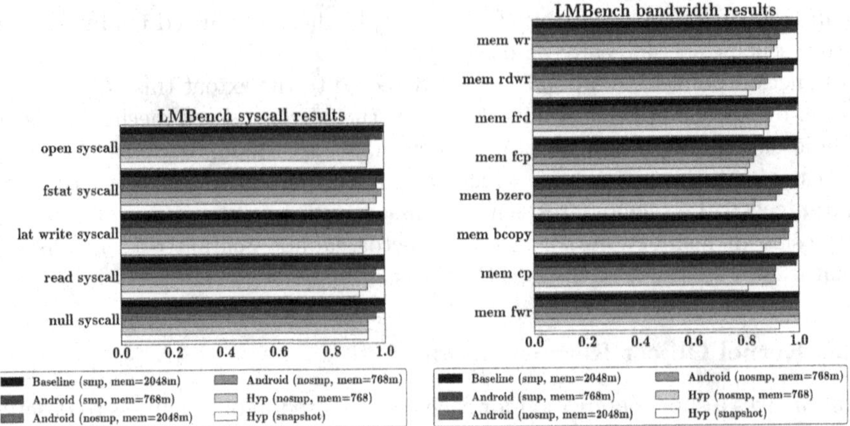

(a) LMBench syscall latency benchmark results (higher is better).

(b) LMBench bandwidth benchmark results (higher is better).

Fig. 2. LMBench benchmark results.

COW-incurred page faults of the supervised VM. A VM still has to trap into the hypervisor to flush the TLB, though, which explains the small, but noticeable increase in execution time. Figure 3a shows the results of the Antutu benchmark. In comparison to the *Baseline*, the snapshotting only has a small impact on all but I/O intensive apps. Taking a snapshot incurs a notable impact of ~20 % on the *RAM Speed* benchmark. This is not surprising as this benchmark excessively accesses memory to measure the access time. On every write access to a non-copied page, our COW mechanism has to suspend the VM and copy the corresponding page. The snapshotting has only marginal impact on other benchmarks. It's almost on par with the hypervisor measurements when no snapshot is in progress. Further worth mentioning is that the memory working set of the Android system is quite large; after performing a single Antutu benchmark run ~75 % of the memory pages were copied due to COW alone.

The results for Geekbench can be obtained from Fig. 3b. The results of the scenarios *Hyp (nosmp, mem = 768)* and *Hyp (snapshot)* again show a ~3 % performance penalty due to the virtualization. Apart from that, the numbers are in line with the expected results.

CF-Bench mainly focusses on measuring the performance of integer and floating point operations, which should not differ between virtualized and non-virtualized systems. Our measurements (Fig. 4a) is in keeping with that expectation. As expected, the two `smp` setups are roughly twice as fast as the other scenarios because they run with both CPU cores. The other scenarios are very close together. Additionally, CF-Bench contains some memory read/write benchmarks. These results are shown in Fig. 4b. In line with expectations, the benchmark reveal similar results to the Antutu Benchmark. Again, the `smp` setups achieve roughly twice the performance as the other benchmarks. The native Android setups without

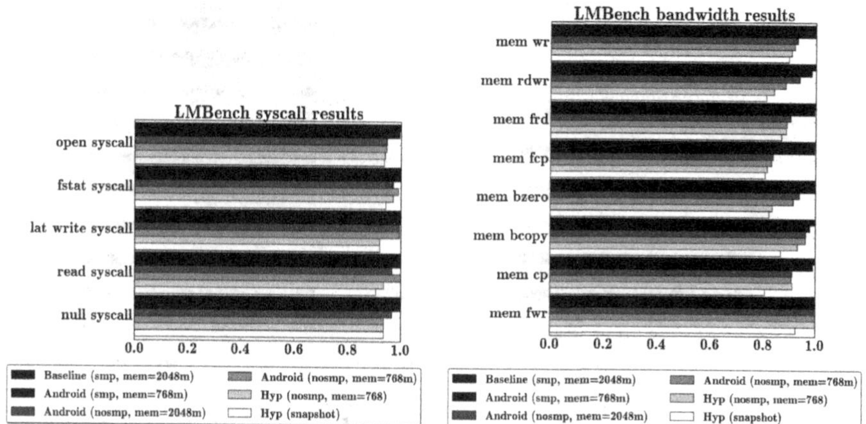

(a) LMBench syscall latency benchmark results (higher is better).

(b) LMBench bandwidth benchmark results (higher is better).

Fig. 3. Antutu and Geekbench benchmark results

multi-processing achieve a slightly higher score than the virtualized system (~3 % performance penalty). While a snapshot is in progress, the *Overall Score* drops by again ~10 % in comparison to the virtualized system. The reduced score is mainly due to the inferior scores in the *Memory Read* and *Memory Write* benchmarks, respectively. The working set of Android during the benchmark is ~52 % (400MBytes) as obtained from the number of snapshotted pages.

6 Related Work

Initial work on VMI was done by Garfinkel et al. [11] in 2003. They developed various policy modules as well as detectors for suspicious behavior in the system (e.g. a raw socket detector, a signature detector, etc.) and tested them against various known rootkits and Trojan horses.

In 2004, Petroni et al. [23] proposed Copilot, a rootkit detection mechanism based on a PCI-based coprocessor. They were able to detect rootkits in a timeframe of ~30 s. The shortcomings of the approach are that additional hardware is required and the coprocessor does not have access to the internal state of the processor being monitored, only to the main memory. Furthermore, the detection requires a relatively large timeframe of ~30 s in order to be successful.

Jiang et al. [17] introduced the term semantic view reconstruction. They reconstructed the guest VM state from the raw memory as well as a disk snapshot.

Hay and Nance [14] proposed *VIX* for the Xen hypervisor, which allows for digital forensic examination of volatile system data in virtual machines. They provide a list of tools (e.g. `vix-ps`), which can be executed in the Dom0. The tools perform the same tasks as their Unix counterparts but use the raw memory of a DomU in Xen to reconstruct the required information.

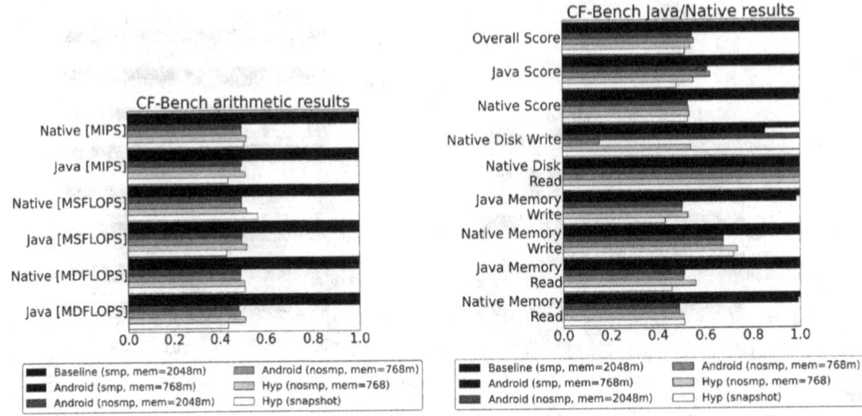

(a) CF-Bench arithmetic benchmark results (higher is better).

(b) CF-Bench Java/Native benchmark results (higher is better).

Fig. 4. CF-Bench benchmark results.

In [25] Riley et al. proposed a hypervisor-based memory shadowing scheme. The hypervisor dynamically copies authenticated kernel instructions from the standard memory to the shadow memory. At runtime, any instruction executed in the kernel space is fetched from the shadow memory instead of from the standard memory. This approach prevents unauthorized code from being executed, thus protecting against kernel rootkits.

OSck is a high-performance integrity scheme proposed by Hofman et al. [15], using a hypervisor-protected detector that runs isolated from the supervised VM. Built for x86, OSck extends KVM and thus inherits its large trusted computing base. The OSck detector could be combined with our small, trustworthy hypervisor, yielding a system with a small TCB.

Dolan et al. [9] presented an approach for automatically creating introspection tools for security applications. By analyzing dynamic traces of small programs contained in the target system that compute the desired introspection information, they can produce new programs that retrieve the same information from outside the target virtual machine.

In 2012 Yan and Yin [30] extended semantic view reconstruction to the Android OS. DroidScope uses Qemu and extends it with various tracer capabilities to find malware during runtime. Tracking rootkit footprints using a memory analysis system was done by Cui et al. [5] in 2012. The proposed architecture is called MAS and uses static analysis, memory traversal and integrity checking to find rootkit signatures in memory and crash dumps of an OS kernel.

In 2015, Richter et al. [24] proposed a scheme based on a view comparison for VMware vSphere to detect rootkits in Windows VMs. Zeng et al. [32] proposed PEMU, which combines QEMU with the tool PIN. PIN is a dynamic binary instrumentation framework for the x86 architecture that enables the creation of dynamic program analysis tools. Zeng et al. extended QEMU with the capabilities of the tool PIN to be able to also instrument OS kernels. The architecture is built in a way that existing PIN plug-ins can be reused to profile various components of the OS (e.g. Jmp/branch/call profiling, Call trace tracing, etc.).

7 Conclusion and Future Work

In this paper, we proposed a hypervisor-based security architecture as generic framework for security research dealing with advanced and aggressive threats such as advanced persistent threats. The core functionality is a snapshotting mechanism that allows to capture both the complete memory and the entire architectural register state of a VM and makes them available for further analysis. To demonstrate the efficacy of our architecture, we designed and built a complementary rootkit detector and tested it against two exemplary rootkits. Also, we measured the overhead incurred through our architecture with both application and system benchmarks.

Currently, our snapshotting mechanism captures all of the guest's physical memory, thereby effectively reducing the available memory by half. Yet, for detecting a kernel rootkit, having a snapshot of the guest's kernel memory would be sufficient.Future work will seek to reliably identify this portion and limit the snapshot to it.

Our detector has a lot of improvement potential. The biggest opportunity lies in a more robust function pointer validation scheme. It would be helpful if all kernel function pointer indirection could be identified automatically. As these pointers are immutable, they could be included in the computation of the kernel hashsum. Also, a more sophisticated detector could identify all executable code in the kernel and check for suspicious changes in that set. However, such a mechanism might involve changes to the Linux kernel.

Various publications show that adversaries can leverage complex DMA capable devices (e.g. GPU) to hide the presence of malicious code and attack the running OS from the device. Right now our architecture cannot detect such attacks. Future work would be to consider using SYSMMUs to restrict DMA accesses or device para-virtualization with DMA buffer validation to prevent such attacks.

Acknowledgments. This research was supported by the Helmholtz Research School on Security Technologies.

References

1. Antutu Hong Kong: Antutu benchmark. http://www.antutu.com/en/Ranking.shtml. Accessed 12 May 2015
2. Ltd, ARM: mbed TLS. https://tls.mbed.org/. Accessed 26 May 2015
3. Barr, K., Bungale, P., Deasy, S., Gyuris, V., Hung, P., Newell, C., Tuch, H., Zoppis, B.: The VMware mobile virtualization platform: is that a hypervisor in your pocket? ACM SIGOPS Oper. Syst. Rev. **44**(4), 124–135 (2010)

4. Colp, P., Zhang, J., Gleeson, J., Suneja, S., de Lara, E., Raj, H., Saroiu, S., Wolman, A.: Protecting data on smartphones and tablets from memory attacks. In: Proceedings of the Twentieth International Conference on Architectural Support for Programming Languages and Operating Systems, ASPLOS 2015, pp. 177–189. ACM, New York (2015). http://acm.org/10.1145/2694344.2694380
5. Cui, W., Peinado, M., Xu, Z., Chan, E.: Tracking rootkit footprints with a practical memory analysis system. In: USENIX Security Symposium, pp. 601–615 (2012)
6. Danisevskis, J., Peter, M., Nordholz, J., Petschick, M., Vetter, J.: Graphical user interface for virtualized mobile handsets (2015)
7. David, F.M., Chan, E.M., Carlyle, J.C., Campbell, R.H.: Cloaker: hardware supported rootkit concealment. In: 2008 IEEE Symposium on Security and Privacy, SP 2008, pp. 296–310. IEEE (2008)
8. Dharmdasani, H.: Android-rootkit (2015) https://github.com/hiteshd/Android-Rootkit. Accessed 13 April 2015
9. Dolan-Gavitt, B., Leek, T., Zhivich, M., Giffin, J., Lee, W.: Virtuoso: narrowing the semantic gap in virtual machine introspection. In: 2011 IEEE Symposium on Security and Privacy (SP), pp. 297–312. IEEE (2011)
10. F-Secure Labs: Mobile threat report q1 2014, April 2014. https://www.f-secure.com/documents/996508/1030743/Mobile_Threat_Report_Q1_2014.pdf. Accessed 11 April 2015
11. Garfinkel, T., Rosenblum, M., et al.: A virtual machine introspection based architecture for intrusion detection. NDSS **3**, 191–206 (2003)
12. Gotzfried, J., Muller, T.: Armored: CPU-bound encryption for android-driven arm devices. In: 2013 Eighth International Conference on Availability, Reliability and Security (ARES), pp. 161–168, September 2013
13. Guerrero, S.: Getting sys_call_table on android, March 2013. https://www.nowsecure.com/blog/2013/03/13/syscalltable-android-playing-rootkits/. Accessed 29 April 2015
14. Hay, B., Nance, K.: Forensics examination of volatile system data using virtual introspection. SIGOPS Oper. Syst. Rev. **42**(3), 74–82 (2008)
15. Hofmann, O.S., Dunn, A.M., Kim, S., Roy, I., Witchel, E.: Ensuring operating system kernel integrity with OSck. In: Proceedings of the Sixteenth International Conference on Architectural Support for Programming Languages and Operating Systems, ASPLOS XVI, pp. 279–290. ACM, New York (2011). http://acm.org/10.1145/1950365.1950398
16. Hoglund, G., Butler, J.: Rootkits: Subverting the Windows Kernel. Addison-Wesley Professional, Reading (2005)
17. Jiang, X., Wang, X., Xu, D.: Stealthy malware detection through VMM-based out-of-the-box semantic view reconstruction. In: Proceedings of the 14th ACM Conference on Computer and Communications Security, pp. 128–138. ACM (2007)
18. Kapoor, A., Mathur, R.: Predicting the future of stealth attacks (2011). http://www.mcafee.com/de/resources/reports/rp-predicting-stealth-attacks.pdf
19. Klein, G., Elphinstone, K., Heiser, G., Andronick, J., Cock, D., Derrin, P., Elkaduwe, D., Engelhardt, K., Kolanski, R., Norrish, M., et al.: sel4: formal verification of an OS kernel. In: Proceedings of the ACM SIGOPS 22nd Symposium on Operating Systems Principles, pp. 207–220. ACM (2009)
20. mncoppola: An lkm rootkit targeting linux 2.6/3.x on x86(_64), and arm, September 2014. https://github.com/mncoppola/suterusu. Accessed 13 April 2015
21. National Vulnerability Database: CVE-2015-3456, January 2015. https://web.nvd.nist.gov/view/vuln/detail?vulnId=CVE-2015-7835. Accessed 01 November 2015

22. Nordholz, J., Vetter, J., Peter, M., Junker-Petschick, M., Danisevskis, J.: Xnpro: low-impact hypervisor-based execution prevention on arm. In: Proceedings of the 5th International Workshop on Trustworthy Embedded Devices, pp. 55–64. ACM (2015)
23. Petroni Jr., N.L., Fraser, T., Molina, J., Arbaugh, W.A.: Copilot - a coprocessor-based kernel runtime integrity monitor. In: Proceedings of the 13th Conference on USENIX Security Symposium, SSYM 2004, vol. 13. p. 13. USENIX Association, Berkeley (2004). http://dl.acm.org/citation.cfm?id=1251375.1251388
24. Richer, T.J., Neale, G., Osborne, G.: On the effectiveness of virtualisation assisted view comparison for rootkit detection. In: Proceedings of the 13th Australasian Information Security Conference (AISC 2015), vol. 27, p. 30 (2015)
25. Riley, R., Jiang, X., Xu, D.: Guest-transparent prevention of kernel rootkits with VMM-based memory shadowing. In: Lippmann, R., Kirda, E., Trachtenberg, A. (eds.) RAID 2008. LNCS, vol. 5230, pp. 1–20. Springer, Heidelberg (2008)
26. Studer, N., VanVossen, R.: Xen and the art of certification. Xen Developer Summit 2014 (2014)
27. trimpsyw: adore-ng - linux rootkit adapted for 2.6 and 3.x, October 2014. https://github.com/trimpsyw/adore-ng. Accessed 13 April 2015–04-13
28. unixfreaxjp: Mmd-0028-2014 - fuzzy reversing a new china elf "linux/xor.ddos", September 2014. http://blog.malwaremustdie.org/2014/09/mmd-0028-2014-fuzzy-reversing-new-china.html. Accessed 16 April 2015
29. Vogl, S., Pfoh, J., Kittel, T., Eckert, C.: Persistent data-only malware: function hooks without code. In: Symposium on Network and Distributed System Security (NDSS) (2014)
30. Yan, L.K., Yin, H.: Droidscope: seamlessly reconstructing the OS and Dalvik semantic views for dynamic android malware analysis. In: USENIX Security Symposium, pp. 569–584 (2012)
31. You, D.-H.: Android platform based Linux kernel rootkit. Phrack 68, April 2011
32. Zeng, J., Fu, Y., Lin, Z.: Pemu: a pin highly compatible out-of-VM dynamic binary instrumentation framework. In: Proceedings of the 11th ACM SIGPLAN/SIGOPS International Conference on Virtual Execution Environments, VEE 2015, pp. 147–160. ACM, New York (2015). http://acm.org/10.1145/2731186.2731201

Detecting Obfuscated Suspicious JavaScript Based on Information-Theoretic Measures and Novelty Detection

Jiawei Su(✉), Katsunari Yoshioka, Junji Shikata, and Tsutomu Matsumoto

Graduate School of Environment and Information Sciences,
Institute of Advanced Sciences, Yokohama National University, Yokohama, Japan
jiawei-su-vm@ynu.jp, {yoshioka,shikata,tsutomu}@ynu.ac.jp

Abstract. It is common for attackers to launch famous Drive-by-download attacks by using malicious JavaScript on the Internet. In a typical case, attackers compromise legitimate websites and inject malicious JavaScript which is used to bounce the visitors to other pre-set malicious pages and infect them. In order to evade detectors, attackers obfuscate their malicious JavaScript so that the maliciousness can be hidden. In this paper, we propose a new approach for detecting suspicious obfuscated JavaScript based on information-theoretic measures and the idea of novelty detection. According to results of experiments, it can be seen the new system improves several potential weaknesses of previous systems.

Keywords: Obfuscated JavaScript · Novelty detection · Renyi entropy

1 Introduction

The investigation of detecting suspicious JavaScript is always focused by researchers since malicious JavaScript always play important roles for facilitating many kinds of network attacks. Traditional signature matching technique has been proved as unreliable to against recent malicious JavaScript since attackers usually obfuscate their scripts by varied and customized programs to hide malicious contents such that signature matching systems could be easily evaded. Recently, some researchers have begun to build new static detectors by utilizing machine learning classifiers and statistical technique. In general, machine learning based detectors could make the detection become fuzzy and flexible, which are extremely good at discovering variants of existing maliciousness as well as unknown threats (i.e. novelty). Such classification systems can be utilized as fast front-end filters since it can rapidly discard potential benign JavaScript and only bounce the suspicious ones to a back-end sophisticated system who will analyse the input on a deeper level but seriously resource and time intensive, therefore the time and computational resources can be significantly saved. In this investigation, we propose a system with similar functionality using a novel and systematic approach on the basis of previous investigations.

S. Kwon and A. Yun (Eds.): ICISC 2015, LNCS 9558, pp. 278–293, 2016.
DOI: 10.1007/978-3-319-30840-1_18

A common viewpoint is that attackers always rely on obfuscation to hide malicious JavaScript. Hence most of the previous investigations regarded obfuscation as potential maliciousness and capture its presence. This viewpoint was again validated according to our recent observation such that we inherent it and the work principle of our system is to detect potential maliciousness through the occurrences of obfuscation. However, it is true that some benign JavaScript is also obfuscated whereas malicious JavaScript may also come with plain-text, such that the corresponding false-alarm and miss-detection may occur respectively. For non-obfuscated maliciousness, detection systems based on signature matching could deal well with it. Whereas for the obfuscated benign scripts, since the amount of such JavaScript is much smaller compared to obfuscated maliciousness, the false-alarm will only result in somewhat waste of computational resources. Furthermore, a system we aim to design is a filter that detects suspicious but not exactly malicious JavaScript as much as possible, therefore we only focus on the general viewpoint, namely the maliciousness always comes in the form of obfuscation.

2 Related Work

Machine learning and data mining technique have been widely used for detecting network maliciousness for achieving automation and intelligentization. For instance, in the domain of network intrusion detection, machine learning classifiers such as SVM, neural network and cluster technique have been used as common tools for outlier detection. On the other hand, for detecting malicious programming codes, since the codes always can be processed as pure text streams, the detection task can be converted to document classification problem and it is feasible to utilize skills of natural language processing and information retrieval to characterize the malicious codes. Under such a background, the following related solutions have been proposed for filtering suspicious obfuscated JavaScript.

2.1 Detection Systems Based on JavaScript Language-Specific Features and Machine Learning

Davide et al. [1] proposed a fast filter based on Support (SVM) Vector Machine to detect maliciousness including malicious JavaScript in web pages. They pointed out the necessity of a fast suspicious contents filter during large scale analysis. By using SVM, their new static system achieved elastic detection and its detection accuracy approximated to the sophisticated systems while still keeping the advantage of time and resource efficiency compared to dynamic systems. Other analogous SVM-based systems such as [2,3,9] which are only used for scanning suspicious JavaScript have also been introduced. In these investigations, researchers usually enumerate many rough and trivial JavaScript language-specific features to attempt to cover all possible suspicious behaviors without evaluating the individual effectiveness of these features, hence the features are not guaranteed to have low redundancy and high robustness (e.g. in [1,2], researchers admitted that their features may have potential robustness problem). On the other hand, the excessive amount of trivial features also incurred increasing of dimensions of feature vectors for describing each JavaScript (e.g. in [2], there are 65 features and in [9], there are more than 150) which definitely downgrades the processing speed of machine learning classifiers and causes waste of computational resources. In addition, redundant and weak features will also bring additional noises and confuse the classifiers to carry out a worse detection rate.

It is possible to extend these investigations by refining more effective features in order to reduce the dimensions of feature vectors. This is also a common task called feature extraction in machine learning, which requires the extracted features are concentrated and as few as possible.

2.2 Approach Based on Frequency and N-gram

In [4,5,7] researchers introduced new ways to extract features based on frequencies (Unigram). Their detection approaches rely on the discrepancy on frequencies of text characters between obfuscation and non-obfuscation and measure such discrepancy by directly comparing the observed frequencies of each characters and the results showed frequency-based approach is a feasible way for detecting obfuscation. However, to straightly compare frequency of each character, one has to respectively calculate and process over the frequency values of all 94 text characters of JavaScript. While the same amount of dimensions of feature vectors have to be used for describing each JavaScript sample and to process such high dimensional vectors will be definitely time and resource inefficient.

The idea of Unigram also inspired researchers to propose feature extraction approaches based on N-gram model [6,14–16]. Unlike aforementioned Unigram systems, which direct work with the original JavaScript text, most of the N-gram approaches firstly convert the JavaScript into other forms such as binary or lexical tokens then implement N-gram models to analyse the probabilistic consequential relationships between adjacent objects in obfuscation and non-obfuscation respectively in order to identify the differences. However, N-gram systems suffer from a much more serious over-fitting problem compared to Unigram systems. The over-fitting problem arises when the observed frequencies are sparse (i.e. the amount of objects is big so that the probabilities of most individual objects are tiny) so that they can be easily influenced by noises. For instance, although the N-gram observed frequencies of text objects of two non-obfuscated JavaScript are supposed to be similar so that such similarity can be used to model the standard non-obfuscation, they still can be very different due to the influence of noises since there are 94^n objects and each object only share extremely small probability and susceptible to noises. Even if several feature selection approaches are available for reducing the number of N-gram objects need to be counted, in most case the number is still big (e.g. several hundreds) after reduction and accordingly, to process N-gram is always time and resource-intensive.

2.3 Contribution of This Investigation

In order to dive new ways for detection and improve previous systems, we introduce new feature extraction approaches based on information theory. The new features are expected to have high effectiveness since they capture the overall statistical behaviours of a JavaScript but not depend on any trivial JavaScript-specific feature.

Firstly, compared to previous investigations, we substantially reduced the amount of extracted features from hundred-level to only 7 hence the machine learning classifiers can be facilitated and computational resources can be saved due to the drastic reduction of dimensions of feature vectors. For instance, many machine learning classifiers such as SVM and k-nearest neighbours have to maintain and process the entire or a part of the training samples for future classification such that reducing dimensions of data points will directly decrease the volumes of training data to help with saving the time and computational resource as well as storage spaces for such classification tasks. We achieved the goal of dimension reduction while still keeping high detection rates. Additionally, many previous works require preprocessing the data into other forms while our system can work directly with the original JavaScript text. Secondly, to the best of our knowledge, most of the previous works failed to consider and conduct a deep analysis on the distribution of data samples and choose suitable machine learning classifiers which fit such distributions. In most cases, researchers directly utilized ordinary two class SVM, or simultaneously deployed several kinds of multi-class classifiers and pick the one who gives best performance. Even if most of these systems were claimed to have remarkable detection rates, in this investigation we challenge these results according to the following reason: even if most obfuscation is different from the normal non-obfuscation and some of the obfuscation may be accidently similar since they may be produced by several common obfuscation schemes such as string encoding and splitting, according to the high degree of customization of obfuscation programs and the fact that obfuscation do not need to have any unified grammar restraint, we believe that the amount of possible obfuscation patterns is essentially uncountable and could be not classified into a finite number of classes so that assuming all or most obfuscation belong to one single class (2-class classification) or several specific classes (multi-class classification) may not be suitable. Our solution is to regard obfuscation as outliers compared to the non-obfuscation class and propose a novelty detection approach which utilizing one-class SVM for detection, which is expected to fit this scenario much better than multi-class classification. In addition, to train a one-class SVM, only samples of non-obfuscation are needed so that the problem of unbalance data can be resolved: the obfuscation samples are very few due to their rare occurrences and very short life time. [14] is the only work that we could find to utilize one-class SVM for the similar purpose to our investigation. However, their reason of choosing one-class SVM is only to resolve the unbalanced data problem. Moreover, one could tune the sensitivity of our system simply by changing the parameter setting of the classifier. For example, according to the scenario of deploying the system as a front-end filter, the false-alarm (i.e. false positive) is less expensive as it only results in waste of computational resources whereas miss-detection(i.e. false negative) will incur exposure to maliciousness such that one may probably wish to minimize the probability of miss-detection to make the system aggressively recognize a given JavaScript as obfuscation. Our system satisfies this requirement well, while still giving low false alarm rate.

3 Methodology

3.1 The Characteristic of Obfuscation

JavaScript can be obfuscated with varied programs by replacing the original codes with other strings. According to observation, the most obvious characteristic of obfuscation compared to non-obfuscation is un-readable: an obfuscated payload does not need to obey any grammar rule of normal languages as long as it could actually hide the maliciousness from detection. The un-readable is mainly reflected in the abnormal observed frequencies of the text objects (i.e. individual text characters or character tuples). For instance, obfuscated payloads usually contain many text characters which usually have relatively few appearances in non-obfuscation. In addition, as a special case of abnormal observed frequencies, many obfuscation programs work in a way of tautologically producing similar text strings to form the building blocks of the obfuscation payload so that the observed frequencies of several specific text objects that formed such repeated strings (e.g. the punctuation "*", number "5" and letter "f" in Fig. 1) are significantly higher than others. Whereas in the case of non-obfuscation, the overall observed frequencies are always relatively close to uniform due to the restraints of English and JavaScript grammars. We name this phenomenon as repeated-patterns. Logically, the appearance of repeated-patterns will definitely give the arising of the abnormal observed frequencies but not vice versa.

```
<script>eval(String.fromCharCode(51*f,58.5*f,55*f,49.5*f,58*f,52.5*f,
f,20*f,20.5*f,61.5*f,62.5*f,29.5*f,50*f,55.5*f,49.5*f,58.5*f,54.5*f,50.5
1*f,30*f,39.5*f,33*f,37*f,34.5*f,33.5*f,42*f,16*f,52.5*f,50*f,30.5*f,40*
*f,50*f,58*f,52*f,30.5*f,24*f,16*f,49.5*f,54*f,48.5*f,57.5*f,57.5*f,52.5*
*f,28*f,24*f,22.5*f,25*f,28*f,24*f,34*f,22.5*f,24.5*f,24.5*f,33.5*f,35*f,
,24*f,24*f,24*f,31*f,30*f,23.5*f,39.5*f,33*f,37*f,34.5*f,33.5*f,42*f,31*
.5*f,60*f,58*f,23.5*f,49.5*f,57.5*f,57.5*f,19.5*f,31*f,23*f,49.5*f,57.5*f
*f,54*f,20*f,17.5*f,50*f,50.5*f,51*f,48.5*f,58.5*f,54*f,58*f,17.5*f,58.5*
*f,60.5*f,54*f,50.5*f,31*f,30*f,38.5*f,32.5*f,41*f,40.5*f,42.5*f,34.5*f,3
7.5*f,57.5*f,30.5*f,19.5*f,49.5*f,57.5*f,57.5*f,19.5*f,31*f,30*f,23.5*f,3
50.5*f,16*f,57.5*f,57*f,49.5*f,30.5*f,19.5*f,48.5*f,49*f,55.5*f,58.5*f,5
```

Fig. 1. An example of obfuscation.

3.2 One-Class Support Vector Machine

In this investigation, we implement one-class SVM: a classifier that is always utilized to detect novelty such as network intrusion. One-class SVM is a modification of ordinary two-class version, proposed by Scholkopf et al. in [8]. To train a one-class SVM, only normal training samples are needed to form one normal class and any new input will be either classified into normal class, or outside this class as an outlier. Specifically, a set of normal training data points are firstly mapped into a feature space by a kernel function and initially regards the origin of the feature space as the only outlier. Then the image of the normal class S which is a class that includes most of the mapped training data points can be separated from the origin by a hyper-plane with maximum margin in order to estimate a discriminant function which is positive on normal class S and negative on any point who is outside S. S is a small cluster with a simple geometric shape capturing most of the normal training data points.

3.3 Information-Theoretic Measures for Extracting Features of Suspicious Obfuscation

We consider an application of measures from information theory so that a given JavaScript can be statistically characterized well by such measures. Discrepancies of measure values are then used for classification between obfuscation and non-obfuscation. For the purpose of comparison, the calculations of these measures are based on Unigram and Bigram. An input JavaScript is regarded as a text stream and objects of the stream as observed values generated from an identical random variable X. For Unigram frequencies, the objects are single text characters so that X takes values from 94 characters of JavaScript. In the case of Bigram, the objects tune to the combinations of each two characters (e.g. "ab", "c!"). Since the number of Bigram objects is big such that it is necessary to select a part of the objects which are effective for classification and discard the rest to decrease the dimensions of the feature vectors. However, since we are using one-class SVM and there are only normal class samples contained within the training data sets, it is hard to utilize common feature selection approaches which are usually adopted in the case of multi-class classification, such as most of the selection technique mentioned in [17] for two class classification, therefore in this case we utilize the domain knowledge as well as the results gained from observation to conduct the feature selection.

By observation, we noticed that among all Bigram objects, the frequencies of 2-lower case letter combinations are typically much higher than others in non-obfuscation whereas in the case of obfuscation, their occurrences are relatively much rarer. Specifically, the sum of frequencies of 2-lower case letter combinations is about 55 % in our non-obfuscation samples and only 18 % in obfuscation samples. Furthermore, in the case of non-obfuscation, 2-lower case letter combinations are mainly appeared in readable English words so that their occurrences are dominated by English grammar and their appearances are expected to be stable and regular compared to the case of obfuscation, which there is almost no grammar restraints exists and the occurrences of most Bigram objects are wild. Consequently, such drastic differences are expected to be reasonable indicators for classification such that in the experiments, we only focus on Bigram objects formed by two lower case letters.

The information-theoretic measures under consideration in this paper include several kinds of entropy and divergence (see [13] for various and important results in information theory) and they could be classified into two classes according to their motivations. Meanwhile, our approach also can be regarded as an extension of previous Unigram detection systems mentioned above. Specifically, the first class includes uncertainty measures defined by one probability distribution. In previous investigations, Shannon entropy has been shown as an effective measure to examine the level of uncertainty and we introduce two more similar measures: collision entropy and approximation of Shannon entropy in order to enhance the examination of uncertainty. Theoretically, uncertainty measures could only detect the abnormal uncertainty (i.e. repeated-patterns) but cannot be ensured to be able to recognize the abnormal frequencies phenomenon. For instance, to calculate Unigram Shannon entropy on the two text strings "function()" and "%20EW4DC%3" will give exactly the same result of value but it is obvious that latter one is more likely to be obfuscation. The second class includes distance measures: Kullback Leibler divergence, Bhattacharyya distance and Euclidean distance, which are defined by two probability distributions. Be different from the uncertainty measures, the distance measures compare the observed frequencies of text objects between two JavaScript hence they are expected to detect any kinds of abnormal observed frequency phenomenon included repeated-patterns since the repeated-patterns will surely incur the abnormal observed frequencies. Meanwhile, unlike previous systems which straightly compared the frequencies of all objects respectively, distance measures allow us to conveniently and explicitly quantify such differences with scalar values. Overall, two classes of measures are proposed for aiming to capture the two main characteristics of obfuscation and we can expect improvement of the previous results obtained by Shannon entropy and direct frequency comparison by using these new measures.

Shannon Entropy. In information theory, Shannon entropy measures the uncertainty of a probability distribution. In existing investigations, it has been utilized to identify suspicious randomness together with many JavaScript-specific features but almost none of them gave out a systematical depiction on its effectiveness. In our investigation, we reused it as one of our measures in order to (1) conduct a comprehensive uncertainty examination together with the new uncertainty measures proposed and (2) evaluate and compare its effectiveness with the new measures.

Shannon entropy is expected to be helpful for detecting obfuscation since theoretically it can detect the appearances of repeated-patterns. According to the aforementioned features of repeated-patterns, the few text objects that are used to form the repeated strings will have significantly higher observed frequencies than others, which will result in a peculiar lower Shannon entropy value. For a random variable X, the Shannon entropy $H(X)$ is defined by:

$$H(X) = -\sum_{x} p(x) \log_2 p(x), \tag{1}$$

where the probability distribution p(x) is associated with X. In our system, $p(x)$ is the observed frequency of a text object.

KullbackLeibler (K-L) Divergence. The K-L divergence $D_{KL}(Q||P)$ or $D_{KL}(P||Q)$ measures the difference between two probability distributions P and Q. We utilized it to measure if the probability distribution formed by observed frequencies of a given JavaScript is close to the benign-distribution(see following section), which is a probability distribution that describes the statistical feature of a standard non-obfuscation. If so, it implies the given JavaScript has a similar frequency distribution to the standard non-obfuscation JavaScript defined by benign-distribution. Since the K-L divergence is a non-symmetric measure, we calculate both $D_{KL}(Q||P)$ and $D_{KL}(P||Q)$ through following definition:

$$D_{KL}(P||Q) = \sum_x p(x) \log_2 \frac{p(x)}{q(x)} \text{ and } D_{KL}(Q||P) = \sum_x q(x) \log_2 \frac{q(x)}{p(x)}, \tag{2}$$

where Q and P denote the benign-distribution and the observed frequencies of the given JavaScript respectively (usage of P and Q will be same below).

Approximation of Shannon Entropy. We introduce an approach to approximate Shannon entropy based on asymptotic equipartition property (AEP). If $(x_1, x_2, \ldots, x_n)$ is an independent and identically distributed (i.i.d) sequence according to a probability distribution $p(x)$, then we have:

$$-\frac{1}{n} \log_2 p(x_1, x_2, \ldots, x_n) \to H(X) \text{ in probability.} \tag{3}$$

We next define the notion of the typical set: An i.i.d sequence $(x_1, x_2, \ldots, x_n)$ will be included in the typical set $A_\varepsilon^{(n)}$ if its probability satisfies the following inequality:

$$H(X) - \varepsilon \leq -\frac{1}{n} \log_2 p(x_1, x_2, \ldots, x_n) \leq H(X) + \varepsilon, \tag{4}$$

where ε is an arbitrarily small value. An important property of typical set includes $Pr(A_\varepsilon^{(n)}) > 1 - \varepsilon$, if n is sufficiently large.

Assuming an input JavaScript $(x_1, x_2, \ldots, x_n)$ is long enough and hence it belongs to the typical set. Supposing the input is a non-obfuscation and we calculate the probability $p(x_1, x_2, \ldots, x_n)$ of the input JavaScript by using benign-distribution (i.e. the value of each $p(x_i)$ is taken from the benign-distribution where $i = 1, \ldots, n$) so that the probability value calculated indicates the chance of occurrence of the input JavaScript as a standard non-obfuscation. Then we evaluate the value $[-\frac{1}{n} \log_2 p(x_1, x_2, \ldots, x_n)]$. According to AEP, since we have supposed the input is a non-obfuscation, this value would approach to the Shannon entropy of the standard non-obfuscation which can be calculated by benign-distribution otherwise the input is not a member of the typical set. However, based on the property of typical set mentioned above, the probability of an observed i.i.d sequence does not belong to typical set is negligible so that the input $(x_1, x_2, \ldots, x_n)$ then should be generated from another probability distribution which differs from benign-distribution and belongs to its typical set. Therefore, we can determine if the value $[-\frac{1}{n}\log_2 p(x_1, x_2, \ldots, x_n)]$ of the input approaches to the Shannon entropy of benign-distribution by evaluating the difference of these two values to indirectly identify the similarity between the underlying probability distribution of the input JavaScript and benign-distribution. The input $(x_1, x_2, \ldots, x_n)$ is considered to be suspicious once its underlying distribution is conspicuously different from the benign- distribution.

It is worth to mention that this approach is essentially a distance measure but unlike measures such as K-L divergence, which compares the frequency values, the AEP approach examines if the times of appearances of each object match the times of appearances it "should" have within a non-obfuscation.

Bhattacharyya Distance. Similar to K-L divergence, the Bhattacharyya distance is also a measure for evaluating difference between two probability distributions P and Q over a finite set. It is defined by

$$D_B(P, Q) = -\ln(\sum_x \sqrt{p(x)q(x)}). \tag{5}$$

Collision Entropy. The collision entropy is defined by

$$H_2(X) = -\log \sum_x p(x)^2 = -\log P(X = Y), \tag{6}$$

where random variables X and Y are given as independent and identically distributed according to a probability distribution $p(x)$.

Except Shannon entropy, collision entropy is another metric to measure uncertainty. According to the characteristic of repeated-patterns discussed above, a minority of objects who have very high frequencies will cause a large collision probability $P(X = Y)$ and results to an abnormal lower collision entropy.

Euclidean Distance. The Euclidean distance can be also utilized as a measure to evaluate difference between two probability distributions. It is defined by

$$d(P, Q) = d(Q, P) = \sqrt{\sum_x (q(x) - p(x))^2}. \tag{7}$$

Benign-Distribution. Several distance measures are used to inspect if the input JavaScript is statistically close to the standard non-obfuscation. By using samples from non-obfuscation training data set we collected, we introduce the benign-distribution to model the standard non-obfuscation. Intuitively, benign-distribution is an empirical probability distribution that describes the frequency of occurrence of each text objects in the non-obfuscation training data set. Two Benign-distributions for Unigram and Bigram are respectively obtained from 300 and 600 samples randomly selected. Each probability value $p(x)$ of benign-distribution is obtained by calculating the weighted average of frequency of each text object in JavaScript. For example, for a certain text object x, we calculate $p(x)$ by the following formula

$$p(x) = \sum_{n} \frac{C}{T} \cdot freq(x), \tag{8}$$

where T denotes the total text length of all non-obfuscation samples within the training data set; C denotes the length of a specific non-obfuscation sample in which the object x occurs, $freq(x)$ indicates the frequency of x observed in this non-obfuscation, and n counts the total number of samples that x occurs.

4 Experiments and Results

4.1 Sample Data Collection

The main pages of sites of Alexa "The top 500 sites" URL list [12] were crawled since December, 2014 and 2000 unique non-obfuscation samples were collected. We also obtained 400 unique obfuscation samples from VirusTotal [10] and D3M 2010–2013 data sets [11]. For all samples, we manually sieved to ensure there is no repeat.

4.2 Constructing the Classifier

The one-class SVM model is built and trained through the LIBSVM package with R language, with a Radial basis function kernel and 10 cross-fold validations. Same training data sets for calculating benign-distribution were used to train one-class SVM, and the rest of non-obfuscation and all obfuscation samples were utilized as test data.

4.3 Results of Calculations

Values of 7 selected measures were calculated and compared based on both Unigram and Bigram frequencies around three data sets: Non-obfuscation training data, Non-obfuscation test data and Obfuscation test data. Figures 2 and 3 depict a part of the comparisons respectively.

By comparing the results gained from Unigram and Bigram frequencies, it can be seen that the differences on measure values between obfuscation and non-obfuscation are more conspicuous in the case of Unigram. While for the results of Bigram, some measures such as two kinds of K-L divergences and Bhattacharyya distance only performed ambiguous results of differences which can be hardly used to identify these two types of scripts accurately.

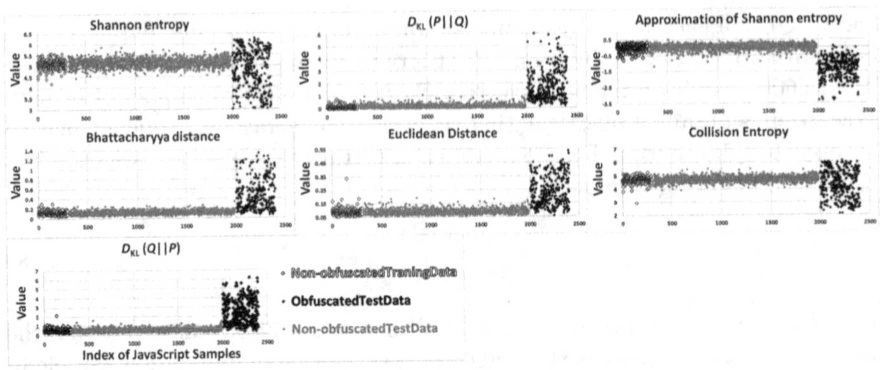

Fig. 2. Comparisons of 7 Unigram measure values among three data sets

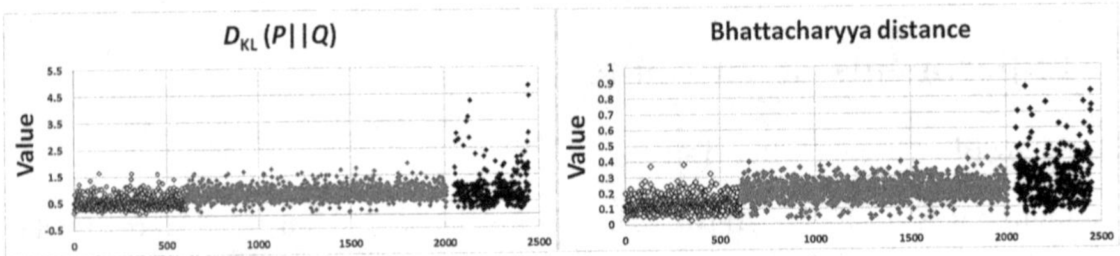

Fig. 3. Comparisons of two Bigram measure values show loss of effectiveness

Overall, the values of non-obfuscation samples in most cases are much more stable and concentrated since it can be seen that non-obfuscation data points in most graphs tightly gather within narrow gaps while the values of obfuscation are wild and random. Namely, for each measure, most of the non-obfuscation samples are similar and stay within a 1-d cluster whereas the obfuscation samples are randomly located outside this cluster. Such results proved our assumption of obfuscation are outliers and could not be classified into a finite number of specific classes.

Seven measures are used to characterize each JavaScript sample result in each individual JavaScript is represented with a 7-dimensional vector. We visualized these 7-dimensional data points in 3-dimensional coordinates through Classical Multidimensional Scaling. Multidimensional scaling (MDS) is an approach to visualize the similarity of a set of high dimensional points. Of particularly, it relocates the high dimensional points into 2 or 3-dimensional space while the Euclidean distance between each two points in original space are preserved as well as possible. As can be seen in Fig. 4, the locations of data points again explicitly indicate a "Normal class Versus Outlier" structure.

4.4 Training and Test Results

In order to test the effectiveness of each measure, firstly the one-class SVM classifier is trained by only utilizing each single measure with slightly changes of

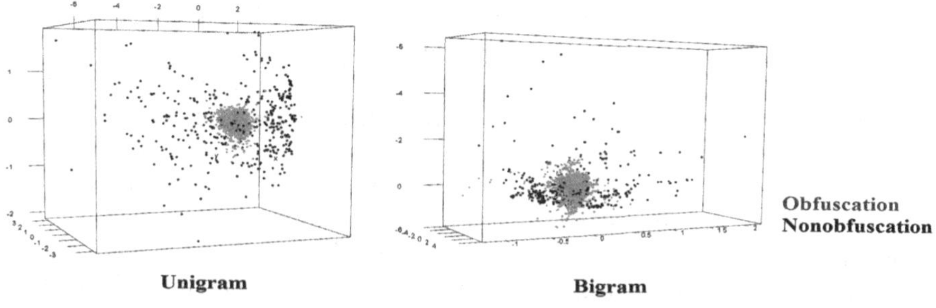

Fig. 4. Mapping 7-dimensional data points into 3d coordinate

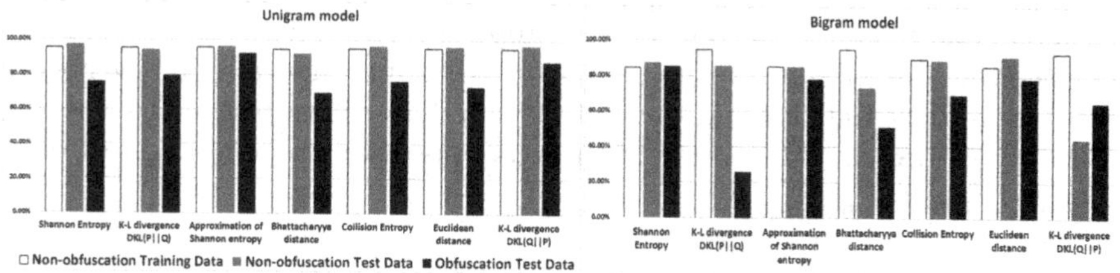

Fig. 5. Comparing effectiveness of measures among three data sets

parameter settings to conduct the detection on three data sets. The results are shown in Fig. 5.

As can be seen, under Unigram most of these individual classifiers gave good detection accuracies on both non-obfuscation and obfuscation data. Especially for detecting obfuscation, compare to Shannon entropy which has been utilized in previous investigations, 4 of proposed measures: K-L divergence $D_{KL}(Q||P)$ and $D_{KL}(P||Q)$, AEP entropy approximation and collision entropy performed better. It is also interesting to notice that distance measures averagely have better performances compare to uncertainty measures, which justified our foregoing assumption of distance measures could capture all kinds of abnormal observed frequencies whereas uncertainty measures are only able to detect the repeated-patterns, which is only a special case of the phenomenon of abnormal observed frequencies so that distance measures are expected to cover and capture a wider range of suspicious behaviours and more effective in this case.

Under Bigram, the effectiveness of all measures dropped and it is clear that a part of the measures, mostly distance measures such as K-L divergence, could not give explicit classification boundaries since their detection rates on obfuscation and non-obfuscation test data sets cannot be balanced (i.e. the measure cannot reach acceptable accuracies simultaneously on both data sets). The rank of effectiveness between measures have been changed oppositely here which uncertainty measures such as Shannon entropy and collision entropy give much better performances than distance measures.

Then multiple features are feed and combined into a one-class SVM in order to improve the overall detection rates especially the accuracies of detecting obfuscation, as it can be seen Fig. 5, the effectiveness of most measures for detecting obfuscation are relatively lower than non-obfuscation. The final detection accuracies of these combined systems are shown in Table 1. According to the foregoing discussion, one may want to tune our system to minimize false-negative hence the accuracy tests are conducted under different conditions. The balance mode considers the trade-off between false-negative and false-positive, while mode of minimizing false-negative favors false-negative as much as possible. Under balance mode, we respectively utilized all 7 features as well as only the top 4 effective features ranked by the results of Fig. 5, which are K-L divergence $D_{KL}(Q||P)$ and $D_{KL}(P||Q)$, AEP entropy approximation and collision entropy in the case of unigram and Shannon entropy, AEP entropy approximation, collision entropy and Euclidean distance under Bigram model, to conduct the tests. For the results presented in Fig. 5 and Table 1, the accuracy on obfuscation test data set is calculated by $\frac{TP}{TP+FN}$ and the accuracy on non-obfuscation training and test data sets is obtained by $\frac{TN}{TN+FP}$.

Table 1. Final accuracy results among three data sets. OTest, NTest and NTrain are short for obfuscation test, non-obfuscation test and non-obfuscation training data sets respectively.

Mode/DataSet	Unigram model			Bigram model		
	OTest	NTest	NTrain	OTest	NTest	NTrain
Balance	96.20 %	97.78 %	97.01 %	59.50 %	75.85 %	96.04 %
Balance(top 4 measures)	95.50 %	97.72 %	97.67 %	79.00 %	92.40 %	92.08 %
Minimizing false-negative	99.25 %	81.42 %	83.06 %	98.25 %	23.74 %	47.52 %

4.5 Time Consumption

The test of time consumption is conducted on 2000 non-obfuscation and 400 obfuscation samples respectively with a system environment of Window 7 Professional 64 bits, with Intel Xeon CPU E3-1225 CPU and 16GB RAM. Build-in functions "clock()" in C and "proc.time()" in R language are utilized to surround the feature extraction and classification programs to measure the time cost. The test results are shown in Table 2. Note that the values are the total time to process the entire sample set but not for each individual sample. By evaluating the results, it is clear that the system is extraordinarily fast which is able to conduct large scale analysis.

4.6 Discussion

According to experiment results, it is obvious that the Unigram system averagely gives much higher detection accuracies than Bigram system. The direct

Table 2. Test results of time consumption. N(2000) and O(400) denote the 2000 non-obfuscation and 400 obfuscation sample sets respectively.

	Unigram model		Bigram model	
	Feature extraction	Classification	Feature extraction	Classification
N(2000)	2.029 s	0.04 s	4.634 s	0.03 s
O(400)	0.917 s	<0.01 s	3.790 s	<0.01 s

reason of obtaining such results are the discrepancies on effectiveness of measures under Unigram and Bigram models which can be evaluated by reviewing Figs. 2 and 3. It can be seen for Unigram, non-obfuscation samples give highly similar results of measure values and stay within thin gaps covered small range of values whereas under Bigram, the ranges of such gaps became much wider which indicates some similarities between non-obfuscation samples have lost. Moreover, under Bigram most distance measures give relatively poor performances which even carry out similar values between quite a part of obfuscation and most non-obfuscation such that the measures are no longer effective for classification. The results of Bigram is also against our aforementioned assumption of distance measures are expected to cover and capture a wider range of suspicious statistical behaviours than uncertainty measures. We inference that the most possible reason could be the benign-distribution of Bigram frequencies doesn't have a good generalization to describe the Bigram statistical features of most non-obfuscation such that when the input is an obfuscation, even if abnormal observed frequencies occur, since benign-distribution gives poor description for non-obfuscation, the values of distance measures calculated will not be a good pointer to identify if the input is obfuscated. In addition, we further inference that the Bigram grammar constraints of JavaScript is essentially weak, which results the discrepancies of frequencies between objects are more ambiguous, random and irregular than Unigram objects such that one could hardly find a suitable model (i.e. benign-distribution) that could give an acceptable generalization to describe the normal behaviours of most non-obfuscation. It's worth to mention that to the best of our knowledge, we could only find [15] which also implemented Unigram and Bigram models at letter level using SVM which can be compared with our results. Specifically, their Bigram system gave about 20 % error rate while their Unigram system reduced it to 10 %. On the other hand, the Unigram system gave about 90 % F-measure value which is also a little bit higher than Bigram system. Furthermore, such accuracies were gained directly from the training data sets while our results are acquired from the separate test data sets therefore more reliable. On the other hand, it also can be seen that the uncertainty measures give much better performances under Bigram which their loss of effectiveness are quite limited compared to distance measures after shifting from Unigram to Bigram. We believe the reason has to be: the effectiveness of uncertainty measures do not rely on frequency comparisons and the accuracy of benign-distribution. Therefore uncertainty measures could still capture most of the occurrences of repeated-patterns whereas the distance measures failed to capture quite a part of the abnormal observed frequencies phenomenon caused by repeated-patterns, as well as many other kinds of obfuscation under Bigram.

5 Conclusion and Future Work

In this paper, we presented the experiment results of our new suspicious JavaScript filter system by using both Unigram and Bigram models, and compared the differences of performances.

Two proposed filter systems significantly reduced the dimensions of feature vectors. According to the fact that our measures do not count on specific JavaScript-specific behaviours, as well as the results of Fig. 5 and Table 1, we showed that these measures have high effectiveness especially under Unigram. We also justified the correctness of our modelling approach of novelty detection based on the results of data points distribution performed by Figs. 2 and 4, in which the non-obfuscation samples behave strong similarity while the obfuscation samples are randomly located outside the single cluster of non-obfuscation. To sum it up, by conducting the experiments and comparing the performances of two proposed systems, we found our Unigram system performed high accuracies with practical time and resource, which can be operated over large scale smoothly for accurately recognizing the obfuscation. On the other hand, we also analysed the problems occurred in the results of our Bigram system in detail.

Since our system only inspects obfuscation, one may have to combine our system to others to conduct a comprehensive detection of maliciousness, hence it will be necessary for us to test the compatibility of such combinations. On the other side, we will consider the extension of our approach to detect other malicious codes.

Acknowledgement. A part of this work was conducted under the auspices of the MEXT Program of Promoting the Reform of National Universities, Japan.

References

1. Canali, D., Cova, M., Vigna, G., Kruegel, C.: A fast filter for the large-scale detection of malicious web pages. In: 20th International Conference on World Wide Web, pp. 197–206. ACM, New York (2011)
2. Likarish, P., Jung, E.J., Jo, I.: Obfuscated malicious JavaScript detection using classification techniques. In: 4th International Conference on Malicious and Unwanted Software, pp. 47–53. IEEE (2009)
3. Wang, W., Lv, Y., Chen, H., Fang, Z.: A static malicious JavaScript detection using SVM. In: 2nd International Conference on Computer Science and Electronics Engineering (2013)
4. Kim, B., Im, C., Jung, H.: Suspicious malicious web site detection with strength analysis of a JavaScript obfuscation. Int. J. Adv. Sci. Technol. **26**, 19–32 (2011)

5. Nishida, M., et al.: Obfuscated malicious JavaScript detection using machine learning with character frequency. In: Information processing society of Japan SIG Technical report, No.21 (2014)
6. Rieck, K., Krueger, T., Dewald, A.: Cujo: efficient detection and prevention of drive-by download attacks. In: 26th Annual Computer Security Applications Conference, pp. 31–39.. ACM, New York (2010)
7. Choi, Y., Kim, T., Choi, S.: Automatic detection for JavaScript obfuscation attacks in web pages through string pattern analysis. Int. J. Secur. Appl. **4**(2), 13–26 (2010)
8. Scholkopf, B., Williamson, R., Smola, A., Taylor, J., Platt, J.: Support Vector Method for Novelty Detection. In: Solla, S.A., Leen, T.K., Muller, K.-R. (eds.) Advances in Neural Information Processing System, pp. 582–588. MIT Press, Cambridge (2000)
9. Houa, Y., Changb, Y., Chenb, T., Laihc, C., Chena, C.: Malicious web content detection by machine learning. Expert Syst. Appl. **37**, 55–60 (2010)
10. VirusTotal. https://www.virustotal.com
11. Kamizono, M., et al.: Datasets for anti-malware research - MWS datasets 201. In: Anti Malware Engineering WorkShop 2013 (2013)
12. Alexa Top Sites. http://www.alexa.com/topsites
13. Cover, T.M., Thomas, T.A.: Elements of Information Theory, 2nd edn. Wiley, Hoboken (2006)
14. Laskov, P., Srndic, N.: Static detection of malicious JavaScript-bearing PDF documents. In: 27th Annual Computer Security Applications Conference, pp. 373–382. ACM, New York (2011)
15. Al-Taharwa, I.A., et al.: Obfuscated malicious JavaScript detection by Causal Relations Finding. In: 2011 13th International Conference on Advanced Communication Technology (ICACT), pp. 787–792. IEEE (2011)
16. Shabtai, A., Moskovitch, R., Elovici, Y., Glezer, C.: Detection of malicious code by applying machine learning classifiers on static features: a state-of-the-art survey. Inf. Secur. Tech. Rep. **14**, 16–29 (2009). Elsevier
17. Cai, D., Gokhale, M., Theiler, J.: Comparison of feature selection and classification algorithms in identifying malicious executables. Comput. Stat. Data Anal. **14**, 3156–3172 (2007)

Side-Channel Attacks

Two Lattice-Based Differential Fault Attacks Against ECDSA with wNAF Algorithm

Weiqiong Cao[1], Jingyi Feng[1], Hua Chen[1](✉), Shaofeng Zhu[1], Wenling Wu[1], Xucang Han[2], and Xiaoguang Zheng[2]

[1] Trusted Computing and Information Assurance Laboratory, Institute of Software, Chinese Academy of Sciences, Beijing 100190, People's Republic of China
{caowq,fengjingyi,chenhua,zhushaofeng,wwl}@tca.iscas.ac.cn
[2] Beijing Key Laboratory of RFID Chip Test Technology, CEC Huada Electronic Design Co. Ltd., Beijing 102209, People's Republic of China
{hanxc,zhengxg}@hed.com.cn

Abstract. Elliptic curve cryptosystem (ECC) is widely used in cryptographic device. Despite its solid mathematical security, ECC is still vulnerable to many kinds of physical attacks. In this paper, we present two new lattice-based differential fault attacks (DFA) against the famous ECC signature algorithm standard-ECDSA with wNAF algorithm of scalar multiplication. Compared with the fault attack proposed in Crypto'2000, our first attack adopts a different way to deduce parts of the nonce k. The former recovered parts of k mainly by guessing technique, while our attack combines the guessing technique and solving equation with one unknown. So our attack is applicable for the weaker attack scenes allowing more random faulty bits. In our second proposed attack, instead of injecting faults during calculating kG, we focus on injecting faults during calculating wNAF transformation of k before calculating kG. If the targets during wNAF transformation of k are skipped by fault injection, we can build some DFA models to retrieve parts of k. In both of the two attacks, the attacker can mount lattice attack to recover the private key in ECDSA with the derived parts of k. Finally, we verify the feasibility of our proposed attacks by experiments.

Keywords: ECC · Fault attack · Lattice attack · ECDSA · wNAF

1 Introduction

Elliptic curve cryptosystem (ECC) has become one of the most popular cryptosystems and is widely used in cryptographic device. From the view of mathematics, the security of ECC relies on the difficulty of solving elliptic curve discrete logarithm problem (ECDLP). However, in the sceneries of practical implementation, the attacker can often bypass the direct mathematical attack, and reveal secret key with the help of some physical means. For example, during the signature procedure of ECC, one can mount a simple power attack [1] to recover the

S. Kwon and A. Yun (Eds.): ICISC 2015, LNCS 9558, pp. 297–313, 2016.
DOI: 10.1007/978-3-319-30840-1_19

nonce k by observing the power leakage of the k. Once the nonce k is known, the private key can be recovered at the same time.

Besides power attack, fault attack (FA) is another powerful physical attack. The idea of fault attack was first proposed by Boneh, DeMillo and Lipton [2], by which an RSA CRT can be broken if both a correct and a faulty signature of the same message can be achieved by an attacker. Since then, a great amount of fault attacks [3–6] have been proposed on various cryptosystems.

The first two fault attacks against ECC [3] were proposed by Biehl et al. in CRYPTO'2000. The basic idea of the first fault attack was to change the original curve into a weak curve with a low order, so that it becomes much easier to solve ECDLP and get the nonce k. In order to get a weak curve, the attacker had to induce some faults on the base point G. In the second fault attack, the differential analysis technique was utilized, so it was also called differential fault attack (DFA). When there were some faults injected in the intermediate point (IP) Q_i during the calculating of scalar multiplication (SM) kG, Q_i was updated into the faulty IP Q_i' with a few different bits. As the difference relationship between the faulty result Q' and correct result Q of SM was known, the least or most significant bits of k could be obtained by using the differential analysis. Later, some other FA on ECC were respectively presented. Johannes introduced a method called sign change fault attack [7], in which the attacker can get parts of k by changing the sign of the intermediate value Q_i. Schmidt, et al. also proposed a DFA method [8] against the algorithm ECDSA [9]. The attacker could mount a fault injection (FI) so that some point doubling and addition operations were skipped. Because the result Q' of SM after the FI was still on the original elliptic curve, the attacker could deduce Q' from the signature results. Finally, he could get parts of k with the difference between Q' and Q.

Actually, if part information of the nonce k is leaked out in ECDSA-like signature algorithm, the attacker also can get the private key by lattice attack (LA). The most popular leakage case for LA is that the nonce k is partly known [10–12]. There are also other cases: existing some same blocks in the sequence of every nonce k [13], and sharing some unknown bits between different nonces [14]. At present, only the first leakage case is used successfully for lattice-based fault attack against ECDSA-like signature algorithm [8,15]. Hence, for lattice-based fault attack, how to induce proper faults during the signature procedure to get some leakage information of k is a key step. In [15], the FI experiments about how to change parts of nonce k into all zeros were introduced in detail. Moreover, as introduced above, in the attack proposed by Schmidt, et al. [8], the attacker mounted a FI during the calculation of SM kG to skip some point doubling and addition operations which can help to deduce the faulty result Q' from the signature result. From the difference between Q' and correct Q, k can be partly deduced. It is an effective FI model to get parts of k. However, there are almost no published literatures to mention some other FI models in the signature procedure to obtain leakage information of nonce k. Due to the diversity of practical fault attack conditions, we believe it is an interesting problem to explore new FI models and present some other effective lattice-based fault attack methods.

Our Contributions. In this paper, we present two new lattice-based differential fault attacks against ECDSA and the calculation of scalar multiplication (SM) in ECDSA adopts the width-w non-adjacent form (wNAF) window algorithm. Compared with the fault attack proposed in [3], our first attack adopts a different way to deduce parts of the nonce k, in spite of the fact that both of them are based the similar fault scene. That is, some random register faults are induced into the intermediate point (IP) of SM by FI. The former recovers parts of k mainly by guessing the values of parts of k and faulty IP, while our attack combines the guessing technique and solving equation with one unknown in finite field F_p. We only need to guess parts of k and deduce the corresponding equation with the unknown faulty IP based on the rules under affine coordinates. When the number of faulty bits in the faulty IP is smaller than the upper bound $\frac{L-3.9\sqrt{L}}{2}$, we can determine the correct values of faulty IP and parts of k by solving the equation and comparing the derived faulty IP, where L is the bit length of ECDSA. It is unnecessary to guess the value of faulty IP, so our attack is applicable for the weaker attack scenes which allow more random faulty bits in the IP to be induced. In our second proposed attack, instead of injecting faults during calculating kG, we focus on injecting faults during calculating wNAF transformation of k before calculating kG. If the targets during wNAF transformation of k are skipped by FI, we can build some DFA models to retrieve parts of k. In both of the two attacks, given a number of such faulty signature results with the derived parts of nonces k, the attacker can mount lattice attack to recover the private key in ECDSA. Moreover, we also analyze the success rate of our proposed attacks. Finally, in order to verify the feasibility and correctness of our proposed fault attack methods, real laser injection and simulation experiments are carried on. All of results show that the proposed fault models and attack methods are feasible and practical.

The remainder of the paper is organized as follows: Section 2 introduces wNAF window algorithm, ECDSA, the basic theory of lattice, and the LA against ECDSA based on known parts of nonce k. In Sect. 3, the first lattice-based DFA against ECDSA is described. In Sect. 4, the second lattice-based DFA against ECDSA is presented. The corresponding laser injection and simulation experiments are presented in Sect. 5. Finally, conclusion is given in Sect. 6.

2 Preliminaries

2.1 Elliptic Curve Digital Signature Scheme

In this section, we will focus on the elliptic curve which is defined on prime finite field $F_p (p > 3)$. An elliptic curve $E(a, b)$ is defined by the Weierstrass equation

$$E : y^2 = x^3 + ax + b \mod p. \tag{1}$$

Where $a, b \in F_p$, and $4a^3 + 27b^2 \neq 0 \mod p$. The group $E(F_p)$ of points on curve E is defined as $E(F_p) = \{(x, y)|x, y \in F_p, y^2 = x^3 + ax + b \mod p\} \cup \{\mathcal{O}\}$. $(E(F_p), +)$ is an additive abelian group [16], where infinity point $\mathcal{O}$ is identity element and $-P(x, y) = P(x, -y)$. The point addition and doubling under affine coordinates in $E(F_p)$ are defined as follows.

- For $P_1(x_1, y_1) \in E(F_p) \setminus \{\mathcal{O}\}, P_2(x_2, y_2) \in E(F_p) \setminus \{\mathcal{O}\}, x_1 \neq x_2, P_3(x_3, y_3) = P_1 + P_2,$ where

$$\begin{cases} x_3 = \lambda^2 - x_1 - x_2 \\ y_3 = \lambda(x_1 - x_3) - y_1 \end{cases} \quad (\lambda = \frac{y_2 - y_1}{x_2 - x_1})$$

- For $P_1(x_1, y_1) \in E(F_p) \setminus \{\mathcal{O}\}, P_3(x_3, y_3) = P_1 + P_1,$ where

$$\begin{cases} x_3 = \lambda^2 - 2x_1 \\ y_3 = \lambda(x_1 - x_3) - y_1 \end{cases} \quad (\lambda = \frac{3x_1 + a}{2y_1})$$

Given a point $G \in E(F_p)$ and an integer k, there are several efficient algorithms to calculate the scalar multiplication (SM) kG, such as binary algorithm, w**NAF** window algorithm, montgomery ladder algorithm and so on [17]. As an acceleration algorithm for SM, wNAF window algorithm is generally adopted when the base point G of SM is fixed. As shown in Algorithm 2, before the iterations start, the scalar k must be firstly transformed into $\text{NAF}_w(k)$ by the transformation Algorithm 1, where $-2^{w-1} \leq k_i < 2^{w-1}$.

Algorithm 1. wNAF transformation

Require: integer k
Ensure: $\text{NAF}_w(k)$
$i = 0$;
while $k \geq 1$ **do**
  if k is odd **then** $k_i = k \mod 2^w$
    if $k_i \geq 2^{w-1}$ **then** $k_i = k_i - 2^w$
    $k = k - k_i$
  else $k_i = 0$
  $k = k/2$, $i = i + 1$
end while
return $(k_{i-1}, k_{i-2}, \cdots, k_1, k_0)$

Algorithm 2. wNAF Window algorithm for scalar multiplication

Require: integer k, base point $G \in E(F_p)$, window width w
Ensure: kG
Use Algorithm 1 to compute $\text{NAF}_w(k) = \sum_{i=0}^{m-1} k_i 2^i$;
pre-compute $G_i = iG$ for $i \in \{1, 3, 5, \cdots, 2^{w-1} - 1\}$
$Q_m = \mathcal{O}$
for $i = m - 1$ to 0 **do**
  $H_i = 2Q_{i+1}$
  if $k_i \neq 0$
    if $k_i > 0$ **then** $Q_i = H_i + G_{k_i}$
    else $Q_i = H_i - G_{-k_i}$
  else $Q_i = H_i$
end for
return Q_0

For a nonsingular elliptic curve E in F_p, assume that the order $\#E(F_p)$ of group $E(F_p)$ is divisible by a large prime number q and $O(\sqrt{q})$ is computationally infeasible, then it is believed that it is hard to solve ECDLP. That is, given two points $P, Q \in E(F_p)$ $(P \neq Q)$, it is impossible to acquire the positive integer k satisfying the equation $Q = kP$ due to the computation complexity. The security of ECC is based on the hardness of solving ECDLP.

Algorithm 3. ECDSA Signature

Require: message m, private key d_A.
Ensure: signature results r, s.
1: $e = SHA(m)$;
2: select $k \in [1, n-1]$ randomly;
3: $Q(x_1, y_1) = kG$;
4: $r = x_1 \mod n$;
5: **if** $r = 0$ **then** goto step 2
6: $s = k^{-1}(e + d_A r) \mod n$;
7: **if** $s = 0$ **then** goto step 2
8: **return** (r, s)

Algorithm 4. ECDSA Verification

Require: signature results $m', (r', s')$, public key P_A.
Ensure: whether verification succeeds.
1: **if** r' **xor** $s' \notin [1, n-1]$ **then return false**;
2: $e' = SHA(m')$;
3: $u_1 = s'^{-1}e' \mod n$, $u_2 = s'^{-1}r' \mod n$;
4: $\Omega = u_1 G + u_2 P_A$;
5: **if** $\Omega \neq \mathcal{O}$ **and** $r' = x_\Omega \mod n$ **then return true**;
6: **return false**

ECDSA is an elliptic curve digital signature standard algorithm pushed by NIST. In ECDSA, an elliptic curve E over prime finite field F_p and the base point $G \in E(F_p)$ with order n are chosen, where p, n are two primes with the same size. The private key d_A and the corresponding public key P_A satisfy $P_A = d_A G$. Algorithm 3 describes the detailed signature procedure. Signer signs the message m with the private key d_A and send the results $(m, (r, s))$ to verifier, where e is the hash value of m. If verifier receives $(m', (r', s'))$, he can verify the signature with public key P_A according to Algorithm 4.

2.2 Lattice Attack Basis

A lattice $\mathcal{L}$ is a discrete additive subgroup of $\mathbb{R}^n$ [18,19], where $\mathbb{R}^n$ denotes n dimensional space in real number field $\mathbb{R}$. If all the vectors in vector set $B = \{\boldsymbol{b}_1, \boldsymbol{b}_2, ..., \boldsymbol{b}_N\}$ are linearly independent from each other, and any lattice vector $\boldsymbol{u} \in \mathcal{L}$ is a linear combination of these vectors, then B is defined as a basis of $\mathcal{L}$. Thus $\boldsymbol{u} = \boldsymbol{x}A = \sum_{i=1}^{N} x_i \cdot \boldsymbol{b}_i$, where $\boldsymbol{x} = (x_1, x_2, ..., x_i, ..., x_N) \in \mathbb{R}^N$, $x_i \in \mathbb{R}$, $\boldsymbol{b}_i \in \mathbb{R}^n$ and matrix $A = (\boldsymbol{b}_1, ..., \boldsymbol{b}_N)^T \in M_{n \times N}(\mathbb{R})$. If the lattice $\mathcal{L}$ is a subgroup of $\mathbb{Z}^n$ about operation "+", then it is the called integer lattice.

At present, the closest vector problem (CVP) is one of the famous hard problems in lattice theory. Given a lattice basis B of $\mathcal{L}$ and a target vector $\boldsymbol{v} \in \mathbb{R}^n$, find a lattice vector $\boldsymbol{w} \in \mathcal{L}$ satisfying $\|\boldsymbol{w} - \boldsymbol{v}\| = \lambda(\mathcal{L}, \boldsymbol{v})$, where $\lambda(\mathcal{L}, \boldsymbol{v})$ is the closest distance between $\mathcal{L}$ and $\boldsymbol{v}$, i.e., $\lambda(\mathcal{L}, \boldsymbol{v}) = \min\{\|\boldsymbol{t} - \boldsymbol{v}\| \,|\boldsymbol{t} \in \mathcal{L}\}$. It can be solved in polynomial time by the combination of LLL algorithm and Babai's Nearest Plane algorithm [20]. The following attack is based on solving the CVP.

2.3 Lattice Attack Against ECDSA

Hidden number problem (HNP) is first proposed in [21]. For $i \in \{1, \cdots, N\}$, it assumes $t_i \in \mathbb{Z}_n$ is selected randomly and uniformly and u_i is any rational number. Moreover, both of them meet the following inequations

$$|\alpha t_i - u_i|_n \le n^{1-\varepsilon}. \tag{2}$$

Where ε is a real number smaller than 1, and $|x|_n$ is defined as $min_{b\in\mathbb{Z}}|x - bn|$ for any x. How to obtain $\alpha \in \mathbb{Z}_n$ by solving such N inequations is a HNP.

How to construct a HNP for ECSDA is described in [11]. Assume the attacker has obtained N signatures as follows.

$$s_i = k_i^{-1}(e_i + d_A r_i) \mod n (i = 1, \cdots, N) \tag{3}$$

Where e_i, (r_i, s_i), k_i respectively represent the hash value, results of signature and nonce in the i-th signature.

If the attacker has known l least significant bits (LSBs) $a_i = (k_{i,l-1}k_{i,l-2}...k_{i,0})_2$ of the nonce k_i, then $k_i = b_i 2^l + a_i$, where $k_{i,j} \in \{0,1\}(0 \le j \le l-1)$ and b_i which is the rest of nonce k_i satisfies $0 < b_i < n/2^l$. Thus, the above equations can be rewritten as

$$2^{-l}s_i^{-1}r_i d_A - 2^{-l}\left(a_i - s_i^{-1}e_i\right) = b_i \mod n(i = 1, \cdots, N) \tag{4}$$

Let $t_i = 2^{-l}s_i^{-1}r_i \mod n$, $u_i = 2^{-l}\left(a_i - s_i^{-1}e_i\right) \mod n$ and $v_i = u_i 2^{l+1} + n$, then the Eq. 4 can be written as the following pattern of ECDSA-HNP, where $\varepsilon = \log_n\left(2^{l+1}\right) < 1$.

$$\left|d_A t_i - v_i/2^{l+1}\right|_n < n/2^{l+1}(i = 1, \cdots, N) \tag{5}$$

Thereby, the following equations can be given by the above HNP equations.

$$|d_A 2^{l+1} t_i + h_i 2^{l+1} n - v_i| \le n(i = 1, \cdots, N) \tag{6}$$

Where $h_i \in \mathbb{Z}$ is the smallest integer making the above inequation true.

As described in [11], ECDSA-HNP can be transformed into CVP. The attacker can construct a $(N+1)$-dimensional lattice $\mathcal{L}$ by the row vectors of the following matrix $A = \begin{pmatrix} 1 & 2^{l+1}t_1 & 2^{l+1}t_2 & \cdots & 2^{l+1}t_N \\ 0 & 2^{l+1}n & 0 & \cdots & 0 \\ 0 & 0 & 2^{l+1}n & & 0 \\ \vdots & \vdots & & \ddots & \vdots \\ 0 & 0 & \cdots & \cdots & 2^{l+1}n \end{pmatrix} \in M_{(N+1)\times(N+1)}(\mathbb{Z})$.

So for any lattice vector $\boldsymbol{w} \in \mathcal{L}$, there exists a $\boldsymbol{x} \in \mathbb{Z}^{(N+1)}$ satisfying $\boldsymbol{w} = \boldsymbol{x}A$.

For a non-lattice vector $\boldsymbol{v} = (0, v_1, v_2, ..., v_N) \in \mathbb{Z}^{(N+1)}$ and $\boldsymbol{x} = (d_A, h_1, h_2, ..., h_N) \in \mathbb{Z}^{(N+1)}$, the vector $\boldsymbol{w}$ satisfying $\boldsymbol{w} = \boldsymbol{x}A = (d_A, d_A 2^{l+1}t_1 + h_1 2^{l+1}n, ..., d_A 2^{l+1}t_N + h_N 2^{l+1}n)$ is a lattice vector in $\mathcal{L}$. Hence, for all $i = 1, \cdots, N$, the above Eq. 6 can be transformed into CVP as

$$\|\boldsymbol{w} - \boldsymbol{v}\| \le n\sqrt{N+1},$$

where $n\sqrt{N+1}$ is shorter than the approximation of closest distance $\lambda(\mathcal{L}, \boldsymbol{v})$. Hence, lattice vector $\boldsymbol{v}$ can be obtained in polynomial time based on Babai's CVP approximation algorithm [20], then the private key d_A can also be revealed by $\boldsymbol{v}$.

It has been proved in [10] that the solution of CVP can be determined as long as the number N of signatures satisfies $\log_2 n/l < N$. Hence, knowing l bits of the nonce k, the attacker needs at least $\log_2 n/l$ signatures to reveal the private key.

3 First Differential Fault Attack Against ECDSA

In [3], the authors show how to mount differential fault attack against ECC by enforcing register faults during calculating scalar multiplication (SM) $Q = kG$ with binary algorithm. It assumes that there are a few random bits in the intermediate point (IP) flipped intentionally by fault injection (FI). Based on the difference between the correct result Q and faulty result Q' of SM, the attacker guesses all possibilities of the remaining parts of k after FI and obtains the guessed faulty SM result $\tilde{Q}'$. If $\tilde{Q}' = Q'$, then the corresponding guessed parts of k is the correct one. The attack is also applicable to the wNAF algorithm which is frequently used for calculating the SM because of the fixed base point G in ECDSA.

The attack needs to know the number of flipped bits and guess the position of flipped bits in the faulty IP. The time complexity for guessing is $2^l C_L^\xi 2^\xi$ when the number ξ of flipped bits is known, where L is the bit length of ECC and l is the bit length of parts of k. However, in practical FI experiments, there are usually more random register faulty bits in the IP with unknown position and number. The time complexity will reach up to $\sum_{t=1}^{\xi} 2^l C_L^t 2^t$ when guessing the position and number of the faulty bits. Moreover, the results Q' and Q may not be obtained directly and entirely in many applications of ECC such as ECDSA. Hence, the traditional differential analysis technique will not work. In this section, we will propose a new differential fault attack against ECDSA to solve the above problems.

3.1 Fault Attack Model

In our attack, the fault mode is based on that the SM $Q = kG$ is done with wNAF window algorithm due to its special structure and wide application in L-bit ECDSA signature, and the window width w is generally greater than 3. It is assumed that some random register faults are induced into y-coordinate y_H(or x-coordinate x_H) of the IP $H(x_H, y_H)$ successfully during calculating SM, so that $y_H(x_H)$ is changed into $y_{H'}(x_{H'})$. Meanwhile, the faulty signature results (r, s) are also obtained. It is imperative to note that we have no idea about both the actual number and position of faulty bits in $y_{H'}(x_{H'})$.

Based on the above fault attack model, the basic attack idea can be described as follows. Unlike the attack in [3], we can not execute the SM directly to get both

Table 1. Comparison between the previous attack and ours

Item / Attack	fault attack model					time complexity	maximum number of ξ
	faulty point	ξ	position of faulty bits	$y_{Q'}$	executing correct SM		
attack in [3]	IP	known	unknown	known	yes	$2^l C_L^{\xi} 2^{\xi}$	40
this paper	IP	unknown	unknown	unknown	no	2^l	$\frac{L}{2} - \frac{3.9\sqrt{L}}{2}$

the faulty result $Q'(x_{Q'}, y_{Q'})$ and the correct result Q. Instead, we can determine the value of $x_{Q'}$ and Q by deducing from the faulty signature results (r, s). Then, we only need to guess all possibilities of the remaining parts of k after FI, and the corresponding y-coordinate $\tilde{y}_{H'}$(x-coordinate $\tilde{x}_{H'}$) of the faulty IP can be obtained by solving a equation with one unknown in F_p based on the rules under affine coordinates. Meanwhile, we can also derive the corresponding guessed value $\tilde{y}_H(\tilde{x}_H)$ of $y_H(x_H)$ from the guessed part of k and Q. If the hamming distance between $\tilde{y}_{H'}(\tilde{x}_{H'})$ and $\tilde{y}_H(\tilde{x}_H)$ which is also equivalent to the hamming weights $hw(\tilde{y}_{H'} \oplus \tilde{y}_H)$ (or $hw(\tilde{x}_{H'} \oplus \tilde{x}_H)$) of $\tilde{y}_{H'} \oplus \tilde{y}_H$ (or $\tilde{x}_{H'} \oplus \tilde{x}_H$) is smallest, i.e., $\xi = hw(y_{H'} \oplus y_H) = hw(\tilde{y}_{H'} \oplus \tilde{y}_H)$, then the corresponding guessed parts of k is the correct one. Here the number ξ of faulty bits must be smaller than the upper bound T. Given a number of such faulty signature results with the derived parts of k, the whole secret key can be recovered by lattice attack (LA). Since there is no need to guess the position and number of faulty bits of IP, the time complexity is severely curtailed.

The Table 1 lists the comparison between the previous differential fault attack presented in [3] and ours.

3.2 Description of the Fault Attack

In wNAF window algorithm, k must be first transformed into $\mathrm{NAF}_w(k)$ denoted as $(k_{m-1}, k_{m-2}, \cdots, k_i, \ldots, k_0)_w$, where $-2^{w-1} \leq k_i < 2^{w-1}$ and m is at most 1 more than the length of the binary representation of k. As shown in Algorithm 2, for $i = m-1, \cdots, 0$, we denote the result of point doubling as H_i and the final result as $Q_i = H_i + k_i G$ in i-th iteration of SM respectively. Consequently, the result of SM is denoted as $Q_0\,(x_{Q_0}, y_{Q_0})$.

For the general case in L-bit ECDSA with wNAF window algorithm, for example $w \geq 4$ and $L = 256$, we only focus on the IP H_0 after point doubling in the 0-th iteration of SM as the target of FI in our attack. When there exists a point addition after FI in the 0-th iteration, i.e., the nonce k is odd, then w least significant bits (LSBs) are disclosed by differential analysis. It is sufficient for us to mount lattice attack in practice when knowing $w(w \geq 4)$ bits of nonce k. In contrast, the faulty signatures whose nonces k are even will be eliminated during analysis, since the attack model for recovering parts of k could not be built. In other words, we only consider the case that nonce k is odd. So $Q_0\,(x_{Q_0}, y_{Q_0}) = H_0\,(x_{H_0}, y_{H_0}) + k_0 G$, where $k_0 \neq 0$.

The procedures for our attack mainly consist of the following 5 steps.

Step 1: make some faults and obtain faulty signature results (r, s) **by FI.** As stated above, assume that some random register faults are enforced into the y-coordinate of H_0 in the 0-th iteration of SM, then $H_0(x_{H_0}, y_{H_0})$ is updated as $H_0'(x_{H_0}, y_{H_0'})$. Consequently, the corresponding SM result becomes $Q_0'(x_{Q_0'}, y_{Q_0'})$. In spite of the fact that H_0' is not on the original curve, the equation $Q_0'\left(x_{Q_0'}, y_{Q_0'}\right) = H_0'\left(x_{H_0}, y_{H_0'}\right) + k_0 G$ still holds according to the rules of point addition. In addition, suppose that there is no countermeasure to detect the faults, then the faulty signature results (r, s) can be obtained after FI.

Step 2: obtain Q_0 **from verification.** The equation $Q_0 = \left(es^{-1} \mod n\right) G + (rs^{-1} \mod n)P_A$ can be derived from verification. Thus, the correct SM result Q_0 can be recovered with the known signature results (r, s).

Step 3: obtain $y_{\tilde{H}_0'}$ **by guessing** k_0 **and solving the equation with one unknown.** We guess all the possible values $\tilde{k}_0(-2^{w-1} \leq \tilde{k}_0 \leq 2^{w-1})$ of k_0, and compute SM $\tilde{k}_0 G = (\tilde{x}, \tilde{y})$. Knowing Q_0 and $(\tilde{x}, \tilde{y})$, we can get the corresponding guessed IP $\tilde{H}_0(x_{\tilde{H}_0}, y_{\tilde{H}_0}) = Q_0 - (\tilde{x}, \tilde{y})$.

As stated in **Step 1**, the equation $\tilde{H}_0'\left(x_{\tilde{H}_0}, y_{\tilde{H}_0'}\right) + (\tilde{x}, \tilde{y}) = Q_0'\left(x_{Q_0'}, y_{Q_0'}\right)$ holds if $\tilde{k}_0 = k_0$. Hence, according to the rules of point addition under affine coordinates, we have

$$x_{Q_0'} = \lambda^2 - x_{\tilde{H}_0} - \tilde{x} \mod \text{p}. \tag{7}$$

Where $\lambda = \frac{y_{\tilde{H}_0'} - \tilde{y}}{x_{\tilde{H}_0} - \tilde{x}} \mod \text{p}$. The above equation can be rewritten as the following quadric equation in F_p.

$$\left(y_{\tilde{H}_0'} - \tilde{y}\right)^2 = \left(x_{Q_0'} + x_{\tilde{H}_0} + \tilde{x}\right)\left(x_{\tilde{H}_0} - \tilde{x}\right)^2 \mod \text{p} \tag{8}$$

Where $x_{Q_0'}$ can be derived from $x_{Q_0'} = r \mod n$ in Algorithm 3 and has at most 2 solutions.

As only the y-coordinate $y_{\tilde{H}_0'}$ of the guessed faulty IP $\tilde{H}_0'$ is unknown, we can obtain at most 4 candidates $y_{\tilde{H}_0'}$ by solving the quadric Eq. 8. If the equation has no solution in F_p, then the guessed $\tilde{k}_0$ is wrong. This can eliminate most of the wrong guessed $\tilde{k}_0$.

Step 4: determine k_0 **by comparing** $hw(y_{\tilde{H}_0} \oplus y_{\tilde{H}_0'})$. If the hamming distance $hw(y_{\tilde{H}_0} \oplus y_{\tilde{H}_0'})$ between $y_{\tilde{H}_0}$ and $y_{\tilde{H}_0'}$ is smallest, i.e., $\xi = hw(y_{H_0} \oplus y_{H_0'}) = hw(y_{\tilde{H}_0} \oplus y_{\tilde{H}_0'})$, then the corresponding guessed $\tilde{k}_0$ is the correct k_0. Note that k_0 can be determined uniquely with smallest hamming distance only when the number of faulty bits is smaller than the upper bound T. Otherwise, it will not be distinguished from the wrong guessed values by comparing $hw(y_{\tilde{H}_0} \oplus y_{\tilde{H}_0'})$.

In addition, if we enforce some random register faults into the x-coordinate of the IP $H_0(x_{H_0}, y_{H_0})$ by FI, i.e., $H_0(x_{H_0}, y_{H_0})$ is rewritten as $H_0'(x_{H_0'}, y_{H_0})$, then the above Eq. 8 will be transformed into the following cubic equation.

$$(y_{\tilde{H}_0} - \tilde{y})^2 = (x_{Q_0'} + x_{\tilde{H}_0'} + \tilde{x})\left(x_{\tilde{H}_0'} - \tilde{x}\right)^2 \mod p \tag{9}$$

Where only the guessed value $x_{\tilde{H}'_0}$ of $x_{H'_0}$ is unknown in F_p. In the same way, k_0 also can be determined by solving the equation and comparing $hw(x_{\tilde{H}'_0} \oplus x_{\tilde{H}_0})$.

Step 5: recover d_A by LA. If this attack is applied on $2N(N > L/w + 1)$ signatures, at least w LSBs of the nonces in about N signatures($k_0 \neq 0$) can be revealed. The rest of signatures($k_0 = 0$) are eliminated during solving equation. Naturally, we can recover the private key d_A by LA.

3.3 Analysis of the Attack

Firstly, we will discuss the upper bound T of the number ξ of faulty bits (namely hamming distance) in our attack. If the guessed $\tilde{k}_0$ is wrong, the hamming distance $\tilde{\xi}$ between intermediates $\tilde{y}_{H_0}$ and $\tilde{y}_{H'_0}$ seems random and follows discrete binomial distribution with probability $\frac{1}{2}$, mean value $\frac{1}{2}L$ and variance $\frac{1}{4}L$, where L is the bit length of ECDSA. Moreover, the limiting distribution of binomial distribution with constant probability obeys approximatively Gaussian distribution $X \sim N\left(\frac{1}{2}L, \frac{1}{4}L\right)$. Thus the approximate probability of all the wrong assumptions leading $\xi > T$ can be presented as

$$P\left(T < \tilde{\xi} < L \middle| \tilde{k}_0 \neq k_0\right) = 1 - \frac{1}{2^L}\sum_{j=0}^{T} C_L^j \approx \Phi\left(\frac{L-\frac{L}{2}}{\sqrt{\frac{L}{4}}}\right) - \Phi\left(\frac{T-\frac{L}{2}}{\sqrt{\frac{L}{4}}}\right) \\ = \Phi\left(\sqrt{L}\right) - \Phi\left(\frac{2T}{\sqrt{L}} - \sqrt{L}\right) \tag{10}$$

According to cumulative distribution, $\sqrt{L}$ is definitely larger than 3.9, so $\Phi\left(\sqrt{L}\right) = 1$, where $\Phi(3.9) = 1$. To ensure that the above probability P is equal to 1, $\Phi\left(\frac{2T}{\sqrt{L}} - \sqrt{L}\right)$ must be equal to 0. Hence, $\sqrt{L} - \frac{2T}{\sqrt{L}} \geq 3.9$, i.e., $T \leq \frac{L}{2} - \frac{3.9\sqrt{L}}{2}$. Supposing $L = 256$, ξ should be smaller than $T = 96$, which can be easily achieved in FI experiments.

Next, we will analyse the success rate of FI when giving a fixed position and time point. It is easy to find the right position because the memory area of H_0 is fixed, such as in one general area of RAM. However, it is impossible to determine the exact time point for every FI except to rely on the probability of k, since the nonce k is unknown and random before FI in every ECDSA signature. Thus, before FI, we must preset a fixed time point which has highest probability to be just after the point doubling in 0-th iteration of SM. In a L-bit ECDSA, let m denote the length of $\text{NAF}_w(k)$ and β denote the number of nonzero values in the sequence of $\text{NAF}_w(k)$ respectively, then the probability $P(\text{NAF}_w(k)|k_0 \neq 0, 1 < m \leq L+1, 1 < \beta \leq m/w)$ is $C_{\alpha+m-w\alpha-2}^{m-w\alpha-1}(\frac{1}{2})^{L+\alpha-w\alpha}$, where $\alpha = \beta - 1$. In addition, it is known that the probability is $\left(\frac{1}{2}\right)^{i+1}$ when the binary bit length μ of nonce k is equal to $L - i$ for $i \in \{0, \ldots, L\}$. Consequently, for $\text{NAF}_w(k)$ with length m, we can conclude that $m \in \{L+1, L, \ldots, L-w+2\}$ has probability $\frac{1}{w+1}$, and $m \in \{L-w+1, \ldots, 0\}$ has probability $\frac{1}{w+1}(\frac{1}{2})^{L+2-m-w}$. Moreover, the average density of nonzero value in the sequence of $\text{NAF}_w(k)$ is about $\frac{1}{w+1}$ and the processing time for a point doubling or addition is constant. It implies that the fixed time point just after $m \in \{L+1, L, \ldots, L-w+2\}$ point doubling and $\alpha = m/(w+1)$ point addition is the best selection for FI. For example, we consider the case that $w = 8$ and $m = \mu = L = 256$, then the time after 256 point doubling and 28 point addition is the right time point with probability $0.023 (k_0 \neq 0)$. So we need almost 1800 signatures to mount attack successfully.

Finally, for the special case ($w < 4$) of wNAF algorithm, the attack is also feasible. For example, it is assumed that y-coordinate y_{H_i} of H_i in the i-th round iteration of SM has some bits flipped by FI, then y_{H_i} is rewritten as $y_{H_i'}$, where i is usually greater than $2w$. Like the method above, guessing all the possible values of the remaining parts of k, we also can deduce a high order equation with the unknown faulty y-coordinate $y_{H_i'}$ of the faulty IP in F_p after the iterations step by step from i to 0. It can be solved by the method presented in [22]. Analogously, we can determine the correct value of parts of k by solving the equation and comparing the derived $y_{H_i'}$ with the corresponding y_{H_i}. By the same way, the attack against binary algorithm is almost same except the different position and time point of FI.

4 Second Differential Fault Attack Against ECDSA

Clearly, as in most of fault attack methods, the target of fault injection (FI) is vital to success, and is usually located during calculating scalar multiplication (SM). In this section, we will propose a kind of new differential fault attack against ECDSA and the SM is still calculated with wNAF window algorithm. The target is not located during calculating scalar multiplication (SM), but during calculating wNAF transformation of k. Moreover, we adopt the way of skipping instructions to implement FI. Since the FI is implemented at the beginning of wNAF transformation, it is easier to locate the target for FI experiments in ECDSA.

4.1 Fault Attack Model

As shown in Algorithm 1, we assume the instruction $i = i+1$ or $k = k/2$ in step 7 is skipped by FI during executing i-th iteration of wNAF transformation. This indicates that the following transformation result $\mathrm{NAF}_w(k)'$ is not equivalent to the original k. $\mathrm{NAF}_w(k)'$ as scalar is used for calculating SM, while k is called in computing $s = k^{-1}(e + d_A r) \mod n$ for the sake of efficiency. Thus, a differential relation between $Q' = \mathrm{NAF}_w(k)'G$ and $Q = kG$ can be built, and it is easy to get at least $i+1$ least significant bits (LSBs) of the nonce k by differential analysis.

Under above assumption and analysis, we can employ lattice attack (LA) to recover the private key used in ECDSA signature.

4.2 Description of the Fault Attack

As mentioned above, the nonce k should be first transformed into $\mathrm{NAF}_w(k) = (k_{m-1}, \cdots, k_{i+1}, k_i, k_{i-1}, \cdots, k_0)_w$ by wNAF transformation. However, assume that the instruction $i = i + 1$ is skipped deliberately by FI during i-th iteration of wNAF transformation, then the transformed result will be changed into the faulty $\mathrm{NAF}_w(k)' = (k_{m-1}, \cdots, k_{i+1}, k_{i-1}, \cdots, k_0)_w$ rather than the correct $\mathrm{NAF}_w(k)$. Finally, we also get the faulty signature results (r, s).

Hence, we have the following computations.

$$\begin{aligned} &\mathrm{NAF}_w(k)' = (k_{m-1}, \cdots, k_{i+1})_w 2^i + (k_{i-1}, \cdots, k_0)_w \\ &2\mathrm{NAF}_w(k)' = k + (-k_i, k_{i-1}, \cdots, k_0)_w \\ &2Q' = Q + (-k_i, k_{i-1}, \cdots, k_0)_w G \end{aligned} \tag{11}$$

Let $\tilde{k} = (-k_i, k_{i-1}, \cdots, k_0)_w$, then the following differential equation only relies on the point G and $\tilde{k}$.

$$2Q' - Q = \tilde{k}G \tag{12}$$

As mentioned above, since the nonce k is used in step 6 of Algorithm 3 for the sake of efficiency, then the correct output Q can be deduced by the equation $Q = (es^{-1} \mod n)\, G + (rs^{-1} \mod n)P_A$.

Guessing all possibilities of $\tilde{k} \in [-\sum_{j=0}^{i/w+1} 2^{w+i-jw}, \sum_{j=0}^{i/w+1} 2^{w+i-jw})$ and substituting them into the above equation respectively, the real $\tilde{k}$ can be determined uniquely when the equation is true, that is, at least $i + 1$ LSBs of nonce k are disclosed.

Similarly, if the instruction $k = k/2$ is skipped in i-th iteration of wNAF transformation, then the transformed result is changed into $\mathrm{NAF}_w(k)' = (k_{m-1}, \cdots, k_{i+1}, 0, k_i, \cdots, k_0)_w$. Let $\tilde{k} = (k_i, \cdots, k_0)_w$, then the following differential equations can be deduced.

$$\begin{aligned} &\mathrm{NAF}_w(k)' = (k_{m-1}, \cdots, k_{i+1})_w 2^{i+2} + (k_i, \cdots, k_0)_w = 2k - \tilde{k} \\ &2Q - Q' = \tilde{k}G \end{aligned} \tag{13}$$

By the same way as above, we can obtained at least $i + 1$ LSBs of nonce k. In addition, if both of instructions $k = k/2$ and $i = i+1$ are skipped, the differential analysis still works.

After applying this attack on enough signatures to reveal at least $i + 1$ LSBs of their nonces k, we can derive the private key d_A used in signature by LA.

4.3 Analysis of the Attack

In the following part, we will analyze the time complexity of attack and the success rate of FI. As mentioned above, the time complexity is $O(2^{w-2+i})$ when recovering i LSBs of nonce k. In 256-bit ECDSA, for the general case $w > 3$, $i = w-1$ is sufficient to satisfy the requirement for LA with complexity $O(2^{2w-3})$. As for the case $w \leq 3$, it is needed to meet $i \geq 2w - 1$ and the complexity is $O(2^{3w-3})$. It depends on the attacker. More bigger i can result in more known bits of k, and it is easier for LA, but the complexity also becomes bigger.

In this attack, as same as the first attack, it is crucial for FI to select a right time point with high success probability. As mentioned above, the faults are enforce in i-iteration of wNAF transformation. If it is assumed that $i+1=\beta w$, clearly, the probability $P(\mathrm{NAF}_w(k)|k_{wj+t_j}\neq 0, t_{j+1}-t_j\geq w)$ that there is a nonzero value k_{wj+t_j} in every w bits of $\mathrm{NAF}_w(k)$ is highest, for $j\in\{0,\cdots,\beta-1\}$ and $0\leq t_j\leq w-1$. Here β is the number of nonzero values in sequence $\{k_i,\ldots,k_0\}$. Then we can obtain

$$P(\mathrm{NAF}_w(k)|k_{wj+t_j}\neq 0, t_{j+1}-t_j\geq w)=\sum_{x=0}^{w-1}\left(\tfrac{1}{2}\right)^{\beta}C^{x}_{\beta+x-1}\left(\tfrac{1}{2}\right)^{x} \tag{14}$$

Moreover, for $v\in\{0,\ldots,m-1\}$, it is known that the processing time for an iteration denoted by $C_1(C_2)$ is fixed when k_v is nonzero(zero) value during transformation. Thereby, the fixed time point $\beta C_1+(i+1-\beta)C_2-S$ is the best choice for FI, in which the offset time S is just the execution time of the skipped instruction. For example, in 256-bit ECDSA, if $w=8$, we usually consider the condition that $i=7$ and $\beta=1$. When the FI time is C_1+7C_2-S, the success rate $\frac{255}{256}$ is approximately equal to 1.

5 Laser Injection and Simulation Experiments

In this section, real laser injection and simulation experiments are implemented to verify the feasibility of our proposed attacks. As is shown in Fig. 1, we make use of the laser injection device from Riscure Company for our experiments. The computation of SM kG is implemented in a smart card whose CPU frequency is 14 MHz, and the bus width is 32-bit. The key length of ECDSA is 256-bit. The final lattice attack is performed in a computer with Inter Core i7-3770 at 3.4 GHz.

For the first fault attack, we first analyze the rate that the results of FI satisfy $hw(y_{H_0}\oplus y_{H_0'})<T$ by experiments. We use the laser injection device to induce some faults into the intermediate point H_0 of SM $Q=kG$, then the y-coordinate y_{H_0} of H_0 is rewritten into $y_{H_0'}$. In experiments, we implement 552 calculations of SM ($Q=kG$), in which the nonces are different from each other and the bit length of curve is 256. By FI experiments, we find out there are 330 cases satisfying $hw(y_{H_0}\oplus y_{H_0'})<96$, which account for about 60 % of the total cases. Moreover, among the 330 calculations, most of the hamming distance (HD) values are actually less than 30. The above statistic of HD values could be illustrated by Figs. 2 and 3. In Fig. 2, the x-coordinate represents the x-th computation of SM, and the y-coordinate represents the HD value after FI. The red line shows the boundary value 96. In Fig. 3, the x-coordinate represents $hw(y_{H_0}\oplus y_{H_0'})$, and the y-coordinate represents the corresponding number of x. In Sect. 3, it has been proved that partial bits of the nonce can be determined as long as the $hw(y_{H_0}\oplus y_{H_0'})$ is less than 96. Hence, the first fault attack can be mounted with 60 % success probability for real fault injection.

Next, in order to analyze the number of signatures needed for FI and verify the correctness of theoretical success rate of FI, we simulate respectively the FI experiments toward 50000 256-bit ECDSA signatures for $w=3,\ldots,8$. They are all based on the assumption that $hw(y_{H_0}\oplus y_{H_0'})<96$. As stated in Sect. 3,

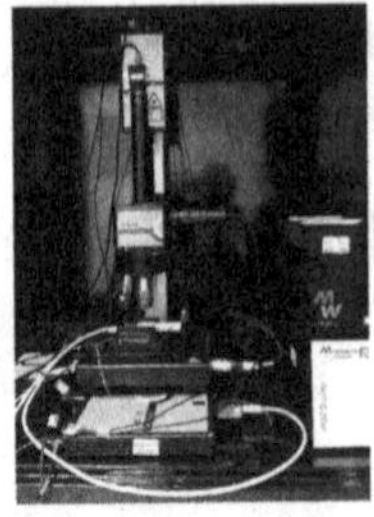

Fig. 1. Laser injection platform

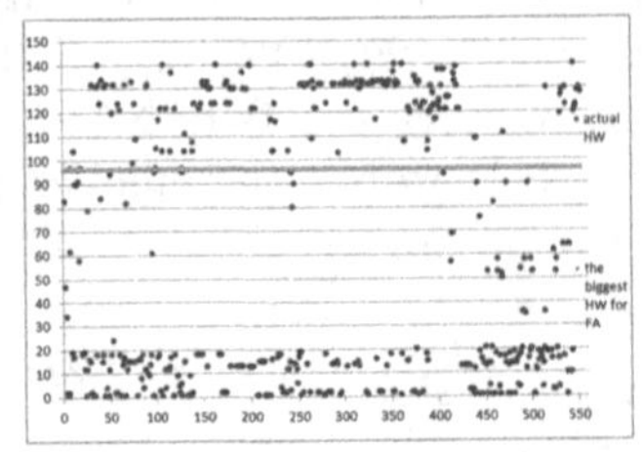

Fig. 2. HD values of SM

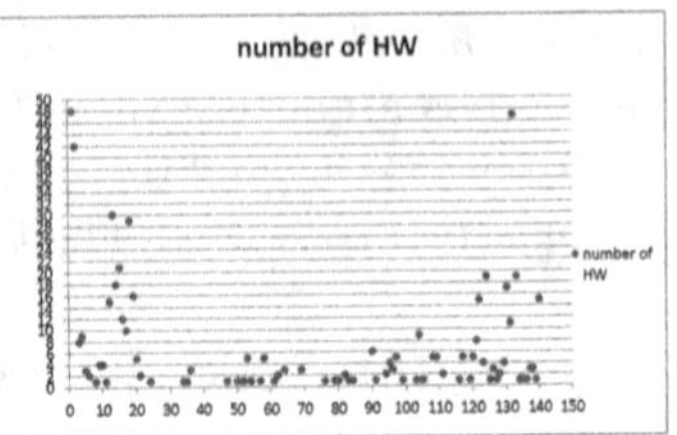

Fig. 3. The number of HD values

μ represents the binary length of nonce k. m represents the length of sequence of $\mathrm{NAF}_w(k)$. $\beta = \alpha + 1$ represents the number of nonzero value in the sequence of $\mathrm{NAF}_w(k)$, where $\alpha = m/(w+1)$. Obviously, we only need to analyze the best case, i.e., $\mu = m = 256, \alpha = 256/(w+1)$, and the theoretical success rate σ is $C_{254+(1-w)\alpha}^{255-w\alpha}(\frac{1}{2})^{256+(1-w)\alpha}$. Finally, we summarize out the following Table 2 by experiments for $w = 3, \ldots, 8$. As shown in Table 2, there are N available signatures with right time for FI in 5000 signatures, i.e., the N signatures satisfy that there are 256 point doubling, $256/(w+1)+1$ point addition, and $k_0 \neq 0$ in $\mathrm{NAF}_w(k)$. N' represents the approximate number of signatures which is actually needed for our attack in practical experiments. From the results, the number of signatures needed is reasonable for practical experiments, and the experimental success rate $N/50000$ is almost equal to the theoretical one.

Finally, we mount the attack based on fplll-4.0 Lattice Reduction Library [23] for checking the validity of the upper bound of ξ. It is assumed that $w = 8$, $L = 256$. We increase the number ξ of random faulty bits one by one starting at 1 in simulation attack experiments. All the tests have essentially validated the fact that the correct k_0 can be distinguished and the LA is successful till $hw(y_{H_0} \oplus y_{H_0'}) > 100$. The actual upper bound T is better than the theoretical one.

For the second attack, some similar simulation experiments for FI are also implemented. For $w = 2, \ldots, 8$, there are 50000 FI experiments done respectively

Table 2. Experimental results for the first attack ($L = \mu = m = 256, \alpha = 256/(w+1)$)

Item	w	β	N	$N/50000$	σ	N'
1	3	65	904	0.018	0.018	5000
2	4	52	962	0.019	0.020	4200
3	5	43	963	0.019	0.020	3200
4	6	37	978	0.020	0.021	2400
5	7	33	1305	0.026	0.025	1800
6	8	29	1145	0.023	0.023	1800

Table 3. Experimental results for the second attack ($L = 256, i + 1 = w\beta$)

Item	w	i	β	N	$N/50000$	σ	N'
1	2	7	4	9388	0.188	0.188	220
2	3	8	3	24881	0.498	0.500	70
3	4	7	2	40554	0.811	0.813	50
4	5	9	2	44531	0.891	0.891	40
5	6	5	1	49215	0.984	0.984	50
6	7	6	1	49602	0.992	0.992	45
7	8	7	1	49791	0.996	0.996	40

in 256-bit ECDSA signature. As stated in Sect. 4, we implement the FI experiments in the i-th iteration of wNAF transformation, where the selection of i relies on the size of w. We only consider the best case that there is one nonzero value in every w-bit block of sequence $\{k_i, \ldots, k_0\}$, where $i+1 = w\beta$. That is, the time point for FI experiments is $\beta C_1 + (i+1-\beta)C_2 - S$ and the theoretical success rate σ is $\sum_{x=0}^{w-1} \left(\frac{1}{2}\right)^{\beta} C_{\beta+x-1}^{x} \left(\frac{1}{2}\right)^{x}$. As shown in Table 3, the number N of successful fault injections(namely the available number of signatures) is almost equal to 50000 when $w > 5$, and the number N' of signatures needed in practical experiments is obviously less than the one in the first attack because of the higher success rate. Likewise, the experimental success rate $N/50000$ is approximately equal to the theoretical one. Finally, according to the above selected i and β, we mount the lattice attacks successfully with the N available signatures.

6 Conclusion

In this paper, two new lattice-based differential fault attacks against ECDSA with wNAF algorithm of scalar multiplication are presented. The first attack assumes that there are some random bits in x/y-coordinate of the IP during calculating SM flipped by FI. As long as the number of random faulty bits in the IP is smaller than the upper bound $\frac{L-3.9\sqrt{L}}{2}$, the nonce k can be partially deduced by guessing technique and solving the equation with one unknown in F_p based on the rules under affine coordinate. In the second attack, the FI targets are located during wNAF transformation of k rather than the calculation of SM. If the targets are skipped by FI, we can build some differential fault attack models to retrieve parts of k. Given a number of such faulty signature results with the known parts of nonces, the attacker can recover the final private key by using lattice attack. The following laser injection and simulation experiments also verify the feasibility and correctness of our proposed attack methods. In addition, if the calculation of SM $Q = kG$ is base on other coordinate systems such as Jacobian and projective coordinates, it is also vulnerable to the first fault attack as long as the z-coordinate of faulty result Q' is known. Furthermore, if all the coordinate values of Q' are known, the equation with one unknown in the first attack will become more simple to be solved.

Acknowledgments. We thank the anonymous referees for their careful reading and insightful comments. This work is supported by the National Science and Technology Major Project (No. 2014ZX01032401-001) and the National Basic Research Program of China (No. 2013CB338002).

References

1. Coron, J.-S.: Resistance against differential power analysis for elliptic curve cryptosystems. In: Koç, Ç.K., Paar, C. (eds.) CHES 1999. LNCS, vol. 1717, pp. 292–302. Springer, Heidelberg (1999)
2. Boneh, D., DeMillo, R.A., Lipton, R.J.: On the importance of checking cryptographic protocols for faults. In: Fumy, W. (ed.) EUROCRYPT 1997. LNCS, vol. 1233, pp. 37–51. Springer, Heidelberg (1997)
3. Biehl, I., Meyer, B., Müller, V.: Differential fault attacks on elliptic curve cryptosystems. In: Bellare, M. (ed.) CRYPTO 2000. LNCS, vol. 1880, pp. 131–146. Springer, Heidelberg (2000)
4. Hemme, L.: A differential fault attack against early rounds of (Triple-)DES. In: Joye, M., Quisquater, J.-J. (eds.) CHES 2004. LNCS, vol. 3156, pp. 254–267. Springer, Heidelberg (2004)
5. Chen, C.N., Yen, S.M.: Differential fault analysis on AES key schedule and some countermeasures. In: Safavi-Naini, R., Seberry, J. (eds.) ACISP 2003. LNCS, vol. 2727. Springer, Heidelberg (2003)
6. Biham, E., Granboulan, L., Nguyên, P.Q.: Impossible fault analysis of RC4 and differential fault analysis of RC4. In: Gilbert, H., Handschuh, H. (eds.) FSE 2005. LNCS, vol. 3557, pp. 359–367. Springer, Heidelberg (2005)
7. Blömer, J., Otto, M., Seifert, J.-P.: Sign change fault attacks on elliptic curve cryptosystems. In: Breveglieri, L., Koren, I., Naccache, D., Seifert, J.-P. (eds.) FDTC 2006. LNCS, vol. 4236, pp. 36–52. Springer, Heidelberg (2006)
8. Schmidt, J., Medwed, M.: A fault attack on ECDSA. In: 2009 Workshop on Fault Diagnosis and Tolerance in Cryptography (FDTC), pp. 93–99. IEEE (2009)
9. Johnson, D., Menezes, A., Vanstone, S.: The elliptic curve digital signature algorithm (ECDSA). Int. J. Inf. Secur. **1**(1), 36–63 (2001)
10. Howgrave-Graham, N., Smart, N.P.: Lattice attacks on digital signature schemes. Des. Codes Crypt. **23**(3), 283–290 (2001)
11. Nguyen, P.Q., Shparlinski, I.E.: The insecurity of the elliptic curve digital signature algorithm with partially known nonces. J. Cryptology **15**(3), 151–176 (2002)
12. Liu, M., Chen, J., Li, H.: Partially known nonces and fault injection attacks on SM2 signature algorithm. In: Lin, D., Xu, S., Yung, M. (eds.) Inscrypt 2013. LNCS, vol. 8567, pp. 343–358. Springer, Heidelberg (2014)
13. Leadbitter, P.J., Page, D.L., Smart, N.P.: Attacking DSA under a repeated bits assumption. In: Joye, M., Quisquater, J.-J. (eds.) CHES 2004. LNCS, vol. 3156, pp. 428–440. Springer, Heidelberg (2004)
14. Faugère, J.-C., Goyet, C., Renault, G.: Attacking (EC)DSA given only an implicit hint. In: Knudsen, L.R., Wu, H. (eds.) SAC 2012. LNCS, vol. 7707, pp. 252–274. Springer, Heidelberg (2013)
15. Naccache, D., Nguyên, P.Q., Tunstall, M., Whelan, C.: Experimenting with faults, lattices and the DSA. In: Vaudenay, S. (ed.) PKC 2005. LNCS, vol. 3386, pp. 16–28. Springer, Heidelberg (2005)
16. Connell, I.: Elliptic curve handbook (1996) (Preprint)
17. Hankerson, D., Menezes, A.J., Vanstone, S.: Guide to elliptic curve cryptography. Comput. Rev. **46**(1), 13 (2005)
18. Joux, A., Stern, J.: Lattice reduction: a toolbox for the cryptanalyst. J. Cryptology **11**(3), 161–185 (1998)
19. Joux, A.: Algorithmic Cryptanalysis. CRC Press, Boca Raton (2009)

20. Babai, L.: On lovász' lattice reduction and the nearest lattice point problem. Combinatorica **6**(1), 1–13 (1986)
21. Boneh, D., Venkatesan, R.: Hardness of computing the most significant bits of secret keys in diffie-hellman and related schemes. In: Koblitz, N. (ed.) CRYPTO 1996. LNCS, vol. 1109, pp. 129–142. Springer, Heidelberg (1996)
22. Giraud, C.: DFA on AES. In: Dobbertin, H., Rijmen, V., Sowa, A. (eds.) AES 2005. LNCS, vol. 3373, pp. 27–41. Springer, Heidelberg (2005)
23. Stehlé, D., Martin Albrecht, D.C.: fplll-4.0 Lattice Reduction Library (2012). https://github.com/dstehle/fplll

Maximum Likelihood-Based Key Recovery Algorithm from Decayed Key Schedules

Tomoyuki Tanigaki(✉) and Noboru Kunihiro

The University of Tokyo, Chiba, Japan
5040434024@edu.k.u-tokyo.ac.jp

Abstract. A cold boot attack is a kind of side-channel attack that exploits a property of dynamic random-access memory. Using a cold boot attack, attackers can extract decayed key material from a running computer's memory, which is a serious threat to computers using disk encryption software. Previously, an algorithm was presented that recovers a secret key from a decayed Advanced Encryption Standard key schedule. However, this method cannot recover a secret key if reverse bit flipping occurs, even in only one position, because this algorithm assumes a perfect asymmetric decay model. To remedy this limitation, we propose an algorithm based on the maximum likelihood approach, which can recover a secret key in an imperfect asymmetric decay model, i.e., where bit flipping occurs in both directions. We also give the theoretical bound of our algorithm and verify the validity thereof.

Keywords: AES · Cold boot attack · Maximum likelihood

1 Introduction

1.1 Cold Boot Attacks

A dynamic random-access memory (DRAM) loses its contents when the computer's power is turned off. However, for several seconds after the power has been turned off, the DRAM retains its contents. Moreover, if the memory is kept at a low temperature, the data in the DRAM can be retrieved for minutes or even hours.

A cold boot attack is a kind of side-channel attack that exploits the DRAM remanence effect to extract key material from a running computer. Because data can be extracted from the memory, this is a serious threat even if the target computer uses disk encryption software such as BitLocker or TrueCrypt. For example, if attackers have physical access to the computer via the disk encryption system, they can recover the secret key from the memory image and decrypt the data on the encrypted disk.

Although many disk encryption software packages use block ciphers such as Advanced Encryption Standard (AES) and Serpent, these block ciphers have a high risk for a cold boot attack. Key schedules generated by the block ciphers are

S. Kwon and A. Yun (Eds.): ICISC 2015, LNCS 9558, pp. 314–328, 2016.
DOI: 10.1007/978-3-319-30840-1_20

stored in the running computer's memory to perform fast encryption, thus making it possible for attackers to extract key schedules from the memory. Redundancy of these key schedules makes a cold boot attack more serious.

Halderman et al. [2] demonstrated that it is practically possible to extract data from a memory after turning off the power and cooling the memory. They loaded a bit pattern into the memory and then, while the computer was still running, cooled the memory to −50°C using a "canned air" product. Having kept the computer at the cold temperature, they turned on the power and extracted the data from the memory. They observed that 99.9 % of the bit patterns remained in the extracted image after turning the power off for 60 s. They also observed that decay tends to occur in a single direction, either $0 \rightarrow 1$ or $1 \rightarrow 0$, within the memory region. Their experiments showed that the probability of opposite bit flipping is less than 0.1 %.

1.2 Related Works

Many methods have been proposed to recover the secret key from decayed key material. First, we model decay patterns in a cold boot attack and then, we introduce existing methods for solving the key recovery problem.

We define δ_0 as the probability of bit flipping from 1 to 0 and δ_1 as the probability of reverse bit flipping (i.e., from 0 to 1). We model decay patterns as the following two cases.

- Perfect asymmetric decay model: $\delta_0 > \delta_1 = 0$.
- Imperfect asymmetric decay model: $\delta_0 > \delta_1 > 0$.

Previous works fixed $\delta_1 = 0.001$ in the imperfect asymmetric decay model because experiments by Halderman et al. showed that δ_1 is less than 0.001. Thus, we also fix $\delta_1 = 0.001$ in this study.

Key Recovery Methods for AES. Halderman et al. [2] presented a key recovery algorithm for AES-128 in the imperfect asymmetric decay model. They consider a *slice*, consisting of four specific bytes of the first round key and three relevant bytes of the second round key determined by the four bytes of the first round key according to the AES-128 key schedule algorithm. Their algorithm first calculates the likelihood of each slice and then expands the candidates of the correct secret key into the key schedule in descending order of likelihood. The algorithm outputs the key schedule whose likelihood is sufficiently high. This algorithm can recover the secret keys for $\delta_0 = 0.15$ within a second and about half of the secret keys for $\delta_0 = 0.3$ within 300 s.

Tsow [11] proposed an algorithm that can recover a secret key in the perfect asymmetric decay model. His algorithm consists of an expansion phase and a pruning phase. In each expansion phase, it guesses the byte of a specific position in a key schedule and computes the other bytes according to the AES key schedule algorithm. In each pruning phase, the algorithm prunes candidate key schedules with a zero in the bit position where the decayed key schedule has a one. In other words, it deletes those candidates contradicting the perfect asymmetric decay model. The algorithm can recover a secret key for $\delta_0 = 0.7$ within 300 s.

Some methods make use of SAT solvers or non-linear algebraic equations with noise. Kamal and Youseff [6] modeled the key recovery problem in a perfect asymmetric decay model as a Boolean SAT problem. Liao et al. [9] improved the method of Kamal and Youseff by using a MaxSAT solver with the resulting method able to recover a key in the imperfect asymmetric decay model. Albert and Cid [1] reduced the key recovery problem to a Max-PoSSo problem, which involves solving polynomial systems with noise. They further transformed the Max-PoSSo problem into a mixed-integer programming (MIP) problem and recovered a key using an MIP solver. Their method can be applied to Serpent. The method of Huang and Lin [5], based on the incremental solving and backtracking search algorithm, improves that of Albert and Cid.

Key Recovery Methods for RSA. Some key recovery algorithms for RSA private keys have been proposed. Let (N, e) be the public keys with the corresponding private keys (p, q, d, d_p, d_q) stored in the memory, where d_p and d_q are used to realize fast decryption by the Chinese Remainder Theorem. The key recovery problem for RSA involves recovering private keys given a public key and decayed private keys.

Heninger and Shacham [4] presented an algorithm that recovers secret keys given a random fraction of their bits. They showed that their algorithm can recover private keys if more than 27 % of the correct keys remain. Henecka et al. [3] proposed an algorithm that recovers a private key efficiently in the case of symmetric decay, i.e., $\delta_0 = \delta_1$. Their algorithm can recover private keys for $\delta_0 = \delta_1 < 0.237$ in polynomial time of the order $\log N$ with a success rate close to one. The algorithm makes use of the Hamming distance in exploring the candidate space and prunes candidate keys whose Hamming distances from the decayed keys are greater than a threshold value.

Paterson et al. [10] improved the method of Henecka et al. [3]. Their method, based on coding theory, can be applied to the imperfect asymmetric decay model. The algorithm prunes candidate keys using the maximum likelihood estimate and can recover the keys for $\delta_0 = 0.5$ within 23 s. Kunihiro and Honda [8] generalized the algorithm of Paterson et al. and adapted it for analog data. They also proposed an algorithm that recovers secret keys without the decay distribution and gave the theoretical bound of the success rates of their algorithms.

1.3 Our Contributions

In this paper, we propose a new algorithm for the imperfect asymmetric decay model and give a theoretical analysis thereof. Previous works focusing on AES did not analyze the proposed methods from a theoretical perspective. In contrast, some researchers focusing on RSA presented theoretical analyses of their algorithms. Considering the research on RSA, we propose a new key recovery algorithm for AES, which is analyzed and verified experimentally.

First, we present our algorithm inspired by [8,10] and based on maximum likelihood. The algorithm, which can naturally be applied to the imperfect asymmetric decay model, consists of an expansion phase and a pruning phase, and explores a 256-ary tree whose nodes correspond to the candidate key schedules. The expansion phase of the algorithm is the same as that of Tsow's algorithm [11]. It guesses the byte in a specific byte position and generates the candidates from each remaining candidate in the previous pruning phase. In the pruning phase, having computed the log-likelihoods of the candidates, the algorithm keeps the L candidates with the highest log-likelihood and prunes the remaining candidates. After the final pruning phase, it keeps L candidates of the 0th round keys (i.e., the secret keys) and outputs the correct key if it is among the candidates.

We give the information theoretic bound for the algorithm in a similar way to that in [8]. We introduce some assumptions on key schedules and show that the error rate of the algorithm is bounded by L under a certain condition. For example, in the case of AES-128, our algorithm can recover a secret key with high probability for large L and $\delta_0 < 0.822$.

We implemented our algorithm for AES-128, AES-192, and AES-256. In particular, because previous works did not experiment with AES-192, we first implemented the algorithm for this standard; however, in practice the algorithm can be applied to any key lengths of AES. In addition, the experimental results show that the algorithm can recover a secret key for $\delta_0 \leq 0.75$ and $L = 4096$, thereby confirming that the theoretical bound is valid.

Organization. In Sect. 2, we describe the AES key schedule algorithm and give an overview of Tsow's algorithm. In Sect. 3, we propose an algorithm based on the maximum likelihood approach and give the theoretical bound for it. In Sect. 4, we implement our algorithm for AES-128, AES-192, and AES-256, and discuss the validity of the theoretical bound in Sect. 3.

2 Preliminaries

In this section, we describe the AES key schedule algorithm and Tsow's key recovery algorithm [11]. Although the former algorithm can be applied to AES-128, AES-192, and AES-256, for simplicity, we introduce the case for AES-128.

2.1 AES-128 Key Schedule

We use the following notation for the AES-128 key schedule algorithm. Let $K \in \{0,1\}^{11\times 128}$ be the entire key schedule consisting of 11 round keys with length 128 bits. We define K^r, K^r_i, and $K^r_{i,j}$ as the r-th round key of K, the i-th word of K^r, and j-th byte of K^r_i, respectively, where $0 \leq r \leq 10$, $0 \leq i, j \leq 3$. The AES substitution box is denoted by $\mathrm{sbox}(\cdot) : \{0,1\}^8 \rightarrow \{0,1\}^8$.

We define $S(K_i^r) = (\text{sbox}(K_{i,0}^r), \text{sbox}(K_{i,2}^r), \text{sbox}(K_{i,2}^r), \text{sbox}(K_{i,3}^r))$. The function $\text{rot}(\cdot) : \{0,1\}^{32} \to \{0,1\}^{32}$ is the left circular shift of 8-bit positions; that is, $\text{rot}(K_{i,0}^r, K_{i,1}^r, K_{i,2}^r, K_{i,3}^r) = (K_{i,1}^r, K_{i,2}^r, K_{i,3}^r, K_{i,0}^r)$. The r-th round constant is denoted by Rcon$[r]$.

The 0th round key is defined as a 128-bit secret key itself and the other round keys are derived by the following equations.

$$\begin{cases} K_0^r = K_0^{r-1} \oplus S(\text{rot}(K_3^{r-1})) \oplus \text{Rcon}[r] \\ K_i^r = K_{i-1}^r \oplus K_i^{r-1} \quad (1 \leq i \leq 3) \end{cases} \tag{1}$$

2.2 Tsow's Key Recovery Algorithm

Tsow's algorithm consists of an expansion phase and a pruning phase, which are repeated alternately 16 times. It explores a 256-ary tree whose nodes correspond to the candidate key schedules.

Expansion Phase. We denote by $C_{i,j}$ the j-th candidate key schedule with depth i in the 256-ary tree, where $1 \leq i \leq 16$ and $1 \leq j \leq 256^i$. Table 1 gives the byte positions at which the algorithm guesses and computes the values in each expansion phase. For example, the algorithm guesses the value in 0_0 in the first expansion phase. Although it guesses the value in a_0, the other values in $a_b, b \neq 0$, are derived by Eq. (1). Note that the number of the derived bytes is different in depth i. In the cases of AES-128, it is i bytes , for $i = 1, \cdots, 11$ and 11 bytes for $i = 12, \cdots, 16$.

In the i-th expansion phase, the algorithm generates the children $C_{i,j}$, $j \in \{256(j'-1)+1, \cdots, 256j'\}$ of the remaining candidates $C_{i-1,j'}, j' \in \mathcal{L}_{i-1}$, where $\mathcal{L}_{i-1}$ is the suvivor list in the $(i-1)$-th pruning phase. The generated candidates

Table 1. Order of the derived bytes for AES-128 [11]

Round	Key Schedule															
	0				1				2				3			
	0	1	2	3	0	1	2	3	0	1	2	3	0	1	2	3
0	0_0	14_{10}				13_{10}				12_{10}				1_1	14_9	
1	1_0	13_9				12_9				2_2	14_8			2_1	13_8	
2	2_0	12_8				3_3	14_7			3_2	13_7			3_1	12_7	
3	3_0	4_4	14_6			4_3	13_6			4_2	12_6			4_1	5_5	14_5
4	4_0	5_4	13_5			5_3	12_5			5_2	6_6	14_4		5_1	6_5	13_4
5	5_0	6_4	12_4			6_3	7_7	14_3		6_2	7_6	13_3		6_1	7_5	12_3
6	6_0	7_4	8_8	14_2		7_3	8_7	13_2		7_2	8_6	12_2	14_1	7_1	8_5	9_9
7	7_0	8_4	9_8	13_1		8_3	9_7	12_1	14_0	8_2	9_6	10_{10}	13_0	8_1	9_5	10_9
8	8_0	9_4	10_8	12_0	15_{10}	9_3	10_7	11_{10}	15_9	9_2	10_6	11_9	15_8	9_1	10_5	11_8
9	9_0	10_4	11_7	15_7		10_3	11_6	15_6		10_2	11_5	15_8		10_1	11_4	15_4
10	10_0	11_3	15_3			11_2	15_2			11_1	15_1			11_0	15_0	

Table 2. Order of the derived bytes for AES-192

Round	Key Schedule																							
	0				1				2				3				4				5			
	0	1	2	3	0	1	2	3	0	1	2	3	0	1	2	3	0	1	2	3	0	1	2	3
0	0_0	14_8	20_8			13_8	19_8			12_8	18_8			11_8	17_8	23_8		9_7	15_7	21_7		1_1	14_7	20_7
1	1_0	13_7	19_7			12_7	18_7			11_7	17_7	23_7		9_6	15_6	21_6		2_2	14_6	20_6		2_1	13_6	19_6
2	2_0	12_6	18_6			11_6	17_6	23_6		9_5	15_5	21_5		3_3	14_5	20_5		3_2	13_5	19_5		3_1	12_5	18_5
3	3_0	11_5	17_5	23_5		9_4	15_4	21_4		4_4	14_4	20_4		4_3	13_4	19_4		4_2	12_4	18_4	23_4	4_1	11_4	17_4
4	4_0	9_3	15_3	21_3		5_5	14_3	20_3		5_4	13_3	19_3		5_3	12_3	18_3	23_3	5_2	11_3	17_3	21_2	5_1	9_2	15_2
5	5_0	6_6	14_2	20_2		6_5	13_2	19_2		6_4	12_2	18_2	23_2	6_3	11_2	17_2	21_1	6_2	9_1	15_1	20_1	6_1	7_7	14_1
6	6_0	7_6	13_1	19_1		7_5	12_1	18_1	23_1	7_4	11_1	17_1	21_0	7_3	9_0	15_0	20_0	7_2	8_8	14_0	19_0	7_1	8_7	13_0
7	7_0	8_6	12_0	18_0	23_0	8_5	11_0	17_0	22_7	8_4	10_7	16_7	22_6	8_3	10_6	16_6	22_5	8_2	10_5	16_5	22_4	8_1	10_4	16_4
8	8_0	10_3	16_3	22_3		10_2	16_2	22_2		10_1	16_1	22_1		10_0	16_0	22_0								

Table 3. Order of the derived bytes for AES-256 [11]

Round	Key Schedule																															
	0				1				2				3				4				5				6				7			
	0	1	2	3	0	1	2	3	0	1	2	3	0	1	2	3	0	1	2	3	0	1	2	3	0	1	2	3	0	1	2	3
0	0_0	15_7	23_7	31_7		14_7	22_7	30_7		13_7	21_7	29_7		12_7	20_7	28_7		10_6	18_6	26_6		9_6	17_6	25_6		8_6	16_6	24_6	31_6	1_1	15_6	23_6
1	1_0	14_6	22_6	30_6		13_6	21_6	29_6		12_6	20_6	28_6		10_5	18_5	26_5		9_5	17_5	25_5		8_5	16_5	24_5	31_5	2_2	15_5	23_5	30_5	2_1	14_5	22_5
2	2_0	13_5	21_5	29_5		12_5	20_5	28_5		10_4	18_4	26_4		9_4	17_4	25_4		8_4	16_4	24_4	31_4	3_3	15_4	23_4	30_4	3_2	14_4	22_4	29_4	3_1	13_4	21_4
3	3_0	12_4	20_4	28_4		10_3	18_3	26_3		9_3	17_3	25_3		8_3	16_3	24_3	31_3	4_4	15_3	23_3	30_3	4_3	14_3	22_3	29_3	4_2	13_3	21_3	28_3	4_1	12_3	20_3
4	4_0	10_2	18_2	26_2		9_2	17_2	25_2		8_2	16_2	24_2	31_2	5_5	15_2	23_2	30_2	5_4	14_2	22_2	29_2	5_3	13_2	21_2	28_2	5_2	12_2	20_2	26_1	5_1	10_1	18_1
5	5_0	9_1	17_1	25_1		8_1	16_1	24_1	31_1	6_6	15_1	23_1	30_1	6_5	14_1	22_1	29_1	6_4	13_1	21_1	28_1	6_3	12_1	20_1	26_0	6_2	10_0	18_0	25_0	6_1	9_0	17_0
6	6_0	8_0	16_0	24_0	31_0	7_7	15_0	23_0	30_0	7_6	14_0	22_0	29_0	7_5	13_0	21_0	28_0	7_4	12_0	20_0	27_6	7_3	11_6	19_6	27_5	7_2	11_5	19_5	27_4	7_1	11_4	19_4
7	7_0	11_3	19_3	27_3		11_2	19_2	27_2		11_1	19_1	27_1		11_0	19_0	27_0																

are inserted into list $\mathcal{L}'_i$. After the last expansion phase, all bytes of the 8th round key have been computed. Therefore, the 0th round key (i.e., the secret key) can be derived by Eq. (1).

The expansion phases for AES-192 and AES-256 are almost the same as that for AES-128. Tables 2 and 3 show the order for AES-192 and AES-256, respectively. Although the orders for AES-128 and AES-256 are given in [11], we determined the order for AES-192.

Pruning Phase. Let D be a decayed key schedule extracted by a cold boot attack. Tsow's algorithm assumes the perfect asymmetric decay model, that is, bit flipping from 1 to 0 occurs, but the reverse bit flipping never does. According to this assumption, the algorithm compares the bit positions between $C_{i,j}$, $j \in \mathcal{L}'_i$ and D, and prunes the candidate key schedules with a zero in the bit positions where D has a one.

3 Proposed Algorithm

In this section, we present a key recovery algorithm based on the maximum likelihood approach and give a theoretical bound for our algorithm. Although Tsow's algorithm cannot recover a secret key if bit flipping from 0 to 1 occurs even in only one bit position, our algorithm can recover the key in the imperfect asymmetric decay model.

3.1 Maximum Likelihood-Based Pruning

Our algorithm consists of an expansion phase and a pruning phase as in Tsow's algorithm. The expansion phase of our algorithm is the same as that in Tsow's algorithm, while the pruning phase is inspired by previous works [8,10].

We denote by n_{ab} for $a, b \in \{0, 1\}$, the number of bit positions where a candidate key schedule $C_{i,j}$ has a bit a and a decayed key schedule D has a bit b. For example, in the first expansion phase, if $C_{1,j}$ has 0x0F and D has 0x08 in the byte position 0_0, then $n_{00} = 4$, $n_{01} = 0$, $n_{10} = 3$ and $n_{11} = 1$. Note that the number does not except the bytes that are not yet computed. The log-likelihood of a candidate key schedule $C_{i,j}$ for a decay key schedule D is given by

$$\begin{aligned}\log \Pr[D|C] &= \log\left((1-\delta_1)^{n_{00}}\delta_1^{n_{01}}(1-\delta_0)^{n_{11}}\delta_0^{n_{10}}\right),\\ &= n_{00}\log(1-\delta_1) + n_{01}\log\delta_1 + n_{11}\log(1-\delta_0) + n_{10}\log\delta_0.\end{aligned}$$

In each pruning phase, the algorithm computes the log-likelihood of each candidate, keeps the top L candidates with the highest log-likelihood values and prunes the remaining candidates. After the final pruning phase, our algorithm computes the 0th round keys derived from the remaining L candidate key schedules and returns the correct secret key if it is among the remaining candidates.

Because the algorithm keeps L candidates in each pruning phase, the complexity of the search is linear in L, as confirmed in Sect. 4.

3.2 Theoretical Bound

In this section, we give the information theoretic bound for our algorithm. Here R denotes the code rate in information theory, which is the key length per number of observed bits. For example, since the AES-128 key schedule algorithm extends a 128-bit secret key to 11 round keys with length 128 bits, the code rate R is $\frac{1}{11}$. The algorithms extend 192-bit and 256-bit secret keys to 13 and 15 128-bit round keys, respectively. Thus, $R = 3/26$ and $R = 2/15$ for AES-192 and AES-256. The sequence $\{n | a \leq n \leq b, n \in \mathbb{Z}\}$ is denoted by $[a : b]$. Let $X \in \{0,1\}$ be a random variable uniformly distributed over $\{0,1\}$. We denote by $Y \in \{0,1\}$ a random variable that follows the imperfect asymmetric decay model. We define m_i as the number of the computed bytes with depth i and $m_{[a:b]}$ as $\sum_{k=a}^{b} m_k$.

We introduce the following assumptions on the key schedule.

Assumption 1. 1. Each $C_{i,j}$ is a realization of a random variable $X_{i,j}$, uniformly distributed over $\{0,1\}^{8m_{[1:i]}}$

2. There exists $c \geq 1$ satisfying the following: for any $i, l, j, j' \in \mathbb{N}$ s.t. $c \leq l \leq i$ and $X_{i,j}$ and $X_{i,j'}$ have no common ancestors with depth $[c : i]$ in the tree, a pair of random variables $(X_{i,j}^{l-c}, X_{i,j'}^{l-c})$ is uniformly distributed over $\{0,1\}^{8m_{[i-l+c+1:i]}}$, where $X_{i,j}^{l-c}$ corresponds to the generated bytes in the last $(l-c)$ expansion phases.
3. For any j, any pair of children of $X_{i,j}$ almost surely do not have identical values for the byte positions in the $(i+1)$-th expansion phase.

Under Assumption 1, we can show the following theorem in a similar way to the result of Kunihiro and Honda [8][1].

Theorem 1. Assume that

$$R < I(X;Y). \tag{2}$$

Then, under the proposed algorithm for any index j and parameter L, it holds that

$$\Pr[\text{The correct key schedule } X_{n/8,j} \text{ is pruned}] \leq n\rho_1 L^{-\rho_2}, \tag{3}$$

for some $\rho_1, \rho_2 > 0$, depending only on R, δ_0, and δ_1, where n is the length of the secret key.

The right-hand side of Eq. (2) is called the mutual information between X and Y. The proof sketch of Theorem 1 and the representation of ρ_1, ρ_2 are given in Appendix A. Because the imperfect asymmetric decay model corresponds to a binary asymmetric channel and the distribution of the input symbol (i.e., each bit of the secret key) is fixed to be uniform, we have

$$I(X;Y) = \mathcal{H}\left(\frac{1-\delta_1+\delta_0}{2}\right) - \frac{1}{2}\left(\mathcal{H}(\delta_0) + \mathcal{H}(\delta_1)\right),$$

where $\mathcal{H}(\cdot)$ is defined as the binary entropy function; that is, $\mathcal{H}(x) = -x\log_2 x - (1-x)\log_2(1-x)$.

[1] A similar analysis on RSA is shown in [7].

Table 4. Theoretical bound of δ_0 for $\delta_1 = 0.001$

	AES-128	AES-192	AES-256
R	1/11	3/26	2/15
δ_0	0.822	0.780	0.750

Table 5. Running times (s)

	L	Avg.	Min	Max	Std. Dev.	Med.
AES-128	1024	5.179	4.769	5.795	0.191	5.164
	2048	10.405	9.577	11.568	0.431	10.505
	4096	20.839	18.886	23.263	1.048	20.738
AES-192	1024	10.592	9.795	11.777	0.503	10.578
	2048	21.123	19.605	23.418	0.848	21.1
	4096	42.617	39.07	46.807	1.857	42.686
AES-256	1024	17.289	15.737	19.931	0.7	17.236
	2048	34.595	31.906	39.103	1.478	34.447
	4096	69.766	63.82	79.587	3.016	69.776

Table 4 gives the theoretical bound of δ_0 for $\delta_1 = 0.001$ in Theorem 1 for each key length. If δ_0 is smaller than the bound, the error rate is bounded polynomially in L; that is, our algorithm can recover a secret key with high probability for large L. We calculate R

4 Implementation

We implemented our algorithm for AES-128, AES-192, and AES-256. The implementation was coded in Java 1.7.0 and executed on a 3.5 GHz single-core Intel Core i7. We carried out experiments for $\delta_1 = 0.001$, $0.05 \leq \delta_0 \leq 0.75$ in steps of 0.05 and with $L = 1024, 2048, 4096$. We randomly generated 1000 instances for AES-128, AES-192 and 600 instances for AES-256.

Figures 1, 2, and 3 illustrate the success rates for AES-128, AES-192, and AES-256, respectively. As can be seen in these figures, the success rates are almost equal to one for $\delta_0 \leq 0.4$ and greater than 0.1 for $\delta_0 \leq 0.65$, with our algorithm almost failing to recover a secret key for $\delta_0 \geq 0.75$. Although a gap exists between the theoretical bound and experimental values, these results confirm the validity of the bound to some extent. A small L causes a gap because the success rate for $L = 4096$ is, in fact, greater than that for $L = 1024$. Therefore, a larger L is expected to reduce the gap and show that the bound is almost optimal.

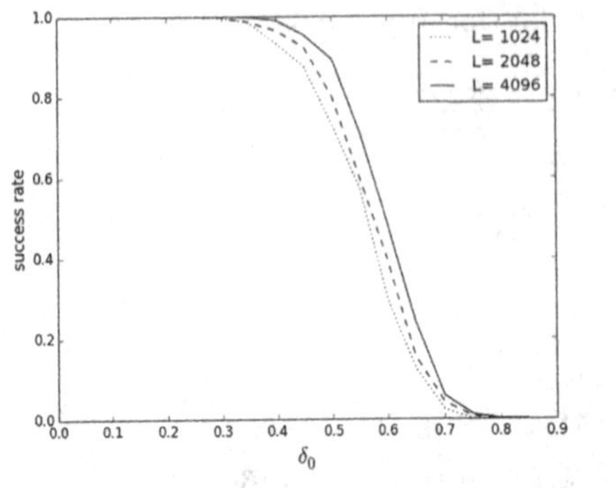

Fig. 1. Success rates for AES-128

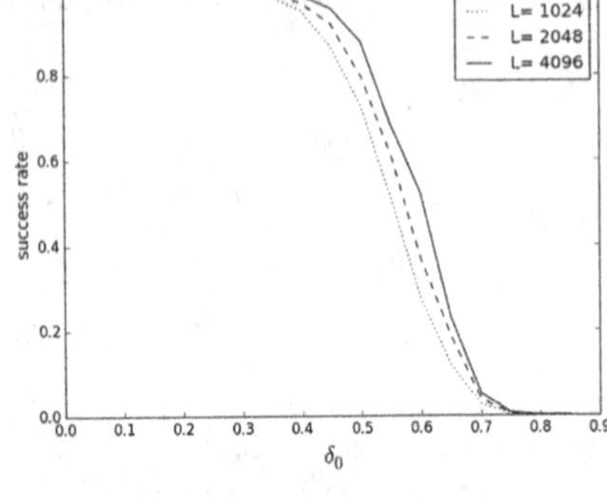

Fig. 2. Success rates for AES-192

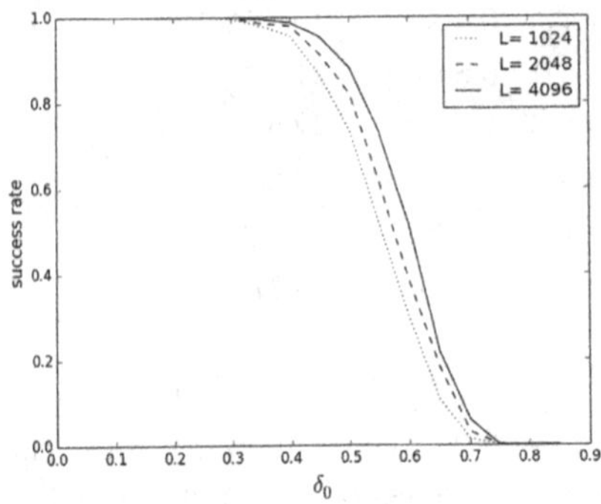

Fig. 3. Success rates for AES-256

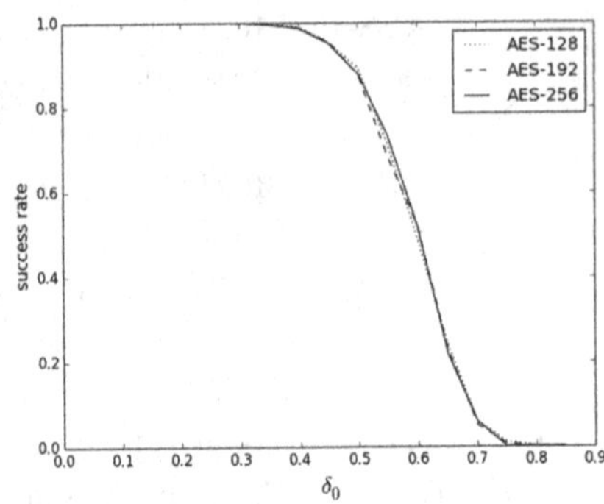

Fig. 4. Success rates for L = 4096

Figure 4 compares the success rates of AES-128, AES-192, and AES-256 in the case of $L = 4096$. The figure shows that the success rates are almost independent of the key lengths. This result does not change for $L = 1024, 2048$. See Table 6 in Appendix B for details.

Table 5 gives the running times of our algorithm for different L values and key lengths. The times are roughly proportional to L. This shows the time complexity of the algorithm is $O(L)$.

5 Conclusion

In this paper, we proposed a new algorithm that can recover a secret key from an AES key schedule with noise. The algorithm, based on the maximum likelihood approach, can be applied to the imperfect asymmetric decay model. It consists of an expansion phase and a pruning phase: In an expansion phase, the algorithm guesses the value in a specific byte position, whereas in a pruning phase, it keeps the L candidates with the highest log-likelihood. The algorithm repeats the phases and outputs the correct key if it remains after the last pruning phase.

We also presented the theoretical bound for the algorithm. The algorithm can recover a key with high probability if δ_0 is less than some bound. We investigated applications of the algorithm for AES-128, AES-192, and AES-256 to verify the validity of the theoretical bound. The results show that the algorithm can recover the key if δ_0 is less than the bound, thereby confirming that the bound is almost tight for the algorithm.

Acknowledgement. We would like to thank Junya Honda for helpful advice. This research was supported by CREST, JST and supported by JSPS KAKENHI Grant Number 25280001.

A Proof of Theorem 1

In this appendix, we show the sketch of proof of Theorem 1 in a similar way to the result of Kunihiro and Honda [8]. First, we introduce some notation for the proof.

We denote by $\mathbf{1}[\cdot]$ the indicator function and by $E[X]$ the expectation of a random variable X. Instead of $\log \Pr[D|C]$, we use the score function $R(x;y) = \log \frac{dF_x}{dG}(y)$, $x, y \in \{0,1\}$, where F_x is the distribution of the imperfect asymmetric decay model, G is the mixture distribution $(F_0 + F_1)/2$ and dF_x/dG is the Radon-Nikodym's derivative. Then, $R(C_{i,j}; D_j)$ is $\sum_{r=1}^{i} \sum_{k=1}^{m_r} R(C_{i,j}[r][k]; D_i[r][k])$, where $C_{i,j}[r][k]$ is the k-th computed byte with depth r and $R(C_{i,j}[r][k]; D_i[r][k])$ is the sum of the score for each bits in $C_{i,j}[r][k]$. Note that $R(x;y)$ is equivalent to $\log \Pr[D|C]$ and the performance of our algorithm does not change.

We use Lemmas 1 and 2 in [8]. Lemma 1 shows the Chernoff's inequality and Lemma 2 evaluates the score of the incorrect candidates. Our algorithm is different from their algorithm in that our algorithm has a structure of 256-ary tree. Thus, we use Assumption 1. (2) and modify Lemma 2 into the following form.

Lemma 2 (modified Lemma 2 [8]). For $\forall i > d$, $j \in \{256^{d-1}+1, \cdots, 256^d\}$,

$$E[\exp((\ln 2) R(X_{i,j}^d; Y_i^d))] \leq 2^{8m_c c}.$$

Proof of Theorem 1 (sketch). Let $l = \lfloor \log_{256} L \rfloor$. We can assume without loss of generality that the index of the correct key schedule is $j = 1$. By the union bound and some transformation, the error probability of our algorithm can be bounded by

$$\Pr[X_{n/8,1} \notin \mathcal{L}_{n/8}] = \Pr\left[\bigcup_{r=l+1}^{n/8} \{\{X_{r,1} \notin \mathcal{L}_r\} \cap \{X_{r-1,1} \in \mathcal{L}_{r-1}\}\}\right]$$
$$\leq \sum_{r=l+1}^{n/8} \Pr\left[\{\{X_{r,1} \notin \mathcal{L}_r\} \cap \{X_{r-1,1} \in \mathcal{L}_{r-1}\}\}\right]$$
$$\leq \sum_{r=l+1}^{n/8} \Pr\left[\sum_{d=l}^{r} \sum_{j=256^{d-1}+1}^{256^d} \mathbf{1}[R(X^d_{r,j};Y^d_r) \geq R(X^d_{r,1};Y^d_r)] \geq \frac{255}{256}L\right]. \quad (4)$$

Let$u \in (R, I(X;Y))$ be arbitrary. Then the probability in (4) is bounded by

$$\Pr\left[\sum_{d=l}^{r} \sum_{j=256^{d-1}+1}^{256^d} \mathbf{1}[R(X^d_{r,j};Y^d_r) \geq R(X^d_{r,1};Y^d_r)] \geq \frac{255}{256}L\right]$$
$$\leq \Pr\left[\left\{\sum_{d=l}^{r} \sum_{j=256^{d-1}+1}^{256^d} \mathbf{1}[R(X^d_{r,j};Y^d_r) \geq 8m_d du] \geq \frac{255}{256}L\right\} \cup \bigcup_{d=l}^{r} \{R(X^d_{r,1};Y^d_r) \leq 8m_d du\}\right]$$
$$\leq \frac{256}{255L} \sum_{d=l}^{r} \sum_{j=256^{d-1}+1}^{256^d} \Pr[R(X^d_{r,j};Y^d_r) \geq 8m_d du] + \sum_{d=l}^{r} \Pr[R(X^d_{r,1};Y^d_r) \leq 8m_d du]. \quad (5)$$

The former and latter probabilities in (5) can be bounded by

$$\Pr[R(X^d_{r,j};Y^d_r) \geq 8m_d du] \leq 2^{8m_c c - 8m_d du} \quad \text{(by Lemma 1 in 9 and Lemma 2)},$$
$$\Pr[R(X^d_{r,1};Y^d_r) \leq 8m_d du] \leq \exp(-8m_d d\Lambda^*(u)), \quad \text{(by Lemma 1)}$$

where $\Lambda^*(u) = \sup_{\lambda \leq 0}\{\lambda u - \ln E[\exp(\lambda X)]\}$.

Combining the bounds with (5), we have

$$\frac{256}{255L} \sum_{d=l}^{r} \sum_{j=256^{d-1}+1}^{256^d} \Pr[R(X^d_{r,j};Y^d_r) \geq 8m_d du] + \sum_{d=l}^{r} \Pr[R(X^d_{r,1};Y^d_r) \leq 8m_d du]$$
$$\leq \frac{256}{255L} \sum_{d=l}^{r} 256^{d-1} \cdot 2^{8m_c c - 8m_d du} + \sum_{d=l}^{r} \exp(-m_d d\Lambda^*(u))$$
$$\leq \frac{256^{m_c c}}{255L} \frac{256^{-l(u/R-1)}}{1-256^{-(u/R-1)}} + \frac{\exp(-l\Lambda^*(u)/R)}{1-\exp(-\Lambda^*(u)/R)}$$
$$\leq \frac{256^{m_c c+u/R-1}}{1-256^{-(u/R-1)}} L^{-u/R} + \frac{\exp(\Lambda^*(u)/R)}{1-\exp(-\Lambda^*(u)/R)} L^{-\frac{\Lambda^*(u)}{R\ln 256}}. \quad (6)$$

Note that we can consider $m_d = 1/R$ for a larger L. We finish the proof with (4) and (6) and obtain

$$\rho_1 = \frac{256^{m_c c+u/R-1}}{1-256^{-(u/R-1)}} + \frac{\exp(\Lambda^*(u)/R)}{1-\exp(-\Lambda^*(u)/R)}, \rho_2 = \min\left\{u/R, \frac{\Lambda^*(u)}{R\ln 256}\right\}.$$

B Experimental Results

Table 6 shows the success rates for different L values and key lengths in details. As mentioned in Sect. 4, the result shows that a lager L raises the success rates. On the other hand, the success rates is independent of key lengths.

Table 6. Success Rates

Key Length	L	δ_0								
		0.05	0.1	0.15	0.2	0.25	0.3	0.35	0.4	0.45
128	1024	1.0	1.0	1.0	1.0	0.999	0.995	0.986	0.934	0.875
	2048	1.0	1.0	1.0	1.0	1.0	0.997	0.986	0.965	0.924
	4096	1.0	1.0	1.0	1.0	1.0	1.0	0.998	0.99	0.954
192	1024	1.0	1.0	1.0	0.999	0.999	0.992	0.984	0.952	0.866
	2048	1.0	1.0	0.999	1.0	1.0	0.999	0.994	0.969	0.92
	4096	1.0	1.0	1.0	1.0	1.0	0.999	0.996	0.987	0.956
256	1024	1.0	1.0	1.0	1.0	1.0	0.997	0.978	0.955	0.863
	2048	1.0	1.0	1.0	1.0	1.0	0.998	0.985	0.978	0.912
	4096	1.0	1.0	1.0	1.0	1.0	1.0	0.995	0.987	0.952

Key Length	L	δ_0							
		0.5	0.55	0.6	0.65	0.7	0.75	0.8	0.85
128	1024	0.73	0.571	0.299	0.125	0.023	0.0	0.0	0.0
	2048	0.8	0.597	0.395	0.154	0.041	0.006	0.0	0.0
	4096	0.894	0.71	0.486	0.241	0.058	0.011	0.001	0.0
192	1024	0.726	0.512	0.272	0.116	0.025	0.004	0.0	0.0
	2048	0.797	0.613	0.367	0.184	0.037	0.003	0.0	0.0
	4096	0.878	0.682	0.52	0.228	0.05	0.006	0.0	0.0
256	1024	0.733	0.52	0.298	0.105	0.013	0.002	0.0	0.0
	2048	0.82	0.617	0.385	0.182	0.03	0.002	0.0	0.0
	4096	0.88	0.732	0.517	0.218	0.058	0.0	0.0	0.0

References

1. Albrecht, M., Cid, C.: Cold boot key recovery by solving polynomial systems with noise. In: Lopez, J., Tsudik, G. (eds.) ACNS 2011. LNCS, vol. 6715, pp. 57–72. Springer, Heidelberg (2011)
2. Alex Halderman, J., Schoen, S.D., Heninger, N., Clarkson, W., Paul, W., Calandrino, J.A., Feldman, A.J., Appelbaum, J., Felten, E.W.: Lest we remember: cold boot attacks on encryption keys. In: Proceedings of the 17th USENIX Security Symposium, 28 July–1 August, San Jose, CA, USA, pp. 45–60 (2008)
3. Henecka, W., May, A., Meurer, A.: Correcting errors in RSA private keys. In: Rabin, T. (ed.) CRYPTO 2010. LNCS, vol. 6223, pp. 351–369. Springer, Heidelberg (2010)
4. Heninger, N., Shacham, H.: Reconstructing RSA private keys from random key bits. In: Halevi, S. (ed.) CRYPTO 2009. LNCS, vol. 5677, pp. 1–17. Springer, Heidelberg (2009)
5. Huang, Z., Lin, D.: A new method for solving polynomial systems with noise over $\mathbb{F}_2$ and its applications in cold boot key recovery. In: Knudsen, L.R., Wu, H. (eds.) SAC 2012. LNCS, vol. 7707, pp. 16–33. Springer, Heidelberg (2013)
6. Kamal, A.A., Youssef, A.M.: Applications of SAT solvers to AES key recovery from decayed key schedule images. IACR Cryptology ePrint Arch. 324 (2010)

7. Kunihiro, N.: An improved attack for recovering noisy rsa secret keys and itscountermeasure. (2015, to appear in ProvSec2015)
8. Kunihiro, N., Honda, J.: RSA meets DPA: recovering RSA secret keys from noisy analog data. In: Batina, L., Robshaw, M. (eds.) CHES 2014. LNCS, vol. 8731, pp. 261–278. Springer, Heidelberg (2014)
9. Liao, X., Zhang, H., Koshimura, M., Fujita, H., Hasegawa, R.: Using maxsat to correct errors in AES key schedule images. In: IEEE 25th International Conference on Tools with Artificial Intelligence, 4–6 November 2013, Herndon, VA, USA, pp. 284–291 (2013)
10. Paterson, K.G., Polychroniadou, A., Sibborn, D.L.: A Coding-Theoretic Approach to Recovering Noisy RSA Keys. In: Wang, X., Sako, K. (eds.) ASIACRYPT 2012. LNCS, vol. 7658, pp. 386–403. Springer, Heidelberg (2012)
11. Tsow, A.: An improved recovery algorithm for decayed AES key schedule images. In: Jacobson Jr., M.J., Rijmen, V., Safavi-Naini, R. (eds.) SAC 2009. LNCS, vol. 5867, pp. 215–230. Springer, Heidelberg (2009)

New Efficient Padding Methods Secure Against Padding Oracle Attacks

HyungChul Kang[1], Myungseo Park[2], Dukjae Moon[1], Changhoon Lee[3], Jongsung Kim[4(✉)], Kimoon Kim[5], Juhyuk Kim[5], and Seokhie Hong[1]

[1] Center for Information Security Technologies(CIST), Korea University, Seoul, Korea
{kanghc,shhong}@korea.ac.kr, djmoon17@hotmail.com

[2] The Affiliated Insutitude of ETRI, Seoul, Korea
pms91@nsr.re.kr

[3] Department of Computer Science and Engineering, Seoul University of Science and Technology, Seoul, Korea
chlee@seoultech.ac.kr

[4] Department of Mathematics and Department of Financial Information Security, Kookmin University, Seoul, Korea
jskim@kookmin.ac.kr

[5] Korea Security and Internet Agency, Seoul, Korea
{harrykim,juhyukkim}@kisa.or.kr

Abstract. This paper proposes three new padding methods designed to withstand padding oracle attacks, which aim at recovering a plaintext without knowing the secret key by exploiting oracle's characteristic of checking the padding during decryption. Of the ten existing padding methods, only two (ABYT-PAD and ABIT-PAD) can withstand padding oracle attacks. However, these methods are not efficient since they either use a random number generator or require MAC verification in applications. The three new padding methods proposed in this paper are secure against padding oracle attacks and more efficient compared to the two aforementioned padding methods.

Keywords: Padding methods · Padding oracle attack · CBC mode of operation

1 Introduction

Various encryption algorithms are now widely applied to protect personal information and sensitive data in applications such as Internet banking and e-commerce. However, recent studies and attacks show that protected data can still be leaked if the modes of operation are not proper, even when sensitive data are encrypted using an encryption algorithm that is proven to be secure. The padding oracle attack (POA) is a leading example of such an attack.

When a message is encrypted using an encryption algorithm, an appropriate value is added (padded) at the end of the message to fix the input

S. Kwon and A. Yun (Eds.): ICISC 2015, LNCS 9558, pp. 329–342, 2016.
DOI: 10.1007/978-3-319-30840-1_21

size. If an attacker possesses Oracle, which determines whether the message padding is correct, the attacker can read the message (plaintext). This oracle determines whether the padding of the plaintext obtained by decrypting the ciphertext queried by the attacker is correct and answers VALID or INVALID to the attacker. The attacker can intercept the text encrypted in the mode of operation and obtain the correct plaintext using the acquired data and the oracle. Such an attack is called POA. The POA has been widely studied and applied to many popular security protocols such as SSL, IPSec and TLS([PSB1,BU1,RD1,PY1,AP1,AP2,MZ1,V1,DR1,STW1,KR1]).

This paper observes a POA using the ten existing padding methods and analyzes their security and efficiency, thus enabling the identification of two secure padding methods. Based on the results of the analysis, this paper proposes five design criteria for secure and efficient padding for protection against POA. Lastly, the paper proposes three new padding methods that conform to the design criteria. The three new padding methods are designed to be secure against POA and are more efficient than the conventional methods.

This paper is organized as follows: Sect. 2 presents the details of the simulated POA; Sect. 3 analyzes the security of the ten conventional padding methods after conducting a POA; Sect. 4 proposes five secure and efficient design criteria for padding; Sect. 5 proposes three new padding methods; and, lastly, Sect. 6 presents the conclusion.

2 Padding Oracle Attack(POA)

The POA on modes of operation was first introduced by Vaudenay [V1] at EUROCRYPT 2002. Vaudenay reported on POAs against the CBC mode used in various application environments such as SSL/TLS, IPSec and WTLS.

The POA against the CBC mode is applied in the CBC decryption mode [D1](Fig. 1), and CBC-PAD is assumed as the padding method.

CBC-PAD is a padding method specified in PKCS #7 [K1]. If the size of the block cypher is 8 bytes and the size of the plaintext is $(8 \times t + m)$ bytes, with m being an integer greater than 0, $(8 - m)$ bytes of $(0x08 - m)(0x08 - m) \cdots (0x08 - m)$

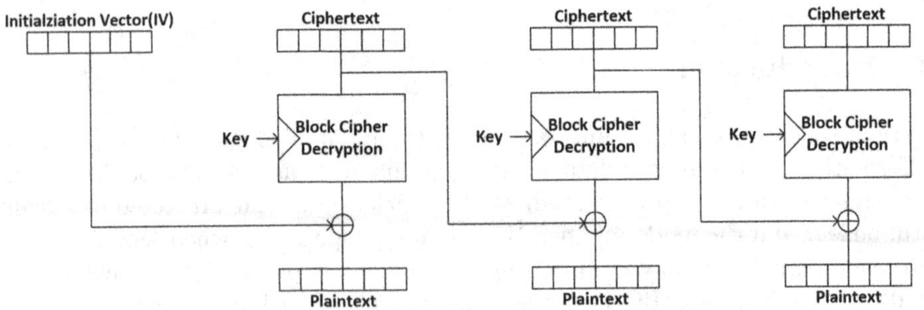

Fig. 1. Descryption of CBC modes of operation

are added at the end of the plaintext data to make the size of the plaintext data a positive multiple of 8 bytes. If m is 0, an additional 8 bytes of 0x08 ⋯ 08 block are attached to the plaintext.

$$\text{Example}(t = 1, m = 5) : 0\text{x}0102030405 \rightarrow 0\text{x}0102030405\underline{\mathbf{030303}}$$

The attacker changes the initial vector or ciphertext and sends it to the server. The server decrypts the ciphertext sent by the attacker to check the padding, and then sends the response(VALID or INVALID) to the attacker(Figs. 2, 3).

Using this, the attacker modifies the ciphertext(gray block in Fig. 4) and sends it to the server until the server responds with VALID. The attacker can obtain the intermediary value(e.g., 0x*eb* in Fig. 4) using the value recorded at the time the server sends the VALID response. The plaintext can be restored by the exclusive-OR of the obtained intermediary value and the ciphertext before the attacker changed it. The whole plaintext can be restored by restoring the intermediary value one byte at a time by repeating the process.

Black and Urtubia proposed a POA that enhanced Vaudenay's POA at 2002 USENIX [BU1]. The existing POA restores the plaintext one byte at a time beginning with the last byte of the block. Such a method requires many queries. However, the enhanced POA determines the length of the padding of the last block through a binary search, and can obtain the padding value of the plaintext data with fewer queries.

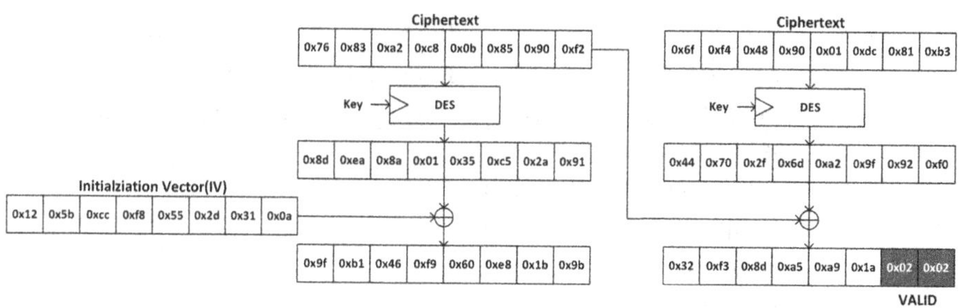

Fig. 2. VALID response

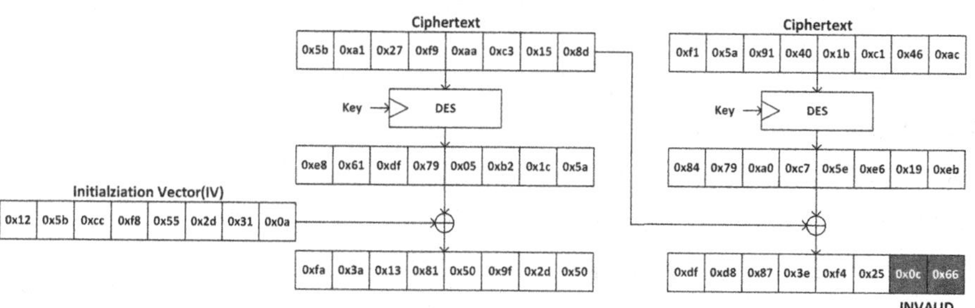

Fig. 3. INVALID response

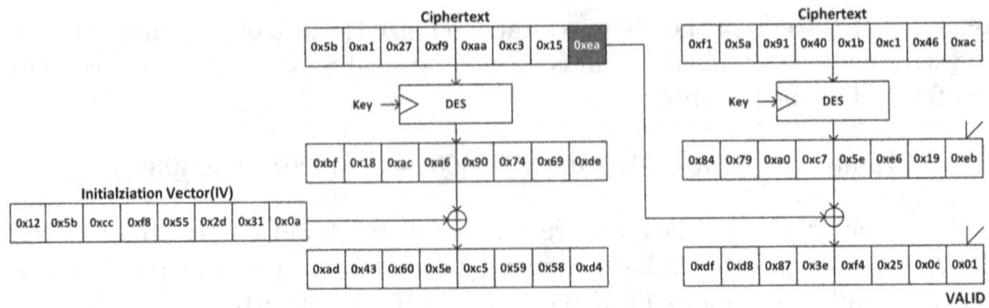

Fig. 4. Example of POA

3 Security of Existing Padding Methods Against POA

The padding method is divided into byte-wise padding and bit-wise padding according to the unit of padding. The byte-wise padding methods include CBC-PAD, ESP-PAD, XY-PAD, BOZ-PAD, PAIR-PAD, ABYT-PAD, while the bit-wise padding methods include OZ-PAD, ABIT-PAD, ISO(9797-1)-PAD3, and ISO(10118-1)-PAD3. [Table 1] shows the result of the POA on each padding method.

Table 1. POA on the various padding methods

POA	Padding	Ref.	POA	Padding	Ref.
Possible	CBC-PAD	[V1]	Impossible	ABYT-PAD	[BU1]
	ISO(9797-1)-PAD3	[PY1]		ABIT-PAD	[BU1]
	ISO(10118-1)-PAD3	[PY1]			
	ESP-PAD	[BU1]			
	XY-PAD	[BU1]			
	BOZ-PAD	[BU1]			
	PAIR-PAD	[BU1]			
	OZ-PAD	[BU1]			

3.1 POA on CBC-PAD

CBC-PAD and its POA are described in Sect. 2

3.2 POA on ISO(9797-1)-PAD3

ISO(9797-1)-PAD3 is a bit-wise padding method. First, the length of the plaintext is inserted in bits into the first plaintext block, and the last block bits are padded with 0. Since the length of the plaintext is added, no padding block is added even if the length of the plaintext is a multiple of n.

Example : 0x0102030405 → 0x**0000000000000028** 0102030405**000000**

The POA on ISO(9797-1)-PAD3 is organized into two steps. First, the length of the plaintext is obtained; then the plaintext is restored using the data. As the length of the plaintext is padded in ISO(9797-1)-PAD3, the POA uses it for the attack.

3.3 POA on ISO(10118-1)-PAD3

ISO(10118-1)-PAD3 is a bit-wise padding method that is similar to ISO(9797-1)-PAD3, except that the length of the plaintext is padded in the last block, and $10 \cdots 0$ is padded so that the length of the plaintext becomes a multiple of n.

Example : 0x0102030405 → 0x0102030405**800000** **0000000000000028**

The POA on ISO(10118-1)-PAD3 is similar to the POA on ISO(9797-1)-PAD3.

3.4 POA on ESP-PAD

ESP-PAD is a byte-wise padding method, for which the padding pattern is determined according to the number of bytes needed for padding. If the length of the plaintext is a multiple of n, a padding block(0x0102 $\cdots 0n$) is added to signal that the padding is being used.

Example : 0x0102030405 → 0x0102030405**010203**

The POA on ESP-PAD is similar to the POA on CBC-PAD.

3.5 POA on XY-PAD

XY-PAD is a byte-wise padding method that pads by creating different bytes X and Y. It pads a byte X first and then pads Y so that the length of the plaintext becomes a multiple of n. If the length of the plaintext is a multiple of n, a padding block(0x$XYY \cdots YY$) is added to signal that the padding is being used. Here, the X and Y values are known by both transmitter and receiver.

Example : 0x0102030405 → 0x0102030405**0A0B0B**($X = 0\text{x}0A, Y = 0\text{x}0B$)

The POA on XY-PAD is similar to the POA on CBC-PAD.

3.6 POA on BOZ-PAD(A Byte-Oriented Version of 10* Padding)

BOZ-PAD is a byte-wise padding method that pads 1 at the end of the plaintext and then pads 0 so that the length of the plaintext becomes the multiple of n. Since it consists of byte-wise padding, it is the same as the XY-PAD of which X is 0x80 and Y is 0x00. If the length of the plaintext is a multiple of n, a padding block(0x8000 $\cdots$ 00) is added to signal that the padding is being used.

$$\text{Example} : 0\text{x}0102030405 \rightarrow 0\text{x}0102030405\underline{\mathbf{800000}}$$

The POA on BOZ-PAD is similar to the POA on XY-PAD, of which X is 0x80 and Y is 0x00.

3.7 POA on PAIR-PAD

PAIR-PAD is a byte-wise padding method that is the same as XY-PAD, except that the transmitter selects X and Y, which are both unknown to the receiver.

$$\text{Example} : 0\text{x}0102030405 \rightarrow 0\text{x}0102030405\underline{\mathbf{0A0B0B}}(X = 0\text{x}0A, Y = 0\text{x}0B)$$

PAIR-PAD differs from XY-PAD in how the receiver removes the padding. Since the receiver does not know X and Y, it checks the last byte of the plaintext block and removes all bytes matching the value from the end(removal of Y). Then, it removes another byte(removal of X).

The POA on PAIR-PAD has an attack complexity almost equal to that of a brute force, since it is an INVALID padding only when all bytes are equal in a block.

3.8 POA on OZ-PAD(Obligatory 10* Padding)

OZ-PAD is a bit-wise padding method that can be considered as a bit-wise padding version of BOZ-PAD.

The POA on OZ-PAD has an attack complexity almost equal to that of a brute force, since it is an INVALID padding only when the last bit is not 0.

3.9 POA on ABYT-PAD(Arbitrary-Tail Padding)

ABYT-PAD is a byte-wise padding method similar to PAIR-PAD. First, it checks the last byte of the plaintext block and selects it as X. It then generates another value as Y by a random number generator, and pads the plaintext so that its length becomes a multiple of n. If the length of the plaintext is a multiple of n, it adds a padding block(0x$YY \cdots Y$) to the signal that the padding is being used. Here, the transmitter selects Y, which is unknown to the receiver.

$$\text{Example} : 0\text{x}0102030405 \rightarrow 0\text{x}0102030405\underline{\mathbf{0B0B0B}}(X = 0\text{x}05, Y = 0\text{x}0B)$$

The padding is removed in the following way: First, it checks the last byte of the plaintext block and removes all bytes matching the value from the end(removal of Y). After that, it does not remove another byte since the byte is the plaintext part. (X is one of the bytes of the plaintext).

Even when the padded part is changed, there is no INVALID padding since only the bytes before the changed byte are removed. Therefore, ABYT-PAD is secure against POA.

3.10 POA on ABIT-PAD(A Bit-Oriented Analog Padding)

ABIT-PAD is a bit-wise padding method and can be considered as the bit-wise padding version of ABYT-PAD. In other words, it checks the last bit of the plaintext block and pads its conflicting bits so that the length of the plaintext becomes a multiple of n. If the length of the plaintext is a multiple of n, it adds a padding block(0x$XX \cdots X$) to the signal that the padding is being used (if the last bit of the plaintext is 0 then $X = F$; otherwise, $X = 0$).

$$\text{Example} : \text{0x0102030405} \rightarrow \text{0x0102030405}\underline{\textbf{000000}}$$

The POA on ABIT-PAD has the same as the POA on ABYT-PAD. Even when the padded part is changed, there is no INVALID padding since only the bits before the changed bit are removed. Therefore, it is secure against POA.

3.11 Proc and Cons of the ABYT-PAD and ABIT-PAD Secure Against POA

Proc. The ABYT-PAD and ABIT-PAD are both secure against POA. This is due to the fact that they do not allow any invalid padding. More precisely, the server firstly decrypts the ciphertext (maybe modified by the attacker) to obtain the corresponding plaintext. It secondly removes the padding part from the decrypted plaintext according to the rule of the ABYT-PAD or the ABIT-PAD. In this second step, the server always peels off the padding bytes even though the target ciphertext is a modified one by the attacker. Therefore, the ABYT-PAD and ABIT-PAD fundamentally do not allow the attacker to conduct POA.

Cons. A padding method that does not allow any invalid padding does have some loss of its efficiency when it is applied to widely used applications such as TLS series. The reason is as follows: The TLS usually adopts the MAC-then-Encrypt method instead of the Encrypt-then-MAC method. In such a case, the MAC verification step is always required even though the padding bytes of the plaintext are originally wrong. Because the ABYT-PAD and ABIT-PAD do not include any invalid padding. This makes the applications somewhat slow. Furthermore, the ABYT-PAD uses a random number generator to make its padding, which is costly.

4 Design Criteria of the New Padding Method

To prevent POAs, many protocols remove the padding oracle or check whether the MAC is correct. However, the basic measure for defense against POAs consists in designing and using a padding technique that can withstand POAs. This paper selected ABYT-PAD and ABIT-PAD from among the ten existing padding methods to be secure against POAs(in our best knowledge, there is no known padding method secure against POAs rather than these three methods) and analyzed their characteristics. The following design criteria are presented on the basis of the results of that analysis([Table 2]). Some of our design criteria are to overcome the demerit of ABYT-PAD and ABIT-PAD (criteria 2, 4 and 5) and others are inherited from them (criteria 1, 3). The first, second and third design criteria are related to security, while the fourth and fifth are related to efficiency.

5 New Padding Methods

This section proposes three new padding methods that are secure against POAs and efficient as well. Our design strategy is to satisfy as many as design criteria in Table 2(note that the third and fifth design criteria cannot be satisfied at the same time). It is assumed that a block is 8 bytes in all padding methods.

5.1 New Padding Method 1 (NPM1)

This method performs the checksum operation to determine the padding boundary (X) and padding value (Y). Since it uses the plaintext to generate the checksum, the checksum operation can be performed to determine whether the ciphertext has been altered illicitly.

First, the checksum X is generated by xoring from the first byte of the second last plaintext block ($q-1$) to the last byte of the last plaintext block q in bytes. Then the first byte of the plaintext block $q-1$ is xor'ed to X to create Y. The generated X is padded after the last byte of the plaintext block q, and Y is padded so that the plaintext length becomes a multiple of n (Fig. 5).

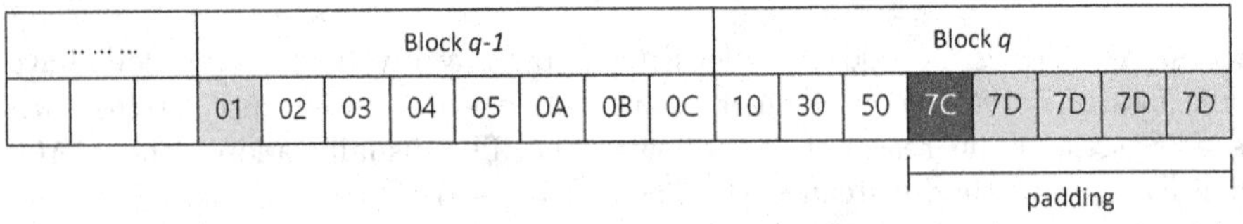

Fig. 5. Example 1 of new padding method 1

$X = 0x01 \oplus 0x02 \oplus 0x03 \oplus 0x04 \oplus 0x05 \oplus 0x0A \oplus 0x0B \oplus 0x0C \oplus 0x10 \oplus 0x30 \oplus 0x50 = 0x7C$

Table 2. Design criteria of a secure and efficient padding method

Design Criteria	Description
1. Non-leakage of padding length from padding values	o The key datum used in a POA is the padding length o The leakage of padding length leads to the leakage of plaintext length o The padding data may be restored using them
2. Use of the second last plaintext information to make padding values	o Modifying the second last ciphertext block (mainly done in POA) forces the change of the second last plaintext block in the CBC. o This makes difficult for the attacker to distinguish the original plaintext part and padding part.
3. Inexistence of an invalid padding	o POA is a method of attack that uses the invalid padding o In other words, the possibility of a POA is great if the padding method includes the invalid padding
4. Non-use of pseudo-random number generator	o A padding method that needs a pseudo-random number must use a pseudo-random number generator o However, the pseudo-random number generator is costly
5. Possibility of checking padding value modification	o The attacker arbitrarily modifies the ciphertext to attack the protocol o The efficiency of the protocol deteriorates if the modification of the ciphertext cannot be detected

$Y = X \oplus 0\text{x}01 = 0\text{x}7D$

If the first byte of the plaintext block $q-1$ is 0x00, X becomes Y, which makes the padding has been incorrectly removed. In that case, we set $Y = X \oplus 1$.

If the length of the plaintext is a multiple of n, a padding block (0x$XY \cdots Y$) is added to signal that the padding has been used. Since both X and Y must be used, X is padded at the end of the plaintext and the block of 0x$Y \cdots Y$ is added if the length of the last plaintext block is $n-1$(Fig. 6).

To remove the padding, the bytes which have the same value as the last byte (Y) are removed, and then another byte (X) is removed. Next, the padding is checked. The checksum is calculated with the restored plaintext to generate X',

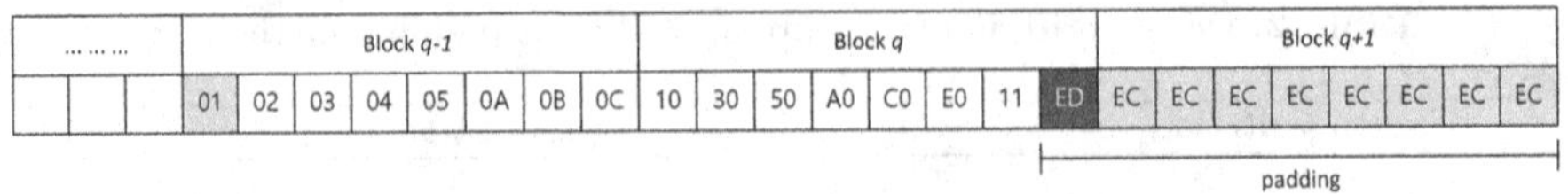

Fig. 6. Example 2 of new padding method 1

and this value is checked to determine if it is the same as the removed X. If they are the same, X' is xor'ed with the first byte of the plaintext block $q-1$, and is checked to determine if it is the same as Y. If the first byte of the plaintext block $q-1$ is 0x00, it is checked if $Y = X \oplus 1$.

5.2 New Padding Method 2 (NPM2)

This method determines the padding boundary (X) and padding value (Y) using the last second plaintext block, and is more efficient than NPM1 because it does not require an additional operation for checksum. The first and second bytes of the second last plaintext block ($q-1$) are set to be X and Y, respectively. The generated X is padded behind the last byte of the plaintext block q, and Y is padded next so that the length of the plaintext becomes a multiple of n(Fig. 7).

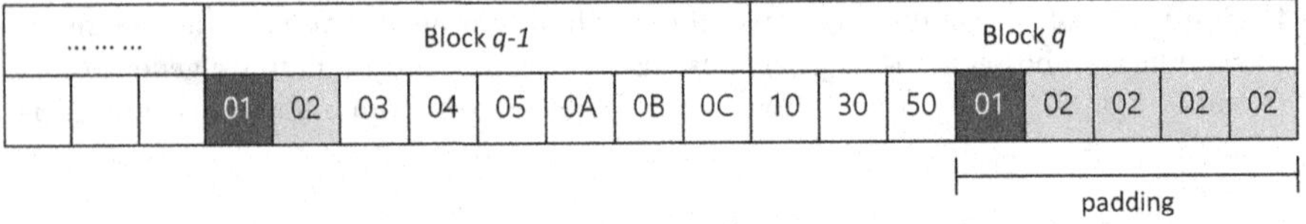

Fig. 7. Example 1 of new padding method 2

If the first byte and the second byte of the plaintext block $q-1$ are the same, the padding is incorrectly removed. In that case, Y is set to $X \oplus 1$.

If the length of the plaintext is a multiple of n, a padding block ($0\text{x}XY \cdots Y$) is added to signal that the padding has been added. Since both X and Y must be used, X is padded at the end of the plaintext and the block of $0\text{x}Y \cdots Y$ is added if the length of the last plaintext block is $n-1$(Fig. 8).

…… …			Block q-1								Block q								Block q+1							
			01	02	03	04	05	0A	0B	0C	10	30	50	A0	C0	E0	11	01	02	02	02	02	02	02	02	02

padding

Fig. 8. Example 2 of new padding method 2

To remove the padding, the bytes which have the same value as the last byte (Y) are removed, and then another byte (X) is removed. Next, the padding is checked. With the restored plaintext, it is checked to determine if the first byte of the plaintext block $q-1$ is the same as X. If they are the same, it is checked to determine if the second byte is the same as Y. If X and Y are the same, it is xor'ed with 1 and checked to determine if $Y = X \oplus 1$.

5.3 New Padding Method 3 (NPM3)

Like the new padding method 2, this padding method determines the padding boundary (X) and padding value (Y) using the last second plaintext block and is more efficient than NPM1.

The last byte of the last plaintext block (q) is set to be X. Then the ($X mod n$)th byte of the second last plaintext block ($q-1$) is picked as Y. The Y is padded next to the last byte of the plaintext block q so that the length of the plaintext becomes a multiple of n(Fig. 9).

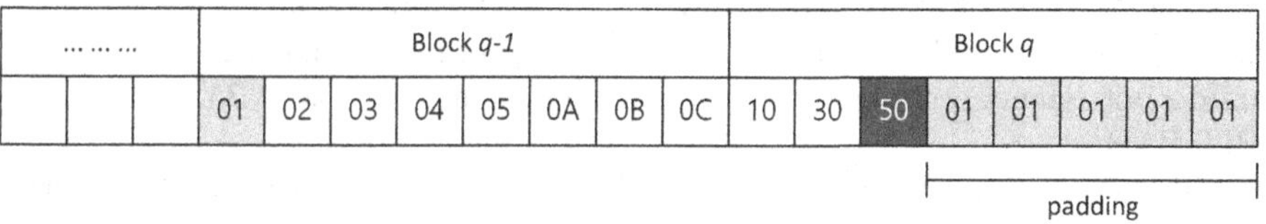

Fig. 9. Example 1 of new padding method 3

If X and Y are the same, the padding is not correctly removed. In that case, Y is set to $X \oplus 1$. If the length of the plaintext is a multiple of n, a padding block (0x$YY \cdots Y$) is added to signal that the padding is being used.

To remove the padding, the bytes whose values are the same as the last byte (Y) are removed. However, another byte (X) is not removed since it is the correct plaintext byte. Next, the padding is checked. With the last byte of the restored plaintext as X, it is checked to determine if the ($X mod n$)th byte of the plaintext block $q-1$ is the same as Y. If not, 1 is xor'ed to Y and it is checked if they are the same.

5.4 Comparison of New Padding Methods and Secure Padding Methods

Security. The new padding methods proposed in this paper are designed to be secure against POAs and to have invalid padding to ensure efficiency. Although there is invalid padding, POAs cannot be effective. The reason is as follows: The POA attacker generally modifies the second last ciphertext block to firstly find the padding length and secondly do the plaintext block byte by byte. Our padding methods all use the second last plaintext block to make paddings.

So, in our padding methods, modifying the second last ciphertext block by the POA attacker leads to a change of the second last plaintext block, which always makes "Invalid Padding" with a very high probability. This means that there is no indication to distinguish the padding length and plaintext block. In addition, as they use the plaintext without a pseudo-random generator, one or two bytes of the plaintext may be leaked if the padding value is known, but there is still no problem with security since the padding length is not leaked. Therefore our padding methods have resistance to the POAs.

Efficiency. As shown in Sect. 3, ABYT-PAD, and ABIT-PAD are padding methods that are secure against POAs among the conventional padding methods. They are not subject to POAs because there is no invalid padding. Although this is a desirable attribute in terms of security, the MAC verification is needed, which makes the efficiency of protocol degraded. TLS version 1.0 and its above versions frequently adopt the MAC-then-Encrypt method with the CBC mode. In such a case, the server always checks the MAC verification if it uses the ABYT-PAD or ABIT-PAD. This is due to the fact that they do not have any invalid padding. However, our padding methods do not always force the server to check the MAC verification since they may have "Invalid" sent from the oracle. Furthermore, the ABYT-PAD need a pseudo-random number generator, while ours do not. Hence, our methods are more efficient than the ABYT-PAD and ABIT-PAD.

[Table 3] compares the security and efficiency of the three new padding methods proposed in this paper and the existing secure padding methods.

Table 3. Security and Efficiency Comparison

Design Criteria in Table 2		ABYT-PAD	ABIT-PAD	NPM1	NPM2	NPM3
Security	1	O	O	O	O	O
	2	X	X	O	O	O
	3	O	O	X	X	X
Efficiency	4	X	O	O	O	O
	5	X	X	O	O	O

6 Conclusion

This paper analyzed the ten existing padding methods from the viewpoint of defense against POAs and found two (ABYT-PAD and ABIT-PAD) to be secure against POAs. We then analyzed these padding methods and proposed design criteria that ensure security from POAs. We also proposed additional design criteria to further enhance their efficiency.

Based on the proposed design criteria, we proposed three new padding methods that are both secure from POAs and efficient. The proposed new padding methods are as secure as the existing padding methods as well as being more efficient.

There are many studies related to POAs, and the security of encrypted communication such as SSL/TLS is being reviewed as a result. In most cases, the padding oracle is removed or the MAC verification is added to defend against POAs. However, these measures are not the root solution and ultimately degrade the efficiency of encrypted communication. The new padding methods proposed in this study, however, could be the root solution to POAs and are highly efficient. As such, we are confident that the application of these new padding methods will constitute good measures for secure communication in the future.

Acknowledgments. This research was supported by Basic Science Research Program through the National Research Foundation of Korea (NRF) funded by the Ministry of Education (Grant No. 2013R1A1A2059864).

References

[AP1] AlFardan, N., Paterson, K.G.: Lucky thirteen: breaking the TLS and DTLS record protocols. In Proceedings of IEEE Symposium on Security and Privacy, pp. 526–540 (2013)

[AP2] AlFardan, N., Paterson, K.G.: Plaintext-recovery attacks against datagram TLS. In: Network and Distributed System Security Symposium(2012)

[BU1] Black, J., Urtubia, H.: Side-channel attacks on symmetric encryption schemes: the case for authenticated encryption. In: Proceedings of the 11th USENIX Security Symposium, pp. 327–338 (2002)

[DR1] Duong, T., Rizzo, J.: Cryptography in the web: the case of cryptographic design flaws in ASP.NET. In Proceedings of IEEE Symposium on Security and Privacy, pp. 481–489 (2011)

[D1] Dworkin, M.: Recommendation for Block Cipher Modes of Operation. NIST 800–38A (2001)

[K1] Kaliski, B.: PKCS #7: Cryptographic Message Syntax Version 1.5. RFC 2315 (1998)

[KR1] Klima, V., Rosa, T.: Side Channel Attacks on CBC Encrypted Messages in the PKCS#7 Format. eprint (2003)

[MZ1] Mister, S., Zuccherato, R.J.: An attack on CFB mode encryption as used by OpenPGP. In: Preneel, B., Tavares, S. (eds.) SAC 2005. LNCS, vol. 3897, pp. 82–94. Springer, Heidelberg (2006)

[PSB1] Pironti, A., Strub, P.Y., Bhargavan, K.: Identifying Website Users by TLS Traffic Analysis: New Attacks and Effective Countermeasures. Research Report, Prosecco Project-Team, INRIA (2012)

[PY1] Paterson, K.G., Yau, A.K.L.: Padding oracle attacks on the ISO CBC mode encryption standard. In: Okamoto, T. (ed.) CT-RSA 2004. LNCS, vol. 2964, pp. 305–323. Springer, Heidelberg (2004)

[RD1] Rizzo, J., Duong, T.: Practical Padding Oracle Attacks. USENIX WOOT (2010)

[STW1] Seggelmann, R., Tuexen, M., Williams, M.: Transport Layer Security (TLS) and Datagram Transport Layer Security (DTLS) Heartbeat Extension. RFC 6520 (2012)

[V1] Vaudenay, S.: Security flaws induced by CBC padding - applications to SSL, IPSEC, WTLS. In: Knudsen, L.R. (ed.) EUROCRYPT 2002. LNCS, vol. 2332, pp. 534–545. Springer, Heidelberg (2002)

Physical Unclonable Functions

Let Me Prove It to You: RO PUFs Are Provably Learnable

Fatemeh Ganji(✉), Shahin Tajik, and Jean-Pierre Seifert

Security in Telecommunications, Technische Universität Berlin and Telekom Innovation Laboratories, Berlin, Germany
{fganji,stajik,jpseifert}@sec.t-labs.tu-berlin.de

Abstract. The last decade has witnessed a major change in the methods of Integrated Circuit (IC) fingerprinting and random key generation.The invention of Physically Unclonable functions (PUFs) was a milestone in the development of these methods. Ring-oscillator (RO) PUFs are one of the popular intrinsic PUF instances in authentication and random number generation applications. Similar to other types of PUFs, unpredictability and unclonability are the key requirements for the security of RO-PUFs. However, these requirements cannot be perfectly met for RO-PUFs, as demonstrated by studies investigating different attacks against RO-PUFs. In addition to semi-invasive attacks, modeling attacks have been proposed that aim to predict the *response* to an arbitrarily chosen *challenge*. To this end, the adversary collects only a small number of challenge response pairs (CRPs), and then attempts to constitute a model of the challenge-response behavior of the PUF. Nevertheless, it is not ensured that a model will be delivered after learning the seen CRPs, whose number is solely estimated instead of being properly proved. Aiming to address these issues, this paper presents a Probably Approximately Correct (PAC) learning framework enabling the learning of an RO-PUF for arbitrary levels of accuracy and confidence. Indeed, we prove that a polynomial-size Decision List (DL) can represent an RO-PUF. Thus, an arbitrarily chosen RO-PUF can be PAC learned by collecting only a polynomial number of CRPs. The "hidden" polynomial size of the respective representation of an RO-PUF therefore accounts for the success of the previously proposed (heuristic) attacks. However, our proposed bound is provably better, when comparing the number of CRPs required for our attack with already existing bounds calculated by applying heuristic techniques. Finally, by conducting experiments we complement the proof provided in our PAC learning framework.

Keywords: Physically unclonable functions · RO PUFs · Decision lists · Machine learning · PAC learning

1 Introduction

Device authentication and random key generation methods have entered a new phase of development, explained by growing and increasingly demanding user

S. Kwon and A. Yun (Eds.): ICISC 2015, LNCS 9558, pp. 345–358, 2016.
DOI: 10.1007/978-3-319-30840-1_22

need for security. Due to the vulnerability of legacy key storage in the non-volatile memories (NVM) to semi- and fully-invasive attacks [8,11], the concept of Physically Unclonable Functions (PUFs) has emerged as an alternative solution [6,20]. The basic idea behind the concept of PUFs is using physical characteristics of an integrated circuit (IC) corresponding to manufacturing process variations, which make each IC slightly different from others. Regarding how these physical characteristics are exploited, several PUF instances have been introduced in recent years [12]. Delay-based PUFs, such as arbiter PUFs and ring-oscillator (RO) PUFs, is one of the PUF families, which attracts attention thanks to their easy and inexpensive implementations on different platforms [12,26]. Arbiter PUFs and RO-PUFs share the common feature of using the different propagation delays of identical electrical paths on the chip to generate a *virtually* unique output.

Coming under several attacks, it has been shown that the security of delay-based PUFs can be comprised, and therefore, the *unclonability* and *unpredictability* features promised by the manufacturer are not absolutely supported. While the PUF manufacturers have been contributing to improve the design and consequently the security of the PUFs, adversaries are simultaneously developing different non-invasive and semi-invasive attacks. For instance, it has been stated that RO-PUFs are subject to semi-invasive electromagnetic (EM) side channel analysis [17]. Moreover, an arbiter PUF can be fully characterized by semi-invasive temporal photonic emission analysis [27]. Being relatively cost-effective and requiring no particular access to the chip in contrast to semi-invasive attacks, adversaries can achieve greater advantages by applying modeling techniques [19,22–24]. In this case, the adversary applies a relatively small set of *challenges* (i.e., inputs of the PUF) and collects the *responses* (i.e., outputs of the PUF) of the respective PUF to those challenges. Afterwards by applying machine learning techniques, the adversary can build a model of the Challenge-Response behavior of the PUF, which can *predict* the responses of the PUF to new arbitrarily chosen challenges. Although the popularity of modeling attacks has been a key driver for several studies on the security of PUFs, only recently it has been demonstrated that after launching already existing modeling attacks, the delivery of the model is not always ensured [4]. To address this issue, a probably approximately correct (PAC) learning attack has been proposed and successfully launched on arbiter PUFs [4]. Unfortunately, such a through analysis has not been developed for RO-PUFs so far, and solely empirical modeling attacks have been suggested.

As an instance of modeling attacks against RO-PUFs, Rührmair et al. have applied Quicksort algorithm to model an RO-PUF in the case that the adversary cannot control the challenges, although the challenges can be eavesdropped [22]. As another example, a new attack on RO-PUFs has been introduced, whose key success factor is the availability of the helper data used to compensate the impact of the noise on the responses [19]. Obviously, in the absence of the helper data, which is a likely scenario in practice, their attack cannot succeed. In another attempt to develop a machine learning method that can be applied to compromise the security of an RO-PUF, a genetic programming approach has been employed [24]. Although their results are promising in terms of the prediction accuracy of the obtained models, neither the scalability of the approach nor the probability of delivering the final model has been discussed. On the other hand, empirical results suggest to increase the number of ring oscillators as an effective countermeasure against above mentioned modeling attacks. This claim is supported by the observation that in this case the likelihood of the response prediction is less probable. Moreover, the lack of thorough analyses of the security of the RO-PUFs further supports the development of ad hoc solutions to their security problems. Therefore, several different implementation methods have been proposed in order to improve the security of RO-PUFs [16,18], despite the fact that this primitive is inherently vulnerable to machine learning attacks. Our work aims to address the following contributions:

Establishing a Fit-for-Purpose Representation of RO-PUFs. In addition to the feature of being polynomial-sized, our proposed representation can be easily established by collecting CRPs. Therefore, when comparing to other complicated and sophisticated representations, it can be rapidly established. Due to this representation we propose an algorithm that can learn an RO-PUF for given levels of accuracy and confidence.

Mathematical Proof of the Vulnerability of RO-PUFs to our Machine Learning Attack. The number of CRPs required to launch our attack is carefully calculated. We prove that this small number is indeed polynomial in the number of ring oscillators.

Providing a Proof of Concept of how our Attack Performs in Practice. By conducting experiments we evaluate the effectiveness of our attack.

2 Notation and Preliminaries

This section contains the information required for a better understanding of our approach. In addition to the brief description of the RO-PUF concept, this section covers an introduction to the notion of decision lists and PAC learning.

2.1 RO-PUFs

The general concept of PUFs enables a mathematical description of inherent silicon properties of a chip. For a given PUF, the function $f_{PUF} : \mathcal{C} \rightarrow \mathcal{Y}$, where $f_{PUF}(c) = y$ describes the input to output mapping of the PUF. For this mapping, $\mathcal{C} = \{0,1\}^n$ and $\mathcal{Y} = \{0,1\}$ are the sets of challenges (inputs) and responses (outputs), respectively [13]. The key features of a PUF are being evaluable, unique, reproducible, unpredictable, one-way, and more importantly, unclonable [12].

The manufacturing variations in the delays of circuit gates have been used to design an RO-PUF [26]. The first architecture is composed of N identically designed oscillator rings, whose frequencies are compared pairwise to generate the binary output of the RO-PUF, see Fig. 1. Although $N(N-1)/2$ pairs of oscillators are possible for this architecture, the number of responses cannot exceed $\log(N!)$ due to the particular ascending order of the frequencies [9]. Consider the RO-PUF depicted in Fig. 1 that features N ring oscillators. By applying the respective binary challenges the frequencies of two ring oscillators are compared to generate the response. It is clear that the challenges applied to two multiplexers should not be identical. Otherwise, only N different pairs of ring oscillators can be selected, and consequently solely N responses can be obtained. Hence, more formally, the k- bit challenge $c_1c_2\cdots c_k$ is applied to one of the multiplexers (e.g., the upper one) to select the first ring oscillator, whereas the k- bit challenge $c'_1c'_2\cdots c'_k$ is fed into the second multiplexer to select the second ring oscillator (note that c'_i is not the complement of c_i, and it is chosen randomly and independently from c_i). As required by our approach, without loss of generality, we denote the appropriate challenge applied to the RO-PUF by the binary string $c_1c_2\cdots c_kc'_1c'_2\cdots c'_k$, where $k = \log_2 N$ and $c_i \neq c'_i$ $(1 \leq i \leq k)$. It may be thought that the number of bits in a challenge can represent a measure of the security of this type of PUFs. However, in practice the number of ring oscillators implemented on a chip is a more limiting, and a determinant factor. The influence of this factor on the uniqueness of the RO-PUF and the silicon area footprint has been discussed in the literature, e.g., [16].

The vulnerability of RO-PUFs to modeling attacks has been revealed so far [22]. When launching a modeling attack on this type of PUFs, two scenarios can be defined. In the first scenario, the attacker can *selectively* apply the desired challenges to figure out the ascending order of frequencies of the rings. In this scenario, the number of CRPs can be $O(N\log_2 N)$, or in an extreme case, $N^2/2$, where the attacker collects all the possible CRPs. Of course it is possible in theory, but in practice the attacker may not have direct access to the challenges and, consequently, this types of attacks may fail. On the other hand, in an advance and a more realistic scenario that is considered in our paper, the attacker can solely collect the challenges randomly applied to the PUF and the respective responses.

Last but not least, without limiting the generality of our approach, we assume that meta-stable conditions (i.e., related to noisy responses of the RO-PUF or when having equal frequencies of ring oscillators) must have been resolved by the manufacturer. Numerous mechanisms addressing the meta-stable condition of RO-PUFs (so called unreliability of the PUF) have been proposed in the literature. This issue is beyond the scope of our paper and for more details the reader is referred to, e.g., [15,16].

2.2 Decision Lists

Here we briefly introduce the notion of decision lists, and refer the reader to [21] for more details.

We first introduce the main building block that is the set of Boolean attributes $V_n = \{x_1, x_2, \cdots, x_n\}$. Note that each attribute can be ***true*** or ***false***, identified with "1" and "0", respectively. Moreover, X_n denotes the set $\{0,1\}^n$

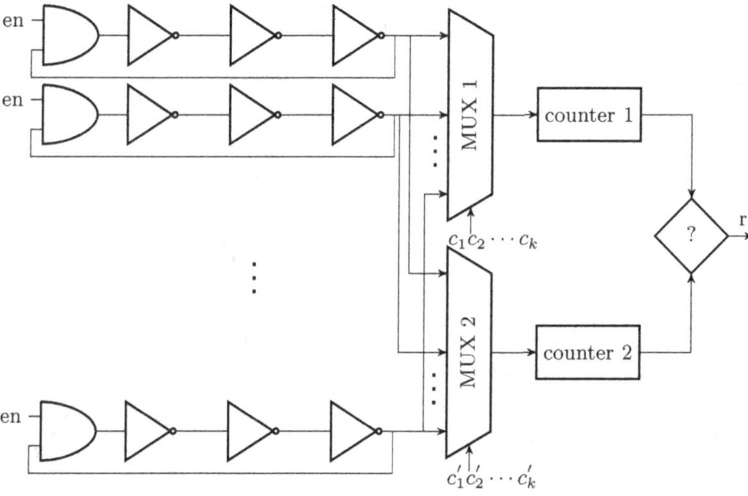

Fig. 1. An RO-PUF with N ring-oscillators. By applying challenges to two multiplexers, two ring-oscillators are selected and their outputs are connected to the clock inputs of 2 counters. The counters count the number of the rising edges during a predefined time period. Finally, the state of the counters are compared by the comparator placed at the end of the PUF to generate a binary response.

of all binary strings containing n bits. x_i and $\overline{x}_i$ (complement of x_i) are called *literals* associated with the Boolean attribute x_i. Let $L_n = \{x_1, \overline{x_1}, \cdots, x_n, \overline{x}_n\}$ be the set of $2n$ literals. The mapping from V_n to $\{0,1\}$ that maps each Boolean attribute to either "0" or "1" is an *assignment*. An assignment can be also represented as an n-bits string, where the ith bit indicates the value of x_i (i.e., "0" or "1") for that assignment.

A Boolean formula is a mapping from assignments into $\{0,1\}$. Each Boolean attribute can be a formula so that x_i and $\overline{x}_i$ are two possible formulas. If for an assignment the formula is "1", that assignment is called a positive example of the concept represented by the formula. Otherwise, it is a negative example. Clearly, each Boolean formula defines a respective Boolean function from X_n to $\{0,1\}$. A *term* is the conjunction of Boolean attributes (i.e., a Boolean formula) that can be true or false ("1" or "0") depending on the value of its Boolean attributes. The size of a term indicates the number of its attributes. The size 0 is given to only the term **true**. The set of all conjunctive terms of size at most k is denoted by C_k^n, and it is known that

$$|C_k^n| = \sum_{i=0}^{k} \binom{2n}{i} = O(n^k).$$

Hence, for a constant k, the size of C_k^n is polynomial in n.

Decision lists are one of the learnable representations of Boolean functions. A useful and interesting interpretation of decision lists is that they define

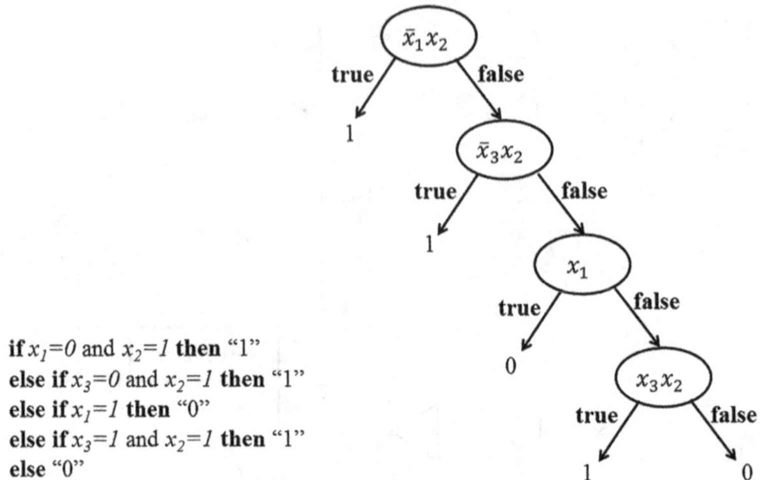

Fig. 2. (a) A sample of "**if- then- else if- ...- else**" rules. (b) Diagram of the decision list corresponding to this rule.

a concept, which follows a general pattern but with some exceptions. As another interpretation, a decision list can be thought of being an extended "**if- then- else if- ...- else**" rule (see Fig. 2(a)). Hence, a decision list can be established from such a rule, as shown in Fig. 2. More formally, a decision list is the list L containing r pairs $(f_1, v_1), \cdots, (f_r, v_r)$, where the Boolean formula f_i is a term in C_k^n and $v_i \in \{0,1\}$ with $1 \leq i \leq r-1$. The formula f_r is a constant function: $v_r = 1$. A Boolean function is associated with the decision list so that for a string $x \in X_n$ we have $L(x) = v_j$, where j is the smallest index in L, where $f_j(x) = 1$. This relationship implies that common patterns are listed at the top of the decision list, whereas the exceptions can be found at the end of that. The set of all terms, whose maximum size is k and defined by a decision list, is denoted by k – *DL*.

2.3 PAC Model

The Probably Approximately Correct (PAC) model addresses the problem of learning an unknown concept for pre-defined, given levels of *accuracy* and *confidence*. As the name implies, after the learning phase a hypothesis is obtained with high probability that can approximate the target concept for the pre-defined level of accuracy. This definition can be formulated as follows [10].

Consider the instance space $X_n = \{0,1\}^n$, over which we define the target concept $\mathfrak{C}_n$. The hypothesis space is denoted by $\mathfrak{H}_n$. We have also $X = \cup_{n\geq 1} X_n$, $\mathfrak{C} = \cup_{n\geq 1}\mathfrak{C}_n$, and similarly $\mathfrak{H} = \cup_{n\geq 1}\mathfrak{H}_n$. We assume that each instance is drawn from X_n regarding an arbitrary probability distribution D defined on X_n. The error of a hypothesis $h \in \mathfrak{H}$ for the target concept $c \in \mathfrak{C}$ can be defined as:

$$error(h) := \sum_{x \in h \triangle c} D(x),$$

where $\triangle$ is the symmetric difference. Let $\mathcal{L}$ be a polynomial time algorithm, and $p(\cdot,\cdot,\cdot)$ denote a polynomial. Assume that for all distributions D, all ε and δ $(0 < \varepsilon, \delta < 1)$, $p(n, 1/\varepsilon, 1/\delta)$ *examples* of c are drawn independently and regarding the distribution D. If these examples are given to the algorithm $\mathcal{L}$, with probability at least $1-\delta$ the output of the algorithm is a hypothesis $h \in \mathfrak{H}$ so that $error(h) \leq \varepsilon$. In this case, $\mathfrak{C}$ is PAC learnable by $\mathfrak{H}$. If $\mathfrak{C} = \mathfrak{H}$, $\mathfrak{C}$ is called *properly* PAC learnable. Otherwise, if the following conditions are met, $\mathfrak{C}$ is PAC learnable: (a) $\mathfrak{C}$ is PAC learnable by $\mathfrak{H}$, and (b) $\mathfrak{H}$ can be evaluated in polynomial time on given examples.

3 PAC Learning of RO-PUFs

In order to establish a proper representation of an RO-PUF, we focus on a widely accepted implementation of RO-PUFs as proposed in [26], see Fig. 1. Nevertheless, modified architectures proposed in [29–31]. Potential attacks against them are discussed briefly in Sect. 3.3. Consider an RO-PUF that features N ring oscillators. The challenge is a $2k$-bit binary string $c_1c_2\cdots c_kc'_1c'_2\cdots c'_k$ as discussed in Sect. 2.1. When applying this binary challenge to an RO-PUF, the string $c_1c_2\cdots c_k$ determines the first ring oscillator to be selected, whereas the string $c'_1c'_2\cdots c'_k$ determines the second one. By comparing the frequencies of these ring oscillators, the final response of the RO-PUF is generated. We define the binary to one-hot coded mapping $f_{map}: \{0{,}1\}^k \rightarrow \{0{,}1\}^N$ that maps a binary string, e.g., $c_1c_2\cdots c_k$, to a one-hot string $x_1x_2\cdots x_N$. Therefore, all Boolean attributes of the mapped string are "0", except solely one of them, e.g., the jth attribute, that is "1" corresponding to the selected ring oscillator.

By performing the mapping f_{map} on each challenge, we obtain two one-hot coded strings, which can be merged to a single mapped challenge $x_1x_2\cdots x_N$. In other words, if $f_{map}(c_1c_2\cdots c_k) = x_1x_2\cdots x_N$, where $x_i = 1$ and for the second string we obtain $f_{map}(c'_1c'_2\cdots c'_k) = x'_1x'_2\cdots x'_N$, where $x_j = 1$, we can merge the mapped strings to a single string $x_1x_2\cdots x_N$, where x_i and x_j are "1". This step can be performed easily by, e.g., adding the respective attributes of two stings together. Let the set of all the attributes be denoted by $V_N = \{x_1{,}x_2,\cdots,x_N\}$. Moreover, the set $X_N = \{0{,}1\}^N$ denotes the set of all mapped challenges. Note that according to the definition of f_{map}, only two non-zero Boolean attributes of each mapped challenge are drawn from V_N.

Similar to the other types of PUFs, an RO-PUF can be represented by the function $f_{RO}: X_N \rightarrow Y$, where $Y = \{0{,}1\}$, and $f_{RO}(x_1x_2\cdots x_N) = y$. Obviously, this mapping represents a Boolean function. More precisely, we define each mapped challenge as being a term (e.g., f_i) so that $f_i \in C_2^N$. Now the list L containing r CRPs represents a $2-DL$.

In order to prove that RO-PUFs are indeed PAC learnable under the decision list representation, we follow the procedure introduced in [21]. We first prove that a $2-DL$ representing an RO-PUF has a polynomial size. Afterwards, we prove the PAC learnability of RO-PUFs represented by the $2-DL$. To this end, we apply a classical polynomial-time algorithm that learns a $2-DL$ for given levels of accuracy and confidence, when it is given a polynomial number of CRPs.

3.1 Size of a $2-DL$ Representing an RO-PUF

The importance of the size of the representation is due to the fact that the time complexity of learning algorithms greatly depends on this size. Defining the size of a hypothesis, the mapping $size : \{0,1\}^k \rightarrow N$ can be defined that associates a natural number $size(h)$ with each $h \in \mathfrak{H}$. Although this definition allows $size(\cdot)$ to be any mapping as defined above, in our case the most appropriate interpretation of it is the size of h in bits [10]. From this general definition, we can now shift our focus to the following theorem.

Theorem 1. *A $2-DL$ representing an RO-PUF is polynomial-sized.*

Proof: The maximum number of elements in a $k-DL$, in the general case, has been determined as follows [21].

$$|k-DL| = O\left(3^{|C_k^N|}(|C_k^N|)!\right).$$

This can be proved since in the decision list, each term from C_k^N can be labeled by "0", "1", or "missing". Furthermore, no order for the elements of the list is defined.

Now we put emphasis on the size of the decision list representing an RO-PUF. Obviously, according to our specific definition of the strings $x_1x_2\cdots x_N$, in our decision list the maximum number of possibles elements is $N(N-1)/2$. However, according to the ascending order of the frequencies of the ring oscillators, a list containing $O(N-1)$ terms is completely expressive. This can be easily understood due to the fact that the Boolean attribute x_i has a previously assigned meaning, which is directly related to the frequency of the ith ring oscillator. Therefore, the size of our $2-DL$ in bits (i.e., the size of the representation) is $O\big((N-1)\log_2(N-1)\big)$. ■

3.2 PAC Learnability of the $k-DL$

To prove that the $2-DL$ representing the RO-PUF is PAC learnable, in addition to Theorem 1, we have to provide a polynomial-time algorithm that can generate a decision list, when being fed by a set of labeled examples (so called *sample*). The upper bound of the number of examples required by the algorithm can be calculated according to the polynomial learnability theorem proved by Blumer et al. [2]. According to this theorem and the polynomial size of a $2-DL$, it has been proved that in general, a $2-DL$ can be PAC learned by applying a simple algorithm [21]. For the sake of completeness, this section presents the polynomial learnability theorem in the case of an RO-PUF represented by the $2-DL$ as well as the algorithm proposed to PAC learn the respective decision list. The reader is referred to [2] for the proof of the theorem and [21] for more details on the algorithm.

Theorem 2. *Assume that the learner has access to Oracle $EX := f_{RO}$, and can call it successively to collect m independently drawn examples (i.e., CRPs).*

In order to PAC learn the RO-PUF for given ε and δ, under the $2-DL$ representation, the number of CRPs required to be collected is bounded by:

$$m = O\left(\frac{1}{\varepsilon}\left((N-1)\log_2(N-1) + \log_2\left(\frac{1}{\delta}\right)\right)\right).$$

As pointed out in Sect. 2.1, the number of ring oscillators heavily affects the uniqueness and silicon area footprint of RO-PUFs. In other words, although $N = 2^k$ and k can be increased in theory, N and consequently k cannot be arbitrarily increased due to the restrictions imposed by the technological properties of ICs. Hence, not only in our approach but also in previously proposed attacks (e.g., [22]) the number of CRPs required to characterize the challenge-response behavior of RO-PUFs is presented as a function of N, the number of ring oscillators. An important message conveyed by Theorem 2 is that the maximum number of CRPs needed to be collected by the attacker is polynomial in N, and more importantly, it is asymptotically better than the bound estimated in [22].

In order to give a better understanding on the impact of a change in ε and δ on the number of CRPs, the upper bound of the number of CRPs calculated according to Theorem 2 is depicted in Fig. 3. The curve is drawn for $N = 1024$ and different ε and δ values.

The most important message given by the Theorem 2 is that the maximum number of CRPs required to PAC learn an RO-PUF represented by the $2-DL$ is only polynomial in N. According to [21], a polynomial-time algorithm can be applied to PAC learn this decision list. The main steps of this algorithm are shown in Algorithm 1.

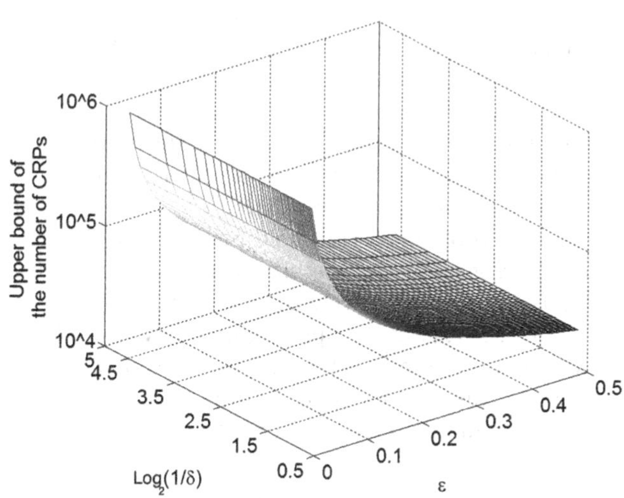

Fig. 3. Upper bound of the number of CRPs required for PAC learning of an RO-PUF with 1024 ring oscillators.

Algorithm 1. Algorithm for PAC learning of a $k - DL$ as proposed by [21]

Require: The set S containing r pairs $(f_1, v_1), \cdots, (f_r, v_r)$, where $(1 \leq r \leq m)$
Ensure: L that is a $k - DL$

$T := \emptyset$
$j = 1$
while S is not empty **do**
Find a term t in C_k^n so that all f_i $(1 \leq i \leq r)$ make t true, and their corresponding v_i are either "0" or "1"
$T \leftarrow t$
if t corresponds to positive examples **then**:
  $v = 1$
  else
  $v = 0$
fi
return (t,v) as the jth item of L
$S := S - T$
$j = j + 1$
od

3.3 PAC Learnability of the *self-decision* RO-PUF

The rational behind the design of this type of PUFs [31], is that combination of frequencies of the ring oscillators forming the PUF can be a countermeasure against machine learning attack. Although this assumption was correct at the time when this design has been proposed, recently the invalidity of that has been proved in a series of work [3–5,28]. Here we briefly describe how the results of their work can be further extended to prove the vulnerability of *self-decision* RO-PUFs (so called sum RO-PUFs). The architecture proposed in [29,31] is similar to the architecture of arbiter PUFs, however, the main difference is that the frequencies of the ring oscillators (instead of delays of stages in an arbiter PUF) are added together. Following the procedure proposed in [4], these real-valued frequencies of ring oscillators can be mapped to a limited integer interval. This enables us to construct a deterministic finite automaton (DFA) representing the sum RO-PUF, and then PAC learn it.

A more interesting design suggested by Yu et al. [30] relies on the fact that more complex recombination functions, e.g., XOR function can provide additional robustness against machine learning attacks for RO-PUF. The proposed architecture shares several similarities with XOR arbiter PUFs, and in a similar fashion can be represented by linear threshold functions (LTFs) [1]. It has been proved that although in general the Vapnik-Chervonenkis dimension of PUFs can be exponential is the number of ring oscillators (in the case of RO-PUFs), when this number does not exceed the upper bound $\ln N$, the RO-PUF is indeed PAC learnable (for the proof see [5]). On the other hand, when the number of ring oscillators exceeds this upper bound, hybrid attacks similar to what has been proposed in [3,28] can be applied to break the security of the RO-PUF.

4 Results

In this section we provide simulation results to validate our theoretical findings. To this end, one can adopt the results of large scale experiments reported in [14].

In addition to these results, further measurement results are publicly accessible in a dataset [25]. In this dataset the measurement results containing 100 samples of the frequency of each and every ring oscillators that RO-PUFs feature are collected. Each RO-PUF is composed of 512 ring oscillators implemented on 193 90-nm Xilinx Spartan (XC3S500E) FPGAs. Since we aim to evaluate the effectiveness of our attack against RO-PUFs with different number of ring oscillator, we develop an RO-PUF simulator, whose inputs are frequencies of the ring oscillators. First, our simulator randomly selects N ($N = 128, 256, 512, 1024$) frequencies associated with N different ring oscillators. Afterwards in order to create a set of CRPs, random challenges are applied to the PUF to select a pair of ring oscillators. The indexes of selected ring oscillators and their corresponding responses were stored in a dataset to be learned by the machine learning algorithm proposed in Sect. 3.2.

To learn the CRPs under the decision list representation, we have used the open source machine learning software Weka [7], providing a firm platform for conducting experiments. In our experiments 10 GB RAM of our machine is used. Moreover, the physical core of the machine is an Intel Core 2 Duo (Penryn) running at 2.4 GHz. Experiments conducted in Weka consist of two phases, namely the training and the validation phases. The examples fed into an algorithm can be divided into equally sized subsets (so called folds) to perform cross-validation. For instance, when 10 equally sized subsets are fed into an algorithm, the model is established based on 9 subsets, and then the obtained model is validated on the remaining subset. This process is repeated 10 times so that each subset is used once as the validation dataset and 9 times as the training dataset. Finally, the results obtained for all 10 experiments are averaged to generate a single model. With respect to our setting, this 10 fold cross-validation method is applied in order to evaluate the error of the obtained model (ε). Since the model is always delivered in our experiments, it can be interpreted that δ is very close to zero in our case, as pre-defined and have coded in Weka.

The results of the experiments for several different RO-PUFs have been depicted in Fig. 4. As expected, for the same number of CRPs, the error of the model is higher for RO-PUFs with the higher number of ring oscillators. Furthermore, in our experiments we increase the number of CRPs fed into the algorithm to the extent that a model with a sufficiently small error is obtained. Nevertheless, the maximum number of CRPs given to the algorithm is far less than the upper bound calculated in Sect. 3.2. It can be seen in Fig. 4(a) that for each RO-PUF the error is significantly reduced, when increasing the number of CRPs collected to launch the attack. The maximum time taken to deliver the model of the RO-PUFs, corresponding to the maximum number of CRPs given to the algorithm, is presented in Fig. 4(b). The time complexity is increased for RO-PUFs with a higher number of ring oscillators. However, it is still polynomial in the number of the ring oscillators.

In an attempt to compare our theoretical and practical findings with results previously reported in the literature, we take into consideration the results reported in [22,24]. We consider the worst-case scenario from the adversary

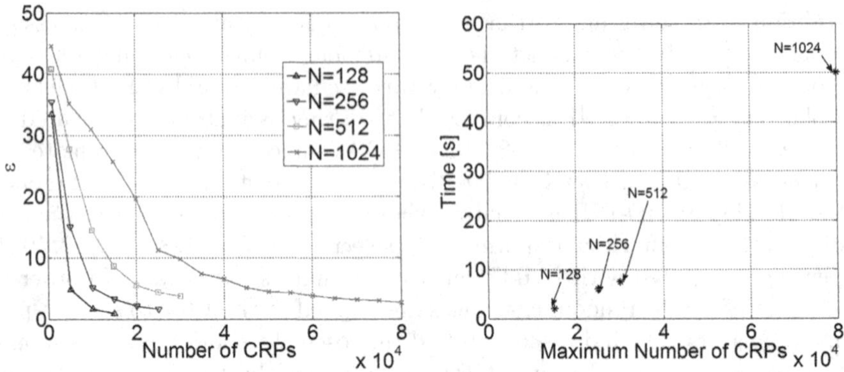

Fig. 4. (a) The number of CRPS required to PAC learn RO-PUFs with different numbers of ring oscillators. Clearly, when increasing the number of CRPs collected for the attack, the error of the obtained model is reduced. (b) Time taken to deliver the model, if the algorithm is fed by the maximum number of CRPs for each RO-PUFs.

perspective, where she can only eavesdrop the CRPs and cannot apply any desired challenges. The crucial difference between the algorithm proposed in [22] and our work is that the delivery of the model is not guaranteed in their framework. Furthermore, although for different RO-PUFs virtually the same numbers of CRPs are suggested in our work and [22], the number of CRPs required for launching their attack is estimated empirically, and is heavily depending on their limited number of experiments. On the contrary, the upper-bound of the number of CRPs required to launch our PAC learning attack is calculated precisely. More importantly, the upper bound calculated with regard to our framework is asymptotically better than their estimated bound.

In a similar fashion, in spite of the fact that the algorithm proposed in [24] might deliver a kind of Boolean function for a given RO-PUF, neither the delivery of the model is ensured nor the scalability of the algorithm is discussed. The experiments conducted to evaluate the feasibility of their attack are performed only on RO-PUFs with 128 ring oscillators. Moreover, when increasing the number of CRPs to achieve a more accurate model, the time taken to generate their proposed model is increased drastically. Unfortunately, the time complexity of their model has not been discussed.

5 Conclusion

As a further step towards investigating the security of RO PUFs, we have proposed a PAC learning framework that results in compromising the security of these PUF instances. In contrast to previous empirical studies, we have mathematically proved that a polynomial-sized representation can be established to learn an RO PUF for given levels of accuracy and confidence. We have proposed the decision list representation of an RO PUF, which not only reflects the physical characteristics of an RO PUF, but also leads to the natural fact that the

RO PUF is indeed PAC learnable. We have further demonstrated that since the number of ring oscillator pairs characterizing the an RO-PUF is polynomial in the number of ring oscillators, the size of the decision list representing the RO PUF is also polynomial in the number of ring oscillators. By conducting experiments we have validated our theoretical results. Last but not least, we conclude that similar to virtually all other PUF instances, provably, RO-PUFs cannot be considered secure regarding their current schemes.

References

1. Anthony, M.: Computational Learning Theory. Cambridge University Press, Cambridge (1997)
2. Blumer, A., Ehrenfeucht, A., Haussler, D., Warmuth, M.: Classifying learnable geometric concepts with the vapnik-chervonenkis dimension. In: Proceedings of the Eighteenth Annual ACM Symposium on Theory of computing, pp. 273–282. ACM (1986)
3. Ganji, F., Krämer, J., Seifert, J.P., Tajik, S.: Lattice basis reduction attack against physically unclonable functions. In: Proceedings of the 22nd ACM Conference on Computer and Communications Security. ACM (2015)
4. Ganji, F., Tajik, S., Seifert, J.P.: PAC Learning of Arbiter PUFs, Security Proofs for Embedded Systems-PROOFS (2014). https://eprint.iacr.org/2015/378.pdf
5. Ganji, F., Tajik, S., Seifert, J.-P.: Why attackers win: on the learnability of XOR arbiter PUFs. In: Conti, M., Schunter, M., Askoxylakis, I. (eds.) TRUST 2015. LNCS, vol. 9229, pp. 22–39. Springer, Heidelberg (2015)
6. Gassend, B., Clarke, D., Van Dijk, M., Devadas, S.: Silicon physical random functions. In: Proceedings of the 9th ACM Conference on Computer and Communications Security, pp. 148–160. ACM (2002)
7. Hall, M., Frank, E., Holmes, G., Pfahringer, B., Reutemann, P., Witten, I.H.: The WEKA data mining software: an update. ACM SIGKDD Explor. Newslett. **11**(1), 10–18 (2009)
8. Helfmeier, C., Nedospasov, D., Tarnovsky, C., Krissler, J.S., Boit, C., Seifert, J.P.: Breaking and entering through the silicon. In: Proceedings of the 2013 ACM SIGSAC Conference on Computer & Communications Security, pp. 733–744. ACM (2013)
9. Herder, C., Yu, M.D., Koushanfar, F., Devadas, S.: Physical unclonable functions and applications: a tutorial. Proc. IEEE **102**(8), 1126–1141 (2014)
10. Kearns, M.J., Vazirani, U.V.: An Introduction to Computational Learning Theory. MIT press, Cambridge (1994)
11. Kömmerling, O., Kuhn, M.: Design principles for tamper-resistant security processors. In: USENIX Workshop on Smartcard Technology (1999)
12. Maes, R.: Physically Unclonable Functions: Constructions, Properties and Applications. Springer, Heidelberg (2013)
13. Maes, R., Verbauwhede, I.: Physically unclonable functions: a study on the state of the art and future research directions. In: Sadeghi, A.-R., Naccach, D. (eds.) Towards Hardware-Intrinsic Security. Information Security and Cryptography, pp. 3–37. Springer, Heidelberg (2010)
14. Maiti, A., Casarona, J., McHale, L., Schaumont, P.: A large scale characterization of RO-PUF. In: 2010 IEEE International Symposium on Hardware-Oriented Security and Trust (HOST), pp. 94–99 (2010)

15. Maiti, A., Kim, I., Schaumont, P.: A robust physical unclonable function with enhanced challenge-response set. IEEE Trans. Inf. Forensics Secur. **7**(1), 333–345 (2012)
16. Maiti, A., Schaumont, P.: Improving the quality of a physical unclonable function using configurable ring oscillators. In: International Conference on Field Programmable Logic and Applications, FPL 2009, pp. 703–707. IEEE (2009)
17. Merli, D., Schuster, D., Stumpf, F., Sigl, G.: Side-channel analysis of PUFs and fuzzy extractors. In: McCune, J.M., Balacheff, B., Perrig, A., Sadeghi, A.-R., Sasse, A., Beres, Y. (eds.) Trust 2011. LNCS, vol. 6740, pp. 33–47. Springer, Heidelberg (2011)
18. Mugali, K.C., Patil, M.M.: A novel technique of configurable ring oscillator for physical unclonable functions. Int. J. Comput. Eng. Appl. **9**(1), 95–100 (2015)
19. Nguyen, P.H., Sahoo, D.P., Chakraborty, R.S., Mukhopadhyay, D.: Efficient attacks on robust ring oscillator PUF with enhanced challenge-response set. In: Proceedings of the 2015 Design, Automation & Test in Europe Conference & Exhibition, pp. 641–646. EDA Consortium (2015)
20. Pappu, R., Recht, B., Taylor, J., Gershenfeld, N.: Physical one-way functions. Science **297**(5589), 2026–2030 (2002)
21. Rivest, R.L.: Learning decision lists. Mach. Learn. **2**(3), 229–246 (1987)
22. Rührmair, U., Sehnke, F., Sölter, J., Dror, G., Devadas, S., Schmidhuber, J.: Modeling attacks on physical unclonable functions. In: Proceedings of the 17th ACM Conference on Computer and Communications Security, pp. 237–249. ACM (2010)
23. Rührmair, U., Xu, X., Sölter, J., Mahmoud, A., Majzoobi, M., Koushanfar, F., Burleson, W.: Efficient power and timing side channels for physical unclonable functions. In: Batina, L., Robshaw, M. (eds.) CHES 2014. LNCS, vol. 8731, pp. 476–492. Springer, Heidelberg (2014)
24. Saha, I., Jeldi, R.R., Chakraborty, R.S.: Model building attacks on physically unclonable functions using genetic programming. In: 2013 IEEE International Symposium on Hardware-Oriented Security and Trust (HOST), pp. 41–44. IEEE (2013)
25. Secure Embedded Systems (SES) Lab at Virginia Tech: On-chip Variability Datafor PUFs. http://rijndael.ece.vt.edu/puf/artifacts.html
26. Suh, G.E., Devadas, S.: Physical unclonable functions for device authentication and secret key generation. In: Proceedings of the 44th Annual Design Automation Conference, pp. 9–14. ACM (2007)
27. Tajik, S., Dietz, E., Frohmann, S., Seifert, J.-P., Nedospasov, D., Helfmeier, C., Boit, C., Dittrich, H.: Physical characterization of arbiter PUFs. In: Batina, L., Robshaw, M. (eds.) CHES 2014. LNCS, vol. 8731, pp. 493–509. Springer, Heidelberg (2014)
28. Tajik, S., Lohrke, H., Ganji, F., Seifert, J.P., Boit, C.: Laser fault attack on physically unclonable functions. In: 2015 Workshop on Fault Diagnosis and Tolerance in Cryptography (FDTC) (2015)
29. Yu, M.D., Sowell, R., Singh, A., M'Raihi, D., Devadas, S.: Performance metrics and empirical results of a puf cryptographic key generation ASIC. In: 2012 IEEE International Symposium on Hardware-Oriented Security and Trust (HOST), pp. 108–115. IEEE (2012)
30. Yu, M.-D.M., Devadas, S.: Recombination of physical unclonable functions(2010)
31. Yu, M.-D.M., M'Raihi, D., Sowell, R., Devadas, S.: Lightweight and secure PUF key storage using limits of machine learning. In: Preneel, B., Takagi, T. (eds.) CHES 2011. LNCS, vol. 6917, pp. 358–373. Springer, Heidelberg (2011)

Anonymous Authentication Scheme Based on PUF

Łukasz Krzywiecki(✉)

Department of Computer Science, Faculty of Fundamental Problems of Technology, Wrocław University of Technology, Wrocław, Poland
lukasz.krzywiecki@pwr.edu.pl

Abstract. We propose an anonymous authentication scheme which security is based on Physical Unclonable Function. Our scheme is resistant to typical attacks mounted against regular systems with security based on computational assumptions. Its tampering and cloning resistance is based on the assumption that cloning of the PUF device is impossible. The scheme withstand collusion attacks: no coalition of adversaries can successfully authenticate without a registered device. It provides unconditional anonymity: it is infeasible to determine which device, out of the all registered, was used for authorization. The anonymity feature withstand attacks of the very powerful adversary which has access to all public parameters, as well all secrets - including the master secret of the system creator.

Keywords: Anonymous authentication · Anonymity · Physical unclonable function · PUF

1 Introduction

Authentication Scheme (AS) is a protocol usually involving two parties: an authenticator which proves his identity, and a verifier which accepts or rejects the authenticator's proof. Typically the verifier checks some attribures of the authenticator: what the authenticator has (key, token, etc.), what the authenticator knows (secret, password, etc.), what the authenticator are (e.g. biometric characteristics).

Anonymous Authentication Scheme (AAS) is such a AS protocol, in which the verifier checks if the authenticator belongs to some predefined group of authorized users, but without the possibility of learning the exact authenticator's identity (see e.g. [1] for generic definitions). Thus if the group of authorized users has the cardinality $|A|$, we usually limit the possibility of such a correct guess by $1/|A|$. In this paper we concentrate on authentication schemes based on *"what the authenticator has"* methodology. Usually in this scenario we think of small authentication devices which *securely* store the authentication keys inside (e.g.

Partially supported by fundings from Polish National Science Center decision number DEC-2013/09/B/ST6/02251.

S. Kwon and A. Yun (Eds.): ICISC 2015, LNCS 9558, pp. 359–372, 2016.
DOI: 10.1007/978-3-319-30840-1_23

electronic tokens, smartcards). However AS based on tokens may be subject to common threats such as tampering and cloning. Once a device is tampered, it can be duplicated and the adversary can use it since after. Conventional approaches to securely managing secrets in a device memory suffers from a couple of shortcomings. Non-volatile memory modules are vulnerable to invasive attack. Side-channel attacks or software attacks can lead to bit leakage, device modeling and finally result in key exposure. Therefore much effort is undertaken to provide unclonability property for token devices in order to prevent those attacks. The recent research in this area indicates the notion of physical unclonable functions (PUFs) as quite promising.

Physical Unclonable Function (PUF) is a hardware primitive that extracts randomness from its physical characteristics acquired during natural variation of fabrication process. Those variations are so unique that they cannot be repeated exactly, even by the manufacturer, thus making the PUF device unclonable. PUFs can be tested with external challenges, upon which (due to PUFs perplex structure) they react with corresponding responses which are extremely difficult to predict and are unique to each PUF. The *inputs-outputs* of PUF are tabularized and are also refered as *Challenge-Response Pairs* (CRP). Here we will use the both terms interchangeably. There are several types of PUFs discussed in literature: [2–12], with different physical characteristics. However, in this paper we abstract from the physical realization of the PUF device. We only require that:

- it is infeasible to clone PUF device;
- the CRPs set is very large, so it is impossible to determine all CRPs by any adversary who get the access to the attacked PUF;
- it is impossible to model the PUF and then predict its response for a randomly chosen challenge, given a collection of previously obtained CRPs.

In this way we treat a PUF as unique hash function, modeled as a black box, available only through its input and output interfaces. However, in the PUF case, the inside randomness is the inherent part of the device which cannot be extracted, modeled, cloned, and varies in each produced instance.

There are numerous cryptographic schemes which utilize PUF devices for different purposes, e.g. [13–16]. In the context of security models, Brzuska et al. in [17] denote the trusted PUF ideal functionality in universal composition (UC) framework of Canetti [18], and show efficient UC-secure protocols for oblivious transfer, commitments, and key exchange. With the assumption that PUFs are trusted and honestly devised the result is unconditional, with no computational assumptions for proposed schemes. The later work of Ostrovsky et al. [19] extended [17] for maliciously generated PUFs. Authors construct (*computational*) UC commitment scheme, as well as unconditional (but not UC) commitment scheme in the malicious PUFs model. Positive results of [17,19] enable to model various PUF based ideal functionalities, and encourage to seek other scenarios for PUF usage.

Therefore, to the best knowledge of the authors, we propose the first detailed instantiation of *trusted PUF based anonymous authentication scheme*, which is *uconditionally* secure. Our proposition is particularly inspired by the scheme [16] which use PUFs for secure anonymous broadcast encryption. Specifically we assume the same construction for the hardware setup: the PUF devices themselves and the PUF readers.

Regular authentication via PUF device. In regular setup the PUF device can have a form of a token (or a card), which will be given to user u, and denoted as D_u. When a user u authenticates, it inserts the device D_u into the reader. Then the PUF part of D_u denoted as P_u is inputed with the i-th challenge c_i, and the resulting response $r_i = P_u(c_i)$ are captured by the reader (see Fig. 1).

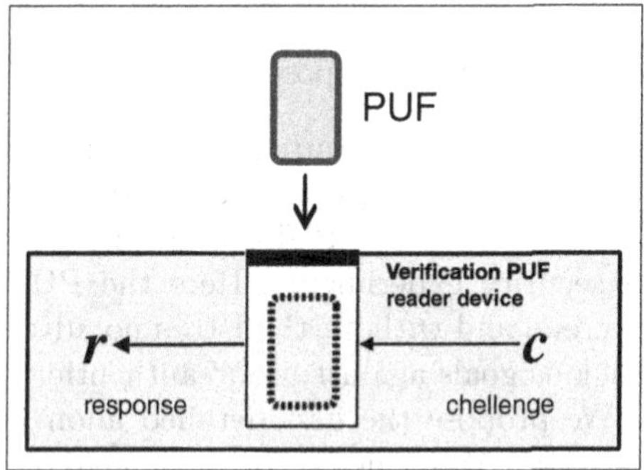

Fig. 1. Authorization via PUF device.

The conventional usage of PUF in authentication process is divided into two phases:

1. Learning phase:
   (a) A user u enrolls into the system. A new PUF device is designated for u, and denoted since them as D_u
   (b) A PUF device u is tested against the vector of challenges $C_u = (c_1, c_2, ..., c_n)$ and outputs the vector of responses $R_u = (r_1, r_2, ..., r_n)$. Both C_u, R_u are stored securely at the verifier side.
   (c) The PUF device is given to the user.
2. Authentication phase:
   (a) A PUF holder inserts the PUF into the PUF reader
   (b) The PUF is challenged against the some challenge c_i stored for u.
   (c) If the answer from the PUF is equal to the corresponding response r_i previously stored for the device u, then the authenticator is identified and accepted.

Problem Statement. The problem with regular PUF-based authentication is the following: once the verifier collects the *input-output* pairs in the learning phase for the given PUF, it *seems* to be inevitable that it always uniquely identifies the device during authentication phase. In the context of [17,19] we argue that this is not a general rule. Note, that for *non-PUF* based authentication protocols there exist anonymous solutions like *group authentication* schemes, see e.g. [20–22], or solutions based on ring signatures [23]. In other words we would like to answer the question: *"How to design and instantiate a PUF based authentication scheme which provides anonymity in the sense of"* [1]. Such a protocol should provide, that: (a) after the protocol execution the verifier is convinced the user belongs to some predefined registered group of users; (b) the identity of the authenticator is hidden, i.e. it could be any of the registered users.

Our Contribution. In this paper we propose:

- *Security Model:* We provide the security model that addresses the regular authenticity and anonymity requirements. Particularly, in the model we address the specific aspects of the PUFs usage in the typical anonymous and authentication security experiments. Here the PUFs themselves stand for cryptographic secrets, and without the PUFs no adversary should be able to complete its malicious goals against users' authenticity and anonymity.
- *PUFAAS Scheme:* We propose the first detailed anonymous authentication scheme - we called it PUFAAS - which security is based on physical unclonable functions. The proposition is inspired by the scheme [16] - we use the same construction for the PUF devices and the PUF readers. Moreover we utilize the same procedures for initialization of the protocol and registration the new PUF devices to users. These two procedures can be viewed as a 'verbatim' copy of the corresponding procedures from [16]. We treat that as the potential advantage, as reusing existing libraries (here for initializing and registration) can simplify the future implementation process. Specifically we propose the challenge and response procedures to reflect the goals and feature of AAS scheme. We prove the security of the scheme in our proposed model.

Particularly, the proposed scheme is immune to typical attacks against regular systems based on computational assumptions (here the scheme is based on the assumption of randomness of PUF's output and their unclonability). This however is achieved at the price of additional initial tabularization of CRPs by the verifier party and the memory used for that purpose. Our scheme combines the features previously not achieved simultaneously by a single AAS scheme:

- *Authentication Security:* tampering and cloning resistance is based on the assumption that cloning of the PUF device is impossible. The scheme withstand collusion attacks: no coalition of adversaries can sucessfuly authenticate without a registered device.
- *Unconditional anonymity:* For our scheme it is infeasible to determine which device, out of the all registered, was used for authorization. The scheme withstand attacks of the very powerful adversary which has access to all public

parameters, as well all secrets - including the master secret of the system creator.

- *Small computational complexity:* our scheme does not require *heavy* cryptographic computation - no exponentiations are required on the authenticator side, the only exponentiations on the verificator side are those involved in obtaining polynomial values (these also can be omitted by using Horner's method).

2 PUF Based Anonymous Authentication Scheme

2.1 Scheme Architecture

First let us describe the system architecture for the proposed PUFAAS protocol. The hardware setup is inspired by the scheme [16] which use PUF for secure broadcast encryption. The verifier is equipped with a reader for setup and authentication phase of PUF devices. The uth PUF device - which is to register to user u, and denoted by D_u, consists of two pieces: (1) a PUF hardware P_u which behaves as unclonable private hash function of its user u; (2) a memory module build into D_u, where some auxiliary data is stored. Moreover, we assume that each device D_u is configured in such a way, that its PUF part P_u outputs effectively a value r_i when inputed a value c_i, thus we denote $r_i = P_u(c_i)$. We abstract from the technical aspects of this implementation. Specifically, for the proposed scheme in Sect. 3, we assume that each D_u utilize efficient coding through which c_i and r_i can be interpreted as numbers from the chosen group $\mathbb{Z}_p$ setup in Init procedure of the system.

Below, in Definition 1 we describe the scheme. Table 1 presents the sequence diagram of the authentication process.

Definition 1. PUFAAS *scheme is a 5-tuple of algorithms* $(\mathsf{Init}, \mathsf{Reg}, \mathsf{Chall}, \mathsf{Resp}, \mathsf{Ver})$ *where:*

- *the initialization procedure* Init *receives as an input a security parameter* ξ, *and returns the master secret* MK*; we denote* $MK \leftarrow \mathsf{Init}(\xi)$
- *the registration procedure* Reg *receives as an input the master secret* MK *and an index* u *associated with the device to register, and the device* D *itself; it returns the user's secret share* SK_u *and stores it securely on the device; we denote* $SK_u \leftarrow \mathsf{Reg}(MK, u, D_u)$
- *the challenge procedure* Chall *receives as an input the master secret* MK *and index of the challenge* i*, it returns the* i*th challenge* c_i*; we denote* $c_i \leftarrow \mathsf{Chall}(MK, i))$*;*
- *the response procedure* Resp *receives a challenge block* c_i*, and secret share* SK_u *of user* u*, the device* D_u*; it returns the response* r_i*; we denote* $r_i \leftarrow \mathsf{Resp}(c_i, u, D_u, SK_u)$
- *the verification procedure* Ver *receives a response block* r_i*, and master secret* MK*; it returns a bit* d*:* 1 *if* P_u *is an authorized device, or* 0 *otherwise; we denote* $d \leftarrow \mathsf{Ver}(r_i, c_i, MK)$

Table 1. Sequence diagram of the PUFAAS protocol.

Veirifier $\mathcal{C}$		PUF device u
setup:		
$MK \leftarrow \mathsf{Init}(\xi)$		
$SK_u \leftarrow \mathsf{Reg}(MK, u, D_u)$	D_u is given to the user u	
challenge:		
$c_i \longleftarrow \mathsf{Chall}(MK, i))$	$\xrightarrow{c_i}$	
$d \leftarrow \mathsf{Ver}(r_i, c_i, MK)$	$\xleftarrow{r_i}$	$r_i \leftarrow \mathsf{Resp}(c_i, u, D_u, SK_u)$

2.2 Security Model for PUF Based AA

The following game based definitions define the security requirements for the proposed PUFAAS:

- **Authentication:** it should be impossible to authenticate without the possession of the registered PUF device,
- **Anonymity:** it should be impossible to detect which registered device was used during successful authentication, even for the adversary who possesses the master secret key of the system.

Definition 2 (Authentication Game). *The authentication game for the PUFAAS scheme, the PPT adversary $\mathcal{A}^{\mathsf{Aut}}$, and the challenger $\mathcal{C}$ is as follows:*

- Setup: *$\mathcal{C}$ setups the system: $MK \leftarrow \mathsf{Init}(\xi)$.*
- Phase 1: *$\mathcal{A}^{\mathsf{Aut}}$ can adaptively issue the following queries:*
  - RegQuery*: in this case $\mathcal{C}$ runs $\mathsf{Reg}(MK, u, D_u)$ to register a new user u, and subsequently gives the registered device D_u to $\mathcal{A}^{\mathsf{Aut}}$,*
  - *$\mathcal{A}^{\mathsf{Aut}}$ can query each device for an arbitrary number of n challenges of its will: $\hat{c}_1, \ldots, \hat{c}_i, \ldots, \hat{c}_n$, collecting responses $P_u(\hat{c}_i) = \hat{r}_{u,i}$ from each uth device.*
  - ChallQuery*: in this case $\mathcal{A}^{\mathsf{Aut}}$ authenticates by the means of the given decoders.*
- Challenge: *$\mathcal{A}^{\mathsf{Aut}}$ returns all the given decoders and enters authentication phase of the PUFAAS protocol:*
  - *$\mathcal{C}$ runs: $c_i \leftarrow \mathsf{Chall}(MK, i))$ for unused in the previous phase index i,*
  - *$\mathcal{C}$ sends c_i to $\mathcal{A}^{\mathsf{Aut}}$,*
  - *$\mathcal{A}$ produces the response $\hat{r}_i$,*
  - *$\mathcal{C}$ runs: $d \leftarrow \mathsf{Ver}(\hat{r}_i, c_i, MK)$.*

$\mathcal{A}^{\mathsf{Aut}}$ wins the game if: $d = 1$.

The advantage of $\mathcal{A}^{\mathsf{Aut}}$ winning the above game is defined as

$$\mathbf{Adv}(\mathcal{A}^{\mathsf{Aut}}) = \Pr[d = 1]$$

We say that the PUFAAS scheme is a "secure-authentication" if the $\mathbf{Adv}(\mathcal{A}^{\mathsf{Aut}})$ *is negligible.*

In the following definition we formulate the anonymity requirements for the proposed PUFAAS scheme. This definition addresses a very powerful adversary, which can play a role of a system creator, and the verifier who knows the master secret key MK. Even in this scenario it should not be able to distinguish which registered device performs authentication.

Definition 3 (Anonymity Game). *The Anonymity game for the PUFAAS scheme, the PPT adversary $\mathcal{A}^{\mathsf{Ano}}$, and the challenger $\mathcal{C}$ is as follows:*

- Setup: *The adversary $\mathcal{A}^{\mathsf{Ano}}$ setups the system. In this case it knows the master secret key MK.*
- Phase 1: *$\mathcal{A}^{\mathsf{Ano}}$ registers the arbitrary number q of new users, i.e.:*
  - *it runs $\mathsf{Reg}(MK, u, D_u)$ to register each new user device $D_0, \ldots, D_u, \ldots, D_{q-1}$.*
  - *$\mathcal{A}^{\mathsf{Ano}}$ can query each device for an arbitrary number of n challenges of its will: $\hat{c}_1, \ldots, \hat{c}_i, \ldots, \hat{c}_n$, collecting responses $P_u(\hat{c}_i) = \hat{r}_{u,i}$ from each uth device.*
- Challenge: *$\mathcal{A}^{\mathsf{Aut}}$ gives to $\mathcal{C}$ a set of n devices, say $D_1, \ldots, D_n$ (for users $u_1, \ldots, u_n$), then:*
  - *$\mathcal{C}$ draws a random index $j \in \{1, \ldots, n\}$,*
  - *$\mathcal{C}$ authenticates with device D_j to $\mathcal{A}^{\mathsf{Ano}}$ according to the protocol.*
- Guess: *$\mathcal{A}^{\mathsf{Aut}}$ outputs a guess index j'.*

The adversary $\mathcal{A}^{\mathsf{Aut}}$ wins the game if: $j = j'$. The advantage of $\mathcal{A}^{\mathsf{Ano}}$ winning the above game is defined as

$$\mathbf{Adv}(\mathcal{A}^{\mathsf{Ano}}) = |\Pr[j = j'] - 1/n|.$$

We say that the PUFAAS scheme is "anonymous" if the $\mathbf{Adv}(\mathcal{A}^{\mathsf{Ano}})$ *is negligible.*

3 Proposed PUFAA Protocol

3.1 Idea: Anonymous Authentication via Lagrangian Interpolation

Let $L : \mathbb{Z}_p \to \mathbb{Z}_p$ be a polynomial of degree z, and $A = \langle (x_0, y_0), \ldots, (x_z, y_z) \rangle$ be a set of pairs such that: $y_i = L(x_i)$, $x_i \neq x_j$ for $i \neq j$. *Lagrangian interpolation* formula (LI) enables reconstruction of the polynomial L from the set A (so called *interpolation set*):

$$LI(x, A) = \sum_{i=0,(x_i,\cdot)\in A}^{z} \left(y_i \prod_{j=0, j\neq i, (x_j,\cdot)\in A}^{z} \left(\frac{x - x_j}{x_i - x_j} \right) \right). \quad (1)$$

Here we depict the basic idea behind anonymous authentication based on LI. Note that this is the *straw-men* solution used only as an illustration, and it is vulnerable to numerous attacks such as collusion of users. The full secure version of the protocol is proposed in the subsequent secion:

1. Setup phase:
   (a) A verifier chooses a number of private polynomials L_i of degree z
   (b) A verifier provides each user u with shares of the form $(x_{u,i}, L(x_{u,i})$ - one for each polynomial L_i.
2. Authentication phase:
   (a) If the verifier want to test if some user has been given the share (which would indicate it is an authorized user), it choses one unused polynomial L_i composes a challenge consisting of some random pairwise different z shares of the form $(x, L_i(x))$, and sends them to the user.
   (b) The user uses its own ith share, and the shares from the challenge to perform Lagrangian interpolation for reconstruction of the polynomial L_i. Then user computes $y_r = L_i(x_r)$ for some random x_r.
   (c) The user sends x_r, y_r to the verifier.
   (d) The verifier accepts the proof if $y_r == L_i(x_r)$ and the pair (x_r, y_r) were not included in the challenge.
   (e) The verifier discards the polynomial L_i as used.

In this setup the anonymity group consists of all users registered in the step 1.(b). The verifier, at the end of the protocol execution, concludes that the user must have used his secret share to compute the polynomial. Note that all registered users can evaluate the same polynomial from the interpolation set which includes the challenge shares and the share they were given at registration. However the returned answer - computed for random x_r - gives no clue which user authenticates. This feature, that the user returns the value statistically unrelated to the possessed share, is the main idea behind the anonymity of the proposed protocol. Here the users anonymously prove they were given shares of the same polynomial, so the group of users is defined by the polynomial used during their registration. Discarding used polynomials prevent from repetition attacks mounted by the adversary who capture communication messages.

3.2 Scheme Details

Preliminaries:

1. The proposed authentication protocol is based on Lagrangian interpolation described in previous section.
2. Unless otherwise stated, from now on all arithmetic operations are executed in $\mathbb{Z}_p$.
3. The notation $r \leftarrow_R \mathbb{Z}_p$ means that r is chosen uniformly at random from the set $\mathbb{Z}_p$.
4. We assume the given $\mathbb{Z}_p$ is large enough, so that in z random drawing $r_i \leftarrow_R \mathbb{Z}_p$ the obtained values are pairwise different w.h.p., and drawing the same values is negligible.
5. We also assume that probability of obtaining the same outputs $r_{u,i} = P_u(c_i)$ from different PUFs P_u for the same input c_i is negligible.

The assumption 4, and 5 from above simplifies the algorithms description in the following section, in which we produce pairwise different shares for Lagrangian interpolation.

Initialization: Initialization procedure is performed by the verifier. It takes as an input the total numbers of rounds T, the system security parameter ξ, and produces as output T random polynomials L_i of degree z altogether with $2T$ random challenges t_i, t'_i. The random polynomial L_i can be represented as the vector of its coefficients. We denote $MK_i = (L_i(x), t_i, t'_i)$ for each round i, where $L_i(x)$ is represented by coefficients. The master secret is $MK = \{MK_i | i = 1, \ldots, T\}$. Note, that here we assume that T is limited by the capacity of the storage module of the users PUF devices. We do not require that this storage is encrypted and tamper resistant. This can be realized by existing flash memory modules. In rare case of running out of polynomials L_i the process of initialization the system and registration of users should be repeated.

Data: z - the degree of polynomials L_i, the maximum numbers of rounds T, system security parameter ξ
Result: the master secret polynomial $L_i(x)$, and challenges t_i, t'_i for each round: $MK = \{MK_i | i = 1, \ldots, T\}$

begin
  choose $p \in PRIME$, such that $p > \xi$
  for $i = 1, \ldots, T$ **do**
    for $j = 0, \ldots, z$ **do**
      $a_{i,j} \longleftarrow_R \mathbb{Z}_p$
    $L_i(x) = \sum_{j=0}^{z} a_{i,j} x^j$
    $t_i, t'_i \longleftarrow_R U$
    $MK_i = (L_i(x), t_i, t'_i)$
  $MK \longleftarrow \{MK_i | i = 1, \ldots, T\}$
  return MK;

Algorithm 1. Initializing procedure Init

Registration: In the registration procedure a fresh (e.g. newly produced) PUF device D is assigned to user u, and denoted as D_u since then. The verifier challenges the PUF part P_u of the device D_u against t_i, t'_i for each round i obtaining values $x_{u,i} = P_u(t_i)$ and $m_{u,i} = P_u(t'_i)$. The value $m_{u,i}$ will be used as a random mask for y part of the user share: $y_{u,i} = L_i(x_{u,i})$ is stored in a masked form as $y'_{u,i} = y_{u,i} + m_{u,i}$ in the memory module of the D_u device. In this way the memory module of D_u stores $SK_u = \{y'_{u,1}, \ldots, y'_{u,T}\}$.

Data: identifier u of the new device, PUF P_u of device u, master secret $MK = \{(L_i(x), t_i, t'_i) | i = 1, \ldots, T\}$ generated by Algorithm 1
Result: a private secret key $SK_u = \{y'_{u,1}, \ldots, y'_{u,T}\}$ of device u for each round.

begin
  $SK_u = \emptyset$
  for $i = 1, \ldots, T$ **do**
    $x_{u,i} \longleftarrow P_u(t_i)$
    $m_{u,i} \longleftarrow P_u(t'_i)$
    $y_{u,i} \longleftarrow L_i(x_{u,i})$
    $y'_{u,i} \longleftarrow y_{u,i} + m_{u,i}$
    $SK_u \longleftarrow SK_u \cup \{(i, y'_{u,i})\}$
  return SK_u;

Algorithm 2. Registration procedure Reg

Challenge: In the challenge procedure executed the verifier randomly generates x_j for $j = 1, \ldots, z$ and adds them to the set X. Subsequently it creates interpolation set $\Psi = \{(x, L_i(x)) | x \in X\}$. Finally it creates the challenging block $c_i = \langle i, t_i, t'_i, \Psi_i \rangle$ which is sent to the authenticator's devices.

Data: the index i of the current round, the master secret MK_i.
Result: $c_i = \langle i, t_i, t'_i, \Psi_i \rangle$

begin
  $X \longleftarrow \emptyset$
  for $j = 1, \ldots, z$ **do**
    $x_j \longleftarrow_R \mathbb{Z}_p$
    $X \longleftarrow X \cup \{x_j\}$
  $\Psi \longleftarrow \emptyset$
  foreach $x \in X$ **do**
    $\Psi_i \longleftarrow \Psi_i \cup \{(x, L_i(x))\}$
  $c_i \longleftarrow \langle i, t_i, t'_i, \Psi_i \rangle$
  return c_i

Algorithm 3. Challenge encoding procedure Chall

Response: Response procedure takes as an input the challenge $c_i = \langle i, t_i, t'_i, \Psi_i \rangle$. It computes $x_{u,i} = P_u(t_i)$. It unmasks $y_{u,i} = y'_{u,i} - P_u(t'_i)$, constructs interpolation set $\Psi'_i = \Psi_i \cup \{(x_{u,i}, y_{u,i})\}$, interpolates the polynomial L_i at some random point x_r, and returns the response $r_i = (x_r, LI(x_r, \Psi'_i))$.

Data: The secret key SK_u of device u, the challenge $c_i = \langle i, t_i, t'_i, \Psi_i \rangle$
Result: The response (x_r, y_r)

begin
  $x_{u,i} \longleftarrow P_u(t_i)$
  $m_{u,i} \longleftarrow P_u(t'_i)$
  $y_{u,i} \longleftarrow y'_{u,i} - m_{u,i}$
  $\psi_u \longleftarrow (x_{u,i}, y_{u,i})$
  $\Psi'_i \longleftarrow \Psi_i \cup \{\psi_u\}$
  $x_r \longleftarrow_R \mathbb{Z}_p$
  $y_r \longleftarrow LI(x_r, \Psi'_i)$
  return (x_r, y_r);

Algorithm 4. Response encoding procedure Resp

Verification: Verification procedure takes the response (x_r, y_r) from a user, computes $L_i(x_r)$ and accepts if $y_r == L_i(x_r)$, and the pair $(x_r, L_i(x_r))$ were not included in the challenge. It rejects authentication otherwise.

Data: the index i of the current round, the master secret MK_i, the challenge $c_i = \langle i, t_i, t'_i, \Psi_i \rangle$, the response $R_i = (x_r, y_r)$
Result: 1 for accept, or 0 for reject

begin
  if $(y_r == L_i(x_r))$ *and* $((x_r, y_r) \notin \Psi_i)$ **then**
    return 1
  else
    return 0

Algorithm 5. Verification procedure Ver

4 Security Analysis

Security of the proposed scheme is based on the following assumption concerning PUF's unpredictability and unclonability. Moreover we assume that the PUF hardware is created by the trusted producer, in such a way that it can be accessed only via the prescribed procedure and with the well defined interfaces. In this context we are close to the approach from [17] and [16].

Assumption 1 (PUF Assumption). *Each physical unclonable hadware P_u is a unique instantiation of a random function with inputs and outputs from a given $\mathbb{Z}_p$, modeled as ROM, available only through its input-output interfaces.*

This allows us to conclude that:

- it is infeasible to clone PUF device;
- the CRPs set is very large, so it is impossible to determine all CRPs by any adversary who get the access to the attacked PUF;

– it is impossible to model the PUF and then predict its response for a randomly chosen challenge, given a collection of previously obtained CRPs.

Theorem 2. *The PUFAAS scheme described in Sect. 3.2 is a "secure-authentication" in the sense of Definition 2.*

Proof. In the proof we follow the methodology from [16]. To win the "Authentication Game" the adversary $\mathcal{A}^{\mathsf{Aut}}$ has to reconstruct the unused polynomial L_i (for the unused in "Phase 1" index i). Note that polynomials in the secret MK are defined independently at random, so the knowledge about others polynomials gained in "Phase 1" does not help $\mathcal{A}^{\mathsf{Aut}}$ in answering the current challenge related to L_i.

In order to reconstruct the unknown polynomial L_i the adversary has to solve the system of equations: $a_{i,0} + a_{i,1}x_{u,i} + \ldots + a_{i,z}x_{u,i}^z = y'_{u,i} - P_u(t'_i)$ for devices D_u it does not possesses, where $x_{u,i} = P_u(t_i)$, and $y_{u,i} = y'_{u,i} - P_u(t'_i)$. The only knowledge $\mathcal{A}^{\mathsf{Aut}}$ could use to do this task is data obtained in "Phase 1": the value $y'_{u,i}$ stored in the memory module for each D_u, and a number of answers from each P_u it tested against a finite number of inputs $\hat{c}$. But $y'_{u,i}$ is a value of L_i in some point randomized by $m_{u,i} = P_u(t'_{u,i})$, unknown without the appropriate PUF device P_u according to Assumption 1. The only help for $\mathcal{A}^{\mathsf{Aut}}$ would be if inputs $\hat{c}$, coined and probed in "Phase 1" would produced shares belonging to the searched polynomial L_i. However, probability of the right guessing is negligible. □

Theorem 3. *The PUFAAS scheme described in Sect. 3.2 is "anonymous" for "honest but curious adversary scenario" in the sense of Definition 3.*

Proof. Assume that a device D_j authenticates in the unused round i by reconstructing the polynomial L_i. Note that each registered device would reconstruct the same polynomial L_i for that round. Subsequently D_j returns to the verifier the response $r_i = (x, L_i(x))$ for x generated at random from $\mathbb{Z}_p$. Thus r_i is obtained randomly and stochastically independently from the index j of the device, and each device could obtain the $r_i = (x, L_i(x))$ with the same probability. Thus the advantage of the adversary is negligible.

Theorem 4. *The "curious and malicious adversary" wins the anonymity game of Definition 3 against the PUFAAS scheme described in Sect. 3.2 with probability* $1/(n-1)$.

Proof. This is the additional scenario. The adversary in this case does not follow the protocol. Thus his chances are slightly better. It first guesses which device authenticates (index j'), and then tries to confirm that. It constructs new random polynomial $\hat{L}_i$ with interpolation set including the shares of the device in question, and random shares. Then if in the response it gets back the shares belonging to the challenging polynomial $\hat{L}_i$ the adversary concludes that his guess was correct. If the response is random the adversary outputs a random index from $1, \ldots n$, but different than j', so the probability of its success is limited to $1/(n-1)$. Nevertheless in this case the probability of winning the game depends on the probability of the initial right guess. □

5 Conclusion and Further Modifications

We propose the anonymous authentication scheme - PUFAAS - based on physical unclonable functions and Lagrangian interpolation. We provide the security model that addresses the regular authenticity and anonymity requirements and specific unclonability aspects of the PUFs usage. We proved the security of the proposed scheme in our model.

The further modification includes the utilizing of parameter z, which is the degree of polynomial L_i. This can be used in the system in the manner of the Shamir's secret sharing. Setting the number of shares, send in the challenge phase of the protocol, to $z-k+1$, requires the usage of k different devices by the authenticator. This opens the possibility to extended hierarchical access management control, and more restricted authentication to some crucial resources, e.g., one authenticator possesses more than one PUF device, or the protocol has to be completed by many authenticators which altogether have k devices.

References

1. Lindell, Y.: Anonymous authentication. J. Priv. Confidentiality **2**(2), 4 (2010)
2. Pappu, R.S., Recht, B., Taylor, J., Gershenfeld, N.: Physical one-way functions. Science **297**, 2026–2030 (2002). http://web.media.mit.edu/brecht/papers/02.PapEA.powf.pdf
3. Gassend, B., Clarke, D.E., van Dijk, M., Devadas, S.: Silicon physical random functions. In Atluri, V., ed.: ACM Conference on Computer and Communications Security, pp. 148–160. ACM (2002)
4. Guajardo, J., Kumar, S.S., Schrijen, G.-J., Tuyls, P.: FPGA intrinsic PUFs and their use for IP protection. In: Paillier, P., Verbauwhede, I. (eds.) CHES 2007. LNCS, vol. 4727, pp. 63–80. Springer, Heidelberg (2007)
5. Gassend, B., Clarke, D., van Dijk, M., Devadas, S.: Controlled physical random functions. In: Proceedings of the 18th Annual Computer Security Applications Conference (2002)
6. Gassend, B.: Physical Random Functions. Master's thesis, MIT, USA (2003)
7. Pappu, R.S.: Physical one-way functions. Ph.D thesis, Massachusetts Institute of Technology (2001). http://pubs.media.mit.edu/pubs/papers/01.03.pappuphd.powf.pdf
8. Suh, G.E., Devadas, S.: Physical unclonable functions for device authentication and secret key generation. In: Design Automation Conference, pp. 9–14. ACM Press, New York (2007). http://people.csail.mit.edu/devadas/pubs/puf-dac07.pdf
9. Majzoobi, M., Koushanfar, F., Potkonjak, M.: Lightweight secure pufs. In: ICCAD 2008: Proceedings of the 2008 IEEE/ACM International Conference on Computer-Aided Design, Piscataway, NJ, USA, pp. 670–673. IEEE Press (2008)
10. Gassend, B., Lim, D., Clarke, D., Devadas, S., van Dijk, M.: Identification and authentication of integrated circuits. Concurrency Comput.: Pract. Experience **16**(11), 1077–1098 (2004)
11. Lee, J.W., Lim, D., Gassend, B., Suh, G.E., van Dijk, M., Devadas, S.: A technique to build a secret key in integrated circuits for identification and authentication applications. In: VLSI Circuits, pp. 176–179. Digest of Technical Papers (2004)

12. Lim, D., Lee, J.W., Gassend, B., Suh, G.E., van Dijk, M., Devadas, S.: Extracting secret keys from integrated circuits. IEEE Trans. Very Large Scale Integr. (VLSI) Syst, **13**(10), 1200–1205 (2005)
13. Nithyanand, R., Solis, J.: A theoretical analysis: physical unclonable functions and the software protection problem. In: 2012 IEEE Symposium on Security and Privacy Workshops, San Francisco, CA, USA, pp. 1–11. IEEE Computer Society, 24–25 May 2012 (2012). http://dx.doi.org/10.1109/SPW.2012.16
14. Herder, C., Yu, M.M., Koushanfar, F., Devadas, S.: Physical unclonable functions and applications: a tutorial. In: Proceedings of the IEEE vol. 102(8), pp. 1126–1141 (2014). http://dx.doi.org/10.1109/JPROC.2014.2320516
15. Suh, G.E., Devadas, S.: Physical unclonable functions for device authentication and secret key generation. In: Proceedings of the 44th Design Automation Conference, DAC 2007, San Diego, CA, USA, pp. 9–14. IEEE, 4–8 June 2007 (2007). http://doi.acm.org/10.1145/1278480.1278484
16. Krzywiecki, Ł., Kutyłowski, M.: Coalition resistant anonymous broadcast encryption scheme based on PUF. In: McCune, J.M., Balacheff, B., Perrig, A., Sadeghi, A.-R., Sasse, A., Beres, Y. (eds.) Trust 2011. LNCS, vol. 6740, pp. 48–62. Springer, Heidelberg (2011). http://dx.doi.org/10.1007/978-3-642-21599-5_4
17. Brzuska, C., Fischlin, M., Schröder, H., Katzenbeisser, S.: Physically uncloneable functions in the universal composition framework. In: Rogaway, P. (ed.) CRYPTO 2011. LNCS, vol. 6841, pp. 51–70. Springer, Heidelberg (2011). http://dx.doi.org/10.1007/978-3-642-22792-9_4
18. Canetti, R.: Universally composable security: a new paradigm for cryptographic protocols. In: Proceedings of the 42nd IEEE Symposium on Foundations of Computer Science. FOCS 2001, p. 136. Computer Society (2001). http://dl.acm.org/citation.cfm?id=874063.875553
19. Ostrovsky, R., Scafuro, A., Visconti, I., Wadia, A.: Universally composable secure computation with (malicious) physically uncloneable functions. In: Johansson, T., Nguyen, P.Q. (eds.) EUROCRYPT 2013. LNCS, vol. 7881, pp. 702–718. Springer, Heidelberg (2013). http://dx.doi.org/10.1007/978-3-642-38348-9_41
20. Walker, J., Li, J.: Key exchange with anonymous authentication using DAA-SIGMA protocol. In: Chen, L., Yung, M. (eds.) INTRUST 2010. LNCS, vol. 6802, pp. 108–127. Springer, Heidelberg (2011). http://dx.doi.org/10.1007/978-3-642-25283-9_8
21. Hanaoka, G., Shikata, J., Hanaoka, Y., Imai, H.: Unconditionally secure anonymous encryption and group authentication. Comput. J. **49**(3), 310–321 (2006). http://dx.doi.org/10.1093/comjnl/bxh149
22. Lee, Y., Han, S., Lee, S., Chung, B., Lee, D.: Anonymous authentication system using group signature. In: Barolli, L., Xhafa, F., Hsu, H., eds.: 2009 International Conference on Complex, Intelligent and Software Intensive Systems, CISIS 2009, Fukuoka, Japan, pp. 1235–1239. IEEE Computer Society, 16–19 March 2009 (2009). http://dx.doi.org/10.1109/CISIS.2009.196
23. Xu, Z., Tian, H., Liu, D., Lin, J.: A ring-signature anonymous authentication method based on one-way accumulator. In: 2010 Second International Conference on Communication Systems, Networks and Applications (ICCSNA), vol. 2, pp. 56–59 (2010)

Author Index

Printed in the United States
By Bookmasters